Materials excerpted from

Windows Server® 2008 Applications Infrastructure Configuration

Microsoft Certified Technology Specialist
Exam 70-643

Craig T. Zacker

Microsoft® Exchange Server® 2007 Configuration

Microsoft Certified Technology Specialist
Exam 70-236

Jason W. Eckert, triOS College

WILEY Custom
LEARNING SOLUTIONS

The content of this text has been taken from

Microsoft ® Official Academic Course

Windows Server® 2008 Applications Infrastructure Configuration

Microsoft Certified Technology Specialist Exam 70-643

And

Microsoft® Official Academic Course

Microsoft® Exchange Server® 2007 Configuration

Microsoft Certified Technology Specialist Exam 70-236

Since this custom text is based on excerpts of the full Microsoft® Official Academic Course textbooks for 70-643 and 70-236, it is not intended to cover the entire objective domain for these two Microsoft® certification exams. In that way, this custom text is not meant to be a preparatory text for these two Microsoft certification exams.

Custom Contents

PART 1

Excerpts from

Microsoft® Official Academic Course

Windows Server® 2008 Applications Infrastructure Configuration

Microsoft Certified Technology Specialist Exam 70-643

Microsoft® Official Academic Course

Windows Server® 2008 Applications Infrastructure Configuration (70-643)

Craig Zacker

WILEY

Credits

EXECUTIVE EDITOR	John Kane
DIRECTOR OF MARKETING AND SALES	Mitchell Beaton
MICROSOFT STRATEGIC RELATIONSHIPS MANAGER	Merrick Van Dongen of Microsoft Learning
DEVELOPMENT AND PRODUCTION	Custom Editorial Productions, Inc.
EDITORIAL ASSISTANT	Jennifer Lartz
PRODUCTION MANAGER	Micheline Frederick
PRODUCTION EDITOR	Kerry Weinstein
CREATIVE DIRECTOR	Harry Nolan
COVER DESIGNER	Michael St. Martine
TECHNOLOGY AND MEDIA	Lauren Sapira/Elena Santa Maria

This book was set in Garamond by Aptara, Inc. and printed and bound by Bind Rite Graphics.
The covers were printed by Phoenix Color.

ISBN 978-0-470-22513-4

Printed in the United States of America

10 9 8 7 6 5 4 3 2 1

Foreword from the Publisher

Wiley's publishing vision for the Microsoft Official Academic Course series is to provide students and instructors with the skills and knowledge they need to use Microsoft technology effectively in all aspects of their personal and professional lives. Quality instruction is required to help both educators and students get the most from Microsoft's software tools and to become more productive. Thus our mission is to make our instructional programs trusted educational companions for life.

To accomplish this mission, Wiley and Microsoft have partnered to develop the highest quality educational programs for Information Workers, IT Professionals, and Developers. Materials created by this partnership carry the brand name "Microsoft Official Academic Course," assuring instructors and students alike that the content of these textbooks is fully endorsed by Microsoft, and that they provide the highest quality information and instruction on Microsoft products. The Microsoft Official Academic Course textbooks are "Official" in still one more way—they are the officially sanctioned courseware for Microsoft IT Academy members.

The Microsoft Official Academic Course series focuses on *workforce development*. These programs are aimed at those students seeking to enter the workforce, change jobs, or embark on new careers as information workers, IT professionals, and developers. Microsoft Official Academic Course programs address their needs by emphasizing authentic workplace scenarios with an abundance of projects, exercises, cases, and assessments.

The Microsoft Official Academic Courses are mapped to Microsoft's extensive research and job-task analysis, the same research and analysis used to create the Microsoft Certified Technology Specialist (MCTS) exam. The textbooks focus on real skills for real jobs. As students work through the projects and exercises in the textbooks they enhance their level of knowledge and their ability to apply the latest Microsoft technology to everyday tasks. These students also gain resume-building credentials that can assist them in finding a job, keeping their current job, or in furthering their education.

The concept of life-long learning is today an utmost necessity. Job roles, and even whole job categories, are changing so quickly that none of us can stay competitive and productive without continuously updating our skills and capabilities. The Microsoft Official Academic Course offerings, and their focus on Microsoft certification exam preparation, provide a means for people to acquire and effectively update their skills and knowledge. Wiley supports students in this endeavor through the development and distribution of these courses as Microsoft's official academic publisher.

Today educational publishing requires attention to providing quality print and robust electronic content. By integrating Microsoft Official Academic Course products, *WileyPLUS*, and Microsoft certifications, we are better able to deliver efficient learning solutions for students and teachers alike.

Bonnie Lieberman

General Manager and Senior Vice President

Welcome to the Microsoft Official Academic Course (MOAC) program for Microsoft Windows Server 2008. MOAC represents the collaboration between Microsoft Learning and John Wiley & Sons, Inc. publishing company. Microsoft and Wiley teamed up to produce a series of textbooks that deliver compelling and innovative teaching solutions to instructors and superior learning experiences for students. Infused and informed by in-depth knowledge from the creators of Windows Server 2008, and crafted by a publisher known worldwide for the pedagogical quality of its products, these textbooks maximize skills transfer in minimum time. Students are challenged to reach their potential by using their new technical skills as highly productive members of the workforce.

Because this knowledgebase comes directly from Microsoft, architect of the Windows Server operating system and creator of the Microsoft Certified Technology Specialist and Microsoft Certified Professional exams (www.microsoft.com/learning/mcp/mcts), you are sure to receive the topical coverage that is most relevant to students' personal and professional success. Microsoft's direct participation not only assures you that MOAC textbook content is accurate and current; it also means that students will receive the best instruction possible to enable their success on certification exams and in the workplace.

■ The Microsoft Official Academic Course Program

The *Microsoft Official Academic Course* series is a complete program for instructors and institutions to prepare and deliver great courses on Microsoft software technologies. With MOAC, we recognize that, because of the rapid pace of change in the technology and curriculum developed by Microsoft, there is an ongoing set of needs beyond classroom instruction tools for an instructor to be ready to teach the course. The MOAC program endeavors to provide solutions for all these needs in a systematic manner in order to ensure a successful and rewarding course experience for both instructor and student—technical and curriculum training for instructor readiness with new software releases; the software itself for student use at home for building hands-on skills, assessment, and validation of skill development; and a great set of tools for delivering instruction in the classroom and lab. All are important to the smooth delivery of an interesting course on Microsoft software, and all are provided with the MOAC program. We think about the model below as a gauge for ensuring that we completely support you in your goal of teaching a great course. As you evaluate your instructional materials options, you may wish to use the model for comparison purposes with available products.

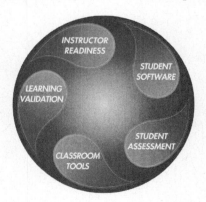

▪ Pedagogical Features

The MOAC textbook for Windows Server 2008 Applications Infrastructure Configuration is designed to cover all the learning objectives for that MCTS exam, which is referred to as its "objective domain." The Microsoft Certified Technology Specialist (MCTS) exam objectives are highlighted throughout the textbook. Many pedagogical features have been developed specifically for *Microsoft Official Academic Course* programs.

Presenting the extensive procedural information and technical concepts woven throughout the textbook raises challenges for the student and instructor alike. The Illustrated Book Tour that follows provides a guide to the rich features contributing to *Microsoft Official Academic Course* program's pedagogical plan. Following is a list of key features in each lesson designed to prepare students for success on the certification exams and in the workplace:

- Each lesson begins with an **Objective Domain Matrix.** More than a standard list of learning objectives, the Domain Matrix correlates each software skill covered in the lesson to the specific MCTS "objective domain."

- Concise and frequent **Step-by-Step** instructions teach students new features and provide an opportunity for hands-on practice. Numbered steps give detailed, step-by-step instructions to help students learn software skills. The steps also show results and screen images to match what students should see on their computer screens.

- **Illustrations:** Screen images provide visual feedback as students work through the exercises. The images reinforce key concepts, provide visual clues about the steps, and allow students to check their progress.

- **Key Terms:** Important technical vocabulary is listed at the beginning of the lesson. When these terms are used later in the lesson, they appear in bold italic type and are defined. The Glossary contains all of the key terms and their definitions.

- Engaging point-of-use **Reader aids,** located throughout the lessons, tell students why this topic is relevant (*The Bottom Line*), provide students with helpful hints (*Take Note*), or show alternate ways to accomplish tasks (*Another Way*). Reader aids also provide additional relevant or background information that adds value to the lesson.

- **Certification Ready?** features throughout the text signal students where a specific certification objective is covered. They provide students with a chance to check their understanding of that particular MCTS objective and, if necessary, review the section of the lesson where it is covered. MOAC offers complete preparation for MCTS certification.

- **Knowledge Assessments** provide three progressively more challenging lesson-ending activities.

▪ Lesson Features

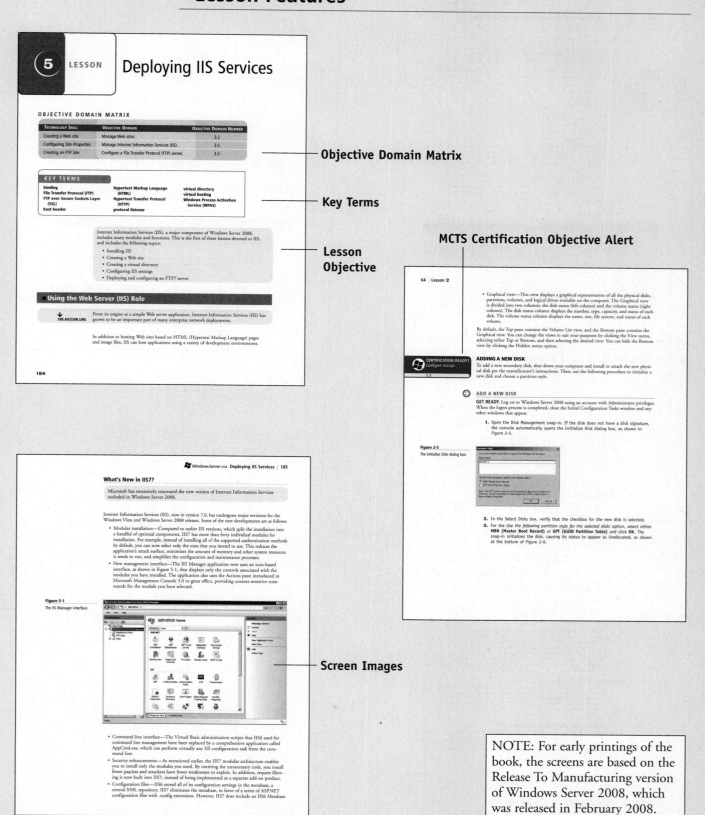

Objective Domain Matrix

Key Terms

Lesson Objective

MCTS Certification Objective Alert

Screen Images

NOTE: For early printings of the book, the screens are based on the Release To Manufacturing version of Windows Server 2008, which was released in February 2008.

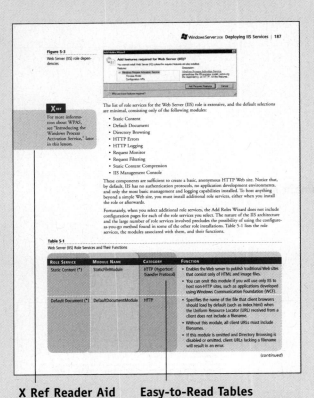

X Ref Reader Aid

Easy-to-Read Tables

The Bottom Line Reader Aid

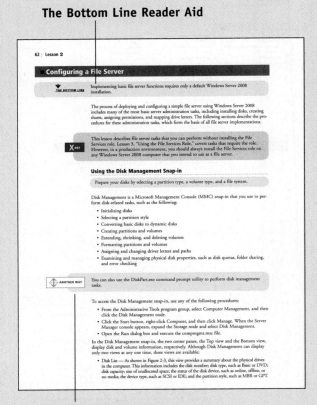

Another Way Reader Aid

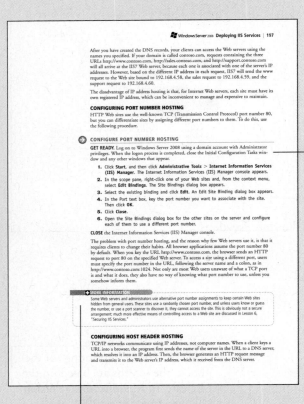

Hands-on Practice

More Information Reader Aid

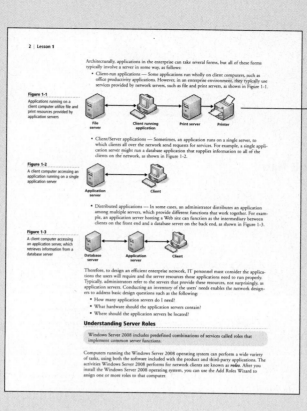

Informative Diagrams

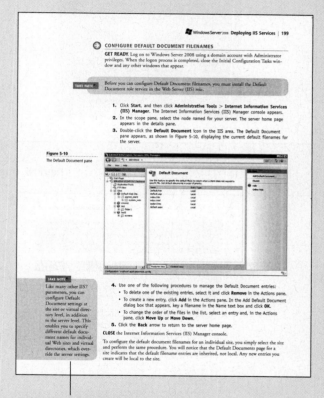

Take Note Reader Aid

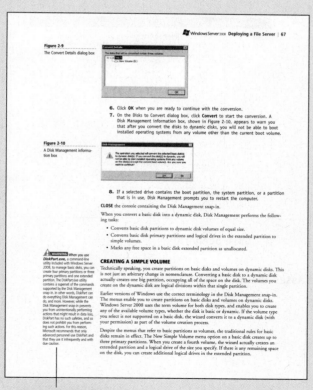

Warning Reader Aid

Summary Skill Matrix

Review Questions

Case Scenarios

Knowledge Assessment Questions

Conventions and Features Used in This Book

This book uses particular fonts, symbols, and heading conventions to highlight important information or to call your attention to special steps. For more information about the features in each lesson, refer to the Illustrated Book Tour section.

CONVENTION	MEANING
NEW FEATURE	This icon indicates a new or greatly improved Windows feature in this version of the software.
↓ THE BOTTOM LINE	This feature provides a brief summary of the material to be covered in the section that follows.
CLOSE	Words in all capital letters and in a different font color than the rest of the text indicate instructions for opening, saving, or closing files or programs. They also point out items you should check or actions you should take.
CERTIFICATION READY?	This feature signals the point in the text where a specific certification objective is covered. It provides you with a chance to check your understanding of that particular MCTS objective and, if necessary, review the section of the lesson where it is covered.
TAKE NOTE	Reader aids appear in shaded boxes found in your text. *Take Note* provides helpful hints related to particular tasks or topics.
ANOTHER WAY	*Another Way* provides an alternative procedure for accomplishing a particular task.
X REF	These notes provide pointers to information discussed elsewhere in the textbook or describe interesting features of Windows Server 2008 that are not directly addressed in the current topic or exercise.
Alt + Tab	A plus sign (+) between two key names means that you must press both keys at the same time. Keys that you are instructed to press in an exercise will appear in the font shown here.
A *shared printer* can be used by many individuals on a network.	Key terms appear in bold italic.
Key **My Name is**.	Any text you are asked to key appears in color.
Click **OK**.	Any button on the screen you are supposed to click on or select will also appear in color.

The *Microsoft Official Academic Course* programs are accompanied by a rich array of resources that incorporate the extensive textbook visuals to form a pedagogically cohesive package. These resources provide all the materials instructors need to deploy and deliver their courses. Resources available online for download include:

- The **MSDN Academic Alliance** is designed to provide the easiest and most inexpensive developer tools, products, and technologies available to faculty and students in labs, classrooms, and on student PCs. A free 3-year membership is available to qualified MOAC adopters.

  Note: Microsoft Windows Server 2008 can be downloaded from MSDN AA for use by students in this course

- The **Instructor's Guide** contains Solutions to all the textbook exercises as well as chapter summaries and lecture notes. The Instructor's Guide and Syllabi for various term lengths are available from the Book Companion site (http://www.wiley.com/college/microsoft) and from *WileyPLUS*.

- The **Test Bank** contains hundreds of questions in multiple-choice, true-false, short answer, and essay formats and is available to download from the Instructor's Book Companion site (http://www.wiley.com/college/microsoft) and from *WileyPLUS*. A complete answer key is provided.

- **PowerPoint Presentations and Images.** A complete set of PowerPoint presentations is available on the Instructor's Book Companion site (http://www.wiley.com/college/micro-soft) and in *WileyPLUS* to enhance classroom presentations. Tailored to the text's topical coverage and Skills Matrix, these presentations are designed to convey key Windows Server concepts addressed in the text.

  All figures from the text are on the Instructor's Book Companion site (http://www.wiley.com/college/microsoft) and in *WileyPLUS*. You can incorporate them into your PowerPoint presentations, or create your own overhead transparencies and handouts.

  By using these visuals in class discussions, you can help focus students' attention on key elements of Windows Server and help them understand how to use it effectively in the workplace.

- When it comes to improving the classroom experience, there is no better source of ideas and inspiration than your fellow colleagues. The Wiley Faculty Network connects teachers with technology, facilitates the exchange of best practices, and helps to enhance instructional efficiency and effectiveness. Faculty Network activities include technology training and tutorials, virtual seminars, peer-to-peer exchanges of experiences and ideas, personal consulting, and sharing of resources. For details visit www.WhereFacultyConnect.com.

WileyPLUS

Broad developments in education over the past decade have influenced the instructional approach taken in the Microsoft Official Academic Course program. The way that students learn, especially about new technologies, has changed dramatically in the Internet era. Electronic learning materials and Internet-based instruction is now as much a part of classroom instruction as printed textbooks. *WileyPLUS* provides the technology to create an environment where students reach their full potential and experience academic success that will last them a lifetime!

WileyPLUS is a powerful and highly-integrated suite of teaching and learning resources designed to bridge the gap between what happens in the classroom and what happens at home and on the job. *WileyPLUS* provides instructors with the resources to teach their students new technologies and guide them to reach their goals of getting ahead in the job market by having the skills to become certified and advance in the workforce. For students, *WileyPLUS* provides the tools for study and practice that are available to them 24/7, wherever and whenever they want to study. *WileyPLUS* includes a complete online version of the student textbook, PowerPoint presentations, homework and practice assignments and quizzes, image galleries, test bank questions, gradebook, and all the instructor resources in one easy-to-use Web site.

Organized around the everyday activities you and your students perform in the class, *WileyPLUS* helps you:

- **Prepare & Present** outstanding class presentations using relevant PowerPoint slides and other *WileyPLUS* materials—and you can easily upload and add your own.
- **Create Assignments** by choosing from questions organized by lesson, level of difficulty, and source—and add your own questions. Students' homework and quizzes are automatically graded, and the results are recorded in your gradebook.
- **Offer context-sensitive help to students, 24/7.** When you assign homework or quizzes, you decide if and when students get access to hints, solutions, or answers where appropriate—or they can be linked to relevant sections of their complete, online text for additional help whenever—and wherever they need it most.
- **Track Student Progress:** Analyze students' results and assess their level of understanding on an individual and class level using the *WileyPLUS* gradebook, or export data to your own personal gradebook.
- **Administer Your Course:** *WileyPLUS* can easily be integrated with another course management system, gradebook, or other resources you are using in your class, providing you with the flexibility to build your course, your way.

Please view our online demo at **www.wiley.com/college/wileyplus**. Here you will find additional information about the features and benefits of *WileyPLUS*, how to request a "test drive" of *WileyPLUS* for this title, and how to adopt it for class use.

MSDN ACADEMIC ALLIANCE—FREE 3-YEAR MEMBERSHIP AVAILABLE TO QUALIFIED ADOPTERS!

The Microsoft Developer Network Academic Alliance (MSDN AA) is designed to provide the easiest and most inexpensive way for universities to make the latest Microsoft developer tools, products, and technologies available in labs, classrooms, and on student PCs. MSDN AA is an annual membership program for departments teaching Science, Technology, Engineering, and Mathematics (STEM) courses. The membership provides a complete solution to keep academic labs, faculty, and students on the leading edge of technology.

Software available in the MSDN AA program is provided at no charge to adopting departments through the Wiley and Microsoft publishing partnership.

As a bonus to this free offer, faculty will be introduced to Microsoft's Faculty Connection and Academic Resource Center. It takes time and preparation to keep students engaged while giving them a fundamental understanding of theory, and the Microsoft Faculty Connection is designed to help STEM professors with this preparation by providing articles, curriculum, and tools that professors can use to engage and inspire today's technology students.

* Contact your Wiley rep for details.

For more information about the MSDN Academic Alliance program, go to:

http://msdn.microsoft.com/academic/

Note: Microsoft Windows Server 2008 can be downloaded from MSDN AA for use by students in this course.

Important Web Addresses and Phone Numbers

To locate the Wiley Higher Education Rep in your area, go to the following Web address and click on the "*Who's My Rep?*" link at the top of the page.

http://www.wiley.com/college

Or Call the MOAC Toll Free Number: 1 + (888) 764-7001 (U.S. & Canada only).

To learn more about becoming a Microsoft Certified Professional and exam availability, visit www.microsoft.com/learning/mcp.

Student Support Program

Book Companion Web Site (www.wiley.com/college/microsoft)

The students' book companion site for the MOAC series includes any resources, exercise files, and Web links that will be used in conjunction with this course.

WileyPLUS

WileyPLUS is a powerful and highly-integrated suite of teaching and learning resources designed to bridge the gap between what happens in the classroom and what happens at home and on the job. For students, *WileyPLUS* provides the tools for study and practice that are available 24/7, wherever and whenever they want to study. *WileyPLUS* includes a complete online version of the student textbook, PowerPoint presentations, homework and practice assignments and quizzes, image galleries, test bank questions, gradebook, and all the instructor resources in one easy-to-use Web site.

WileyPLUS provides immediate feedback on student assignments and a wealth of support materials. This powerful study tool will help your students develop their conceptual understanding of the class material and increase their ability to answer questions.

- A **Study and Practice** area links directly to text content, allowing students to review the text while they study and answer.
- An **Assignment** area keeps all the work you want your students to complete in one location, making it easy for them to stay on task. Students have access to a variety of interactive self-assessment tools, as well as other resources for building their confidence and understanding. In addition, all of the assignments and quizzes contain a link to the relevant section of the multimedia book, providing students with context-sensitive help that allows them to conquer obstacles as they arise.
- A **Personal Gradebook** for each student allows students to view their results from past assignments at any time.

Please view our online demo at www.wiley.com/college/wileyplus. Here you will find additional information about the features and benefits of *WileyPLUS*, how to request a "test drive" of *WileyPLUS* for this title, and how to adopt it for class use.

Wiley Desktop Editions

Wiley MOAC Desktop Editions are innovative, electronic versions of printed textbooks. Students buy the desktop version for 50% off the U.S. price of the printed text, and get the added value of permanence and portability. Wiley Desktop Editions provide students with numerous additional benefits that are not available with other e-text solutions.

Wiley Desktop Editions are NOT subscriptions; students download the Wiley Desktop Edition to their computer desktops. Students own the content they buy to keep for as long as they want. Once a Wiley Desktop Edition is downloaded to the computer desktop, students have instant access to all of the content without being online. Students can also print out the sections they prefer to read in hard copy. Students also have access to fully integrated resources within their Wiley Desktop Edition. From highlighting their e-text to taking and sharing notes, students can easily personalize their Wiley Desktop Edition as they are reading or following along in class.

Preparing to Take the Microsoft Certified Technology Specialist (MCTS) Exam

The Microsoft Certified Technology Specialist (MCTS) certifications enable professionals to target specific technologies and to distinguish themselves by demonstrating in-depth knowledge and expertise in their specialized technologies. Microsoft Certified Technology Specialists are consistently capable of inplementing, building, troubleshooting, and debugging a particular Microsoft Technology.

For organizations, the new generation of Microsoft certifications provides better skills verification tools that help with assessing not only in-demand skills on Windows Server, but also the ability to quickly complete on-the-job tasks. Individuals will find it easier to identify and work towards the certification credential that meets their personal and professional goals.

To learn more about becoming a Microsoft Certified Professional and exam availability, visit www.microsoft.com/learning/mcp.

Microsoft Certifications for IT Professionals

The new Microsoft Certified Technology Specialist (MCTS) and Microsoft Certified IT Professional (MCITP) credentials provide IT professionals with a simpler and more targeted framework to showcase their technical skills in addition to the skills that are required for specific developer job roles.

The Microsoft Certified Database Administrator (MCDBA), Microsoft Certified Desktop Support Technician (MCDST), Microsoft Certified System Administrator (MCSA), and Microsoft Certified Systems Engineer (MCSE) credentials continue to provide IT professionals who use Microsoft SQL Server 2000, Windows XP, and Windows Server 2003 with industry recognition and validation of their IT skills and experience.

Microsoft Certified Technology Specialist

The new Microsoft Certified Tehnology Specialist (MCTS) credential highlights your skills using a specific Microsoft technology. You can demonstrate your abilities as an IT professional or developer with in-depth knowledge of the Microsoft technology that you use today or are planning to deploy.

The MCTS certifications enable professionals to target specific technologies and to distinguish themselves by demonstrating in-depth knowledge and expertise in their specialized technologies. Microsoft Certified Technology Specialists are consistently capable of implementing, building, troubleshooting, and debugging a particular Microsoft technology.

You can learn more about the MCTS program at www.microsoft.com/learning/mcp/mcts.

Microsoft Certified IT Professional

The new Microsoft Certified IT Professional (MCITP) credential lets you highlight your specific area of expertise. Now, you can easily distinguish yourself as an expert in database administration, database development, business intelligence, or support.

By becoming certified, you demonstrate to employers that you have achieved a predictable level of skill not only in the use of the Windows Server operating system, but with a comprehensive set of Microsoft technologies. Employers often require certification either as a condition of employment or as a condition of advancement within the company or other organization.

You can learn more about the MCITP program at www.microsoft.com/learning/mcp/mcitp.

The certification examinations are sponsored by Microsoft but administered through Microsoft's exam delivery partner Prometric.

Preparing to Take an Exam

Unless you are a very experienced user, you will need to use a test preparation course to prepare to complete the test correctly and within the time allowed. The *Microsoft Official Academic Course* series is designed to prepare you with a strong knowledge of all exam topics, and with some additional review and practice on your own, you should feel confident in your ability to pass the appropriate exam.

After you decide which exam to take, review the list of objectives for the exam. You can easily identify tasks that are included in the objective list by locating the Objective Domain Matrix at the start of each lesson and the Certification Ready sidebars in the margin of the lessons in this book.

To take the MCTS test, visit www.microsoft.com/learning/mcp/mcts to locate your nearest testing center. Then call the testing center directly to schedule your test. The amount of advance notice you should provide will vary for different testing centers, and it typically depends on the number of computers available at the testing center, the number of other testers who have already been scheduled for the day on which you want to take the test, and the number of times per week that the testing center offers MCTS testing. In general, you should call to schedule your test at least two weeks prior to the date on which you want to take the test.

When you arrive at the testing center, you might be asked for proof of identity. A driver's license or passport is an acceptable form of identification. If you do not have either of these items of documentation, call your testing center and ask what alternative forms of identification will be accepted. If you are retaking a test, bring your MCTS identification number, which will have been given to you when you previously took the test. If you have not prepaid or if your organization has not already arranged to make payment for you, you will need to pay the test-taking fee when you arrive.

About the Author

Craig Zacker is a writer, editor, and networker whose computing experience began in the days of teletypes and paper tape. After making the move from minicomputers to PCs, he worked as an administrator of Novell NetWare networks and as a PC support technician while operating a freelance desktop publishing business. After earning a Master's Degree in English and American Literature from New York University, Craig worked extensively on integrating Microsoft Windows operating systems into existing internetworks, supported fleets of Windows workstations, and was employed as a technical writer, content provider, and webmaster for the online services group of a large software company. Since devoting himself to writing and editing full-time, Craig has authored or contributed to dozens of books on networking topics, operating systems, and PC hardware, including *Microsoft Official Academic Course: Windows Vista Configuration Exam 70-620* and *Windows XP Pro: The Missing Manual.* He developed educational texts for college courses, designed online training courses for the Web, and published articles with top industry publications.

Acknowledgments

MOAC Instructor Advisory Board

We would like to thank our Instructor Advisory Board, an elite group of educators who has assisted us every step of the way in building these products. Advisory Board members have acted as our sounding board on key pedagogical and design decisions leading to the development of these compelling and innovative textbooks for future Information Workers. Their dedication to technology education is truly appreciated.

Charles DeSassure, Tarrant County College

Charles DeSassure is Department Chair and Instructor of Computer Science & Information Technology at Tarrant County College Southeast Campus, Arlington, Texas. He has had experience as a MIS Manager, system analyst, field technology analyst, LAN Administrator, microcomputer specialist, and public school teacher in South Carolina. DeSassure has worked in higher education for more than ten years and received the Excellence Award in Teaching from the National Institute for Staff and Organizational Development (NISOD). He currently serves on the Educational Testing Service (ETS) iSkills National Advisory Committee and chaired the Tarrant County College District Student Assessment Committee. He has written proposals and makes presentations at major educational conferences nationwide. DeSassure has served as a textbook reviewer for John Wiley & Sons and Prentice Hall. He teaches courses in information security, networking, distance learning, and computer literacy. DeSassure holds a master's degree in Computer Resources & Information Management from Webster University.

Kim Ehlert, Waukesha County Technical College

Kim Ehlert is the Microsoft Program Coordinator and a Network Specialist instructor at Waukesha County Technical College, teaching the full range of MCSE and networking courses for the past nine years. Prior to joining WCTC, Kim was a professor at the Milwaukee School of Engineering for five years where she oversaw the Novell Academic Education and the Microsoft IT Academy programs. She has a wide variety of industry experience including network design and management for Johnson Controls, local city fire departments, police departments, large church congregations, health departments, and accounting firms. Kim holds many industry certifications including MCDST, MCSE, Security+, Network+, Server+, MCT, and CNE.

Kim has a bachelor's degree in Information Systems and a master's degree in Business Administration from the University of Wisconsin Milwaukee. When she is not busy teaching, she enjoys spending time with her husband Gregg and their two children—Alex, 14, and Courtney, 17.

Penny Gudgeon, Corinthian Colleges, Inc.

Penny Gudgeon is the Program Manager for IT curriculum at Corinthian Colleges, Inc. Previously, she was responsible for computer programming and web curriculum for twenty-seven campuses in Corinthian's Canadian division, CDI College of Business, Technology and Health Care. Penny joined CDI College in 1997 as a computer programming instructor at one of the campuses outside of Toronto. Prior to joining CDI College, Penny taught productivity software at another Canadian college, the Academy of Learning, for four years. Penny has experience in helping students achieve their goals through various learning models from instructor-led to self-directed to online.

Before embarking on a career in education, Penny worked in the fields of advertising, marketing/sales, mechanical and electronic engineering technology, and computer programming. When not working from her home office or indulging her passion for lifelong learning, Penny likes to read mysteries, garden, and relax at home in Hamilton, Ontario, with her Shih-Tzu, Gracie.

Margaret Leary, Northern Virginia Community College

Margaret Leary is Professor of IST at Northern Virginia Community College, teaching Networking and Network Security Courses for the past ten years. She is the co-Principal Investigator on the CyberWATCH initiative, an NSF-funded regional consortium of higher education institutions and businesses working together to increase the number of network security personnel in the workforce. She also serves as a Senior Security Policy Manager and Research Analyst at Nortel Government Solutions and holds a CISSP certification.

Margaret holds a B.S.B.A. and MBA/Technology Management from the University of Phoenix, and is pursuing her Ph.D. in Organization and Management with an IT Specialization at Capella University. Her dissertation is titled "Quantifying the Discoverability of Identity Attributes in Internet-Based Public Records: Impact on Identity Theft and Knowledge-based Authentication." She has several other published articles in various government and industry magazines, notably on identity management and network security.

Wen Liu, ITT Educational Services, Inc.

Wen Liu is Director of Corporate Curriculum Development at ITT Educational Services, Inc. He joined the ITT corporate headquarters in 1998 as a Senior Network Analyst to plan and deploy the corporate WAN infrastructure. A year later he assumed the position of Corporate Curriculum Manager supervising the curriculum development of all IT programs. After he was promoted to the current position three years ago, he continued to manage the curriculum research and development for all the programs offered in the School of Information Technology in addition to supervising the curriculum development in other areas (such as Schools of Drafting and Design and Schools of Electronics Technology). Prior to his employment with ITT Educational Services, Liu was a Telecommunications Analyst at the state government of Indiana working on the state backbone project that provided Internet and telecommunications services to the public users such as K-12 and higher education institutions, government agencies, libraries, and healthcare facilities.

Wen Liu has an M.A. in Student Personnel Administration in Higher Education and an M.S. in Information and Communications Sciences from Ball State University, Indiana. He used to be the director of special projects on the board of directors of the Indiana Telecommunications User Association, and used to serve on Course Technology's IT Advisory Board. He is currently a member of the IEEE and its Computer Society.

Jared Spencer, Westwood College Online

Jared Spencer has been the Lead Faculty for Networking at Westwood College Online since 2006. He began teaching in 2001 and has taught both on-ground and online for a variety of institutions, including Robert Morris University and Point Park University. In addition to his academic background, he has more than fifteen years of industry experience working for companies including the Thomson Corporation and IBM.

Jared has a master's degree in Internet Information Systems and is currently ABD and pursuing his doctorate in Information Systems at Nova Southeastern University. He has authored several papers that have been presented at conferences and appeared in publications such as the Journal of Internet Commerce and the Journal of Information Privacy and Security (JIPC). He holds a number of industry certifications, including AIX (UNIX), A+, Network+, Security+, MCSA on Windows 2000, and MCSA on Windows 2003 Server.

MOAC Windows Server Reviewers

We also thank the many reviewers who pored over the manuscript, providing invaluable feedback in the service of quality instructional materials.

Windows Server® 2008 Applications Infrastructure Configuration Exam 70-643

Chris Aburime, Inver Hills Community College

Ron Handlon, Remington College — Tampa

Steve Strom, Butler Community College

Bonnie Willy, Ivy Tech

Focus Group and Survey Participants

Finally, we thank the hundreds of instructors who participated in our focus groups and surveys to ensure that the Microsoft Official Academic Courses best met the needs of our customers.

Jean Aguilar, Mt. Hood Community College

Konrad Akens, Zane State College

Michael Albers, University of Memphis

Diana Anderson, Big Sandy Community & Technical College

Phyllis Anderson, Delaware County Community College

Judith Andrews, Feather River College

Damon Antos, American River College

Bridget Archer, Oakton Community College

Linda Arnold, Harrisburg Area Community College–Lebanon Campus

Neha Arya, Fullerton College

Mohammad Bajwa, Katharine Gibbs School–New York

Virginia Baker, University of Alaska Fairbanks

Carla Bannick, Pima Community College

Rita Barkley, Northeast Alabama Community College

Elsa Barr, Central Community College–Hastings

Ronald W. Barry, Ventura County Community College District

Elizabeth Bastedo, Central Carolina Technical College

Karen Baston, Waubonsee Community College

Karen Bean, Blinn College

Scott Beckstrand, Community College of Southern Nevada

Paulette Bell, Santa Rosa Junior College

Liz Bennett, Southeast Technical Institute

Nancy Bermea, Olympic College

Lucy Betz, Milwaukee Area Technical College

Meral Binbasioglu, Hofstra University

Catherine Binder, Strayer University & Katharine Gibbs School–Philadelphia

Terrel Blair, El Centro College

Ruth Blalock, Alamance Community College

Beverly Bohner, Reading Area Community College

Henry Bojack, Farmingdale State University

Matthew Bowie, Luna Community College

Julie Boyles, Portland Community College

Karen Brandt, College of the Albemarle

Stephen Brown, College of San Mateo

Jared Bruckner, Southern Adventist University

Pam Brune, Chattanooga State Technical Community College

Sue Buchholz, Georgia Perimeter College

Roberta Buczyna, Edison College

Angela Butler, Mississippi Gulf Coast Community College

Rebecca Byrd, Augusta Technical College

Kristen Callahan, Mercer County Community College

Judy Cameron, Spokane Community College

Dianne Campbell, Athens Technical College

Gena Casas, Florida Community College at Jacksonville

Jesus Castrejon, Latin Technologies

Gail Chambers, Southwest Tennessee Community College

Jacques Chansavang, Indiana University–Purdue University Fort Wayne

Nancy Chapko, Milwaukee Area Technical College

Rebecca Chavez, Yavapai College

Sanjiv Chopra, Thomas Nelson Community College

Greg Clements, Midland Lutheran College

Dayna Coker, Southwestern Oklahoma State University–Sayre Campus

Tamra Collins, Otero Junior College

Janet Conrey, Gavilan Community College

Carol Cornforth, West Virginia Northern Community College

Gary Cotton, American River College

Edie Cox, Chattahoochee Technical College

Rollie Cox, Madison Area Technical College

David Crawford, Northwestern Michigan College

J.K. Crowley, Victor Valley College

Rosalyn Culver, Washtenaw Community College

Sharon Custer, Huntington University

Sandra Daniels, New River Community College

Anila Das, Cedar Valley College

Brad Davis, Santa Rosa Junior College

Susan Davis, Green River Community College

Mark Dawdy, Lincoln Land Community College

Jennifer Day, Sinclair Community College

Carol Deane, Eastern Idaho Technical College

Julie DeBuhr, Lewis-Clark State College

Janis DeHaven, Central Community College

Drew Dekreon, University of Alaska–Anchorage

Joy DePover, Central Lakes College

Salli DiBartolo, Brevard Community College

Melissa Diegnau, Riverland Community College

Al Dillard, Lansdale School of Business

Marjorie Duffy, Cosumnes River College

Sarah Dunn, Southwest Tennessee Community College

Shahla Durany, Tarrant County College– South Campus

Kay Durden, University of Tennessee at Martin

Dineen Ebert, St. Louis Community College–Meramec

Donna Ehrhart, State University of New York–Brockport

Larry Elias, Montgomery County Community College

Glenda Elser, New Mexico State University at Alamogordo

Angela Evangelinos, Monroe County Community College

Angie Evans, Ivy Tech Community College of Indiana

Linda Farrington, Indian Hills Community College

Dana Fladhammer, Phoenix College

Richard Flores, Citrus College

Connie Fox, Community and Technical College at Institute of Technology West Virginia University

Wanda Freeman, Okefenokee Technical College

Brenda Freeman, Augusta Technical College

Susan Fry, Boise State University

Roger Fulk, Wright State University–Lake Campus

Sue Furnas, Collin County Community College District

Sandy Gabel, Vernon College

Laura Galvan, Fayetteville Technical Community College

Candace Garrod, Red Rocks Community College

Sherrie Geitgey, Northwest State Community College

Chris Gerig, Chattahoochee Technical College

Barb Gillespie, Cuyamaca College

Jessica Gilmore, Highline Community College

Pamela Gilmore, Reedley College

Debbie Glinert, Queensborough Community College

Steven Goldman, Polk Community College

Bettie Goodman, C.S. Mott Community College

Mike Grabill, Katharine Gibbs School– Philadelphia

Francis Green, Penn State University

Walter Griffin, Blinn College

Fillmore Guinn, Odessa College

Helen Haasch, Milwaukee Area Technical College

John Habal, Ventura College

Joy Haerens, Chaffey College

Norman Hahn, Thomas Nelson Community College

Kathy Hall, Alamance Community College

Teri Harbacheck, Boise State University

Linda Harper, Richland Community College

Maureen Harper, Indian Hills Community College

Steve Harris, Katharine Gibbs School–New York

Robyn Hart, Fresno City College

Darien Hartman, Boise State University

Gina Hatcher, Tacoma Community College

Winona T. Hatcher, Aiken Technical College

BJ Hathaway, Northeast Wisconsin Tech College

Cynthia Hauki, West Hills College – Coalinga

Mary L. Haynes, Wayne County Community College

Marcie Hawkins, Zane State College

Steve Hebrock, Ohio State University Agricultural Technical Institute

Sue Heistand, Iowa Central Community College

Heith Hennel, Valencia Community College

Donna Hendricks, South Arkansas Community College

Judy Hendrix, Dyersburg State Community College

Gloria Hensel, Matanuska-Susitna College University of Alaska Anchorage

Gwendolyn Hester, Richland College

Tammarra Holmes, Laramie County Community College

Dee Hobson, Richland College

Keith Hoell, Katharine Gibbs School–New York

Pashia Hogan, Northeast State Technical Community College

Susan Hoggard, Tulsa Community College

Kathleen Holliman, Wallace Community College Selma

Chastity Honchul, Brown Mackie College/ Wright State University

Christie Hovey, Lincoln Land Community College

Peggy Hughes, Allegany College of Maryland

Sandra Hume, Chippewa Valley Technical College

John Hutson, Aims Community College

Celia Ing, Sacramento City College

Joan Ivey, Lanier Technical College

Barbara Jaffari, College of the Redwoods

Penny Jakes, University of Montana College of Technology

Eduardo Jaramillo, Peninsula College

Barbara Jauken, Southeast Community College

Susan Jennings, Stephen F. Austin State University

Leslie Jernberg, Eastern Idaho Technical College

Linda Johns, Georgia Perimeter College

Brent Johnson, Okefenokee Technical College

Mary Johnson, Mt. San Antonio College

Shirley Johnson, Trinidad State Junior College–Valley Campus

Sandra M. Jolley, Tarrant County College

Teresa Jolly, South Georgia Technical College

Dr. Deborah Jones, South Georgia Technical College

Margie Jones, Central Virginia Community College

Randall Jones, Marshall Community and Technical College

Diane Karlsbraaten, Lake Region State College

Teresa Keller, Ivy Tech Community College of Indiana

Charles Kemnitz, Pennsylvania College of Technology

Sandra Kinghorn, Ventura College

Bill Klein, Katharine Gibbs School–Philadelphia

Bea Knaapen, Fresno City College

Kit Kofoed, Western Wyoming Community College

Maria Kolatis, County College of Morris

Barry Kolb, Ocean County College

Karen Kuralt, University of Arkansas at Little Rock

Belva-Carole Lamb, Rogue Community College

Betty Lambert, Des Moines Area Community College

Anita Lande, Cabrillo College

Junnae Landry, Pratt Community College

Karen Lankisch, UC Clermont

David Lanzilla, Central Florida Community College

Nora Laredo, Cerritos Community College

Jennifer Larrabee, Chippewa Valley Technical College

Debra Larson, Idaho State University

Barb Lave, Portland Community College

Audrey Lawrence, Tidewater Community College

Deborah Layton, Eastern Oklahoma State College

Larry LeBlanc, Owen Graduate School– Vanderbilt University

Philip Lee, Nashville State Community College

Michael Lehrfeld, Brevard Community College

Vasant Limaye, Southwest Collegiate Institute for the Deaf – Howard College

Anne C. Lewis, Edgecombe Community College

Stephen Linkin, Houston Community College

Peggy Linston, Athens Technical College

Hugh Lofton, Moultrie Technical College

Donna Lohn, Lakeland Community College

Jackie Lou, Lake Tahoe Community College

Donna Love, Gaston College

Curt Lynch, Ozarks Technical Community College

Sheilah Lynn, Florida Community College– Jacksonville

Pat R. Lyon, Tomball College

Bill Madden, Bergen Community College

Heather Madden, Delaware Technical & Community College

Donna Madsen, Kirkwood Community College

Jane Maringer-Cantu, Gavilan College

Suzanne Marks, Bellevue Community College

Carol Martin, Louisiana State University– Alexandria

Cheryl Martucci, Diablo Valley College

Roberta Marvel, Eastern Wyoming College

Tom Mason, Brookdale Community College

Mindy Mass, Santa Barbara City College

Dixie Massaro, Irvine Valley College

Rebekah May, Ashland Community & Technical College

Emma Mays-Reynolds, Dyersburg State Community College

Timothy Mayes, Metropolitan State College of Denver

Reggie McCarthy, Central Lakes College

Matt McCaskill, Brevard Community College

Kevin McFarlane, Front Range Community College

Donna McGill, Yuba Community College

Terri McKeever, Ozarks Technical Community College

Patricia McMahon, South Suburban College

Sally McMillin, Katharine Gibbs School–Philadelphia

Charles McNerney, Bergen Community College

Lisa Mears, Palm Beach Community College

Imran Mehmood, ITT Technical Institute–King of Prussia Campus

Virginia Melvin, Southwest Tennessee Community College

Jeanne Mercer, Texas State Technical College

Denise Merrell, Jefferson Community & Technical College

Catherine Merrikin, Pearl River Community College

Diane D. Mickey, Northern Virginia Community College

Darrelyn Miller, Grays Harbor College

Sue Mitchell, Calhoun Community College

Jacquie Moldenhauer, Front Range Community College

Linda Motonaga, Los Angeles City College

Sam Mryyan, Allen County Community College

Cindy Murphy, Southeastern Community College

Ryan Murphy, Sinclair Community College

Sharon E. Nastav, Johnson County Community College

Christine Naylor, Kent State University Ashtabula

Haji Nazarian, Seattle Central Community College

Nancy Noe, Linn-Benton Community College

Jennie Noriega, San Joaquin Delta College

Linda Nutter, Peninsula College

Thomas Omerza, Middle Bucks Institute of Technology

Edith Orozco, St. Philip's College

Dona Orr, Boise State University

Joanne Osgood, Chaffey College

Janice Owens, Kishwaukee College

Tatyana Pashnyak, Bainbridge College

John Partacz, College of DuPage

Tim Paul, Montana State University–Great Falls

Joseph Perez, South Texas College

Mike Peterson, Chemeketa Community College

Dr. Karen R. Petitto, West Virginia Wesleyan College

Terry Pierce, Onandaga Community College

Ashlee Pieris, Raritan Valley Community College

Jamie Pinchot, Thiel College

Michelle Poertner, Northwestern Michigan College

Betty Posta, University of Toledo

Deborah Powell, West Central Technical College

Mark Pranger, Rogers State University

Carolyn Rainey, Southeast Missouri State University

Linda Raskovich, Hibbing Community College

Leslie Ratliff, Griffin Technical College

Mar-Sue Ratzke, Rio Hondo Community College

Roxy Reissen, Southeastern Community College

Silvio Reyes, Technical Career Institutes

Patricia Rishavy, Anoka Technical College

Jean Robbins, Southeast Technical Institute

Carol Roberts, Eastern Maine Community College and University of Maine

Teresa Roberts, Wilson Technical Community College

Vicki Robertson, Southwest Tennessee Community College

Betty Rogge, Ohio State Agricultural Technical Institute

Lynne Rusley, Missouri Southern State University

Claude Russo, Brevard Community College

Ginger Sabine, Northwestern Technical College

Steven Sachs, Los Angeles Valley College

Joanne Salas, Olympic College

Lloyd Sandmann, Pima Community College–Desert Vista Campus

Beverly Santillo, Georgia Perimeter College

Theresa Savarese, San Diego City College

Sharolyn Sayers, Milwaukee Area Technical College

Judith Scheeren, Westmoreland County Community College

Adolph Scheiwe, Joliet Junior College

Marilyn Schmid, Asheville-Buncombe Technical Community College

Janet Sebesy, Cuyahoga Community College

Phyllis T. Shafer, Brookdale Community College

Ralph Shafer, Truckee Meadows Community College

Anne Marie Shanley, County College of Morris

Shelia Shelton, Surry Community College

Merilyn Shepherd, Danville Area Community College

Susan Sinele, Aims Community College

Beth Sindt, Hawkeye Community College

Andrew Smith, Marian College

Brenda Smith, Southwest Tennessee Community College

Lynne Smith, State University of New York–Delhi

Rob Smith, Katharine Gibbs School–Philadelphia

Tonya Smith, Arkansas State University–Mountain Home

Del Spencer – Trinity Valley Community College

Jeri Spinner, Idaho State University

Eric Stadnik, Santa Rosa Junior College

Karen Stanton, Los Medanos College

Meg Stoner, Santa Rosa Junior College

Beverly Stowers, Ivy Tech Community College of Indiana

Marcia Stranix, Yuba College

Kim Styles, Tri-County Technical College

Sylvia Summers, Tacoma Community College

Beverly Swann, Delaware Technical & Community College

Ann Taff, Tulsa Community College

Mike Theiss, University of Wisconsin–Marathon Campus

Romy Thiele, Cañada College

Sharron Thompson, Portland Community College

Ingrid Thompson-Sellers, Georgia Perimeter College

Barbara Tietsort, University of Cincinnati–Raymond Walters College

Janine Tiffany, Reading Area Community College

Denise Tillery, University of Nevada Las Vegas

Susan Trebelhorn, Normandale Community College

Noel Trout, Santiago Canyon College

Cheryl Turgeon, Asnuntuck Community College

Steve Turner, Ventura College

Sylvia Unwin, Bellevue Community College

Lilly Vigil, Colorado Mountain College

Sabrina Vincent, College of the Mainland

Mary Vitrano, Palm Beach Community College

Brad Vogt, Northeast Community College

Cozell Wagner, Southeastern Community College

Carolyn Walker, Tri-County Technical College

Sherry Walker, Tulsa Community College

Qi Wang, Tacoma Community College

Betty Wanielista, Valencia Community College

Marge Warber, Lanier Technical College–Forsyth Campus

Marjorie Webster, Bergen Community College

Linda Wenn, Central Community College

Mark Westlund, Olympic College

Carolyn Whited, Roane State Community College

Winona Whited, Richland College

Jerry Wilkerson, Scott Community College

Joel Willenbring, Fullerton College

Barbara Williams, WITC Superior

Charlotte Williams, Jones County Junior College

Bonnie Willy, Ivy Tech Community College of Indiana

Diane Wilson, J. Sargeant Reynolds Community College

James Wolfe, Metropolitan Community College

Marjory Wooten, Lanier Technical College

Mark Yanko, Hocking College

Alexis Yusov, Pace University

Naeem Zaman, San Joaquin Delta College

Kathleen Zimmerman, Des Moines Area Community College

We also thank Lutz Ziob, Jim DiIanni, Merrick Van Dongen, Jim LeValley, Bruce Curling, Joe Wilson, Rob Linsky, Jim Clark, and Scott Serna at Microsoft for their encouragement and support in making the Microsoft Official Academic Course programs the finest instructional materials for mastering the newest Microsoft technologies for both students and instructors.

Brief Contents

Contents

Lesson 11: Using Network Application Services 384

Lesson 12: Using High Availability Technologies 432

Deploying an Application Server

OBJECTIVE DOMAIN MATRIX

TECHNOLOGY SKILL	OBJECTIVE DOMAIN	OBJECTIVE DOMAIN NUMBER
Installing Windows Deployment Services	Deploy images by using Windows Deployment Services.	1.1
Activating Windows	Configure Microsoft Windows activation.	1.2

KEY TERMS

application
application services
client machine ID (CMID)
directory services
feature
infrastructure services
Key Management Service (KMS)

KMS activation threshold
MAK Independent Activation
MAK Proxy Activation
Multiple Activation Key (MAK)
preboot execution environment (PXE)
role
ServerManagerCmd.exe

thin client
virtual server
Windows Deployment Services (WDS)
Windows PE (Preinstallation Environment) 2.1

■ Introducing Windows Server 2008 Application Services

THE BOTTOM LINE

Windows Server 2008 includes support services that enable administrators to deploy applications in several different ways.

Two basic types of computers can be on an enterprise network: clients and servers. In computer networking, a server is, by definition, a system that responds to requests for resources originating from clients on the same network. The resources provided by a server can take many forms, including information, document files, Web pages, and security services.

Designing an enterprise network is a complex undertaking that must consider many factors, not all of them technical. Certainly, technical elements such as hardware platforms and operating systems are important, but the designers of a large network also have to consider other elements, including management, political, and economic factors.

One of the primary considerations in the enterprise network design process is what the users of the network need to do with their computers. After all, companies supply their employees with computers so that they can get work done, and to accomplish this goal, the users need computer programs designed to aid them in the performance of specific tasks. These programs are also known as *applications*.

Architecturally, applications in the enterprise can take several forms, but all of these forms typically involve a server in some way, as follows:

- Client-run applications — Some applications run wholly on client computers, such as office productivity applications. However, in an enterprise environment, they typically use services provided by network servers, such as file and print servers, as shown in Figure 1-1.

Figure 1-1

Applications running on a client computer utilize file and print resources provided by application servers

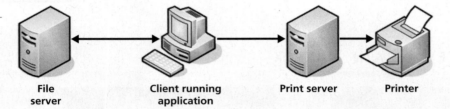

File
server

Client running
application

Print server

Printer

- Client/Server applications — Sometimes, an application runs on a single server, to which clients all over the network send requests for services. For example, a single application server might run a database application that supplies information to all of the clients on the network, as shown in Figure 1-2.

Figure 1-2

A client computer accessing an application running on a single application server

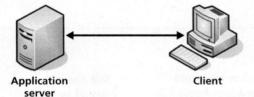

Application
server

Client

- Distributed applications — In some cases, an administrator distributes an application among multiple servers, which provide different functions that work together. For example, an application server hosting a Web site can function as the intermediary between clients on the front end and a database server on the back end, as shown in Figure 1-3.

Figure 1-3

A client computer accessing an application server, which retrieves information from a database server

Database
server

Application
server

Client

Therefore, to design an efficient enterprise network, IT personnel must consider the applications the users will require and the server resources those applications need to run properly. Typically, administrators refer to the servers that provide these resources, not surprisingly, as application servers. Conducting an inventory of the users' needs enables the network designers to address basic design questions such as the following:

- How many application servers do I need?
- What hardware should the application servers contain?
- Where should the application servers be located?

Understanding Server Roles

Windows Server 2008 includes predefined combinations of services called roles that implement common server functions.

Computers running the Windows Server 2008 operating system can perform a wide variety of tasks, using both the software included with the product and third-party applications. The activities Windows Server 2008 performs for network clients are known as *roles*. After you install the Windows Server 2008 operating system, you can use the Add Roles Wizard to assign one or more roles to that computer.

The roles provided by the Add Roles Wizard fall into three basic categories, as follows:

- *Directory services* — Store, organize, and supply information about a network and its resources.
- *Infrastructure services* — Provide support services for network clients.
- *Application services* — Provide communications services, operating environments, or programming interfaces for specific applications.

> **TAKE NOTE***
>
> The Add Roles Wizard and the Add Features Wizard are accessible from the Initial Configuration Tasks window or the Server Manager application. You can also install and remove roles and features from the command line, using the ServerManagerCmd.exe utility.

Table 1-1 lists the specific roles that Microsoft has supplied with Windows Server 2008. This book is devoted to the roles providing the Windows Server 2008 application services, but the directory and infrastructure services also play a part in providing network clients with access to the applications they need.

Table 1-1

Windows Server 2008 Server Roles

DIRECTORY SERVICES	INFRASTRUCTURE SERVICES	APPLICATION SERVICES
Active Directory Certificate Services — Implements certification authorities (CAs) and other services that facilitate the creation and management of the public key certificates employed by the identity and access control elements of the Windows Server 2008 security infrastructure.	DHCP (Dynamic Host Configuration Protocol) Server — Provides network clients with dynamically-assigned IP addresses and other TCP/IP configuration settings, such as subnet masks, default gateway addresses, DNS (Domain Name system) server addresses, and WINS (Windows Internet Naming System) server addresses.	Application Server — Provides an integrated environment for deploying and running server-based business applications designed within (or expressly for) the organization, such as those requiring the services provided by Internet Information Services (IIS), Microsoft.NET Framework 2.0 and 3.0, COM+, ASP.NET, Message Queuing, or Windows Communication Foundation (WCF).
Active Directory Domain Services — Configures the server to function as an Active Directory domain controller, which stores and manages a distributed database of network resources and application-specific information.	DNS Server — Provides name-to-address and address-to-name resolution services for Active Directory and Internet clients. The Windows Server 2008 DNS server implementation also supports dynamic DNS and DHCP integration.	Fax Server — Enables administrators to manage fax devices and clients to send and receive faxes over the network.
Active Directory Federation Services — Creates a single sign-on environment by implementing trust relationships that enable users on one network to access applications on other networks without providing a secondary set of logon credentials.	Network Policy and Access Services (NPAS) — Implements services such as Routing and Remote Access (RRAS), Network Policy Server (NPS), Health Registration Authority (HRA), and Host Credential Authorization Protocol (HCAP), which provide network connectivity and secure network access to local and remote users.	File Services — Installs tools and services that enhance Windows Server 2008's basic ability to provide network clients with access to files stored on server drives, including Distributed File System (DFS), DFS Replication, Storage Manager for Storage Area Networks (SANs), fast file searching, and file services for UNIX clients.

(continued)

Table 1-1 (*continued*)

DIRECTORY SERVICES	INFRASTRUCTURE SERVICES	APPLICATION SERVICES
Active Directory Lightweight Directory Services — Implements a Lightweight Directory Access Protocol (LDAP) directory service that provides support for directory-enabled applications without incurring the extensive overhead of Active Directory Domain Services.	Windows Deployment Services (WDS) — Enables administrators to remotely install Windows operating systems on computers throughout the enterprise.	Print Services — Provides clients with access to printers attached to the server or to the network, as well as centralized network printer and print server management, and printer deployment using Group Policy.
Active Directory Rights Management Services (AD RMS) — Client/server system that uses certificates and licensing to implement persistent usage policies, which can control access to information, no matter where a user moves it.		Streaming Media Services — Enables the server to transmit digital media content to network clients in real time. (This role is not included with Windows Server 2008, but it is available as a free download from Microsoft's Web site.)
		Terminal Services — Enables clients on the network or on the Internet to remotely access server-based applications or the entire Windows desktop, using server resources.
		UDDI Services — Implements Universal Description, Discovery, and Integration (UDDI), which enables the organization to publish information about its Web services for use by intranet, extranet, and/or Internet clients.
		Web Server (IIS) — Installs Internet Information Services (IIS) 7.0, which enables the organization to publish Web sites and ASP.NET, WCF, or Windows SharePoint-based applications for use by intranet, extranet, and/or Internet clients.

Understanding Server Features

Windows Server 2008 includes a large collection of individual modules called *features,* which you can install in any combination.

In addition to its roles, Windows Server 2008 includes a collection of features, which you can select individually. You can also augment a given role by adding features that increase its capabilities.

The features that are installable using the Add Features Wizard are as follows:

- .NET Framework 3.0 — A software package containing code that provides solutions to a large number of common programming requirements, including user interface, database access, cryptographic security, and network communications routines. Software developers can utilize these routines, with their own code, to build Windows applications more easily.
- BitLocker Drive Encryption — Encrypts entire hard disk volumes, allowing access to the volumes only after validating the integrity of the computer's boot components and confirming that no one has moved the drive to another computer.

- BITS Server Extensions — The Background Intelligent Transfer Service (BITS) enables client computers to transmit and receive files without utilizing resources needed by other processes. These server extensions enable the Windows Server 2008 computer to receive files uploaded by BITS clients.
- Connection Manager Administration Kit (CMAK) — Enables administrators to create customized service profiles for the Connection Manager client dialer application.
- Desktop Experience — Implements a collection of Windows Vista features on the Windows Server 2008 computer, including Windows Media Player and desktop themes.
- Failover Clustering — Enables multiple servers to work together at performing the same tasks, to provide high availability for applications and services.
- Group Policy Management — Installs the Group Policy Management Console, a Microsoft Management Console snap-in that simplifies the process of deploying, managing, and troubleshooting Group Policy Objects (GPOs).
- Internet Printing Client — Enables users to send print jobs to remote Web server-based printers, using an Internet connection.
- Internet Storage Name Server (iSNS) — Provides discovery services for clients accessing storage area networks running the Internet Small Computer System Interface (iSCSI), including registration, deregistration, and queries.
- LPR (Line Printer Remote) Port Monitor — Enables the computer to send print jobs to a UNIX computer with a compatible line printer daemon (LPD) implementation running on it.
- Message Queuing — Provides a variety of messaging services that enable applications to communicate, even when they run on different operating systems, use different types of networks, run at different times, or are temporarily offline.
- Multipath I/O (MPIO) — Provides multiple data paths to a single server storage device.
- Network Load Balancing (NLB) — Distributes incoming client traffic evenly among servers running the same application, enabling administrators to scale the application up or down by adding or removing servers as needed.
- Peer Name Resolution Protocol (PNRP) — A name resolution service that enables computers to register their peer names and associate them with their IPv6 addresses. Other computers on the network can then use the service to resolve a name into an address, enabling them to establish a connection to the named computer.
- Quality Windows Audio Video Experience (qWave) — Provides flow control and traffic prioritization services for applications that stream audio and video content over a network.
- Remote Assistance — Enables one user to provide technical support or training to another user at a remote computer by observing the remote user's desktop or by taking control of it.
- Remote Differential Compression (RDC) — Enables applications to conserve network bandwidth by determining what parts of a file have changed and transmitting only the modifications over the network.
- Remote Server Administration Tools — Enables administrators to access management tools on remote computers running Windows Server 2003 and Windows Server 2008.
- Removable Storage Manager (RSM) — Creates catalogs of removable media and operates drives that use removable media.
- RPC Over HTTP Proxy — Enables objects to receive Remote Procedure Calls (RPC) messages using the Hypertext Transfer Protocol (HTTP), even if someone has moved the object to another server on the network.
- Simple TCP/IP Services — Implements the Character Generator, Daytime, Discard, Echo, and Quote of the Day services, as defined in the TCP/IP standards.
- SMTP Server — The Simple Mail Transfer Protocol (SMTP) provides communication between email servers, and between email clients and servers.

- SNMP Services — Installs support for the Simple Network Management Protocol (SNMP), which enables network management applications to communicate with the agents for managed devices on the network.
- Storage Manager for SANs — Enables administrators to create and manage logical unit numbers (LUNs) for storage subsystems on a storage area network (SAN).
- Subsystem for UNIX-based Applications — Enables Windows Server 2008 to compile and run UNIX-based applications.
- Telnet Client — Enables the computer to connect to a Telnet server and access a command-line administration interface.
- Telnet Server — Enables remote users running Telnet clients to connect to the computers and access a command-line administration interface.
- TFTP (Trivial File Transfer Protocol) Client — Enables the computer to send files to and receive them from a TFTP server on the network, without the need for authentication.
- Windows Internal Database — Implements a relational data store that other Windows Server 2008 roles and features can utilize.
- Windows PowerShell — Implements a command-line shell and scripting language that provides improved administration and automation capabilities.
- Windows Process Activation Service (WPAS) — Implements an environment that generalizes the IIS process model by removing the dependency on HTTP, thus enabling WCF applications to use non-HTTP protocols. This feature is required to run the Web Server (IIS) role.
- Windows Server Backup Features — Enables administrators to perform full or partial server backups at scheduled intervals.
- Windows System Resource Manager (WSRM) — Enables administrators to allocate specific amounts of CPU and memory resources to specific applications, services, or processes.
- WINS Server — Provides NetBIOS name registration and resolution services for down level Windows clients.
- Wireless LAN Service — Implements the Wireless LAN (WLAN) AutoConfig service, which detects and configures wireless network adapters, and manages wireless networking profiles and connections.

■ Planning an Enterprise Application Server Deployment

THE BOTTOM LINE

Planning an enterprise server deployment requires an understanding of the Windows Server 2008 roles and how they interact.

A Windows Server 2008 computer can perform one role or many roles, depending on the requirements of the organization. A small business might have only one server that fulfills all of the roles the company requires. A large enterprise network, on the other hand, typically has many servers and distributes the required roles among them. It is also possible to separate roles by deploying multiple virtual machines on a single computer and installing a different role on each one.

Assigning Multiple Roles

Windows Server 2008 computers can perform multiple roles at the same time.

The concept of assigning multiple roles to a single Windows Server 2008 computer makes it possible to utilize each computer's hardware resources more efficiently. For example, a computer that is functioning only as a DHCP server will probably only utilize a small percentage of its

CPU resources, as shown in Figure 1-4. This is because the only thing the DHCP service has to do is assign TCP/IP configuration settings to computers as they start, and then renew those settings, usually several days later. Most of the time, the service is idle.

Figure 1-4

Running a single role on a server can often be a waste of system resources

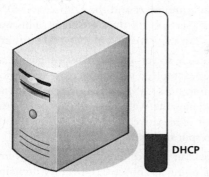

DHCP

To take full advantage of that DHCP server, a designer can assign other roles to it as well. The number of roles a server can perform depends on the computer's hardware configuration, the hardware requirements of the role, and the size and scope of the enterprise. For example, on a large enterprise network hosting 10,000 clients, a dedicated DHCP server would make sense. However, in a small to medium-sized enterprise, that DHCP server might also be able to function as a DNS server and an Active Directory domain controller without overtaxing its hardware, as shown in Figure 1-5.

Figure 1-5

Many servers can support several roles simultaneously

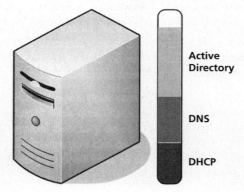

Active Directory

DNS

DHCP

In fact, the computer might have the hardware capacity to function as a Web server also. However, before adding that role, you must consider some other factors. Will the Web server be hosting a low-volume intranet Web site or a high-traffic Internet site? A greater amount of Web client traffic requires more resources.

With that consideration in mind, you might think it is a good idea to purchase the most powerful computer you can find, one with sufficient hardware resources to run all of the server roles the enterprise needs. For some organizations, this is a viable option, but distributing server roles among several computers has several distinct advantages, including the following:

- Fault tolerance — A single server provides a single point of failure. If one computer is performing all of the roles your enterprise needs to function, and that computer malfunctions, then you lose all of the services. Running multiple servers enables the business to better tolerate a single failure.

- Resource allocation — The hardware resources needed by specific server roles can fluctuate wildly, depending on a number of factors. A Web server, for example, might require more server resources during periods of heavy incoming network traffic, which occur at certain times of the day. If the Web server's peak utilization period happens to coincide with the peak utilization of the computer's other roles, the server could become a bottleneck, forcing performance of all the roles to suffer.

- Availability — Distributing roles among several computers enables you to build high availability into your network design. For example, you might configure one computer with the Web server role, and another computer to perform infrastructure roles, such as DHCP and DNS. To add high availability to the design, you would install the Web server role on the infrastructure server and the DHCP and DNS roles on the Web server, disabling the redundant services for the time being. This way, in the event that either server fails, the other one can take over its roles at a few minutes notice.

- Scalability — Having multiple servers on the network enables administrators to reallocate resources as needed. If, for example, a sudden increase in traffic to the company's Internet Web server causes that computer's CPU utilization to consistently spike at 100 percent, you could conceivably redeploy the Web server role on one of the company's other servers, one with a faster processor. Alternatively, you could add a second Web server and configure the two computers to split the traffic load between them.

- Security — Different roles can have different security requirements. For example, you might have a server functioning as an Active Directory domain controller that has sufficient resources to take on another role, but it would be a bad idea to use that computer as an Internet Web server. Computers exposed to the Internet are points of vulnerability, and for that reason, many enterprises put them on perimeter networks, isolated from internal resources, such as infrastructure servers. Generally speaking, the more roles a server has to perform, the more ports it has to leave open for incoming network traffic, and more open ports increase the attack surface of the computer.

- Network traffic — Running a variety of roles on a single server can consolidate a lot of network traffic onto a single subnet. Even if the server is capable of handling many different types of requests from clients all over the enterprise, the network might become a serious performance bottleneck. Distributing roles among servers on different subnets can prevent too much traffic from converging on a single location.

- Update management — It is far easier to keep servers updated with the latest operating system patches if each computer is running as few roles as is practical. In addition, fewer problems occur if an update has deleterious side effects.

TAKE NOTE

Another factor to consider when allocating roles to servers is the dependencies between many of the Windows Server 2008 roles and services. The Add Roles Wizard and the Add Features Wizard both enforce these dependencies by prompting you to install the correct antecedents with your selected roles and features.

Selecting Application Server Roles

Most Windows Server 2008 roles include a variety of options that you can use to customize the installation.

As mentioned earlier in this lesson, the complexity of the design and implementation process for an enterprise network's application servers is largely dependent on the types of applications the users need. The first step of the design process is to inventory those needs. Then, you can consider the various ways of providing for those needs.

The application services Microsoft includes with Windows Server 2008 provide administrators with several ways to deploy even the simplest applications. The method you choose depends on several factors, including economy, security, and ease of administration. The following sections examine the major application service roles listed earlier in this lesson, list the services that compose each one, and discuss how to use them to implement applications on an enterprise network.

USING THE FILE SERVICES ROLE

Virtually all enterprise networks have some (or maybe all) users who spend much of their time working with standard, off-the-shelf productivity applications, such as word processors, spreadsheets, email clients, and so forth. Even though the simplest way to deploy these applications is to install them on the users' individual workstations, employees can use application servers on the network in several ways.

The first consideration is where the users will store their documents. Storing document files on local workstation drives is a simple solution, but one with significant drawbacks. If users have to collaborate on documents, they would have to create shares on their local drives. This could result in dozens or hundreds of additional shares on the network, making navigation difficult. This practice also creates access control problems; the users would have to either set their own permissions or rely on administrators to do so. Finally, storing documents on workstation drives complicates the process of backing them up on a regular basis.

The more common, and more practical, solution is to have users store their documents on network servers, which means deploying one or more file servers on the network. Windows Server 2008 does not need a special role to provide basic file services. Administrators can share folders on any server drive and make them available to users by assigning the appropriate permissions.

However, installing the File Services role on a Windows Server 2008 computer provides additional capabilities that can aid in the management of document storage, such as the following:

- Distributed File System — Consists of two role services: DFS Namespace, which enables administrators to create a virtual directory tree consisting of folders stored on different servers, and DFS Replication, which maintains duplicate copies of the DFS namespace in remote locations.

- File Server Resource Manager (FSRM) — Enables administrators to create and enforce storage quotas, specify file types that are permitted on network volumes, and generate storage reports.

- Services for Network File System — Implements the Network File System (NFS) on the Windows Server 2008 computer. NFS is the standard file-sharing solution for UNIX-based operating systems, so this service enables UNIX clients to access files stored on a Windows server.

- Single Instance Store (SIS) — Conserves disk space on Windows servers by creating a single master copy of duplicate files stored in several locations, and deleting the duplicates.

- Windows Search Service — Creates an index that enables clients to rapidly search for files stored on server drives, without having to access each drive in turn.

- Windows Server 2003 File Services — Provides down level replication and indexing services that enable the server to participate on legacy networks with Windows Server 2003 storage services.

- Share and Storage Management — A new snap-in for Microsoft Management Console (MMC) that provides a centralized administration tool for file server resources.

In addition to the services provided by the File Services role, additional Windows Server 2008 applications and services provide management capabilities for storage area network (SAN) technology, including the following:

- Storage Manager for SANs — Provides configuration and management capabilities for SANs implemented using Fibre Channel or iSCSI networking technologies.

- Storage Explorer — An MMC snap-in that generates a tree view of a SAN and provides access to the configuration interfaces of individual SAN devices.

- iSCSI Initiator — Internet Small Computer System Interface (iSCSI) is an open standard SAN technology that provides a lower cost alternative to Fibre Channel. The iSCSI Initiator enables a Windows Server 2008 computer to access storage devices connected with a standard Gigabit Ethernet switch.

- iSCSI Remote Boot — Enables a Windows Server 2008 computer (or a group of Windows Server 2008 computers) to boot from a remote disk on a SAN.

X REF

For more information on the File Services role and other Windows Server 2008 storage technologies, see Lesson 2, "Deploying a File Server."

- iSNS Server — The Internet Storage Naming Service (iSNS) associates iSCSI initiators with specific SAN storage devices, thus emulating an iSCSI SAN function built into Fibre Channel switches.
- Multipath I/O — Provides an additional level of fault tolerance for storage technologies, such as Redundant Array of Independent Disks (RAID) arrays, that are designed to provide high availability.

USING THE TERMINAL SERVICES ROLE

Installing productivity applications on an individual workstation is a simple task, unless you have to repeat the process on hundreds or thousands of computers. In addition, after you have installed the applications, you must consider the prospect of upgrading and maintaining them as needed. Methods for automating the deployment and maintenance of applications on large groups of computers can require extensive planning and preparation, as well as the additional expense of a management software product.

Windows Server 2008 provides an alternative to individual workstation installations in the form of Terminal Services. Terminal Services is a technology that enables users working at another computer on the company network or on the Internet to establish a connection to a server and open an application or desktop session there.

Deploying applications using Terminal Services offers several advantages to the network administrator, including the following:

TAKE NOTE *

Microsoft provides the Remote Desktop feature, based on Terminal Services, with the Windows XP Professional and Windows Vista desktop operating systems.

- Single application installation — Because the applications run on the Terminal Services server, it is only necessary to install them on that one computer. This ensures that all of the users are running the same application versions, and simplifies maintenance and upgrade tasks for the administrators, because they only have to work on a single installation.
- Low bandwidth consumption — Unlike virtual private network (VPN) or direct dial-up connections, a Terminal Services connection uses relatively little network bandwidth because the applications are running on the server computer. The only data exchanged by the Terminal Services client and the server is data needed to relay the keyboard, mouse, and display information.
- Broad-based client support — A user connecting to the Terminal Services server only has to run a simple client program because the resources needed to run the applications are on the server. This means that the client workstations can be low-end computers, non-Windows computers, or even *thin client* devices, which are minimal computers designed only for server communication.

TAKE NOTE *

Using Terminal Services might yield savings on application licenses, but a computer connecting to a terminal server requires a Terminal Server client access license (CAL) as well. The only exceptions to this are the two client licenses included with Windows Server 2008 for Remote Desktop administration purposes.

- Conservation of licenses — Instead of purchasing application licenses for individual workstations, which might or might not be in use at any given time, you can maintain a pool of licenses on the Terminal Services server, which the system allocates to users as they log on. For example, an office with 100 workstations would require 100 licenses for an application installed on each computer, even if there were never more than 50 users running the application at any one time. Using Terminal Services, 50 application licenses would be sufficient, because only the users actually connected to the server need a license.

The Terminal Services role included in Windows Server 2008 implements the following role services:

- Terminal Server — Implements the service that enables remote users to connect to the computer and run applications or a full desktop session.
- TS Licensing — Manages the client access licenses that remote computers need to access the Terminal Server.
- TS Session Broker — On enterprise networks with multiple, load-balanced Terminal Servers, enables clients to reconnect to an existing session on a specific Terminal Server.
- TS Gateway — Enables remote users on the Internet to access a Terminal Server on an enterprise network using HTTP.
- TS Web Access — Enables remote users to access Terminal Servers using a Web-based client.

X REF

For more information on the Terminal Services role and other Windows Server 2008 remote access technologies, see Lesson 8, "Using Terminal Services," Lesson 9, "Configuring Terminal Services Clients," and Lesson 10, "Using the Terminal Services Gateway."

USING THE WEB SERVER (IIS) ROLE

Originally, Web servers were designed to respond to requests for Hypertext Markup Language (HTML) files generated by client browsers. These HTML files, when interpreted by the browser, display Web page content. Eventually, Web pages grew in complexity, incorporating images into their content, and then audio and video, and finally applications. Today, organizations use Web servers for a huge variety of applications, servicing clients on intranets, extranets, and the Internet.

While standalone applications certainly have their uses, many applications rely on the client/ server model, particularly when many users have to access the same resources. For example, it would be possible to create a standalone database application that runs entirely on a single workstation and enables the user to access the company's customer list. However, to add a new customer, it would be necessary to update the database on each user's workstation, as shown in Figure 1-6, which would be highly impractical.

Figure 1-6

Running standalone applications with duplicate databases on every workstation is not a practical solution

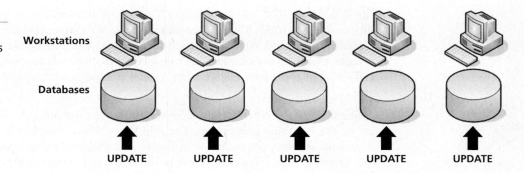

It makes far more sense to store a single copy of the customer list in a database on a central server and have each of the users run a client program that sends requests to the server, as shown in Figure 1-7. This way, administrators only have to make modifications to a single copy of the database, and all of the users can obtain the updated information immediately.

Figure 1-7

Running a single database application enables all of the workstations to retrieve updated information

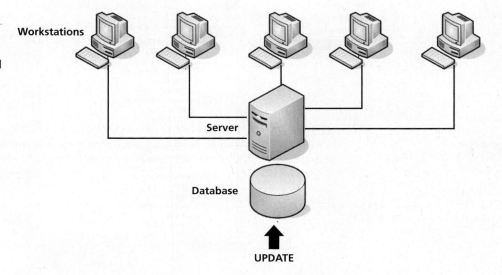

The question remains, however, of where a Web server fits into this client/server model. The simple answer is that Web servers and Web browsers eliminate the need for application developers to reinvent existing technologies. Web browsers are clients that send requests for information to Web servers, which respond by sending the requested information. To implement the client/server database application described earlier from scratch, developers would have to create a client program that generates database requests and a server program that processes those requests, accesses the desired information in the database, and generates replies.

By using the existing IIS Web server and Internet Explorer Web browser applications already incorporated in the Windows operating systems, database application developers can concentrate on the back end server application, which manages the database itself. They do not have to create a client interface or a server to receive and interpret the client requests.

The client/server model implemented by IIS and Internet Explorer can support many types of applications other than databases. Custom-designed business applications can run on the same computer as the Web server, on a different server, or on the client workstation itself.

Therefore, the client/server model in this type of arrangement consists of three elements:

- An Internet Explorer client browser running on the workstation
- An IIS server running on a Windows Server 2008 computer
- An application that makes use of the services provided by the Web server and the client browser

The Web Server (IIS) role in Windows Server 2008 implements, as its core, Internet Information Services 7.0. IIS 7 provides the basic Web server functionality that enables you to publish a standard Web site on the Internet or on a private network. However, IIS 7 also includes a large number of optional role services that provide support for virtually any type of Web-based application deployment, as well as management, diagnostic, and security functions.

Unlike some of the other Windows Server 2008 roles, installing the Web Server (IIS) role is not an all-or-nothing proposition. The Add Roles Wizard enables you to select a combination of optional role services, as shown in Figure 1-8, while enforcing any dependencies that might exist between them. This enables you to install the capabilities that your applications require, without wasting server resources running a lot of unnecessary code.

Figure 1-8

Selecting role services for the Web Server (IIS) role

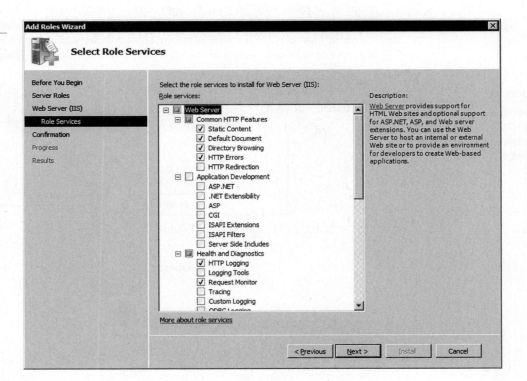

The following sections describe the various role services that you can install as part of the Web Server (IIS) role. The modules marked with an asterisk (*) are those the operating system installs with the role by default.

SELECTING IIS 7 WEB SERVER ROLE SERVICES

The Web Server role services provide basic HTTP server functionality, plus optional features that enhance the Web server's ability to support custom Web server settings, specific application environments, Web server logging functions, client access control capabilities, and Web server performance controls. The features you can select within the Web Server role service are as follows.

- Common HTTP Features — Provides support for standard Web server features, including the following:

  - Static Content (*) — Enables the Web server to publish Web sites that consist only of HTML and image files.

  - Default Document (*) — Specifies the name of the file that client browsers should load by default (such as index.html) when the Uniform Resource Locator (URL) received from a client does not include a filename.

  - Directory Browsing (*) — Enables clients to view a listing of the files in a particular directory and navigate up and down through the directory tree.

  - HTTP Errors (*) — Enables the Web server administrator to create customized messages for specific HTTP errors.

  - HTTP Redirection — Enables the Web server to forward incoming requests for a specific URL to another URL, such as when a site changes domain names.

- Application Development — Provides infrastructure support for applications developed using the following programming tools:

  - ASP.NET — Implements a server side, object-oriented programming environment based on the .NET framework.

  - .NET Extensibility — Enables developers to modify the functionality of the Web server, using the ASP.Net extensibility model and the .NET application programming interfaces (APIs).

  - ASP (Active Server Pages) — Provides a server-side scripting environment that supports both VBScript (Microsoft Visual Basic Scripting Edition) and Jscript for the development of Web sites and applications.

  - Common Gateway Interface (CGI) — Provides a scripting interface that enables a Web server to pass incoming information to another program.

  - Internet Server Application Programming Interface (ISAPI) Extensions — Enables the Web server to execute compiled ISAPI applications.

  - ISAPI Filters — Provides support for applications that use ISAPI filters to modify the functionality of the IIS Web server.

  - Server Side Includes (SSI) — Provides support for a scripting language that enables the Web server to dynamically generate HTML pages.

- Health and Diagnostics — Enables IIS to capture information that administrators can use to manage, monitor, and troubleshoot the Web server, using tools like the following:

  - Custom Logging — Enables administrators to log Web server activity using a customized format.

  - HTTP Logging (*) — Enables the Web server to maintain logs of all Web site activity.

  - Logging Tools — Provides tools for managing activity logs and automating logging tasks.

  - Open Database Connectivity (ODBC) Logging — Enables the Web server to save its logs to an ODBC-compliant database.

  - Request Monitor (*) — Captures information about HTTP requests that administrators can use to monitor the Web server's health and troubleshoot performance problems.

  - Tracing — Enables the Web server to save information about failed application requests for troubleshooting purposes.

- Security — Enables administrators to restrict access to the Web server, using tools like the following:
  - Basic Authentication — Provides support for a highly compatible and relatively unsecured form of authentication using Windows user names and passwords.
  - Client Certificate Mapping Authentication — Provides certificate-based authentication using Active Directory for one-to-one certificate mapping.
  - Digest Authentication — Authenticates users by sending a password hash to a domain controller on the network.
  - IIS Client Certificate Mapping Authentication — Provides certificate-based authentication using IIS for one-to-one or many-to-one certificate mapping.
  - IP and Domain Restrictions — Enables administrators to restrict access to the Web server by allowing only computers with certain IP addresses or domain names to connect.
  - Request Filtering (*) — Enables the Web server to block malicious traffic by filtering incoming requests based on rules the administrator creates.
  - URL Authorization — Enables administrators to restrict access to specific URLs by authorizing only specific users or groups.
  - Windows Authentication — Provides a secure NTLM- or Kerberos-based authentication method for domain users.
- Performance — Enables administrators to conserve network bandwidth by using the following data compression techniques:
  - Dynamic Content Compression — Enables the Web server to conserve network bandwidth by compressing dynamic Web site content before transmitting it to the client, at the cost of increased Web server CPU utilization.
  - Static Content Compression (*) — Enables the Web server to conserve network bandwidth by compressing static Web site content before transmitting it to the client.

SELECTING IIS 7 MANAGEMENT TOOLS

The Management Tools role service provides a variety of interfaces to the Web server administration controls, including MMC snap-ins, command-line tools, and scripting capabilities. The individual services you can select are as follows:

- IIS 6 Management Compatibility — Enables administrators to manage an IIS 7 Web server using IIS 6 tools and scripts.
  - IIS 6 Management Console — Provides the ability to manage remote IIS 6 Web servers.
  - IIS 6 Metabase Compatibility — Translates interfaces and scripts designed for the IIS 6 metabase to the new IIS 7 format.
  - IIS 6 Scripting Tools — Enables administrators to use IIS 6 scripting tools to manage IIS 7 Web servers.
  - IIS 6 WMI Compatibility — Provides support for IIS 6 Windows Management Instrumentation (WMI) scripts.
- IIS Management Console (*) — An MMC snap-in that enables administrators to manage local or remote IIS 7 Web servers.
- IIS Management Scripts and Tools — Enables administrators to automate IIS 7 management tasks using command-line tools and scripts.
- Management Service — Enables administrators to manage the Web server remotely using the IIS Management Console.

SELECTING FTP PUBLISHING SERVICES

The FTP Publishing Service included with Windows Server 2008 provides an alternative, directory-based interface that clients can use to upload and download files and perform basic file management tasks. The service, which is the same as the one included with IIS 6, consists of the following elements:

- FTP Server — Enables the Web server to host FTP sites and respond to FTP client requests.
- FTP Management Console — Enables administrators to manage local and remote IIS 7 FTP sites.

A new FTP Publishing Service for IIS7 is available as a free download from Microsoft's Web site. FTP7 is compatible with the IIS7 Management console, as well as other new IIS7 features, such as XML-based configuration files with .config extensions, shared configurations, and modular extensibility.

SELECTING ROLE SERVICES

Microsoft designed the Web server role services to support a wide variety of application development environments and administration requirements. Unless you plan to run a large number of applications that require different development environments, you will not need all of the role services that Web Server (IIS) role provides. In fact, Microsoft includes some of the role services, particularly some of those in the Application Development category, primarily to support legacy applications. If your organization is creating new applications for the server deployment, then it makes sense to select a single development environment and install only the role services needed to support those applications.

X REF

For more information on the Web Server (IIS) role, see Lesson 5, "Deploying IIS Services," Lesson 6, "Securing IIS Servers," and Lesson 7, "Deploying Web Applications."

USING THE UDDI SERVICES ROLE

Originally designed to be the basis for a worldwide directory of Internet sites and services, it is now more common for large organizations to use Universal Description, Discovery, and Integration (UDDI) as an internal catalog of their available Web services. Clients on the company intranet or a protected extranet can use a Web interface to access the catalog and search for the services the company's Web servers provide.

The UDDI Services role in Windows Server 2008 consists of the following role services:
- UDDI Services Database — Provides a central storage location for the UDDI catalog and the service's configuration settings.
- UDDI Services Web Application — Implements a Web site with which users and applications can access the UDDI catalog to search for Web services on the network.

X REF

For more information on deploying the UDDI Services role, see Lesson 7, "Deploying Web Applications."

USING THE APPLICATION SERVER ROLE

The Web Server (IIS) role provides a number of technologies that enable organizations to develop and deploy their own custom applications, using IIS to handle incoming requests from clients. The Application Server role is essentially a superset of the Web Server (IIS) role that enables IIS to host Web services developed using environments such as Windows Communication Foundation (WCF) and .NET Framework 3.0.

Installing the Application Server role automatically installs .NET Framework 3.0, and the Add Roles Wizard enables you to select from the following role services:

- Application Server Foundation — Implements the core technologies needed to support .NET 3.0 applications, including WCF, Windows Presentation Foundation (WPF), and Windows Workflow Foundation (WWF). This is the only role service installed with the role by default.

+ MORE INFORMATION

Microsoft server applications, such as Exchange Server and SQL Server, do not require the Application Server role for their own functions. However, custom applications that use the services provided by Exchange and SQL Server might require the role.

- Web Server (IIS) Support — Enables the application server to host internal or external Web sites, as well as Web applications and services using technologies such as ASP.NET and WCF.
- COM+ Network Access — Enables the application server to host applications built with COM+ or Enterprise Services components.
- TCP Port Sharing — Enables multiple applications to share a single TCP port, so that they can coexist on a single computer.
- Windows Process Activation Service Support — Enables the Application Server to invoke applications remotely over the network, so that the applications can start and stop dynamically in response to incoming traffic. The individual traffic types WAS supports are as follows:
  - HTTP Activation — Enables applications to start and stop dynamically in response to incoming HTTP traffic.
  - Message Queuing Activation — Enables applications to start and stop dynamically in response to incoming Message Queuing traffic.
  - TCP Activation — Enables applications to start and stop dynamically in response to incoming TCP traffic.
  - Named Pipes Activation — Enables applications to start and stop dynamically in response to incoming named pipes traffic.
- Distributed Transactions — Implements services that help to ensure the successful completion of transactions involving multiple databases hosted by different computers. The individual services are as follows:
  - Incoming Remote Transactions — Provides support for transactions that applications on remote servers propagate.
  - Outgoing Remote Transactions — Enables the server to propagate the transactions that it generates itself to remote servers.
  - WS-Atomic Transactions — Provides support for applications that use two-phase commit transactions based on Simple Object Access Protocol (SOAP) exchanges.

X REF

For more information on using the Application Server role, see Lesson 11, "Using Network Application Services."

USING THE PRINT SERVICES ROLE

Sharing printers was one of the original applications that inspired the development of local area networks (LANs), and it is a common requirement on enterprise networks today. You can share a printer connected to a Windows Server 2008 computer without installing the Print Services role, but the role provides centralized tools that enable an administrator to monitor printer activities all over the network. The Print Services role includes the following optional role services:

- Print Server — Installs the Print Management snap-in for MMC, which provides centralized printer management for an entire enterprise network.
- LPD Service — Enables UNIX client computers running the line printer remote (LPR) application to send jobs to Windows Server 2008 printers.
- Internet Printing — Implements a Web-based printer management interface and enables remote users on the Internet to send print jobs to Windows Server 2008 printers.

X REF

For more information on using the Print Services and Fax Server roles, see Lesson 4, "Deploying Print and Fax Servers."

USING THE FAX SERVER ROLE

Sending and receiving faxes through the network can be an enormous convenience and Windows Server 2008 includes a Fax Server role that includes the Fax Service Manager application, which enables administrators to monitor fax devices, create fax rules and policies, and manage all of the faxes for the organization. The Fax Server role has no optional role services from which to choose. However, it does require the installation of the Print Services role.

USING THE STREAMING MEDIA SERVICES ROLE

The Streaming Media Services role enables an application server to provide digital audio and video content to network clients in real time, using HTTP or the Real Time Streaming Protocol (RTSP). The clients run a media player application that processes the content as they receive it from the server.

Unlike earlier versions of Windows Server, the Streaming Media Services role is not included with the operating system. You must download an update from the Microsoft Web site to add the role to the Server Manager application. When you install the role, you can choose from the following role services:

- Windows Media Server — Enables the application server to stream media to clients on the network.
- Web-based Administration — Provides a Web-based interface for managing media server functions.
- Logging Agent — Enables the media server to maintain logs of statistics received from clients.

X REF

For more information on using the Streaming Media Services role, see Lesson 11, "Using Network Application Services."

Selecting Application Server Hardware

Choosing the correct hardware for an application server requires an understanding of the roles it will perform.

Not until you have decided how you will deploy your applications and what roles an application server will perform should you begin selecting the hardware that goes into the computer. For example, suppose your organization decides to deploy an application suite such as Microsoft Office on all of the company's workstations. If you decide to install the applications on each individual workstation, each of the computers must have sufficient memory and processor speed to run them efficiently. The application servers on the network will then only have to perform relatively simple roles, such as file and print services, which do not require enormous amounts of server resources.

By contrast, if you decide to deploy the applications using Terminal Services, you can use workstations with a minimal hardware configuration, because the terminal servers will take most of the burden. In this case, you will need an application server that is more powerful, in terms of processor and memory, or perhaps even several servers sharing the client load.

Server roles can also dictate requirements for specific subsystems within the application server computers, as in the following examples.

X REF

For more information on storage area networking, see Lesson 2, "Deploying a File Server." For more information on network load balancing and server clustering, see Lesson 12, "Using High Availability Technologies."

- Servers hosting complex applications might require more memory and faster processors.
- File servers can benefit from hard drives with higher speeds and larger caches, or even a high performance drive interface, such as SATA (Serial Advanced Technology Attachment) or SCSI (Small Computer System Interface).
- Web servers receiving large amounts of traffic might need higher-end network adapters or multiple adapters to connect to different subnets.
- Streaming media servers require sufficient hardware in all subsystems, because any performance bottleneck in the server can interrupt the client's media experience.

Finally, enterprises with extensive application server requirements might want to consider specialized server hardware, such as a storage area network, network attached storage, or server cluster.

Selecting Application Server Software

Microsoft provides several alternative software deployments for Windows Server 2008 computers.

Microsoft provides a number of additional products and alternative installation practices that you might be able to use to minimize the cost and maximize the efficiency of your application server deployment. These alternatives are not suitable for all installations, but they can be viable solutions for some.

The following sections discuss software alternatives that require either a different Windows Server 2008 installation procedure, the installation of additional software, or the purchase of a different software product.

USING TERMINAL SERVICES

As mentioned earlier in this lesson and discussed at length later in this book, Terminal Services can provide a number of benefits in an enterprise application deployment, including substantial savings in the cost of workstation hardware and conservation of network bandwidth. Windows Server 2008 includes all of the software needed to implement a terminal server, plus new features, such as the Terminal Services Gateway.

With Windows Server 2008, Windows Vista Service Pack 1, and Windows XP Service Pack 3, Microsoft includes the Remote Desktop Connection 6.1 client application that workstations need to connect to a terminal server and utilize all of its capabilities. The license that each client needs to connect to a terminal server is the only Terminal Services component that Microsoft does not include with the operating system or make available as a free download.

Windows Server 2008 includes a two-user client license so that administrators can use Remote Desktop to configure servers from other computers, but clients using Terminal Services to run applications or desktop sessions must have additional licenses. This is an additional purchase and an additional cost that you must not forget when calculating your network deployment costs.

USING WEB EDITION

The Windows Server 2008 Standard, Enterprise, and Datacenter editions include all of the roles and features discussed in this lesson. However, another viable alternative is available for some installations: Windows Server 2008 Web Edition. Microsoft has designed the Web Edition of Windows Server 2008 for computers dedicated solely to hosting Web sites, applications, and services.

The Web Edition is essentially a subset of Windows Server 2008 Standard Edition, available at a reduced cost. When compared to the Standard edition, the Web Edition product has the following limitations:

- Windows Server 2008 Web Edition supports two-way symmetric multiprocessing (SMP), a maximum of 2 gigabytes of RAM, and 10 inbound Server Message Block (SMB) connections.
- Windows Server 2008 Web Edition can host only Web-based applications; applications that do not use IIS Web serving capabilities are prohibited.
- A Windows Server 2008 Web Edition server can be a member of an Active Directory domain, but it cannot function as a domain controller or run any of the Active Directory server roles.
- Windows Server 2008 Web Edition does not support the UDDI Services server role.
- Windows Server 2008 Web Edition cannot run Microsoft SQL Server, although it can run SQL Server 2005 Express Edition.
- Windows Server 2008 Web Edition is not available as a retail product. It is available only to Microsoft customers with an Enterprise, Select, Open, or Service Provider licensing agreement, or through Microsoft original equipment manufacturers (OEMs) and System Builder partners.

USING A SERVER CORE INSTALLATION

Computer users today have become so accustomed to graphical user interfaces (GUIs) that many are unaware that there is any other way to operate a computer. When the first version of Windows NT Server appeared, many network administrators complained about wasting the server's system resources on graphical displays and other elements that they deemed unnecessary. Until that point, server displays were usually minimal, character-based, monochrome affairs. In fact, many servers had no display hardware at all, relying instead on text-based remote administration tools, such as Telnet.

Many enterprise networks today use many servers, with each server performing one or two roles. You learned about the advantages to this arrangement earlier in this lesson. However, when a server is devoted to performing a single role, does it really make sense to have so many other processes running that contribute nothing to that role?

INTRODUCING SERVER CORE

Windows Server 2008 includes an installation option that addresses those old complaints. By using the Windows Server Core installation option of Windows Server 2008, you get a stripped-down version of the operating system. There is no Start menu, no desktop Explorer shell, no MMC console, and virtually no graphical applications. All you see when you start the computer is a single window with a command prompt.

In addition to omitting most of the graphical interface, a Server Core installation omits some of the server roles and features found in a full installation. Tables 1-2 and 1-3 list the roles and features that are available and not available in a Server Core installation.

> **TAKE NOTE***
>
> Server Core is not a separate product. It is an installation option included with the Windows Server 2008 Standard, Enterprise, and Datacenter Editions, in both the x86 and x64 versions.

Table 1-2

Windows Server 2008 Server Core Roles

Roles Available in Server Core Installation	Roles Not Available in Server Core Installation
Active Directory Domain Services	Active Directory Certificate Services
Active Directory Lightweight Directory Services	Active Directory Federation Services
DHCP Server	Active Directory Rights Management Services
DNS Server	Network Policy and Access Services
File Services	Windows Deployment Services
Print Services	Application Server
Web Server (IIS)	Fax Server
	Terminal Services
	UDDI Services

Table 1-3

Windows Server 2008 Server Core Features

Features Available in Server Core Installation	Features Not Available in Server Core Installation
BitLocker Drive Encryption	.NET Framework 3.0
Failover Clustering	BITS Server Extensions
Multipath I/O	Connection Manager Administration Kit
Network Load Balancing	Desktop Experience
QoS (Quality of Service) (qWave)	Internet Printing Client

(continued)

Table 1-3 (continued)

FEATURES AVAILABLE IN SERVER CORE INSTALLATION	FEATURES NOT AVAILABLE IN SERVER CORE INSTALLATION
Removable Storage Manager	Internet Storage Name Server
SNMP Services	LPR Port Monitor
Subsystem for UNIX-based Applications	Message Queuing
Telnet Client	Peer Name Resolution Protocol
Windows Server Backup	Remote Assistance
Windows Internet Name Service (WINS) Server	Remote Server Administration Tools
	RPC Over HTTP Proxy
	Simple TCP/IP Services
	SMTP Server
	Storage Manager for SANs
	Telnet Server
	Trivial File Transfer Protocol Client
	Windows Internal Database
	Windows Process Activation Service
	Windows System Resource Manager
	Wireless LAN Service

ADMINISTERING SERVER CORE

Obviously, with so much of the operating system missing, a computer running Server Core can devote more of its resources to its server functions. However, the missing elements provide most of the traditional Windows Server management and administration tools. To work with a Server Core computer, you must rely primarily on either the extensive collection of command prompt tools Microsoft includes with Windows Server 2008 or use MMC consoles on another system to connect to the server.

A few graphical applications can still run on Server Core. Notepad still works, so you can edit scripts and batch files. Task Manager runs, enabling you to load programs and monitor processes. Some elements of the Control Panel work as well, including the Date and Time application and the Regional and Language Options.

JUSTIFYING SERVER CORE

The next logical question to ask about Server Core is whether it is worth the inconvenience of learning a completely new management paradigm and giving up so much server functionality to save some memory and processor clock cycles. The answer is that there are other benefits to using Server Core besides hardware resource conservation.

As mentioned earlier, many Windows Server computers on enterprise networks are dedicated to a single role, but they still have a great many other applications, services, and processes running on them all the time. You can take it as an axiom that the more complex a system is, the more ways it can go wrong. Despite the fact that all of those extra software elements are performing no useful purpose, it is still necessary to maintain and update them, and that introduces the potential for failure. By removing many of these elements and leaving only the functions needed to perform the server's role, you diminish the failure potential, reduce the number of updates you need to apply, and increase the computer's reliability.

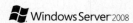

Another drawback to having all of those unnecessary processes running on a server is that they provide an increased attack surface for the computer. The more processes a computer is running, the more avenues there are for attacks to exploit. Removing the unneeded software elements makes the server more secure as well.

USING SERVER CORE FOR APPLICATION SERVERS

It is clear from the Tables 1-2 and 1-3, earlier in this section, that the Server Core configuration is limited when it comes to application services. The removal of the Application Server and Terminal Services roles means that you cannot use Server Core to deploy some applications or Terminal Services connections. However, the Server Core option provides a viable alternative for file and print servers, as well as streaming media servers.

USING VIRTUAL APPLICATION SERVERS

As discussed earlier in this lesson, running a large number of server roles on a single computer has distinct disadvantages, and yet distributing roles among many servers can be expensive and wasteful. However, a compromise between these two extremes is becoming an increasingly popular enterprise networking solution.

A ***virtual server*** is a complete installation of an operating system that runs in a software environment emulating a physical computer. Applications such as Microsoft Virtual Server 2005 and the Windows Server virtualization technology in Windows Server 2008 make it possible for a single computer to host multiple virtual machines, each of which runs in a completely independent environment.

The advantages of virtualization include the following:

- Fault tolerance — Any type of software failure on a virtual server affects only that server.
- Security — Virtual servers appear to the network as separate computers, so an attack on a virtual server has no effect on the other virtual machines or the host computer.
- Disaster recovery — Virtual servers are hardware independent, so in the event of a hardware failure, you can easily restore a backup copy of a virtual server on another computer and have it running in minutes.
- Resource allocation — As resource requirements for individual servers change, you can easily redeploy them onto other computers or adjust the physical computer resources allocated to them.
- Training and testing — Virtual servers simplify the task of creating an isolated laboratory environment in which you can test software products and train users and administrators.

For more information on Microsoft virtualization technologies and using them to deploy application servers, see Lesson 12, "Using High Availability Technologies."

■ Deploying Servers

↓
THE BOTTOM LINE
Windows Deployment Services enables administrators to perform attended and unattended operating system installations on remote computers.

After you have selected the application servers you need on your network and created a plan specifying the roles you will install on your servers, it is time to think about the actual server deployment process. For small networks, manual server installations, in which you run the Windows Server 2008 DVD on each computer separately, might be the most practical solution. However, if you have many servers to install, you might benefit from automating the installation process using Windows Deployment Services.

Windows Deployment Services (WDS) is a role included with Windows Server 2008, which enables you to perform unattended installations of Windows Server 2008 and other operating systems on remote computers, using network-based boot and installation media. This means that you can deploy a new computer with no operating system or local boot device on it, by installing image files stored on a server running Windows Deployment Services.

WDS is a client/server application in which the server supplies operating system image files to clients on the network. However, unlike most client/server applications, the WDS server is also responsible for providing the remote computer with the boot files it needs to run and the client side of the application.

For this to be possible, the client computer must have a network adapter that supports a **preboot execution environment (PXE)**. In a PXE, the computer, instead of booting from a local drive, connects to a server on the network and downloads the boot files it needs to run. In the case of a WDS installation, the client downloads a boot image that loads **Windows PE (Preinstallation Environment) 2.1**, after which it installs the operating system using another image file.

+ MORE INFORMATION

The image files that WDS uses are highly compressed archives with a .wim extension. Unlike most image file formats, WIM images are file-based, not bit-based, which means that you can modify the image by adding or removing files as needed. For example, you can add an application or an updated device driver to an operating system image without recreating it from scratch.

Installing Windows Deployment Services

To use WDS, you must install the Windows Deployment Services role, configure the service, and add the images you want to deploy.

CERTIFICATION READY?
Deploy images by using Windows Deployment Services
1.1

WDS is a standard role that you can install from the Initial Configuration Tasks window or the Server Manager console. The Windows Deployment Services role includes the following two role services:

- Deployment Server
- Transport Server

The Deployment Server role service provides a full WDS installation and requires the installation of the Transport Server role service as well. If you select Transport Server by itself, you install only the core networking elements of WDS, which you can use to create namespaces that enable you to transmit image files using multicast addresses. You must choose the Deployment Server role service to perform full remote operating system installations.

The Add Roles Wizard enforces no other dependencies for the Windows Deployment Services role, but the Wizard has several other requirements, as follows:

- Active Directory — The Windows Deployment Services computer must be a member of, or a domain controller for, an Active Directory domain.
- DHCP — The network must have an operational DHCP server that is accessible by the WDS clients.
- DNS — A DNS server must be on the network for the WDS server to function.
- NTFS — The WDS server must have an NTFS drive to store the image files.

The process of installing the Windows Deployment Services role does not add configuration pages to the Add Roles Wizard, but you must configure the server before clients can use it, as discussed in the following sections.

CONFIGURING THE WDS SERVER

After you install Windows Deployment Services, it remains inactive until you configure the service and add the images that the server will deploy to clients. To configure the server, use the following procedure.

 CONFIGURE A WDS SERVER

GET READY. Log on to Windows Server 2008 using an account with Administrative privileges. When the logon process is completed, close the Initial Configuration Tasks window and any other windows that appear.

1. Click **Start**, and then click **Administrative Tools** > **Windows Deployment Services**. The Windows Deployment Services console appears, as shown in Figure 1-9.

Figure 1-9

The Windows Deployment Services console

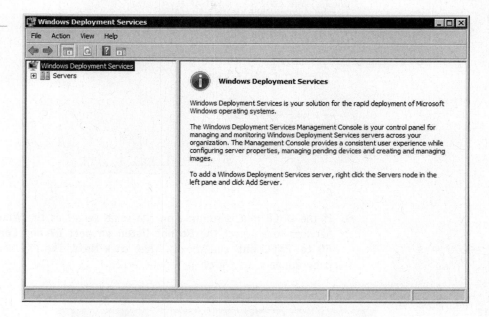

2. In the scope (left) pane, expand the **Servers** node. Right-click your server and, from the context menu, select **Configure Server**. The Windows Deployment Services Configuration Wizard appears.

3. Click **Next** to bypass the Welcome page. The Remote Installation Folder Location page appears, as shown in Figure 1-10.

Figure 1-10

The Remote Installation Folder Location page

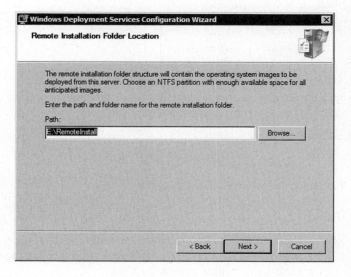

4. In the Path text box, key or browse to the folder where you want to locate the WDS image store. The folder you select must be on an NTFS drive and must have sufficient space to hold all of the images you want to deploy. Microsoft also recommends that the image store not be located on the system drive.

5. Click **Next** to continue. The DHCP Option 60 page appears, as shown in Figure 1-11.

Figure 1-11

The DHCP Option 60 page

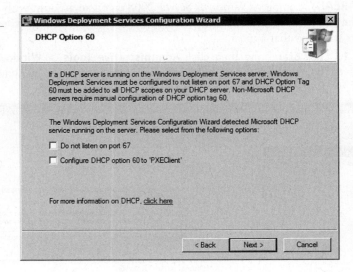

6. If the DHCP role is running on the same server as the Windows Deployment Services role, select the **Do not listen on port 67** and **Configure DHCP option 60 to 'PXEClient'** checkboxes. Then click **Next**. The PXE Server Initial Settings page appears, as shown in Figure 1-12.

Figure 1-12

The PXE Server Initial Settings page

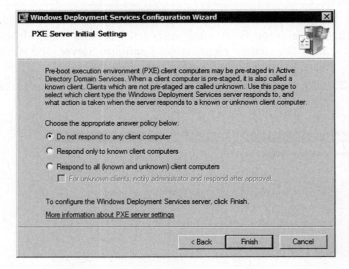

7. Select one of the following options:

  a. Do not respond to any client computer — Prevents the WDS from providing boot access to any clients.

  b. Respond only to known client computers — Configures the WDS server to provide boot access only to clients that you have prestaged in Active Directory by creating computer objects for them.

  c. Respond to all (known and unknown) client computers — Configures the WDS server to provide access to all clients, whether you have prestaged them or not. Selecting the *For unknown clients, notify administrator and respond after approval* checkbox requires an administrator to approve each client connection attempt before the server provides it with boot access.

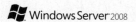

8. Click **Next** to complete the configuration process. The Configuration Complete page appears, as shown in Figure 1-13.

Figure 1-13

The Configuration Complete page

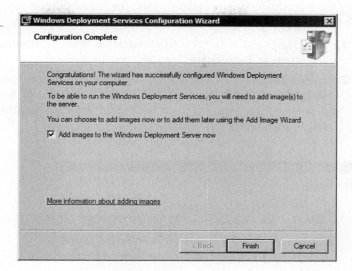

9. Select the **Add images to the Windows Deployment Server now** checkbox to launch the Add Image Wizard. Then click **Finish** to complete the Windows Deployment Services Configuration Wizard.

CLOSE the Windows Deployment Services console.

After the Windows Deployment Services Configuration Wizard has completed its tasks, the server has the proper environment to store image files and listen for incoming requests from clients. However, you still must populate the image store with image files, as described in the next section.

ADDING IMAGE FILES

Windows Deployment Services requires two types of image files to perform remote client installations: a boot image and an install image. The boot image contains the files needed to boot the computer and initiate an operating system installation. The Windows Server 2008 installation DVD includes a boot image file called boot.wim, located in the \Sources folder, which loads Windows PE 2.1 on the client computer. You can use this image file for virtually any operating system deployment without modification.

⊕ **MORE INFORMATION**

If you want to deploy an operating system to a computer that is not PXE-enabled, you can add a boot image to the store, and then convert it to a discover boot image by right-clicking the image and selecting Create a Discover Image from the context menu. A discover image is an image file that you can burn to a CD-ROM or other boot medium. When you boot the client computer using the discover image disk, the computer loads Windows PE, connects to a specified WDS server, and proceeds with the operating system installation process.

The image file contains the operating system that WDS will install on the client computer. Windows Server 2008 includes an install image in the \Sources folder on the installation DVD as well, called install.wim. This file performs a standard Windows Server 2008 setup, just as if you used the DVD to perform a manual installation.

To add the image files into the Windows Deployment Services console, use the following procedure.

⊕ **ADD IMAGE FILES**

GET READY. Log on to Windows Server 2008 using an account with Administrative privileges. When the logon process is completed, close the Initial Configuration Tasks window and any other windows that appear.

1. Click **Start**, and then click **Administrative Tools** > **Windows Deployment Services**. The Windows Deployment Services console appears.

2. Expand the Server node and the node for your server. Then, right-click the **Boot Images** folder and, from the context menu, select **Add Boot Image**. The Windows Deployment Services – Add Image Wizard appears, showing the Image File page, as shown in Figure 1-14.

Figure 1-14

The Image File page in the Windows Deployment Services – Add Image Wizard

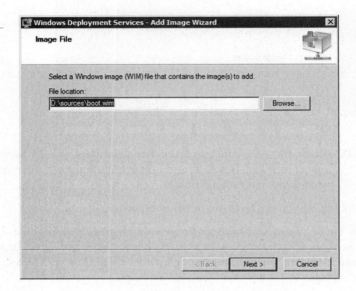

3. Key or browse to the location of the boot image you want to add to the store and then click **Next**. The Image Metadata page appears, as shown in Figure 1-15.

Figure 1-15

The Image Metadata page

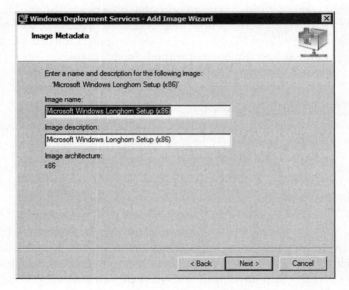

4. Specify different Image Name and Image Description values for the image file you selected, if desired. Then click **Next** to continue. The Summary page appears.

5. Click **Next** to continue. The Task Progress page appears, as the wizard adds the image to the store.

6. When the operation is complete, click **Finish**. The image appears in the detail pane of the console.

7. Right-click the **Install Images** folder and, from the context menu, select **Add Install Image**. The Windows Deployment Services – Add Image Wizard appears, showing the Image Group page, as shown in Figure 1-16.

Figure 1-16

The Image Group page in the Windows Deployment Services – Add Image Wizard

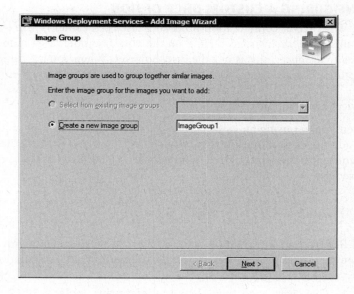

8. With the default *Create a new image group* option selected, supply a name for the group, if desired, and then click **Next**. The Image File page appears.

9. Key or browse to the location of the boot image you want to add to the store and then click **Next**. The List of Available Images page appears, as shown in Figure 1-17, containing a list of the images in the file you selected.

Figure 1-17

The List of Available Images page

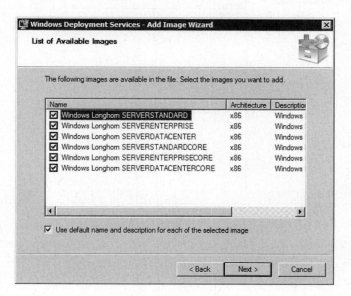

10. Select the images you want to add to the store and then click **Next**. The Summary page appears.

11. Click **Next** to continue. The Task Progress page appears, as the wizard adds the image to the store.

12. When the operation is complete, click **Finish.** The image group you created and the images you selected appear in the detail pane of the console.

CLOSE the Windows Deployment Services console.

At this point, the WDS server is ready to service clients.

CONFIGURING A CUSTOM DHCP OPTION

The WDS server configuration procedure discussed earlier in this lesson assumes that an administrator has installed DHCP on the same computer as Windows Deployment Services. In many instances, this is not the case, however. When you are using another computer as your DHCP server, you should clear the *Do not listen on port 67* and *Configure DHCP option 60 to 'PXEClient'* checkboxes on the DHCP Option 60 page of the Windows Deployment Services Configuration Wizard.

When you are using an external DHCP server, you must also configure it manually to include the custom option that provides WDS clients with the name of the WDS server. To configure this option on a Windows Server 2008 DHCP server, use the following procedure.

 CONFIGURE A CUSTOM DHCP OPTION

GET READY. Log on to Windows Server 2008 using an account with Administrative privileges. When the logon process is completed, close the Initial Configuration Tasks window and any other windows that appear.

1. Click **Start**, and then click **Administrative Tools** > **DHCP.** The DHCP console appears, as shown in Figure 1-18.

Figure 1-18

The DHCP console

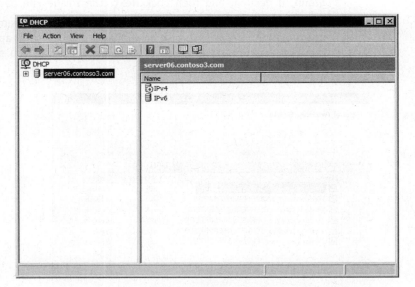

2. In the scope pane, expand the node for your server. Then, right-click the **IPv4** node and, from the context menu, select **Set Predefined Options.** The Predefined Options and Values dialog box appears, as shown in Figure 1-19.

Figure 1-19

The Predefined Options and Values dialog box

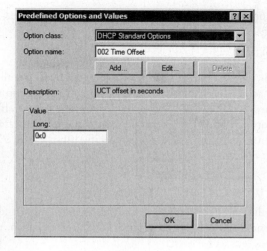

3. Click **Add**. The Option Type dialog box appears, as shown in Figure 1-20.

Figure 1-20

The Option Type dialog box

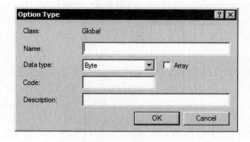

4. In the Name text box, key **PXEClient**.
5. From the Data Type drop-down list, select **String**.
6. In the Code text box, key **060**.
7. Click **OK**.
8. Click **OK** again to close the Predefined Options and Values dialog box.
9. In the scope pane, right-click the **Server Options** node and, from the context menu, select **Configure Options**. The Server Options dialog box appears.
10. In the Available Options list box, scroll down and select the **060 PXEClient** option you just created, as shown in Figure 1-21.

Figure 1-21

The Server Options dialog box

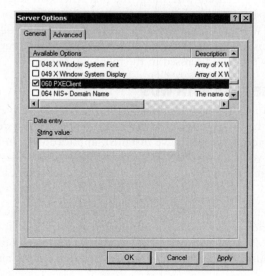

11. In the String Value text box, key the name or IP address of your WDS server. Then, click **OK.**

CLOSE the DHCP console.

This procedure adds the 060 custom option value you defined to all of the DHCPOFFER packets the DHCP server sends out to clients. When a client computer boots from a local device, such as a hard drive or CD-ROM, the 060 option has no effect. However, when a client performs a network boot, after receiving and accepting an offered IP address from the DHCP server, it connects to the WDS server specified in the 060 PXEClient option and uses it to obtain the files it needs to boot.

PERFORMING A WDS CLIENT INSTALLATION

After you have installed and configured your WDS server and added images to the store, it is ready to service clients. In a properly configured WDS installation, the client operating system deployment proceeds as follows:

1. The client computer starts and, finding no local boot device, attempts to perform a network boot.
2. The client computer connects to a DHCP server on the network, from which it obtains a DHCPOFFER message containing an IP address and other TCP/IP configuration parameters, plus the 060 PXEClient option, containing the name of a WDS server.
3. The client connects to the WDS server and is supplied with a boot image file, which it downloads using the Trivial File Transfer Protocol (TFTP).
4. The client loads Windows PE and the Windows Deployment Services client from the boot image file onto a RAM disk (a virtual disk created out of system memory) and displays a boot menu containing a list of the install images available from the WDS server.
5. The user on the client computer selects an install image from the boot menu, and the operating system installation process begins.
6. From this point, setup proceeds just like a manual installation.

Customizing WDS Client Installations

WDS enables you to deploy customized image files and use unattend scripts to perform unattended installations.

As mentioned earlier, the install.wim image file that Microsoft supplies on the Windows Server 2008 DVD performs a basic operating system installation on the client. However, the real strength of WDS in an enterprise environment is in the ability to create and deploy custom image files using unattended procedures. To do this, you must create your own image files and unattend scripts, as discussed in the following sections.

CREATING IMAGE FILES WITH WDS

An install image is basically a snapshot of a computer's hard drive taken at a particular moment in time. The image file contains all of the operating system files on the computer, plus any updates and drivers you have installed, applications you have added, and configuration changes you have made. Creating your own image files is essentially a matter of setting up a computer the way you want it and then capturing an image of the computer to a file.

You can use several tools to create image files, including the ImageX.exe command-line utility Microsoft provides in the Windows Automated Installation Kit (Windows AIK), which is available from the Microsoft Downloads Center at http://microsoft.com/downloads. To use ImageX.exe, you must boot the target computer to Windows PE and run the tool from the

command line. However, the Windows Deployment Center console provides another method for creating image files, using the same WDS infrastructure you used to install images.

WDS enables you to create your own image files by modifying an existing boot image, such as the boot.wim image Microsoft provides with Windows Server 2008, and turning it into a tool that boots the target computer and runs the Windows Deployment Service Capture Utility instead of an operating system's Setup program. The utility then creates an image file and writes it out to the computer's drive, after which you can copy it to the WDS server and deploy it to other computers in the usual manner.

MODIFYING A BOOT IMAGE

To modify a boot image to create image file captures, use the following procedure.

 MODIFY A BOOT IMAGE

GET READY. Log on to Windows Server 2008 using an account with Administrative privileges. When the logon process is completed, close the Initial Configuration Tasks window and any other windows that appear.

1. Click **Start**, and then click **Administrative Tools** > **Windows Deployment Services**. The Windows Deployment Services console appears.

2. Expand the **Server** node and the node for your server. Then, select the **Boot Images** folder.

3. If you have not done so already, add the Windows Server 2008 boot.wim image to the Boot Images store, using the procedure described earlier in this lesson.

4. In the detail pane, right-click the boot image and select **Create Capture Boot Image** from the context menu. The Windows Deployment Services – Create Capture Image Wizard appears, as shown in Figure 1-22.

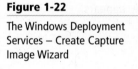

Figure 1-22

The Windows Deployment Services – Create Capture Image Wizard

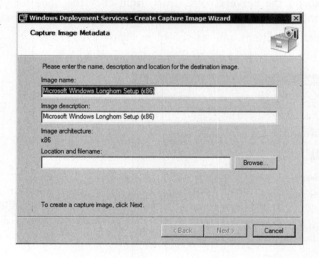

5. On the Capture Image Metadata page, specify a name and description for the new image, and a location and filename for the new image file.

6. Click **Next**. The Task Progress page appears as the wizard creates the new image file.

7. When the image is created successfully, click **Finish**.

CLOSE the Windows Deployment Services console.

You can now add the new capture image to the Boot Image store in the normal manner. To complete the imaging process, you must prepare the target computer with the Sysprep.exe utility and then reboot the system using the capture image. A wizard then appears on the computer that guides you through the process of capturing an image of the computer and uploading it to the WDS server.

DEPLOYING UNATTEND FILES

WDS by itself enables you to perform a standard operating system installation, but the setup process is still interactive, requiring someone at the workstation, like an installation from the DVD. To perform an unattended installation using WDS, you must use unattend files. An unattend file is a script containing responses to all of the prompts that appear on the client during the installation process. To create unattend files, Microsoft recommends using the Windows System Image Manager (Windows SIM) tool in the Windows AIK.

To install an operating system on a client using WDS with no interactivity, you must have two unattend files, as follows:

- WDS client unattend file — This unattend file automates the WDS client procedure that begins when the client computer loads the boot image file.
- Operating system unattend file — This is an unattend file for a standard operating system installation, containing responses to all of the prompts that appear after the client computer loads the install image file.

To use unattend files during a WDS operating system deployment, use the following procedure.

 DEPLOY AN UNATTEND FILE

GET READY. Log on to Windows Server 2008 using an account with Administrative privileges. When the logon process is completed, close the Initial Configuration Tasks window and any other windows that appear.

1. Copy your WDS client unattend file to the \RemoteInstall\WDSClientUnattend folder on the WDS server.
2. Click **Start**, and then click **Administrative Tools** > **Windows Deployment Services**. The Windows Deployment Services console appears.
3. Expand the **Servers** node. Then, right-click the node for your server and, from the context menu, select **Properties**. The server's Properties sheet appears.
4. Click the **Client** tab, as shown in Figure 1-23.

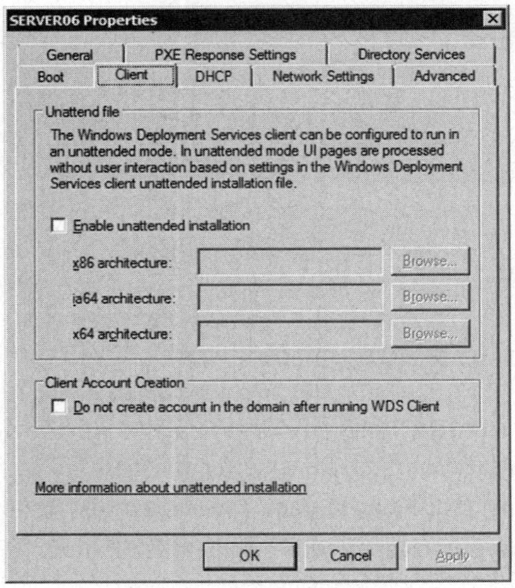

Figure 1-23

The Client tab of a WDS server's Properties sheet

5. Select the **Enable unattended installation** checkbox.
6. Click the **Browse** button corresponding to the processor architecture of the client computer.
7. Browse to your unattend file and then click **Open**.

8. Click **OK** to close the server's Properties sheet.

9. Expand the node for your server and the **Install Images** node and locate the image you want to associate with an unattend file.

10. Right-click the image file and, from the context menu, select **Properties**. The Image Properties sheet appears, as shown in Figure 1-24.

Figure 1-24

The Image Properties sheet

11. Select the **Allow image to install in unattended mode** checkbox.

12. Click **Select File**. The Select Unattend File dialog box appears, as shown in Figure 1-25.

Figure 1-25

The Select Unattend File dialog box

13. Key or browse to the unattend file you want to use and then click **OK**.

14. Click **OK** to close the Image Properties sheet.

CLOSE the Windows Deployment Services console.

At this point, if your unattend files are properly configured, the entire operating system installation process on the client should require no interaction, except for turning on the computer.

■ Activating Windows

THE BOTTOM LINE

You must activate Windows Server 2008 computers within 30 days of installing them. For organizations with volume license agreements, Microsoft has designed a new program called Volume Activation 2.0, which simplifies the process of activating computers on enterprise networks.

Retail versions of Microsoft Windows include a product key that you must supply during installation. After you have installed the operating system, you must activate the product key by contacting Microsoft, either online or by telephone. Activation is the establishment of a relationship between a product key and a copy of the Windows operating system installed on a specific computer.

Enterprise networks, on the other hand, typically do not purchase retail copies of Windows. Instead, they enter into a volume licensing agreement with Microsoft that enables them to run the operating system on a specific number of computers. Until Windows Vista and Windows Server 2008, volume license keys required no activation. However, Microsoft has determined that the vast majority of counterfeit Windows installations are using volume license keys that personnel have illegally shared, whether by accident or intent. As a result, corporate customers must now activate all Windows Vista and Windows Server 2008 computers using volume license keys.

Volume Activation (VA) 2.0 is Microsoft's program for automating and managing the activation of products obtained using volume licenses. VA 2.0 does not alter the terms of your license agreement with Microsoft in any way; it is simply a tool to simplify the activation process. For end users, the activation process is completely transparent, and administrators do not have to supply individual product keys when installing Windows.

Volume licenses for Windows Vista and Windows Server 2008 now include two types of keys, which are designed to support the following two activation services:

- *Key Management Service (KMS)* — An activation service that runs on the local network, enabling clients to activate without communicating with Microsoft.
- *Multiple Activation Key (MAK)* — Enables a specified number of computers to activate using Microsoft's hosted activation services.

Using KMS

KMS enables Windows Server 2008 and Windows Vista computers to activate themselves using a KMS host on the local network.

The Key Management Service is the activation method that Microsoft recommends for medium to large networks with volume licensing agreements. To use KMS, you install the KMS key you receive with your volume license on a computer, which turns it into a KMS host. You then perform a one-time activation of the host with Microsoft, using Microsoft's online services or the telephone. The system resources consumed by the KMS host service are negligible, so you can install it on almost any Windows Vista or Windows Server 2008 computer, and a single host can support a virtually unlimited number of clients.

After you have activated a KMS host on your network, other computers running volume editions of Windows Vista and Windows Server 2008 can activate themselves by contacting the host using their built-in KMS client capabilities. These clients, therefore, do not have to communicate directly with Microsoft.

UNDERSTANDING KMS ACTIVATION

For a KMS host to activate KMS clients, it must receive a certain number of activation requests within the last 30 days. This is called the *KMS activation threshold*, and it is designed to prevent pirated KMS keys from functioning on small networks or individual computers. For a KMS host to activate a Windows Server 2008 client, it must receive at least five client activation requests within 30 days. For a host to activate a Windows Vista client, it must receive 25 activation requests within 30 days.

By default, KMS clients locate KMS hosts by an auto-discovery process that uses DNS queries. When you install a KMS host, the computer creates an SRV resource record on its local DNS server. The SRV record contains the fully-qualified domain name (FQDN) of the com-

puter functioning as a KMS host, and the port number it uses for network communications, which defaults to TCP port 1688.

For the KMS host to successfully create or modify the SRV record, your DNS server must support dynamic updates (Dynamic DNS), like all Windows DNS servers using Windows 2000 Server or better. The host computer must also have appropriate permissions to create and modify DNS records.

When clients attempt to activate, which they do every 120 minutes until an activation is successful, they first query their local DNS server and obtain the SRV records specifying the KMS hosts on the network. The client then selects one of the hosts at random and sends an activation request to it, using the Remote Procedure Call (RPC) protocol. The KMS host counts the number of activation requests it receives within the past 30 days and sends that value back to the client. If the count is sufficient to exceed the activation threshold, the client activates itself for a period of 180 days.

While activated, the client continually attempts to renew its activation by connecting to the host every seven days. When the renewal succeeds, the client pushes its activation period forward to a full 180 days. If the client is unable to contact the host for 180 days, it begins to display recurring messages to the user, specifying the need to activate Windows, until it is able to reactivate.

On the host computer, KMS records the unique ***client machine ID (CMID)*** of each successful activation in a protected table for 30 days, after which it purges the record. When a client successfully renews its activation, the host removes the old CMID entry and creates a new one. As a safety precaution, the host caches twice the number of CMIDs it needs to meet the activation threshold, that is, ten Windows Server 2008 computers or 50 Windows Vista computers. This helps to ensure that clients on a network meeting the activation threshold are always able to activate themselves.

CONFIGURING KMS

KMS often does not require any manual configuration after you install and activate a KMS key on a computer. The host automatically creates an SRV record on the DNS server and volume editions of Windows Vista and Windows Server 2008 automatically attempt to contact the host to authenticate themselves. However, it is possible to modify the default behavior of KMS clients and hosts as needed for your environment.

KMS does not have a graphical interface; you use a script called Slmgr.vbs, which you run from the command-prompt with the Cscript.exe utility, to modify the operational parameters of clients and hosts. The Slmgr.vbs syntax is as follows:

```
Cscript C:\windows\system32\slmgr.vbs [/ipk key] [/ato] [/sprt port]
[/cdns] [/sdns] [/sai interval] [/sri interval] [/skms server{:port}]
[/ckms]
```

- /ipk *key* — Installs the specified KMS key on the computer, turning it into a KMS host.
- /ato — On a host, performs an online activation with Microsoft. On a client, triggers the local activation process.
- /sprt *port* — Configures the KMS host to use the specified TCP port, rather than the default port 1688.
- /cdns — Disables automatic DNS publishing.
- /sdns — Enables automatic DNS publishing.
- /sai *interval* — Specifies a time interval between client activation attempts other than the default 120 minutes.

- /sri *interval* — Specifies a time interval between client activation renewal attempts other than the default 7 days.
- /skms *server:port* — Disables auto-discovery on a KMS client and specifies the name or address (and, optionally, the port number) of the KMS host it will use to activate. The *server* variable can be an FQDN, a NetBIOS name, an IPv4 address, or an IPv6 address.
- /ckms — Re-enables auto-discovery on a KMS client.

Using MAK

> MAK enables individual computers to activate themselves by contacting Microsoft hosts or using a proxy.

Microsoft intends the use of Multiple Activate Keys for networks that do not have a sufficient number of computers to support KMS, or for computers that do not connect to the organization's network on a regular basis, such as laptops issued to traveling users. A MAK is a single key that enables a specified number of computers to activate, using one of the following two types of activation:

- MAK Independent Activation — Clients contact the Microsoft hosts directly, using an Internet connection or a telephone.
- MAK Proxy Activation — Multiple clients send their activation requests to a proxy called the Volume Activation Management Tool (VAMT).

MAK Independent Activation is similar to the standard retail product key activation, except that you use the same key for multiple computers. At its simplest, MAK deployment is a matter of supplying the MAK key during the operating system installation, using the standard setup interface. You can also enter a MAK key on an existing Windows installation through the Control Panel. You can install the MAK key on clients individually, or include the key as part of an image file and deploy it on multiple computers.

After you have installed a MAK on a client computer, the activation proceeds in the usual manner, with the client either contacting a Microsoft host automatically on the Internet, or activating manually, using a telephone call. After installation, the client computer stores the MAK key in encrypted form, so that it is inaccessible to the end user.

For ***MAK Proxy Activation***, you must download the Volume Activation Management Tool (VAMT) from the Microsoft Download Center (at http://microsoft.com/downloads) and install it on a computer with access to the Internet. VAMT collects the activation requests from the clients on the network, uses a single connection to the Microsoft hosts to activate them all at the same time, and then distributes the resulting activation codes to the clients using the Windows Management Instrumentation (WMI) interface. With VAMT, you can also redeploy existing activation codes to clients you have re-imaged or rebuilt.

■ Using Server Manager

THE BOTTOM LINE Server Manager is an MMC console that provides a selection of the most commonly used Windows Server 2008 management tools.

When you start a Windows Server 2008 computer for the first time after installing the operating system, the Initial Configuration Tasks window displays, as shown in Figure 1-26. This window presents a consolidated view of the post-installation tasks that, in previous Windows Server versions, you had to perform using various interfaces presented during and after the OS setup process.

After you complete the configuration tasks in sections 1 and 2 of the Initial Configuration Tasks window, you can use the links in the Customize This Server section to install roles

Figure 1-26

The Initial Configuration Tasks window

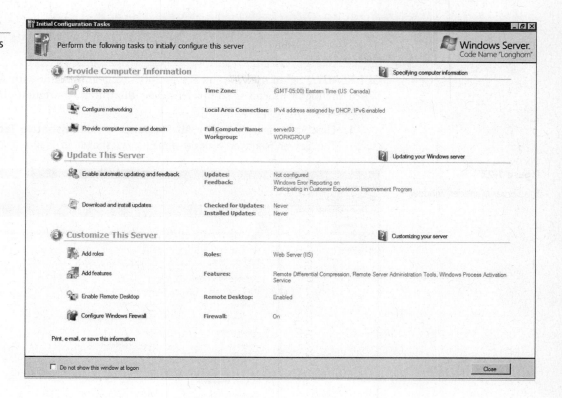

and features on the computer. The Add Roles and Add Features links launch the Add Roles Wizard and the Add Features Wizard, respectively.

You can also install and manage roles and features using the Server Manager console. Server Manager is an MMC console that contains a collection of snap-ins most commonly used by Windows Server 2008 administrators. The Server Manager console integrates the following snap-ins into a single interface:

- Component Services
- Device Manager
- Disk Management
- Event Viewer
- Local Users and Groups
- Reliability and Performance Monitor
- Routing and Remote Access
- Services
- Share and Storage Management
- Task Scheduler
- Terminal Services Configuration
- Terminal Services Manager
- Windows Firewall with Advanced Security
- Windows Server Backup
- WMI Control

Adding Roles

The Add Roles Wizard enables you to select multiple roles and role services for installation.

To add roles using Server Manager, use the following procedure.

 ADD ROLES

GET READY. Log on to Windows Server 2008 using an account with Administrative privileges. When the logon process is completed, close the Initial Configuration Tasks window and any other windows that appear.

1. Click **Start**, and then click **All Programs** > **Administrative Tools** > **Server Manager**. The Server Manager window appears, as shown in Figure 1-27.

Figure 1-27

The Server Manager window

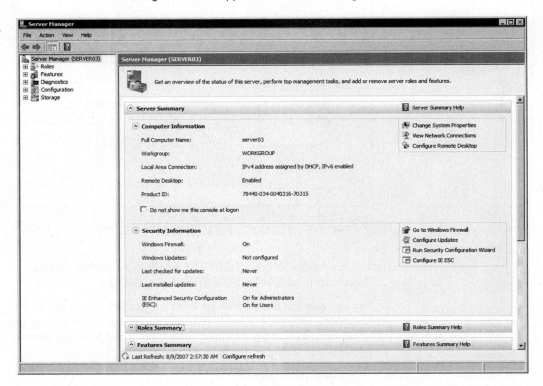

2. In the scope (left) pane, click the **Roles** node, and then click **Add Roles**. The Add Roles Wizard appears, as shown in Figure 1-28.

Figure 1-28

The Add Roles Wizard

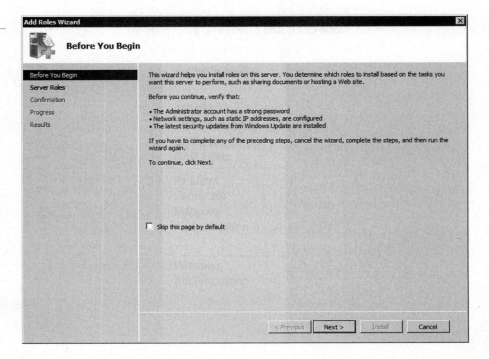

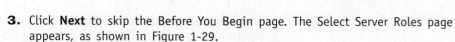

3. Click **Next** to skip the Before You Begin page. The Select Server Roles page appears, as shown in Figure 1-29.

Figure 1-29

The Select Server Roles page

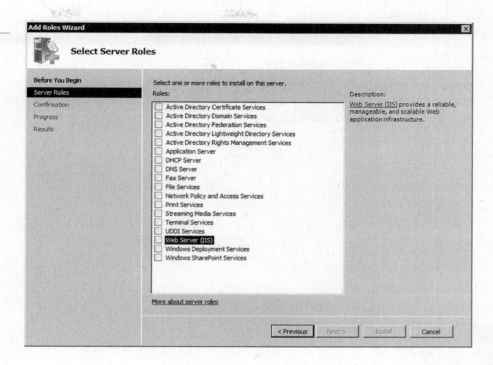

4. Select the checkbox for the role (or roles) you want to install. If the role you select is dependent on other roles or features, the Add Features Required For Web Server (IIS) dialog box appears, as shown in Figure 1-30.

Figure 1-30

The Add Features Required For Web Server (IIS) page

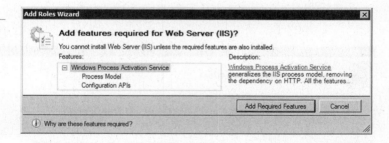

5. Click **Add Required Features**, and then click **Next**. A role-specific Introduction page appears, explaining the function of the role and providing installation notes and links, as shown in Figure 1-31.

Figure 1-31

The Introduction to Web Server (IIS) page

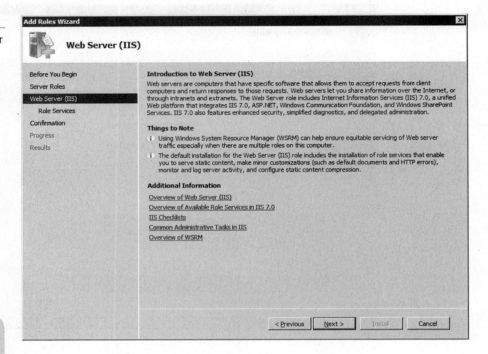

TAKE NOTE*

If you choose to install multiple roles, or if you agree to install antecedent roles required by your selection, the wizard will present the configuration pages for each role it is installing.

6. Click **Next**. Additional role-specific pages might appear, providing access to configuration settings or enabling you to select the role services you want to install.

7. Click **Next**. The Confirm Installation Selections page appears, as shown in Figure 1-32.

Figure 1-32

The Confirm Installation Selections page

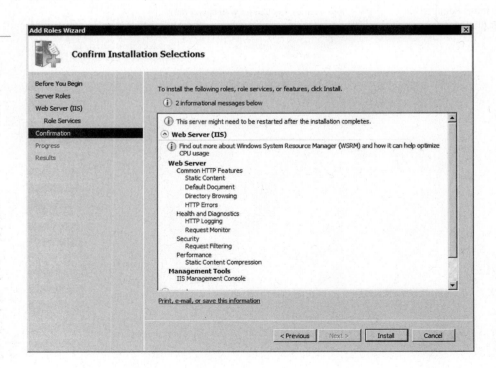

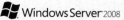

8. Click **Install**. The Installation Progress page appears as the wizard installs the selected roles, role services, and features. When the installation is completed, the Installation Results page appears, as shown in Figure 1-33.

Figure 1-33

The Installation Results page

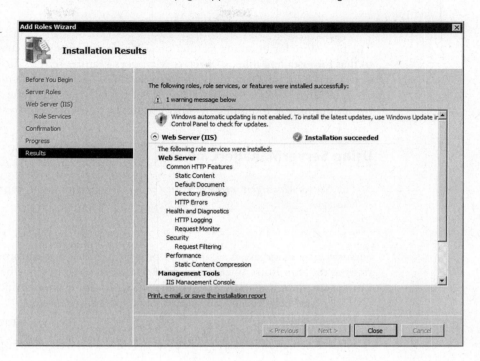

9. After you confirm that all of the installations have completed successfully, click **Close**.

CLOSE the Server Manager console.

After you have completed the Add Roles Wizard, which installed roles on the server, the Roles screen in Server Manager displays a detailed summary of the roles installed on the computer, including a list of all the role services and a status indicator, as shown in Figure 1-34.

Figure 1-34

The Roles screen in Server Manager

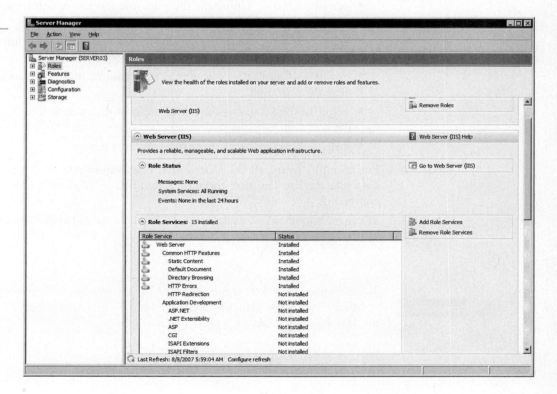

Adding Features

> The Add Features Wizard enables you to select multiple server features for installation.

The procedure for installing features on a Windows Server 2008 computer is almost identical to that for installing roles. On Server Manager's Features screen, click Add Features. The Add Features Wizard takes you through the process of selecting and configuring features. As with the Add Roles Wizard, the Add Features Wizard preserves all of the necessary dependencies by prompting you to install any other features or roles that are necessary.

Using ServerManagerCmd.exe

> The **ServerManagerCmd.exe** utility provides a command prompt alternative to Server Manager.

ServerManagerCmd.exe is a command prompt tool that can perform many of the same functions as the Add Roles Wizard and the Add Features Wizard. The benefit of the command prompt interface is that you can install roles and features from scripts or batch files. The syntax for ServerManagerCmd.exe is as follows:

```
ServerManagerCmd [-query][-install name][-remove name]

[-inputPath answer.xml][-restart][-resultPath result.xml[-help]
```

- -query — Displays a complete list of all the roles, role services, and features supported by the computer and indicates which ones are currently installed.
- -install *name* [-setting *name=value*] [-allSubFeatures] — Installs the role, role service, or feature specified by the *name* variable. Use the — setting parameter to specify values for required role settings. Use the — allSubFeatures parameter to install all of the subordinate roles, role services, or features associated with the module it is installing.
- -remove *name* — Uninstalls the role, role service, or feature specified by the *name* variable.
- -inputPath *answer.xml* — Installs or removes all of the roles, role services, or features listed in the XML file specified by the *answer.xml* variable.
- -restart — Causes the computer to restart automatically, if a restart is needed to complete the operation.
- -resultPath *result.xml* — Saves the results of the operation to an XML file specified by the *result.xml* variable.
- -help — Displays help information for the program.

For example, to install the Distributed File System role service with all of its subordinate role services and save the results to a file called dfsoutput.xml, use the following command:

```
servermanagercmd -install FS-DFS -allsubfeatures -resultpath dfsoutput
.xml
```

TAKE NOTE*

To determine the correct abbreviation to use on the command line for a role, role service, or feature, run ServerManagerCmd.exe with the -query parameter. It shows the abbreviations in square brackets on each line of output.

SUMMARY SKILL MATRIX

IN THIS LESSON YOU LEARNED:

- Applications in the enterprise can take several forms, including client-run applications, client/server applications, and distributed applications.

- The Add Roles Wizard provides roles that fall into three basic categories: directory services, infrastructure services, and application services.

- Windows Server 2008 includes a collection of features, which you can select individually. You can also augment a given role by adding features that increase its capabilities.

- The number of roles a server can perform depends on the computer's hardware configuration, the hardware requirements of the role, and the size and scope of the enterprise.

- Distributing server roles among several computers has several distinct advantages, including fault tolerance, ease of resource allocation, high availability, server scalability, security configuration, dispersed network traffic, and simpler update management.

- Not until you have decided how you will deploy your applications and the roles an application server will perform should you begin selecting the hardware that goes into the computer.

- Terminal Services can provide a number of benefits in an enterprise application deployment, including substantial savings in the cost of workstation hardware and conservation of network bandwidth.

- The Windows Server Core installation option of Windows Server 2008 gives you a stripped-down version of the operating system. There is no Start menu, no desktop Explorer shell, no MMC console, and virtually no graphical applications. All you see when you start the computer is a single window with a command prompt.

- A virtual server is a complete installation of an operating system that runs in a software environment emulating a physical computer. Applications such as Microsoft Virtual Server 2005 and the Windows Server virtualization technology in Windows Server 2008 make it possible for a single computer to host multiple virtual machines, each of which runs in a completely independent environment.

- Windows Deployment Services (WDS) is a role included with Windows Server 2008, which enables you to perform unattended installations of Windows Server 2008 and other operating systems on remote computers, using network-based boot and installation media.

- Volume Activation (VA) 2.0 is Microsoft's program for automating and managing the activation of products obtained using volume licenses. VA 2.0 does not alter the terms of the license agreement with Microsoft in any way; it is simply a tool to simplify the activation process. For end users, the activation process is completely transparent, and administrators do not have to supply individual product keys when installing Windows.

- Volume licenses for Windows Vista and Windows Server 2008 now include two types of keys, which Microsoft designed to support the following two activation services: Key Management Service (KMS) and Multiple Activation Key (MAK).

■ Knowledge Assessment

Fill in the Blank

Complete the following sentences by writing the correct word or words in the blanks provided.

1. The storage area networking technology supported by Windows Server 2008 as a lower cost alternative to Fibre Channel is called _____.

2. The only server roles discussed in this lesson that are not included with the Windows Server 2008 product are _____ and _____.

3. DHCP and DNS are known as _____ services.

4. To create a searchable catalog of Web services on your network, you would install the _____ role.

5. To create Web sites that people can use to collaborate on documents and tasks, you must install the _____ role.

6. The feature that enhances fault tolerance by providing multiple data paths to a single server storage device is called _____.

7. The Windows Server 2008 file server element that conserves disk space by eliminating duplicate copies of files is called _____.

8. The Application Server role is essentially a superset of the _____ role.

9. To implement Windows Vista desktop themes on a Windows Server 2008 computer, you must install the _____ feature.

10. The type of activation recommended by Microsoft for medium to large networks with volume licensing agreements is _____.

Multiple Choice

Select the correct answer for each of the following questions. Choose all answers that are correct.

1. Which of the following *cannot* be installed from the command line by the ServerManagerCmd.exe utility?
   - **a.** Features
   - **b.** Applications
   - **c.** Roles
   - **d.** Role services

2. Which of the following provide(s) UNIX clients with Windows printing capabilities?
   - **a.** Internet Printing Client
   - **b.** Multipath I/O (MPIO)
   - **c.** LPR Port Monitor feature
   - d. LPD Service role service

3. Which of the following roles must you install with the Fax Server role on a Windows Server 2008 computer?
   - **a.** Active Directory Certificate Services
   - **b.** UDDI Services
   - **c.** Print Services
   - **d.** Web Server

4. When a client runs an application on a terminal server, which of the client computer's resources does the application utilize?
   - **a.** The client computer's memory resources
   - **b.** The client computer's processor resources
   - **c.** The client computer's hard drive resources
   - **d.** None of the above

5. Windows Server 2008 requires that you install which of the following features for the Application Server role?
   - **a.** .NET Framework 3.0 feature
   - **b.** Network Load Balancing (NLB)
   - **c.** Windows System Resource Manager (WSRM)
   - **d.** Windows Process Activation Service (WPAS)

6. Which of the following is a true statement about limitations Microsoft places on the number of roles a Windows Server 2008 computer can support?
   - **a.** There are no limitations placed on the number of roles a Windows Server 2008 computer can perform.
   - **b.** The number of roles that a Windows Server 2008 computer can run is limited only to the amount of hardware resources available to the server.
   - **c.** A Windows Server 2008 computer can perform only one role.
   - **d.** None of the above.

7. Which of the following is *not* true in reference to using the Server Manager console?
   a. The Add Roles Wizard and the Add Features Wizard are both accessible from the Server Manager.
   b. You must run a separate instance of the Add Roles Wizard for each role you want to install.
   c. Server Manager can install multiple roles at once.
   d. You must download an update from the Microsoft Downloads Web site to add the Streaming Media Services role to the Server Manager console.

8. Which feature(s) must you install when you install the Web Server (IIS) role?
   a. Windows Process Activation Service (WPAS)
   b. Telnet Client
   c. Message Queuing
   d. Peer Name Resolution Protocol (PNRP)

9. The TS Gateway role service enables clients on the Internet to access which type of server?
   a. Windows Server 2008
   b. SMTP Server
   c. Telnet Server
   d. Windows Server 2008 Terminal Server

10. Which of the following services does a Windows Deployment Services client computer use to locate a WDS server?
    a. DHCP
    b. DNS
    c. Active Directory
    d. WINS

Review Questions

1. List three reasons why it might not be a good idea to purchase the most powerful server computer you can find and install all of the roles your organization needs on that one machine. Explain your answers.

2. Explain how a distributed application works.

■ Case Scenarios

Scenario 1-1: Installing Roles with a Batch File

Mark Lee is an IT technician whose supervisor has assigned the task of configuring twenty new servers, which Mark is to ship to the company's branch offices around the country. He must configure each server to function as a file server with support for DFS and UNIX clients, a print server with support for Internet and UNIX printing, a fax server, and a secured, intranet Web/FTP server for domain users. Write a batch file that Mark can use to install all of the required software elements on a server.

Scenario 1-2: Hosting Applications with Terminal Services

Your company is planning to open a second office in another city, and you are part of the team that is designing the new network. The employees in the new office will be performing a wide variety of tasks, and they need a large number of applications installed on their computers. Ralph, your IT director, is having trouble meeting his budget for the new network, due to the high cost of the applications, processor, memory, and disk space resources the workstations will need to run the applications. He is also concerned about supporting and maintaining the workstations because there will be no full-time IT personnel at the new site.

You suggest using Terminal Services to host the applications. Ralph, however, knows nothing about Terminal Services. Explain how using Terminal Services can resolve all of the network design problems Ralph is experiencing.

5 LESSON

Deploying IIS Services

OBJECTIVE DOMAIN MATRIX

TECHNOLOGY SKILL	OBJECTIVE DOMAIN	OBJECTIVE DOMAIN NUMBER
Creating a Web site	Manage Web sites.	3.2
Configuring Site Properties	Manage Internet Information Services (IIS).	3.5
Creating an FTP Site	Configure a File Transfer Protocol (FTP) server.	3.3

KEY TERMS

binding
File Transfer Protocol (FTP)
FTP over Secure Sockets Layer
  (SSL)
host header

Hypertext Markup Language
  (HTML)
Hypertext Transfer Protocol
  (HTTP)
protocol listener

virtual directory
virtual hosting
Windows Process Activation
  Service (WPAS)

Internet Information Services (IIS), a major component of Windows Server 2008, includes many modules and functions. This is the first of three lessons devoted to IIS, and includes the following topics:

- Installing IIS
- Creating a Web site
- Creating a virtual directory
- Configuring IIS settings
- Deploying and configuring an FTP7 server

■ Using the Web Server (IIS) Role

THE BOTTOM LINE

From its origins as a simple Web server application, Internet Information Services (IIS) has grown to be an important part of many enterprise network deployments.

In addition to hosting Web sites based on HTML (Hypertext Markup Language) pages and image files, IIS can host applications using a variety of development environments.

What's New in IIS7?

Microsoft has extensively renovated the new version of Internet Information Services included in Windows Server 2008.

Internet Information Services (IIS), now in version 7.0, has undergone major revisions for the Windows Vista and Windows Server 2008 releases. Some of the new developments are as follows:

- Modular installation—Compared to earlier IIS versions, which split the installation into a handful of optional components, IIS7 has more than forty individual modules for installation. For example, instead of installing all of the supported authentication methods by default, you can now select only the ones that you intend to use. This reduces the application's attack surface, minimizes the amount of memory and other system resources it needs to run, and simplifies the configuration and maintenance processes.

- New management interface—The IIS Manager application now uses an icon-based interface, as shown in Figure 5-1, that displays only the controls associated with the modules you have installed. The application also uses the Actions pane introduced in Microsoft Management Console 3.0 to great effect, providing context-sensitive commands for the module you have selected.

Figure 5-1

The IIS Manager interface

- Command line interface—The Virtual Basic administration scripts that IIS6 used for command line management have been replaced by a comprehensive application called AppCmd.exe, which can perform virtually any IIS configuration task from the command line.

- Security enhancements—As mentioned earlier, the IIS7 modular architecture enables you to install only the modules you need. By omitting the unnecessary code, you install fewer patches and attackers have fewer weaknesses to exploit. In addition, request filtering is now built into IIS7, instead of being implemented as a separate add-on product.

- Configuration files—IIS6 stored all of its configuration settings in the metabase, a central XML repository. IIS7 eliminates the metabase, in favor of a series of ASP.NET configuration files with .config extensions. However, IIS7 does include an IIS6 Metabase

Compatibility role service, which enables administrators to continue using any management scripts they created for the IIS6 metabase. IIS7 also provides a variety of configuration options that can help to replicate servers in a Web farm.

- Error handling—IIS7 is able to capture more information about failed requests than previous versions. The IIS log file format includes new error subcodes that provide more detailed reasons for a failure, and Failed Request Tracing capabilities, which enable IIS7 to log additional diagnostic information when an application meets specified status code, time elapsed, or error type conditions.

- Extensibility—In addition to providing control over the IIS7 modules you install, the Web server's modular architecture enables developers to create modules that plug into the same pipeline as the IIS7 components.

Selecting IIS Role Services

Internet Information Service includes a large collection of role services that you can use to customize the server installation.

As mentioned earlier, IIS7 uses a modularized architecture that enables you to install only the functions that you need for your Web sites. When you add the Web Server (IIS) role on a Windows Server 2008 computer, the Add Roles Wizard displays the Role Services page shown in Figure 5-2, in which you can select from the many role services provided with IIS.

Figure 5-2

The Select Role Services page for the Web Server (IIS) role

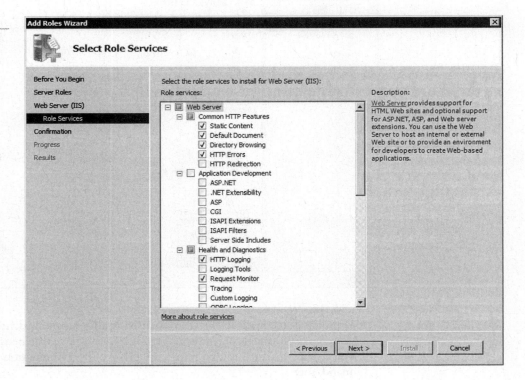

When you select the Web Server (IIS) role for installation, the wizard displays the message box shown in Figure 5-3, asking if you want to install the Windows Process Activation Service (WPAS) feature that the role requires. The default Web server (IIS) role installation requires WPAS with its Process Model and Configuration APIs components. If you select the ASP.NET or .NET Extensibility role services, the WPAS.NET Environment component is required as well.

Figure 5-3

Web Server (IIS) role dependencies

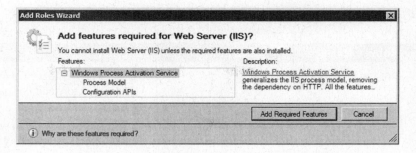

XREF

For more information about WPAS, see "Introducing the Windows Process Activation Service," later in this lesson.

The list of role services for the Web Server (IIS) role is extensive, and the default selections are minimal, consisting only of the following modules:

- Static Content
- Default Document
- Directory Browsing
- HTTP Errors
- HTTP Logging
- Request Monitor
- Request Filtering
- Static Content Compression
- IIS Management Console

These components are sufficient to create a basic, anonymous HTTP Web site. Notice that, by default, IIS has no authentication protocols, no application development environments, and only the most basic management and logging capabilities installed. To host anything beyond a simple Web site, you must install additional role services, either when you install the role or afterwards.

Fortunately, when you select additional role services, the Add Roles Wizard does not include configuration pages for each of the role services you select. The nature of the IIS architecture and the large number of role services involved precludes the possibility of using the configure-as-you-go method found in some of the other role installations. Table 5-1 lists the role services, the modules associated with them, and their functions.

Table 5-1

Web Server (IIS) Role Services and Their Functions

ROLE SERVICE	MODULE NAME	CATEGORY	FUNCTION
Static Content (*)	StaticFileModule	HTTP (Hypertext Transfer Protocol)	• Enables the Web server to publish traditional Web sites that consist only of HTML and image files. • You can omit this module if you will use only IIS to host non-HTTP sites, such as applications developed using Windows Communication Foundation (WCF).
Default Document (*)	DefaultDocumentModule	HTTP	• Specifies the name of the file that client browsers should load by default (such as index.html) when the Uniform Resource Locator (URL) received from a client does not include a filename. • Without this module, all client URLs must include filenames. • If this module is omitted and Directory Browsing is disabled or omitted, client URLs lacking a filename will result in an error.

(*continued*)

Table 5-1 (continued)

ROLE SERVICE	MODULE NAME	CATEGORY	FUNCTION
Directory Browsing (*)	DirectoryListingModule	HTTP	• Enables clients to view a listing of the files in a particular directory and navigate up and down through the directory tree. • Select this module if you want to provide Web site users with directory-based access to the files on your Web sites. • After installation, you can enable or disable this module for individual sites, as needed.
HTTP Errors (*)	CustomErrorModule	HTTP	• Enables the Web server administrator to create customized messages for specific HTTP errors. • Install this module if you want to provide specific information to clients when they experience an error, such as the email address or telephone number of the company help desk.
HTTP Redirection	HttpRedirect	HTTP	• Enables the Web server to forward incoming requests for a specific URL to another URL, such as when a site changes domain names. • This module is useful when you move a Web site to a new domain due to a product name change, company merger, or sale of a product line, and you want the Web server to automatically forward user traffic to the new URL.
ASP.NET	ASP.NET	Application Development	• Implements a server side, object-oriented programming environment, based on the .NET framework.
.NET Extensibility	NetFxExtensibility	Application Development	• Enables developers to modify the functionality of the Web server, using the ASP.Net extensibility model and the .NET application programming interfaces (APIs).
Active Server Pages (ASP)	ASP	Application Development	• Provides a server side scripting environment for the development of Web sites and applications that supports VBScript and JScript.
Common Gateway Interface (CGI)	CGIModule	Application Development	• Provides a scripting interface that enables a Web server to pass incoming information to another program.
Internet Server Application Programming Interface (ISAPI) Extensions	ISAPIModule	Application Development	• Enables the Web server to execute compiled ISAPI applications.
ISAPI Filters	ISAPIFilterModule	Application Development	• Provides support for applications that use ISAPI filters to modify the functionality of the IIS Web server.
Server Side Includes (SSI)	ServerSideIncludeModule	Application Development	• Provides support for a scripting language that enables the Web server to dynamically generate HTML pages.

(continued)

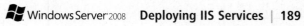

Table 5-1 (*continued*)

ROLE SERVICE	MODULE NAME	CATEGORY	FUNCTION
HTTP Logging (*)	HttpLoggingModule	Health and Diagnostics	• Enables the Web server to maintain logs of all Web site activity. • Virtually all Web sites can benefit from detailed examination of activity logs for troubleshooting, traffic analysis, market research, and other statistical purposes.
Logging Tools	LoggingLibraries	Health and Diagnostics	• Provides tools for managing activity logs and automating logging tasks.
Request Monitor (*)	RequestMonitorModule	Health and Diagnostics	• Captures information about HTTP requests that administrators can use to monitor the Web server's health and troubleshoot performance problems.
Tracing	HTTPTracingModule	Health and Diagnostics	• Enables the Web server to save information about failed application requests for troubleshooting purposes.
Custom Logging	CustomLoggingModule	Health and Diagnostics	• Enables administrators to log Web server activity using a customized format. • Many tools are available to analyze and interpret Web server logs in their standard format, but if you plan to use tools that require a different format, this module enables you to alter the default logs.
Open Database Connectivity (ODBC) Logging	ODBCLogging	Health and Diagnostics	• Enables the Web server to save its logs to an ODBC-compliant database. • Web server logs are typically saved as text files, but database logging can provide more advanced and automated statistical capabilities.
Basic Authentication	BasicAuthModule	Security	• Provides support for a highly compatible and relatively unsecured form of authentication, using Windows user names and passwords. • Suitable for relatively small intranet Web sites, but not for Internet sites, because it is easy to capture and decrypt the user passwords. • Use with Secure Sockets Layer (SSL).
Windows Authentication	WindowsAuthModule	Security	• Provides a secure NTLM- or Kerberos-based authentication method for domain users. • Not suitable for Web sites with clients that are not members of the domain, or who must access the site through a firewall or proxy server.
Digest Authentication	DigestAuthModule	Security	• Authenticates users by sending a password hash to a domain controller on the network. • Provides better security than Basic Authentication. • Suitable for Web sites with clients who must access the site through a firewall or proxy server.
Client Certificate Mapping Authentication	CertificateMapping-AuthenticationModule	Security	• Provides certificate-based authentication using Active Directory for one-to-one certificate mapping.

(*continued*)

Table 5-1 (*continued*)

ROLE SERVICE	MODULE NAME	CATEGORY	FUNCTION
IIS Client Certificate Mapping Authentication	IISCertificateMapping-AuthenticationModule	Security	• Provides certificate-based authentication using IIS for one-to-one or many-to-one certificate mapping.
URL Authorization	UrlAuthorizationModule	Security	• Enables administrators to restrict access to specific URLs by authorizing only specific users, groups, or HTTP verbs (such as GET or POST). • Suitable only for protecting intranet sites because the authorized users and groups must have a domain account or a local account on the Web server.
Request Filtering (*)	RequestFilteringModule	Security	• Enables the Web server to block malicious traffic by filtering incoming requests based on rules created by the administrator. • Replaces the URLScan utility from earlier IIS versions.
IP and Domain Restrictions	IPSecurityModule	Security	• Enables administrators to restrict access to the Web server by allowing only computers with certain IP addresses or domain names to connect.
Static Content Compression (*)	HTTPStaticCompression	Performance	• Enables the Web server to conserve network bandwidth by compressing static Web site content before transmitting it to the client.
Dynamic Content Compression	HTTPDynamic Compression	Performance	• Enables the Web server to conserve network bandwidth by compressing dynamic Web site content before transmitting it to the client, at the cost of increased Web server CPU utilization.
IIS Management Console (*)	ManagementConsole	Management Tools	• Enables administrators to manage local or remote IIS7 Web servers.
IIS Management Scripts and Tools	ManagementScripting	Management Tools	• Enables administrators to automate IIS7 management tasks using command-line tools and scripts.
Management Service	ManagementService	Management Tools	• Enables the Web server to be managed remotely using the IIS Management Console.
IIS 6 Metabase Compatibility	Metabase	Management Tools	• Translates interfaces and scripts designed for the IIS 6 metabase to the new IIS7 format.
IIS 6 WMI Compatibility	WMICompatibility	Management Tools	• Provides support for IIS 6 Windows Management Instrumentation (WMI) scripts.
IIS 6 Scripting Tools	LegacyScripts	Management Tools	• Enables administrators to use IIS 6 scripting tools to manage IIS7 Web servers.
IIS 6 Management Console	LegacySnap-in	Management Tools	• Provides the ability to manage remote IIS 6 Web servers.
FTP Server	FTPServer	FTP Publishing	• Enables the Web server to host FTP sites and respond to FTP client requests.
FTP Management Console	FTPManagement	FTP Publishing	• Enables administrators to manage local and remote IIS7 FTP sites.

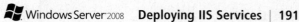

Introducing the Windows Process Activation Service

WPAS enables IIS to respond to a variety of incoming message types, not just HTTP.

A Web server is essentially a program that listens for incoming requests from clients and responds to those requests by supplying data or executing an instruction. Originally, Web servers listened only for messages sent using the ***Hypertext Transfer Protocol (HTTP),*** the standard application layer protocol for Web communications, which client browsers generated when a user keyed or clicked a link for a Uniform Resource Locator (URL). On receiving such a request, the server responded by transmitting a file back to the client, coded using ***Hypertext Markup Language (HTML)***, a simple coding language that provides the client browser with instructions on displaying the text in the file and embedding the accompanying image files.

Today, however, Web servers can also listen for types of requests other than HTTP and respond by executing programs and sending the resulting data back to the client in any number of different forms. This means that several modules other than the HTTP listener are listening for client requests. In previous versions of IIS, the World Wide Web Publishing Service (W3SVC) managed all requests; the process was essentially HTTP-centric.

In IIS7, the modular architecture extends into the request handling process as well. Instead of a monolithic, HTTP-based request pipeline with support for additional request types tacked on to it, IIS7 uses a generic request pipeline that is modular in nature. When you select the role services that provide support for various types of applications, IIS7 plugs those modules into the pipeline.

The component that manages the request pipeline, the server's application pools, and the worker processes running in them is called the ***Windows Process Activation Service (WPAS)***. As mentioned earlier in this lesson, you must install the WPAS feature, with its subfeatures, to run the Web Server (IIS) role. Because WPAS now handles incoming requests instead of the W3SVC service, those requests do not have to be based on HTTP. Therefore, you can use IIS7 to implement applications through HTTP or non-HTTP Web sites.

■ Publishing IIS Web Sites

↓
THE BOTTOM LINE   IIS creates a default Web site when you install it, but you can create as many additional sites as you wish.

After you have installed the Web Server (IIS) role, you can use the Internet Information Services (IIS) Manager application to create, configure, and secure sites, and deploy applications, if desired. These procedures are covered in the following sections, as well as in Lesson 6, "Securing IIS Services," and Lesson 7, "Deploying Web Applications."

Creating a Web Site

Any additional Web sites you create on an IIS7 server inherit the default server settings unless you modify them manually.

CERTIFICATION READY?
Manage Web sites

3.2

When you install the Web Server (IIS) role on a Windows Server 2008 system, IIS7 automatically creates a default Web site, using the modules you selected for installation with the role. You can use that default site to publish your content, reconfiguring it as needed, or you can create additional sites on the server.

To create a new IIS7 Web site, use the following procedure.

➔ **CREATE A WEB SITE**

GET READY. Log on to Windows Server 2008 using a domain account with Administrator privileges. When the logon process is completed, close the Initial Configuration Tasks window and any other windows that appear.

1. Click **Start**, and then click **Administrative Tools** > **Internet Information Services (IIS) Manager.** The Internet Information Services (IIS) Manager console appears, as shown in Figure 5-4.

Figure 5-4

The Internet Information Services (IIS) Manager console

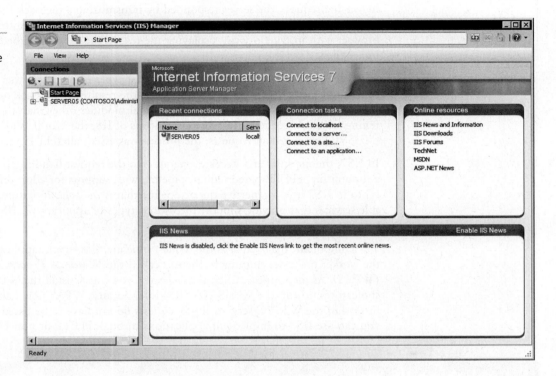

2. In the scope pane, expand the local server. Then, right-click the **Sites** node and, from the context menu, select **Add Web Site**. The Add Web Site dialog box appears, as shown in Figure 5-5.

Figure 5-5

The Add Web Site dialog box

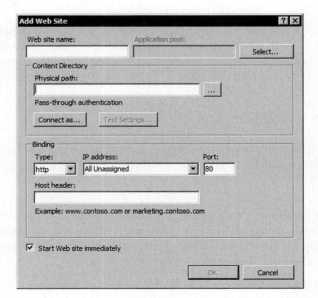

3. In the Web Site Name text box, key the name you want to use for the site.

4. In the Physical Path text box, key or browse to the folder containing the content files for the Web site.

   If the content files are located in a folder that requires authentication for access, click **Connect as** and supply the credentials needed. Remember that IIS requires access to the content files, whether you are logged on to the computer or not.

5. In the Binding box, specify the IP Address, Port, and/or Host Header settings that IIS will use to uniquely identify this Web site.

6. To make the site active as soon as it is created, leave the *Start Web site immediately* checkbox selected.

7. Click **OK** to create the site. The name you selected appears under the Sites node.

CLOSE the Internet Information Services (IIS) Manager console.

If you have selected the *Start Web site immediately* checkbox during the Web site creation process, the site is immediately available to clients supplying the correct URL. If you have not, you must start the site by selecting Start from the actions pane.

Creating a Virtual Directory

> Virtual directories enable you to use a Web site to publish files located anywhere on the network.

When you create a Web site in IIS7, all of the files and folders in the home folder you specify in the Physical Path text box become available on the new site. However, IIS7 also enables you to create virtual directories on your sites. A ***virtual directory*** is an alias that points to a folder in another physical location, essentially a shortcut that enables you to publish content found on different drives or different computers, without copying or moving it.

For example, your company might want to host some of the same documents on several different Web sites. Rather than copy the documents to each content folder, you can create a virtual directory on each site, pointing to a central location where you stored the documents. This way, you can conserve disk space by maintaining a single copy of each document file, and you don't have to replicate the documents to each site when anyone modifies them.

In addition to providing access to content located anywhere on your network, virtual directories also hide the actual locations of your files from the Web clients, which helps to secure your server. To create a virtual directory on one of your sites, use the following procedure.

 CREATE A VIRTUAL DIRECTORY

GET READY. Log on to Windows Server 2008 using a domain account with Administrator privileges. When the logon process is completed, close the Initial Configuration Tasks window and any other windows that appear.

1. Click **Start**, and then click **Administrative Tools** > **Internet Information Services (IIS) Manager**. The Internet Information Services (IIS) Manager console appears.

2. In the scope pane, expand the local server. Then, expand the **Sites** node, right-click a site and, from the context menu, select **Add Virtual Directory**. The Add Virtual Directory dialog box appears, as shown in Figure 5-6.

Figure 5-6

The Add Virtual Directory dialog box

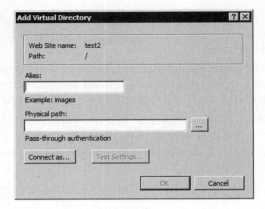

3. In the Alias text box, key the name for the virtual directory on your Web site.

4. In the Physical Path text box, key or browse to the physical location of the folder you want to add to the site as a virtual directory.

5. If the Web server needs credentials to access the folder you specified, click **Connect as**, supply a user name and password, and then click **OK**.

6. Click **OK** to close the Add Virtual Directory dialog box. The new virtual directory appears beneath the site you selected.

CLOSE the Internet Information Services (IIS) Manager console.

After you have created a virtual directory, you can configure it with its own settings for many IIS7 modules, including Default Document, Directory Browsing, and Error Pages. These settings override those the virtual directory inherits from its parent site or server.

Configuring Site Properties

The modular architecture of IIS7 provides an icon-based interface that you can use to configure a Web site's many properties.

CERTIFICATION READY?
Manage Internet Information Services (IIS)
3.5

Assuming that you leave the *Start Web site immediately* checkbox selected, each new Web site that you create in IIS7 should be immediately accessible from a Web browser. However, you might want to configure a number of other site properties before you consider it ready for your users.

TAKE NOTE*

The following sections discuss some of the most basic Web site configuration tasks you are likely to perform in IIS7. Remember, however, that many of these tasks are dependent on selecting the appropriate role services when you install the Web Server (IIS) role. If the controls for a particular feature do not appear in your IIS Manager console, it is probably because the dependent role service is not installed.

X REF

For information on configuring Web site permissions and other security issues, see Lesson 6, "Securing IIS Services." For information on configuring Web sites to host applications, see Lesson 7, "Deploying Web Applications."

CONFIGURING SITE BINDINGS

IIS7 is capable of hosting many separate Web sites simultaneously. However, for the Web sites to be accessible to clients, the HTTP ***protocol listener***, Http.sys, must have some way of associating each incoming request with one particular Web site. The ***binding*** for each site determines how the listener will identify its requests.

IIS7 supports three HTTP binding options, as described in the following sections:

- IP address—You can assign multiple IP addresses to a single network connection on the Web server and use a different address for each site hosted by IIS7. For this method to function practically, you must register each IP address in a DNS domain with a different host name.

- Port number—HTTP Web sites use the well-known port number 80, but you can differentiate sites by assigning different port numbers to them. However, client browsers use the port number 80 by default, so to access the sites with alternative ports, users must specify the port number in the URL, following the server name and a colon, as in the example http://www.contoso.com:1024.
- Host header—HTTP request messages contain a Host: field containing a server name, which IIS7 uses to associate the request with one of the sites it is hosting. For this method to function, you must register each of the host header names you specify in your Web site bindings in a DNS domain, using the IP address of the server. Sometimes known as *virtual hosting*, this method enables the Web server to host multiple Web sites using a single IP address and port number, without requiring any special information from clients.

CONFIGURING IP ADDRESS HOSTING

You can assign multiple IP addresses to a single network connection on the Web server, and use a different address for each site hosted by IIS7. To set this up, use the following procedure.

 CONFIGURE IP ADDRESS HOSTING

GET READY. Log on to Windows Server 2008 using a domain account with Administrator privileges. When the logon process is completed, close the Initial Configuration Tasks window and any other windows that appear.

1. Click **Start**, and then **Control Panel**. Open the **Network and Sharing Center** and click **Manage Network Connections**. The Network Connections window appears.
2. Right-click the connection you want to modify and, from the context menu, select **Properties**. The connection's Properties sheet appears.
3. Select **Internet Protocol Version 4 (TCP/IPv4)** and click **Properties**. The Internet Protocol Version 4 (TCP/IPv4) Properties sheet appears.
4. Click **Advanced**. The Advanced TCP/IP Settings dialog box appears, as shown in Figure 5-7.

Figure 5-7

The Advanced TCP/IP Settings sheet

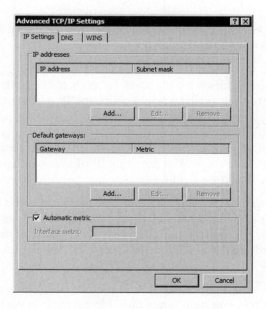

5. Click **Add**. The TCP/IP Address dialog box appears.
6. Key an IP address and subnet mask in the text boxes provided and click **OK**. The address appears in the IP Addresses box on the Advanced TCP/IP Settings sheet.
7. Create additional IP address entries as needed.

IP addresses identify computers serving as hosts on a network. Port numbers identify specific applications running on a host.

8. Click **OK** three times to close the dialog boxes. At this point, all of the IP addresses appearing in the Advanced TCP/IP Properties sheet are equally valid addresses for the computer.

9. Click **Administrative Tools** > **Internet Information Services (IIS) Manager**. The Internet Information Services (IIS) Manager console appears.

10. In the scope pane, right-click one of the Web sites on the server and, from the context menu, select **Edit Bindings**. The Site Bindings dialog box appears, like the one shown in Figure 5-8.

Figure 5-8

The Site Bindings dialog box

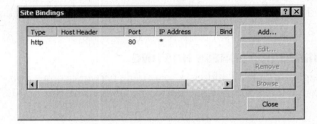

11. Select the existing binding and click **Edit**. An Edit Site Binding dialog box appears, as shown in Figure 5-9.

Figure 5-9

The Edit Site Binding dialog box

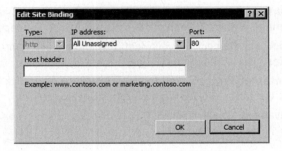

12. Using the IP Address dropdown list, select one of the IP addresses you assigned to the network connection. Click **OK**.

13. Click **Close**.

14. Open the Site Bindings dialog boxes for each of the other sites hosted by IIS7 and configure their bindings to use different IP addresses.

CLOSE the Network Connections window.

IIS7 configures the Default Web Site to use the All Unassigned setting for the IP Address binding. When you create a new Web site using IP address hosting, you must configure it with its own unique IP address binding.

After you have changed the bindings for your sites, users can access each of the Web sites on the IIS7 by keying a URL containing the appropriate IP address in a Web browser, as in http://192.168.4.58. For clients to be able to use server names in their URLs, you must create a Host (A) record in your DNS domain for each IP address, associating it with a different server name.

For example, if you have created three Web sites on an IIS7 Web server, and bound each one to a different IP address, you must create three Host records in your DNS domain, using information such as the following:

```
www          192.168.4.58
sales        192.168.4.59
support      192.168.4.60
```

After you have created the DNS records, your clients can access the Web servers using the names you specified. If your domain is called contoso.com, requests containing the three URLs http://www.contoso.com, http://sales.contoso.com, and http://support.contoso.com will all arrive at the IIS7 Web server, because each one is associated with one of the server's IP addresses. However, based on the different IP address in each request, IIS7 will send the www request to the Web site bound to 192.168.4.58, the sales request to 192.168.4.59, and the support request to 192.168.4.60.

The disadvantage of IP address hosting is that, for Internet Web servers, each site must have its own registered IP address, which can be inconvenient to manage and expensive to maintain.

CONFIGURING PORT NUMBER HOSTING

HTTP Web sites use the well-known TCP (Transmission Control Protocol) port number 80, but you can differentiate sites by assigning different port numbers to them. To do this, use the following procedure.

 ### CONFIGURE PORT NUMBER HOSTING

GET READY. Log on to Windows Server 2008 using a domain account with Administrator privileges. When the logon process is completed, close the Initial Configuration Tasks window and any other windows that appear.

1. Click **Start**, and then click **Administrative Tools** > **Internet Information Services (IIS) Manager**. The Internet Information Services (IIS) Manager console appears.

2. In the scope pane, right-click one of your Web sites and, from the context menu, select **Edit Bindings**. The Site Bindings dialog box appears.

3. Select the existing binding and click **Edit**. An Edit Site Binding dialog box appears.

4. In the Port text box, key the port number you want to associate with the site. Then click **OK**.

5. Click **Close**.

6. Open the Site Bindings dialog box for the other sites on the server and configure each of them to use a different port number.

CLOSE the Internet Information Services (IIS) Manager console.

The problem with port number hosting, and the reason why few Web servers use it, is that it requires clients to change their habits. All browser applications assume the port number 80 by default. When you key the URL http://www.contoso.com, the browser sends an HTTP request to port 80 on the specified Web server. To access a site using a different port, users must specify the port number in the URL, following the server name and a colon, as in http://www.contoso.com:1024. Not only are most Web users unaware of what a TCP port is and what it does, they also have no way of knowing what port number to use, unless you somehow inform them.

 **MORE INFORMATION**

Some Web servers and administrators use alternative port number assignments to keep certain Web sites hidden from general users. These sites use a randomly chosen port number, and unless users know or guess the number, or use a port scanner to discover it, they cannot access the site. This is obviously not a secure arrangement; much more effective means of controlling access to a Web site are discussed in Lesson 6, "Securing IIS Services."

CONFIGURING HOST HEADER HOSTING

TCP/IP networks communicate using IP addresses, not computer names. When a client keys a URL into a browser, the program first sends the name of the server in the URL to a DNS server, which resolves it into an IP address. Then, the browser generates an HTTP request message and transmits it to the Web server's IP address, which it received from the DNS server.

However, the HTTP request message also contains a ***Host header*** field, which contains the name of the Web server to which the client is sending the request. IIS7 can use this Host field to associate the request with one of the Web sites it is hosting. For example, IIS7 might be hosting three Web sites, each with a different server name, as follows:

```
www.contoso.com
sales.contoso.com
support.contoso.com
```

All three names resolve to the same IP address in the DNS database, so no matter which name clients use in their URLs, the HTTP request messages all go to the same Web server. When IIS7 receives the messages, it checks the contents of the Host field, and sends the request message to the Web site associated with the server name it finds there. This is the most commonly used method for creating multiple virtual Web servers on a single computer.

To configure IIS7 sites to use host header hosting, use the following procedure.

 CONFIGURE HOST HEADER HOSTING

GET READY. Log on to Windows Server 2008 using a domain account with Administrator privileges. When the logon process is completed, close the Initial Configuration Tasks window and any other windows that appear.

1. Click **Start**, and then click **Administrative Tools** > **Internet Information Services (IIS) Manager**. The Internet Information Services (IIS) Manager console appears.
2. In the scope pane, right-click one of your Web sites and, from the context menu, select **Edit Bindings**. The Site Bindings dialog box appears.
3. Select the existing binding and click **Edit**. An Edit Site Binding dialog box appears.
4. In the *Host header* text box, key the server name that you want IIS7 to associate with that site. Then click **OK**.
5. Click **Close**.
6. Open the Site Bindings dialog boxes for the other sites on the server and configure each of them to use a different *Host header* value.

CLOSE the Internet Information Services (IIS) Manager console.

For this hosting method to function, you must register each of the host header names you specify in the Web site bindings in your DNS domain, using the IP address of the server. Sometimes known as virtual hosting, this method enables a Web server to host multiple Web sites using a single IP address and port number, without the clients requiring any special knowledge.

CONFIGURING THE DEFAULT DOCUMENT FILENAMES

The URLs that clients key into their browsers usually do not include a filename; they contain only server and directory names. When a Web server receives an HTTP request, it parses the URL and locates the directory it specifies. When the URL does not specify a filename, the Web server replies to the request with the default file specified for the Web site. When you install the Default Document role service in IIS7, you can specify default filenames for the entire Web server, and for each of the server's Web sites, individually.

The original default filename for the Web was index.html, but Web servers running on Windows computers were then constrained to the 8.3 file naming format, and frequently used index.htm instead. IIS has traditionally used the filename default.htm. The Default Document module in IIS7 includes all of the filenames, plus others supporting Active Server Pages (ASP). When the server processes a request, it checks the directory specified in the URL for each file-name in the list sequentially and replies to the client with the first named file that it finds.

In IIS7, you can configure default document filenames for the entire Web server or for indi-vidual Web sites. Each Web site inherits the Default Document settings from the server, until you modify them.

To configure default document filenames, use the following procedure.

CONFIGURE DEFAULT DOCUMENT FILENAMES

GET READY. Log on to Windows Server 2008 using a domain account with Administrator privileges. When the logon process is completed, close the Initial Configuration Tasks window and any other windows that appear.

> **TAKE NOTE***
>
> Before you can configure Default Document filenames, you must install the Default Document role service in the Web Server (IIS) role.

1. Click **Start**, and then click **Administrative Tools** > **Internet Information Services (IIS) Manager.** The Internet Information Services (IIS) Manager console appears.
2. In the scope pane, select the node named for your server. The server home page appears in the details pane.
3. Double-click the **Default Document** icon in the IIS area. The Default Document pane appears, as shown in Figure 5-10, displaying the current default filenames for the server.

Figure 5-10

The Default Document pane

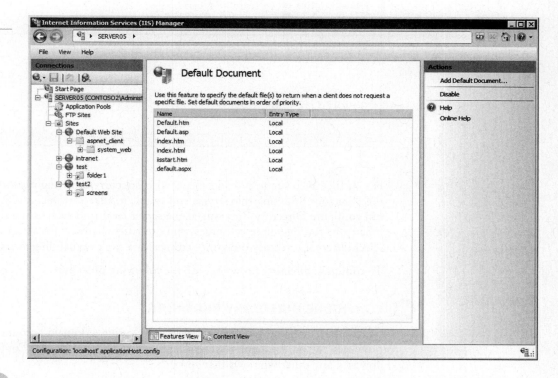

TAKE NOTE*

Like many other IIS7 parameters, you can configure Default Document settings at the site or virtual directory level, in addition to the server level. This enables you to specify different default document names for individual Web sites and virtual directories, which override the server settings.

4. Use one of the following procedures to manage the Default Document entries:
   - To delete one of the existing entries, select it and click **Remove** in the Actions pane.
   - To create a new entry, click **Add** in the Actions pane. In the Add Default Document dialog box that appears, key a filename in the Name text box and click **OK**.
   - To change the order of the files in the list, select an entry and, in the Actions pane, click **Move Up** or **Move Down**.
5. Click the **Back** arrow to return to the server home page.

CLOSE the Internet Information Services (IIS) Manager console.

To configure the default document filenames for an individual site, you simply select the site and perform the same procedure. You will notice that the Default Documents page for a site indicates that the default filename entries are inherited, not local. Any new entries you create will be local to the site.

CONFIGURING DIRECTORY BROWSING

When IIS7 receives an HTTP request containing a URL with no filename, and none of the default document filenames exist in the specified folder, the Web server has two choices: it can generate an error message, or it can display a directory listing, as shown in Figure 5-11. The directory listing enables the user to browse the site's directory structure and select files to display in the browser.

Figure 5-11

An IIS Web site directory display

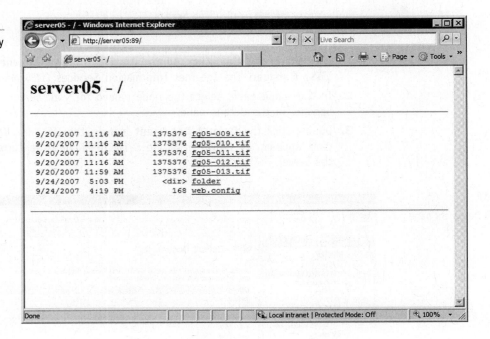

```
server05 - / - Windows Internet Explorer
      http://server05:89/                    Live Search
      server05 - /                                    Page    Tools

server05 - /
_____

 9/20/2007  11:16 AM       1375376  fg05-009.tif
 9/20/2007  11:16 AM       1375376  fg05-010.tif
 9/20/2007  11:16 AM       1375376  fg05-011.tif
 9/20/2007  11:16 AM       1375376  fg05-012.tif
 9/20/2007  11:59 AM       1375376  fg05-013.tif
 9/24/2007   5:03 PM        <dir>   folder
 9/24/2007   4:19 PM          168   web.config
_____

Done                          Local intranet | Protected Mode: Off       100%
```

For an IIS7 Web site to provide clients with directory browsing capability, you must install the Directory Browsing role service and enable it. Like the Default Directory settings, you can configure Directory Browsing at the server level, and each of the sites on the server will inherit the setting you select, unless you explicitly change it for a particular site. You can also select different directory browsing settings for a site's virtual directories.

To configure directory browsing, use the following procedure.

 CONFIGURE DIRECTORY BROWSING

GET READY. Log on to Windows Server 2008 using a domain account with Administrator privileges. When the logon process is completed, close the Initial Configuration Tasks window and any other windows that appear.

TAKE NOTE *

Before you can configure Directory Browsing, you must install the Directory Browsing role service in the Web Server (IIS) role.

1. Click **Start**, and then click **Administrative Tools** > **Internet Information Services (IIS) Manager**. The Internet Information Services (IIS) Manager console appears.
2. In the scope pane, select a server, site, or virtual directory node. The home page for the element you selected appears in the details pane.
3. Double-click the **Directory Browsing** icon in the IIS area. The Directory Browsing pane appears, as shown in Figure 5-12, displaying the current Directory Browsing settings.

Figure 5-12

The Directory Browsing pane

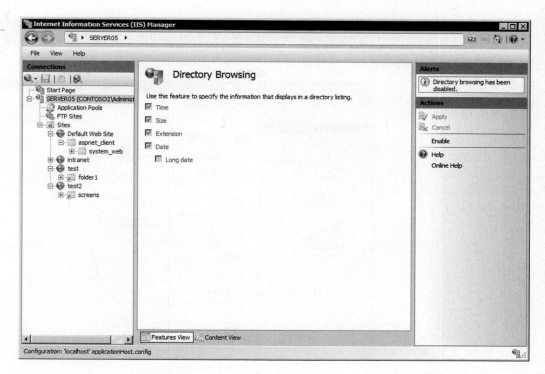

4. Use one of the following procedures to manage the Default Document entries:

- To enable or disable directory browsing, click **Enable** or **Disable** in the Actions pane.
- To specify the information the clients should see in the directory listing, select or clear the checkboxes in the Directory Browsing pane.

5. Click the **Back** arrow to return to the server home page.

CLOSE the Internet Information Services (IIS) Manager console.

For Internet Web sites, enabling directory browsing is usually considered a security breach, albeit a minor one, because it provides users with direct access to the site's files. However, for certain types of files, such as large collections of images, it can be easier to enable directory browsing than to create a page containing links to all of the images.

CONFIGURING WEB SITE LOGGING

HTTP Logging is one of the role services that Windows Server 2008 installs by default with the Web Server (IIS) role. You can configure the log format and other parameters, using the following procedure.

 CONFIGURE WEB SITE LOGGING

GET READY. Log on to Windows Server 2008 using a domain account with Administrator privileges. When the logon process is completed, close the Initial Configuration Tasks window and any other windows that appear.

TAKE NOTE * Before you can configure Web Site Logging, you must install the HTTP Logging role service in the Web Server (IIS) role.

1. Click **Start**, and then click **Administrative Tools** > **Internet Information Services (IIS) Manager**. The Internet Information Services (IIS) Manager console appears.

2. In the scope pane, select a server, site, or virtual directory node. The home page for the server you selected appears in the details pane.

3. Double-click the **Logging** icon in the IIS area. The Logging pane appears, as shown in Figure 5-13, displaying the current Logging settings.

Figure 5-13

The Logging pane

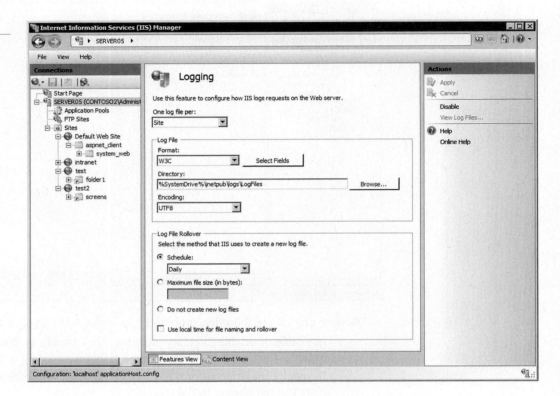

4. Using the *One log file per* dropdown list, specify whether you want IIS to create a single log for the entire server or separate logs for each site.

Selecting the Site option propagates the server's logging settings to all of the individual sites as defaults. You can then configure the logging settings for individual sites, to override the defaults.

5. Using the Format dropdown list, select the format you want IIS to use for the log files from the following options:

- Binary—Creates a single binary log file for all of the sites on the server. This option is not available for individual sites. If you select this option for the server and configure a site to use a different format, you must specify a different log filename for the site. To access binary logs, you must use a product such as Microsoft Log Parser.

- W3C—Configures the server or site to use the World Wide Web Consortium's log file format, which is space-delimited and records time stamps in Coordinated Universal Time (UTC). You can specify the information IIS saves to the log by clicking **Select Fields**, to open the W3C Logging Fields dialog box, as shown in Figure 5-14.

Figure 5-14

The W3C Logging Fields dialog box

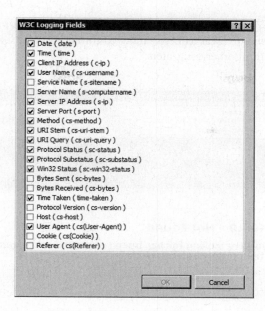

- IIS—Configures the site to use the native IIS log file format, which is comma-delimited, uses local time for time stamps, and is not customizable.
- NCSA—Configures the site to use the National Center for Supercomputing Applications log file format, which is space-delimited, uses UTC time for time stamps, and is not customizable.
- Custom—Disables the IIS logging capability, so that you can use a custom logging module.

6. In the Directory text box, key or browse to the folder where you want IIS7 to create the log files.

7. In the Encoding dropdown list, select the encoding scheme you want to use for the log files, from the following options:
   - UTF-8—Supports single-byte and multibyte characters, providing support for non-English language logging.
   - ANSI—Supports only single-byte characters.

8. In the Log File Rollover box, specify how and when you want IIS7 to create new log files by selecting from the following options:
   - Schedule—Configures IIS to create a new log file at the interval you specify: hourly, daily, weekly, or monthly.
   - Maximum file size—Configures IIS7 to create a new log file when the old file reaches a specified size, in bytes.
   - Do not create new log files—Configures IIS7 to use a single log file.

9. In the actions pane, click **Apply** to save your changes.

CLOSE the Internet Information Services (IIS) Manager console.

Web server logs are text files containing raw information about the activities of the server or a particular site. With this raw data, you can use third-party products to display detailed information about your site or server traffic, often in graphical form.

CONFIGURING ERROR PAGES

When a Web server cannot process a client request, it generates an error code, which specifies the reason for the problem. For example, if a client sends a request for a filename that does not exist, the server generates an HTTP 404.0 — Not Found. The code numbers for the errors are standardized in the HTTP specifications, but how the error messages are presented is left up to the Web server implementation.

By default, when IIS7 generates a 404 error, it sends a detailed error page, like the one shown in Figure 5-15, in response to local requests, and a custom error page, like the one in Figure 5-16, for requests coming from other computers.

Figure 5-15

An IIS7 detailed error page

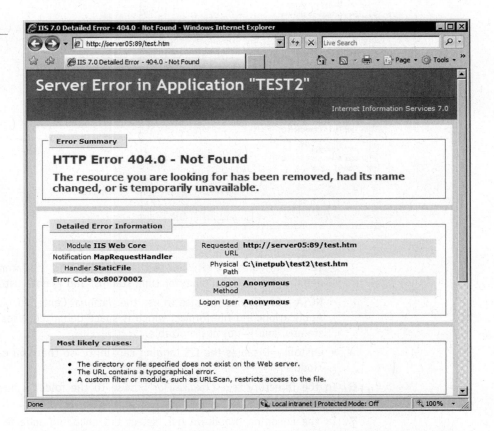

Figure 5-16

An IIS7 custom error page

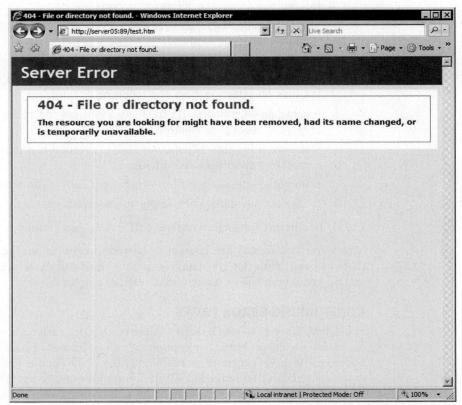

The detailed error page is designed to provide debugging information for administrators and Web site developers. For remote clients, the server uses a simpler error page that does not disclose any potentially sensitive information to outside users.

The HTTP Errors role service enables administrators to control which type of error page the server should use and specify alternatives to IIS7's preconfigured custom error pages. Like most of the other modules, the settings you configure for the server are inherited by the individual sites on that server, unless you override them by configuring the sites separately.

To configure the error pages for a server or site, use the following procedure.

➔ CONFIGURE ERROR PAGES SETTINGS

GET READY. Log on to Windows Server 2008 using a domain account with Administrator privileges. When the logon process is completed, close the Initial Configuration Tasks window and any other windows that appear.

1. Click **Start**, and then click **Administrative Tools** > **Internet Information Services (IIS) Manager**. The Internet Information Services (IIS) Manager console appears.

2. In the scope pane, select a server, site, or virtual directory node. The home page for the server you selected appears in the details pane.

3. Double-click the **Error Pages** icon in the IIS area. The Error Pages pane appears, as shown in Figure 5-17, displaying the current page entries.

TAKE NOTE

Before you can configure error pages, you must install the HTTP Errors role service in the Web Server (IIS) role.

Figure 5-17

The Error Pages pane

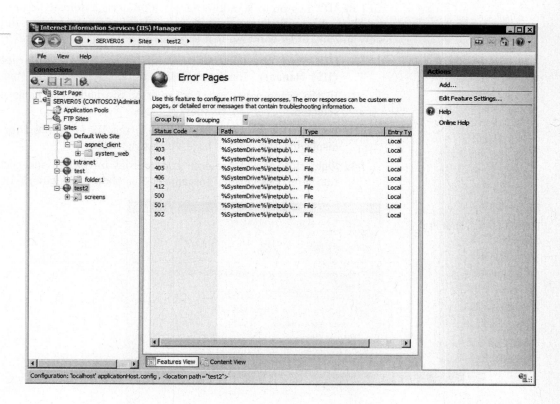

4. In the Actions pane, click **Edit Feature Settings**. The Edit Error Pages Settings dialog box appears.

5. In the Error Responses box, select one of the following options:
   - Custom error pages—Displays custom error pages for all types of requests, disabling detailed errors.

- Detailed errors—Displays detailed errors for all types of requests, disabling custom error pages.
- Detailed errors for local requests and custom error pages for remote requests— Displays detailed errors for requests generated by the local computer and custom error pages for all requests from other computers. This is the default setting.

6. In the Path text box, specify a path or URL for the custom error page you want the server to display.

7. In the Path Type dropdown list, select the type of path you specified in the Path text box, choosing from the following options:

- File—Specifies a full path to a static page, such as an HTML file.
- Execute URL—Specifies a URL to a file providing dynamic content, such as an ASP file.
- Redirect—Species the full URL of a Web page containing a custom error page.

8. Click **OK**.

CLOSE the Internet Information Services (IIS) Manager console.

Completing this procedure configures the basic settings for all of the error pages generated by a server, site, or virtual directory. To configure the custom page for a specific error code, use the following procedure.

 CONFIGURE INDIVIDUAL ERROR PAGES

GET READY. Log on to Windows Server 2008 using a domain account with Administrator privileges. When the logon process is completed, close the Initial Configuration Tasks window and any other windows that appear.

1. Click **Start**, and then click **Administrative Tools** > **Internet Information Services (IIS) Manager**. The Internet Information Services (IIS) Manager console appears.

2. In the scope pane, select a server or site node. The home page for the server you selected appears in the details pane.

3. Double-click the **Error Pages** icon in the IIS area. The Error Pages pane appears, displaying the current page entries.

4. Right-click one of the error code entries in the list and click **Edit**. The Edit Custom Error Page dialog box appears, as shown in Figure 5-18.

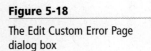

Figure 5-18

The Edit Custom Error Page dialog box

5. In the Response Action box, select and configure one of the following options:

- Insert content from a static file into the error response—Specifies a path to an HTML file containing content that you want to appear on the custom error page

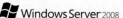

for the selected code. To support multiple languages, create a separate content folder for each language and select the *Try to return the error file in the client language* checkbox.

- Execute a URL on this site—Specifies a relative path to another page on the same site containing content that you want to appear on the custom error page for the selected code.

- Respond with a 302 redirect—Specifies a full URL to a page on another site containing content that you want to appear on the custom error page for the selected code.

6. Click **OK** to save your changes.

CLOSE the Internet Information Services (IIS) Manager console.

By creating custom error pages, you can provide users with information about the problem they are experiencing or specify how they can contact the technical support staff.

■ Deploying an FTP Server

THE BOTTOM LINE   FTP7 does not ship with Windows Server 2008, but it is available as a free download.

Windows Server 2008 ships with an FTP Publishing Service role service, but if you install it, you will find that it is virtually identical to the one included in Windows Server 2003. It even requires you to use the old IIS6 Management console to create and configure FTP sites; it is not compatible with the IIS7 Management console. However, an FTP Publishing Service for IIS7 is available as a free download from Microsoft's Web site. FTP7 is compatible with the IIS7 Management console, as well as other new IIS7 features, such as XML-based configuration files with .config extensions, shared configurations, and modular extensibility.

➕ MORE INFORMATION

FTP7 is being released at the same time as Windows Server 2008, but development schedules made it impossible to include it on the Windows Server 2008 installation DVD.

What's New in FTP7?

FTP7 is fully integrated with IIS7.

File Transfer Protocol (FTP) is an application layer protocol that enables a client to connect to a remote server, perform rudimentary file management tasks, and copy files in either direction between the two computers. FTP is defined by the RFC 114 document, which the Internet Engineering Task Force (IETF) published in 1971, making it one of the oldest TCP/IP protocols still in use. Originally implemented as command-line applications, FTP clients now most often use a graphical interface and are integrated into most browser applications, including Internet Explorer.

Some of the new features in FTP7 are as follows:

- IIS7 integration—FTP7 eliminates the need for the old IIS6 FTP Management console and metabase, as it is fully integrated with the modular IIS7 Manager console and its new configuration architecture.

- *FTP over Secure Sockets Layer (SSL)*—The original FTP standard has no provision for password protection or data encryption; the client transmits user names and passwords to the server in clear text, which in today's environment is highly insecure. FTP7 can use SSL to encrypt its authentication traffic before transmission, providing protection for sensitive passwords, as well as the file data itself.

TAKE NOTE ✱

Virtually all of the operating systems in use today, including Windows Server 2008 and all of the other Windows operating systems, include a command-line FTP client. In Windows, the client is called Ftp.exe.

- Combined FTP and Web hosting—Because FTP is now integrated into IIS7, you can allow Web and FTP access to the same site, simply by adding an FTP binding to an existing Web site.
- Virtual host naming—FTP7 supports host name hosting, just like IIS7 Web sites, enabling you to publish multiple FTP sites on a single computer, using one IP address and port number.
- Improved logging and error handling—FTP7 can now provide detailed error messages for local clients, and its logs include additional fields, session tracking, and sub-status codes.

Installing FTP7

> To use FTP7, you must install it in a Windows Server 2008 computer that is already running the Web Server (IIS) role.

Before you install FTP7, make sure that IIS7 is not running the FTP Publishing Service role services that ship with Windows Server 2008. If these role services are installed, be sure to uninstall them before you install FTP7.

To install FTP7, use the following procedure.

 INSTALL FTP7

GET READY. Log on to Windows Server 2008 using a domain account with Administrator privileges. When the logon process is completed, close the Initial Configuration Tasks window and any other windows that appear.

1. Download Microsoft FTP Publishing Service for IIS 7.0 from the IIS Web site at www.iis.net/downloads.
2. Run the Windows Installer package you downloaded by double-clicking it in any Windows Explorer window. The Welcome to the Microsoft FTP Publishing Service for IIS 7.0 Setup Wizard page appears.
3. Click **Next**. The End User License Agreement page appears.
4. Select the **I accept the terms in the license agreement** checkbox and click **Next**. The Custom Setup page appears, as shown in Figure 5-19.

Figure 5-19

The Custom Setup page in the Microsoft FTP Publishing Service for IIS 7.0 RCO Setup Wizard

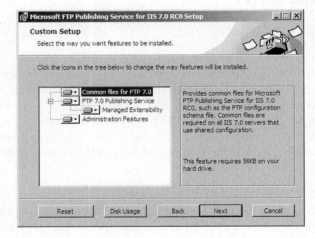

5. Modify the default setup settings to omit features, if desired, and click **Next**. The Ready to install Microsoft FTP Publishing Service for IIS 7.0 page appears.
6. Click **Install**. The Completed the Microsoft FTP Publishing Service for IIS 7.0 Setup Wizard page appears.
7. Click **Finish**.

After you have installed FTP7, the Internet Information Services (IIS) Manager console receives an FTP section, as shown in Figure 5-20, which contains the icons you use to configure the individual FTP parameters.

Figure 5-20

FTP7 icons in the Internet Information Services (IIS) Manager console

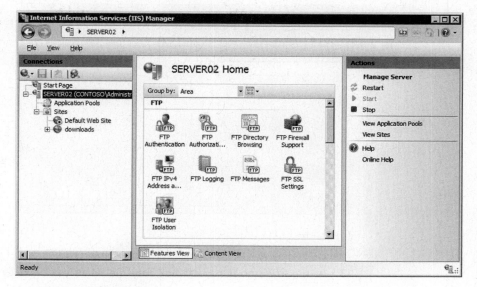

Creating an FTP Site

You can use FTP capabilities on existing Web sites or create new, independent FTP sites.

CERTIFICATION READY?
Configure a File Transfer Protocol (FTP) server
3.3

After you have installed FTP7, you can create an FTP site on your server in one of two basic ways: you can create an entirely new site, devoted to FTP, or you can add FTP capabilities to an existing Web site.

To create a new, dedicated FTP site, use the following procedure.

 CREATE AN FTP SITE

GET READY. Log on to Windows Server 2008 using a domain account with Administrator privileges. When the logon process is completed, close the Initial Configuration Tasks window and any other windows that appear.

1. Click **Start**, and then click **Administrative Tools** > **Internet Information Services (IIS) Manager.** The Internet Information Services (IIS) Manager console appears.

2. In the scope pane, expand the server node. Then, right-click the **Sites** node and, from the context menu, select **Add FTP Site.** The Add FTP Site wizard appears, displaying the Site Information page, as shown in Figure 5-21.

Figure 5-21

The Site Information page of the Add FTP Site wizard

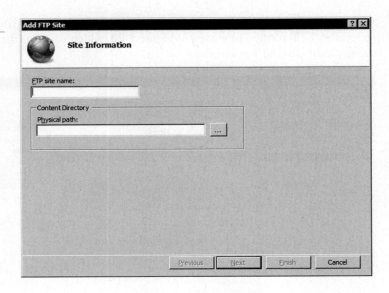

3. In the *FTP site name* text box, key the name you want to use to identify the site.

4. In the *Physical path* text box, key or browse to the folder that will be the root directory for the FTP site. Then click **Next**. The Binding and SSL Settings page appears, as shown in Figure 5-22.

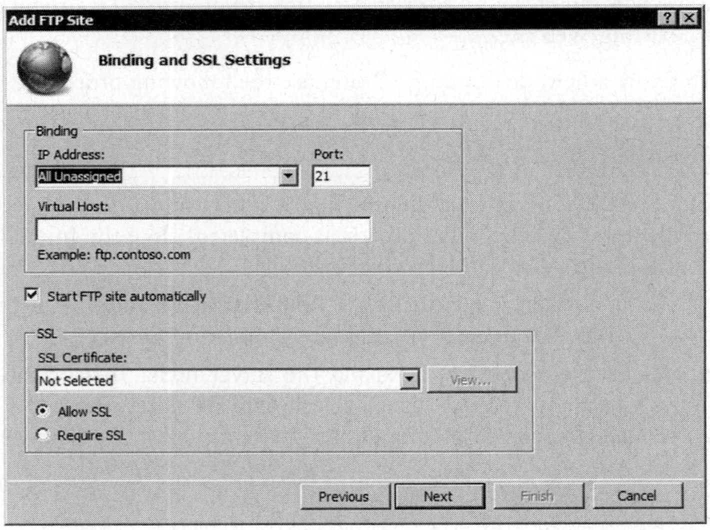

Figure 5-22

The Binding and SSL Settings page of the Add FTP Site wizard

5. If you plan to host other FTP sites on the same server, use the IP Address, Port, and Host Name fields to create a unique binding for the site, just as you did in the "Configuring Site Bindings" procedures, earlier in this lesson.

6. If you want to use SSL to secure the FTP site, select the SSL Certificate you want the server to use for this site and specify whether you want to allow clients to use SSL or require them to do so. If you do not want to use SSL, leave the default values in place.

7. Click **Next**. The Authentication and Authorization Information page appears, as shown in Figure 5-23.

Figure 5-23

The Authentication and Authorization Information page of the Add FTP Site wizard

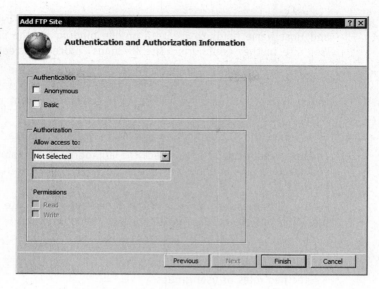

8. In the Authentication box, select the appropriate checkboxes to specify whether you want to allow anonymous access to the site, use Basic Authentication, or both.

 REF   For more information on FTP security issues, including authentication, authorization, and using SSL to secure FTP sites, see Lesson 6, "Securing IIS Services."

9. In the Authorization box, specify who can access the site by selecting one of the following options in the *Allow access to* dropdown list:
  - All users
  - Anonymous users
  - Specified roles or user groups
  - Specified users

  If you select one of the last two options, use the text box provided to specify the name(s) of one or more users, roles, or groups.

10. Specify whether users should have Read or Write access to the site, or both.

11. Click **Finish**. The new site appears in the scope pane.

CLOSE the Internet Information Services (IIS) Manager console.

The Add FTP Site wizard enables you to create only one binding and one authorization rule. However, you can create additional bindings and rules as needed, using the Internet Information Services (IIS) Manager console.

To add FTP access to an existing Web site, use the following procedure.

 ADD FTP TO A WEB SITE

GET READY. Log on to Windows Server 2008 using a domain account with Administrator privileges. When the logon process is completed, close the Initial Configuration Tasks window and any other windows that appear.

1. Click **Start**, and then click **Administrative Tools** > **Internet Information Services (IIS) Manager**. The Internet Information Services (IIS) Manager console appears.

2. In the scope pane, right-click a site node and, from the context menu, select **Add FTP Publishing**. The Add FTP Site Publishing wizard appears, displaying the Binding and SSL Settings page.

3. If you plan to host other FTP sites on the same server, use the IP Address, Port, and Host Name fields to create a unique binding for the site, just as you did for a Web site in the "Configuring Site Bindings" procedures, earlier in this lesson.

4. If you want to use SSL to secure the FTP site, select the SSL Certificate you want the server to use for this site and specify whether you want to allow clients to use SSL or require them to do so. If you do not want to use SSL, leave the default values in place.

5. Click **Next**. The Authentication and Authorization Information page appears.

6. In the Authentication box, select the appropriate checkboxes to specify whether you want to allow anonymous access to the site, use Basic Authentication, or both.

7. In the Authorization box, specify who can access the site by selecting one of the following options in the *Allow access to* dropdown list:
   - All users
   - Anonymous users
   - Specified roles or user groups
   - Specified users

   If you select one of the last two options, use the text box provided to specify the name(s) of one or more users, roles, or groups.

8. Specify whether users should have Read or Write access to the site, or both.

9. Click **Finish**. A message box appears, stating that FTP publishing was successfully added to the site.

10. Click **OK**.

CLOSE the Internet Information Services (IIS) Manager console.

Like Web sites, you can create virtual directories on FTP sites, which are aliases pointing to folders in other locations, by right-clicking a site and selecting Add Virtual Directory from the context menu.

Configuring FTP Properties

After you have created an FTP site or added FTP publishing to an existing Web site, you can configure a number of properties.

Many of the properties of an FTP7 site are security related, and are discussed in Lesson 6, "Securing IIS Servers." Some of the non-security properties you can configure are covered in the following sections.

CONFIGURING FTP DIRECTORY BROWSING

The FTP Directory Browsing feature in FTP7 controls the format that the server uses when sending directory listing information to a client. The original format for FTP directory listings was based on the format used by the UNIX operating systems of the time, as follows:

```
-rwxrwxrwx 1  owner  group  577189 Sep 29 23:36 fg05-0000.tif
-rwxrwxrwx 1  owner  group  577189 Sep 29 23:36 fg05-0001.tif
-rwxrwxrwx 1  owner  group  577189 Sep 29 23:36 fg05-0002.tif
-rwxrwxrwx 1  owner  group  577189 Sep 29 23:37 fg05-0003.tif
-rwxrwxrwx 1  owner  group  577189 Sep 29 23:37 fg05-0004.tif
-rwxrwxrwx 1  owner  group  577189 Sep 29 23:38 fg05-0005.tif
drwxrwxrwx 1  owner  group  0 Oct 1 14:54 files
226-Directory has 33,985,671,168 bytes of disk space available.
226 Transfer complete.
```

You can specify whether to use that format, or one corresponding to MS-DOS directory listings, as follows.

```
09-29-07  11:36PM  577189  fg05-0000.tif
09-29-07  11:36PM  577189  fg05-0001.tif
09-29-07  11:36PM  577189  fg05-0002.tif
09-29-07  11:37PM  577189  fg05-0003.tif
09-29-07  11:37PM  577189  fg05-0004.tif
09-29-07  11:38PM  577189  fg05-0005.tif
10-01-07  02:54PM  <DIR>   files
226-Directory has 33,985,708,032 bytes of disk space available.
226 Transfer complete.
```

The primary difference between the two formats is the inclusion of UNIX-style permissions and ownership information in the former. To configure FTP Directory Browsing, use the following procedure.

 CONFIGURE FTP DIRECTORY BROWSING

GET READY. Log on to Windows Server 2008 using a domain account with Administrator privileges. When the logon process is completed, close the Initial Configuration Tasks window and any other windows that appear.

1. Click **Start**, and then click **Administrative Tools** > **Internet Information Services (IIS) Manager**. The Internet Information Services (IIS) Manager console appears.

2. In the scope pane, expand the server node and the Sites node. Then, select an FTP site node and double-click the **FTP Directory Browsing** icon. The FTP Directory Browsing pane appears, as shown in Figure 5-24.

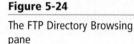

Figure 5-24

The FTP Directory Browsing pane

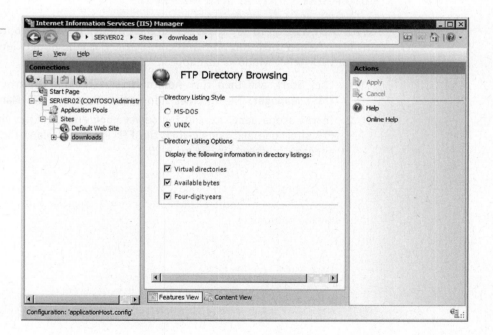

3. In the Directory Listing Style box, select either the **MS-DOS** or **UNIX** option.

4. Select any combination of the following checkboxes.
   - Virtual directories—When selected, IIS7 includes the site's virtual directories in all directory listings. When cleared, virtual directories do not appear in the listings, but are accessible to users that know of them.
   - Available bytes—Causes IIS7 to include the amount of usable storage space left on the site in all directory listings. The usable storage space can be the amount

of physical space left on the hard disk or the amount of space remaining before reaching a storage quota.

- Four digit years—Causes IIS7 to display the last modified date of all files and folders using four-digit year designations. When cleared, IIS7 uses two-digit year designations.

   5. In the Actions pane, click **Apply**.

CLOSE the Internet Information Services (IIS) Manager console.

Please note that the FTP Directory Browsing settings only control the format that the server uses when transmitting directory listings. If you access an IIS7 FTP site using Internet Explorer, you will not see any changes as a result of altering these settings. This is because the browser is responsible for interpreting and displaying the directory listings it receives from FTP servers. The same is true for most graphical FTP clients. To see the changes that result from alterations of the settings, you must use a command-line client, such as Ftp.exe, which displays the server output without modification.

CONFIGURING CUSTOM SITE MESSAGES

When a client first connects to an FTP server, the server transmits a banner message announcing itself before it authenticates the user, a welcome message after a successful authentication, and an exit message when the client disconnects. The server also displays a message when a client attempting to connect to the server exceeds the maximum number of allowed connections.

You can configure FTP7 to display custom messages in place of (or in addition to) the default ones, using the following procedure.

 CONFIGURE CUSTOM SITE MESSAGES

GET READY. Log on to Windows Server 2008 using a domain account with Administrator privileges. When the logon process is completed, close the Initial Configuration Tasks window and any other windows that appear.

   1. Click **Start**, and then click **Administrative Tools** > **Internet Information Services (IIS) Manager**. The Internet Information Services (IIS) Manager console appears.

   2. In the scope pane, expand the server node and the Sites node. Then, select an FTP site node and double-click the **FTP Messages** icon. The FTP Messages pane appears, as shown in Figure 5-25.

Figure 5-25

The FTP Messages pane

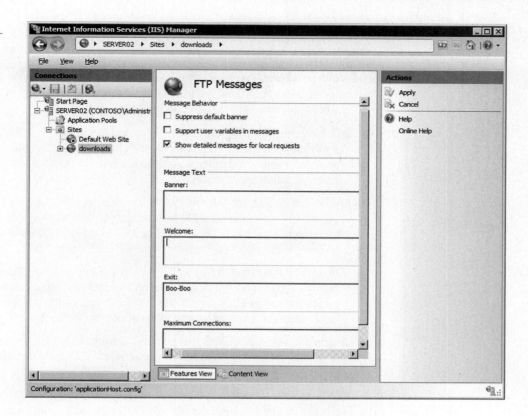

3. Select the **Suppress default banner** checkbox to prevent IIS7 from displaying its default FTP messages.

4. Select the **Support user variables in messages** checkbox to enable the use of the following variables in your custom messages:

- %BytesReceived%
- %BytesSent%
- %SessionID%
- %SiteName%
- %UserName%

5. Select the **Show detailed messages for local requests** checkbox to configure FTP7 to display additional error information when connecting from a client on the local host.

6. In the Message Text box, key the messages you want FTP7 to display in the Banner, Welcome, Exit, and Maximum Connections text boxes.

7. In the Actions pane, click **Apply**.

CLOSE the Internet Information Services (IIS) Manager console.

When you complete the procedure, the customized messages you specified take effect in all subsequent client sessions, but not in sessions that are already running.

CONFIGURING FTP LOGGING

FTP7 sites have the same logging configuration capabilities as IIS7 Web sites. To configure FTP7 logging in the Internet Information Services (IIS) Manager console, select a site and double-click the FTP Logging icon. In the FTP Logging pane, you can configure the controls using the same procedures described in "Configuring Web site Logging," earlier in this lesson.

SUMMARY SKILL MATRIX

IN THIS LESSON YOU LEARNED:

- Internet Information Services (IIS), now in version 7.0, has undergone major revisions for the Windows Vista and Windows Server 2008 releases.

- IIS7 has over forty individual modules that you can select for installation. Selecting only the modules you intend to use reduces the application's attack surface, minimizes the amount of memory and other system resources it needs to run, and simplifies the configuration and maintenance processes.

- The default Web server (IIS) role installation requires you to also install the Windows Process Activation Server (WPAS) feature, with its Process Model and Configuration APIs components. If you select the ASP.NET or .NET Extensibility role services, the WPAS .NET Environment component is required as well.

- When you install the Web Server (IIS) role on a Windows Server 2008 system, IIS7 automatically creates a default Web site, using the modules you selected for installation with the role. You can use that default site to publish your content, reconfiguring it as needed, or you can create any number of additional sites on the server.

- A virtual directory is an alias that points to a folder in another physical location, enabling you to publish content found on different drives or different computers, without copying or moving it.

- IIS7 is capable of hosting many separate Web sites simultaneously. It is the binding for each site that determines how the protocol listener will identify incoming requests and send them to the correct site. IIS7 supports three hosting methods: IP addresses, port numbers, or host headers.

- The Internet Information Services (IIS) Manager in Windows Server 2008 uses icons to configure individual modules, rather than tabbed dialog boxes.

Knowledge Assessment

Fill in the Blank

Complete the following sentences by writing the correct word or words in the blanks provided.

1. The component that manages the IIS7 request pipeline, the server's application pools, and the worker processes running in them is called the _____.

2. The IIS component that enables the computer to recognize and react to incoming HTTP messages is called a(n) _____.

3. Web browsers typically connect to Web servers using a protocol called _____.

4. The techniques that enable multiple Web sites to run on a single computer are called _____.

5. A(n) _____ is an alias that points to a folder in another physical location.

6. The only virtual hosting method you can use for multiple sites using the same IP address and port number is called _____ hosting.

7. For clients to perform file management tasks on an IIS server, they must connect to a(n) _____ server.

8. The original coding language used for the files transmitted to client browsers by Web servers is called _____.

9. FTP7 can secure its communications by using _____.

10. To add FTP capabilities to a Web site requires that you create an additional
_____.

Multiple Choice

Select the correct answer for each of the following questions. Choose all answers that are correct.

1. Which of the following statements about IIS7 hosting is/are true?
   a. IIS7 is not capable of hosting many separate Web sites simultaneously.
   b. IIS7 is limited to hosting ten Web sites simultaneously.
   c. IIS7 is not capable of hosting more than one Web site at a time.
   d. IIS7 is capable of hosting many separate Web sites simultaneously.

2. Which of the following statements is/are true about IIS7 and virtual directories?
   a. Virtual directories cannot help share information across several Web sites.
   b. Virtual directories can help share information across several Web sites, thus conserving disk space.
   c. Virtual directories replicate shared information to each Web site.
   d. Virtual directories are not capable of hiding the actual locations of shared files and folders from Web clients.

3. IIS7 stores all of its configuration settings in
   a. files with a .config extension.
   b. a central location called a metabase.
   c. a central location file you name for security purposes.
   d. files with an .iis7 extension.

4. Which of the following statements is/are true about the default IIS7 error pages?
   a. By default, IIS7 displays custom error pages for local requests.
   b. By default, IIS7 displays detailed error pages for local requests.
   c. By default, IIS7 displays custom error pages for remote requests.
   d. By default, IIS7 displays detailed error pages for remote requests.

5. Client browsers attempting to access a Web site receive an error message when the following conditions are in place:
   a. When Directory Browsing is enabled and a Web site does not have any of the default filenames in its root directory.
   b. When Directory Browsing is enabled and a Web site has a default filename in its root directory.
   c. When Directory Browsing is disabled and a Web site does not have any of the default filenames in its root directory.
   d. When Directory Browsing is disabled and a Web site has a default filename in its root directory.

6. Which of the following IIS7-supported formats can you configure by selecting fields?
   a. FTP Directory Browsing log formatting
   b. Binary log formatting
   c. HTTP log format
   d. W3C log format

7. Which of the following statements is/are true about HTTP Logging?
   a. HTTP Logging is one of the role services that Windows Server 2008 installs by default with the Web Server (IIS) role.
   b. HTTP Logging is not one of the role services that Windows Server 2008 installs by default with the Web Server (IIS) role.
   c. You must configure IIS7 to install HTTP Logging.
   d. HTTP Logging is not included with Windows Server 2008. You must download it from the Microsoft Web site.

8. Which of the following statements about File Transfer Protocol 7 (FTP7) is/are true?
   a. FTP7 enables a client to connect to a remote server.
   b. FTP7 is a transport layer protocol.
   c. FTP7 eliminates the need for the old IIS6 FTP Management console and metabase.
   d. FTP7 has no provision for password protection or data encryption.

9. IIS7 does not support which of the following hosting methods?
   a. IP addresses
   b. Proxy server filtering
   c. Port numbers
   d. Host headers

10. Which of the following IIS role services is/are not included in the HTTP category?
    a. Default Document
    b. Static Content
    c. Directory Browsing
    d. HTTP Logging

Review Questions

1. IIS7 supports three site binding solutions, which enable a single server to host multiple Web sites simultaneously. Of the three, host header hosting is the most popular. Explain why this is so, giving a specific reason why each of the other two solutions is less desirable.

2. Explain the role of the Windows Process Application Service (WPAS) with regard to how IIS7 processes incoming requests from clients.

■ Case Scenarios

Scenario 5-1: Host Header Hosting

Ralph has just installed the Web Server (IIS) role on a Windows Server 2008 computer, and has created five intranet Web sites for various departments in his company. To differentiate the sites, he has configured the bindings with five different host header values, as follows:

- sales.contoso.com
- marketing.contoso.com
- legal.contoso.com
- it.contoso.com
- hr.contoso.com

After starting up all five sites, Ralph emails the various departments to inform them that their intranet Web servers are up and running. Within minutes, emails and phone calls start coming in from users complaining that they cannot access the new Web sites. What is most likely the cause of the problem?

Scenario 5-2: Web Server Publishing

The content files for your company Web server are currently stored on the D drive of a Windows Server 2008 computer with IIS7 installed on it. The server is named Web1, and its URL is *http://intranet.contoso.com*. You have been instructed to create an IIS solution that will enable the Human Resources department to publish documents containing company benefit and policy information on the Web site, using the URL *http://intranet.contoso.com/hr*. These documents are stored on the HR department's own server and change frequently. What would be the most efficient way to make this possible?

Securing IIS Services

OBJECTIVE DOMAIN MATRIX

TECHNOLOGY SKILL	OBJECTIVE DOMAIN	OBJECTIVE DOMAIN NUMBER
Enabling and Configuring Authentication Methods	Configure Web site authentication and permissions.	3.7
Assigning Standard and Special NTFS Permissions	Configure Web site authentication and permissions.	3.7
Configuring Certificates	Configure SSL Security.	3.6

KEY TERMS

Anonymous Authentication
authentication
Basic Authentication
certification authority (CA)

Digest Authentication
digital certificate
Kerberos
NTLMv2

public key infrastructure
Windows Authentication

A Web server is, by definition, a doorway into your network, but this does not mean that the doorway has to be unprotected. This lesson examines some of the many security mechanisms included in IIS7, including:

- IP address and domain name restrictions
- Authentication methods
- Authorization rules
- Handler mappings
- NTFS permissions
- Secure Sockets Layer (SSL)

■ Understanding IIS Security

THE BOTTOM LINE Configuring the various security mechanisms provided by IIS7 and Windows Server 2008 is an essential element of Web server administration.

Internet Information Services (IIS) has become a key component of the Windows Server products over the years, due to the ever increasing importance of the Internet in the business world, and the increasing use of Web server technologies to deploy applications internally and externally. The primary role of an IIS server is to listen for incoming requests from clients of various types and then respond by performing some action or supplying some piece of information.

Because IIS functions, metaphorically, as an open door to a private network, it is also a potential avenue for attack. As a result, the server administrator must secure IIS against such attacks.

Attacks against an IIS server can come in many different forms and for many different reasons. Some attackers might try to use the services provided by IIS to gain access to files or data for which they are not authorized, while others might try to use the server to access the organization's internal network. Still others might only be intent on inhibiting IIS' functionality to prevent other users from accessing its services.

Because of these varied threats, IIS7 has many built-in security mechanisms and makes use of Windows Server 2008's own security features. This lesson discusses how to use these features to protect your IIS7 server against attack.

■ Configuring Web Site Security

THE BOTTOM LINE

IIS7 has many security mechanisms you can use to protect your Web servers individually or in combinations. Each of these mechanisms has its own configuration interface.

As mentioned earlier, IIS7 Web sites are designed to listen for incoming requests from clients and respond to those requests. However, before IIS7 processes a request and issues a response, it must determine whether the client issuing the request has the privileges needed to use the Web site. In essence, IIS7 evaluates each incoming request by asking the following questions:

- Are the client's IP address and domain name allowed access to the site?
- Who is the client sending the request?
- Is the client authorized to access the requested resource?
- Does the client have the permissions needed to access the resource?

These questions all correspond to IIS7 or Windows Server 2008 security mechanisms that administrators can use to protect their Web sites and server resources from unauthorized access.

TAKE NOTE *

While the FTP6 role services included with Windows Server 2008 are relatively limited in their security capabilities, the FTP7 module is fully integrated with IIS7 and supports most of the same security mechanisms, including IP address and domain name restrictions, Anonymous and Basic Authentication, and Secure Sockets Layer (SSL) encryption.

Configuring IP Address and Domain Name Restrictions

To restrict Web site or FTP site access to specific computers or companies, you can create a list of IP addresses and domain names to which the server will grant or deny access.

IIS7 retains a security feature from earlier IIS versions enabling you to specify IP addresses or domain names that the server should allow or deny access to a server, Web or FTP7 site, virtual directory, folder, or file. To configure IP address restrictions, use the following procedure.

TAKE NOTE *

Before you can configure IP address and domain name restrictions, you must install the IP and Domain Restrictions role service in the Web Server (IIS) role.

 CONFIGURE IP ADDRESS RESTRICTIONS

GET READY. Log on to Windows Server 2008 using a domain account with Administrator privileges. When the logon process is completed, close the Initial Configuration Tasks window and any other windows that appear.

1. Click **Start**, and then click **Administrative Tools** > **Internet Information Services (IIS) Manager**. The Internet Information Services (IIS) Manager console appears, as shown in Figure 6-1.

Figure 6-1

The Internet Information Services (IIS) Manager console

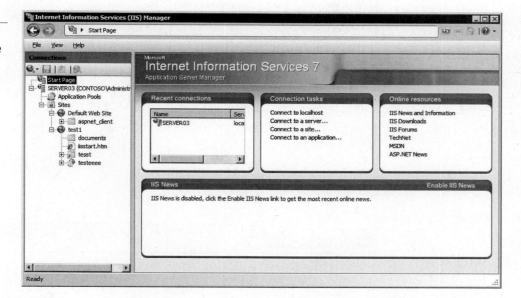

2. In the scope pane, select a server, site, folder, or virtual directory. The Home pane for the selected element appears, like the one shown in Figure 6-2.

Figure 6-2

The Home pane for an IIS7 server

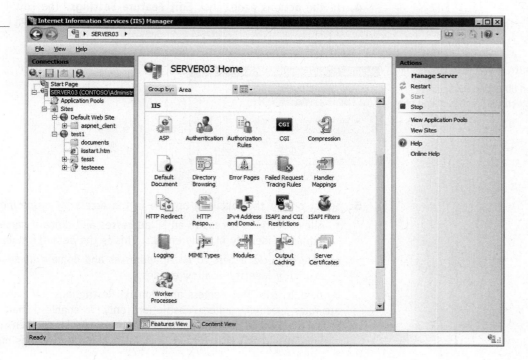

3. Double-click the **IPv4 Address and Domain Restrictions** icon. The IPv4 Address and Domain Restrictions pane appears, as shown in Figure 6-3.

Figure 6-3

The IPv4 Address and Domain Restrictions pane

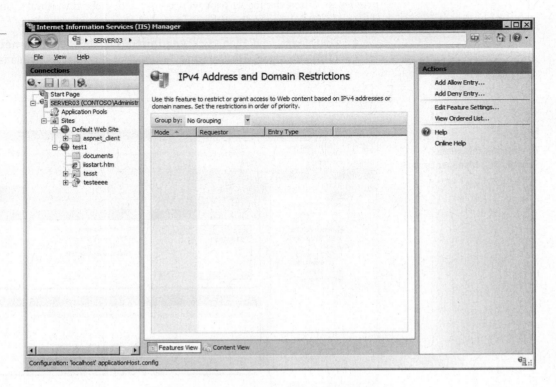

> **TAKE NOTE** *
>
> To configure a folder that is not a virtual directory or an individual file, select a Web site and click Content View. Then, double-click the desired folder or file, return to Features View, and double-click the IPv4 Address and Domain Restrictions icon.

4. In the actions pane, click **Edit Feature Settings**. The Edit IP and Domain Restrictions Settings dialog box appears, as shown in Figure 6-4.

Figure 6-4

The Edit IP and Domain Restrictions Settings dialog box

5. Select one of the following options in the *Access for unspecified clients* dropdown list:

- Allow—Permits access to all IP addresses and domain names except for those you explicitly identify in deny entries. This is the default value.
- Deny—Blocks access to all IP addresses and domain names except for those you explicitly identify in allow entries.

By default, the IPv4 Address and Domain Restrictions role service enables you to create rules specifying address restrictions only. To enable domain name restriction rules, select the **Enable domain name restrictions** checkbox. Then, confirm your action by clicking **Yes** in the **Edit** IP and Domain Restrictions Settings message box that appears.

6. Click **OK** to close the Edit IP and Domain Restrictions Settings dialog box.

7. In the actions pane, click **Add Allow Entry**. The Add Allow Restriction Rule dialog box appears, as shown in Figure 6-5.

Figure 6-5

The Add Allow Restriction Rule dialog box

8. Select one of the following options and key an appropriate entry in the accompanying text box:

   • Specific IPv4 address—Enables you to specify one IP address that will be allowed or denied access to the selected element.

   • IPv4 Address Range—Enables you to specify a range of IP addresses and a subnet mask, identifying a group of systems that you will be allowed or denied access to the selected element.

   • Domain name—Enables you to specify a domain name that will be allowed or denied access to the selected element.

9. Click **OK**. The new entry appears in the IPv4 Address and Domain Restrictions pane.

CLOSE the Internet Information Services (IIS) Manager console.

Although they are easy to understand and use, IP address and domain name restrictions are not particularly useful security tools. For example, if you have an intranet Web site that you want to restrict to a certain group of users, you can configure the site to deny access to all IP addresses except those of specified users. However, it is not difficult to spoof IP addresses, so this practice is not particularly secure. You can also use this feature to deny access to specific Internet addresses or domains that are the sources of attacks, but most installations have a firewall that is better at this sort of thing.

You should also consider carefully the consequences of creating domain name restrictions. As IIS7 mentions in its warning when you enable domain restrictions, this practice can slow the Web server down significantly. HTTP communications are based on IP addresses, not domain names. When you create domain name restrictions, IIS7 must perform a reverse name lookup of the IP address where each incoming request originated to determine its domain name. This adds a substantial additional burden on the server, which can negatively affect its performance.

 **MORE INFORMATION**

DNS servers typically perform name resolutions, in which they take a fully qualified domain name and resolve it into an IP address. A reverse name lookup occurs when a DNS server receives a request containing an IP address and must determine its domain name. You must configure a DNS server to perform reverse name resolutions, by creating a reverse lookup zone and creating Pointer (PTR) records for the addresses you want the server to resolve.

Enabling and Configuring Authentication Methods

The authentication methods you use for your Web sites depend on the types of clients you must support and the sensitivity of your site content.

CERTIFICATION READY?
Configure Web site authentication and permissions
3.7

Authentication is the process of confirming a user's identity, usually by requiring the user to supply some sort of token, such as a password or certificate. By identifying the user sending a request, IIS7 can determine the system resources the user should be permitted to access. Even though it might not seem so in the case of public Web sites accessible through the Internet, IIS7 does authenticate every incoming request to determine the sender. In the case of a public site, the server uses Anonymous Authentication, which does not identify users by name, but still completes the formality of the authentication process.

IIS7 supports several authentication methods, which are listed in Table 6-1, with the role services they require to run, and their intended uses. You must install the appropriate role services using the Add Role Services Wizard in Server Manager before you can enable or configure these authentication methods.

Table 6-1

Authentication Methods Supported by IIS7

AUTHENTICATION METHOD	ADDITIONAL ROLE SERVICES REQUIRED	BEST USED FOR:
Active Directory Client Certificate Authentication	Client Certificate Mapping Authentication	Intranet Web sites on networks already using Active Directory and with a server functioning as a certification authority (CA)
Anonymous Authentication	None	Internet Web or FTP sites that are open to the public with no access restrictions
ASP.NET Impersonation	ASP.NET .NETExtensibility ISAPI Extensions ISAPI Filters	Web sites with ASP.NET applications that require a non-default security context
Basic Authentication	Basic Authentication	Private Web or FTP sites with clients on the other side of firewalls or proxy servers, or that do not support any other type of non-anonymous authentication
Digest Authentication	Digest Authentication	Intranet Web servers with clients that are members of the same Active Directory domain and separated by a firewall or proxy server
Forms Authentication	ASP.NET .NET Extensibility ISAPI Extensions ISAPI Filters	High-traffic Web sites with ASP.NET applications that include application-based authentication capabilities
IIS Client Certificate Authentication	IIS Client Certificate Mapping Authentication	One-to-one and one-to-many certificate mapping on intranet Web sites not using Active Directory certificate mapping and with a server functioning as a certification authority (CA)
Windows Authentication	Windows Authentication	Intranet Web servers with clients that are members of the same Active Directory domain or who have user accounts on the IIS7 server, and are not separated by a firewall or proxy server.

TAKE NOTE★

Generally, using different authentication strategies for various parts of a single site can be more trouble than it is worth, from an administrative standpoint. It is usually easier to create a separate site for content that requires a different authentication method.

Of the methods listed in the table, only Anonymous Authentication is integrated into an IIS7 installation by default. All of the other authentication methods require the selection of additional role services during the installation of the Web Server (IIS) role.

Even when you install the role services required for additional authentication methods, IIS7 leaves those methods disabled by default until you explicitly enable them. You can enable and disable authentication methods for any IIS7 server, application, site, folder, virtual directory, or individual file. For example, if you want the root folder of a site to be available to anyone, and a virtual directory beneath the root to be available only to specific users, you can enable anonymous access at the site level, and then disable it for the virtual directory. Of course, you must also enable some other form of authentication for the virtual directory, if you want anyone to be able to access it.

As is usual in IIS7, the authentication settings you configure at a particular level are inherited by all subordinate levels. IIS7 enables Anonymous Authentication at the server level by default when you install it, so all of the sites you create on the server also have Anonymous Authentication enabled. If you modify the authentication settings at the server level, you must explicitly configure each site that you want to use different settings.

To enable and disable authentication methods that you have already installed in IIS7, use the following procedure.

 ENABLE AUTHENTICATION METHODS

GET READY. Log on to Windows Server 2008 using a domain account with Administrator privileges. When the logon process is completed, close the Initial Configuration Tasks window and any other windows that appear.

1. Click **Start**, and then click **Administrative Tools** > **Internet Information Services (IIS) Manager**. The Internet Information Services (IIS) Manager console appears.

2. In the scope pane, select a server, site, or virtual directory. The Home pane for the selected element appears.

3. Double-click the **Authentication** icon. The Authentication pane appears, as shown in Figure 6-6.

Figure 6-6

The Authentication pane in the Internet Information Services (IIS) Manager console

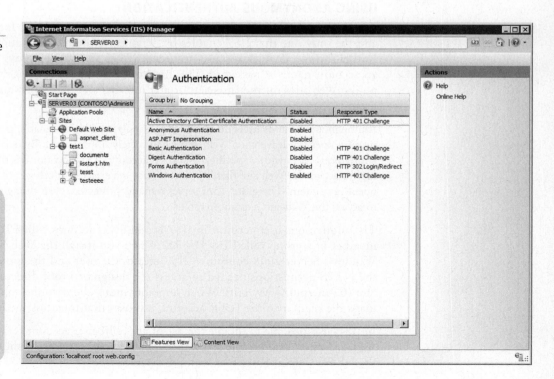

TAKE NOTE★

To configure a folder that is not a virtual directory or an individual file, select a Web site and click Content View. Then double-click the desired folder or file, return to Features View, and double-click the Authentication icon.

TAKE NOTE *

Before you can enable an authentication method, you must install the appropriate role service in the Web Server (IIS) role.

4. Select the authentication method you want to modify and, in the actions pane, click **Enable** or **Disable**. The Status indicator for the authentication method changes.

CLOSE the Internet Information Services (IIS) Manager console.

You can enable as many authentication methods for an IIS7 element as you need to support your clients. When a client connects to a site configured to use multiple authentication methods, it always attempts to establish an anonymous connection first. If either the client or the server does not allow Anonymous Authentication, the systems attempt to authenticate again, using the other methods from most to least secure. Therefore, IIS7 uses its various methods to authenticate clients in the following order:

1. Anonymous Authentication
2. Windows Authentication
3. Digest Authentication
4. Basic Authentication

 REF Active Directory Client Certificate Authentication, ASP.NET Impersonation, and Forms Authentication do not fall within this authentication order. These authentication methods have special requirements that cause IIS7 to handle them differently. For more information, see the individual sections for these methods, later in this lesson.

TAKE NOTE *

FTP7 supports only Anonymous Authentication and Basic Authentication. For greater security, however, you can use SSL with FTP7 to encrypt the authentication traffic as it passes over the network.

If all of the authentication methods fail, as in an improperly configured site with no methods enabled, the client receives the following error message:

```
HTTP Error 401.2 - Unauthorized: Access is denied due to server
configuration
```

The following sections examine the various authentication methods supported by IIS7, including when (or if) you should use them, and how to configure their properties.

USING ANONYMOUS AUTHENTICATION

Anonymous Authentication is the only authentication method integrated into IIS7, and the only one that IIS7 enables by default. As the name implies, Anonymous Authentication enables any user to access a Web site that employs it, without supplying an account name or password. This method of authentication is designed primarily for public Web sites on the Internet, or any internal site that you want to be available to all users.

Although anonymous users do not have to supply credentials, enabling Anonymous Authentication does not leave your Web server completely unprotected. By default, IIS7 authenticates anonymous users with a specifically created account. This account has the permissions necessary to access the Web site files, but it does not have access to other files or sensitive areas of the operating system. Therefore, your server remains protected, even though you are allowing users to access the Web site files anonymously.

The anonymous user account in IIS7 is a built-in account called IUSR, which is a member of a group called IIS_IUSRS. When you install the Web Server (IIS) role on a Windows Server 2008 computer, IIS7 creates the user and the group and assigns the group the NTFS permissions needed to access the designated root directory of the Default Web Site (C:\inetpub\wwwroot). When an anonymous client connects to the Web site, IIS7 maps the request to the IUSR account and uses that to access the necessary files.

In IIS7, it is possible to disable the use of a specific user account for Anonymous Authentication, and use the application pool identity instead. Application pools run under the NETWORKSERVICE account by default.

CHANGING THE ANONYMOUS AUTHENTICATION USER

Although IIS7 uses the IUSR account for anonymous access by default, you can change it. For example, if your Web site uses content files located elsewhere on the network, you might want to use a different account with network privileges for anonymous access. The IUSR account is local, and does not have such privileges. To change the account that IIS7 uses for Anonymous Authentication, use the following procedure.

CHANGE THE ANONYMOUS AUTHENTICATION USER

GET READY. Log on to Windows Server 2008 using a domain account with Administrator privileges. When the logon process is completed, close the Initial Configuration Tasks window and any other windows that appear.

1. Click **Start**, and then click **Administrative Tools** > **Internet Information Services (IIS) Manager**. The Internet Information Services (IIS) Manager console appears.

2. In the scope pane, select a server, site, application, or virtual directory. The Home pane for the selected element appears.

3. Double-click the **Authentication** icon. The Authentication pane appears.

> **TAKE NOTE** *
>
> To configure a folder that is not a virtual directory or an individual file, select a Web site and click Content View. Then double-click the desired folder or file, return to Features View, and double-click the Authentication icon.

> **TAKE NOTE** *
>
> Before you can configure Anonymous Authentication, you must install the Anonymous Authentication role service in the Web Server (IIS) role.

4. Select **Anonymous Authentication** and, in the actions pane, click **Edit**. The Edit Anonymous Authentication Credentials dialog box appears, as shown in Figure 6-7.

Figure 6-7

The Edit Anonymous Authentication Credentials dialog box

5. Click **Set**. The Set Credentials dialog box appears, as shown in Figure 6-8. You can also select the *Application pool identity* option to override the anonymous user account.

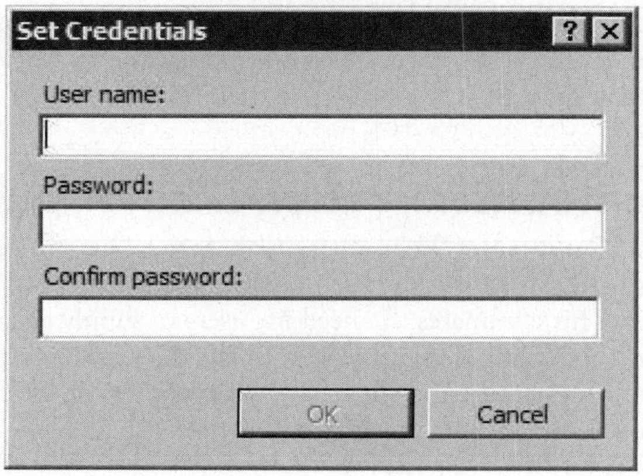

Figure 6-8

The Set Credentials dialog box

6. In the User Name text box, key the name of the account you want IIS7 to use for anonymous access to the element you selected.

7. In the Password and Confirm Password text boxes, key the password associated with the account you specified.

8. Click **OK** to close the Set Credentials dialog box.

9. Click **OK** to close the Edit Anonymous Authentication Credentials dialog box.

10. Restart the Web site.

CLOSE the Internet Information Services (IIS) Manager console.

After the Web site restarts, the server authenticates all anonymous users connecting to the site using the account you specified.

UNDERSTANDING IIS7 ANONYMOUS AUTHENTICATION

The IIS7 anonymous access user and group accounts differ from those of IIS6 and earlier versions. IIS6 uses a standard local user account called IUSR_*computername* and a built-in group called IIS_WPG. The IIS6 elements function in much the same way as IIS7's as far as anonymous request handling is concerned. However, they have caused some administrative problems, particularly in the area of scalability.

Many organizations run multiple, redundant IIS servers to support heavy traffic or provide fault tolerance. To create a duplicate Web site on another IIS server, administrators typically copy the configuration files and content files from one computer to the other, using a utility that retains the access control list (ACL) information for each file and folder, such as the Xcopy.exe program with the /O parameter. The ACL information contains the NTFS permissions that provide the anonymous user account with access to the content files.

The problem with IIS6 arises when the destination computer attempts to parse configuration metabase file and the ACL information on the copied content files. Because anonymous user accounts on the two computers have different names (due to the inclusion of the computer name), the metabase cannot function on the new server without modification.

The problem with the ACL information in the content files results from the fact that each local user and group in Windows Server has a unique security identifier (SID) that the system assigns when creating the account. ACLs use only the SIDs to reference security principals, not the user and group names. The anonymous user and group accounts on the destination computer have different SIDs than the source computer, so the ACLs are useless on the destination computer. Therefore administrators must modify the metabase for each new IIS6 Web server and recreate the NTFS permissions for the content files.

IIS7 addresses these problems in two ways. First, the anonymous user account name (IUSR) no longer includes the computer name, so it is now identical on each IIS7 computer. This makes the configuration files completely compatible, without modifications. Second, the IUSR account is now a built-in account, just like the LOCALSERVICE and NETWORKSERVICE accounts. This type of account does not need a password, which eliminates potential password expiration problems, and is not subject to the SID conflict problems that affect the IIS6 accounts. As a result, administrators can copy IIS7 configuration and content files to multiple servers and use them as is.

ENABLING ACTIVE DIRECTORY CLIENT CERTIFICATE AUTHENTICATION

If you are running an intranet Web server on an Active Directory network with its own certification authority, you can configure IIS7 to automatically authenticate domain users that have client certificates. This eliminates the need for users to supply account names and passwords, while providing a high level of security. Obviously, this form of authentication is not suitable for Internet Web sites because the clients are not members of the Active Directory domain.

To use Active Directory Client Certificate Authentication, your network must meet the following prerequisites:

- Active Directory—The network must have an Active Directory domain controller installed. All of the clients who will access the Web sites using Active Directory Client Certificate Authentication must have Active Directory user accounts.

X REF

For more information on configuring IIS7 sites to use SSL, see "Using Secure Sockets Layer," later in this lesson.

- Certification Authority—The network must have a server functioning as a certification authority (CA), as implemented in the Active Directory Certificate Services role. Certificates issued by a third-party, commercial CA can be used for this purpose, but because all of the systems involved are internal to the organization, this would be an unnecessary expense.
- Secure Sockets Layer (SSL)—To protect the certificates, you must configure all of the Web sites on the IIS7 server to require SSL communications. To do this, you must create an HTTPS binding and enable SSL in the SSL Settings pane.
- Domain server certificate—The server must have a domain server certificate, obtained from a CA.
- Map client certificates—You must map certificates to the domain user objects for the clients that will be accessing the Web sites. To map client certificates, you must obtain certificates from a CA, and then use Active Directory Users and Computers, with Advanced Features enabled, to map the certificates to specific users.

To configure IIS7 to use Active Directory Client Certificate Authentication, use the following procedure.

 ENABLE ACTIVE DIRECTORY CLIENT CERTIFICATE AUTHENTICATION

GET READY. Log on to Windows Server 2008 using a domain account with Administrator privileges. When the logon process is completed, close the Initial Configuration Tasks window and any other windows that appear.

1. Click **Start**, and then click **Administrative Tools** > **Internet Information Services (IIS) Manager**. The Internet Information Services (IIS) Manager console appears.
2. In the scope pane, select a server. The Home pane for the selected element appears.
3. Double-click the **Authentication** icon. The Authentication pane appears.

> **TAKE NOTE*** Active Directory Client Certificate Authentication only appears in the Authentication pane at the server level. You cannot configure individual sites or other IIS7 elements to use this authentication method.

TAKE NOTE*

Before you can configure Active Directory Client Certificate Authentication, you must install the Client Certificate Mapping Authentication role service in the Web Server (IIS) role.

4. Select **Active Directory Client Certificate Authentication** and, in the actions pane, click **Enable**.
5. Disable any other authentication methods that show a status of Enabled.
6. Restart the IIS7 service.

CLOSE the Internet Information Services (IIS) Manager console.

Because Active Directory Client Certificate Authentication requires the use of SSL with client certificates, it is not compatible with any of the other authentication methods IIS7 supports and, therefore, does not fall into any of the authentication methods listed earlier in this lesson. If, for any reason, the IIS7 server cannot authenticate a client, it generates an error message such as the following:

```
HTTP Error 403.7 - Forbidden: The page you are attempting to access
requires your browser to have a Secure Sockets Layer (SSL) client
certificate that the Web server recognizes.
```

MORE INFORMATION

IIS7 also supports its own form of client certificate authentication that does not use Active Directory. The IIS Client Certificate Mapping Authentication role service enables you to create two types of mappings, as follows:

- One-to-one mappings—Each client must have a copy of its own certificate stored on the IIS7 server.

- Many-to-one mappings—Uses wildcard matching rules to ensure that certificates submitted by clients contain specific information.

However, you cannot configure this authentication method using the Internet Information Services (IIS) Manager console. You can only configure IIS client certificate mapping by editing the IIS7 configuration files directly or by using Windows Management Instrumentation (WMI).

USING WINDOWS AUTHENTICATION

Of the three traditional, challenge/response authentication methods supported by IIS7, **Windows Authentication** is the most secure. Known by several other names in previous versions of IIS, the technology that Windows Authentication uses stretches all the way back to the NTLM authentication method in the original Microsoft LAN Manager product of the late 1980s.

IIS7's Windows Authentication module supports two authentication protocols:

- *NTLMv2*—A challenge/response authentication protocol used by Windows computers that are not members of an Active Directory domain. The client initiates the authentication process by sending a message to the server specifying its encryption capabilities and containing the user's account name. The server replies with a message containing information about its own capabilities, plus a random challenge string. The client then uses the challenge string and its password to calculate a response, which it transmits to the server. The server performs the same calculations and, if its results match the client's, the authentication is successful.

- *Kerberos*—A ticket-based authentication protocol used by Windows computers that are members of an Active Directory domain. Unlike NTLM, which involves only the IIS7 server and the client, Kerberos authentication involves an Active Directory domain controller as well. The client begins the authentication process by sending an Authentication Service Request message to the Kerberos Key Distribution Center (KDC) running on the domain controller. This message contains pre-authentication data, which the client encrypts with its user key. The KDC decrypts the data with its own copy of the user key, created when the client specified a password for the user account. If the decryption is successful, then the identity of the client is confirmed, and the KDC responds by sending a ticket granting ticket (TGT) and an encrypted session key that the client will use for all subsequent communications with the ticket granting service (TGS) on the domain controller. After authentication, the client can initiate additional exchanges with the TGS to obtain service tickets that provide access to network services, such as an IIS7 Web site.

Notice that both of these protocols are capable of authenticating clients without transmitting passwords over the network in any form. This is an extremely secure form of authentication, because even if someone with a protocol analyzer is capturing the packets transmitted over the network, no data that would be useful to them is in the packets, even if they could decrypt it.

Windows Authentication is designed for use with intranet Web sites only, because it would not be practical for Internet clients to be members of the Active Directory domain or have accounts on the Web server. In addition, the use of Windows Authentication is also subject to the following restrictions.

- Clients must be running Internet Explorer version 3.01 or later.
- The clients and Web server must be members of the same domain.
- To use Kerberos, the clients and Web server should not be separated by a firewall.
- To use Kerberos, both clients and Web server must have continuous access to an Active Directory domain controller.

- To use NTLMv2, the clients must have user accounts on the Web server.
- To use NTLMv2, the clients should not require the use of a proxy server to access the Web server.

When clients that are not members of an Active Directory domain attempt to access an IIS7 Web site using Windows Authentication, a Connect To dialog box appears, in which the user must specify an account name and password. The IIS7 server then authenticates the client using NTLMv2.

If the client and the IIS7 server are both members of a domain, the client authentication that occurs when the user logs on to the domain is usually sufficient to provide access to the Web sites on the server that is using Windows Authentication. If the client uses the server's computer name in the browser URL, such as http://*servername*, Windows recognizes the server as an internal resource and performs a Kerberos message exchange with the TGS to obtain a service ticket for IIS7. This process is invisible to the user working on the client computer, who receives access to the Web site with no further interaction.

If the client uses the server's IP address or DNS name in its URL, such as http://192.168.3.76 or http://*servername*.contoso.com, Windows might interpret the connection attempt as coming from an outside system and generate a Connect To dialog box for another authentication.

⊕ MORE INFORMATION

On an IIS7 server using Windows Authentication with Active Directory, Kerberos usually makes it possible for clients to access Web site content stored on servers other than the Web server, no matter how you integrate the content into the site. However, in the absence of Active Directory and Kerberos, you must consider how you integrate the remote content, if you want to avoid forcing users to perform an additional authentication. For example, if you map a drive to a share on another server, and publish the mapped drive on a Web site, Kerberos will provide clients with access to the remote content invisibly by obtaining an extra service ticket from the TGS in the background. NTLMv2, however, will not forward the user's credentials to the remote server, so the user will have to log on again to re-authenticate. To avoid this, use virtual directories instead of mapped drives and click the Connect As button in the Add Virtual Directory dialog box to supply alternative credentials that IIS7 should always use when accessing the remote content.

ENABLING DIGEST AUTHENTICATION

TAKE NOTE✱

The Digest Authentication method in IIS7 is comparable to the Advanced Digest Authentication method from IIS6.

Digest Authentication is also designed for use with intranet Web servers in an Active Directory environment. Unlike Windows Authentication, Digest Authentication works through firewalls and proxy servers because it actually transmits passwords over the network. However, the protocol protects the passwords using a strong MD5 encryption scheme.

The use of Digest Authentication is subject to the following restrictions:

- Clients must be running Internet Explorer version 5 or later.
- The clients and Web server must be members of the same Active Directory domain.
- All clients must have user accounts in the Active Directory domain.
- If Anonymous Authentication is installed in IIS7, it must be disabled for Digest Authentication to work.

To configure and enable Digest Authentication, use the following procedure.

 ENABLE DIGEST AUTHENTICATION

GET READY. Log on to Windows Server 2008 using a domain account with Administrator privileges. When the logon process is completed, close the Initial Configuration Tasks window and any other windows that appear.

1. Click **Start**, and then click **Administrative Tools** > **Internet Information Services (IIS) Manager**. The Internet Information Services (IIS) Manager console appears.

2. In the scope pane, select a server, site, application, or virtual directory. The Home pane for the selected element appears.

3. Double-click the **Authentication** icon. The Authentication pane appears.

TAKE NOTE*

To configure a folder that is not a virtual directory or an individual file, select a Web site and click Content View. Then, double-click the desired folder or file, return to Features View, and double-click the Authentication icon.

4. Select **Digest Authentication** and, in the actions pane, click **Edit.** The Edit Digest Authentication Settings dialog box appears, as shown in Figure 6-9.

Figure 6-9

The Edit Digest Authentication Settings dialog box

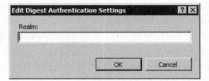

TAKE NOTE*

Before you can configure Digest Authentication, you must install the Digest Authentication role service in the Web Server (IIS) role.

5. In the Realm text box, key the name of the Active Directory domain of which the Web server is a member. Then click **OK.**
6. Select **Digest Authentication** and, in the actions pane, click **Enable.**

TAKE NOTE*

To force clients to use Digest Authentication, disable Anonymous Authentication. All clients attempt to authenticate anonymously first and, failing that, move on to alternative authentication methods.

7. Restart the IIS7 service.

CLOSE the Internet Information Services (IIS) Manager console.

Digest Authentication functions well as a backup for Windows Authentication when some clients on the network cannot use that method. Also, because it uses stronger encryption algorithms, Digest Authentication is significantly more secure than Basic Authentication.

TAKE NOTE*

Some earlier versions of IIS required clients using Basic Authentication to have the Log On Locally user right. However, in IIS6 and IIS7, it is no longer necessary to assign this user right to clients.

ENABLING BASIC AUTHENTICATION

Basic Authentication is the weakest of the challenge/response authentication methods supported by IIS7. When a client authenticates to an IIS7 server using Basic Authentication, the client transmits its credentials unencrypted, using Base64 encoding, so anyone capturing the network packets can read the user's credentials. In addition, the server caches clients' user tokens for 15 minutes, so it is possible to read the credentials from the server hard disk during that time.

To enable Basic Authentication, use the following procedure.

 ENABLE BASIC AUTHENTICATION

GET READY. Log on to Windows Server 2008 using a domain account with Administrator privileges. When the logon process is completed, close the Initial Configuration Tasks window and any other windows that appear.

1. Click **Start**, and then click **Administrative Tools** > **Internet Information Services (IIS) Manager**. The Internet Information Services (IIS) Manager console appears.
2. In the scope pane, select a server, site, application, or virtual directory. The Home pane for the selected element appears.
3. Double-click the **Authentication** icon. The Authentication pane appears.

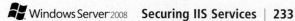

TAKE NOTE *

To configure a folder that is not a virtual directory or an individual file, select a Web site and click Content View. Then, double-click the desired folder or file, return to Features View, and double-click the Authentication icon.

4. Select **Basic Authentication** and, in the actions pane, click **Edit.** The Edit Basic Authentication Settings dialog box appears, as shown in Figure 6-10.

Figure 6-10

The Edit Basic Authentication Settings dialog box

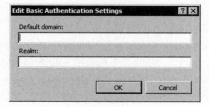

TAKE NOTE *

Before you can configure Basic Authentication, you must install the Basic Authentication role service in the Web Server (IIS) role.

5. In the Default Domain text box, key the name of the Active Directory domain in which you want the clients to be authenticated. The default value, if you leave the field blank, is the IIS7 server's domain. Leave the Realm text box blank, or key the name value as the Default Domain text box, and click **OK.**

6. Select **Basic Authentication** and, in the actions pane, click **Enable.**

7. Restart the IIS7 service.

CLOSE the Internet Information Services (IIS) Manager console.

The advantages of Basic Authentication are that it is defined in the HTTP standard, so virtually all browsers support it, and that it works through firewalls and proxy servers. If you must use Basic Authentication, you should use it in conjunction with SSL, so that the authentication traffic is properly encrypted.

ENABLING ASP.NET IMPERSONATION

ASP.NET Impersonation is not an authentication protocol in itself, unlike most of the other options in the Authentication pane. Instead, ASP.NET is a way to configure an ASP.NET application to run in a security context different from the application's default context. To enable ASP.NET Impersonation, use the following procedure.

 ENABLE ASP.NET IMPERSONATION

GET READY. Log on to Windows Server 2008 using a domain account with Administrator privileges. When the logon process is completed, close the Initial Configuration Tasks window and any other windows that appear.

1. Click **Start**, and then click **Administrative Tools** > **Internet Information Services (IIS) Manager.** The Internet Information Services (IIS) Manager console appears.

2. In the scope pane, select a server, site, application, or virtual directory. The Home pane for the selected element appears.

3. Double-click the **Authentication** icon. The Authentication pane appears.

TAKE NOTE *

To configure a folder that is not a virtual directory or an individual file, select a Web site and click Content View. Then, double-click the desired folder or file, return to Features View, and double-click the Authentication icon.

4. Select **ASP.NET Impersonation** and, in the actions pane, click **Edit.** The Edit ASP.NET Impersonation Settings dialog box appears, as shown in Figure 6-11.

Figure 6-11

The Edit ASP.NET Impersonation Settings dialog box

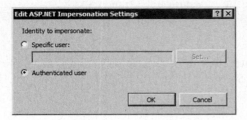

5. Select one of the following options and click **OK:**
   - Specific user—Clicking **Set** opens a Set Credentials dialog box, in which you can specify the credentials you want the ASP.NET application to use.
   - Authenticated user—Causes IIS7 to use the client's current security context when running the ASP.NET application. For example, if the client connects using Anonymous Authentication, the application runs using the IUSR account (unless you have changed the default Anonymous Authentication settings).

6. Select **ASP.NET Impersonation** and, in the actions pane, click **Enable.**

7. Restart the IIS7 service.

CLOSE the Internet Information Services (IIS) Manager console.

Once IIS7 restarts, users accessing the ASP.NET application connect to the server using the credentials you specified, instead of the application's default credentials.

ENABLING FORMS AUTHENTICATION

Windows Authentication, Digest Authentication, and Basic Authentication are all challenge-based authentication methods. An IIS7 server configured to use these methods transmits a challenge message to clients attempting to connect, and the client must reply with the correct response for the authentication to succeed. Forms Authentication, on the other hand, is a login/redirection-based method.

Clients attempting to connect to a site using Forms Authentication are redirected to an alternative Web page containing a logon interface. The advantage of this method is that the authentication process occurs at the application level, instead of the operating system level like challenge-based methods. If you are running a heavily trafficked intranet site or an Internet site with publicly available applications, Forms Authentication can significantly reduce the load on the operating system, diverting it to your application instead.

To configure and enable Forms Authentication, use the following procedure.

 ENABLE FORMS AUTHENTICATION

GET READY. Log on to Windows Server 2008 using a domain account with Administrator privileges. When the logon process is completed, close the Initial Configuration Tasks window and any other windows that appear.

1. Click **Start**, and then click **Administrative Tools** > **Internet Information Services (IIS) Manager.** The Internet Information Services (IIS) Manager console appears.

2. In the scope pane, select a server, site, application, or virtual directory. The Home pane for the selected element appears.

> **TAKE NOTE** *
>
> To configure a folder that is not a virtual directory or an individual file, select a Web site and click Content View. Then, double-click the desired folder or file, return to Features View, and double-click the Authentication icon.

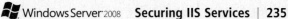

3. Double-click the **Authentication** icon. The Authentication pane appears.

4. Select **Forms Authentication** and, in the actions pane, click **Edit.** The Edit Forms Authentication Settings dialog box appears, as shown in Figure 6-12.

Figure 6-12

The Edit Forms Authentication Settings dialog box

5. Configure the following parameters and click **OK**.
   - Login URL—Specify the URL of the Web page containing the authentication interface.
   - Authentication cookie time-out—Specify the length of time (in minutes) that the cookie containing the Forms Authentication ticket should remain on the client computer before timing out.
   - Mode—Specifies whether the client computer should use cookies to store the Forms Authentication ticket.
   - Name—Specifies the name of the Forms Authentication cookie.
   - Protection mode—Specifies whether the systems should protect the Forms Authentication cookie using data encryption, data validation, both, or neither.
   - Requires SSL—Specifies whether the server should require an SSL connection before transmitting the Forms Authentication cookie. This option is disabled by default.
   - Extend cookie expiration on every request—Enables sliding expiration, which causes the server to reset a client's Forms Authentication cookie each time the client issues a new request during an active session. This option is enabled by default.

6. Select **Forms Authentication** and, in the actions pane, click **Enable.**

7. Disable any other authentication methods that show a status of Enabled.

8. Restart the IIS7 service.

CLOSE the Internet Information Services (IIS) Manager console.

Forms Authentication is designed for use instead of challenge-based authentication methods, not in addition to them. Therefore, you must disable all of the other authentication methods when you enable Forms Authentication.

Creating URL Authorization Rules

Authorization rules specify what clients are able to do on a Web site after the server has authenticated them.

Authentication is the process of identifying users and confirming that they are who they claim to be. After the IIS7 server has authenticated a client, the next step is authorization, which determines what resources the client is allowed to access.

In previous versions of IIS, the primary authorization mechanism is NTFS permissions, which Web administrators can use to control access to site content, in the same way that file server administrators use permissions. NTFS permissions are still a viable authorization tool in IIS7, but they are complex to configure and they can complicate the process of deploying redundant IIS servers due to the unique SIDs assigned to every user and group.

IIS7 provides an alternative to NTFS permissions called URL Authorization, which enables administrators to create authorization rules for individual URLs, not for the underlying file system. IIS7 stores URL Authorization rules in the IIS configuration files, which simplifies the process of copying them to another server on the network. Therefore, URL Authorization rules can function as a replacement for NTFS permissions, providing clients with access to the resources they need and protecting everything else.

IIS7 URL Authorization uses two major guidelines to evaluate the rules that apply to a specific element:

- Deny rules supersede allow rules—If you create conflicting rules at the same level, one of which denies access and one of which allows access, the deny rule will take precedence.

- Parent rules supersede child rules—If you create a rule at one level, and a conflicting rule at a subordinate level, the high-level rule takes precedence.

To create your own URL Authorization rules, use the following procedure.

CREATE URL AUTHORIZATION RULES

GET READY. Log on to Windows Server 2008 using a domain account with Administrator privileges. When the logon process is completed, close the Initial Configuration Tasks window and any other windows that appear.

1. Click **Start**, and then click **Administrative Tools** > **Internet Information Services (IIS) Manager**. The Internet Information Services (IIS) Manager console appears.

2. In the scope pane, select a server, site, application, or virtual directory. The Home pane for the selected element appears.

3. Double-click the **Authorization Rules** icon. The Authorization Rules pane appears, as shown in Figure 6-13.

TAKE NOTE

To configure a folder that is not a virtual directory or an individual file, select a Web site and click Content View. Then double-click the desired folder or file, return to Features View, and double-click the Authorization Rules icon.

Figure 6-13

The Authorization Rules pane

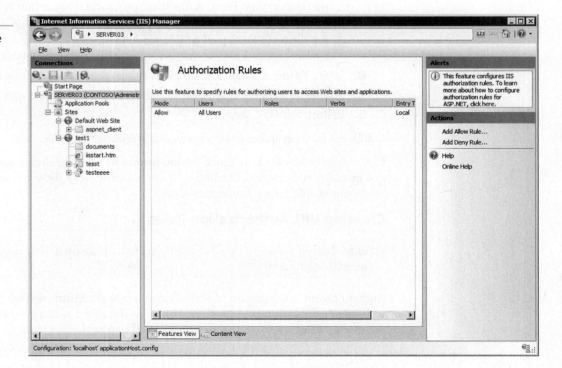

4. In the actions pane, click **Add Allow Rule** or **Add Deny Rule**. The Add Allow Authorization Rule or Add Deny Authorization Rule dialog box appears, as shown in Figure 6-14.

Figure 6-14

The Add Allow Authorization Rule dialog box

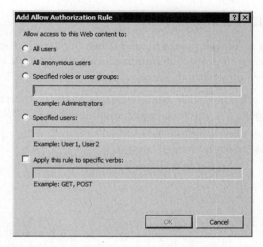

5. Specify to whom you want to apply the rule by using one of the following options:
- All users—Allows or denies access to all clients, regardless of how they are authenticated.
- All anonymous users—Allows or denies access only to clients using Anonymous Authentication.
- Specified roles or user groups—Allows or denies access to the user groups or .NET roles you specify (separated by commas).
- Specified users—Allows or denies access to the users you specify (separated by commas).

6. To limit the rule to specific types of requests, select the **Apply this rule to specific verbs** checkbox and specify the HTTP Method values to which you want the rule to apply. Common values include GET, PUT, POST, REPLY, and DELETE.

7. Click **OK**. The new rule appears in the Authorization Rules pane.

CLOSE the Internet Information Services (IIS) Manager console.

You can create URL Authorization rules for virtually every IIS7 element, including servers, sites, applications, virtual directories, folders, and individual files. By default, IIS7 creates an authorization rule at the server level, granting all users access to the Web content. All of the subordinate elements on the server inherit this rule, so you might have to delete or modify it at any subordinate element where you want to create your own, more restrictive, rules.

Configuring Handler Mappings

In previous versions of IIS, when you specified the home directory that would form the root of a Web site, you could grant clients any combination of read, write, script, and execute permissions for the site. In IIS7, this capability has been moved to a feature called Handler Mappings, which provides additional, more granular, configuration capabilities.

In addition to the general permissions, the Handler Mappings module also enables you to limit client access to specific file types in several different ways. You can limit the application of a handler mapping based on the HTTP verb specified in the request or based on whether the client request is for a file or a folder. You can also specify the permission required by the handler: read, write, script, execute, or none.

To configure handler mappings, use the following procedure.

 CONFIGURE HANDLER MAPPINGS

GET READY. Log on to Windows Server 2008 using a domain account with Administrator privileges. When the logon process is completed, close the Initial Configuration Tasks window and any other windows that appear.

1. Click **Start**, and then click **Administrative Tools** > **Internet Information Services (IIS) Manager**. The Internet Information Services (IIS) Manager console appears.

2. In the scope pane, select a server, site, application, or virtual directory. The Home pane for the selected element appears.

3. Double-click the **Handler Mappings** icon. The Handler Mappings pane appears, as shown in Figure 6-15.

TAKE NOTE*

To configure a folder that is not a virtual directory or an individual file, select a Web site and click Content View. Then, double-click the desired folder or file, return to Features View, and double-click the Handler Mappings icon.

Figure 6-15

The Handler Mappings pane

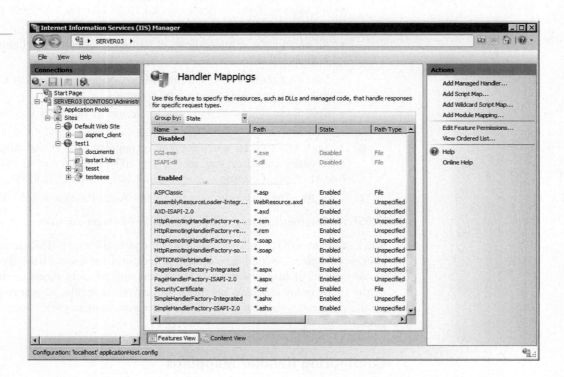

4. In the actions pane, click **Edit Feature Permissions**. The Edit Feature Permissions dialog box appears, as shown in Figure 6-16.

Figure 6-16

The Edit Feature Permissions dialog box

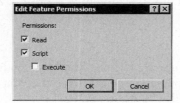

5. Select the checkboxes indicating the default permissions you want clients to have for the selected element. Then click **OK**.

6. Select one of the handlers listed in the pane and, in the actions pane, click **Edit**. An Edit dialog box for the selected handler appears, as shown in Figure 6-17.

Figure 6-17

The Edit dialog box for a handler

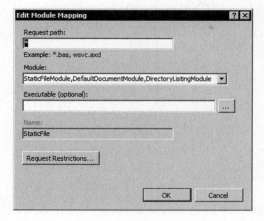

7. Click **Request Restrictions**. A Request Restrictions dialog box appears, as shown in Figure 6-18.

Figure 6-18

The Request Restrictions dialog box

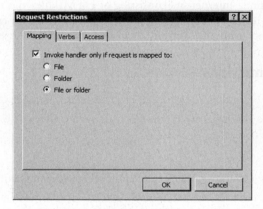

8. To limit the application of the handler, select the **Invoke handler only if request is mapped to** checkbox on the Mapping tab and specify whether you want IIS7 to invoke the handler when the request is for a file (the default), a folder, or both.

9. Click the **Verbs** tab, as shown in Figure 6-19.

Figure 6-19

The Verbs tab of the Request Restrictions dialog box

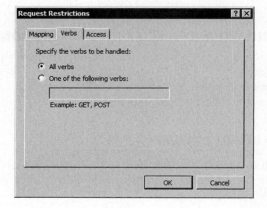

10. To limit the HTTP verbs that the handler can process, select the **One of the following verbs** option and, in the text box, key the verbs you want to permit.

11. Click the **Access** tab, as shown in Figure 6-20.

Figure 6-20

The Access tab of the Request Restrictions dialog box

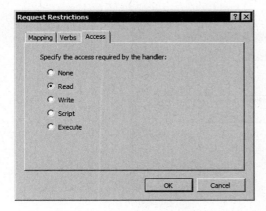

12. Select the permission you want to assign to the handler.

13. Click **OK**.

CLOSE the Internet Information Services (IIS) Manager console.

Limiting the types of client access to a Web site makes the server more secure. If, for example, you are running a simple Internet site consisting of HTML files and images, clients do not need anything other than read access. By denying the clients all access other than read, you eliminate all possibility of clients using the Web site to write to the server or execute programs and scripts.

Using NTFS Permissions

Although URL authorization rules provide an excellent alternative, NTFS permissions still factor into the IIS7 security picture, and they are still a viable means of regulating access to Web site contents.

For a client to access a Web site, the user account with which it is authenticated must have the proper NTFS permissions for the site's content files. This applies to clients that use Anonymous Authentication as well, in which case the IUSR user must have the right permissions.

 Before you begin working with NTFS permissions, it is important to understand how the Windows permission system works. To review the basic principles of permission management, see "Understanding the Windows Permission Architecture" in Lesson 2, "Deploying a File Server."

CERTIFICATION READY?
Configure Web site authentication and permissions
3.7

ASSIGNING STANDARD AND SPECIAL NTFS PERMISSIONS

Most desktop technicians and Windows system administrators work with standard NTFS permissions almost exclusively because you do not need to work directly with special permissions for most common access control tasks. To assign standard NTFS permissions for a Web site element, use the following procedure.

 ASSIGN STANDARD NTFS PERMISSIONS

GET READY. Log on to Windows Server 2008 using a domain account with Administrator privileges. When the logon process is completed, close the Initial Configuration Tasks window and any other windows that appear.

TAKE NOTE *

To configure a folder that is not a virtual directory or an individual file, select a Web site and click Content View. Then, double-click the desired folder or file, return to Features View, and double-click the Authentication icon.

1. Click **Start**, and then click **Administrative Tools** > **Internet Information Services (IIS) Manager**. The Internet Information Services (IIS) Manager console appears.

2. In the scope pane, select a site, application, or virtual directory. The Home pane for the selected element appears.

3. In the actions pane, click **Edit Permissions**. The Properties sheet for the file or folder corresponding to the selected element appears.

4. Click the **Security** tab. The top half of the resulting display lists all of the security principals currently possessing permissions to the file or folder. The bottom half lists the permissions held by the selected security principal.

5. Click **Edit.** A Permissions dialog box for the file or folder appears, as shown in Figure 6-21. The interface is the same as that of the previous dialog box, except that the permissions are now represented by checkboxes, indicating that you can modify their states.

Figure 6-21

A Permissions dialog box

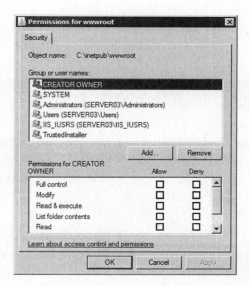

6. Click **Add.** The Select Users, Computers, or Groups dialog box appears, as shown in Figure 6-22.

Figure 6-22

The Select Users, Computers, or Groups dialog box

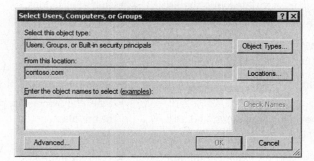

TAKE NOTE *

When you assign permissions on a stand-alone computer, you select local user and group accounts to be the security principals that receive the permissions. However, if the computer is a member of an Active Directory domain, you can also assign permissions to domain users, groups, and other objects.

7. In the *Enter the object names to select* text box, key the name of the user or group to which you want to assign permissions and then click **OK.** The user or group appears in the Permissions dialog box in the *Group or user names* list.

8. Select the user or group you just added and then, in the Permissions box, select or clear the checkboxes to Allow or Deny the user any of the standard permissions.

9. Click **OK** twice to close the Permissions dialog boxes and the Properties sheet.

CLOSE the Internet Information Services (IIS) Manager console.

The standard NTFS permissions have slightly different functions, depending on whether you apply them to a file or a folder. Table 6-2 lists all of the NTFS standard permissions and their effects on files and folders.

 Assigning permissions to the single folder you created takes only a moment, but for a folder with a large number of files and subfolders subordinate to it, the process can take a long time because the system must modify the ACL of each folder and file.

Table 6-2

NTFS Standard Permissions

STANDARD PERMISSION	WHEN APPLIED TO A FOLDER, ENABLES A SECURITY PRINCIPAL TO:	WHEN APPLIED TO A FILE, ENABLES A SECURITY PRINCIPAL TO:
Full Control	• Modify the folder permissions. • Take ownership of the folder. • Delete subfolders and files contained in the folder. • Perform all actions associated with all of the other NTFS folder permissions.	• Modify the file permissions. • Take ownership of the file. • Perform all actions associated with all of the other NTFS file permissions.
Modify	• Delete the folder. • Perform all actions associated with the Write and the Read & Execute permissions.	• Modify the file. • Delete the file. • Perform all actions associated with the Write and the Read & Execute permissions.
Read & Execute	• Navigate through restricted folders to reach other files and folders. • Perform all actions associated with the Read and List Folder Contents permissions.	• Perform all actions associated with the Read permission. • Run applications.
List Folder Contents	• View the names of the files and subfolders contained in the folder.	• Not applicable.
Read	• See the files and subfolders contained in the folder. • View the ownership, permissions, and attributes of the folder.	• Read the contents of the file. • View the ownership, permissions, and attributes of the file.
Write	• Create new files and subfolders inside the folder. • Modify the folder attributes. • View the ownership and permissions of the folder.	• Overwrite the file. • Modify the file attributes. • View the ownership and permissions of the file.

If you ever have to work with NTFS special permissions directly, Windows Server 2008 provides the tools. To view and manage the special NTFS permissions for a file or folder, use the following procedure.

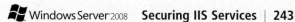

 ASSIGN SPECIAL NTFS PERMISSIONS

GET READY. Log on to Windows Server 2008 using a domain account with Administrator privileges. When the logon process is completed, close the Initial Configuration Tasks window and any other windows that appear.

1. Click **Start**, and then click **Administrative Tools** > **Internet Information Services (IIS) Manager**. The Internet Information Services (IIS) Manager console appears.

2. In the scope pane, select a site, application, or virtual directory. The Home pane for the selected element appears.

3. In the actions pane, click **Edit Permissions**. The Properties sheet for the file or folder corresponding to the selected element appears.

4. Click the **Security** tab, and then click **Advanced**. An Advanced Security Settings page for the selected file or folder appears. This dialog box is as close as the Windows graphical interface can come to displaying the contents of an ACL. Each line in the *Permission entries* list is essentially an ACE and includes the following information:

   • Type—Specifies whether the entry allows or denies the permission.

   • Name—Specifies the name of the security principal receiving the permission.

   • Permission—Specifies the name of the standard permission being assigned to the security principal. If the entry is used to assign special permissions, the word *Special* appears in this field.

   • Inherited From—Specifies whether the permission is inherited and if so, where it is inherited from.

   • Apply To—Specifies whether the permission is inherited by subordinate objects and if so, by which ones.

5. Click **Edit**. Another Advanced Security Settings dialog box appears. This one is editable, as shown in Figure 6-23. This dialog box also contains the following two checkboxes:

Figure 6-23

The editable Advanced Security Settings dialog box

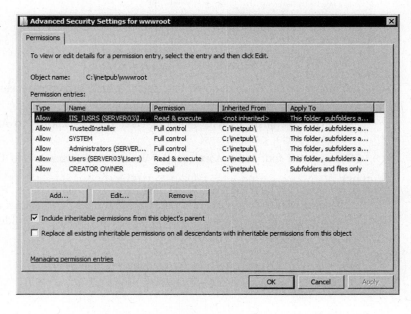

   • Include inheritable permissions from this object's parent—Specifies whether the file or folder should inherit permissions from parent objects. This checkbox is selected by default. Deselecting it causes a Windows Security message box to appear, enabling you to choose whether to remove all of the inherited ACEs from the list or copy the inherited permissions from the parent to the file or folder. If you choose the latter, the effective permissions stay the same, but the file or folder no longer depends on the parent for permission inheritance. If you change the permissions on the parent objects, the file or folder remains unaffected.

- Replace all existing inheritable permissions on all descendents with inheritable permissions from this object—Causes subordinate objects to inherit permissions from this file or folder, to the exclusion of all permissions explicitly assigned to the subordinate objects.

6. Click **Add**. The Select User, Computer, or Group dialog box appears.

7. In the *Enter the object names to select* text box, key the name of the user or group to which you want to assign permissions and then click **OK**. A Permission Entry dialog box for the file or folder appears, as shown in Figure 6-24.

Figure 6-24

A Permission Entry dialog box

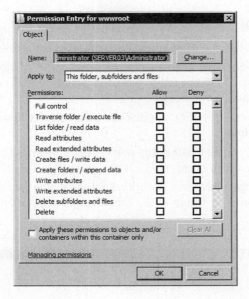

8. In the *Apply to* dropdown list, select which subordinate elements should receive the permissions you assign using this dialog box.

9. In the Permissions list, select or clear the checkboxes to Allow or Deny the user any special permissions.

10. Click **OK** four times to close the various dialog boxes and the Properties sheet.

CLOSE the Internet Information Services (IIS) Manager console.

Special permissions are slightly different from standard permissions, in that they have different names, depending on whether you apply them to a file or a folder. Table 6-3 lists all of the special permissions, along with their functions.

Table 6-3

NTFS Special Permissions

SPECIAL PERMISSION	FUNCTIONS
Traverse Folder/Execute File	• The Traverse Folder permission allows or denies security principals the ability to move through folders that they do not have permission to access to reach files or folders that they do have permission to access. This permission applies to folders only. • The Execute File permission allows or denies security principals the ability to run program files. This permission applies to files only.
List Folder/Read Data	• The List Folder permission allows or denies security principals the ability to view the file and subfolder names within a folder. This permission applies to folders only. • The Read Data permission allows or denies security principals the ability to view the contents of a file. This permission applies to files only.
Read Attributes	Allows or denies security principals the ability to view the NTFS attributes of a file or folder.
Read Extended Attributes	Allows or denies security principals the ability to view the extended attributes of a file or folder.
Create Files/Write Data	• The Create Files permission allows or denies security principals the ability to create files within the folder. This permission applies to folders only. • The Write Data permission allows or denies security principals the ability to modify the file and overwrite existing content. This permission applies to files only.
Create Folders/Append Data	• The Create Folders permission allows or denies security principals to create subfolders within a folder. This permission applies to folders only. • The Append Data permission allows or denies security principals the ability to add data to the end of the file but not to modify, delete, or overwrite existing data in the file. This permission applies to files only.
Write Attributes	Allows or denies security principals the ability to modify the NTFS attributes of a file or folder.
Write Extended Attributes	Allows or denies security principals the ability to modify the extended attributes of a file or folder.
Delete Subfolders and Files	Allows or denies security principals the ability to delete subfolders and files, even if the Delete permission has not been granted on the subfolder or file.
Delete	Allows or denies security principals the ability to delete the file or folder.
Read Permissions	Allows or denies security principals the ability to read the permissions for the file or folder.
Change Permissions	Allows or denies security principals the ability to modify the permissions for the file or folder.
Take Ownership	Allows or denies security principals the ability to take ownership of the file or folder.
Synchronize	Allows or denies different threads of multithreaded, multiprocessor programs to wait on the handle for the file or folder and synchronize with another thread that might signal it.

As mentioned earlier in this lesson, standard permissions are combinations of special permissions designed to provide frequently needed access controls. Table 2-8 in Lesson 2, "Deploying a File Server," lists all of the standard permissions, and the special permissions that compose them.

■ Using Secure Sockets Layer

THE BOTTOM LINE Secure Sockets Layer (SSL) is a security protocol that you can use to encrypt the data exchanged by clients and IIS servers.

When you click a link or key a URL containing the prefix https:// in your browser, you are establishing an SSL connection with the server. Virtually all browsers support SSL, and virtually all servers that handle sensitive data, such as e-commerce information, use it.

TAKE NOTE * When a user typing a URL omits the prefix by keying just a domain address, such as www.sitename.com, the browser automatically uses the http://prefix. To connect to the server using SSL, the URL or link must explicitly contain the https://prefix.

To use SSL on an IIS7 server, you must complete the following tasks:

- Obtain and install a server certificate.
- Create an SSL binding for your Website(s).
- Configure the Web site or FTP7 site to use SSL.

These tasks are discussed in the following sections.

Configuring Certificates

To use SSL, you must obtain a digital certificate for each of your Web servers.

CERTIFICATION READY?
Configuring SSL Security
3.6

A *digital certificate* is an electronic credential, issued by a *certification authority (CA)*, which confirms the identity of the party to which it is issued. For example, a digital certificate issued to a user contains identifying information about the individual, as well as a public key, which enables the user to participate in encrypted communications and prove his or her identity. A certificate issued to a server enables clients to verify that this really is the server it claims to be.

Participants in a *public key infrastructure* are issued two keys, one public and one private. The participant keeps the private key secret, while the public key is freely available in the digital certificate. Data encrypted with the private key can only be decrypted using the public key, and data encrypted with the public key can only be decrypted using the private key. Therefore, when a client obtains a Web server's certificate, its ability to decrypt the server's encrypted transmissions using the server's public key confirms that this is the system represented in the certificate. In addition, any data that the client encrypts using the server's public key can only be decrypted and read by the server.

A CA is simply an entity that issues certificates, which is trusted by both parties involved in the encrypted communications. If you want to use SSL on an Internet Web site, you must obtain a certificate for your Web server from a commercial CA, such as VeriSign, which is trusted both by your organization and by your clients. For intranet Web servers, you can run your own CA on a Windows Server 2008 computer and issue your own certificates. Because both the Web server and the clients are internal to the organization, both can trust an internal CA. To deploy your own CA, you must install the Active Directory Certificate Services role.

CREATING A CERTIFICATE REQUEST FILE

To obtain a server certificate for your IIS7 computer, you must either generate a request file and send it to a commercial CA or send an online request to your organization's internal CA.

To generate a request for a commercial CA, use the following procedure.

➔ CREATE A CERTIFICATE REQUEST FILE

GET READY. Log on to Windows Server 2008 using a domain account with Administrator privileges. When the logon process is completed, close the Initial Configuration Tasks window and any other windows that appear.

1. Click **Start**, and then click **Administrative Tools** > **Internet Information Services (IIS) Manager**. The Internet Information Services (IIS) Manager console appears.

2. In the scope pane, select a server. The Home pane for the selected server appears.

3. Double-click the **Server Certificates** icon. The Server Certificates pane appears, displaying any existing certificates, as shown in Figure 6-25.

Figure 6-25

The Server Certificates pane

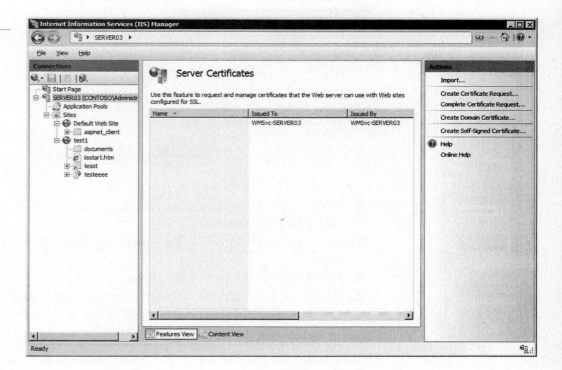

4. In the actions pane, click **Create Certificate Request**. The Request Certificate wizard appears, displaying the Distinguished Name Properties page, as shown in Figure 6-26.

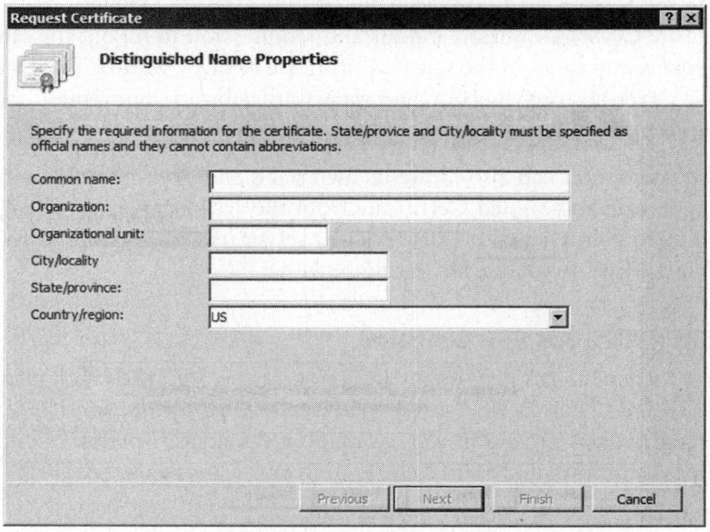

Figure 6-26

The Distinguished Name Properties page of the Request Certificate wizard

5. Fill in each of the text boxes with the requested information about your organization, and then click **Next**. The Cryptographic Service Provider Properties page appears, as shown in Figure 6-27.

Figure 6-27

The Cryptographic Service Provider Properties page of the Request Certificate wizard

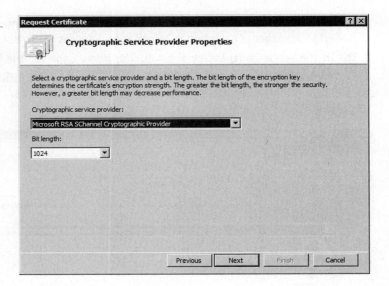

6. In the Cryptographic Service Provider dropdown list, select the provider you want to use for the certificate.

7. In the Bit Length dropdown list, specify the length for the certificate's encryption key.

8. Click **Next**. The File Name page appears.

9. Specify the name you want to use for the certificate request, and click **Finish**. The wizard creates the certificate request and stores it using the filename you specified.

CLOSE the Internet Information Services (IIS) Manager console.

After you create the certificate request file, you must submit it to your CA. The CA will send back a file containing the server certificate, which you must then install by opening the Server Certificates pane again, double-clicking Complete Certificate Request in the action pane, and specifying the name of the file the CA sent you.

If you have your own internal CA on the network, you can request a certificate from it by opening the Server Certificate pane and clicking Create Domain Certificate in the action pane. The Create Certificate wizard appears and requires you to fill out the same Distinguished Name Properties page as in the Create Certificate Request wizard. Then, you specify the name of the server hosting your CA, and the wizard submits your request and installs the certificate it receives in reply.

The computer can also create its own self-signed certificate, which you can request by selecting Create Self-Signed Certificate from the actions pane. A self-signed certificate has no real value to your clients, because it is the server itself that is verifying its own identity, but you can use this capability for testing purposes.

CREATING AN SSL BINDING

For a client to connect to an IIS7 server using SSL, the client must use the https:// prefix in its URL. For an IIS7 server to accept an SSL connection from a client, it must be able to recognize and process a URL containing the https:// prefix. To make this possible, you must create a binding for each Web site that you want to use SSL.

To create an SSL binding, use the following procedure.

⊕ CREATE AN SSL BINDING

GET READY. Log on to Windows Server 2008 using a domain account with Administrator privileges. When the logon process is completed, close the Initial Configuration Tasks window and any other windows that appear.

1. Click **Start**, and then click **Administrative Tools** > **Internet Information Services (IIS) Manager**. The Internet Information Services (IIS) Manager console appears.
2. In the scope pane, right-click one of your Web sites and, from the context menu, select **Edit Bindings**. The Site Bindings dialog box appears.
3. Click **Add**. The Add Site Binding dialog box appears.
4. In the Type dropdown list, select **https**. The Port value changes to 443 and an SSL Certificate dropdown list appears, as shown in Figure 6-28.

Figure 6-28

The modified Add Site Binding dialog box

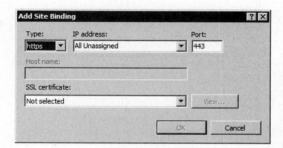

5. In the SSL certificate dropdown list, select the server certificate obtained from your CA.
6. Click **OK**. The new https binding appears in the Site Bindings list.
7. Select the existing http binding and click **Remove**. A Site Bindings message box appears, prompting you to confirm the removal.
8. Click **Yes**.
9. Click **Close**.

CLOSE the Internet Information Services (IIS) Manager console.

As you learned in Lesson 5, "Deploying IIS Services," Web servers use port number 80 by default, but you can select another port number for a site, as long as the clients include that port number in their URLs. The same is true for SSL bindings, except that the default port number for an SSL connection is 443.

ENABLING SSL

With a server certificate installed on the IIS7 server and the https binding in place, you are only required to enable SSL for your Web site, as in the following procedure.

⊕ ENABLE SSL

GET READY. Log on to Windows Server 2008 using a domain account with Administrator privileges. When the logon process is completed, close the Initial Configuration Tasks window and any other windows that appear.

1. Click **Start**, and then click **Administrative Tools** > **Internet Information Services (IIS) Manager**. The Internet Information Services (IIS) Manager console appears.
2. In the scope pane, select a Web site. The Home pane for the selected site appears.

3. Double-click the **SSL Settings** icon. The SSL Settings pane appears, as shown in Figure 6-29.

Figure 6-29

The SSL Settings pane

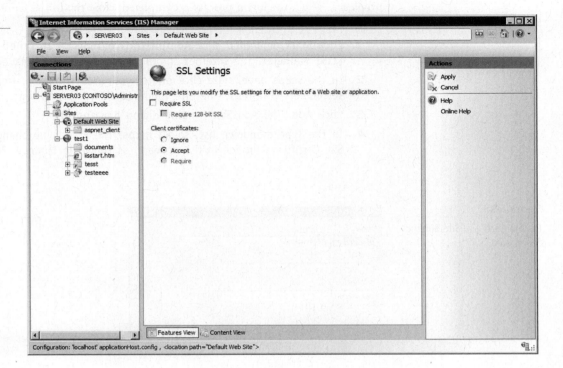

4. Select the **Require SSL** checkbox. If your clients support it, you can also select the **Require 128-bit SSL** checkbox.

5. Select one of the Client Certificates options, indicating whether you want to ignore, accept, or require client certificates.

6. In the action pane, click **Apply**.

CLOSE the Internet Information Services (IIS) Manager console.

After you have completed this procedure, clients can only connect to the Web site using the https:// URL prefix.

Enabling SSL for FTP7

The ability to encrypt FTP traffic using SSL is one of the major advantages of the FTP7 add-on module for Windows Server 2008.

SSL for FTP7 eliminates one of the major shortcomings of FTP: the transmission of passwords in clear text. To use SSL with FTP, you still need a certificate, although you can use a self-signed certificate. You do not need to create a special binding, but you do have to enable SSL for the FTP site, using the following procedure.

ENABLE SSL FOR FTP7

GET READY. Log on to Windows Server 2008 using a domain account with Administrator privileges. When the logon process is completed, close the Initial Configuration Tasks window and any other windows that appear.

1. Click **Start**, and then click **Administrative Tools** > **Internet Information Services (IIS) Manager**. The Internet Information Services (IIS) Manager console appears.

2. In the scope pane, select an FTP site. The Home pane for the selected site appears.

3. Double-click the **FTP SSL Settings** icon. The FTP SSL Settings pane appears, as shown in Figure 6-30.

Figure 6-30

The FTP SSL Settings pane

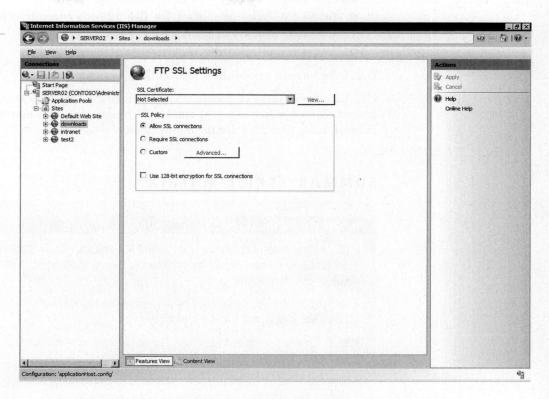

4. In the SSL Certificate dropdown list, select the certificate you want to use.

5. In the SSL Policy box, select the **Custom** option and click **Advanced**. The Advanced SSL Policy dialog box appears, as shown in Figure 6-31.

Figure 6-31

The Advanced SSL Policy dialog box

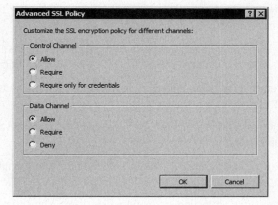

6. In the Control Channel box, select one of the following options:

- Allow—Enables FTP clients that support it to connect to the site using SSL. Clients that do not support SSL can still connect without it.

- Require—Permits only clients supporting SSL to connect to the site.

- Require only for credentials—Permits only clients supporting SSL to connect to the site, but the SSL encryption is limited to authentication traffic.

7. In the Data Channel box, select one of the following options:

- Allow—Enables FTP clients that support it to transfer data files using SSL. Clients that do not support SSL can still transfer files without it.

- Require—Permits only clients supporting SSL to transfer data files.
- Deny—Forbids clients to use SSL encryption for data transfers.

8. Click **OK**.

9. In the SSL Policy box, select the **Use 128-bit encryption for SSL connection** checkbox, if desired.

10. In the action pane, click **Apply**.

CLOSE the Internet Information Services (IIS) Manager console.

FTP uses two separate TCP connections when establishing a client/server connection. The control channel, which uses port number 21 by default, is for commands, while the data channel, using port 23, is for the transmission of data files.

SUMMARY SKILL MATRIX

IN THIS LESSON YOU LEARNED:

- IIS7 retains a security feature from earlier IIS versions that enables you to specify IP addresses or domain names that the server should allow or deny access to a server, site, virtual directory, folder, or file.

- IIS7 supports several password-based authentication methods, including anonymous, Windows, digest, and basic authentication.

- In IIS7, the authentication settings you configure at a particular level are inherited by all subordinate levels.

- When a client connects to a site configured to use multiple authentication methods, it always attempts to establish an anonymous connection first.

- The anonymous user account in IIS7 is a built-in account called IUSR, which is a member of a group called IIS_IUSRS.

- If you are running an intranet Web server on an Active Directory network with its own certification authority, you can configure IIS7 to automatically authenticate domain users that have client certificates.

- Because Active Directory Client Certificate Authentication requires the use of SSL with client certificates, it is not compatible with any of the other authentication methods IIS7 supports.

- Of the three traditional, challenge/response authentication methods supported by IIS7, Windows Authentication is the most secure.

- The Digest Authentication method in IIS7 is comparable to the Advanced Digest Authentication method from IIS6.

- Windows Authentication, Digest Authentication, and Basic Authentication are all challenge-based authentication methods.

- The NTFS permissions protecting a particular file system element are not like the keys to a lock, which provide either full access or no access at all. Permissions are designed to be granular, enabling you to grant specific degrees of access to security principals.

- NTFS permissions are realized as access control lists (ACLs), which consist of two basic types of access control entries (ACEs): Allow and Deny.

- Permissions tend to run down through a hierarchy. This is called permission inheritance.

- A digital certificate contains identifying information about the party to which it is issued, as well as a public key, which enables the issuee to participate in encrypted communications and prove its identity.

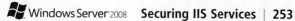

> • If you want to use SSL on an Internet Web site, you must obtain a certificate for your Web server from a commercial CA, such as VeriSign, which is trusted both by your organization and by your clients. For intranet Web servers, you can use a certificate from an internal CA.
>
> • To protect a Web site using SSL, you must have a server certificate and an https binding. Then you must enable SSL for the site.

■ Knowledge Assessment

Fill in the Blank

Complete the following sentences by writing the correct word or words in the blanks provided.

1. The most secure of the challenge/response authentication methods supported by IIS7 is _____ Authentication.

2. IIS7's Windows Authentication module uses the _____ authentication protocol for computers that are members of an Active Directory domain.

3. A(n) _____ is an electronic credential that confirms the identity of the party to which it is issued.

4. The process of confirming a user's identity, usually by requiring the user to supply some sort of token such as a password or certificate, is called _____.

5. The weakest of the challenge/response authentication methods supported by IIS7 is called _____.

6. When clients connect to a Web server using the _____ method, the server logs them on using the IUSR account, by default.

7. _____ Authentication is designed for use with Active Directory Web servers whose clients are on the other side of a proxy server or firewall.

8. Digital certificates are issued by internal or external resources called _____.

9. To authenticate clients that are not members of Active Directory domains, the IIS7 Windows Authentication module uses the _____ protocol.

10. Digital certificates are required for a Web server to participate in a(n) _____ infrastructure.

Multiple Choice

Select the correct answer for each of the following questions. Choose all answers that are correct.

1. Which of the following statements is/are *not* true about the IIS7 Handler Mappings module?
   a. The Handler Mappings module replaces NTFS permissions for IIS Web sites.
   b. The Handler Mappings module enables you to specify the permission required by the handler: read, write, script, execute, or none.
   c. The Handler Mappings module enables you to limit both the general permissions for a Web site and client access to specific file types.
   d. The Handler Mappings module enables you to limit the application of mappings based on the HTTP verb specified in the request.

2. The IIS7 Digest Authentication method
   a. works through firewalls and proxy servers, because it actually transmits passwords over the network.
   b. protects the passwords using a strong Kerberos encryption scheme.
   c. can be used with any version of Internet Explorer.
   d. is new to IIS7 and so is not comparable to authentication methods available in previous IIS versions.

3. Place the following methods that IIS7 uses to authenticate clients in the correct sequence.
   a. Digest Authentication
   b. Windows Authentication
   c. Basic Authentication
   d. Anonymous Authentication

4. Which of the following authentication methods is/are integrated into an IIS7 installation by default?
   a. Basic Authentication
   b. Windows Authentication
   c. Digest Authentication
   d. Anonymous Authentication

5. Anonymous users of an IIS7 Web server are authenticated using a local user account named
   a. Anonymous
   b. Authenticated User
   c. IUSR
   d. IUSR_*computername*

6. Which of the following authentication protocols can the IIS7 Windows Authentication module use?
   a. NTLMv2
   b. KDC
   c. Kerberos
   d. TGS/TGT

7. Which of the following statements about the IIS7 URL authorization rules is/are *not* true?
   a. URL Authorization rules are designed to function on concert with NTFS permissions.
   b. IIS7 stores URL Authorization rules in the IIS configuration files.
   c. Deny rules supersede allow rules.
   d. Parent rules supersede child rules.

8. Which of the following statements about the public key infrastructure is/are true?
   a. Private keys are distributed in digital certificates.
   b. A message encrypted using one user's private key can only be decrypted by another user's private key.
   c. Sending a message encrypted with a private key enables the recipient to confirm that the message actually came from the sender.
   d. Data encrypted using a public key can be decrypted by any user possessing that same public key.

9. Which of the following statements is/are prerequisites for using Active Directory Client Certificate Authentication?
   a. The network must have an Active Directory domain controller installed.
   b. The domain must use the Windows Server 2008 domain functional level.
   c. The network must have a server functioning as a certification authority (CA).
   d. All of the Web sites on the IIS7 server must require SSL communications.

Review Questions

1. List the tasks you must perform to implement SSL encryption for an IIS7 Web site.

2. What is the primary advantage of using Forms Authentication for a high-traffic Web site, rather than Windows, Digest, or Basic Authentication?

■ Case Scenarios

Scenario 6-1: Using Kerberos Authentication

Adam is deploying an intranet Web site on an IIS7 server, to provide company documents to internal users. To secure the site, Adam wants to use the Kerberos authentication capabilities provided by Active Directory, so he installs the Windows Authentication role service. After the site is live, Adam examines the log files and discovers that the clients accessing the server are using Anonymous Authentication, not Windows Authentication. What could be the problem, and what must Adam do to resolve it?

Scenario 6-2: Authorizing Web site Users

Tom is trying to secure the Web sites on his IIS7 server using URL authorization rules instead of NTFS permissions. To do this, he has modified the default rule at the server level to deny all users access. Then, he created new allow rules for each Web site on the server, granting specific users and groups the access they need. When the users attempt to access the sites, they receive error messages. What is the problem, and what changes must Tom make to the rules to correct it?

Deploying Web Applications

OBJECTIVE DOMAIN MATRIX

TECHNOLOGY SKILL	OBJECTIVE DOMAIN	OBJECTIVE DOMAIN NUMBER
Adding an Application to a Site	Configure Web applications.	3.1
Configuring SMTP Settings	Configure Simple Mail Transfer Protocol (SMTP).	3.4

KEY TERMS

Active Server Pages (ASP)
application pool
ASP.NET
Common Gateway Interface (CGI)
FastCGI

Internet Server Application Programming Interface (ISAPI)
ISAPI extensions
ISAPI filters
Server Side Includes (SSI)
Simple Mail Transfer Protocol (SMTP)

Universal Discovery, Description, and Integration (UDDI)
Web garden
worker process
worker process isolation mode

Application hosting is one of the primary areas in which Microsoft has improved Internet Information Services. This lesson examines the application-hosting capabilities built into IIS7, including the following:

- Understanding IIS7 application hosting support
- Creating and configuring application pools
- Deploying UDDI Services
- Deploying SMTP

■ Understanding Web Applications

THE BOTTOM LINE

Applications are now a major part of most Web server implementations. Instead of creating a completely new client, application developers can take advantage of the Web browser's capabilities and use them to access programs deployed on Web servers.

Web servers were originally designed as relatively simple applications that supplied clients with static content, in response to their requests. The static content most often took the form of Hypertext Markup Language (HTML) and image files. HTML is a simple scripting language that uses tags to specify how the client Web browser should display the text in the file and where it should insert images, which the server supplies as separate files. The HTML code is interpreted entirely by the browser application on the client computer. To the Web server, HTML files are simply text files that they supply to clients on demand.

As the Web grew in popularity, it also grew in complexity. Web site owners soon wanted to use their servers to provide more than just static content files. They wanted to perform more complicated tasks. They wanted to provide the information in their company databases to Web clients on demand. They wanted clients to be able to select products from a catalog and pay for them with a credit card. As a result, developers began to create Web servers with application capabilities.

As the years passed, developers devised various ways to implement applications in a Web environment by taking advantage of both clients' and servers' capabilities. Some types of Web-based applications execute scripts or compiled code on the server, while in others, the server supplies the script code to the client. Many Web development solutions combine the two. In any case, the primary advantage of Web applications over traditional client/server applications is that you do not need to develop, install, configure, or maintain complicated application packages on every client computer. Developers wanting to update their applications make all of their changes on the server, instead of distributing new files to hundreds or thousands of clients.

Most of the Web application environments in use today enable a server to dynamically generate Web pages and send them to clients, rather than use static, preconfigured pages. For example, when a user on a client computer keys a term into a search engine, the browser sends a request message containing the term to a Web server. The server cannot possibly hold the millions of static pages it would need to satisfy every possible search term, but it can access a database containing that information. After searching the database using the term supplied by the client, the Web server takes the resulting information, builds a new Web page containing that information, and sends it to the client.

Generally speaking, Web applications use a three-tiered architecture. The first tier is the client browser application running on the end user's computer. The second tier is a Web server with some type of dynamic content generation capability, and the third tier is a database server that stores the information the Web server uses to dynamically generate Web pages.

In addition to the information derived from a database, a dynamically generated Web page might also contain script code that runs on the client and implements dynamic elements on the user interface. Client-side scripting languages such as JavaScript, with other technologies, such as Java and Flash, enable the Web pages on client browsers to emulate virtually any function that a stand-alone client application can perform. Web pages can display virtually any type of content, including audio and video, and provide familiar keyboard and mouse controls, such as drag and drop.

No matter what appears in the client browser, the primary function of the Web server is still to send and receive text-based messages containing requests and replies. The added complexity lies in the technologies that the server uses to create those text messages and the browser uses to interpret them.

Understanding IIS7's Application Hosting Capabilities

IIS7 includes a wide variety of application environments that enable administrators to deploy applications created with many different development tools and languages.

With the increasing demand for Web applications came an increasing demand for Web application development solutions. Products like Microsoft Visual Studio provide simplified application development environments, but many of these products require the Web server to supply an environment in which the applications can run. As a result, Internet Information Systems version 7 (IIS7) includes role services that support a variety of development environments. Some of these role services represent cutting-edge Web development technologies, while others are relatively archaic, included with IIS7 primarily to support legacy applications.

The application role services supplied with IIS7 are discussed in the following sections.

UNDERSTANDING CGI

The *Common Gateway Interface (CGI)* is one of the earliest mechanisms designed to provide Web servers with application hosting capabilities. CGI is essentially a protocol that enables a Web server to run an application specified in a client request and pass the request to

that application for processing. The Web server then receives the output from the application and packages it as a reply to the client in the form of a Web page.

The primary drawback of CGI is that the Web server, in most cases, must launch a separate process to satisfy each request. Depending on the complexity of the program, the language used to write it, and the number of concurrent incoming requests, this can place a substantial burden on the server that increases with the Web site's traffic volume. CGI can also be a security risk, especially on Internet Web servers. By allowing Web pages to call CGI programs, you are essentially permitting anyone on the Internet to run a program on your server.

Developers can create CGI programs using any language that the server is capable of executing. This includes compiled languages, such as C and C++, and scripting languages, such as Perl. Although it is possible to use CGI for major application processes, such as accessing an external database, many CGI programs still in common use on the Internet are small applications that perform relatively simple tasks, such as displaying Web page counters. For more complicated applications that have to run continuously, developers today use other technologies.

Starting with IIS version 5.1, Microsoft provided an alternative to CGI, which overcomes its most serious problem. Called *FastCGI,* this extension to the CGI engine enables the Web server to maintain a pool of processes that new clients can reuse. In standard CGI processing, each client connection causes the operating system on the server to create a new process and map the Standard Input (stdin) and Standard Output (stdout) handles to that client. When the transaction is completed, the client disconnects and the server terminates the process.

In FastCGI, the server allocates each incoming client connection to one of the existing processes in the pool and remaps the stdin and stdout handles to the new client. When the transaction is completed, the server removes the mappings and returns the process to the pool. This eliminates the need for the server to create a new process for each client connection, which boosts CGI performance considerably.

UNDERSTANDING ISAPI

Internet Server Application Programming Interface (ISAPI) was designed to be an alternative to CGI, enabling a Web server to execute applications without spawning a separate process for each incoming request. Written primarily in C++, ISAPI applications can take two forms:

- *ISAPI extensions*—Fully-realized, in-process applications that can generate dynamic HTML pages using information from a database or supplied by the client using a form.
- *ISAPI filters*—A routine that operates between the HTTP server and the HTTP listener, providing additional functionality, such as application-based authentication, encryption, and data compression services. The ISAPI implementation in IIS6 virtually eliminates the need for ISAPI filters, because it can run ISAPI extensions, more efficiently, in their place.

As originally designed, ISAPI programs run in the same address space as the Web server's HTTP engine. ISAPI applications take the form of dynamic link libraries (DLLs) instead of executables (EXEs), which load with the IIS server engine, using the same address space. All of the resources available to the IIS server are also available to the ISAPI DLLs. This eliminates the need for calls between processes, as used in CGI, which enhances performance. It also means that if an ISAPI application crashes, the entire Web server goes with it. Beginning with IIS6, however, ISAPI applications can run in a separate address space, which reduces the danger of crashing the Web server while maintaining its performance levels.

If CGI can be said to represent the first generation of Web application programming, ISAPI must be seen as the second generation. While ISAPI provides improved levels of performance, its reliance on C++ means that developing ISAPI applications requires a high-level programming effort. CGI, by comparison, was more amenable to grass roots programming using Perl and other scripting languages.

In IIS6, ISAPI extensions function as the interface between the IIS engine and other, more flexible, application technologies, such as Active Server Pages (ASP) and ASP.NET. For example, IIS and ASP.NET each maintain their own separate request pipelines, and an ISAPI extension shuttles information between the two. In this arrangement, ISAPI facilitates these other application technologies, but it also constrains them. An application running on an IIS Web site can never run faster than the ISAPI extension that enables it.

IIS7 can use ISAPI in the same way, a compatibility feature that it calls "Classic" mode, but its more efficient "Integrated" mode eliminates the need for ISAPI as the middleman. Instead, IIS, ASP.NET, and other development technologies take the form of modules that plug into a single, generic request pipeline. ISAPI is not needed to provide an interface between IIS and other application types, so the applications are not reliant on, or constrained by, it.

UNDERSTANDING SERVER SIDE INCLUDES

Server Side Includes (SSI) is another relatively old Web server technology that enables HTML pages to contain directives that the server parses and executes. In the original client/server paradigm for the Web, clients, in the form of Web browsers, send requests to a server for specific text files. The server replies to the requests by accessing the appropriate files and sending the text to the client. The server is completely oblivious of the files' contents; it simply packages the text into an HTTP reply and transmits it to the client. The browser is wholly responsible for reading and interpreting the text.

SSI changes this paradigm by forcing the Web server to read the text of the pages it is about to transmit to clients, and act upon specific commands it finds in that text.

SSI consists of two elements:

- a collection of directives that Web designers can include in their HTML pages
- a component that causes the server to scan the outgoing text for directives and take the appropriate action.

For example, to make a Web server insert the contents of a file called filename.txt into a Web page, you insert the following code into the HTML file:

```
<! -#include virtual="filename.txt"- - >
```

The bracketed enclosure is the HTML tag indicating a command, so the browser ignores the contents of the brackets while parsing the file. However, the server does just the opposite, ignoring the rest of the file and paying attention to the SSI directives and their parameters.

SSI is an easy way of updating static HTML files with frequently changing data. For example, if you want to create a Web page that contains mostly static content, but which also specifies the latest price of gold, you can use an #include directive to insert a file containing the gold price into the page. Then, you only have to modify the included file when the price of gold changes. The main Web page file remains unchanged.

SSI, though old, is a useful technology but it does increase the workload on the server. Remember, the server not only has to execute the directives, it also has to scan every outgoing HTTP reply for those directives. If you have only a few Web pages that use SSI, and a great many that do not, it might not be practical to enable SSI for the entire server.

UNDERSTANDING ACTIVE SERVER PAGES

Microsoft designed *Active Server Pages (ASP)*, a server-side script processing engine, to provide dynamic Web content with better performance than CGI and simpler development than ISAPI. ASP files have an .asp extension, and function in much the same way as Server Side Includes, with scripting commands embedded in standard HTML code. Instead of appearing within comment delimiters, however, ASP commands are enclosed within angle brackets and ampersands, such as the following example, which displays the text "Hello, World." in the client browser window:

```
<& Response.Write("Hello, World.") &>
```

Most ASP pages use Microsoft's VBScript scripting language, but it is also possible to use Jscript, Microsoft's version of JavaScript. Third-party products provide support for other active scripting engines.

⊕ MORE INFORMATION

Although designed and implemented by Microsoft for the Windows server operating systems, ASP has been ported to other platforms. For example, a version for Apache Web servers is called Apache::ASP, and uses Perl scripting.

UNDERSTANDING ASP.NET

Much of IIS7's application hosting capability is geared towards the ASP.NET development environment. ASP.NET is the successor to ASP and is still based on server-side scripting, but it is more than just an upgrade. Based on the .NET Framework, *ASP.NET* enables developers to create dynamic Web pages, Web applications, and XML (Extensible Markup Language) Web services, using a wide variety of programming languages and development tools.

ASP.NET files have the extension .aspx, and can contain HTML code, XML code, or scripting code for execution by the server. Now that ASP.NET applications can plug directly into the IIS7 request processing pipeline, instead of using an ISAPI extension like IIS6, the services provided by ASP.NET applications can apply to any type of content handled by the Web server.

Understanding IIS7 Application Hosting

In Windows Server 2008, application hosting has become a primary function of IIS7. As mentioned earlier, previous versions of IIS are HTTP-centric. IIS6 only provides access to application hosting environments such as ASP and ASP.NET by way of ISAPI extensions. The modular architecture of IIS7 enables applications to participate on an equal footing with traditional HTTP request processing.

The fundamental job of an IIS server, or any server, is to receive requests from clients and process them. The server therefore has to "listen" for incoming requests arriving over specific ports. IIS6 introduced a specialized HTTP protocol listener module, called HTTP.sys, which replaced the Windows Sockets API used in earlier IIS versions.

In IIS6, HTTP.sys is responsible for accepting all incoming client requests. If the request is a standard HTTP message, then HTTP.sys hands it off to the World Wide Web Publishing Service (W3SVC) for processing. If the request is directed at an application, HTTP.sys uses ISAPI extensions to pass the request to the appropriate application pipeline. In essence, IIS is enabling multiple applications to share the single TCP port (port 80) dedicated to HTTP traffic.

IIS7 still includes the HTTP.sys module, which now includes support for Secure Sockets Layer (SSL) communications, but as mentioned earlier, there is now a single, generic request pipeline into which W3SVC and the optional application support modules can connect. However, in addition to HTTP.sys, IIS7 also adds three new protocol listeners: NET.TCP, NET.PIPE, and NET.MSMQ. These listeners enable IIS7 to receive client requests using protocols other than HTTP, and ports other than port 80. In other words, it is now possible to use IIS7 to host applications without running the W3SVC service, that is, without a Web server.

UNDERSTANDING APPLICATION POOLS

One of the inherent problems with hosting Web applications on Web sites is the possibility of an unstable application affecting the entire Web server, or worse, the entire computer. This is especially true for a commercial Web hosting operation, in which customers supply their own applications. IIS7, to protect its own server functions, as well as those of other Web sites and Windows Server 2008 itself, can isolate Web applications in separate address spaces called application pools.

An *application pool* is an operational division within IIS7 that consists of a request queue and one or more worker processes. A *worker process* is a host for user-developed application code, which is responsible for processing requests it receives from the protocol listeners and returning the results to the client. Because each application pool occupies its own protected address space, a crashed application cannot affect any process running outside of that pool. This is known as *worker process isolation mode*.

The Windows Process Activation Service (WPAS) is responsible for managing application pools and worker processes. In a typical IIS7 configuration, the request handling process proceeds as follow:

1. An incoming request from a client arrives at the computer.

2. IIS7 forwards the request to the appropriate site, based on its IP address, port number, or host header.

3. If the request contains an application call, such as a URL containing a file with the .aspx extension denoting an ASP.NET application, it goes into the request queue for the application pool associated with the application.

4. WPAS examines the state of the application pool to see if a running worker process can handle the request.

5. If a worker process is available, the request goes directly to that worker process. If no worker process is available, WPAS spawns a new worker process to handle the request.

6. The worker process executes the code and generates the calls necessary to process the request.

7. The worker process packages the results of its activities into a reply message and transmits it to the client.

The configuration of the application pools, worker processes, and applications is highly flexible in IIS7. You can create as many application pools as you need, and configure them in any one of the following three ways:

- Isolated process—A single application, serviced by a single worker process
- Medium (Pooled) process—Multiple applications, serviced by a single worker process
- Web garden—Multiple applications, serviced by multiple worker processes

When you install the Web Server (IIS) role, the wizard creates two application pools in IIS7, called DefaultAppPool and Classic .NET AppPool, both of which are configured to use a single worker process. All applications that you add to the Default Web Site on the server use DefaultAppPool, resulting in a Medium (Pooled) process configuration. When you create a new Web site, IIS7 automatically creates a new application pool with the same name as the site and the same configuration settings as DefaultAppPool. You can modify these pools to use more than one worker process, or create a new pool so configured, to form what is known as a *Web garden*.

UNDERSTANDING MANAGED PIPELINE MODES

As discussed earlier in this lesson, and in more detail in Lesson 5, "Deploying IIS Services," the new modular architecture of IIS7 includes multiple protocol listener modules, all of which can plug into a single, generic request pipeline. This streamlines the application request handling process and eliminates the need for ISAPI extensions linking the HTTP request pipeline with, for example, the ASP .NET pipeline.

However, some legacy applications might not be compatible with the new architecture, and so IIS7 enables you to configure each application pool to use one of the following managed pipeline modes:

- Integrated application pool mode—IIS7 uses the new, generic request pipeline for all protocol listeners and application development environments.
- Classic application pool mode—IIS7 uses the ISAPI-based interface between the HTTP pipeline and the ASP.NET pipeline from IIS6. This mode is intended only for applications that cannot run in Integrated mode.

DefaultAppPool uses the Integrated mode, and Classic .NET AppPool uses Classic mode.

Configuring IIS7 Application Settings

Now that you have learned how IIS7 implements, supports, and processes Web applications, consider how these application development technologies affect you as an administrator of IIS7 Web servers. In many cases, the honest answer is: not very much at all. As the administrator of a Web server, it is your job to provide application developers with the environments they need to run their applications.

You must be familiar with the application hosting capabilities of IIS7 so that you can determine whether it can run a particular application. You must also be familiar with the procedures for implementing and configuring those application hosting capabilities so that you can create Web sites that are appropriately equipped to run the applications that developers supply to you.

The following sections discuss those implementation and configuration procedures.

CREATING AN APPLICATION POOL

Application pools are IIS7 components that you can create as needed, just like you create Web sites and virtual directories. To use an application pool, you then associate it with a particular Web site by adding an application to that site and selecting the appropriate pool.

To create a new application pool, use the following procedure.

 CREATE AN APPLICATION POOL

GET READY. Log on to Windows Server 2008 using a domain account with Administrator privileges. When the logon process is completed, close the Initial Configuration Tasks window and any other windows that appear.

1. Click **Start**, and then click **Administrative Tools** > **Internet Information Services (IIS) Manager**. The Internet Information Services (IIS) Manager console appears.

2. Expand the server node and select the **Application Pools** node. The Application Pools pane appears, as shown in Figure 7-1.

Figure 7-1

The Application Pools pane

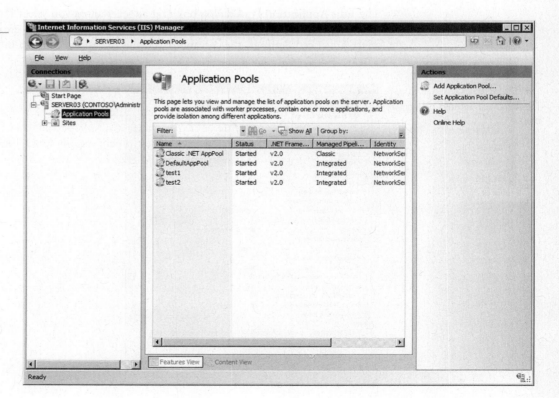

3. Right-click the **Application Pools** node and, from the context menu, select **Add Application Pool**. The Add Application Pool dialog box appears, as shown in Figure 7-2.

Figure 7-2

The Add Application Pool dialog box

4. In the Name text box, key a name for the new application pool.

5. In the *.NET Framework version* dropdown list, select the version of the .NET Framework that you want the application pool to load.

6. In the *Managed pipeline mode* dropdown list, specify whether you want to use Integrated or Classic mode.

7. If you do not want to start the application pool at this time, clear the *Start application pool immediately* checkbox.

8. Click **OK**.

CLOSE the Internet Information Services (IIS) Manager console.

After you have created an application pool, it appears in the Application Pools pane, and you can configure its settings at any time using the IIS Manager console.

CONFIGURING AN APPLICATION POOL

When you select an entry in the Applications Pool pane, you can select either Basic Settings or Advanced Settings from the actions pane.

The Edit Application Pool dialog box that appears when you select Basic Settings contains the same controls as the Add Application Pool dialog box you used to create the pool. When you select Advanced Settings, the Advanced Settings dialog box, shown in Figure 7-3, appears.

Figure 7-3

The Advanced Settings dialog box

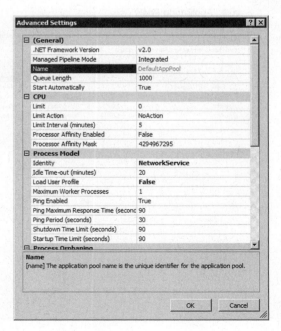

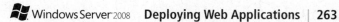

This dialog box, in addition to providing access to the basic settings, enables you to configure the resources allotted to the application pool and the actions IIS7 should take when the pool exceeds those resources. These settings are particularly useful in a commercial Web hosting environment when you want to ensure that one Web site does not monopolize the computer's resources. The parameters you can configure are listed in Table 7-1.

Table 7-1

Application Pool Advanced Settings

Setting	Default Value	Description
(General)		
.NET Framework version	v2.0	Specifies the version of the .NET Framework that the application pool will load.
Managed Pipeline Mode	Integrated	Specifies whether IIS7 will use the new, generic request pipeline for all protocol listeners and application development environments or the IIS6 ISAPI-based interface between the HTTP pipeline and the ASP.NET pipeline.
Queue length	1000	Specifies the number of requests that HTTP.sys can hold in its queue before IIS7 begins returning error messages to clients.
Start automatically	True	Specifies whether the application pool should start when IIS7 starts.
CPU		
Limit	0	Specifies the maximum percentage of CPU time (in 1/1000s of a percent) that the worker processes in the application pool are allowed to consume.
Limit Action	NoAction	Specifies the action that IIS7 should take when the application pool exceeds its CPU time limit. The NoAction value generates an event log entry, and the KillW3wp value shuts down the application pool for a designated time interval and creates an event log entry.
Limit Interval	5	Specifies the time interval (in minutes) during which the Limit value is imposed and the application pool remains shut down in the event of a KillW3p incident.
Processor Affinity Enabled	False	Specifies whether the application pool should be forced to use specific processors on a multi-processor system.
Processor Affinity Mask	[Varies]	Specifies which processor(s) the application pool should use on a multi-processor system.
Process Model Identity	Network Service	Specifies the built-in or user account that the application pool should use to run.
Idle Time-out	20	Specifies the amount of time (in minutes) that a worker process can remain idle before IIS7 shuts it down.
Load User Profile	False	Specifies whether IIS7 should load the user profile for the account specified in the Identity value.
Maximum Worker Processes	1	Specifies the number of worker processes the application pool can use. Specifying a value greater than 1 configures the pool as a Web garden.
Ping Enabled	True	Activates health monitoring, in which IIS7 pings each worker process periodically to ensure that it is active.

(continued)

Table 7-1 (*continued*)

SETTING	DEFAULT VALUE	DESCRIPTION
Ping Maximum Response Time	90	Specifies the amount of time (in seconds) that a worker process has to reply to a ping before IIS7 terminates the worker process.
Ping Period	30	Specifies the interval (in seconds) between health monitoring pings.
Shutdown Time Limit	90	Specifies the amount of time (in seconds) allotted to worker processes to finish processing all outstanding requests and shut down. If a worker process exceeds this time limit, IIS7 terminates it.
Startup Time Limit	90	Specifies the amount of time (in seconds) allotted to worker processes to start up and initialize. If a worker process exceeds this time limit, IIS7 terminates it.
Process Orphaning		
Enabled	False	Specifies whether IIS7 should abandon unresponsive worker processes instead of terminating them.
Executable	[None]	Specifies the name of a program that IIS7 should run when it abandons a worker process.
Executable Parameters	[None]	Specifies parameters that IIS7 should include when running the program specified in the Executable value.
Rapid Fail Protection		
"Service Unavailable" Response Type	HttpLevel	Specifies whether a stopped application pool should cause IIS7 to generate HTTP 503 errors or reset the TCP connection.
Enabled	True	Specifies whether IIS7 should shut down an application pool when a specified number of worker process crashes occur within a specified time interval.
Failure Interval	5	Specifies the time interval (in minutes) during which a specified number of worker process crashes must occur for IIS7 to shut down an application pool.
Maximum Failures	5	Specifies the number of worker process crashes that must occur during the time period specified by the Failure Interval value for IIS7 to shut down an application pool.
Shutdown Executable	[None]	Specifies the name of a program that IIS7 should run when it shuts down an application pool.
Shutdown Executable Parameters	[None]	Specifies parameters that IIS7 should include when running the program specified in the Shutdown Executable value.
Recycling		
Disable Overlapped Recycle	False	Specifies whether the application pool should wait for a worker process to terminate before it creates a new worker process.
Disable Recycling for Configuration Changes	False	Specifies whether the application pool should recycle worker processes when its configuration changes.
Generate Recycle Event Log Entry	[Various]	Specifies whether IIS7 should create event log entries when individual specified recycle events occur.
Private Memory Limit	0	Specifies the amount of private memory (in KB) that a worker process can consume before IIS7 recycles the application pool.

(*continued*)

Table 7-1 (*continued*)

SETTING	DEFAULT VALUE	DESCRIPTION
Regular Time Interval	1740	Specifies the time interval (in minutes) between application pool recycles.
Request Limit	0	Specifies the maximum number of requests an application pool can process before it recycles.
Specific Times	TimeSpan[] Array	Contains a list of specified times that the application pool should recycle.
Virtual Memory Limit	0	Specifies the amount of virtual memory (in KB) that a worker process can consume before IIS7 recycles the application pool.

CERTIFICATION READY?
Configure Web applications
3.1

ADDING AN APPLICATION TO A SITE

After you create an application pool, you must associate it with the applications that will run within it. To add an application to a Web site in IIS7, use the following procedure.

 ADD AN APPLICATION TO A SITE

GET READY. Log on to Windows Server 2008 using a domain account with Administrator privileges. When the logon process is completed, close the Initial Configuration Tasks window and any other windows that appear.

1. Click **Start**, and then click **Administrative Tools** > **Internet Information Services (IIS) Manager**. The Internet Information Services (IIS) Manager console appears.
2. Expand the server node and then expand the Sites folder.
3. Right-click a Web site and, from the context menu, select **Add Application**. The Add Application dialog box appears, as shown in Figure 7-4.

Figure 7-4

The Add Application dialog box

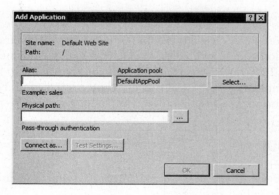

4. In the Alias text box, key the name that you want clients to use in their URLs to access the application.
5. Click **Select**. The Select Application Pool dialog box appears, as shown in Figure 7-5.

Figure 7-5

The Select Application Pool dialog box

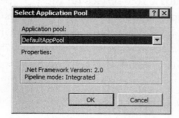

6. In the Application Pool dropdown list, select the application pool in which you want the application to run. Then click **OK**.

7. In the Add Application dialog box, in the Physical Path text box, key or browse to the folder where the application content is located. The folder can be on the local or a remote computer, and you can use drive letter notation (c:\foldername) or Universal Naming Convention (UNC) notation (\\servername\foldername).

8. By default, IIS7 uses the client user account to access application content on other systems. If the client needs alternative credentials to access the application, click **Connect As** and specify a user name and password.

9. Click **OK**.

CLOSE the Internet Information Services (IIS) Manager console.

An application node appears, subordinate to the selected Web site. When requests for the application arrive at the Web site, IIS7 passes them to the specified application pool for processing, and WPAS allocates a worker process to the task.

Deploying UDDI Services

THE BOTTOM LINE
Universal Discovery, Description, and Integration (UDDI) is an XML-based directory service that enables businesses to publish listings about their activities and the services they offer.

Windows Server 2008 includes a UDDI Services role that organizations can use to share information about their Web sites and services with clients on an intranet, extranet, or the Internet.

The UDDI Services role consists of the following two role services:

- UDDI Services Database
- UDDI Services Web Application

You can install both of the role services on one computer, for a stand-alone installation, the only installation type supported on Windows Server 2008 Standard. If you are running Windows Server 2008 Enterprise or Datacenter, you can choose to install the role services on two different computers, which is called a distributed installation. For performance reasons, Microsoft recommends the latter arrangement.

Installing UDDI

The UDDI Services Database is where the service stores information about Web sites, as well as its configuration settings.

The UDDI Services role supplied with Windows Server 2008 can store its database on a computer running Microsoft SQL Server, as long as you perform a distributed installation and install the UDDI Services Database role service on the SQL Server computer. Therefore, when you select only one of the two role services in the Add Roles Wizard, a SQL Server Instance page appears, as shown in Figure 7-6, on which you specify where the SQL Server is installed.

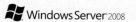

Figure 7-6

The SQL Server Instance page
in the Add Roles Wizard

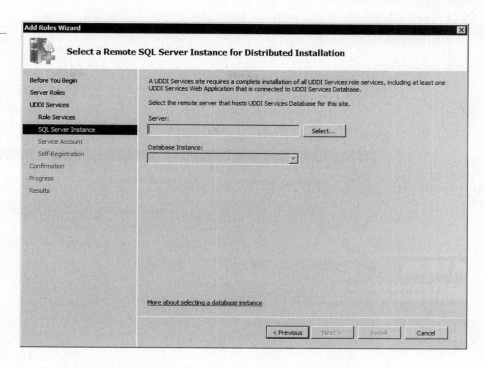

When you select both of the role services to perform a stand-alone installation, there is no
SQL Server Instance page because the UDDI Services Database role service uses the Windows
Internal Database, a version of SQL Server included with Windows Server 2008.

The UDDI Services Web Application role service uses IIS to deploy a Web site providing
access to UDDI functions. Therefore, you must have IIS installed on the same computer
where you install UDDI Services Web Application. On a computer that is not yet running
IIS when you select the UDDI Services Web Application role service, the Add Roles Wizard
prompts you to install the following required role services and features:

- Web Server (IIS) > Common HTTP Features > Static Content
- Web Server (IIS) > Common HTTP Features > Default Document
- Web Server (IIS) > Common HTTP Features > Directory Browsing
- Web Server (IIS) > Common HTTP Features > HTTP Errors
- Web Server (IIS) > Common HTTP Features > HTTP Redirection
- Web Server (IIS) > Application Development > ASP.NET
- Web Server (IIS) > Application Development > .NET Extensibility
- Web Server (IIS) > Application Development > ISAPI Extensions
- Web Server (IIS) > Application Development > ISAPI Filters
- Web Server (IIS) > Health and Diagnostics > HTTP Logging
- Web Server (IIS) > Health and Diagnostics > Logging Tools
- Web Server (IIS) > Health and Diagnostics > Request Monitor
- Web Server (IIS) > Health and Diagnostics > Tracing
- Web Server (IIS) > Security > Basic Authentication
- Web Server (IIS) > Security > Windows Authentication
- Web Server (IIS) > Security > Request Filtering
- Web Server (IIS) > Performance > Static Content Compression
- Web Server (IIS) > Management Tools > IIS Management Console
- Web Server (IIS) > Management Tools > IIS 6 Management Compatibility > IIS 6
  Metabase Compatibility
- Windows Process Activation Service > Process Model

- Windows Process Activation Service > .NET Environment
- Windows Process Activation Service > Configuration APIs

In addition to requiring these modules, selecting the UDDI Services Web Application role service adds the following pages to the wizard, which enable you to configure the basic service parameters:

- SSL Encryption Options—Specifies whether clients publishing data to the UDDI site must use Secure Sockets Layer (SSL) encryption, as shown in Figure 7-7.

Figure 7-7

The Secure Sockets Layer (SSL) Encryption Options page in the Add Roles Wizard

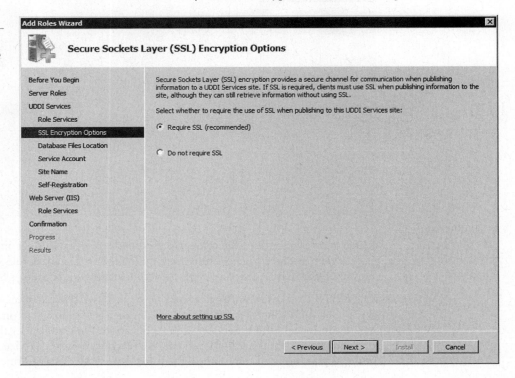

- Database Files Location—On a stand-alone installation, specifies where UDDI Services should store its database and log files, as shown in Figure 7-8.

Figure 7-8

The Specify Database and Log Files Locations page in the Add Roles Wizard

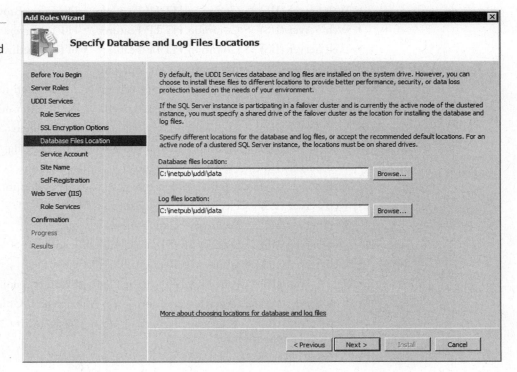

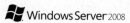

- Service Account—Specifies whether UDDI Services should communicate with other services using the Local Service account (the default) or a user account that you specify, as shown in Figure 7-9.

Figure 7-9

The Choose Service Account page in the Add Roles Wizard

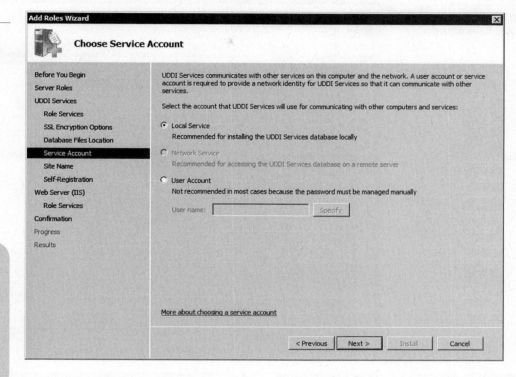

TAKE NOTE *

The combination of the UDDI Services Database and UDDI Services Web Application role services, when the two share the same configuration, is known as a site.

- Site Name—Specifies the name that you want to assign to the UDDI site, as shown in Figure 7-10.

Figure 7-10

The Specify Site Name page in the Add Roles Wizard

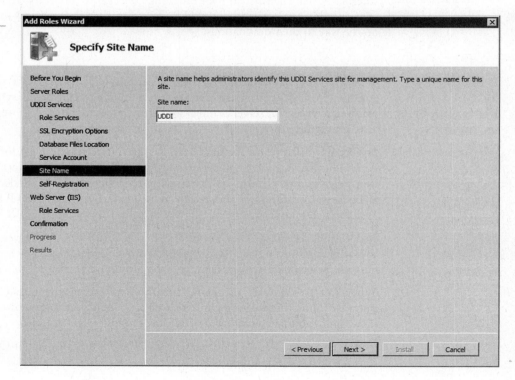

• Self-Registration—Specifies whether you want UDDI Services to enter itself into the UDDI registry, as shown in Figure 7-11.

Figure 7-11

The Set Self-Registration page in the Add Roles Wizard

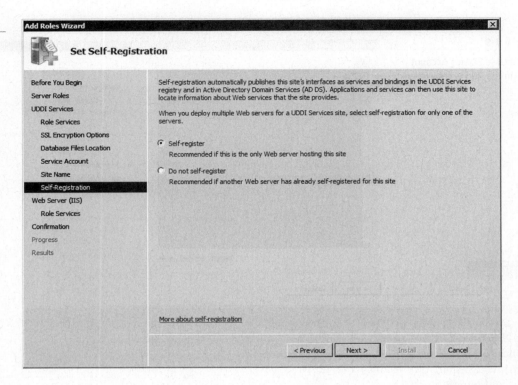

■ Deploying an SMTP Server

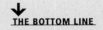

THE BOTTOM LINE

The **Simple Mail Transfer Protocol (SMTP)** is the standard email protocol for the Internet. Email clients send their outgoing messages to an SMTP server specified in their configuration settings, and the SMTP server forwards the messages to other mail servers on the way to their destinations.

Windows Server 2008 includes a feature that implements an SMTP server, which you can configure to handle all of the outgoing email messages sent by the system's various roles and features. The SMTP server is integrated into IIS because the sites you host on a Web server also can require its services.

For example, if your IIS server is hosting a Web page containing a form that clients can use to communicate with the webmaster, the application processing the form accepts the information submitted by clients, packages it as an email message, and sends it to an SMTP server to be forwarded to the webmaster's own mail server. As such, SMTP Server is essentially the Windows counterpart to the sendmail program used by most UNIX Web servers.

In addition, several of the server roles included with Windows Server 2008 have the ability to notify administrators and/or users when certain events occur by sending them automated email messages. The computer can use the SMTP Server feature to send these messages.

When you use the Add Features Wizard in Server Manager to install SMTP Server on a computer with no other roles or features installed, the message box shown in Figure 7-12 appears, informing you that the following additional modules are required:

• Web Server (IIS) > Management Tools > IIS 6 Management Compatibility > IIS 6 Metabase Compatibility

- Web Server (IIS) > Management Tools > IIS 6 Management Compatibility > IIS 6 Management Console
- Remote Server Administration Tools > Feature Administration Tools > SMTP Server Tools

Figure 7-12

The *Add role services and features required for SMTP Server?* message box in the Add Features Wizard

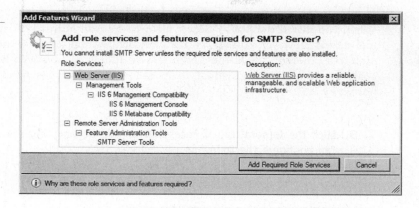

Configuring SMTP Settings

As you might surmise from the IIS6 compatibility modules required, the Windows Server 2008 SMTP Server is essentially unchanged from the Windows Server 2003 version.

 **CERTIFICATION READY?**
Configure Simple Mail
Transfer Protocol (SMTP)
3.4

To configure the SMTP Server, you use the Internet Information Services (IIS) 6.0 Manager, which employs the tabbed Properties sheet interface from IIS6, rather than IIS7's icon-based interface.

To configure the IIS7 SMTP Server module, use the following procedure.

 CONFIGURE SMTP SETTINGS

GET READY. Log on to Windows Server 2008 using a domain account with Administrator privileges. When the logon process is completed, close the Initial Configuration Tasks window and any other windows that appear.

1. Click **Start**, and then click **Administrative Tools** > **Internet Information Services (IIS) 6.0 Manager**. The Internet Information Services (IIS) 6.0 Manager console appears, as shown in Figure 7-13.

Figure 7-13

The Internet Information Services (IIS) 6.0 Manager console

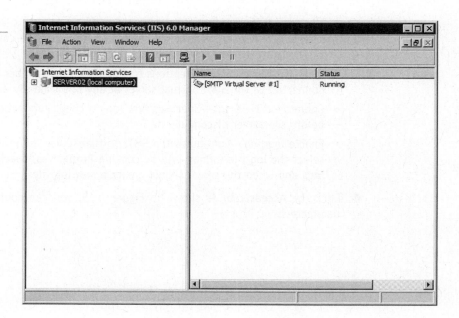

2. In the scope pane, expand the server node. Then, right-click the **SMTP Virtual Server #1** node and, from the context menu, select **Properties.** The SMTP Virtual Server #1 Properties sheet appears.

When you install the SMTP Server feature, the Add Features Wizard creates one virtual server. However, you can create additional virtual servers as needed, assigning each to a different one of the computer's IP addresses. In a Web hosting situation, this enables you to create individual, dedicated SMTP server instances for each Web site hosted by IIS.

3. Click the **General** tab if necessary. On the General tab, shown in Figure 7-14, you can configure the following parameters:

Figure 7-14

The General tab of an SMTP virtual server's Properties sheet

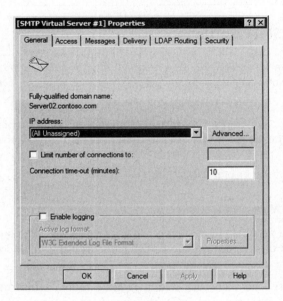

- IP address—Select the address you want clients to use to access the SMTP virtual server. If only one SMTP virtual server is running on the computer, you can leave the default All Unassigned value in place.
- Limit the number of connections to—Specifies the number of clients that can be connected to the SMTP virtual server at any one time. By default, there is no limit.
- Connection time-out—Specifies how long a client connection can remain inactive before the server disconnects it.
- Enable logging—Configures the SMTP virtual server to log its activities. You can select the log file format, and by clicking **Properties**, specify the location for the logs and when the server should create a new log file.

4. Click the **Access** tab. As shown in Figure 7-15, you can configure the following parameters:

Figure 7-15

The Access tab of an SMTP virtual server's Properties sheet

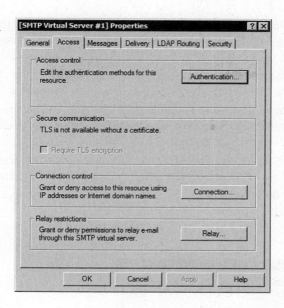

- Authentication—By default, the SMTP virtual server permits anonymous access. Click **Authentication** to enable Basic Authentication or Integrated Windows Authentication.
- Secure Communication—Configures servers with appropriate certificates to require Transport Layer Security (TLS) encryption for all client connections.
- Connection control—Enables you to control access to the SMTP virtual server by specifying IP addresses or domain names.
- Relay restrictions—Enables you to control which systems can relay mail through the SMTP virtual server by specifying IP addresses or domain names.

5. Click the **Messages** tab. As shown in Figure 7-16, you can configure the following parameters:

Figure 7-16

The Messages tab of an SMTP virtual server's Properties sheet

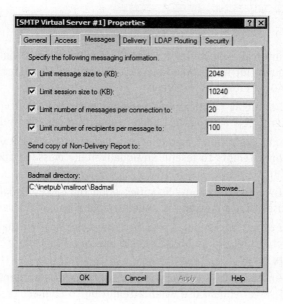

- Limit message size to—Specifies the size (in KB) of the largest message that the SMTP virtual server will accept. The default value is 2048.
- Limit session size to—Specifies the maximum amount of data (in KB) that a client can send to the SMTP virtual server in one session. The default value is 10240.

- Limit number of messages per connection to—Specifies the maximum amount of messages that a client can send to the SMTP virtual server in one connection. The default value is 20.

- Limit number of recipients per message to—Specifies the maximum number of recipients the SMTP virtual server will accept for each message. The default value is 100.

- Send copy of Non-Delivery Report to—Enables you to specify the email address of an administrator who should receive copies of all non-delivery reports the SMTP virtual server sends to users.

- Badmail directory—Specifies the path to the directory where the SMTP virtual server should put all mail that remains undeliverable after the specified number of retries.

6. Click the **Delivery** tab. As shown in Figure 7-17, you can configure the following parameters:

Figure 7-17

The Delivery tab of an SMTP virtual server's Properties sheet

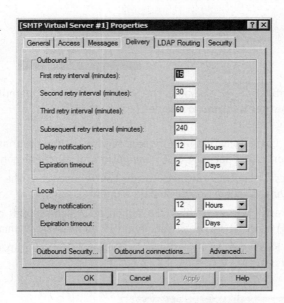

- Retry intervals—Specifies the time intervals between the first, second, third, and subsequent retries of failed message deliveries. The default values are 15, 30, 60, and 240 minutes, respectively.

- Outbound Delay notification—Specifies when the SMTP virtual server should notify the user that a message is undeliverable. The default value is 12 hours.

- Outbound Expiration timeout—Specifies when the SMTP virtual server should abandon attempts to resend an undeliverable message and transmit a non-delivery report to the user.

- Local Delay notification—Specifies when the SMTP virtual server should notify a local user that a message is undeliverable. The default value is 12 hours.

- Local Expiration timeout—Specifies when the SMTP virtual server should abandon attempts to resend an undeliverable message from a local user and transmit a non-delivery report.

- Outbound Security—Enables you to configure the authentication settings the SMTP virtual server should use when attempting to connect to another SMTP server.

- Outbound Connections—Specifies the maximum number of connections permitted and the time-out interval for the SMTP virtual server's communications with other SMTP servers.

- Advanced—Specifies the maximum number of routers for outgoing SMTP traffic, the masquerade domain name the server should insert into all outgoing messages, the fully qualified domain name of the computer, and the name of a smart host that will provide alternate routing options.

7. Click the **LDAP Routing** tab. As shown in Figure 7-18, you can configure the following parameters:

• Enable LDAP routing—Enables the SMTP virtual server to use a Lightweight Directory Access Protocol (LDAP) server to resolve email addresses, instead of a Domain Name System (DNS) server.

Figure 7-18

The LDAP Routing tab of an SMTP virtual server's Properties sheet

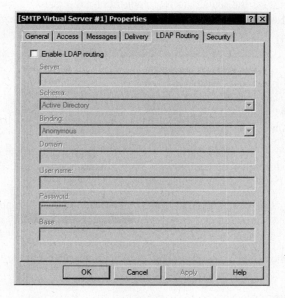

8. Click the **Security** tab. As shown in Figure 7-19, you can configure the following parameters:

• Operators—Enables you to assign operator permissions to specific Windows or domain users.

Figure 7-19

The Security tab of an SMTP virtual server's Properties sheet

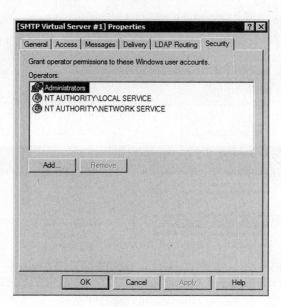

9. Click **OK** to close the Properties sheet.

CLOSE the Internet Information Services (IIS) Manager console.

At this point, the SMTP Server is ready to receive outgoing mail requests from applications running on the server, or from other Windows Server 2008 services.

SUMMARY SKILL MATRIX

IN THIS LESSON YOU LEARNED:

- Internet Information Systems version 7 (IIS7) includes role services that support a variety of development environments.

- CGI is a protocol that enables a Web server to run an application specified in a client request and pass the request to that application for processing. FastCGI is a new variant of CGI that enables IIS7 to provide clients with access to applications without creating a new process for each client.

- Internet Server Application Programming Interface (ISAPI) is designed to be an alternative to CGI, enabling a Web server to execute applications without spawning a separate process for each incoming request.

- Server Side Includes (SSI) is a relatively old Web server technology that enables HTML pages to contain directives that the server parses and executes.

- Active Server Pages (ASP) is a server-side script processing engine designed by Microsoft to provide dynamic Web content with better performance than CGI and simpler development than ISAPI.

- ASP.NET enables developers to create dynamic Web pages, Web applications, and XML (Extensible Markup Language) Web services, using a wide variety of programming languages and development tools.

- An application pool is an operational division within IIS7 that consists of a request queue and one or more worker processes.

- A worker process is a host for user-developed application code, which is responsible for processing requests it receives from the protocol listeners and returning the results to the client.

- IIS7 enables you to configure each application pool to use one of the following managed pipeline modes: Integrated or Classic.

- Universal Discovery, Description, and Integration (UDDI) is an XML-based directory service that enables businesses to publish listings about their activities and the services they offer.

- The Simple Mail Transfer Protocol (SMTP) is the standard email protocol for the Internet. Email clients send their outgoing messages to an SMTP server specified in their configuration settings, and the SMTP server forwards the messages to other mail servers on the way to their destinations.

■ Knowledge Assessment

Matching

Complete the following exercise by matching the terms with their corresponding definitions.

a. Application hosting technology that launches a separate process for each request

b. Provides the interface between IIS and ASP.NET in IIS7's Classic mode

c. The first Web technology to enable servers to process code in HTML files

d. Programming environment based on the .NET Framework 3.0

e. Sends information keyed by clients into Web forms to server administrators

f. Prevents unstable Web applications from crashing the server

g. Created and terminated as needed by Windows Process Activation Service

h. Uses commands enclosed within angle brackets and ampersands

i. An application pool with multiple worker processes

j. Allocates processes to clients from a pool rather than creating new ones

_____   **1.** Active Server Pages (ASP)

_____   **2.** application pool

_____   **3.** ASP.NET

_____   **4.** Common Gateway Interface (CGI)

_____   **5.** Internet Server Application Programming Interface (ISAPI)

_____   **6.** FastCGI

_____   **7.** Server Side Includes (SSI)

_____   **8.** Simple Mail Transfer Protocol (SMTP)

_____   **9.** Web garden

_____   **10.** worker process

Multiple Choice

Select the correct answer for each of the following questions.

1. The primary function of a Web server is to:
   a. store client information
   b. provide data storage for Web-based applications
   c. receive and send text-based messages, using the HTTP protocol syntax
   d. authenticate clients

2. When you install the Web Server (IIS) role in Windows Server 2008, the Add New Roles Wizard creates which application pools in IIS7? (Choose all answers that are correct.)
   a. DefaultNETPool
   b. Classic .NET DefaultAppPool
   c. Classic .NET AppPool
   d. DefaultAppPool

3. The Windows Process Activation Service (WPAS) is responsible for creating and terminating what IIS7 components?
   a. worker processes
   b. directory browsing
   c. request filtering
   d. application pools

4. Web applications typically use a three-tiered architecture. Which of the following is not one of those three tiers?
   a. A Web server with some type of dynamic content generation capability.
   b. A Web server that acts as a database server to store application information.
   c. A database server that stores the information the Web server uses to dynamically generate Web pages.
   d. The client browser application running on the end user's computer.

5. The UDDI Services role consists of which of the following role services? (Choose all answers that are correct.)
   a. UDDI Services Database
   b. UDDI Services Web Application
   c. UDDI Services Database Security
   d. UDDI Services Web Browser

6. The Windows Process Activation Service (WPAS) is responsible for managing application pools and worker processes. In a typical IIS7 configuration, the request handling process proceeds as follows: (Place all five answers in the correct order.)
   a. WPAS examines the state of the application pool to see if there is a worker process running that can handle the request.
   b. A worker process performs the tasks necessary to process the request.
   c. An incoming request from a client arrives at the computer.
   d. IIS7 sends the request to the application pool associated with the application.
   e. The worker process transmits a reply message to the client.

7. Which of the following provides the interface between the IIS request pipeline and the ASP.NET pipeline when an application pool is running in Classic mode?
   a. CGI
   b. .NET Framework
   c. ASP
   d. ISAPI

8. Which of the following authentication methods is not supported by the SMTP Server service in Windows Server 2008?
   a. Anonymous Authentication
   b. Basic Authentication
   c. Digest Authentication
   d. Integrated Windows Authentication

9. Which of the following application pool settings would you modify to create a Web garden?
   a. Managed Pipeline Mode
   b. .NET Framework Version
   c. Maximum Worker Processes
   d. Failure Interval

10. What term is used to describe the combination of the UDDI Services Database and UDDI Services Web Application role services when the two share the same configuration?
   a. site
   b. UDDI pool
   c. worker process
   d. XML

Review Questions

1. Explain how the development of application technologies such as Server Side Includes and Active Server Pages modified the fundamental role of the Web server.

2. List the three types of application pool configurations and describe how they differ.

■ Case Scenarios

Scenario 7-1: Configuring Application Pools

Amanda is the owner and operator of a small Web hosting company. She is using Windows Server 2008 computers as her Web servers, with IIS7 hosting multiple Web sites on each computer. One of Amanda's clients is a game manufacturer who has released a hot new product. Their Web site contains an online demo, created using ASP.NET, which is experiencing a dramatic increase in traffic. Unfortunately, this one site is starting to monopolize the server's resources, to the detriment of the other sites running on the same computer. Which of the following options can prevent the game application from affecting the other sites? Explain your answer.

   A. Increase the maximum number of worker processes allowed in the game site's application pool.
   B. Set a value other than zero for the application pool's Private Memory Limit setting.
   C. Change the application pool's Managed Pipeline Mode setting from Integrated to Classic.
   D. Set a value other than zero for the application pool's Limit setting.

Scenario 7-2: Deploying UDDI

Robert wants to deploy a UDDI site on his company network. He has two Windows Server 2008 computers running IIS7, but he is afraid that neither one has the resources to run both of the UDDI role services. Therefore, he decides to install the UDDI Services Web Application role service on one computer and the UDDI Services Database role service on the other, using the Windows Internal Database to store the UDDI site information.

What is wrong with this plan and what must Robert do to make it work?

11 LESSON

Using Network Application Services

OBJECTIVE DOMAIN MATRIX

TECHNOLOGY SKILL	OBJECTIVE DOMAIN	OBJECTIVE DOMAIN NUMBER
Installing the Streaming Media Services Role	Configure Windows Media® server.	4.1
Installing Windows SharePoint Services	Configure Microsoft Windows SharePoint® Services server options.	4.3
Configuring Email Integration	Configure Windows SharePoint Services email integration.	4.4
Using Digital Rights Management	Configure Digital Rights Management (DRM).	4.2

KEY TERMS

broadcast streams
differential backup
Digital Rights Management
   (DRM)
Fast Streaming
multicast

on-demand streams
protocol rollover
publishing points
Real Time Streaming Protocol
   (RTSP)
unicast

Windows Media Encoder
Windows Media Player
Windows Media Services
Windows SharePoint
   Services 3.0

Windows Server 2008 supports add-on modules that implement network applications you can use to provide multimedia content and workspace collaboration capabilities for users. In this lesson, you learn about the following:

- Deploying multimedia content using Windows Media Services
- Installing and configuring Windows SharePoint Services
- Protecting information resources with Digital Rights Management

■ Using Windows Media Services

THE BOTTOM LINE

Windows Media Services enables a Windows Server 2008 server to stream multimedia content in real time, using either live or pre-recorded content.

In most cases, the role of an application server is to provide data to clients on the network. File servers and Web servers, for example, provide clients with data in the form of files. The server stores the files on its drives, transmits them to the client, and then the client either displays them or stores them on its own drive. In these cases, the client cannot make use of the data until the entire file containing it arrives at the client computer.

Windows Media Services is a Windows Server 2008 role that provides a twist to this formula. With Windows Media Services, a server can stream audio and video content to network clients in real time. A player on the client computer establishes a direct connection with the server and plays the audio or video content as it arrives.

Audio and video content is particularly well-suited to real-time streaming over a network. Unlike application or document files, audio and video data does not have to arrive at the client in bit-perfect condition to be usable. If, for example, a client runs an application from a file server drive, just one lost bit means that the application will not run. On the other hand, a few bits lost from a video data stream will result only in a few bad pixels, or at most a dropped frame or two, not enough to ruin the user experience.

A computer running Windows Media Services is responsible for publishing audio/video content to network users, but it is only one part of the equation. The front end of a Windows Media installation is the Windows Media Player client running on a user's computer, as shown in Figure 11-1. The Media Player client and the Media Services server establish a connection that enables the server to transmit content data to the client and the client to play the content as the data arrives.

Figure 11-1

A Windows Media Services server and a Windows Media Player client

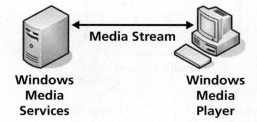

This arrangement seems simple; the server sends the content and the client receives it. However, the process involves other elements as well. The other component visible to the end user is the means by which the systems initiate the client/server connection. In most cases, this is a Web server publishing a home page that contains a link to the audio/video content on the server, as shown in Figure 11-2. In Windows Media Services, the Web server is a completely separate entity and need not be running on the same computer as Windows Media Services. The only role of the Web server is to provide a hyperlink to the streaming content. When a user clicks the link, ***Windows Media Player*** launches on the client and establishes a direct connection to the Windows Media Services server. The Web server is, from this point, out of the picture.

Figure 11-2

A Web server provides users with a link to content published by a Windows Media Services server

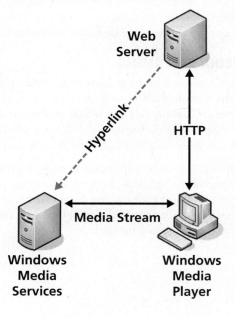

At the back end of the installation, invisible to the end user, there can be a variety of mechanisms that generate the streaming content published by Windows Media Services. The content might be pre-recorded and stored on the Windows Media Services server or located on another server. The content can also be a live event, captured using a digital video camera and sent to a server running *Windows Media Encoder*, which converts it into the Windows Media format and sends it to the Windows Media Services server for real-time distribution, as shown in Figure 11-3.

Figure 11-3

A Windows Media Encoder server, processing live video data and sending it to Windows Media Services for streaming to clients

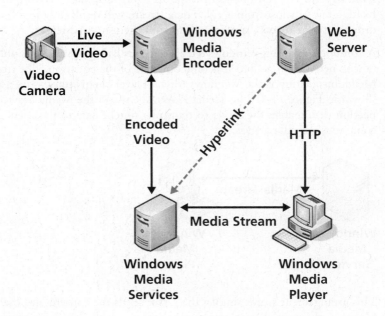

Planning a Windows Media Services Deployment

Deploying Windows Media Services largely consists of managing and regulating the large amounts of bandwidth that multimedia streams can consume.

Setting up a Windows Media Services deployment is not difficult. It can be more difficult, however, to design an effective Media Services deployment for your network. Audio and video streams often consist of large amounts of data; video files can be hundreds or even thousands of megabytes, and they can overwhelm even the fastest networks.

UNDERSTANDING MEDIA STREAMING

Media streaming is always a tradeoff between bandwidth and signal quality. As you increase the quality and/or resolution of the video image, you also increase the amount of bandwidth the stream consumes. A low-bit-rate video that appears in a postage stamp-sized window on the client's monitor might require 100 kilobytes per minute of content, whereas a high-definition, full-screen video might require ten megabytes per minute or more.

As mentioned earlier, network users access applications and documents by downloading them to their computers and then launching them. For audio/video content, network administrators can choose between publishing the files in the usual manner or streaming them. As a general rule, however, you should not use the download method for this type of content. Table 11-1 lists the reasons for this recommendation.

Table 11-1

Differences Between Downloading and Streaming Multimedia Content

DOWNLOADING	STREAMING
Multimedia content cannot begin playing until the file download is complete.	Multimedia content can begin playing soon after the file begins streaming.
The server transmits the file to the clients as quickly as possible, utilizing all of the available network bandwidth and possibly degrading the performance of other network functions.	The server streams the multimedia content to the clients, using only the speed needed to render the content properly, thus conserving network bandwidth.
Cannot be used to publish live multimedia content because the entire file must download before the client can play it.	Can transmit live multimedia content in real time as the event occurs.
Multimedia content always plays at full quality because the client does not begin rendering until it completely downloads the file.	If the bandwidth required to render the content adequately is more than the amount available on the network, the server can drop frames or otherwise thin the stream to keep the content playing on the client computer.

To provide the end user with a smooth, uninterrupted multimedia experience, a media player must receive a continuous stream of data. Because network performance can fluctuate, player applications maintain a data buffer, which is a staging area for the multimedia rendering process. The player stores arriving data in the buffer and feeds it to the rendering engine at a steady rate. In its basic configuration, the player cannot start displaying the content until the buffer is full, but Windows Media Player has a feature called *Fast Streaming*, which includes several techniques that enable the player to begin displaying content more quickly, improving the user experience. These techniques include the following:

- Fast Start—Causes the player to begin streaming data at full network speed until the buffer is filled, at which point the rendering process can begin. Then, the stream slows down to the player's normal rendering speed.
- Advanced Fast Start—The player begins streaming at an accelerated rate and starts rendering as soon as possible, before the buffer is filled. After the buffer is full, the player reverts to its normal rendering speed.
- Fast Cache—The player streams all data at the highest possible speed, filling the buffer first and then storing the rest of the data in a temporary cache on the computer's local drive.
- Fast Recovery—Enables Forward Error Correction (FEC) on the Windows Media Services server, which enables the Windows Media Player client to recover from lost or damaged packets without requesting a resend.
- Fast Reconnect—Enables a client to reconnect to a Windows Media Services server and resume an interrupted stream after a temporary network outage.

CREATING A DEPLOYMENT PLAN

When you plan a Windows Media Services deployment, you must decide how much signal quality you can afford with the bandwidth you have to expend. To do this, consider the following three elements:

- Client bandwidth—How much network bandwidth does each of your clients have available? A client that accesses a Windows Media Services server using a dial-up connection cannot possibly receive the same high-quality media stream as a LAN (local area network) client.
- Number of clients—Multiply the bandwidth required for each of your media streams by the number of concurrent clients you want to serve simultaneously. If the resulting product is near to or greater than your total network bandwidth, then you must reduce the signal quality of your data streams to lower their bandwidth requirements.

- Content requirements—How much signal quality do your media streams require to effectively service your clients? To reduce the bandwidth required for each stream, you can lower the signal resolution or use a different format, such as variable-bit-rate encoding (VBR). How you package your media content directly affects the user experience and the bandwidth the service consumes.

SELECTING A STREAM TYPE

Another important element of a deployment plan should be the type of streams you intend to publish. To publish content on a Windows Media Services server, you create **publishing points**, the components through which clients access specific content streams. Windows Media Services supports two types of publishing points: **on-demand streams** and **broadcast streams**. Table 11-2 summarizes the differences between on-demand and broadcast streams.

Table 11-2

Differences Between On-demand Streams and Broadcast Streams

ON-DEMAND STREAMS	BROADCAST STREAMS
Streaming begins when the user requests it	Streaming begins at a pre-arranged time
Typically used for pre-recorded content	Typically used for live content
Supports unicast transmissions only	Supports unicast or multicast transmissions
End user can employ playback controls to pause, resume, rewind, and fast forward	End user can start and stop the stream playback, but cannot control the transmission, which proceeds uninterrupted from beginning to end
The server establishes a separate connection with each client	The server can use a single transmission to service multiple clients

SELECTING A TRANSMISSION TYPE

The type of transmissions you configure Windows Media Services to use when streaming multimedia content can impact the bandwidth the service consumes. Windows Media Services uses **unicast** transmissions by default. In a unicast transmission, each client establishes its own connection to the Windows Media Services server and has its own data stream, as shown in Figure 11-4.

Figure 11-4

Unicast data streams between Windows Media Services servers and clients

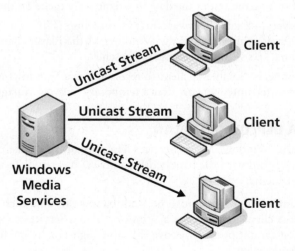

The use of unicast transmissions enables end users to control the playback of the multimedia content. When the user pauses, rewinds, or fast-forwards the playback, the server actually alters the stream by changing its speed or its content. This is possible because these changes in the stream affect only that one user.

The biggest drawback of unicast streaming is the bandwidth it can consume. Because each unicast client has its own separate stream, the Windows Media Services server can use five times the bandwidth for five clients that are playing the same video. Even when multiple clients are playing the same content, the server must transmit a separate stream for each one, with each stream containing the same data.

Multicast transmissions prevent this wastage. Multicasting is a TCP/IP (Transmission Control Protocol/Internet Protocol) feature that provides one-to-many transmission capabilities. In TCP/IP communications, IP addresses typically represent individual systems called unicast addresses. However, a special class of multicast IP addresses is called Class D addresses, each of which represents a group of computers on a network.

When you configure Windows Media Services to use multicast transmissions, the server creates a single stream directed to a single multicast address. Multiple clients can then subscribe to that address and receive the stream, as shown in Figure 11-5. No matter how many clients access the content, only a single stream is provided, which can save a vast amount of bandwidth.

Figure 11-5

Multicast data streams between Windows Media Services servers and clients

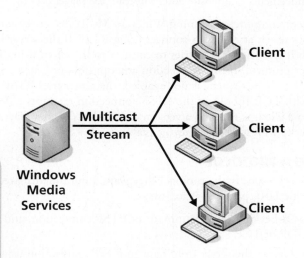

TAKE NOTE*

Windows Media Services only supports multicast streaming when it is running on Windows Server 2008 Enterprise or Windows Server 2008 Datacenter. Multicasting is not supported on Windows Server 2008 Standard or Windows Web Server 2008.

Because many clients rely on a single stream when you use multicast transmissions, individual users cannot manipulate the playback as they can with unicasts. A user can stop the playback by disconnecting from the stream, but the stream continues transmitting to the other clients. When the user restarts the playback, it reconnects to the stream at its current point, skipping any data the server transmitted in the interim.

Because multicast transmissions are designed to service multiple clients simultaneously, you can use them only for broadcast streams, not on-demand streams.

SELECTING A DATA TRANSFER PROTOCOL

Windows Media Services can stream multimedia content, using a variety of protocol combinations, to support different Windows Media Player versions. When you add the Windows Media Services role on a Windows Server 2008 computer, the Select Data Transfer Protocols page enables you to select ***Real Time Streaming Protocol (RTSP)***, Hypertext Transfer Protocol (HTTP), or both.

The Windows Server 2008 version of Windows Media Services uses the RTSP protocol by default. Any client computer running Windows Media Player 9 or later can use RTSP to stream multimedia content, with either TCP or UDP (User Datagram Protocol) at the transport layer. RTSP is actually a control protocol, which carries commands between the client and server using the connection-oriented TCP protocol and port number 554. For the actual data streaming, Windows Media Services uses the Real Time Protocol (RTP).

HTTP is the same protocol that Web servers use to send HTML (Hypertext Markup Language) and image files to client browsers. Windows Media Services includes HTTP primarily to support Windows Media Players prior to version 9, which cannot use RTSP, or clients that must stream content through a firewall. Windows Media Services uses TCP port 80 to stream multimedia content with HTTP, the same port that Web servers use, which is why most firewalls allow traffic using port 80 to pass through them.

USING PROTOCOL ROLLOVER

When you enable both the RTSP and the HTTP protocols on a Windows Media Services server, the clients and the server use a process called *protocol rollover* to negotiate the most efficient protocol they have in common. A client establishing a connection to a Windows Media Services server sends information about the protocols it can use, and the server selects the best protocol it is capable of using. If, for any reason, the client cannot use the selected protocol, the server reverts to the next best protocol in its list.

To use protocol rollover, administrators should publish their multimedia content using URLs with a Microsoft Media Server (MMS) URL moniker (mms:// prefix), as in *mms://servername/video*. If you use announcements to publish content instead, the player uses the mms:// prefix automatically.

When the client computer is running Windows Media Player version 9 or later, a Windows Media Services server attempts to connect using RTSP. If the server is configured to use Fast Cache (which it is by default), it tries to connect to the client using RTSP with the TCP transport layer protocol. If this connection attempt does not succeed, the server then tries RTSP with UDP. If Fast Cache is not enabled, the server tries RTSP with UDP first, and then RTSP with TCP. If both of the RTSP connection attempts fail, the server reverts to HTTP. When a client is running a version of Windows Media Player older than version 9, the server uses HTTP to connect to the player.

SPECIFYING A PROTOCOL

Administrators can specify the protocol they want a multimedia stream to use by employing protocol-specific URL prefixes, as follows:

- rtsp://—Causes the server to initiate an RTSP connection, and then negotiate whether to use UDP or TCP.
- rtspt://—Causes the server to initiate an RTSP connection using TCP.
- rtspu://—Causes the server to initiate an RTSP connection using UDP.
- http://—Causes the server to initiate an HTTP connection.

Installing the Streaming Media Services Role

Originally, the Streaming Media Services role was included with the Windows Server 2008 product. At some point during the development process, however, Microsoft decided to remove the role from the operating system and supply it as a free download instead.

When you find Windows Media Services 2008 at the Microsoft Downloads Center (http://microsoft.com/downloads), you see three Microsoft Standalone Update (MSU) files for each of the x86 and x64 platforms. The contents of the files are as follows:

- Admin—Contains only the Windows Media Services console, enabling you to administer a server running the Streaming Media Services role from another computer.
- Core—Contains the Windows Media Services console and the Streaming Media Services role for the Windows Server Core installation option of Windows Server 2008 Standard or Enterprise Edition.
- Server—Contains the Windows Media Services console and the Streaming Media Services role for a full installation of Windows Server 2008 Standard or Enterprise Edition.

To perform a full Windows Media Services installation on a Windows Server 2008 computer, first you must run the Server or Core MSU file. Executing the file does not activate the

CERTIFICATION READY?
Configure Windows
Media® Server
4.1

Streaming Media Services role, however; it merely installs it on the computer. You must add the role in the usual manner using the Server Manager console.

Use the following complete procedure for installing Windows Media Services on a full installation of Windows Server 2008.

 INSTALL WINDOWS MEDIA SERVICES

GET READY. Log on to Windows Server 2008 using an account with administrative privileges. When the logon process is completed, close the Initial Configuration Tasks window and any other windows that appear.

1. Open Internet Explorer and download the appropriate Windows Media Services 2008 file for your server's architecture (x86 or x64) from http://microsoft.com/downloads.

2. Click **Start**, and then click **Run**. The Run dialog box appears.

3. Browse to the Windows Media Services Server MSU file on your local drive and click **OK**. A Windows Update Standalone Installer message box appears, confirming that you want to install the update.

4. Click **OK**. A Read These License Terms window appears.

5. Click **I Accept** to agree to the terms. A progress indicator page appears.

6. When the Installation Complete page appears, click **Close**.

7. Click **Start**, and then click **Administrative Tools** > **Server Manager**. The Server Manager console appears.

8. Start the Add Roles Wizard. The Streaming Media Services role should now appear on the Select Server Roles page.

9. Select the **Streaming Media Services** role, as shown in Figure 11-6.

Figure 11-6

The Select Server Roles page of the Add Roles Wizard

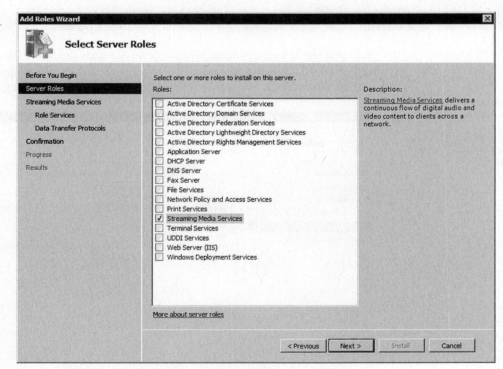

10. Complete the installation, using the procedure documented in Lesson 1, "Deploying an Application Server."

The Streaming Media Services role includes three role services. Table 11-3 lists the dependencies for each role service, the wizard pages each role service adds to the Add Roles Wizard, and the system services and Microsoft Management Console (MMC) snap-ins each role service installs.

Table 11-3

Windows Media Services Role Services

ROLE SERVICES	DEPENDENCIES	WIZARD PAGES	SYSTEM SERVICES	SNAP-INS
Windows Media Server	[None]	• Streaming Media Services > Data Transfer Protocols	• Windows Media Services (WMServer)	• Windows Media Services
Web-Based Administration	• Web Server (IIS) • Windows Process Activation Service > Process Model	• Web Server (IIS) > Role Services	• Application Host Helper Service (apphostsvc) • IIS Admin Service (iisadmin) • Windows Process Activation Service (WAS) • World Wide Web Publishing Service (w3svc)	[None]
Logging Agent	• Web Server (IIS) > ISAPI Extensions • Web Server (IIS) > ISAPI Filters • Windows Process Activation Service > Process Model	• Web Server (IIS) > Role Services	• Application Host Helper Service (apphostsvc) • Windows Process Activation Service (WAS) • World Wide Web Publishing Service (w3svc)	[None]

Selecting the Windows Media Server role service adds the Select Data Transfer Protocols page to the wizard, as shown in Figure 11-7. This page enables you to specify whether you want the Windows Media Services server to support Real Time Streaming Protocol (the default),

Figure 11-7

The Select Data Transfer Protocols page of the Add Roles Wizard

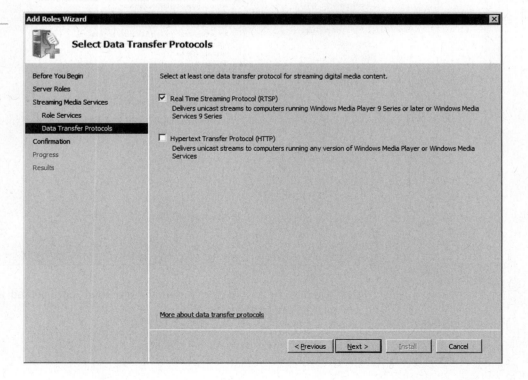

Hypertext Transfer Protocol, or both, for streaming multimedia content. If you are certain that all of your clients are computers on the local network running Windows Media Player version 9 or higher, you can safely select RTSP only. However, if any of your clients are running older versions of Windows Media Player or connecting to the server through a firewall, you should enable HTTP streaming as well.

Creating a Publishing Point

> Installing the Streaming Media Services role creates two default publishing points, but you can add as many additional publishing points as you need.

After you install the Streaming Media Services role, you can begin deploying multimedia content by creating new publishing points that specify the stream and transmission types you want the server to use.

To create a publishing point, use the following procedure.

 CREATE A PUBLISHING POINT

GET READY. Log on to Windows Server 2008 using an account with administrative privileges. When the logon process is completed, close the Initial Configuration Tasks window and any other windows that appear.

1. Click **Start**, and then click **Administrative Tools** > **Windows Media Services**. The Windows Media Services console appears, as shown in Figure 11-8.

Figure 11-8

The Windows Media Services console

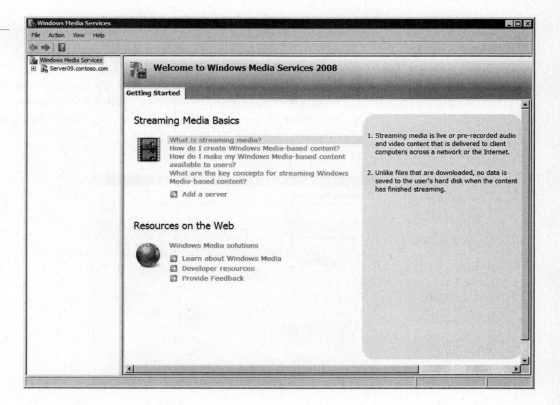

2. In the scope pane, expand the server node and select the **Publishing Points** node. The default on-demand and broadcast publishing points appear in the detail pane, as shown in Figure 11-9.

Figure 11-9

The default publishing points in the Windows Media Services console

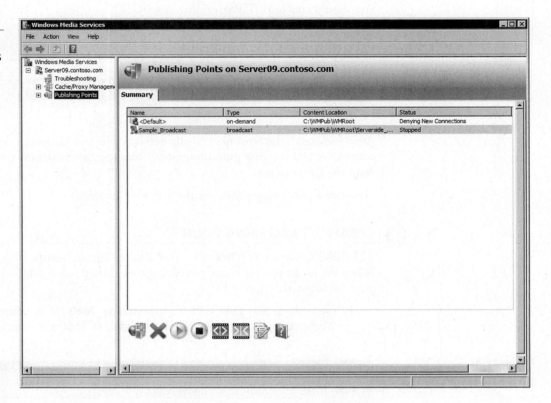

3. Right-click **Publishing Points** and, from the context menu, select **Add Publishing Point (Wizard)**. The Add Publishing Point Wizard appears.

4. Click **Next** to bypass the Welcome page. The Publishing Point Name page appears, as shown in Figure 11-10.

Figure 11-10

The Publishing Point Name page of the Add Publishing Point Wizard

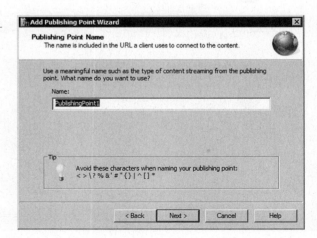

5. Key a name for the publishing point in the Name text box and click **Next**. The Content Type page appears, as shown in Figure 11-11.

Figure 11-11

The Content Type page of the Add Publishing Point Wizard

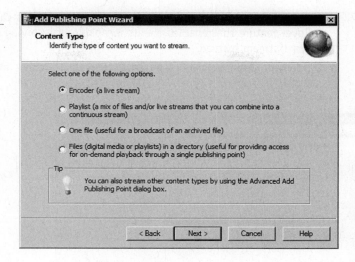

6. Select one of the following options:
   - Encoder—Indicates that the content is a live stream, encoded in real time.
   - Playlist—Indicates that the content is a playlist file containing a collection of files and/or live streams that will play consecutively.
   - One file—Indicates that the content is a single, prerecorded file.
   - Files (digital media or playlists) in a directory—Specifies the name of a single folder containing all of the content files.

7. Click **Next**. The Publishing Point Type page appears, as shown in Figure 11-12.

Figure 11-12

The Publishing Point Type page of the Add Publishing Point Wizard

8. Select one of the following options:
   - Broadcast publishing point—Creates a single, scheduled stream that multiple clients can view simultaneously. If you select this option, an additional Delivery Options for Broadcast Publishing Points page appears in the wizard, enabling you to specify whether the publishing point should use unicast or multicast transmis-

sions, as shown in Figure 11-13. Multicast transmissions can also include a unicast rollover feature that enables clients incapable of receiving multicasts to receive a unicast stream instead.

- On-demand publishing point—Creates individual streams for individual users, as needed.

Figure 11-13

The Delivery Options for Broadcast Publishing Points page of the Add Publishing Point Wizard

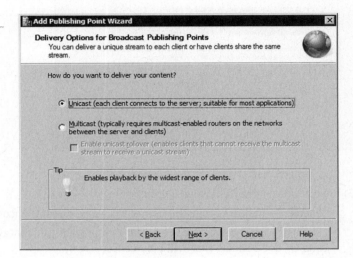

9. Click **Next**. A page appears, prompting you for the location of the content you want to publish. The exact appearance of this and the following pages depends on the Content Type and Publishing Point Type values you selected. For example, if you select Files for the content type, the Directory Location page appears, as shown in Figure 11-14.

Figure 11-14

The Directory Location page of the Add Publishing Point Wizard

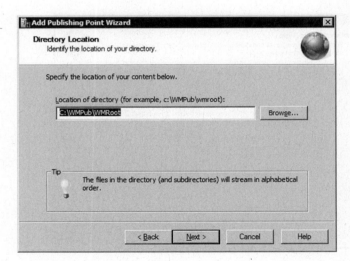

10. Specify the location of the file or folder containing the content and click **Next**. If you selected the *Files in a directory* Content Type option, the Content Playback page appears, as shown in Figure 11-15.

11. Select one of the following options, if desired:
- Loop—Causes the server to replay the content continuously.
- Shuffle—Causes the server to play the various files and/or live streams in the content in random order.

12. Click **Next**. If you are creating a unicast stream, the Unicast Logging page appears, as shown in Figure 11-16.

Figure 11-15

The Content Playback page
of the Add Publishing Point
Wizard

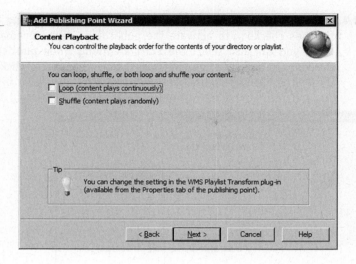

Figure 11-16

The Unicast Logging page
of the Add Publishing Point
Wizard

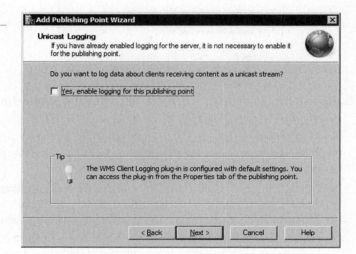

13. Select the **Yes, enable logging for the publishing point** checkbox if you want
the server to log unicast client connections. Then, click **Next**. The Publishing Point
Summary page appears, as shown in Figure 11-17.

Figure 11-17

The Publishing Point Summary
page of the Add Publishing
Point Wizard

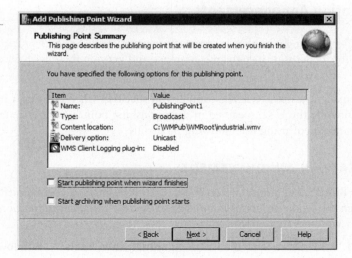

14. For broadcast publishing points, select the **Start publishing point when wizard finishes** checkbox to activate the publishing point immediately; for unicast broadcasts, you can also select the **Start archiving when publishing point starts** checkbox to save the content to an archive file. Then, click **Next**. The Completing the Add Publishing Point Wizard page appears, as shown in Figure 11-18.

Figure 11-18

The Completing the Add Publishing Point Wizard page of the Add Publishing Point Wizard

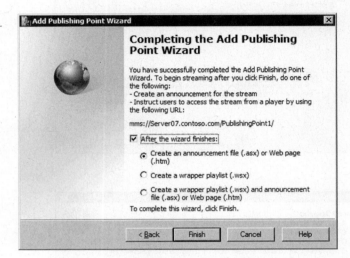

15. To perform additional tasks, select the **After the wizard finishes** checkbox and choose one of the following options:

- Create an announcement file (.asx) or Web page (.htm)—Launches the appropriate announcement wizard for the transmission type, which enables you to create a file that users can click to load the multimedia stream.
- Create a wrapper playlist (.wsx)—Launches the Create Wrapper Wizard, which enables you to create a playlist that includes additional content (such as announcements or advertisements) before and/or after your main content.
- Create a wrapper playlist (.wsx) and announcement file (.asx) or Web page (.htm) —Launches both the announcement wizard and the Create Wrapper Wizard.

16. Click **Finish**. The new publishing point appears in the console's detail pane.

CLOSE the Windows Media Services console.

At this point, the content you specified while creating the publishing point is available for streaming.

Creating Announcements

After creating a publishing point, Windows Media Services provides several ways to inform clients of the stream's existence and provide them with access to it.

To enable users to access the content you specified when creating a publishing point, you can provide the URL specified in the publishing point's Announce tab or you can create an announcement using the following procedure.

 CREATE AN ANNOUNCEMENT

GET READY. Log on to Windows Server 2008 using an account with administrative privileges. When the logon process is completed, close the Initial Configuration Tasks window and any other windows that appear.

1. Click **Start**, and then click **Administrative Tools** > **Windows Media Services**. The Windows Media Services console appears.

2. Add your server to the console, if needed. In the scope pane, expand the server node and the Publishing Points node, and select the publishing point you want to announce.

3. In the detail pane, click the **Announce** tab, as shown in Figure 11-19.

Figure 11-19

A publishing point's Announce tab

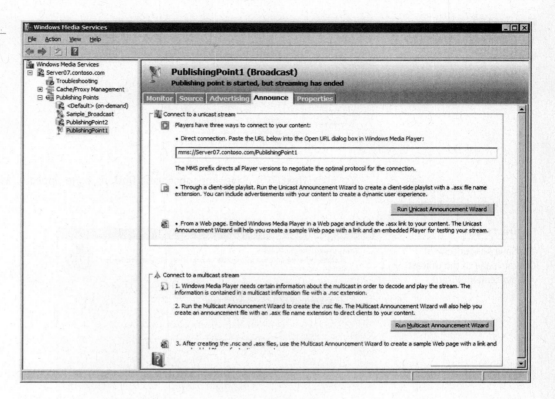

4. Click the **Run Unicast Announcement Wizard** button. The Unicast Announcement Wizard appears.

TAKE NOTE*

This procedure creates an announcement for a unicast stream. To create an announcement for a multicast stream, click the Run Multicast Announcement Wizard button instead.

5. Click **Next** to bypass the Welcome page. The Access the Content page appears, as shown in Figure 11-20.

Figure 11-20

The Access the Content page of the Unicast Announcement Wizard

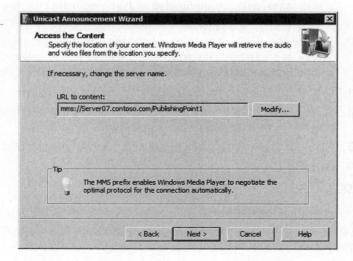

6. If you want the announcement to use a different name for the server or an IP address instead of a name, click **Modify** and, in the Modify Server Name dialog box shown in Figure 11-21, key the name or address. Then, click **OK**.

Figure 11-21

The Modify Server Name dialog box

7. Click **Next**. The Save Announcement Options page appears, as shown in Figure 11-22.

Figure 11-22

The Save Announcement Options page of the Unicast Announcement Wizard

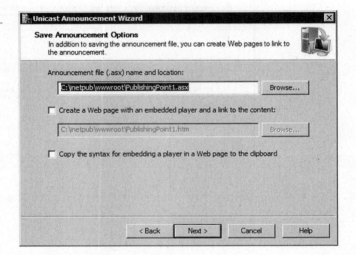

8. In the *Announcement file (.asx) name and location* text box, specify the name you want to assign to the announcement file and the folder where you want to create it.

9. To create an HTML file containing code that embeds the media player interface and a link to the content you specified into the Web page, select the **Create a Web page with an embedded player and a link to the content** checkbox. Specify the name and location for the .htm file.

10. To copy the HTML code that embeds the media player interface into the clipboard so you can paste it into an existing Web page file, select the **Copy the syntax for embedding a player in a Web page to the clipboard** checkbox.

11. Click **Next**. The Edit Announcement Metadata page appears, as shown in Figure 11-23.

12. Specify title, author, copyright, banner, and/or log URL information about the content in the publishing point as desired.

13. Click **Next**. The Completing the Unicast Announcement Wizard page appears.

14. Click **Finish**.

CLOSE the Windows Media Services console.

If you select the *Test files when the wizard finishes* checkbox, the Test Unicast Announcement dialog box appears, as shown in Figure 11-24, with which you can execute both the announcement file and the Web page created by the wizard.

Figure 11-23

The Edit Announcement Metadata page of the Unicast Announcement Wizard

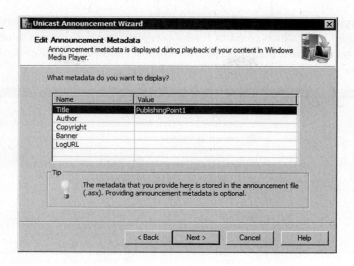

Figure 11-24

The Test Unicast Announcement dialog box

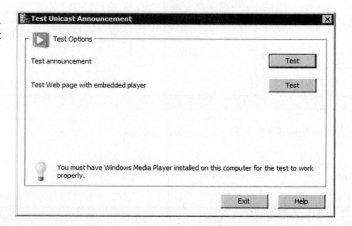

TAKE NOTE* To perform the announcement tests, the computer must have Windows Media Player installed. On a Windows Server 2008 computer, you must add the Desktop Experience feature using Server Manager to install Windows Media Player.

Controlling Bandwidth Utilization

Heavily used multimedia streams can easily consume all of a network's bandwidth. Administrators should understand the impact that streaming media can have on network performance, and be familiar with the controls they can use to regulate the bandwidth that the streams utilize.

Earlier in this lesson, you learned about several factors that can affect the amount of network bandwidth consumed by Windows Media Services. In addition to these design factors, you can specify values for configuration parameters that control bandwidth utilization.

Every component on a Windows Media Services server has a Properties tab, as shown in Figure 11-25, which contains several categories, with properties in each one. The Limits category contains the properties that control bandwidth utilization, which you can configure at the server level or the publishing point level.

Figure 11-25

The Limits parameters for a Windows Media Services server

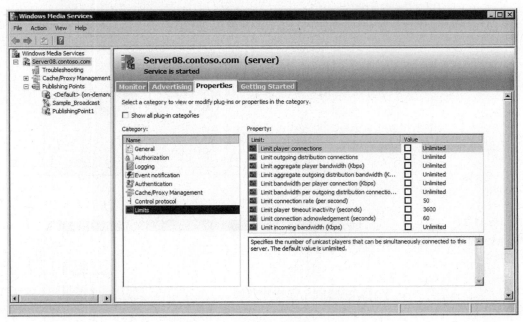

Table 11-4 lists the Limits parameters and their functions.

Table 11-4

Windows Media Services Limits Parameters

PROPERTIES	APPLIES TO	UNIT OF MEASUREMENT	DEFAULT VALUE	DESCRIPTION
Limit player connections	Server and publishing points	Connections	Unlimited	Specifies the maximum number of clients that can establish unicast connections to the server or publishing point at any one time.
Limit outgoing distribution connections	Server and publishing points	Connections	Unlimited	Specifies the maximum number of connections to other servers that the server or publishing point can establish at any one time.
Limit aggregate player bandwidth	Server and publishing points	Kbps	Unlimited	Specifies the total amount of bandwidth that clients connected to the server or publishing point can use at any one time.
Limit aggregate outgoing distribution bandwidth	Server and publishing points	Kbps	Unlimited	Specifies the total amount of bandwidth that the server or publishing point can use for connections to cache/proxy servers at any one time.
Limit bandwidth per player connection	Server and publishing points	Kbps	Unlimited	Specifies the maximum amount of bandwidth that each client connected to the server or publishing point can use when receiving a stream.
Limit bandwidth per outgoing distribution connection	Server and publishing points	Kbps	Unlimited	Specifies the maximum amount of bandwidth that the server or publishing point can use for each connection to another server.

(continued)

Table 11-4 (continued)

Properties	Applies to	Unit of Measurement	Default Value	Description
Limit connection rate	Server only	Per second	50	Specifies the maximum number of connections the server can resolve each second.
Limit player timeout activity	Server only	Seconds	3600	Specifies how long a client can remain connected to the server without activity. After the specified time period expires, the server disconnects the inactive client.
Limit connection acknowledgment	Server only	Seconds	60	Specifies how long the server will wait for an acknowledgment from a client before disconnecting it.
Limit incoming bandwidth	Server only	Kbps	Unlimited	Specifies the maximum amount of bandwidth each incoming connection to the server can use.
Limit Fast Cache content delivery rate	On-demand publishing points only	Multiple of encoded bit rate	5	Specifies the maximum accelerated delivery factor for connections to players. The value (1 to 5) designates a multiple of the encoded bit rate of the content.
Limit Fast Start bandwidth per player connection	Publishing points only	Kbps	3500	Specifies the maximum amount of bandwidth a client supporting Fast Start can use during the initial accelerated buffering phase of a connection.

■ Using Windows SharePoint Services

THE BOTTOM LINE

Windows SharePoint Services 3.0 is, essentially, a database-enabled Web application that runs on an Internet Information Services server.

By accessing the *Windows SharePoint Services 3.0* site, users can employ browser-based workspaces to share information in a variety of ways, such as storing documents, creating calendar appointments and task lists, and contributing to newsgroup-style discussions. You can create individual Web sites for specific projects, departments, or workgroups that contain some or all of these features.

Windows SharePoint Services relies on Microsoft SQL Server 2005 technology to manage the database that stores user documents and information. For small deployments, you can use a single Windows Server 2008 computer to host the IIS Web server and the SQL database, in addition to the Windows SharePoint Services application. Windows Server 2008 includes Windows Internal Database, which is an SQL-based data store for Windows roles and features.

For large organizations, you can scale up the Windows SharePoint Services deployment by creating a server farm that distributes the functions among several computers and replicates the servers using failover clustering. For example, you can run Microsoft SQL Server 2005 on a computer separate from the Web server or even separate the Web server from the SharePoint search service and other application server features.

Installing Windows SharePoint Services

Windows SharePoint Services was included as part of Windows Server 2003, but for Windows Server 2008, Microsoft has released it as a separate product, available as a free download.

Unlike Windows Media Services, Windows SharePoint Services is not a role; it has its own installation program and requires you to install its dependent features manually.

To install a stand-alone Windows SharePoint Services 3.0 server, use the following procedure.

INSTALL WINDOWS SHAREPOINT SERVICES

GET READY. Log on to Windows Server 2008 using an account with administrative privileges. When the logon process is completed, close the Initial Configuration Tasks window and any other windows that appear.

1. Click **Start**, and then click **Administrative Tools** > **Server Manager**. The Server Manager console appears.

2. In the scope pane, right-click the **Features** node and, from the context menu, select **Add Features**. The Add Features Wizard appears, as shown in Figure 11-26.

Figure 11-26

The Add Features Wizard

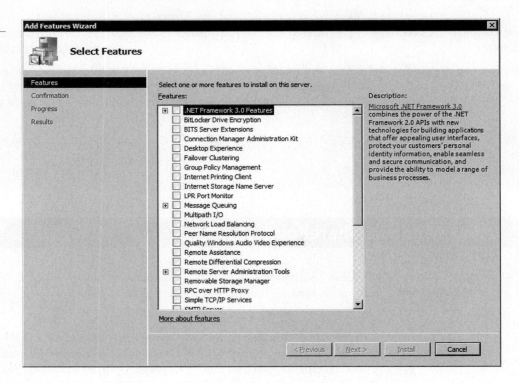

3. On the Select Features page, select the **.NET Framework 3.0 Features** checkbox. The *Add role services and features required for .NET Framework 3.0 Features?* dialog box appears, as shown in Figure 11-27.

Figure 11-27

The *Add role services and features required for .NET Framework 3.0 Features?* dialog box

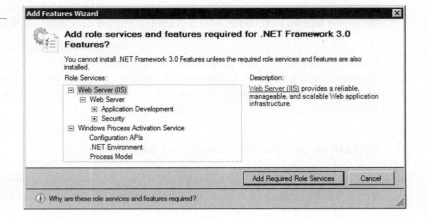

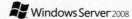

4. Click **Add Required Role Services**.

5. Click **Next**.

6. Click **Next** again to bypass the Web Server (IIS) page. The Select Role Services page appears.

7. Click **Next** to accept the selected Web Server (IIS) role services. The Confirm Installation Selection page appears.

8. Click **Install**.

9. When the installation procedure finishes, click **Close**.

10. Download Windows SharePoint Services 3.0 with Service Pack 1 from the Microsoft Download Center.

TAKE NOTE *

To install Windows SharePoint Services 3.0 on Windows Server 2008, you must download the product with Service Pack 1 integrated into it. Although Windows SharePoint Services 3.0 and Service Pack 1 are available as separate downloads, you cannot install the two separately on Windows Server 2008.

11. Run the SharePoint.exe file you downloaded. An Open File—Security Warning dialog box appears, prompting you to confirm that you want to run the file.

12. Click **Run**. The Microsoft Windows SharePoint Services 3.0 wizard appears, displaying the Read the Microsoft Software License Terms page, as shown in Figure 11-28.

Figure 11-28

The Read the Microsoft Software License Terms page

| Microsoft Windows SharePoint Services 3.0 | ☒ |

Read the Microsoft Software License Terms

To continue you must accept the terms of this agreement. If you do not want to accept the Microsoft Software License Terms, close this window to cancel the installation.

MICROSOFT SOFTWARE SUPPLEMENTAL LICENSE TERMS
MICROSOFT WINDOWS SHAREPOINT SERVICES (WSS) VERSION 3 FOR MICROSOFT WINDOWS SERVER 2003
Microsoft Corporation (or based on where you live, one of its affiliates) licenses this supplement to you. If you are licensed to use Microsoft Windows Server 2003, Standard Edition, Enterprise Edition, Datacenter Edition or Web Edition (each edition, the "software"), you may use this supplement. You may not use it if you do not have a license for the software. You may use a copy of this supplement with each validly licensed copy of the software.
These terms and the license terms for the software apply to your use of the supplement. If there is a conflict, these supplemental license terms apply.
By using this supplement, you accept these terms. If you do not accept them, do not use this supplement.
If you comply with these license terms and the license terms for the software, you have the rights to use the supplement
1. RIGHT TO USE. Use of the supplement on Microsoft Windows Server 2003 Web Edition is limited to front-end web serving tasks. The data storage portion of the supplement may not be installed or used on Microsoft Windows Server 2003 Web Edition.
2. SUPPORT SERVICES FOR SUPPLEMENT. Microsoft provides support services for this software as described at www.support.microsoft.com/common/international.aspx.

EULAID:O12 RTM SRV.0 WSS EN

☐ I accept the terms of this agreement   Continue

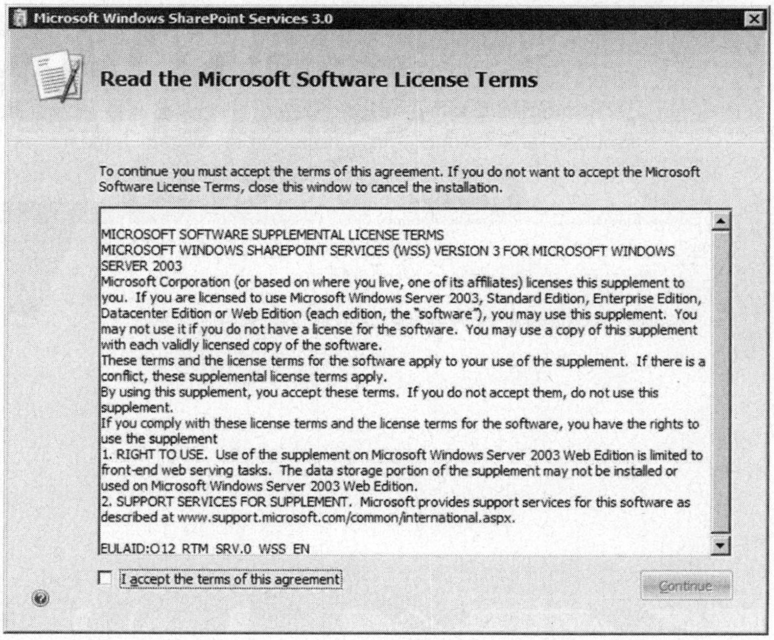

13. Select the **I accept the terms of this agreement** checkbox and click **Continue**. The *Choose the installation you want* page appears, as shown in Figure 11-29.

Figure 11-29

The *Choose the installation you want* page

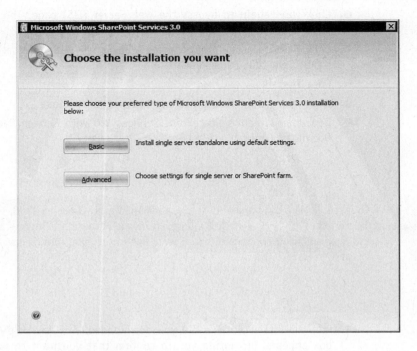

14. Click **Basic**. The Installation Progress page appears.

 TAKE NOTE*

Click Advanced to specify an alternate location for the Windows SharePoint Services files or to install a server farm.

15. When the installation is complete, verify that the **Run the SharePoint Products and Technologies Configuration Wizard** checkbox is selected and click **Close**. The SharePoint Products and Technologies Configuration Wizard appears, as shown in Figure 11-30.

Figure 11-30

The SharePoint Products and Technologies Configuration Wizard

16. Click **Next** to bypass the Welcome page. A SharePoint Products and Technologies Configuration Wizard message box appears, as shown in Figure 11-31, warning you of the services that have to be started or reset during the configuration process.

Figure 11-31

The SharePoint Products and Technologies Configuration Wizard message box

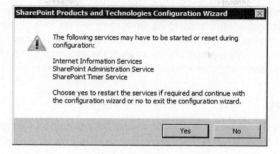

17. Click **Yes.** The configuration process begins. When the process is complete, the Configuration Successful page appears.

18. Click **Finish**.

CLOSE the Server Manager console.

When the configuration process is completed, an Internet Explorer window appears and, after prompting you to log on, displays the server's default Web page, as shown in Figure 11-32. Windows SharePoint Services calls this default Web page the Team Site page. You can, of course, customize this page any way you wish, using standard HTML coding and Web development tools.

Figure 11-32

The Team Site Web page

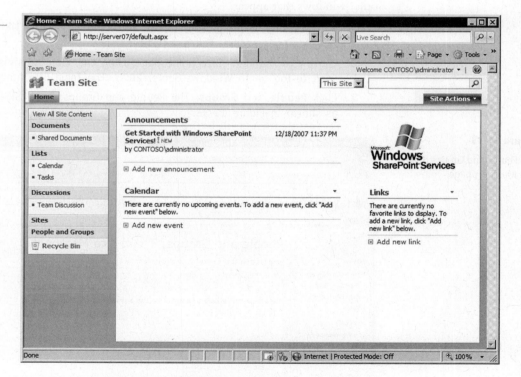

Configuring SharePoint Server Options

After you install and configure Windows SharePoint Services, you can access the administration interface by selecting SharePoint 3.0 Central Administration from the Administrative Tools program group in the Start menu.

Using the Windows SharePoint Services administration interface and the main home page, you can configure a wide array of server settings, as discussed in the following sections.

SharePoint 3.0 Central Administration is a separate Web site running on the same IIS server as the Team Site. During the installation, the Windows SharePoint Services setup program assigns a random port number over 1024 to the administration site to keep it separated from the user site, which uses the standard HTTP port number 80. The SharePoint 3.0 Central Administration shortcut in the Administration Tools program group simply loads Internet Explorer with a URL containing the server name and the assigned port number. While the use of the alternate port number effectively keeps the administrative site hidden from most users, you should not consider it an adequate security measure. Control access to the administrative site using accounts with secure passwords, just as you would any other administrative feature on the server.

ADDING USERS

As you saw when the SharePoint Products and Technologies Configuration Wizard finished running and launched Internet Explorer, you must log on to access the Team Site home page. For other users to access the site, you must add the users to the SharePoint server and assign appropriate permissions. The accounts you add to a SharePoint server can be local users, local groups, domain users, or domain groups, using the form *server\user*, *domain\user*, or *user@domain.com*.

To add users to the default SharePoint Team Site and assign permissions to them, use the following procedure.

 ADD USERS

GET READY. Log on to Windows Server 2008 using an account with administrative privileges. When the logon process is completed, close the Initial Configuration Tasks window and any other windows that appear.

1. Open Internet Explorer and, in the address box, key the URL for your server, such as *http://servername*, and press **Enter**.

2. Log on to the Team Site home page using the same administrative account you used to log on to Windows Server 2008. The Team Site home page appears.

3. Click **People and Groups**. The People and Groups: Team Site Members page appears, as shown in Figure 11-33.

Figure 11-33

The People and Groups: Team Site Members page

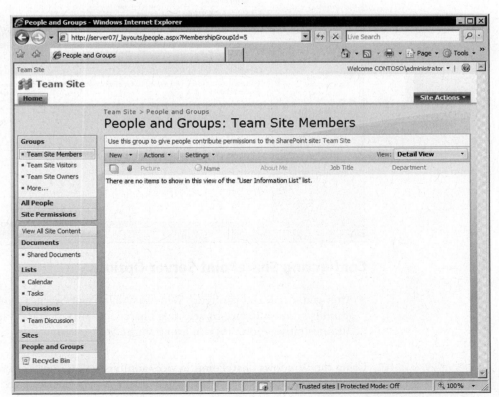

4. Click **New** and, from the context menu, select **Add Users**. The Add Users: Team Site page appears, as shown in Figure 11-34.

Figure 11-34

The Add Users: Team Site page

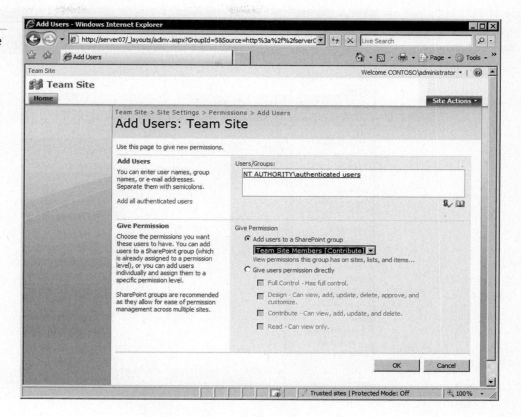

5. In the Users/Groups text box, key the names of the users and/or groups you want to add, separated by semicolons.

6. To add the users/groups you specified to an existing SharePoint group, select the **Add users to a SharePoint group** option and select one of the following groups from the dropdown list:

- Team Site Owners [Full Control]—Provides complete administrative and operational control over the site
- Team Site Visitors [Read]—Provides the user only with view capabilities for the site
- Team Site Members [Contribute]—Provides the user with view, add, update, and delete capabilities for the site

7. To assign permissions to the users/groups you specified, select the **Give users permission directly** option and choose from the following permissions:

- Full Control—Provides complete administrative and operational control over the site
- Design—Provides the user with view, add, update, delete, approve, and customize capabilities for the site
- Contribute—Provides the user with view, add, update, and delete capabilities for the site
- Read—Provides the user only with view capabilities for the site

8. Click **OK**. The People and Groups: Team Site Members page appears, as shown in Figure 11-35.

Figure 11-35

The People and Groups: Team Site Members page

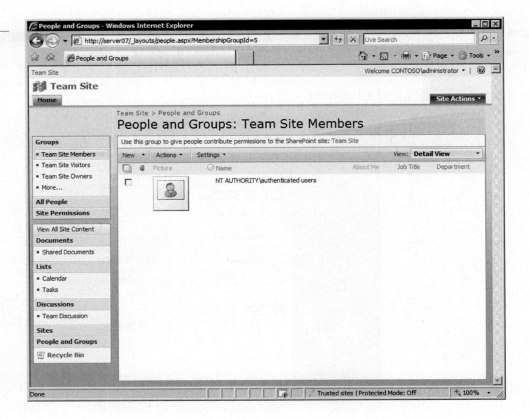

CLOSE the Internet Explorer window.

You can also click the *Add all authenticated users* link to assign permissions to the Authenticated Users special identity, which enables all users who successfully log on to access the Windows SharePoint Services site.

CONFIGURING ANTIVIRUS SETTINGS

Because Windows SharePoint Services is, by nature, a collaboration tool that enables users to share documents, you should consider using an antivirus product to protect against the spread of infections via those documents. When you install an antivirus software product compatible with Windows SharePoint Services, you can use SharePoint 3.0 Central Administration to configure its activity, using the following procedure.

 CONFIGURE ANTIVIRUS SETTINGS

GET READY. Log on to Windows Server 2008 using an account with administrative privileges. When the logon process is completed, close the Initial Configuration Tasks window and any other windows that appear.

1. Click **Start**, and then click **Administrative Tools** > **SharePoint 3.0 Central Administration**. A Connect To dialog box appears, prompting you for administrative credentials.

2. Key an appropriate user name and password in the text boxes provided and click **OK**. An Internet Explorer window appears, displaying the Central Administration home page, as shown in Figure 11-36.

Figure 11-36

The Central Administration
home page

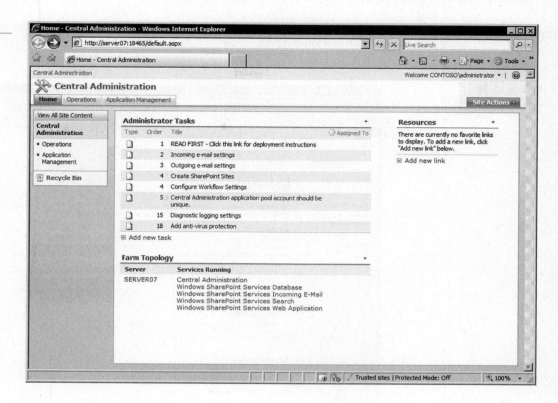

3. Click the **Operations** tab. The Operations page appears, as shown in Figure 11-37.

Figure 11-37

The Operations page

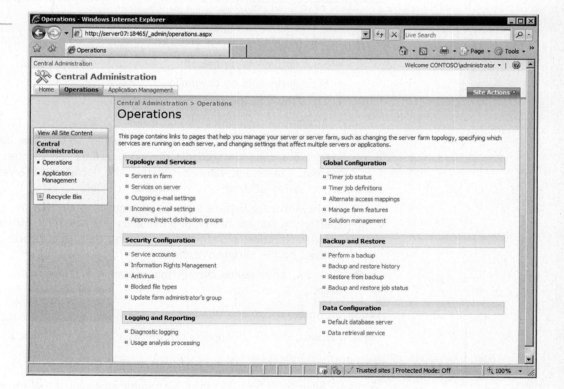

4. Under Security Configuration, click **Antivirus**. The Antivirus page appears, as shown in Figure 11-38.

Figure 11-38

The Antivirus page

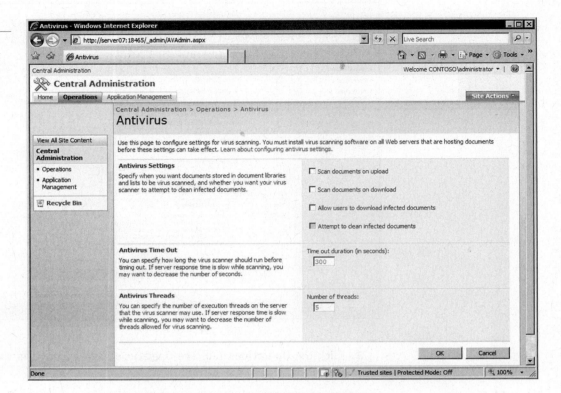

5. In the Antivirus Settings area, select some or all of the following options:

- Scan documents on upload
- Scan documents on download
- Allow users to download infected documents
- Attempt to clean infected documents

6. In the Antivirus Time Out area, key a number in the *Time out duration* box to specify how long (in seconds) the virus scanner should attempt to run before timing out. The default value is 300 seconds. Decreasing the value reduces the processor resources utilized by the antivirus scanner.

7. In the Antivirus Threads area, key a number in the *Number of threads* box to specify the number of execution threads you want the antivirus scanner to use. The default value is 5 threads. Decreasing the value reduces the processor resources utilized by the antivirus scanner.

8. Click **OK**. After saving the settings, Internet Explorer returns to the Operations page.

CLOSE the Internet Explorer window.

Now, Windows SharePoint Services can use your antivirus software to scan user documents.

BACKING UP WINDOWS SHAREPOINT SERVICES

Windows SharePoint Services can easily become an essential tool for your end users, one in which they store large amounts of important data. Like any application of this type, one of the most important administrative tasks is protecting that data by performing regular database backups. Because standard backup programs cannot back up an SQL database while it is running, Windows SharePoint Services includes its own backup function, which copies all or

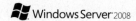

part of the database to an alternate location. Then, you can back up the copy to an alternate medium using your regular network backup utility.

To back up Windows SharePoint Services, use the following procedure.

 BACK UP WINDOWS SHAREPOINT SERVICES

GET READY. Log on to Windows Server 2008 using an account with administrative privileges. When the logon process is completed, close the Initial Configuration Tasks window and any other windows that appear.

1. Click **Start**, and then click **Administrative Tools** > **SharePoint 3.0 Central Administration**. A Connect To dialog box appears, prompting you for administrative credentials.

2. Key an appropriate user name and password in the text boxes provided and click **OK**. An Internet Explorer window appears, displaying the Central Administration home page.

3. Click the **Operations** tab. The Operations page appears.

4. Under Backup and Restore, click **Perform a backup**. The Perform a Backup—Step 1 of 2: Select Component to Backup page appears, as shown in Figure 11-39.

Figure 11-39

The Perform a Backup—Step 1 of 2: Select Component to Backup page

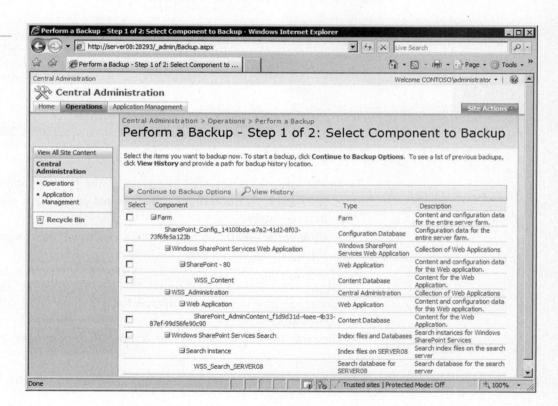

5. Select the component(s) that you want to back up. Selecting the Farm option backs up the entire Windows SharePoint Services installation, including the content database, configuration settings, and search indices. The other options let you select various combinations of individual SharePoint components.

6. Click **Continue to Backup Options**. The Start Backup—Step 2 of 2: Select Backup Options page appears, as shown in Figure 11-40.

Figure 11-40

The Start Backup—Step 2 of 2: Select Backup Options page

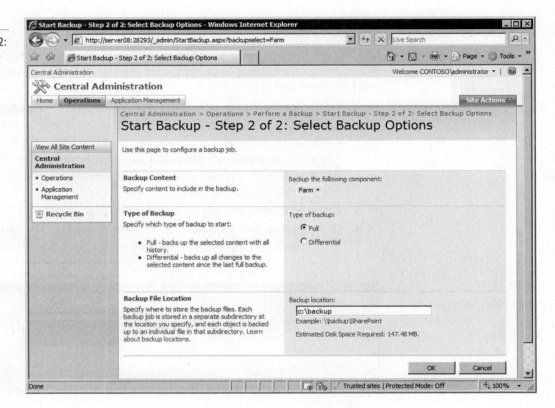

7. In the Type of Backup area, select one of the following options:
   - Full—Backs up the entirety of the selected components, regardless of the previous backup history.
   - *Differential*—Backs up only the data in the selected components that has changed since the last full backup.

8. In the Backup File Location area, in the *Backup location* box, specify the folder where you want the system to place the backups. Use drive letter format, as in *c:\folder*, or Universal Naming Convention (UNC) format, as in *\\server\share*.

9. Click **OK**. The Backup and Restore Status page appears, as shown in Figure 11-41.

CLOSE the Internet Explorer window.

Figure 11-41

The Backup and Restore Status page

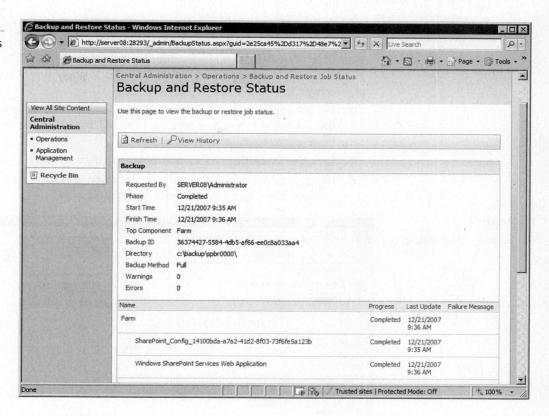

When Windows SharePoint Services performs a backup, it creates a new subdirectory beneath the folder you specified in the Backup File Location box and begins copying the application data to that subdirectory. After the backup is complete, you can back up the subdirectory to magnetic tape or any other storage medium for addition protection.

CONFIGURING EMAIL INTEGRATION

Windows SharePoint Services can integrate with email in a variety of ways, enabling users to set up calendar appointments, post announcements, add documents, and contribute to blogs and discussion forums. To provide users with these email capabilities, you must install a Simple Mail Transfer Protocol (SMTP) server and configure the incoming and outgoing email settings in Windows SharePoint Services.

Windows SharePoint Services uses incoming email to enable users to contribute content to the site. To do this, you must install an SMTP server on the SharePoint computer. Outgoing email enables SharePoint to send email-based alerts, invitations, and notifications to users and administrators. Outgoing email requires an SMTP server as well, but it does not have to be running on the SharePoint computer.

CERTIFICATION READY?
Configure Windows SharePoint Services email integration
4.4

 REF

SMTP Server is a feature included with Windows Server 2008 that you can install using the Add Features Wizard in Server Manager. See "Deploying an SMTP Server" in Lesson 7, "Deploying Web Applications," for more information.

To configure the Windows SharePoint Services incoming and outgoing email settings, use the following procedure.

 CONFIGURE EMAIL INTEGRATION

GET READY. Log on to Windows Server 2008 using an account with administrative privileges. When the logon process is completed, close the Initial Configuration Tasks window and any other windows that appear.

1. If you have not done so already, add the SMTP Server service using the Server Manager console.

2. Click **Start**, and then click **Administrative Tools** > **SharePoint 3.0 Central Administration**. A Connect To dialog box appears, prompting you for administrative credentials.

3. Key an appropriate user name and password in the text boxes provided and click **OK**. An Internet Explorer window appears, displaying the Central Administration home page.

4. Click the **Operations** tab. The Operations page appears.

5. Under Topology and Services, click **Outgoing e-mail settings**. The Outgoing E-Mail Settings page appears, as shown in Figure 11-42.

Figure 11-42

The Outgoing E-Mail Settings page

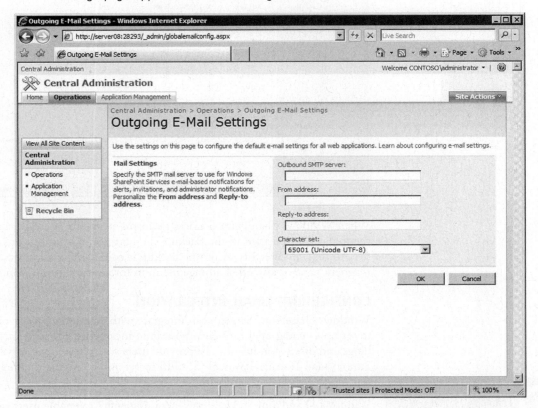

6. In the *Outbound SMTP server* text box, key the name or IP address of a Windows Server 2008 computer running the SMTP Server feature.

TAKE NOTE ✱ For outgoing SMTP traffic, you can use any mail server that conforms to the SMTP standard, whether it runs on Windows or not.

7. In the *From address* text box, key the address that you want email recipients to see as the sender of the message.

8. In the *Reply-to address* text box, key the address that you want email recipients to use when replying to a message.

9. In the *Character set* dropdown list, select the appropriate character set for the language your server is using.

10. Click **OK**. The Operations page reappears.

11. Click **Incoming e-mail settings**. The Configure Incoming E-Mail Settings page appears, as shown in Figure 11-43.

12. In the Enable Incoming E-Mail box, click **Yes** in response to the *Enable sites on this server to receive e-mail?* prompt.

Figure 11-43

The Configure Incoming E-Mail Settings page

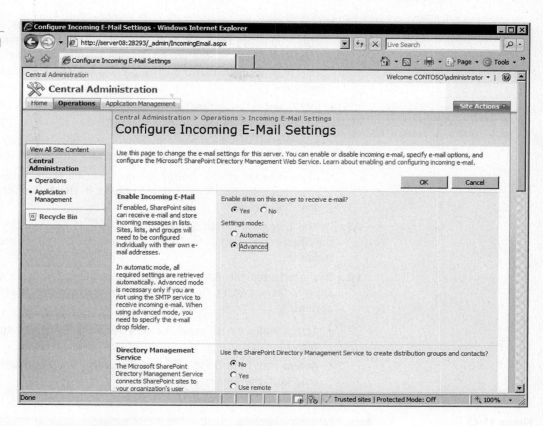

13. For *Settings mode,* select one of the following options:

- Automatic—Select this option if the SMTP Server feature included with Windows Server 2008 is installed on the computer.

- Advanced—Select this option if the computer is running an SMTP server other than the one included with Windows Server 2008.

14. In the Directory Management Service box, shown in Figure 11-44, select **Yes** to enable Windows SharePoint Services to interact with Active Directory. Then, configure the following settings:

Figure 11-44

The Directory Management Service box on the Configure Incoming E-Mail Settings page

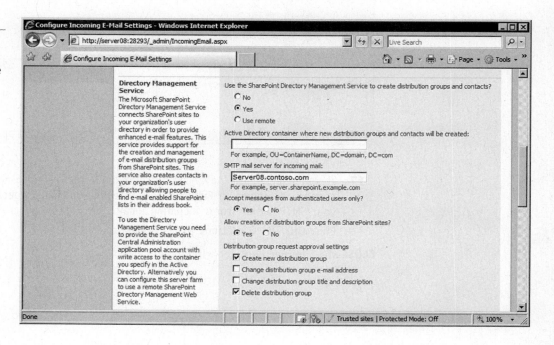

- Active Directory container where new distribution groups and contacts will be created—Specifies the location in the Active Directory hierarchy where SharePoint will create new objects. You must grant the SharePoint Central Administration application pool account with the Write permission for the container you specify in this setting.

- SMTP mail server for incoming mail—Specifies the FQDN of the SMTP server that SharePoint should use for incoming mail.

- Accept messages from authenticated users only—Specifies whether users must log on successfully to send email messages to a SharePoint site.

- Allow creation of distribution groups from SharePoint sites—Enables SharePoint sites to create distribution group objects in the Active Directory container you specified earlier.

15. In the Incoming E-Mail Server Display Address box, specify the email address the SharePoint should display in Web pages when users create incoming mail addresses.

16. If you selected the Automatic Settings mode option, a Safe E-Mail Servers box appears, as shown in Figure 11-45, in which you can select one of the following options:

- Accept mail from all e-mail servers—Enables SharePoint to receive mail from any server

- Accept mail from these safe e-mail servers—Enables SharePoint to receive mail only from the servers you specify

Figure 11-45

The Safe E-Mail Servers box on the Configure Incoming E-Mail Settings page

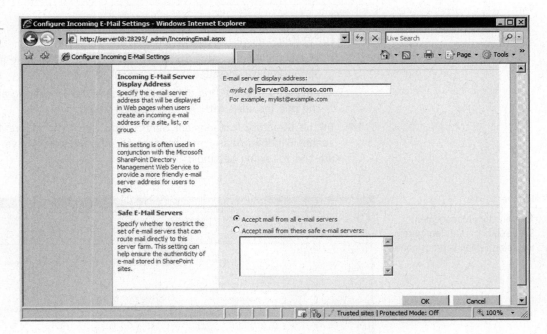

17. If you selected the Advanced Settings mode option, an E-Mail Drop Folder box appears, as shown in Figure 11-46, in which you must specify the location where your SMTP server stores incoming email.

18. Click **OK**. The Operations page reappears.

CLOSE the Internet Explorer window.

Figure 11-46

The E-Mail Drop Folder box on the Configure Incoming E-Mail Settings page

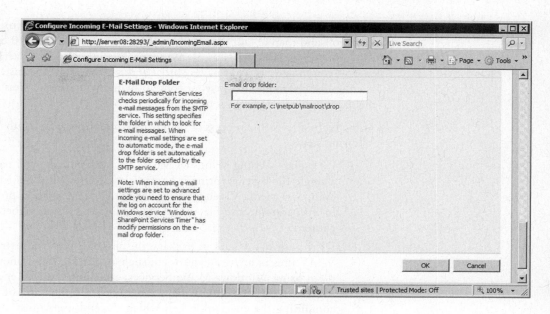

Users can now interact with Windows SharePoint Services by using their email clients to send messages to the server.

Using Digital Rights Management

THE BOTTOM LINE

Digital rights management (DRM) enables administrators to protect specific types of information from unauthorized consumption and distribution, even by users who have the appropriate credentials and permissions to access the information.

Throughout this book, you have learned how to protect applications and data by authenticating users to confirm their identities and authorizing users to allow them access to specific resources. However, security doesn't stop there. How do you protect information after a user has been granted access to it? An administrator might grant a specific user access to a confidential document, but what prevents the user from giving the document to others or printing and distributing copies? Digital rights management is one possible solution to this problem.

CERTIFICATION READY?
Configure Digital Rights
Management (DRM)
4.2

Windows Server 2008 includes several technologies that enable you to restrict access to specific documents by specifying what users can do with them. These components include Windows Media Rights Manager, which you can use to protect multimedia files from unauthorized copying and distribution, and Active Directory Rights Management Services (AD RMS), which is a client/server application that can apply persistent protection to individual documents. The following sections examine these two technologies.

Using Windows Media Rights Manager

In some cases, multimedia content publishers might want to control access to their content by imposing limitations on it, such as who can play it, what devices they can use, how often they can play it, and so forth. To do this, you can use Windows Media Rights Manager (WMRM). WMRM is a Microsoft technology that enables you to package your content in a secure form and issue licenses that provide authorized users with limited access to the content.

To protect your content using WMRM, you must enter into a license agreement with Microsoft and then obtain the Windows Media Rights Manager 10 Software Development Kit (SDK). This SDK contains the Windows Media Rights Manager application, which enables you to package your own content and issue your own licenses. WMRM also functions as an online clearinghouse for your content by receiving users' access requests, authenticating the users, and issuing licenses to them.

At the highest level, the process of deploying content protected with WMRM consists of the following steps:

1. Packaging—Using Windows Media Rights Manager, you package your content into a single file by encrypting it and storing it in a Windows Media Audio (WMA) or Windows Media Video (WMV) format. The encryption process uses a key, stored in a separate license file, which the end users must have before they can play the content.

2. Distribution—After you package the content, you can distribute the WMA or WMV files in any way you wish, such as posting them on a Web site, streaming them using Windows Media Services, attaching them to email messages, or burning them to CD or DVD disks. These distributions do not include the license file containing the encryption key, which the end users must obtain separately. The separate distribution of the content and the license is the basis for the entire DRM security paradigm.

3. Licensing—The user requests a license for the content by establishing contact with your server running Windows Media Rights Manager. The license acquisition process can begin either when users attempt to obtain the content or after they obtain it, when they attempt to open the content file in Windows Media Player. Depending on how you configure Windows Media Rights Manager, the end user might be able to obtain a license invisibly or might be referred to a Web site requiring registration and/or payment of a fee.

4. Playback—After a user has obtained both the content file and the appropriate license file, Windows Media Player can play back the content, limited only by the rights the license terms grant.

Using the licensing capabilities of WMRM, you can restrict access to your content files in many different ways, using a variety of business rules, such as the following:

- Time limits—You can restrict the content to play back only between specific start and end times or specify a license duration limit, which begins when the user obtains the license.

- Count limits—You can limit users to a specified number of content playbacks, after which they must obtain an additional license.

- Transfer limits—You can specify whether users are able to copy the content file to a portable playback device and limit the transfer to a single device by binding the license to a device identifier.

- Copy limits—Users can freely copy the content files to other computers, but each computer requires its own license. You can limit the number of licenses you issue for a particular content file.

- Burn limits—You can specify whether users are able to burn the content to a CD or DVD. Disk-burning software products that support Windows Media content files are required to adhere to the terms of the licenses issued with the content. After the user burns the content to a disk, it is no longer protected by WMRM.

- Multiple licenses—You can create licenses with different rights for a single content file, enabling users to choose between single-playback and unlimited-playback licenses, for example.

Using Active Directory Rights Management Services

> Active Directory Rights Management Services (AD RMS) is a Windows Server 2008 role that enables you to create usage policies for specific types of information that specify what authorized users can do with that information.

With Active Directory Rights Management Services, you can, for example, enable users to read a document, but prevent them from modifying or printing it. The protection provided by AD RMS is persistent, meaning that it remains a part of the document no matter where anyone moves it.

UNDERSTANDING THE AD RMS ARCHITECTURE

AD RMS consists of three components, as follows:

- AD RMS server—A Windows Server 2008 computer responsible for issuing certificates that enable users and services to assign AD RMS protection to documents by creating publishing licenses. The server also functions as a clearinghouse for client access requests.
- AD RMS client—A Windows Vista or Windows Server 2008 computer running an AD RMS-enabled application, such as Internet Explorer 7.0 or 2007 Microsoft Office system applications. When the client attempts to open a protected document, the application sends an access request to the AD RMS server, which issues a user license specifying the limitations of the user's access.
- Database server—A computer running a database manager, such as Microsoft SQL Server 2005, which stores configuration, logging, and directory services information for the AD RMS cluster.

INSTALLING THE ACTIVE DIRECTORY RIGHTS MANAGEMENT SERVICES ROLE

AD RMS is a Windows Server 2008 role that you can install like any other role using the Server Manager console. However, you must consider several prerequisites. Before you begin the installation, you must do the following:

- Add the server to the Active Directory domain that will be hosting the users of the protected content.
- Create a domain user for AD RMS to use as a service account.
- Create an IIS Web site that AD RMS will use for its virtual directory.
- Log on to Windows Server 2008 using an account that is a member of the Enterprise Admins group and that has the permissions needed to create a new database on the database server.

The AD RMS role installation process is one of the most complex in Windows Server 2008. Selecting the role adds many pages to the Add Roles Wizard, which you use to configure the server's database access and security settings. The pages that the AD RMS role adds to the wizard and the options each page provides are as follows:

- Select Role Services—Enables you to select which of the AD RMS role services you want to install, as shown in Figure 11-47, by selecting from the following options:
  - Active Directory Rights Management Server—A required role service that enables the server to identify authorized users and issue the licenses they need to access protected information.
  - Identity Federation Support—Enables AD RMS protection to cross organizational boundaries using trust relationships created with Active Directory Federation Services (AD FS). To install this role service, you must also install the AD FS role. Selecting this role service also adds a Configure Identity Federation Support page to the end of the wizard, on which you specify the name of your federation server.

Figure 11-47

The Select Role Services page of the Add Roles Wizard

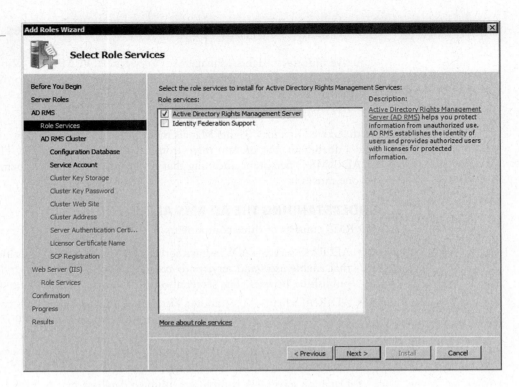

- Create or Join an AD RMS Cluster—Enables you to specify whether you want to create a new AD RMS root cluster or join the server to an existing AD RMS cluster, as shown in Figure 11-48, by selecting one of the following options:

  - Create a New AD RMS Cluster—Configures the computer to be the first server in a new AD RMS cluster. The first AD RMS server in an Active Directory forest is called the root cluster. To scale the AD RMS service, you can add more servers to the root cluster. For larger installations, you can create additional, licensing-only clusters.

  - Join an Existing AD RMS Cluster—Configures the server to be a part of a previously created AD RMS cluster.

Figure 11-48

The Create or Join an AD RMS Cluster page of the Add Roles Wizard

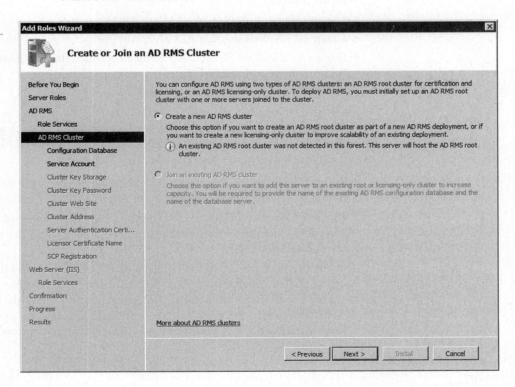

- Select Configuration Database—Enables you to specify the type and location of the database manager that AD RMS will use, as shown in Figure 11-49, by selecting from the following options:

  - Use Windows Internal Database on this server—Installs and enables AD RMS to use Windows Internal Database, a reduced version of SQL Server included with Windows Server 2008. Selecting this option limits AD RMS to a single-server cluster. Microsoft recommends using this option for testing purposes only; production AD RMS deployments should use an external database server.

  - Use a different database server—Enables AD RMS to use an external database server to store AD RMS data. Selecting this option activates the text boxes in which you must specify the name (or IP address) of the database Server and the Database Instance on that server. You must be logged on using an account that has the permissions needed to create a new database.

Figure 11-49

The Select Configuration
Database page of the Add
Roles Wizard

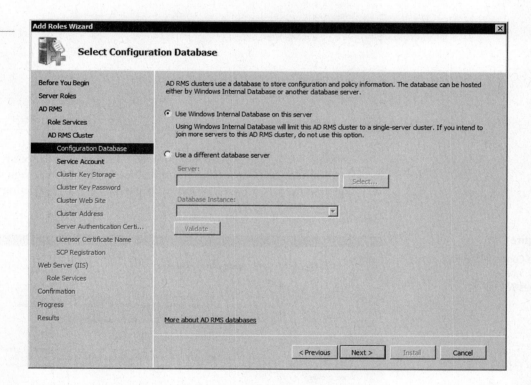

- Specify Service Account—Enables you to specify the domain user account you want AD RMS to use when communicating with other services, as shown in Figure 11-50. You should create a domain user account for this purpose. The account does not require any additional permissions.

Figure 11-50

The Specify Service Account page of the Add Roles Wizard

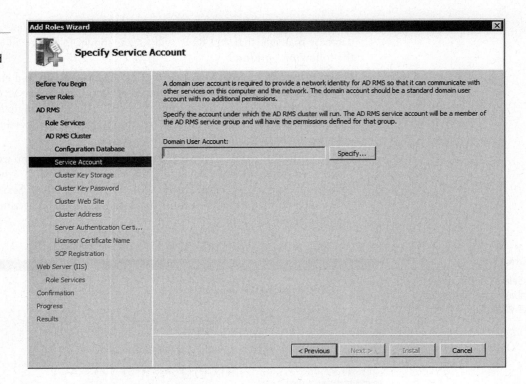

- Configure AD RMS Cluster Key Storage—Enables you to specify what method AD RMS should use to create the cluster key with which it will digitally sign the certificates and licenses it issues, as shown in Figure 11-51, by selecting one of the following options:

Figure 11-51

The Configure AD RMS Cluster Key Storage page of the Add Roles Wizard

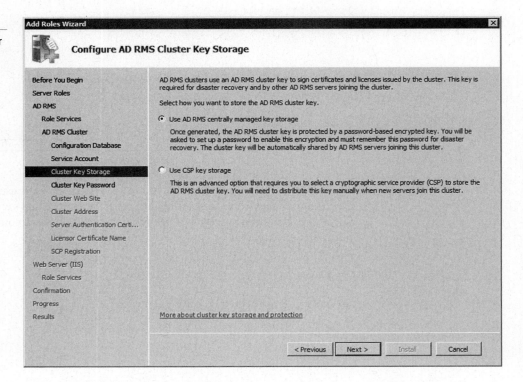

- Use AD RMS centrally managed key storage—Causes AD RMS to create a cluster key using password-based encryption. When you select this option, a Specify AD RMS Cluster Key Password page appears in the wizard, on which you must specify the password you want the server to use when creating the key.

- Use CSP key storage—Causes AD RMS to store the cluster key using a cryptographic service provider (CSP). When you select this option, a Specify AD RMS Cluster Key page appears in the wizard, on which you must select a CSP and specify whether you want to create a new key or use an existing one, as shown in Figure 11-52.

Figure 11-52

The Specify AD RMS Cluster Key Password page of the Add Roles Wizard

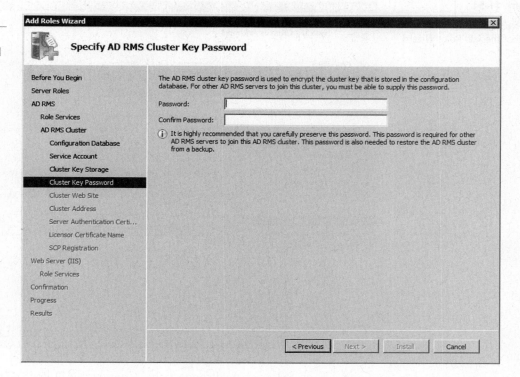

- Select AD RMS Cluster Web Site—Enables you to select the Internet Information Services (IIS) Web site that AD RMS will use to host its virtual directory, as shown in Figure 11-53. The page contains a list of all of the sites currently hosted by IIS, from which you can choose.

Figure 11-53

The Select AD RMS Cluster Web Site page of the Add Roles Wizard

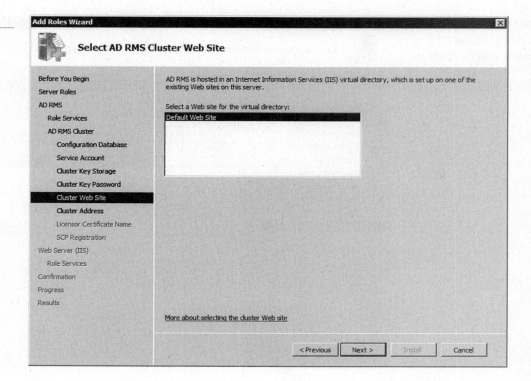

- Specify Cluster Address—Enables you to specify the fully-qualified domain name (FQDN) that clients will use to communicate with the AD RMS cluster, as shown in Figure 11-54. The settings on this page are as follows:

Figure 11-54

The Specify Cluster Address page of the Add Roles Wizard

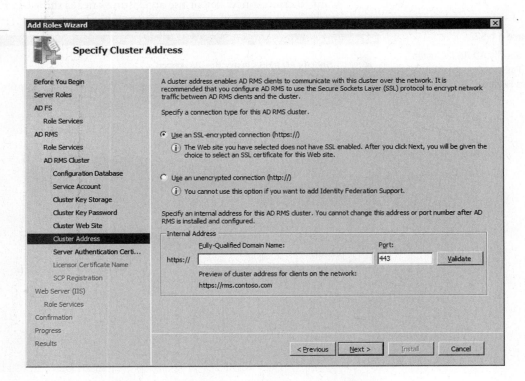

- Use an SSL-encrypted connection—Configures AD RMS to require client connections that are encrypted using Secure Sockets Layer (SSL). If you select this option, a Choose a Server Authentication Certificate for SSL Encryption page appears in the wizard, as shown in Figure 11-55, on which you can select an existing server certificate for SSL encryption or create a new one.

Figure 11-55

The Choose a Server Authentication Certificate for SSL Encryption page of the Add Roles Wizard

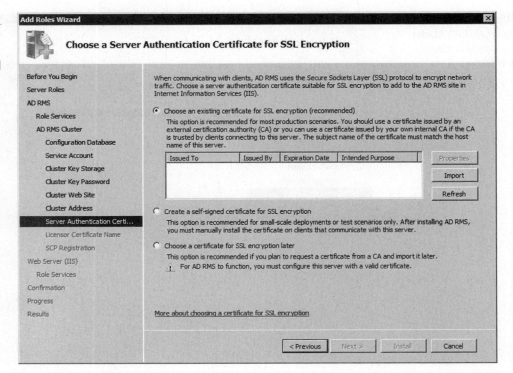

- Use an unencrypted connection—Configures AD RMS to use unencrypted client connections. You cannot select this option if you are installing the Identity Federation Support role service.
- Specify an internal address for this AD RMS cluster—Enables you to specify the FQDN and port number for the AD RMS cluster.
- Name the Server Licensor Certificate—Enables you to specify a name for the certificate that the AD RMS cluster will use to identify itself to clients, as shown in Figure 11-56.

Figure 11-56

The Name the Server Licensor Certificate page of the Add Roles Wizard

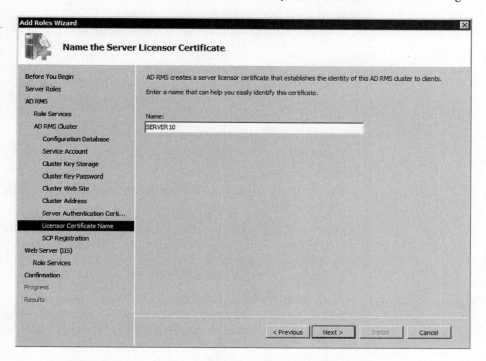

- Register AD RMS Service Connection Point—Enables you to create a service connection point for the AD RMS cluster in the Active Directory domain, either now or later, as shown in Figure 11-57. To create the connection point, you must be logged on using an account that is a member of the Enterprise Admins group.

Figure 11-57

The Register AD RMS Service Connection Point page of the Add Roles Wizard

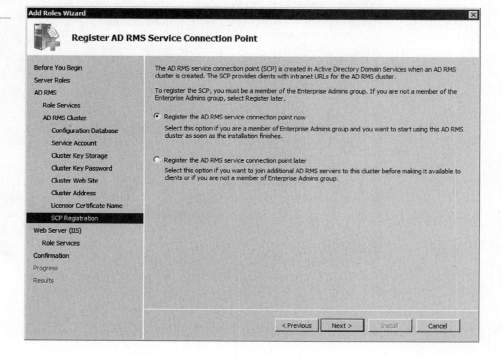

After you complete the installation of the AD RMS role, the server is ready to process AD RMS client requests.

SUMMARY SKILL MATRIX

IN THIS LESSON YOU LEARNED:

- Windows Media Services is a Windows Server 2008 role that enables a server to stream audio and video content to network clients in real time. A player on the client computer establishes a direct connection with the server and plays the audio or video content as it arrives.

- Media streaming is always a tradeoff between bandwidth and signal quality. As you increase the quality and/or resolution of the video image, you also increase the amount of bandwidth the stream consumes.

- Windows Media Player has a feature called Fast Streaming, which includes several techniques that enable the player to begin displaying content more quickly, improving the user experience.

- Windows Media Services supports two types of publishing points: on-demand streams and broadcast streams.

- Windows Media Services uses unicast transmissions by default. In a unicast transmission, each client establishes its own connection to the Windows Media Services server. To conserve bandwidth, use multicast transmissions. Multicasting is a TCP/IP feature that provides one-to-many transmission capabilities.

- Windows Media Services can stream multimedia content using different protocols to support different Windows Media Player versions, including Real Time Streaming Protocol (RTSP) and Hypertext Transfer Protocol (HTTP). When you enable both the RTSP and the HTTP protocols on a Windows Media Services server, the clients and the server use a process called protocol rollover to negotiate the most efficient protocol they have in common.

- To control access to your multimedia content, you can use Windows Media Rights Manager. WMRM is a Microsoft technology that enables you to package your content in a secure form and issue licenses that provide authorized users with limited access to the content.

- Active Directory Rights Management Services (AD RMS) is a Windows Server 2008 role that enables you to create usage policies for specific types of information that specify what authorized users can do with that information.

- Windows SharePoint Services 3.0 is a database-enabled Web application that runs on an Internet Information Services server. By accessing the site, users can employ browser-based workspaces to share information in a variety of ways, such as storing documents, creating calendar appointments and task lists, and contributing to newsgroup-style discussions.

- After you install and configure Windows SharePoint Services, you can access the administration interface by selecting SharePoint 3.0 Central Administration from the Administrative Tools program group.

- Windows SharePoint Services can integrate with email in a variety of ways, enabling users to set up calendar appointments, post announcements, add documents, and contribute to blogs and discussion forums. To provide users with these email capabilities, you must install a Simple Mail Transfer Protocol (SMTP) server and configure the incoming and outgoing email settings in Windows SharePoint Services.

■ Knowledge Assessment

Matching

Complete the following exercise by matching the terms with their corresponding definitions.

    a. Converts live multimedia content for real-time streaming.

    b. Enables media players to start displaying content sooner.

    c. Can only use unicast transmissions.

    d. Can use unicast or multicast transmissions.

    e. Enables users to rewind and fast forward streamed content.

    f. Uses Class D IP addresses.

    g. Requires Windows Media Player version 9 or higher.

    h. Enables any version of Windows Media Player to connect to a Windows Media Services server.

    i. Controls access to Windows Media content.

    j. Uses an SQL server database to store content.

_____ **1.** unicast

_____ **2.** Digital Rights Management (DRM)

_____ **3.** broadcast streams

_____ **4.** protocol rollover

_____ **5.** Fast Streaming

_____ **6.** on-demand streams

_____ **7.** Windows SharePoint Services 3.0

_____ **8.** Real Time Streaming Protocol (RTSP)

_____ **9.** Windows Media Encoder

_____ **10.** multicast

Multiple Choice

Select the correct answer for each of the following questions.

1. Before you install Windows SharePoint Services 3.0, you must install which of the following Windows Server 2008 elements?
    a. The .NET Framework 3.0 feature
    b. The Web Server (IIS) role
    c. Microsoft SQL Server 2005
    d. SharePoint 3.0 Central Administration

2. Which of the following is not a benefit of streaming multimedia content rather than downloading it?
    a. Playback begins sooner with streaming than with downloading.
    b. Streaming uses lower transmission rates than downloading.
    c. Streaming provides better playback quality than downloading.
    d. Streaming supports live content, while downloading does not.

3. Which of the following Fast Streaming technologies does not enable the client playback to begin sooner?
    a. Fast Reconnect
    b. Fast Start
    c. Advanced Fast Start
    d. Fast Cache

4. Which of the following is not true about broadcast streaming?
   a. Broadcast streams can use unicast or multicast transmissions.
   b. Users cannot rewind or fast forward a broadcast stream.
   c. Multiple clients can receive a single broadcast stream.
   d. Streaming can only be used for live content.

5. Which of the following URL prefixes enables a Windows Media Player client and a Windows Media Services server to use protocol rollover to negotiate the most efficient streaming protocol?
   a. rtsp://
   b. mms://
   c. http://
   d. rtspt://

6. To configure a Windows SharePoint Services 3.0 server to receive user content via incoming email, you must do which of the following?
   a. Install the Microsoft SMTP Server feature on the computer running Windows SharePoint Services.
   b. Install the Microsoft SMTP Server feature on any computer on the network.
   c. Install any SMTP server on the computer running Windows SharePoint Services.
   d. Install any SMTP server on any computer on the network.

7. Which of the following is a Windows Media Services parameter that you can adjust to limit the bandwidth utilized by client/server connections?
   a. Limit connection rate
   b. Limit player connections
   c. Limit outgoing distribution connections
   d. Limit connection acknowledgment

8. Which of the following is not true about Windows Media Services and multicast transmissions?
   a. Media streams that use multicast transmissions conserve bandwidth.
   b. Multicast transmissions send streams to multiple IP addresses simultaneously.
   c. Multicast transmissions use Class D IP addresses.
   d. Windows Media Services can only use multicast transmissions for broadcast streams.

9. Which of the following tools do you use to configure Windows SharePoint Services 3.0 settings?
   a. A SharePoint 3.0 Central Administration Web page that uses a different IP address than the Team Site page.
   b. A SharePoint 3.0 Central Administration snap-in for Microsoft Management Console.
   c. A password-protected link on the Team Site home page.
   d. A SharePoint 3.0 Central Administration Web page using a randomly selected port number.

10. During the planning phase of Windows Media Services deployment, which of the following is not one of the elements you should consider when deciding how much signal quality you can afford with the bandwidth you have to expend?
    a. How much network bandwidth your clients have available.
    b. How many clients you must service simultaneously.
    c. How much signal quality your media streams require to effectively service your clients.
    d. How many publishing points you need to create.

Review Questions

1. List the four steps involved in deploying DRM-protected content in the correct order.

2. List and explain five limitations that you can apply to a DRM license to control client access to a protected content file.

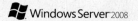

■ Case Scenario

Scenario 11-1: Installing Windows Media Services

Ralph just installed Windows Server 2008 on a new computer that he wants to use to stream training videos to clients on the local network. When he opens Server Manager for the first time, Ralph is surprised to discover that Streaming Media Services is not listed in the Add Roles Wizard. After checking on the Internet, Ralph learns that Windows Media Services no longer ships with Windows Server 2008. Ralph downloads the Windows Media Services files from the Microsoft Download Center and executes the Server file on the computer. After the installation process is completed, however, Ralph can find no indication that Windows Media Services has been installed. There is no console in the Administrative tools group and no new system services running. What must Ralph do to install Windows Media Services on the computer?

Appendix A
Windows Server 2008 Applications Infrastructure Configuration (Exam 70-643)

Matrix Skill	Skill Number	Lesson Number
Deploying Servers		
Deploy images by using Windows Deployment Services.	1.1	1
Configure Microsoft Windows activation.	1.2	1
Configure Windows Server Hyper-V and virtual machines.	1.3	12
Configure high availability.	1.4	12
Configure storage.	1.5	2
Configuring Terminal Services		
Configure Windows Server 2008 Terminal Services RemoteApp (TS RemoteApp).	2.1	8
Configure Terminal Services Gateway.	2.2	10
Configure Terminal Services load balancing.	2.3	12
Configure and monitor Terminal Services resources.	2.4	8
Configure Terminal Services licensing.	2.5	9
Configure Terminal Services client connections.	2.6	9
Configure Terminal Services server options.	2.7	8
Configuring a Web Services Infrastructure		
Configure Web applications.	3.1	7
Manage Web sites.	3.2	5
Configure a File Transfer Protocol (FTP) server.	3.3	5
Configure Simple Mail Transfer Protocol (SMTP).	3.4	7
Manage Internet Information Services (IIS).	3.5	5
Configure SSL security.	3.6	6
Configure Web site authentication and permissions.	3.7	6
Configuring Network Application Services		
Configure Windows Media server.	4.1	11
Configure Digital Rights Management (DRM).	4.2	11
Configure Microsoft Windows SharePoint Services server options.	4.3	11
Configure Windows SharePoint Services email integration.	4.4	11

The *Windows Server 2008 Applications Infrastructure Configuration* title of the Microsoft Official Academic Course (MOAC) series includes two books: a textbook and a lab manual. The exercises in the lab manual are designed for classroom use under the supervision of an instructor or a lab aide.

■ Classroom Setup

This course should be taught in a classroom containing networked computers where students can develop their skills through hands-on experience with Microsoft Windows Server 2008. The exercises in the lab manual require the computers to be installed and configured in a specific manner. Failure to adhere to the setup instructions in this document can produce unanticipated results when the students perform the exercises.

Classroom Configuration

The following configurations and naming conventions are used throughout the course and are required for completing the labs as outlined in the lab manual.

The classroom network consists entirely of computers running Windows Server 2008, including a single classroom server and a number of student servers. The classroom server performs several roles for the student servers, including the following:

- Active Directory Domain Services domain controller
- Domain Name System (DNS) server
- Dynamic host Configuration Protocol (DHCP) server

Use the following information when setting up the classroom server:

- Active Directory domain name: contoso.com
- Computer name: ServerDC
- Fully qualified domain name (FQDN): ServerDC.contoso.com
- Administrator password: P@ssw0rd

The student computers are also servers running Windows Server 2008, which the students will join to the contoso.com domain. Each student computer in the domain is to be named Server##, where ## is a unique number assigned to each computer by the instructor. Each student server will also have a corresponding domain user account called Student##, where ## is the same number assigned to the computer.

As they work through the lab manual, the students will install and remove several different roles and features. In some of the exercises, students will initiate communication with another server on the network. To make this possible, the lab manual is designed to support the following three classroom configurations.

- Dedicated computers—Each student computer has a single instance of Windows Server 2008 installed. To complete the lab exercises that require interaction between two servers, you can provide each student with two computers or assign a lab partner to each student. In the latter case, each student will complete the exercise and provide the services required by his or her partner.

- Local virtual machines—Each student computer has a virtualization product, such as Microsoft Virtual PC, installed, enabling you to create two virtual machines, each running an instance of Windows Server 2008. With this configuration, each student can perform all of the exercises on one computer, using the two virtual machines to perform the required roles.

- Web-hosted virtual machines—Each student computer uses a Web browser to access two Windows Server 2008 virtual machines hosted by a commercial service on the Internet. With this configuration, each student can perform all of the exercises on one computer, using the two virtual machines to perform the required roles.

To support these classroom configurations, students must begin each lab in the manual with the same baseline operating system configuration on the student computers. Therefore, each lab begins with an exercise that sets up the server for that lab and concludes with an exercise that returns the server to the baseline configuration. Depending on your classroom configuration, the students might be able to skip the first and last exercises in each lab.

Classroom Server Requirements

The computer running Windows Server 2008 in the classroom requires the following hardware and software:

Hardware Requirements

- Processor: 1 GHz (minimum); 2 GHz or faster (recommended)
- RAM: 512 MB (minimum); 2 GB or more (recommended)
- Disk space requirements: 10 GB (minimum); 40 GB or more (recommended)
- DVD-ROM drive
- Super VGA (800 × 600) or higher-resolution monitor
- Keyboard and mouse (or other pointing device)
- One network interface adapter

Software Requirements

- Microsoft Windows Server 2008, Standard or Enterprise

Student Computer Requirements

Each student computer requires the following hardware and software:

Hardware Requirements

- Processor: 1 GHz (minimum); 2 GHz or faster (recommended)
- RAM: 512 MB (minimum); 2 GB or more (recommended)
- First hard drive: 50+ GB, sufficient disk space for one 40 GB system partition and at least 10 GB of unpartitioned space
- Second hard drive: 10+ GB with no partitions
- DVD-ROM drive
- Super VGA (800 × 600) or higher-resolution monitor
- Keyboard and mouse (or other pointing device)
- One network interface adapter

SOFTWARE REQUIREMENTS

- Windows Server 2008, Standard or Enterprise

■ Classroom Server Setup Instructions

Before you begin, do the following:

- Read this entire document.
- Verify that you have the course materials provided on the instructor companion site and the installation disk for Microsoft Windows Server 2008.

> **WARNING** By performing the following setup instructions, your computer's hard disks will be repartitioned and reformatted. You will lose all existing data on the system.

Installing Windows Server 2008

Using the following setup procedure, install Windows Server 2008 on ServerDC.

➜ INSTALL WINDOWS SERVER 2008

1. Boot the computer from the Windows Server 2008 Installation disk. When you boot from the disk, the Windows Server 2008 Setup program starts automatically and the Install Windows page appears.

2. Modify the *Language to install, Time and currency format,* and *Keyboard or input method* settings, if necessary. Click **Next**.

3. Click **Install now**. The *Type your product key for activation* page appears.

4. Enter your product key in the *Product key* text box and click **Next**. The *Please read the license terms* page appears.

> **TAKE NOTE** ⁎
> If you plan to use evaluation versions of Windows Server 2008 in the classroom, you can leave the Product key field blank and, in the *Select the edition of Windows that you purchased* window that subsequently appears, select Windows Server 2008 Enterprise (Full Installation) for the version you want to install.

5. Select the **I accept the license terms** checkbox and click **Next**. The *Which type of installation do you want?* page appears.

6. Click **Custom**. The *Where do you want to install Windows?* page appears.

7. Select the disk where you want to install Windows Server 2008 and click **Next**. The *Installing Windows* page appears.

8. When the installation process is complete, the computer restarts and prompts you to change the Administrator password. Click **OK**.

9. Key **P@ssw0rd** in the New Password and Confirm Password text boxes and click the right arrow button. Then click **OK**. Windows Server 2008 starts and the Initial Configuration Tasks window appears.

10. Install any updates needed to keep the operating system current.

> **TAKE NOTE** ⁎
> If your computer supports booting from CD/DVD, the computer might try to boot from the Windows Server 2008 disk after Windows Server 2008 Setup restarts. If this happens, you should be prompted to press a key to boot from the disk. However, if Setup restarts automatically, simply remove the disk and restart the computer.

PROCEED to the following section to continue the server configuration process.

Before you proceed with the server configuration, install any required updates to keep the operating system current. Use Automatic Updates, the Windows Update Web site, or any other mechanism to locate, download, and install the updates.

Completing Post-Installation Tasks on ServerDC

After the installation is complete and the Initial Configuration Tasks window has appeared, complete the following procedures to prepare the computer to function as the classroom server.

PERFORMING INITIAL CONFIGURATION TASKS

Use the following procedure to prepare the server for the course.

PERFORM INITIAL CONFIGURATION TASKS

1. In the Initial Configuration Tasks window, click **Set time zone**. The Date and Time dialog box appears.
2. Verify that the date, time, and time zone shown in the dialog box are correct. If they are not, click **Change date and time** or **Change time zone** and correct them. Then click **OK**.
3. Click **Configure Networking**. The Network Connections window appears.
4. Right-click the **Local Area Connection** icon and, from the context menu, select **Properties**. The Local Area Connection Properties sheet appears.
5. Clear the Internet Protocol Version 6 (TCP/IPv6) checkbox.
6. Select **Internet Protocol Version 4 (TCP/IPv4)** and click **Properties**. The Internet Protocol Version 4 (TCP/IPv4) Properties sheet appears.
7. Configure the TCP/IP parameters using the following values:

   - IP Address: 10.1.1.100
   - Subnet Mask: 255.255.255.0
   - Preferred DNS Server: 127.0.0.1

TAKE NOTE*

The IP addresses supplied in this setup document and in the lab manual are suggestions. You can use any IP addresses for the computers in your classroom, as long as all of the systems are located on the same subnet. If the classroom network is connected to a school network or the Internet, you can specify the address of the router providing the network connection in the Default Gateway field. Otherwise, leave it blank.

8. Click **OK** twice to close the two Properties sheets. Close the Network Connections window.
9. In the Initial Configuration Tasks window, click **Provide computer name and domain**. The System Properties dialog box appears with the Computer Name tab selected.
10. Click **Change**. The Computer Name/Domain Changes dialog box appears.
11. In the Computer name text box, key **ServerDC** and click **OK**. A message box appears, prompting you to restart your computer.
12. Click **OK**, then click **Close** to close the System Properties dialog box. Another message box appears, informing you again that you must restart the computer.
13. Click **Restart Now**. The computer restarts.

The ServerDC computer must be an Active Directory domain controller. After the computer restarts, you can install the Active Directory Domain Services role and the Active Directory Domain Services Installation Wizard.

INSTALL ACTIVE DIRECTORY

To install Active Directory on ServerDC, use the following procedure.

INSTALL ACTIVE DIRECTORY

1. Log on with the local Administrator account, using the password **P@ssw0rd**.
2. When the Initial Configuration Tasks window appears, click **Add Roles**. The Add Roles Wizard appears.

3. Using the Add Roles Wizard, install the Active Directory Domain Services role.

4. When the role installation is complete, click the **Close this wizard and launch the Active Directory Domain Services Installation Wizard (dcpromo.exe)** link. The *Welcome to the Active Directory Installation Wizard* page appears.

5. Click **Next** to proceed with the Active Directory installation.

6. On the *Operating System Compatibility* page, click **Next**.

7. On the *Choose a Deployment Configuration* page, select **Create a new domain in a new forest** and click **Next**.

8. On the *Name the Forest Root Domain* page, key **contoso.com** and click **Next**.

9. On the *Set the Forest Functional Level* page, click **Next** to accept the default setting.

10. On the *Set Domain Functional Level* page, click **Next** to accept the default setting.

11. On the *Additional Domain Controller Options* page, verify that the **DNS server** checkbox is selected and click **Next**. A Static IP Assignment message box appears, warning you that the computer has a dynamically assigned IP address.

12. For the purposes of this manual, you can ignore the warning. Click **Yes, the computer will use a dynamically assigned IP address** to continue. A message box appears, warning you that the system cannot locate an existing DNS infrastructure.

13. Because you will be creating a new DNS infrastructure, you can ignore this warning and click **Yes**.

14. On the *Location for Database, Log Files, and SYSVOL* page, click **Next** to accept the default settings.

15. On the *Directory Services Restore Mode Administrator Password* page, key **P@ssw0rd** in the Password and Confirm Password text boxes and click **Next**.

16. On the *Summary* page, click **Next**.

17. When the installation process is complete, restart the server.

After the server restarts, it functions as the domain controller for the contoso.com domain. Students must log on to the domain in all of the lab exercises.

INSTALLING THE DHCP SERVER ROLE

To install the DHCP server on ServerDC, use the following procedure.

⊙ INSTALL THE DHCP SERVER ROLE

1. Log on with the domain Administrator account using the password **P@ssw0rd**.

2. When the Initial Configuration Tasks window appears, click **Add Roles**. The Add Roles Wizard appears.

3. Using the Add Roles Wizard, install the DHCP Server role.

4. On the *Select Network Connection Bindings* page, click **Next** to accept the default settings.

5. On the *Specify IPv4 DNS Server Settings* page, click **Next** to accept the default settings.

6. On the *Specify IPv4 WINS Server Settings* page, click **Next** to accept the default settings.

7. On the *Add or Edit DHCP Scopes* page, click **Add**.

8. In the Add Scope dialog box, create a scope using the following values:
   - Scope Name: Classroom
   - Starting IP Address: 10.1.1.101
   - Ending IP Address: 10.1.1.199
   - Subnet Mask: 255.255.255.0
   - Subnet Type: Wired

TAKE NOTE*

If the classroom network is connected to a school network or the Internet, you can specify the address of the router providing the network connection in the Default Gateway field. Otherwise, leave it blank.

9. Select the **Activate this scope** checkbox and click **OK**. Then click **Next**.

10. On the Configure DHCPv6 Stateless Mode pane, click **Next** to accept the default settings.

11. On the *Authorize DHCP Server* page, click **Next** to accept the default settings.

12. On the *Confirm Installation Selections* page, click **Install**.

CLOSE the Initial Configuration Tasks window when the installation is complete.

After the DHCP role is installed, all student servers will obtain their IP addresses and other TCP/IP configuration settings via DHCP.

Creating User Accounts

Each student must have a domain user account called Student##, where ## is the same number as the computer the student is using. To create the student accounts, use the following procedure.

 CREATE USER ACCOUNTS

1. Click **Start**, and then select **Administrative Tools** > **Active Directory Users and Computers**. The Active Directory Users and Computers console appears.

2. Expand the contoso.com domain.

3. Right-click the **Users** container and select **New** > **User**. The New Object-User wizard appears.

4. Key **Student##** in the First Name and User Logon Name text boxes, where ## is the number assigned to the first student computer in the classroom. Then click **Next**.

5. In the Password and Confirm Password text boxes, key **P@ssw0rd**.

6. Clear the **User Must Change Password At Next Logon** checkbox and select the **Password Never Expires** checkbox. Then click **Next**.

7. Click **Finish** to create the user account.

8. Repeat Steps 3–7 to create a Student## user account for each computer in the classroom.

9. Right-click the **Users** container and select **New** > **Group**. The New Object-Group wizard appears.

10. In the Group Name text box, key **Students**. Then click **Next**.

11. Click **Finish** to create the group.

12. In the Users container, double-click the Students group you just created. The Students Properties sheet appears.

13. Click the **Members** tab.

14. Click **Add**, key the name of the first Student## user you created, and click **OK**.

15. Repeat Step 14 to add all the Student## accounts you created to the Students group.

16. Click **OK** to close the Students Properties sheet.

17. Using the same procedure, open the Properties sheet for the Domain Admins group and add each of the Student## user accounts you created as members of that group.

CLOSE the Active Directory Users and Computers console.

The students will use these Student## accounts to log on to the domain as they complete the exercises in the lab manual. Their membership in the Students group provides domain administrator privileges, as well as local Administrator privileges on their individual servers.

PREPARING THE FILE SYSTEM

From the Microsoft Web site, download the following add-on modules for Windows Server 2008:

- Windows Media Services 2008 for Windows Server 2008 – Server MSU file
- Windows SharePoint Services 3.0 with Service Pack 1
- Microsoft FTP Publishing Service for IIS 7.0

Windows Media Services 2008 and Windows SharePoint Services 3.0 with Service Pack 1 are available from the Microsoft Download Center at http://microsoft.com/downloads. Microsoft FTP Publishing Service for IIS 7.0 is available from Microsoft's Internet Information Services site at http://iis.net/downloads.

Complete the following procedure to make these modules available to the students and provide the students with storage on the classroom server.

PREPARE THE FILE SYSTEM

1. On the server's C drive, create a new folder called *Install* and three subfolders called *Install\\MediaSvcs*, *Install\\FTP7*, and *Install\\SharePoint*.
2. Copy the add-on modules you downloaded to the appropriate folders.
3. Share the C:\\Install folder using the share name *Install*, and then grant only the Allow Read share permission to the Everyone special identity.
4. Using Windows Explorer, grant the Students group the Allow Read, Allow Read & Execute, and Allow List Folder Contents NTFS permissions for the C:\\Install folder.
5. Also on the server's C drive, create a new folder called *Students* and copy the Lab Manual Worksheets from the book's instructor companion site to the C:\\Students folder.
6. Grant the Students group the Allow Full Control NTFS permission for the C:\\Students folder.
7. Share the C:\\Students folder using the share name Students, and then grant the Everyone special identity the Allow Full Control share permission.

CLOSE the Windows Explorer window.

These folders provide students with the additional software they need to complete the lab exercises and storage space to keep their lab worksheet files.

CONFIGURING FILE REDIRECTION

To complete the lab exercises, each student must be able to store files on the classroom server. Use Group Policy to redirect each user's Documents folder to the classroom server drive, using the following procedure.

CONFIGURE FILE REDIRECTION

1. Click **Start**, and then select **Administrative Tools** > **Group Policy Management**. The Group Policy Management console appears.
2. In the scope (left) pane, expand the console tree to display and select the **Group Policy Objects** node under the contoso.com domain.
3. In the detail (right) pane, right-click the **Default Domain Policy GPO** and, from the context menu, select **Edit**. The Group Policy Management Editor window appears.
4. Navigate to the **User Configuration** > **Policies** > **Windows Settings** > **Folder Redirection** folder. Then, right-click the **Documents** subfolder and, from the context menu, select **Properties**. The Documents Properties sheet appears.
5. From the Setting dropdown list, select **Basic – Redirect Everyone's folder to the same location**.

6. In the Target Folder Location box, verify that the default **Create a folder for each user under the root path option** is selected.

7. In the Root Path text box, key **\\ServerDC\Students**.

8. Click the **Settings** tab and clear the **Grant the user exclusive rights to Documents** checkbox.

9. Click **OK** to close the Documents Properties sheet.

CLOSE the Group Policy Management Editor and Group Policy Management consoles.

The computer is ready to function as the classroom server. You can install the student servers.

Student Server Setup

The setup for the student computers depends on your classroom configuration. The result is a bare Windows Server 2008 installation, which students can configure. However, the tasks you must complete before the students arrive vary, as follows:

- Dedicated computers—If each student computer in your classroom will have a single copy of Windows Server 2008 installed on it, proceed directly to the following Install Windows Server 2008 procedure.

- Local virtual machines—If you plan to use a virtualization product on the student computers to enable each system to run multiple copies of Windows Server 2008, first you must install the virtualization software on each computer according the manufacturer's instructions and create a virtual machine for each copy of Windows Server 2008 you plan to install. Then, install the operating system on each virtual machine, using the following Install Windows Server 2008 procedure.

- Web-hosted virtual machines—If your students will access virtual machines provided by a commercial service over the Web, then your classroom computers can run any operating system that provides the appropriate Web browser application. All of the operating systems are preinstalled, so you can skip the following procedure.

INSTALLING WINDOWS SERVER 2008 ON A STUDENT COMPUTER

Using the following setup procedure, install Windows Server 2008 on the student computers.

 INSTALL WINDOWS SERVER 2008

1. Boot the computer from the Windows Server 2008 Installation disk. When you boot from the disk, the Windows Server 2008 Setup program starts automatically, and the *Install Windows* page appears.

2. Modify the *Language to install*, *Time and currency format*, and *Keyboard or input method* settings, if necessary, and click **Next**.

3. Click **Install now**. The *Type your product key for activation* page appears.

4. Enter your product key in the *Product key* text box and click **Next**. The *Please read the license terms* page appears.

TAKE NOTE*

If you plan to use unregistered evaluation versions of Windows Server 2008 in the classroom, you can leave the Product key field blank and, in the *Select the edition of Windows that you purchased* window that subsequently appears, select Windows Server 2008 Enterprise (Full Installation) for the version you want to install.

5. Select the **I accept the license terms** checkbox and click **Next**. The *Which type of installation do you want?* page appears.

6. Click **Custom**. The *Where do you want to install Windows?* page appears.

TAKE NOTE*

Depending on the capabilities of your virtualization software and the type of licensing your school provides, you can perform a Windows Server 2008 installation on a single virtual machine and then clone multiple instances of that virtual machine, rather than perform each OS installation individually.

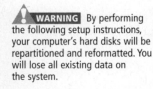 WARNING By performing the following setup instructions, your computer's hard disks will be repartitioned and reformatted. You will lose all existing data on the system.

7. Select the disk where you want to install Windows Server 2008 and click **Drive Options**.

8. Click **New**. In the Size text box, key **40000**. Click **Apply**.

9. Select the partition you just created and click **Next**. The *Installing Windows* page appears.

10. When the installation process is complete, the computer restarts and prompts you to change the Administrator password. Click **OK**.

TAKE NOTE *

If your computer supports booting from CD/DVD, the computer might try to boot from the Windows Server 2008 disk after Windows Server 2008 Setup restarts. If this happens, you should be prompted to press a key to boot from the disk. However, if Setup restarts automatically, simply remove the disk and restart the computer.

---

11. Key **P@ssw0rd** in the New Password and Confirm Password text boxes and click the right arrow button. Then click **OK**. Windows Server 2008 starts and the Initial Configuration Tasks window appears.

12. Install any updates needed to keep the operating system current.

CLOSE the Initial Configuration Tasks window.

The computer is ready for a student to begin working through the lab manual. The student will perform all of the initial configuration tasks that the computer requires.

Glossary

A

access control entry (ACE) An entry in an object's access control list (ACL) that grants permissions to a user or group. Each ACE consists of a security principal (the name of the user, group, or computer being granted the permissions) and the specific permissions assigned to that security principal. When you manage permissions in any of the Windows Server 2008 permission systems, you are creating and modifying the ACEs in an ACL.

access control list (ACL) A collection of access control entries that defines the access that all users and groups have to an object.

Active Directory Microsoft's directory service that automates network management, such as user data, resources, and security.

Active Server Pages (ASP) A server-side script processing engine designed by Microsoft to provide dynamic Web content with better performance than the Common Gateway Interface (CGI) and simpler development than Internet Server Application Programming Interface (ISAPI). ASP files have an .asp extension and function like Server Side Includes, with scripting commands embedded in standard HTML code.

Anonymous Authentication In Internet Information Services, an authentication mechanism that enables any user to access a Web site that employs it, without supplying an account name or password. This authentication method is designed primarily for public Web sites on the Internet or any internal site available to all users.

application Computer program designed to aid users in the performance of specific tasks.

application pool In Internet Information Services, an operational division that consists of a request queue and one or more worker processes.

application services Software components that provide communications services, operating environments, or programming interfaces for specific applications.

Arbitrated loop (FC-AL) A Fibre Channel topology that consists of up to 127 devices, connected in a loop, similar to that of a token ring network. The loop can be physical, with each device connected to the next device, or virtual, with each device connected to a hub that implements the loop.

ASP.NET The successor to Active Server Pages (ASP), ASP.NET is based on server-side scripting and enables developers to create dynamic Web pages, Web applications, and XML (Extensible Markup Language) Web services using a wide variety of programming languages and development tools. ASP.NET files have the extension .aspx, and can contain HTML code, XML code, or scripting code for execution by the server.

ATA (Advanced Technology Attachment) A disk interface that uses parallel communications to connect multiple hard disk drives and other devices to a computer.

authentication The process by which Windows Server 2008 verifies that the user matches the user account employed to gain access.

authorization The process of determining whether an identified user or process is permitted access to a resource and the user's appropriate level of access.

B

Basic Authentication The weakest of the challenge/response authentication methods supported by Internet Information Services. Clients transmit unencrypted credentials using Base64 encoding, so anyone capturing the network packets can read the user's password.

basic disk The default disk type in Windows Server 2008. A basic disk supports up to four partitions, typically three primary and one extended, with logical drives to organize data.

binding In Internet Information Services, the mechanism by which the protocol listener associates each incoming request with one particular Web site hosted by the server.

bitmap caching In Terminal Services, a Windows desktop performance feature that enables a client to store display information in a cache in local memory, so that the server does not have to repeatedly transmit the same data.

block I/O access In storage area networking, a type of storage in which a computer accesses the stored data one block at a time.

broadcast stream In Windows Media Services, a multimedia stream that typically consists of live content delivered according to a prearranged schedule.

C

certification authority (CA) A software component or a commercial service that issues digital certificates. Windows Server 2008 includes a CA as part of the Active Directory Certificate Services role.

client access license (CAL) A document that grants a single client access to a specific software program, such as a Terminal Services server.

client machine ID (CMID) A unique identifier assigned to each computer that the Key Management Service host records when it successfully activates the computer.

client-side caching A Remote Desktop Connection feature that enables a client to store screen elements that remain unchanged from one refresh to the next in a cache on the computer.

Common Gateway Interface (CGI) A protocol that enables a Web server to run an application specified in a client request and pass the request to that application for processing. The Web server then receives the output from the application and packages it as a reply to the client in the form of a Web page.

connection authorization policy (CAP) A Terminal Services Gateway component that specifies the Internet users allowed to use the TS Gateway server.

copy-on-write data sharing A Windows Server 2008 Terminal Services memory management technique used by the operating system that, when a client attempts to write to a shared application file, creates a copy of that file, allocates it for the exclusive use of that client, and writes the changes to the copy.

Credential Security Service Provider (CredSSP) In Terminal Services, the protocol that Network Level Authentication (NLA) uses to confirm clients' identities.

D

differential backup A type of backup that saves only the data in the selected components that has changed since the last full backup.

Digest Authentication In Internet Authentication Services, an authentication protocol designed for use with intranet Web servers in an Active Directory environment. Unlike Windows Authentication, Digest Authentication works through firewalls and proxy servers because it transmits passwords over the network. However, the protocol protects the passwords using a strong MD5 encryption scheme.

digital certificate An electronic credential, issued by a certification authority (CA), which confirms the identity of the party to which it is issued.

Digital Rights Management (DRM) A collection of Windows technologies that enable administrators to protect specific types of information from unauthorized consumption and distribution by all users, including users with the appropriate credentials and permissions to access the information.

direct-attached storage Hard disk drives and other storage media connected to a computer using one of the standard disk interfaces, as opposed to network-connected storage.

directory services Software components that store, organize, and supply information about a network and its resources.

disk duplexing A fault tolerance mechanism in which the computer stores duplicate data on two separate disks, each on a separate host adapter, so the data remains available if one disk fails.

disk mirroring A fault tolerance mechanism in which the computer stores duplicate data on two separate disks so the data remains available if a disk fails.

DiskPart.exe A Windows Server 2008 command-line program that you can use to perform disk management tasks.

Distributed File System (DFS) A Windows Server 2008 File Services role service that includes two technologies: DFS Namespaces and DFS Replication. These technologies enable administrators to create virtual directories for shared network files and automatically copy files and folders between duplicate virtual directories.

DNS round robin A load-balancing technique in which you create an individual resource record for each terminal server in the server farm using the server's IP address and the name of the farm (instead of the server name). When clients attempt to establish a Terminal Services connection to the farm, DNS distributes the incoming name resolution requests among the IP addresses.

domain A set of network resources available for a group of users who can authenticate to the network to gain access to those resources.

domain controller A Windows server with Active Directory directory service installed. Each workstation computer joins the domain and is represented by a computer object. Administrators create user objects that represent human users. A domain differs from a workgroup because users log on to the domain once, rather than to each individual computer.

dynamic disk The alternative to the basic disk type in Windows Server 2008. Dynamic disks can have an unlimited number of volumes using various configurations. The process of converting a basic disk to a dynamic disk creates a single partition that occupies the entire disk. You can create an unlimited number of volumes out of the space in that partition.

E

Easy Print A Windows Server 2008 Terminal Services feature that eliminates the need for the printer driver on the terminal server. Instead, the terminal server has a generic Easy Print driver based on the XML Paper Specification (XPS) document format introduced in Windows Vista and Windows Server 2008.

effective permissions A combination of allowed, denied, inherited, and explicitly assigned permissions that provides a composite view of a security principal's functional access to a resource.

Enhanced Metafile (EMF) A standardized, highly portable print job format that is the default format used by the Windows 2000, Windows XP, and Windows Server 2003 print subsystems.

Execution mode One of two operational modes in Terminal Services; used when running applications.

external drive array Hard disk drives and other storage media connected to a computer using a network medium, such as Ethernet or Fibre Channel.

F

failover cluster A collection of redundant servers configured to perform the same tasks, so that if one server fails, another server can take its place almost immediately.

FastCGI An extension to the Common Gateway Interface (CGI) that enables a Web server to maintain a pool of processes that new clients can reuse.

Fast Streaming A collection of techniques that enables Windows Media Player to begin displaying streamed multimedia content more quickly.

feature An individual Windows Server 2008 component designed to perform a specific administrative function.

Fibre Channel A high-speed serial networking technology that was originally designed for use with supercomputers, but is now associated primarily with storage area networking.

Fibre Channel Protocol (FCP) The protocol that Fibre Channel storage area networks use to transmit SCSI traffic between devices.

file system An operating system component that provides a means for storing and organizing files so that users can easily locate them.

File Transfer Protocol (FTP) An application layer protocol that enables a client to connect to a remote server, perform rudimentary file management tasks, and copy files in either direction between the two computers.

file-based I/O In storage area networking, a type of storage in which a computer accesses the stored data one file at a time.

firewall A software routine that acts as a virtual barrier between a computer and the attached network. A firewall is essentially a filter that enables certain types of incoming and outgoing traffic to pass through the barrier, while blocking other types.

folder redirection A Windows service that enables workstations to store user profile data on a shared network drive instead of a local drive.

font smoothing In Terminal Services, a Windows desktop performance feature that enables the client to display screen fonts without jagged lines. Also called anti-aliasing.

FTP over Secure Sockets Layer (SSL) A method by which computers use the SSL protocol to encrypt FTP communications.

full mesh topology In the Distributed File System, a replication scheme in which every member in a group replicates with every other member.

G

globally unique identifier (GUID) partition table (GPT) You can use GPT as a boot disk if the computer's architecture provides support for an Extensible Firmware Interface (EFI)-based boot partition. Otherwise, you can use it as a non-bootable disk for data storage only. When used as a boot disk, it differs from the master boot record because platform operation critical data is located in partitions rather than unpartitioned or hidden sectors.

H

host header In Internet Information Services, a Web site property that specifies the name of the Web server to which clients send requests. IIS uses this Host field to associate incoming requests with one of the Web sites hosted by the server. See also virtual hosting.

hub/spoke topology In the Distributed File System, a replication scheme in which replication traffic is limited to specific pairs of members.

hybrid virtualization A type of virtualization in which a host OS shares access to the computer's processor with the virtual machine manager, with each taking the clock cycles it needs and passing control of the processor back to the other.

Hypertext Markup Language (HTML) A simple tagged coding language that provides a client Web browser with instructions on how to display the text in the file and embed the accompanying media files into the display.

Hypertext Transfer Protocol (HTTP) The standard application layer protocol for Web communications.

Hyper-V A Windows Server 2008 role that implements hypervisor virtualization on the computer.

hypervisor In virtualization, an abstraction layer that interacts directly with the computer's physical hardware.

I

infrastructure services Software components that provide support functions for network clients.

Install mode One of two operational modes in Terminal Services; used when installing applications.

Internet Server Application Programming Interface (ISAPI) An application processing alternative to the Common Gateway Interface (CGI), which enables a Web server to execute applications without spawning a separate process for each incoming request. ISAPI applications take the form of dynamic link libraries (DLLs) instead of executables (EXEs), which load with the IIS server engine using the same address space.

Internet Storage Name Service (iSNS) In storage area networking, a software component that registers the presence of iSCSI initiators and targets on a SAN and responds to queries from iSNS clients.

IP (Internet Protocol) address A unique 32-bit numeric address used as an identifier for a device, such as a computer, on a TCP/IP network.

ISAPI extension A fully realized, in-process application that can generate dynamic HTML pages using information from a database or a form supplied by the client.

ISAPI filter A routine that operates between the HTTP server and the HTTP listener, providing additional functionality, such as application-based authentication, encryption, and data compression services.

iSCSI initiator In storage area networking, a hardware or software device running on a computer that accesses the storage devices on the SAN.

iSCSI target In storage area networking, a component integrated into a drive array or computer that receives SCSI commands from the initiator and passes them to a storage device.

J

JBOD (Just a Bunch of Disks) A colloquial term for a drive array that is not configured to use RAID or any other type of special fault tolerance mechanism.

K

Kerberos A ticket-based authentication protocol used by Windows computers that are members of an Active Directory domain. Unlike NTLM, which involves only the IIS7 server and the client, Kerberos authentication involves an Active Directory domain controller as well.

Key Management Service (KMS) An activation service that runs on the local network, enabling clients to activate without communicating with Microsoft.

KMS activation threshold The number of activation requests that a Key Management Service host must receive within the last 30 days to activate KMS clients.

L

Licensing server discovery mode A Terminal Services configuration setting that specifies how the terminal server will locate a TS Licensing server.

logical unit number (LUN) An identifier assigned to a specific component within a SCSI device, such as an individual disk drive in an array, which enables the SCSI host adapter to send commands to that component.

M

MAK Independent Activation Clients contact Microsoft hosts directly, using an Internet connection or a telephone, to activate a product. It is similar to the standard retail product key activation, except that a single key activates multiple computers.

MAK Proxy Activation Multiple clients send activation requests to a proxy, the Volume Activation Management Tool (VAMT).

master boot record (MBR) The default partition style used since Windows was released. Supports up to four primary partitions or three primary partitions and one extended partition, with unlimited logical drives on the extended partition.

Mstsc.exe A Windows program that provides command-line access to the Remote Desktop Connection client.

multicast In Windows Media Services, a type of transmission in which a single stream is delivered to multiple clients at the same time.

multimaster replication A technique in which duplicate copies of a file are updated on a regular basis, no matter which copy changes. For example, if a file is duplicated on four different servers, a user can access any of the four copies and modify the file as needed. The replication engine uses the changes made to the modified copy to update the other three copies. Compare to single master replication.

Multiple Activation Key (MAK) A product key that enables a specified number of computers to activate using Microsoft's hosted activation services.

N

namespace In the Distributed File System, a virtual directory tree that contains references to shared folders located on network file servers. This directory tree does not exist as a true copy of the folders on different servers. Instead, it is a collection of references to the original folders, which users can browse like an actual server share.

network attached storage (NAS) A dedicated file server device, containing disk drives, which connects to a network and provides clients with direct, file-based access to storage resources. Unlike a storage area network, NAS devices include a rudimentary operating system and a file system implementation.

Network File System (NFS) An open standard, application layer, file sharing protocol, commonly used by UNIX and Linux operating systems. Windows Server 2008 includes an NFS server implementation, in the form of the Services for Network File System role service, part of the File Services role.

Network Level Authentication (NLA) A Terminal Services feature that confirms the user's identity with the Credential Security Service Provider (CredSSP) protocol before the client and server establish the Terminal Services connection.

network load balancing (NLB) A clustering technology in which a collection of identical servers run simultaneously, sharing incoming traffic equally among them.

NTFS permissions Controls access to the files and folders stored on disk volumes formatted with the NTFS file system. To access a file on the local system or over a network, a user must have the appropriate NTFS permissions.

NTLMv2 A challenge/response authentication protocol used by Windows computers that are not members of an Active Directory domain.

O

Offline Files A Windows feature that enables client computers to maintain copies of server files on their local drives. If the computer's connection to the network is severed or interrupted, the client can continue to work with the local copies until network service is restored, at which time the client synchronizes its data with the data on the server.

on-demand stream In Windows Media Services, a multimedia stream of prerecorded content delivered at the user's request.

P

partition style The method that Windows operating systems use to organize partitions on a disk. Two hard disk partition styles can be used in Windows Server 2008: master boot record (MBR) and GUID partition table (GPT).

preboot execution environment (PXE) A network adapter feature that enables a computer to connect to a server on the network and download the boot files it needs to run, rather than booting from a local drive.

print device The hardware that produces hard copy documents on paper or other print media. Windows Vista supports *local print devices*, which are directly attached to the computer's parallel, serial, Universal Serial Bus (USB), or IEEE 1394 (FireWire) ports; and *network interface print devices*, which are connected to the network directly or through another computer.

print server A computer or stand-alone device that receives print jobs from clients and sends them to print devices that are attached locally or connected to the network.

printer The software interface through which a computer communicates with a print device. Windows Vista supports numerous interfaces, including parallel (LPT), serial (COM), USB, IEEE 1394, Infrared Data Access (IrDA), and Bluetooth ports; and network printing services such as lpr, Internet Printing Protocol (IPP), and standard TCP/IP ports.

printer control language (PCL) A language understood by the printer. Each printer is associated with a printer driver that converts the commands generated by an application into the printer's PCL.

printer driver A device driver that converts the print jobs generated by applications into an appropriate string of commands for a specific print device. Printer drivers are designed for specific print devices and provide applications that access all of the print device's features.

printer pool A single print server connected to multiple print devices. The print server can distribute large numbers of incoming jobs among several identical print devices to provide timely service. Alternatively, you can connect print devices that support different forms and paper sizes to a single print server, which distributes jobs with different requirements to the appropriate print devices.

private key In public key infrastructure (PKI), the secret key in a pair of keys, which is known only to the message or file recipient and used to decrypt the item. When a message is encrypted using the private key, only the public key can decrypt it. The ability to decrypt the message using the public key proves that the message originated from the holder of the private key.

protocol listener In Internet Information Services, the component that awaits incoming requests from clients and forwards them to the appropriate server applications.

protocol rollover In Windows Media Services, the technique by which clients and servers negotiate the most efficient streaming protocol they have in common. A client establishing a connection to a Windows Media Services server sends information about the protocols it can use and the server selects the best protocol it is capable of using. If, for any reason, the client cannot use the selected protocol, the server reverts to the next best protocol in its list.

public key infrastructure (PKI) A security relationship in which participants are issued two keys: public and private. The participant keeps the private key secret, while the public key is freely available in the digital certificate. Data encrypted with the private key can only be decrypted using the public key and data encrypted with the public key can only be decrypted using the private key.

publishing points In Windows Media Services, the components on a server through which clients access specific content streams.

R

Real Time Streaming Protocol (RTSP)
A control protocol, used by default in Windows Media Services running on Windows Server 2008, which carries commands between a client and server using the connection-oriented TCP protocol and port number 554. For the actual data streaming, Windows Media Services uses the Real Time Protocol (RTP).

Redundant Array of Independent Disks (RAID) A series of data storage technologies that use multiple disks to provide computers with increased storage, I/O performance, and/or fault tolerance.

Remote Desktop Connection A program running on a desktop computer that establishes a connection to a terminal server using Remote Desktop Protocol (RDP) and displays a session window containing a desktop or application.

Remote Desktop Protocol (RDP) The protocol used to transmit screen information, keystrokes, and mouse movements between the Remote Desktop Connection client and a Remote Desktop or Terminal Services server.

Remote Differential Compression (RDC) In the Distributed File System, a protocol that conserves network bandwidth by detecting changes in files and transmitting only the modified data to the destination. This conserves bandwidth and greatly reduces the time needed for the replication process.

RemoteApp A Terminal Services feature that enables clients to run terminal server applications within individual, resizable windows.

replication group In the Distributed File System, a collection of servers, known as members, each of which contains a target for a particular DFS folder.

resource authorization policy (RAP) A Terminal Services Gateway component that specifies the terminal servers users are permitted to access on the private network.

role A collection of Windows Server 2008 modules and tools designed to perform specific tasks for network clients.

S

security identifier (SID) A unique value assigned to every Active Directory object when it is created.

security principal The user, group, or computer to which an administrator assigns permissions.

serial ATA (SATA) A newer version of the ATA disk interface that uses serial instead of parallel communications, improves transmission speeds, and provides the ability to queue commands at the drive.

server farm A collection of identical servers used to balance a large incoming traffic load.

ServerManagerCmd.exe A Windows Server 2008 command-line tool used to install roles and features.

Server Message Blocks (SMB) The default application layer, file sharing protocol used by the Windows operating systems.

Server Side Includes (SSI) A relatively old Web server technology that enables HTML pages to contain directives that the server parses and executes.

session In Terminal Services, a collection of client processes that form an individual user environment running on the server.

Session ID In Terminal Services, a unique identifier that a terminal server assigns to each client session to keep the processes for individual clients separate.

Shadow Copies A Windows Server 2008 feature that maintains a library containing multiple versions of selected files. Users can select a version of a file to restore as needed.

Simple Mail Transfer Protocol (SMTP) The standard Transmission Control Protocol/Internet Protocol (TCP/IP) email protocol for the Internet. Email clients send outgoing messages to an SMTP server specified in their configuration settings and the SMTP server forwards the messages to other mail servers on the way to their destinations.

simple volume Consists of space from a single disk. After you create a simple volume, you can extend it to multiple disks to create a spanned or striped volume if it is not a system volume or boot volume.

single master replication. A technique in which duplicate copies of a file are updated on a regular basis from one master copy. For example, if a file is duplicated on four different servers, users can modify one copy and the replication engine propagates the changes to the other three copies. Compare with multimaster replication.

Small Computer System Interface (SCSI) A storage interface that enables computers to transfer data to multiple storage devices connected to a bus.

spanned volume A method for combining the space from multiple (2 to 32) dynamic disks into a single large volume. If a single physical disk in the spanned volume fails, all the data in the volume is lost.

special permissions An element providing a security principal with a specific degree of access to a resource.

spooler A service running on a print server that temporarily stores print jobs until the print device can process them.

standard permissions A common combination of special permissions used to provide a security principal with a level of access to a resource.

stateless Descriptive term for a server that does not maintain information about the client connections or the files opened by individual clients. NFS servers are stateless.

storage area network (SAN) A dedicated, high-speed network that connects block-based storage devices to servers. Unlike NAS devices, SANs do not provide a file system implementation. SANs require a server to provide clients with access to the storage resources.

striped volume A method for combining the space from multiple (2 to 32) dynamic disks into a single large volume. If a single physical disk in the striped volume fails, all the data in the volume is lost. A striped volume differs from a spanned volume in that the system writes data one stripe at a time to each successive disk in the volume.

subnet mask In TCP/IP networking, a 32-bit value that specifies which bits of an IP address form the network identifier and which bits form the host identifier.

Switched fabric (FC-SW) A Fibre Channel topology that consists of up to 16,777,216 (2^{24}) devices, each of which is connected to a Fibre Channel switch.

T

target In the Distributed File System, a physical folder on a shared server drive that is represented by a virtual directory in a DFS namespace.

Terminal Services client access license (TS CAL) A document that grants a single client access to a specific software program, in this case, a Terminal Services server.

Terminal Services Gateway A Terminal Services role service that enables Internet users to access terminal servers on private networks, despite the presence of intervening firewalls and network access translation (NAT) servers.

Terminal Services licensing mode A Terminal Services configuration parameter that specifies whether the terminal server should issue Per Device or Per User licenses to clients.

Terminal Services (TS) Web Access A Terminal Services role service that enables users to launch an application by double-clicking an icon on a Web page.

thin client A software program or hardware device that connects to a terminal server and accesses applications running on the server.

thin client computing A variation on the mainframe computing paradigm, in which clients function only as terminals and servers do all of the application computing.

TS Licensing server A Terminal Services software component that issues client access licenses to Terminal Services clients on a network.

tunneling A networking technique in which one protocol is encapsulated within another protocol. In virtual private networking (VPN), an entire client/server session is tunneled within another protocol. Because the internal, or payload, protocol is carried by another protocol, it is protected from most standard forms of attack.

U

unicast In Windows Media Services, a type of transmission in which each client establishes its own connection to the Windows Media Services server and has its own data stream.

Universal Discovery, Description, and Integration (UDDI) An XML-based directory service that enables businesses to publish listings about their activities and the services they offer.

V

VDS hardware provider In storage area networking, a software component that enables you to use the Storage Manager for SANs snap-in to manage LUNs on an external storage device.

virtual directory In Internet Information Services, an alias that points to a folder in another physical location. This shortcut enables you to publish content found on different drives or different computers without copying or moving it.

virtual hosting In Internet Information Services, a binding method in which each Web site hosted by a server is assigned a unique name, called a host header value, which differentiates it from the server's other sites. This binding method enables the Web server to host multiple Web sites using a single IP address and port number without requiring any special information from clients.

virtual instance A guest OS installed on a virtual machine in a Windows Server 2008 computer using Hyper-V.

virtual machine (VM) In virtualization, one of multiple separate operating environments on a single computer, in which you can install a separate copy of an operating system.

virtual private networking (VPN) A technique for connecting to a network at a remote location using the Internet as a network medium.

virtual server A complete installation of an operating system that runs in a software environment emulating a physical computer.

virtualization The process of deploying and maintaining multiple instances of an operating system on a single computer.

Volume Activation (VA) 2.0 Microsoft's program for automating and managing the activation of products obtained using volume licenses.

Volume Activation Management Tool (VAMT) A Microsoft program that collects activation requests from clients on the network. It uses a single connection to the Microsoft hosts to activate all of the clients at the same time, and then distributes the resulting activation codes to the clients using the Windows Management Instrumentation (WMI) interface.

W

Web garden A Web site with an application pool that uses more than one worker process.

Windows Authentication The most secure of the challenge/response authentication methods supported by Internet Information Services 7. Supports two authentication protocols: NTLMv2 and Kerberos.

Windows CE A real-time, modular operating system designed for devices with minimal amounts of memory. Windows CE is not based on the NT kernel, but it does provide users with a familiar Windows graphical user interface (GUI), and has been adapted to a variety of devices, including handhelds, smart phones, and game consoles.

Windows Deployment Services (WDS) A role included with Windows Server 2008, which enables you to perform unattended installations of Windows Server 2008 and other operating systems on remote computers, using network-based boot and installation media.

Windows Media Encoder A Windows application that converts captured digital content into the Windows Media format and sends it to a Windows Media Services server for real time distribution.

Windows Media Player A client application supplied with the Windows operating system that enables the computer to request, receive, and display multimedia streams.

Windows Media Services A Windows Server 2008 role that can stream audio and video content to network clients in real time. A player on the client computer establishes a direct connection with the server and plays the audio or video content as it arrives.

Windows PE (Preinstallation Environment) 2.1 A subset of Windows Server 2008 that provides basic access to the computer's network and disk drives, making it possible to perform an in-place or a network installation. This eliminates DOS from the installation process by supplying its own preinstallation environment.

Windows Process Activation Service (WAS) Windows Server 2008 feature that manages the Internet Information Services 7 request pipeline, the server's application pools, and the worker processes running in them.

Windows SharePoint Services 3.0 A Microsoft service that enables users to employ browser-based workspaces to share information in a variety of ways, such as storing documents, creating calendar appointments and task lists, and contributing to newsgroup-style discussions.

Windows XPe A full-featured operating system based on the standard Windows XP kernel. Windows XPe terminals include more local computing capabilities than terminals using Windows CE or a proprietary OS, including support for local browsers and Java applications, as well as embedded

Win32 applications. Windows XPe also supports the full range of Windows drivers and peripherals. The result is a powerful and efficient workstation that can continue to function when disconnected from the network.

witness disk In failover clustering, a shared storage medium that holds the cluster configuration database.

worker process In Internet Information Services, a host for user-developed application code, which is responsible for processing requests from the protocol listeners and returning the results to the client.

worker process isolation mode In Internet Information Services, an arrangement in which each application pool occupies its own protected address space. As a result, a crashed application cannot affect any process running outside of that pool.

X

XML Paper Specification (XPS) A new, platform-independent document format included with Windows Server 2008 and Windows Vista, in which print job files use a single XPS format for their entire journey to the print device, rather than being converted first to EMS and then to PCL.

Index

PART 2

Excerpts from

Microsoft® Official Academic Course

Microsoft® Exchange Server® 2007 Configuration

Microsoft Certified Technology Specialist Exam 70-236

Microsoft® Official Academic Course

Microsoft Exchange Server® 2007
Configuration (70-236)

Jason W. Eckert, triOS College

WILEY

Credits

EXECUTIVE EDITOR	John Kane
DIRECTOR OF MARKETING AND SALES	Mitchell Beaton
MICROSOFT STRATEGIC RELATIONSHIPS MANAGER	Merrick Van Dongen of Microsoft Learning
EDITORIAL PROGRAM ASSISTANT	Jennifer Lartz
PRODUCTION MANAGER	Micheline Frederick
PRODUCTION EDITOR	Kerry Weinstein
CREATIVE DIRECTOR	Harry Nolan
COVER DESIGNER	Jim O'Shea
TECHNOLOGY AND MEDIA	Lauren Sapira/Elena Santa Maria

This book was set in Garamond by Aptara, Inc. and printed and bound by Bind Rite Graphics.
The covers were printed by Phoenix Color.

Microsoft, ActiveX, Excel, InfoPath, Microsoft Press, MSDN, OneNote, Outlook, PivotChart, PivotTable, PowerPoint, SharePoint, SQL Server, Visio, Windows, Windows Mobile, Windows Server, and Windows Vista are either registered trademarks or trademarks of Microsoft Corporation in the United States and/or other countries. Other product and company names mentioned herein may be the trademarks of their respective owners.

The example companies, organizations, products, domain names, e-mail addresses, logos, people, places, and events depicted herein are fictitious. No association with any real company, organization, product, domain name, e-mail address, logo, person, place, or event is intended or should be inferred.

The book expresses the author's views and opinions. The information contained in this book is provided without any express, statutory, or implied warranties. Neither the authors, John Wiley & Sons, Inc., Microsoft Corporation, nor their resellers or distributors will be held liable for any damages caused or alleged to be caused either directly or indirectly by this book.

ISBN 978-0-470-38029-1

Printed in the United States of America

10 9 8 7 6 5 4 3 2 1

Foreword from the Publisher

Wiley's publishing vision for the Microsoft Official Academic Course series is to provide students and instructors with the skills and knowledge they need to use Microsoft technology effectively in all aspects of their personal and professional lives. Quality instruction is required to help both educators and students get the most from Microsoft's software tools and to become more productive. Thus our mission is to make our instructional programs trusted educational companions for life.

To accomplish this mission, Wiley and Microsoft have partnered to develop the highest quality educational programs for Information Workers, IT Professionals, and Developers. Materials created by this partnership carry the brand name "Microsoft Official Academic Course," assuring instructors and students alike that the content of these textbooks is fully endorsed by Microsoft, and that they provide the highest quality information and instruction on Microsoft products. The Microsoft Official Academic Course textbooks are "Official" in still one more way—they are the officially sanctioned courseware for Microsoft IT Academy members.

The Microsoft Official Academic Course series focuses on *workforce development*. These programs are aimed at those students seeking to enter the workforce, change jobs, or embark on new careers as information workers, IT professionals, and developers. Microsoft Official Academic Course programs address their needs by emphasizing authentic workplace scenarios with an abundance of projects, exercises, cases, and assessments.

The Microsoft Official Academic Courses are mapped to Microsoft's extensive research and job-task analysis, the same research and analysis used to create the Microsoft Certified Technology Specialist (MCTS) exam. The textbooks focus on real skills for real jobs. As students work through the projects and exercises in the textbooks they enhance their level of knowledge and their ability to apply the latest Microsoft technology to everyday tasks. These students also gain resume-building credentials that can assist them in finding a job, keeping their current job, or in furthering their education.

The concept of life-long learning is today an utmost necessity. Job roles, and even whole job categories, are changing so quickly that none of us can stay competitive and productive without continuously updating our skills and capabilities. The Microsoft Official Academic Course offerings, and their focus on Microsoft certification exam preparation, provide a means for people to acquire and effectively update their skills and knowledge. Wiley supports students in this endeavor through the development and distribution of these courses as Microsoft's official academic publisher.

Today educational publishing requires attention to providing quality print and robust electronic content. By integrating Microsoft Official Academic Course products, *WileyPLUS*, and Microsoft certifications, we are better able to deliver efficient learning solutions for students and teachers alike.

Bonnie Lieberman

General Manager and Senior Vice President

Preface

Welcome to the Microsoft Official Academic Course (MOAC) program for Microsoft Exchange Server 2007. MOAC represents the collaboration between Microsoft Learning and John Wiley & Sons, Inc. publishing company. Microsoft and Wiley teamed up to produce a series of textbooks that deliver compelling and innovative teaching solutions to instructors and superior learning experiences for students. Infused and informed by in-depth knowledge from the creators of Exchange Server 2007, and crafted by a publisher known worldwide for the pedagogical quality of its products, these textbooks maximize skills transfer in minimum time. Students are challenged to reach their potential by using their new technical skills as highly productive members of the workforce.

Because this knowledgebase comes directly from Microsoft, architect of the Exchange Server 2007 operating system and creator of the Microsoft Certified Technology Specialist and Microsoft Certified Professional exams (www.microsoft.com/learning/mcp/mcts), you are sure to receive the topical coverage that is most relevant to students' personal and professional success. Microsoft's direct participation not only assures you that MOAC textbook content is accurate and current; it also means that students will receive the best instruction possible to enable their success on certification exams and in the workplace.

■ The Microsoft Official Academic Course Program

The *Microsoft Official Academic Course* series is a complete program for instructors and institutions to prepare and deliver great courses on Microsoft software technologies. With MOAC, we recognize that, because of the rapid pace of change in the technology and curriculum developed by Microsoft, there is an ongoing set of needs beyond classroom instruction tools for an instructor to be ready to teach the course. The MOAC program endeavors to provide solutions for all these needs in a systematic manner in order to ensure a successful and rewarding course experience for both instructor and student—technical and curriculum training for instructor readiness with new software releases; the software itself for student use at home for building hands-on skills, assessment, and validation of skill development; and a great set of tools for delivering instruction in the classroom and lab. All are important to the smooth delivery of an interesting course on Microsoft software, and all are provided with the MOAC program. We think about the model below as a gauge for ensuring that we completely support you in your goal of teaching a great course. As you evaluate your instructional materials options, you may wish to use the model for comparison purposes with available products.

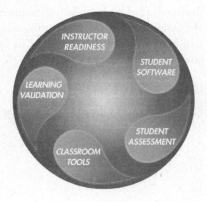

▪ Pedagogical Features

The MOAC textbook for Microsoft Exchange Server 2007 Configuration is designed to cover all the learning objectives for that MCTS exam, which is referred to as its "objective domain." The Microsoft Certified Technology Specialist (MCTS) exam objectives are highlighted throughout the textbook. Many pedagogical features have been developed specifically for *Microsoft Official Academic Course* programs.

Presenting the extensive procedural information and technical concepts woven throughout the textbook raises challenges for the student and instructor alike. The Illustrated Book Tour that follows provides a guide to the rich features contributing to *Microsoft Official Academic Course* program's pedagogical plan. Following is a list of key features in each lesson designed to prepare students for success on the certification exams and in the workplace:

- Each lesson begins with an **Lesson Skill Matrix**. More than a standard list of learning objectives, the Domain Matrix correlates each software skill covered in the lesson to the specific MCTS objective domain.

- Concise and frequent **Step-by-Step** instructions teach students new features and provide an opportunity for hands-on practice. Numbered steps give detailed, step-by-step instructions to help students learn software skills. The steps also show results and screen images to match what students should see on their computer screens.

- **Illustrations:** Screen images provide visual feedback as students work through the exercises. The images reinforce key concepts, provide visual clues about the steps, and allow students to check their progress.

- **Key Terms:** Important technical vocabulary is listed at the beginning of the lesson. When these terms are used later in the lesson, they appear in bold italic type and are defined. The Glossary contains all of the key terms and their definitions.

- Engaging point-of-use **Reader aids**, located throughout the lessons, tell students why this topic is relevant (*The Bottom Line*), provide students with helpful hints (*Take Note*), or show alternate ways to accomplish tasks (*Another Way*). Reader aids also provide additional relevant or background information that adds value to the lesson.

- **Certification Ready?** features throughout the text signal students where a specific certification objective is covered. They provide students with a chance to check their understanding of that particular MCTS objective and, if necessary, review the section of the lesson where it is covered. MOAC offers complete preparation for MCTS certification.

- **Knowledge Assessments** provide progressively more challenging lesson-ending activities.

■ Lesson Features

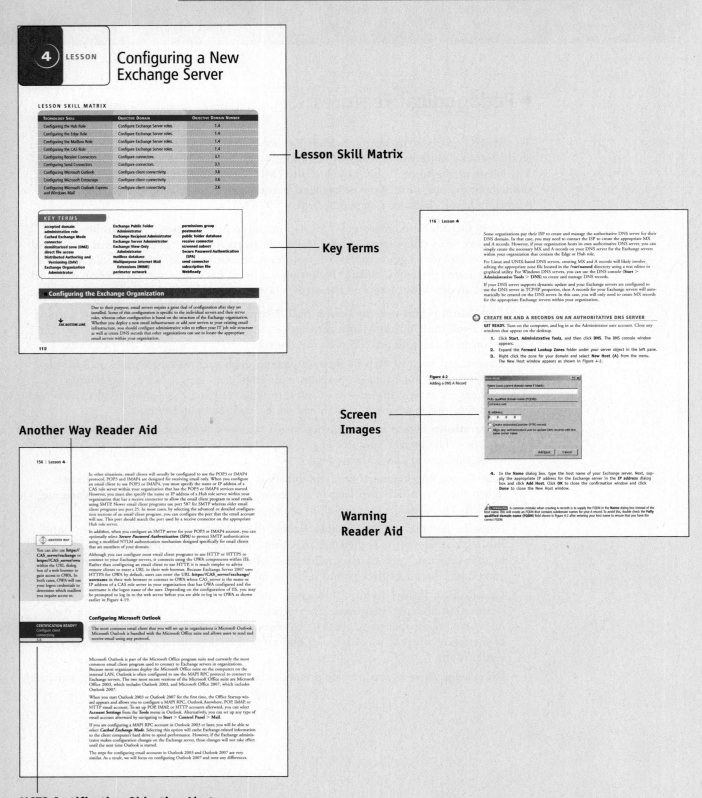

Lesson Skill Matrix

Key Terms

Screen Images

Another Way Reader Aid

Warning Reader Aid

MCTS Certification Objective Alert

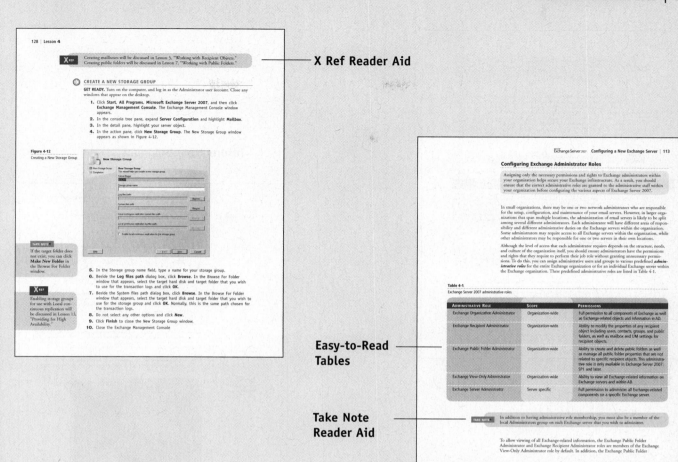

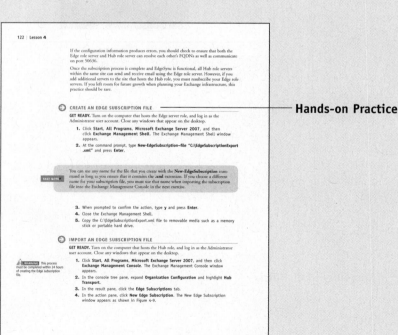

X Ref Reader Aid

Easy-to-Read Tables

Take Note Reader Aid

Hands-on Practice

Informative Diagrams

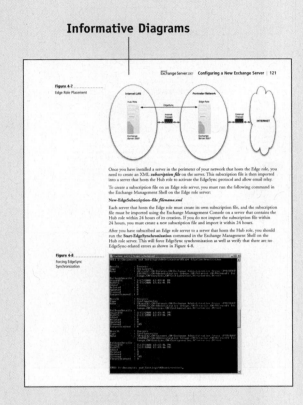

The Bottom Line Reader Aid

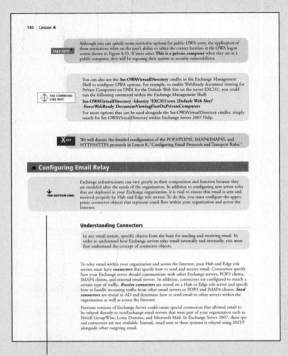

Summary Skill Matrix

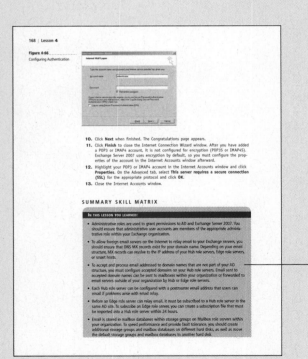

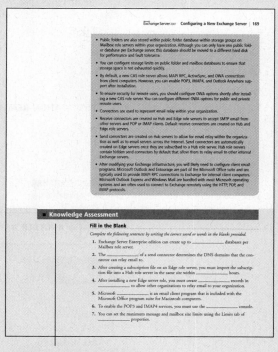

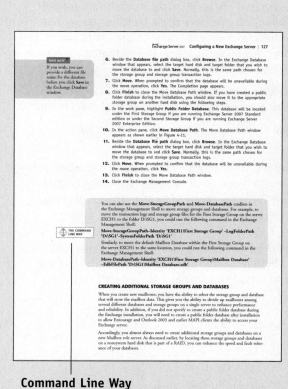

Review Questions

Case Scenarios

Knowledge Assessment Questions

Command Line Way

Conventions and Features Used in This Book

This book uses particular fonts, symbols, and heading conventions to highlight important information or to call your attention to special steps. For more information about the features in each lesson, refer to the Illustrated Book Tour section.

CONVENTION	MEANING
NEW FEATURE ✓	This icon indicates a new or greatly improved Windows feature in this version of the software.
↓ THE BOTTOM LINE	This feature provides a brief summary of the material to be covered in the section that follows.
CLOSE	Words in all capital letters and in a different font color than the rest of the text indicate instructions for opening, saving, or closing files or programs. They also point out items you should check or actions you should take.
CERTIFICATION READY?	This feature signals the point in the text where a specific certification objective is covered. It provides you with a chance to check your understanding of that particular MCTS objective and, if necessary, review the section of the lesson where it is covered.
TAKE NOTE	Reader aids appear in shaded boxes found in your text. *Take Note* provides helpful hints related to particular tasks or topics.
◆ ANOTHER WAY	*Another Way* provides an alternative procedure for accomplishing a particular task.
X REF	These notes provide pointers to information discussed elsewhere in the textbook or describe interesting features of Mircrosoft Exchange Server 2007 that are not directly addressed in the current topic or exercise.
Alt + Tab	A plus sign (+) between two key names means that you must press both keys at the same time. Keys that you are instructed to press in an exercise will appear in the font shown here.
A *shared printer* can be used by many individuals on a network.	Key terms appear in bold italic.
Key **My Name is**.	Any text you are asked to key appears in color.
Click **OK**.	Any button on the screen you are supposed to click on or select will also appear in color.

The *Microsoft Official Academic Course* programs are accompanied by a rich array of resources that incorporate the extensive textbook visuals to form a pedagogically cohesive package. These resources provide all the materials instructors need to deploy and deliver their courses. Resources available online for download include:

- The **MSDN Academic Alliance** is designed to provide the easiest and most inexpensive developer tools, products, and technologies available to faculty and students in labs, classrooms, and on student PCs. A free 3-year membership is available to qualified MOAC adopters.

  Note: Microsoft Exchange Server 2007 can be downloaded from MSDN AA for use by students in this course

- The **Instructor's Guide** contains Solutions to all the textbook exercises as well as chapter summaries and lecture notes. The Instructor's Guide and Syllabi for various term lengths are available from the Book Companion site (www.wiley.com/college/microsoft) and from *WileyPLUS*.

- The **Test Bank** contains hundreds of questions in multiple-choice, true-false, short answer, and essay formats and is available to download from the Instructor's Book Companion site (www.wiley.com/college/microsoft) and from *WileyPLUS*. A complete answer key is provided.

- **PowerPoint Presentations and Images.** A complete set of PowerPoint presentations is available on the Instructor's Book Companion site (www.wiley.com/college/microsoft) and in *WileyPLUS* to enhance classroom presentations. Tailored to the text's topical coverage and Skills Matrix, these presentations are designed to convey key Microsoft Exchange Server concepts addressed in the text.

  All figures from the text are on the Instructor's Book Companion site (www.wiley.com/college/microsoft) and in *WileyPLUS*. You can incorporate them into your PowerPoint presentations, or create your own overhead transparencies and handouts.

  By using these visuals in class discussions, you can help focus students' attention on key elements of Windows Server and help them understand how to use it effectively in the workplace.

- When it comes to improving the classroom experience, there is no better source of ideas and inspiration than your fellow colleagues. The **Wiley Faculty Network** connects teachers with technology, facilitates the exchange of best practices, and helps to enhance instructional efficiency and effectiveness. Faculty Network activities include technology training and tutorials, virtual seminars, peer-to-peer exchanges of experiences and ideas, personal consulting, and sharing of resources. For details visit www.WhereFacultyConnect.com.

WileyPLUS

Broad developments in education over the past decade have influenced the instructional approach taken in the Microsoft Official Academic Course program. The way that students learn, especially about new technologies, has changed dramatically in the Internet era. Electronic learning materials and Internet-based instruction is now as much a part of classroom instruction as printed textbooks. *WileyPLUS* provides the technology to create an environment where students reach their full potential and experience academic success that will last them a lifetime!

WileyPLUS is a powerful and highly-integrated suite of teaching and learning resources designed to bridge the gap between what happens in the classroom and what happens at home and on the job. *WileyPLUS* provides instructors with the resources to teach their students new technologies and guide them to reach their goals of getting ahead in the job market by having the skills to become certified and advance in the workforce. For students, *WileyPLUS* provides the tools for study and practice that are available to them 24/7, wherever and whenever they want to study. *WileyPLUS* includes a complete online version of the student textbook, PowerPoint presentations, homework and practice assignments and quizzes, image galleries, test bank questions, gradebook, and all the instructor resources in one easy-to-use Web site.

Organized around the everyday activities you and your students perform in the class, *WileyPLUS* helps you:

- **Prepare & Present** outstanding class presentations using relevant PowerPoint slides and other *WileyPLUS* materials—and you can easily upload and add your own.

- **Create Assignments** by choosing from questions organized by lesson, level of difficulty, and source—and add your own questions. Students' homework and quizzes are automatically graded, and the results are recorded in your gradebook.

- **Offer context-sensitive help to students, 24/7.** When you assign homework or quizzes, you decide if and when students get access to hints, solutions, or answers where appropriate—or they can be linked to relevant sections of their complete, online text for additional help whenever—and wherever they need it most.

- **Track Student Progress.** Analyze students' results and assess their level of understanding on an individual and class level using the *WileyPLUS* gradebook, or export data to your own personal gradebook.

- **Administer Your Course.** *WileyPLUS* can easily be integrated with another course management system, gradebook, or other resources you are using in your class, providing you with the flexibility to build your course, your way.

Please view our online demo at **www.wiley.com/college/wileyplus.** Here you will find additional information about the features and benefits of *WileyPLUS*, how to request a "test drive" of *WileyPLUS* for this title, and how to adopt it for class use.

MSDN ACADEMIC ALLIANCE—FREE 3-YEAR MEMBERSHIP AVAILABLE TO QUALIFIED ADOPTERS!

The Microsoft Developer Network Academic Alliance (MSDN AA) is designed to provide the easiest and most inexpensive way for universities to make the latest Microsoft developer tools, products, and technologies available in labs, classrooms, and on student PCs. MSDN AA is an annual membership program for departments teaching Science, Technology, Engineering, and Mathematics (STEM) courses. The membership provides a complete solution to keep academic labs, faculty, and students on the leading edge of technology.

Software available in the MSDN AA program is provided at no charge to adopting departments through the Wiley and Microsoft publishing partnership.

As a bonus to this free offer, faculty will be introduced to Microsoft's Faculty Connection and Academic Resource Center. It takes time and preparation to keep students engaged while giving them a fundamental understanding of theory, and the Microsoft Faculty Connection is designed to help STEM professors with this preparation by providing articles, curriculum, and tools that professors can use to engage and inspire today's technology students.

Contact your Wiley rep for details.

For more information about the MSDN Academic Alliance program, go to:

msdn.microsoft.com/academic/

Note: Microsoft Exchange Server 2007 can be downloaded from MSDN AA for use by students in this course.

Important Web Addresses and Phone Numbers

To locate the Wiley Higher Education Rep in your area, go to the following Web address and click on the "*Who's My Rep?*" link at the top of the page.

www.wiley.com/college

Or Call the MOAC Toll Free Number: 1 + (888) 764-7001 (U.S. & Canada only).

To learn more about becoming a Microsoft Certified Professional and exam availability, visit www.microsoft.com/learning/mcp.

Student Support Program

Book Companion Web Site (www.wiley.com/college/microsoft)

The students' book companion site for the MOAC series includes any resources, exercise files, and Web links that will be used in conjunction with this course.

WileyPLUS

WileyPLUS is a powerful and highly-integrated suite of teaching and learning resources designed to bridge the gap between what happens in the classroom and what happens at home and on the job. For students, *WileyPLUS* provides the tools for study and practice that are available 24/7, wherever and whenever they want to study. *WileyPLUS* includes a complete online version of the student textbook, PowerPoint presentations, homework and practice assignments and quizzes, image galleries, test bank questions, gradebook, and all the instructor resources in one easy-to-use Web site.

WileyPLUS provides immediate feedback on student assignments and a wealth of support materials. This powerful study tool will help your students develop their conceptual understanding of the class material and increase their ability to answer questions.

- A **Study and Practice** area links directly to text content, allowing students to review the text while they study and answer.
- An **Assignment** area keeps all the work you want your students to complete in one location, making it easy for them to stay on task. Students have access to a variety of interactive self-assessment tools, as well as other resources for building their confidence and understanding. In addition, all of the assignments and quizzes contain a link to the relevant section of the multimedia book, providing students with context-sensitive help that allows them to conquer obstacles as they arise.
- A **Personal Gradebook** for each student allows students to view their results from past assignments at any time.

Please view our online demo at www.wiley.com/college/wileyplus. Here you will find additional information about the features and benefits of *WileyPLUS*, how to request a "test drive" of *WileyPLUS* for this title, and how to adopt it for class use.

Wiley Desktop Editions

Wiley MOAC Desktop Editions are innovative, electronic versions of printed textbooks. Students buy the desktop version for 50% off the U.S. price of the printed text, and get the added value of permanence and portability. Wiley Desktop Editions provide students with numerous additional benefits that are not available with other e-text solutions.

Wiley Desktop Editions are NOT subscriptions; students download the Wiley Desktop Edition to their computer desktops. Students own the content they buy to keep for as long as they want. Once a Wiley Desktop Edition is downloaded to the computer desktop, students have instant access to all of the content without being online. Students can also print out the sections they prefer to read in hard copy. Students also have access to fully integrated resources within their Wiley Desktop Edition. From highlighting their e-text to taking and sharing notes, students can easily personalize their Wiley Desktop Edition as they are reading or following along in class.

Microsoft Exchange Server 2007 Software

As an adopter of a MOAC textbook, your school's department is eligible for a free three-year membership to the MSDN Academic Alliance (MSDN AA). Through MSDN AA, full versions of Exchange Server 2007 are available for your use with this course. See your Wiley rep for details.

Preparing to Take the Microsoft Certified Technology Specialist (MCTS) Exam

The Microsoft Certified Technology Specialist (MCTS) certifications enable professionals to target specific technologies and to distinguish themselves by demonstrating in-depth knowledge and expertise in their specialized technologies. Microsoft Certified Technology Specialists are consistently capable of implementing, building, troubleshooting, and debugging a particular Microsoft Technology.

For organizations, the new generation of Microsoft certifications provides better skills verification tools that help with assessing not only in-demand skills on Exchange Server, but also the ability to quickly complete on-the-job tasks. Individuals will find it easier to identify and work towards the certification credential that meets their personal and professional goals.

To learn more about becoming a Microsoft Certified Professional and exam availability, visit www.microsoft.com/learning/mcp.

Microsoft Certifications for IT Professionals

The new Microsoft Certified Technology Specialist (MCTS) and Microsoft Certified IT Professional (MCITP) credentials provide IT professionals with a simpler and more targeted framework to showcase their technical skills in addition to the skills that are required for specific developer job roles.

The Microsoft Certified Professional (MCP), Microsoft Certified System Administrator (MCSA), and Microsoft Certified Systems Engineer (MCSE) credentials continue to provide IT professionals who use Microsoft Exchange Server 2003, Windows XP, and Windows Server 2003 with industry recognition and validation of their IT skills and experience.

Microsoft Certified Technology Specialist

The new Microsoft Certified Tehnology Specialist (MCTS) credential highlights your skills using a specific Microsoft technology. You can demonstrate your abilities as an IT professional or developer with in-depth knowledge of the Microsoft technology that you use today or are planning to deploy.

The MCTS certifications enable professionals to target specific technologies and to distinguish themselves by demonstrating in-depth knowledge and expertise in their specialized technologies. Microsoft Certified Technology Specialists are consistently capable of implementing, building, troubleshooting, and debugging a particular Microsoft technology.

You can learn more about the MCTS program at www.microsoft.com/learning/mcp/mcts.

Microsoft Certified IT Professional

The new Microsoft Certified IT Professional (MCITP) credential lets you highlight your specific area of expertise. Now, you can easily distinguish yourself as an expert in engineering, designing, and deploying messaging solutions with Microsoft Exchange Server 2007.

By becoming certified, you demonstrate to employers that you have achieved a predictable level of skill in the use of Microsoft technologies. Employers often require certification either as a condition of employment or as a condition of advancement within the company or other organization.

You can learn more about the MCITP program at www.microsoft.com/learning/mcp/mcitp.

The certification examinations are sponsored by Microsoft but administered through Microsoft's exam delivery partner Prometric.

Preparing to Take an Exam

Unless you are a very experienced user, you will need to use a test preparation course to prepare to complete the test correctly and within the time allowed. The *Microsoft Official Academic Course* series is designed to prepare you with a strong knowledge of all exam topics, and with some additional review and practice on your own, you should feel confident in your ability to pass the appropriate exam.

After you decide which exam to take, review the list of objectives for the exam. You can easily identify tasks that are included in the objective list by locating the Lesson Skill Matrix at the start of each lesson and the Certification Ready sidebars in the margin of the lessons in this book.

To take the MCTS test, visit www.microsoft.com/learning/mcp/mcts to locate your nearest testing center. Then call the testing center directly to schedule your test. The amount of advance notice you should provide will vary for different testing centers, and it typically depends on the number of computers available at the testing center, the number of other testers who have already been scheduled for the day on which you want to take the test, and the number of times per week that the testing center offers MCTS testing. In general, you should call to schedule your test at least two weeks prior to the date on which you want to take the test.

When you arrive at the testing center, you might be asked for proof of identity. A driver's license or passport is an acceptable form of identification. If you do not have either of these items of documentation, call your testing center and ask what alternative forms of identification will be accepted. If you are retaking a test, bring your MCTS identification number, which will have been given to you when you previously took the test. If you have not prepaid or if your organization has not already arranged to make payment for you, you will need to pay the test-taking fee when you arrive.

Student CD

The CD-ROM included with this book contains practice exams that will help you hone your knowledge before you take the MCTS Microsoft Exchange Server 2007 Configuration (Exam 70-236) certification examination. The exams are meant to provide practice for your certification exam and are also good reinforcement of the material covered in the course.

The enclosed Student CD will run automatically. Upon accepting the license agreement, you will proceed directly to the exams. The exams also can be accessed through the Assets folder located within the CD files.

Jason W. Eckert is a technical trainer, consultant, and best-selling author in the Information Technology (IT) industry. With over 20 IT certifications, 20 years of IT experience, and 18 published textbooks covering topics such as UNIX, Linux, Exchange Server, BlackBerry, Windows Server 2003, and Windows Vista, Jason brings his expertise to every class that he teaches at triOS College. Jason is also the triOS College Technology Faculty Head, where he continues to refine and improve the college technology programs. You can find more information about Jason @ http://www.jasoneckert.net.

Acknowledgments

MOAC Instructor Advisory Board

We thank our Instructor Advisory Board, an elite group of educators who has assisted us every step of the way in building these products. Advisory Board members have acted as our sounding board on key pedagogical and design decisions leading to the development of these compelling and innovative textbooks for future Information Workers. Their dedication to technology education is truly appreciated.

Charles DeSassure, Tarrant County College

Charles DeSassure is Department Chair and Instructor of Computer Science & Information Technology at Tarrant County College Southeast Campus, Arlington, Texas. He has had experience as a MIS Manager, system analyst, field technology analyst, LAN Administrator, microcomputer specialist, and public school teacher in South Carolina. DeSassure has worked in higher education for more than ten years and received the Excellence Award in Teaching from the National Institute for Staff and Organizational Development (NISOD). He currently serves on the Educational Testing Service (ETS) iSkills National Advisory Committee and chaired the Tarrant County College District Student Assessment Committee. He has written proposals and makes presentations at major educational conferences nationwide. DeSassure has served as a textbook reviewer for John Wiley & Sons and Prentice Hall. He teaches courses in information security, networking, distance learning, and computer literacy. DeSassure holds a master's degree in Computer Resources & Information Management from Webster University.

Kim Ehlert, Waukesha County Technical College

Kim Ehlert is the Microsoft Program Coordinator and a Network Specialist instructor at Waukesha County Technical College, teaching the full range of MCSE and networking courses for the past nine years. Prior to joining WCTC, Kim was a professor at the Milwaukee School of Engineering for five years where she oversaw the Novell Academic Education and the Microsoft IT Academy programs. She has a wide variety of industry experience including network design and management for Johnson Controls, local city fire departments, police departments, large church congregations, health departments, and accounting firms. Kim holds many industry certifications including MCDST, MCSE, Security+, Network+, Server+, MCT, and CNE.

Kim has a bachelor's degree in Information Systems and a master's degree in Business Administration from the University of Wisconsin Milwaukee. When she is not busy teaching, she enjoys spending time with her husband Gregg and their two children—Alex, 14, and Courtney, 17.

Penny Gudgeon, Corinthian Colleges, Inc.

Penny Gudgeon is the Program Manager for IT curriculum at Corinthian Colleges, Inc. Previously, she was responsible for computer programming and web curriculum for twenty-seven campuses in Corinthian's Canadian division, CDI College of Business, Technology and Health Care. Penny joined CDI College in 1997 as a computer programming instructor at one of the campuses outside of Toronto. Prior to joining CDI College, Penny taught productivity software at another Canadian college, the Academy of Learning, for four years. Penny has experience in helping students achieve their goals through various learning models from instructor-led to self-directed to online.

Before embarking on a career in education, Penny worked in the fields of advertising, marketing/sales, mechanical and electronic engineering technology, and computer programming. When not working from her home office or indulging her passion for lifelong learning, Penny likes to read mysteries, garden, and relax at home in Hamilton, Ontario, with her Shih-Tzu, Gracie.

Margaret Leary, Northern Virginia Community College

Margaret Leary is Professor of IST at Northern Virginia Community College, teaching Networking and Network Security Courses for the past ten years. She is the co-Principal Investigator on the CyberWATCH initiative, an NSF-funded regional consortium of higher education institutions and businesses working together to increase the number of network security personnel in the workforce. She also serves as a Senior Security Policy Manager and Research Analyst at Nortel Government Solutions and holds a CISSP certification.

Margaret holds a B.S.B.A. and MBA/Technology Management from the University of Phoenix, and is pursuing her Ph.D. in Organization and Management with an IT Specialization at Capella University. Her dissertation is titled "Quantifying the Discoverability of Identity Attributes in Internet-Based Public Records: Impact on Identity Theft and Knowledge-based Authentication." She has several other published articles in various government and industry magazines, notably on identity management and network security.

Wen Liu, ITT Educational Services, Inc.

Wen Liu is Director of Corporate Curriculum Development at ITT Educational Services, Inc. He joined the ITT corporate headquarters in 1998 as a Senior Network Analyst to plan and deploy the corporate WAN infrastructure. A year later he assumed the position of Corporate Curriculum Manager supervising the curriculum development of all IT programs. After he was promoted to the current position three years ago, he continued to manage the curriculum research and development for all the programs offered in the School of Information Technology in addition to supervising the curriculum development in other areas (such as Schools of Drafting and Design and Schools of Electronics Technology). Prior to his employment with ITT Educational Services, Liu was a Telecommunications Analyst at the state government of Indiana working on the state backbone project that provided Internet and telecommunications services to the public users such as K-12 and higher education institutions, government agencies, libraries, and healthcare facilities.

Wen Liu has an M.A. in Student Personnel Administration in Higher Education and an M.S. in Information and Communications Sciences from Ball State University, Indiana. He used to be the director of special projects on the board of directors of the Indiana Telecommunications User Association, and used to serve on Course Technology's IT Advisory Board. He is currently a member of the IEEE and its Computer Society.

Jared Spencer, Westwood College Online

Jared Spencer has been the Lead Faculty for Networking at Westwood College Online since 2006. He began teaching in 2001 and has taught both on-ground and online for a variety of institutions, including Robert Morris University and Point Park University. In addition to his academic background, he has more than fifteen years of industry experience working for companies including the Thomson Corporation and IBM.

Jared has a master's degree in Internet Information Systems and is currently ABD and pursuing his doctorate in Information Systems at Nova Southeastern University. He has authored several papers that have been presented at conferences and appeared in publications such as the Journal of Internet Commerce and the Journal of Information Privacy and Security (JIPC). He holds a number of industry certifications, including AIX (UNIX), A+, Network+, Security+, MCSA on Windows 2000, and MCSA on Windows 2003 Server.

We thank Scott Elliott, Christie Digital Systems, Inc., for his diligent review, providing invaluable feedback in the service of quality instructional materials.

Focus Group and Survey Participants

Finally, we thank the hundreds of instructors who participated in our focus groups and surveys to ensure that the Microsoft Official Academic Courses best met the needs of our customers.

Jean Aguilar, Mt. Hood Community College

Konrad Akens, Zane State College

Michael Albers, University of Memphis

Diana Anderson, Big Sandy Community & Technical College

Phyllis Anderson, Delaware County Community College

Judith Andrews, Feather River College

Damon Antos, American River College

Bridget Archer, Oakton Community College

Linda Arnold, Harrisburg Area Community College–Lebanon Campus

Neha Arya, Fullerton College

Mohammad Bajwa, Katharine Gibbs School–New York

Virginia Baker, University of Alaska Fairbanks

Carla Bannick, Pima Community College

Rita Barkley, Northeast Alabama Community College

Elsa Barr, Central Community College–Hastings

Ronald W. Barry, Ventura County Community College District

Elizabeth Bastedo, Central Carolina Technical College

Karen Baston, Waubonsee Community College

Karen Bean, Blinn College

Scott Beckstrand, Community College of Southern Nevada

Paulette Bell, Santa Rosa Junior College

Liz Bennett, Southeast Technical Institute

Nancy Bermea, Olympic College

Lucy Betz, Milwaukee Area Technical College

Meral Binbasioglu, Hofstra University

Catherine Binder, Strayer University & Katharine Gibbs School–Philadelphia

Terrel Blair, El Centro College

Ruth Blalock, Alamance Community College

Beverly Bohner, Reading Area Community College

Henry Bojack, Farmingdale State University

Matthew Bowie, Luna Community College

Julie Boyles, Portland Community College

Karen Brandt, College of the Albemarle

Stephen Brown, College of San Mateo

Jared Bruckner, Southern Adventist University

Pam Brune, Chattanooga State Technical Community College

Sue Buchholz, Georgia Perimeter College

Roberta Buczyna, Edison College

Angela Butler, Mississippi Gulf Coast Community College

Rebecca Byrd, Augusta Technical College

Kristen Callahan, Mercer County Community College

Judy Cameron, Spokane Community College

Dianne Campbell, Athens Technical College

Gena Casas, Florida Community College at Jacksonville

Jesus Castrejon, Latin Technologies

Gail Chambers, Southwest Tennessee Community College

Jacques Chansavang, Indiana University–Purdue University Fort Wayne

Nancy Chapko, Milwaukee Area Technical College

Rebecca Chavez, Yavapai College

Sanjiv Chopra, Thomas Nelson Community College

Greg Clements, Midland Lutheran College

Dayna Coker, Southwestern Oklahoma State University–Sayre Campus

Tamra Collins, Otero Junior College

Janet Conrey, Gavilan Community College

Carol Cornforth, West Virginia Northern Community College

Gary Cotton, American River College

Edie Cox, Chattahoochee Technical College

Rollie Cox, Madison Area Technical College

David Crawford, Northwestern Michigan College

J.K. Crowley, Victor Valley College

Rosalyn Culver, Washtenaw Community College

Sharon Custer, Huntington University

Sandra Daniels, New River Community College

Anila Das, Cedar Valley College

Brad Davis, Santa Rosa Junior College

Susan Davis, Green River Community College

Mark Dawdy, Lincoln Land Community College

Jennifer Day, Sinclair Community College

Carol Deane, Eastern Idaho Technical College

Julie DeBuhr, Lewis-Clark State College

Janis DeHaven, Central Community College

Drew Dekreon, University of Alaska–Anchorage

Joy DePover, Central Lakes College

Salli DiBartolo, Brevard Community College

Melissa Diegnau, Riverland Community College

Al Dillard, Lansdale School of Business

Marjorie Duffy, Cosumnes River College

Sarah Dunn, Southwest Tennessee Community College

Shahla Durany, Tarrant County College–South Campus

Kay Durden, University of Tennessee at Martin

Dineen Ebert, St. Louis Community College–Meramec

Donna Ehrhart, State University of New York–Brockport

Larry Elias, Montgomery County Community College

Glenda Elser, New Mexico State University at Alamogordo

Angela Evangelinos, Monroe County Community College

Angie Evans, Ivy Tech Community College of Indiana

Linda Farrington, Indian Hills Community College

Dana Fladhammer, Phoenix College

Richard Flores, Citrus College

Connie Fox, Community and Technical College at Institute of Technology West Virginia University

Wanda Freeman, Okefenokee Technical College

Brenda Freeman, Augusta Technical College

Susan Fry, Boise State University

Roger Fulk, Wright State University–Lake Campus

Sue Furnas, Collin County Community College District

Sandy Gabel, Vernon College

Laura Galvan, Fayetteville Technical Community College

Candace Garrod, Red Rocks Community College

Sherrie Geitgey, Northwest State Community College

Chris Gerig, Chattahoochee Technical College

Barb Gillespie, Cuyamaca College

Jessica Gilmore, Highline Community College

Pamela Gilmore, Reedley College

Debbie Glinert, Queensborough Community College

Steven Goldman, Polk Community College

Bettie Goodman, C.S. Mott Community College

Mike Grabill, Katharine Gibbs School–Philadelphia

Francis Green, Penn State University

Walter Griffin, Blinn College

Fillmore Guinn, Odessa College

Helen Haasch, Milwaukee Area Technical College

John Habal, Ventura College

Joy Haerens, Chaffey College

Norman Hahn, Thomas Nelson Community College

Kathy Hall, Alamance Community College

Teri Harbacheck, Boise State University

Linda Harper, Richland Community College

Maureen Harper, Indian Hills Community College

Steve Harris, Katharine Gibbs School–New York

Robyn Hart, Fresno City College

Darien Hartman, Boise State University

Gina Hatcher, Tacoma Community College

Winona T. Hatcher, Aiken Technical College

BJ Hathaway, Northeast Wisconsin Tech College

Cynthia Hauki, West Hills College–Coalinga

Mary L. Haynes, Wayne County Community College

Marcie Hawkins, Zane State College

Steve Hebrock, Ohio State University Agricultural Technical Institute

Sue Heistand, Iowa Central Community College

Heith Hennel, Valencia Community College

Donna Hendricks, South Arkansas Community College

Judy Hendrix, Dyersburg State Community College

Gloria Hensel, Matanuska-Susitna College University of Alaska Anchorage

Gwendolyn Hester, Richland College

Tammarra Holmes, Laramie County Community College

Dee Hobson, Richland College

Keith Hoell, Katharine Gibbs School–New York

Pashia Hogan, Northeast State Technical Community College

Susan Hoggard, Tulsa Community College

Kathleen Holliman, Wallace Community College Selma

Chastity Honchul, Brown Mackie College/Wright State University

Christie Hovey, Lincoln Land Community College

Peggy Hughes, Allegany College of Maryland

Sandra Hume, Chippewa Valley Technical College

John Hutson, Aims Community College

Celia Ing, Sacramento City College

Joan Ivey, Lanier Technical College

Barbara Jaffari, College of the Redwoods

Penny Jakes, University of Montana College of Technology

Eduardo Jaramillo, Peninsula College

Barbara Jauken, Southeast Community College

Susan Jennings, Stephen F. Austin State University

Leslie Jernberg, Eastern Idaho Technical College

Linda Johns, Georgia Perimeter College

Brent Johnson, Okefenokee Technical College

Mary Johnson, Mt. San Antonio College

Shirley Johnson, Trinidad State Junior College–Valley Campus

Sandra M. Jolley, Tarrant County College

Teresa Jolly, South Georgia Technical College

Dr. Deborah Jones, South Georgia Technical College

Margie Jones, Central Virginia Community College

Randall Jones, Marshall Community and Technical College

Diane Karlsbraaten, Lake Region State College

Teresa Keller, Ivy Tech Community College of Indiana

Charles Kemnitz, Pennsylvania College of Technology

Sandra Kinghorn, Ventura College

Bill Klein, Katharine Gibbs School–Philadelphia

Bea Knaapen, Fresno City College

Kit Kofoed, Western Wyoming Community College

Maria Kolatis, County College of Morris

Barry Kolb, Ocean County College

Karen Kuralt, University of Arkansas at Little Rock

Belva-Carole Lamb, Rogue Community College

Betty Lambert, Des Moines Area Community College

Anita Lande, Cabrillo College

Junnae Landry, Pratt Community College

Karen Lankisch, UC Clermont

David Lanzilla, Central Florida Community College

Nora Laredo, Cerritos Community College

Jennifer Larrabee, Chippewa Valley Technical College

Debra Larson, Idaho State University

Barb Lave, Portland Community College

Audrey Lawrence, Tidewater Community College

Deborah Layton, Eastern Oklahoma State College

Larry LeBlanc, Owen Graduate School–Vanderbilt University

Philip Lee, Nashville State Community College

Michael Lehrfeld, Brevard Community College

Vasant Limaye, Southwest Collegiate Institute for the Deaf – Howard College

Anne C. Lewis, Edgecombe Community College

Stephen Linkin, Houston Community College

Peggy Linston, Athens Technical College

Hugh Lofton, Moultrie Technical College

Donna Lohn, Lakeland Community College

Jackie Lou, Lake Tahoe Community College

Donna Love, Gaston College

Curt Lynch, Ozarks Technical Community College

Sheilah Lynn, Florida Community College–Jacksonville

Pat R. Lyon, Tomball College

Bill Madden, Bergen Community College

Heather Madden, Delaware Technical & Community College

Donna Madsen, Kirkwood Community College

Jane Maringer-Cantu, Gavilan College

Suzanne Marks, Bellevue Community College

Carol Martin, Louisiana State University–Alexandria

Cheryl Martucci, Diablo Valley College

Roberta Marvel, Eastern Wyoming College

Tom Mason, Brookdale Community College

Mindy Mass, Santa Barbara City College

Dixie Massaro, Irvine Valley College

Rebekah May, Ashland Community & Technical College

Emma Mays-Reynolds, Dyersburg State Community College

Timothy Mayes, Metropolitan State College of Denver

Reggie McCarthy, Central Lakes College

Matt McCaskill, Brevard Community College

Kevin McFarlane, Front Range Community College

Donna McGill, Yuba Community College

Terri McKeever, Ozarks Technical Community College

Patricia McMahon, South Suburban College

Sally McMillin, Katharine Gibbs School–Philadelphia

Charles McNerney, Bergen Community College

Lisa Mears, Palm Beach Community College

Imran Mehmood, ITT Technical Institute–King of Prussia Campus

Virginia Melvin, Southwest Tennessee Community College

Jeanne Mercer, Texas State Technical College

Denise Merrell, Jefferson Community & Technical College

Catherine Merrikin, Pearl River Community College

Diane D. Mickey, Northern Virginia Community College

Darrelyn Miller, Grays Harbor College

Sue Mitchell, Calhoun Community College

Jacquie Moldenhauer, Front Range Community College

Linda Motonaga, Los Angeles City College

Sam Mryyan, Allen County Community College

Cindy Murphy, Southeastern Community College

Ryan Murphy, Sinclair Community College

Sharon E. Nastav, Johnson County Community College

Christine Naylor, Kent State University Ashtabula

Haji Nazarian, Seattle Central Community College

Nancy Noe, Linn-Benton Community College

Jennie Noriega, San Joaquin Delta College

Linda Nutter, Peninsula College

Thomas Omerza, Middle Bucks Institute of Technology

Edith Orozco, St. Philip's College

Dona Orr, Boise State University

Joanne Osgood, Chaffey College

Janice Owens, Kishwaukee College

Tatyana Pashnyak, Bainbridge College

John Partacz, College of DuPage

Tim Paul, Montana State University–Great Falls

Joseph Perez, South Texas College

Mike Peterson, Chemeketa Community College

Dr. Karen R. Petitto, West Virginia Wesleyan College

Terry Pierce, Onandaga Community College

Ashlee Pieris, Raritan Valley Community College

Jamie Pinchot, Thiel College

Michelle Poertner, Northwestern Michigan College

Betty Posta, University of Toledo

Deborah Powell, West Central Technical College

Mark Pranger, Rogers State University

Carolyn Rainey, Southeast Missouri State University

Linda Raskovich, Hibbing Community College

Leslie Ratliff, Griffin Technical College

Mar-Sue Ratzke, Rio Hondo Community College

Roxy Reissen, Southeastern Community College

Silvio Reyes, Technical Career Institutes

Patricia Rishavy, Anoka Technical College

Jean Robbins, Southeast Technical Institute

Carol Roberts, Eastern Maine Community College and University of Maine

Teresa Roberts, Wilson Technical Community College

Vicki Robertson, Southwest Tennessee Community College

Betty Rogge, Ohio State Agricultural Technical Institute

Lynne Rusley, Missouri Southern State University

Claude Russo, Brevard Community College

Ginger Sabine, Northwestern Technical College

Steven Sachs, Los Angeles Valley College

Joanne Salas, Olympic College

Lloyd Sandmann, Pima Community College–Desert Vista Campus

Beverly Santillo, Georgia Perimeter College

Theresa Savarese, San Diego City College

Sharolyn Sayers, Milwaukee Area Technical College

Judith Scheeren, Westmoreland County Community College

Adolph Scheiwe, Joliet Junior College

Marilyn Schmid, Asheville-Buncombe Technical Community College

Janet Sebesy, Cuyahoga Community College

Phyllis T. Shafer, Brookdale Community College

Ralph Shafer, Truckee Meadows Community College

Anne Marie Shanley, County College of Morris

Shelia Shelton, Surry Community College

Merilyn Shepherd, Danville Area Community College

Susan Sinele, Aims Community College

Beth Sindt, Hawkeye Community College

Andrew Smith, Marian College

Brenda Smith, Southwest Tennessee Community College

Lynne Smith, State University of New York–Delhi

Rob Smith, Katharine Gibbs School–Philadelphia

Tonya Smith, Arkansas State University–Mountain Home

Del Spencer – Trinity Valley Community College

Jeri Spinner, Idaho State University

Eric Stadnik, Santa Rosa Junior College

Karen Stanton, Los Medanos College

Meg Stoner, Santa Rosa Junior College

Beverly Stowers, Ivy Tech Community College of Indiana

Marcia Stranix, Yuba College

Kim Styles, Tri-County Technical College

Sylvia Summers, Tacoma Community College

Beverly Swann, Delaware Technical & Community College

Ann Taff, Tulsa Community College

Mike Theiss, University of Wisconsin–Marathon Campus

Romy Thiele, Cañada College

Sharron Thompson, Portland Community College

Ingrid Thompson-Sellers, Georgia Perimeter College

Barbara Tietsort, University of Cincinnati–Raymond Walters College

Janine Tiffany, Reading Area Community College

Denise Tillery, University of Nevada Las Vegas

Susan Trebelhorn, Normandale Community College

Noel Trout, Santiago Canyon College

Cheryl Turgeon, Asnuntuck Community College

Steve Turner, Ventura College

Sylvia Unwin, Bellevue Community College

Lilly Vigil, Colorado Mountain College

Sabrina Vincent, College of the Mainland

Mary Vitrano, Palm Beach Community College

Brad Vogt, Northeast Community College

Cozell Wagner, Southeastern Community College

Carolyn Walker, Tri-County Technical College

Sherry Walker, Tulsa Community College

Qi Wang, Tacoma Community College

Betty Wanielista, Valencia Community College

Marge Warber, Lanier Technical College–Forsyth Campus

Marjorie Webster, Bergen Community College

Linda Wenn, Central Community College

Mark Westlund, Olympic College

Carolyn Whited, Roane State Community College

Winona Whited, Richland College

Jerry Wilkerson, Scott Community College

Joel Willenbring, Fullerton College

Barbara Williams, WITC Superior

Charlotte Williams, Jones County Junior College

Bonnie Willy, Ivy Tech Community College of Indiana

Diane Wilson, J. Sargeant Reynolds Community College

James Wolfe, Metropolitan Community College

Marjory Wooten, Lanier Technical College

Mark Yanko, Hocking College

Alexis Yusov, Pace University

Naeem Zaman, San Joaquin Delta College

Kathleen Zimmerman, Des Moines Area Community College

We also thank Lutz Ziob, Merrick Van Dongen, Jim LeValley, Bruce Curling, Joe Wilson, Rob Linsky, Jim Clark, Jim Palmeri, and Scott Serna at Microsoft for their encouragement and support in making the Microsoft Official Academic Course programs the finest instructional materials for mastering the newest Microsoft technologies for both students and instructors.

Brief Contents

www.wiley.com/college/microsoft or
call the MOAC Toll-Free Number: 1+(888) 764-7001 (U.S. & Canada only)

Contents

Exchange Server 2007 Basics

LESSON SKILL MATRIX

TECHNOLOGY SKILL	OBJECTIVE DOMAIN
Identify the purpose and usage of Exchange Server 2007.	Supplemental
Describe standard email terminology.	Supplemental
Understand email relay and DNS MX record usage.	Supplemental
Explain the various types and uses of email protocols.	Supplemental
Identify previous versions of Exchange Server and their features.	Supplemental
List the new features introduced in Exchange Server 2007.	Supplemental
Describe the function and usage of Exchange Server 2007 server roles.	Supplemental

KEY TERMS

Active Directory (AD)
ActiveSync
Client Access Server (CAS)
cmdlets
Domain Name System (DNS)
Edge Transport Role (Edge)
EdgeSync
Exchange Management Console (EMC)
Exchange Management Shell (EMS)
Extended Simple Mail Transfer Protocol (ESMTP)
Hub Transport Role (Hub)

Hypertext Transfer Protocol (HTTP)
Internet Message Access Protocol Version 4 (IMAP4)
Mail Delivery Agent (MDA)
Mail Transfer Agent (MTA)
Mail User Agent (MUA)
Mailbox Role
MAPI clients
Messaging Application Programming Interface (MAPI)
Messaging Records Management (MRM)
Outlook Anywhere

Outlook Web Access (OWA)
Post Office Protocol Version 3 (POP3)
PowerShell
public folders
round robin
RPC over HTTP/HTTPS
Secure Socket Layer (SSL)
Simple Mail Transfer Protocol (SMTP)
smart host
Transport Layer Security (TLS)
Unified Messaging (UM)

■ Understanding Course Requirements

THE BOTTOM LINE   Exchange Server is a messaging and collaboration software product from Microsoft. Exchange Server 2007 is the most comprehensive and feature-rich version of Exchange Server to date.

Microsoft Exchange Server is a messaging software product that is used in many organizations today. Although its main use is to provide email services, Exchange Server can also be used for collaboration such as scheduling and calendaring.

Exchange Server 2007 provides a new interface that is easier to use and a new role-based structure that is scalable to very large organizations. Whether you are new to Exchange Server or have experience maintaining a previous version of Exchange Server or other email system, you will be introduced to many new concepts and procedures as you learn Exchange Server 2007.

In this course, we examine how email systems work to deliver email across networks and the Internet as well as how Exchange Server 2007 works with the Windows Active Directory service to provide for email delivery within an organization.

You will learn how to install, configure, maintain, and troubleshoot Exchange Server 2007 in a variety of different environments and scenarios. More specifically, you will learn how to configure email clients, user settings, mailboxes, public folders, email protocols, address lists, and the Active Directory service. Additionally, you will learn how to backup, restore, monitor, secure, and cluster email servers.

■ Email Fundamentals

THE BOTTOM LINE

Because email plays an important role in our lives, it is exciting to learn how Microsoft Exchange Server 2007 works within an organization to relay email across the Internet. However, you must first have a solid grasp of email terminology and concepts. Additionally, it is vital to understand how email is sent from your email client to email servers around your organization and the Internet. More specifically, this includes understanding how emails are relayed using the DNS system on the Internet, as well a general knowledge of the various email protocols that work together to relay emails from one computer to another.

How Email Works

Email is one of the oldest applications of the Internet. Understanding how MUAs, MTAs and MDAs work together to relay email will help you understand how Microsoft Exchange Server 2007 relays email in various environments.

Electronic mail (email) consists of written messages that are sent between people on a computer or computer network. Long before the Internet, universities and other academic institutions that had large computer systems used forms of email. Since 1965, Massachusetts Institute of Technology (MIT), for example, used email as a means of collaboration between computer programmers.

When ARPANET became popular as an interuniversity computer network in the 1980s, email was considered its main application. ARPANET eventually became known as the Internet in the 1990s and is the largest interconnected series of networks in the world. Email was its first "killer application."

Today, nearly everyone who has a computer and Internet access from an ***Internet Service Provider (ISP)*** sends email to communicate with friends and family.

More important, email is used by nearly every organization as its main form of internal and external communication. Organizations in the past communicated almost exclusively by meetings or telephone, which can be time consuming for certain tasks that can be quickly communicated via email.

For users who send email (called ***senders***), email is typically created and sent using an email client program called a ***Mail User Agent (MUA)***. Common MUAs include:

- Microsoft Outlook
- Microsoft Outlook Express
- Windows Mail
- Microsoft Entourage
- Mozilla Thunderbird
- Apple Mail
- Eudora
- Web browsers such as Internet Explorer and Mozilla Firefox (if connecting to web-based email systems like Gmail, Hotmail, and Yahoo Mail)

Each of these MUAs has different user interfaces and configuration options. We will examine the configuration of different MUAs in a later lesson.

Once an email is written using an MUA and addressed to a target user (called a ***recipient***), it must be sent to an email server. Common email servers include:

- Microsoft Exchange
- Lotus Domino
- Novell GroupWise
- Sendmail
- Postfix

The email server contains a program called the ***Mail Transfer Agent (MTA)*** that decides where to send the email that it receives from the MUA.

If the email needs to be delivered to a recipient in another organization, then the MTA sends the email across the Internet to the target email server for the other organization (see Figure 1-1). The target email server contains a program called a ***Mail Delivery Agent (MDA)*** that it uses to deliver the mail to the correct mailbox on the email server. Recipients will then use their MUA to obtain the email from their mailbox.

Figure 1-1

Internet Email Relay

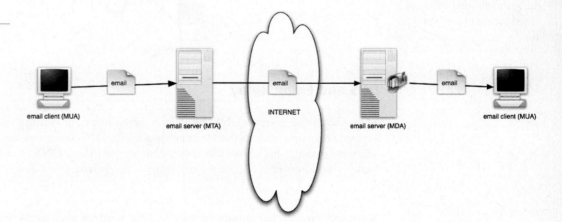

Alternatively, if the email needs to be delivered to a user within the same organization, then the MTA sends the email to its own MDA, which it then uses to deliver the email to the correct mailbox for the recipient. Recipients can then use their own MUA to retrieve the email as shown in Figure 1-2.

Figure 1-2

Internal Email Relay

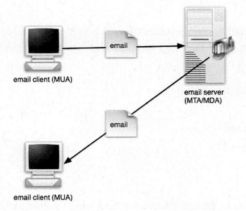

Regardless of whether the MTA and MDA are within the same organization, the process whereby an MTA sends email to an MDA is commonly called **email relay**.

To send email back and forth, email servers typically have both an MTA and an MDA. Furthermore, MUAs can connect across the Internet to an email server to send and receive emails. This is common for remote and home users who connect across the Internet to the email server at their company or ISP. This organization is shown in Figure 1-3.

Figure 1-3

Internet Mail Relay and Access

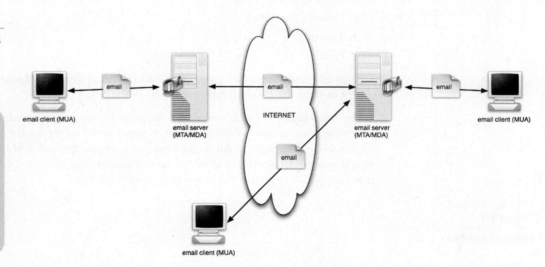

TAKE NOTE*

The process for sending email described in this section is a simplified overview. The actual process is more complex and is explained in more depth throughout this book.

DNS and Email Relay

Domain Name System (DNS) provides a robust means of locating resources on local and remote networks such as the Internet. As a result, DNS is used to locate destination email servers by using special records. Understanding how these DNS records work enables you to understand how email is relayed across networks to remote email servers and smart hosts.

To connect to another computer on a TCP/IP network such as the Internet, you need to obtain the IP address of the destination computer. Unfortunately, IP addresses are numbers, and numbers are hard to remember.

Domain Name System (DNS) provides us with an easy way around this problem. DNS has a hierarchical naming convention (also called a namespace) that starts with an imaginary root (referred to with a period ".") and several top-level domain names that describe the type of organization.

The most common top-level domain names in DNS include:

- com (commercial)
- org (nonprofit organization)
- net (an organization that maintains a network)
- edu (educational institution)
- gov (government)
- *abbr* (a two-letter *abbreviation* for the country; for example *us* refers to the United States and *ca* refers to Canada)

A DNS name also contains a second-level domain name that refers to the actual name of the organization. For example, microsoft.com is the commercial organization called Microsoft.

Under the second-level domain can be other subdomain names or the names of individual computer hosts. For example, www.microsoft.com refers to the computer called www (running the web server service) in the commercial organization called Microsoft. Similarly, server1.north.bell.ca refers to the computer called server1 in the north division of a Canadian organization called Bell. Both www.microsoft.com and server1.north.bell.ca are called *Fully Qualified Domain Names (FQDNs)* because they contain the name of the host computer.

To simplify resource location, each FQDN must be matched to a corresponding IP address on a DNS server on the Internet. The records on a DNS server that match an FQDN to an IP address are called *A (host) records.*

Because the DNS namespace is hierarchal, each domain in DNS has its own DNS server(s). For example, Microsoft will have one or more DNS server that holds the FQDNs and IP addresses for computers within the microsoft.com domain. Furthermore, all DNS servers, including the DNS servers at your company or ISP, know how to query other DNS servers within the DNS hierarchy.

Thus, when you type www.microsoft.com into a web browser, your computer contacts the DNS server listed in TCP/IP properties for your network interface and resolves the name www.microsoft.com to the correct IP address using the appropriate A record. This process is called *DNS name resolution*. Next, your web browser contacts the Microsoft web server by IP address to obtain a web page. The whole process is illustrated in Figure 1-4.

Figure 1-4

DNS Name Resolution

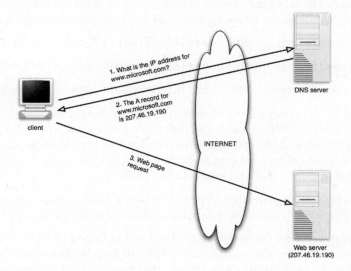

TAKE NOTE✷

You can test DNS name resolution using nslookup.exe at a Windows command prompt.

When configuring an MUA, you need to specify the MTA that it will use by IP address, NetBIOS name, or FQDN. If you specify the MTA using an FQDN, then a DNS server on your network must have an entry that will resolve the name to an IP address.

Alternatively, when sending email, you never address the target email server using an FQDN. Instead, email addresses are typically sent to the target domain and not the target email server. For example, to email Bob Jones at Microsoft, you would use an email such as bob .jones@microsoft.com instead of bob.jones@mailserver1.microsoft.com.

To accommodate this, DNS servers contain **Mail eXchanger (MX) records** that are used to indicate the email server for a particular domain to which email should be forwarded.

When an MUA sends an email (addressed to a recipient such as bob.jones@microsoft.com) to an MTA, the MTA uses the DNS server listed in its own TCP/IP properties to resolve the MX record for the target domain (i.e., microsoft.com). After the MX record has been resolved to the IP address of a target email server using the associated A record, the MTA forwards the email to the MDA on the target email server, which then delivers the email to the correct mailbox based on the recipient's name in the email address (i.e., bob.jones). The recipient can then access the email from his mailbox as shown in Figure 1-5.

Figure 1-5

Resolving MX Records

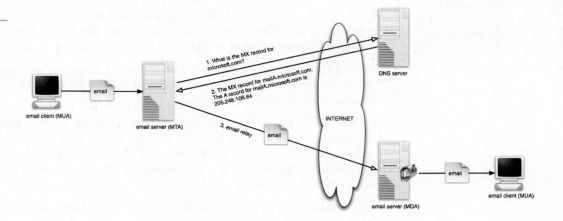

Because there may be more than one email server in a particular organization, domains may have more than one MX record. Each MX record is given a **priority number** when created. The lower the priority number, the greater the chance that it will be a target for email. Consider the following MX records for the microsoft.com domain:

```
microsoft.com    MX    mailA.microsoft.com    priority=10

microsoft.com    MX    mailB.microsoft.com    priority=20

microsoft.com    MX    mailC.microsoft.com    priority=30
```

If an MTA queries a DNS server for the MX record for microsoft.com, the DNS server returns all three MX records and their priority numbers. The MTA then tries to contact the email server with the lowest priority number first (mailA.microsoft.com). If mailA.microsoft .com could not be contacted, then the MTA tries to contact the email server with the second lowest priority (mailB.microsoft.com), and so on.

This is useful in companies that wish to have a backup email server. In the previous example, mailB.microsoft.com would only be contacted if mailA.microsoft.com was unavailable.

Similarly, some organizations use smart hosts to receive email from the Internet. A **smart host** is an email server that receives inbound email and simply forwards it to another email server within the organization. Smart hosts often have antivirus and spam-filtering software that stops malicious and unsolicited email from entering the company.

TAKE NOTE✷

ISPs commonly offer smart host services for many organizations. Email is sent to the smart host at the ISP and forwarded to the organization's email server after being filtered.

The MX record for the smart host should have a lower priority number than other MX records. In the earlier example, mailA.microsoft.com could be the smart host email server and would receive all emails by default. If mailA.microsoft.com was unavailable, then email would be sent to the internal mail server (mailB.microsoft.com) or to the backup internal mail server (mailC.microsoft.com) if mailB.microsoft.com was unavailable.

In larger organizations, there may be several MX records for different email servers that have the same priority:

```
microsoft.com      MX      mailA.microsoft.com      priority=10

microsoft.com      MX      mailB.microsoft.com      priority=10

microsoft.com      MX      mailC.microsoft.com      priority=10
```

Just as before, when the MTA queries a DNS server for the MX record for microsoft.com, the DNS server returns all three MX records. Because the priority numbers are the same on all three records, the MTA tries to contact the email server that is first in the list (mailA.microsoft.com). If mailA.microsoft.com could not be contacted, then the MTA tries to contact the email server that is second in the list (mailB.microsoft.com), and so on.

Although this initially achieves the same result, DNS will rotate the list of MX records each time an MTA sends an MX record query. This feature of DNS is called **round robin**. Thus, the next time an MTA queries the MX records for microsoft.com, it will receive the following list:

```
microsoft.com      MX      mailB.microsoft.com      priority=10

microsoft.com      MX      mailC.microsoft.com      priority=10

microsoft.com      MX      mailA.microsoft.com      priority=10
```

Now, the first email server to be contacted is mailB.microsoft.com. Similarly, the third MX record query will return a list with mailC.microsoft.com at the top of the list and the fourth MX record query will return the original list with mailA.microsoft.com at the top of the list.

By keeping the same priorities on MX records, you can balance the load of traffic evenly across each of the three email servers. These three email servers may be internal email servers, or they may be smart hosts that will forward email to internal mail servers.

Creating MX records in DNS is a common task after installing Exchange Server 2007. As a result, MX record creation is discussed in Lesson 4, "Configuring a New Exchange Server."

TEST DNS NAME RESOLUTION USING NSLOOKUP

GET READY. Log on to Windows Server 2003, and open a command prompt window.

1. Type nslookup at the command prompt and press **Enter**.

2. At the **nslookup** prompt, type **www.yahoo.com** and press **Enter**. Notice the IP address for the Yahoo web server. The nslookup.exe command queries A records by default.

3. At the nslookup prompt, type **set q=mx** and press **Enter**. This tells nslookup.exe to obtain MX records on future queries.

4. At the nslookup prompt, type **yahoo.com** and press **Enter**. Notice that there are several MX records with the same priority (or preference) for the yahoo.com domain. Record the order of the MX records. Also note that the nslookup.exe command returns the IP addresses for each email server from the associated A records.

5. At the nslookup prompt, type **yahoo.com** and press **Enter**. Notice that the order of the MX records for the yahoo.com domain is different from the previous step due to the round robin feature of DNS.

6. Type **exit** at the nslookup prompt and press **Enter**.

7. Type **exit** at the command prompt and press **Enter**.

ANOTHER WAY

You can also type **set type=mx** at the nslookup prompt to tell nslookup .exe to obtain MX records on future queries.

Email Formats and Protocols

Today, email systems are very complex and involve several different technologies for sending and receiving emails. Possessing knowledge of the many protocols used to send and receive emails is a vital asset when examining the structure of Exchange Server 2007.

When you type an email into an MUA, the text itself is either left unformatted (called *plain text*) or formatted using *Hypertext Markup Language (HTML)* or *Rich Text Format (RTF)* to allow different font, colors, and pictures.

Regardless of the email format, MUAs, MTAs, and MDAs must also use specific *email protocols* when sending email across a network. The most common email protocols include:

- SMTP (Simple Mail Transfer Protocol)
- SMTPS (Secure Simple Mail Transfer Protocol)
- ESMTP (Extended Simple Mail Transfer Protocol)
- ESMTPS (Secure Extended Simple Mail Transfer Protocol)
- POP3 (Post Office Protocol Version 3)
- POP3S (Secure Post Office Protocol Version 3)
- IMAP4 (Internet Message Access Protocol Version 4)
- IMAP4S (Secure Internet Message Access Protocol Version 4)
- HTTP (Hypertext Transfer Protocol)
- HTTPS (Secure Hypertext Transfer Protocol)
- RPC (Remote Procedure Call)
- RPC (Remote Procedure Call) over HTTP/HTTPS
- ActiveSync

TAKE NOTE*

All protocols that end with S (SMTPS, ESMTPS, POP3S, IMAP4S, and HTTPS) use *Secure Socket Layer (SSL)* encryption or *Transport Layer Security (TLS)* encryption to protect the contents of emails.

The protocols available depend on whether the email is being sent from an MUA to an MTA, from an MTA to an MDA, or from a mailbox to an MUA as shown in Figure 1-6. For example, when an MUA sends email to an MTA, one of the following protocols may be used:

- SMTP/SMTPS
- ESMTP/ESMTPS
- HTTP/HTTPS
- RPC
- RPC over HTTP/HTTPS
- ActiveSync

Alternatively, when an MUA receives email from a mailbox, it uses only one of the following protocols:

- POP3/POP3S
- IMAP4/IMAP4S
- HTTP/HTTPS
- RPC
- RPC over HTTP/HTTPS
- ActiveSync

Finally, when an MTA relays email to an MDA, it can use one of the following protocols only:

- SMTP/SMTPS
- ESMTP/ESMTPS
- RPC
- RPC over HTTP/HTTPS

Figure 1-6

Email Protocols

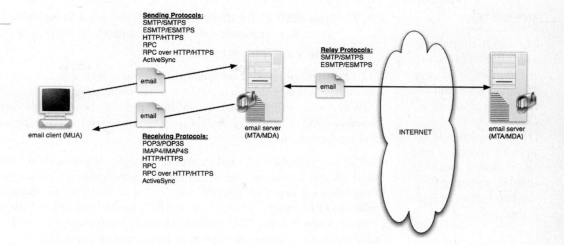

You can optionally con-
figure POP3 to leave a
copy of emails in your
mailbox on the email
server.

The POP3 and IMAP4 protocols are very similar and designed for obtaining emails from the
mailbox on an email server. By default, POP3 downloads and erases the email from the mailbox on the email server, whereas IMAP4 allows you to view emails while leaving a copy in the
mailbox on the email server. In addition, IMAP4 can support larger emails than POP3.

Although IMAP4 was designed as a replacement for POP3, POP3 continues to be one of the
most common email protocols on the Internet between ISPs and home clients.

The SMTP and ESMTP protocols were specifically designed to send emails rather than
obtain them. When you configure a POP3 or IMAP4 email account in an MUA, you must
supply the name or IP address of the email server that hosts the POP3 or IMAP4 service to
receive email, as well as the name or IP address of a server that hosts the SMTP service so
that you can send email.

ESMTP is an improved version of SMTP that has greater support for embedded graphics and
attachments in emails and is the most common form of SMTP used today between email
servers. To see which version of SMTP your email server accepts, you can use the telnet.exe
program from a client computer to connect to the email server on the SMTP/ESMTP port
(25 by default). If the email server accepts the EHLO command in your telnet session, it supports ESMTP. Alternatively, if the email server accepts the HELO command in your telnet
session, it only supports SMTP.

Although email servers and clients use the term SMTP in most of their configuration
options, they actually mean ESMTP. As a result, SMTP is often used when referring to
both SMTP and ESMTP.

 VERIFY ESMTP SUPPORT ON AN EMAIL SERVER

GET READY. Log on to Windows Server 2003, and open a command prompt window.

If you are trying this
exercise on a home
Internet connection and
you do not receive any
response from a target
email server, your ISP
may not allow traffic
from your home com-
puter on port 25.

1. Type **nslookup** at the command prompt and press **Enter**.
2. At the nslookup prompt, type **set q=mx** and press **Enter**.
3. At the nslookup prompt, type **yahoo.com** and press **Enter**. Record the IP address
   of the first Yahoo email server.
4. Type **exit** at the nslookup prompt and press **Enter**.
5. Type **telnet *IP_address* 25** at the nslookup prompt (where ***IP_address*** refers to
   the IP address of the first Yahoo email server from Step 3) and press **Enter**.
6. Type **EHLO** at the command prompt and press **Enter**. Notice that the Yahoo email
   server supports ESMTP.

The OWA interface in a web browser is not as user friendly as the interface in an email client program such as Outlook. As a result, OWA was designed as an easily accessible back-up method of checking email in the event that the email client program is inaccessible.

7. Type **HELO** at the command prompt and press **Enter**. Notice that the Yahoo email server has backwards compatibility support for SMTP.

8. Close your command window.

HTTP is typically used if the email server hosts a Web site that allows you to view and compose emails using your web browser or email client program. Microsoft **Outlook Web Access (OWA)** comes with Exchange Server 2007 and may be used with **Internet Information Services (IIS)** to provide a way for users to connect remotely using a web browser to check and send email.

RPC-based protocols are used to provide a variety of protocols across a network. Microsoft Outlook and Entourage clients can use RPCs alongside the Microsoft **Messaging Application Programming Interface (MAPI)** component of Windows to take advantage of all the features available in Exchange Server. However, RPC-based protocols are not well suited for use with remote clients because RPC traffic is relatively bandwidth intensive compared to other protocols and requires unnecessary ports to be opened on firewalls.

Because Microsoft email clients such as Outlook and Entourage can use MAPI and RPCs to send and receive emails, these clients are often called **MAPI clients** in Exchange Server 2007. Likewise, the term **MAPI RPC** usually refers to the MAPI implementation of the RPC email protocol.

As a result of these limitations, Outlook 2003 and later clients can use RPC over HTTP to connect to a remote Microsoft Exchange server. RPCs are encapsulated in HTTP packets in Outlook before they are sent across the Internet to an RPC over HTTP proxy, which removes the encapsulation and forwards the RPCs to the Microsoft Exchange server. In Microsoft Exchange Server 2007, RPC over HTTP is called **Outlook Anywhere**.

ActiveSync is a protocol based on HTTP and XML that can be used by some browser-enabled cellular telephones (called **smart phones**) to access emails from a Microsoft Exchange server. Any smart phone running the Windows Mobile operating system can use the ActiveSync protocol.

■ Introducing Exchange Server 2007

THE BOTTOM LINE

Now that you have an understanding of email systems, you can apply that knowledge to Exchange Server 2007. In addition to several new features, Exchange Server 2007 introduces a role-based structure that is radically different from the structure used in previous versions of Exchange. Understanding the features and structure of Exchange Server 2007 compared to its predecessors is vital when deploying and configuring Exchange Server 2007 email servers within your organization.

Exchange Server Overview

Prior to Exchange Server 2007, there were three other major versions of Exchange Server. Understanding their features will help you understand how Exchange Server 2007 operates in a mixed environment.

Exchange Server is Microsoft's email server product. In addition to the typical MTA and MDA functions, Exchange Server has several extra features to enhance business productivity (such as personal calendars, scheduling, and contact management) that work with MUAs.

TAKE NOTE*

Only MAPI clients can take full advantage of all the features in Exchange Server.

There are four main versions of Exchange that are used in organizations today:

- Exchange Server 5.5
- Exchange Server 2000
- Exchange Server 2003
- Exchange Server 2007

Microsoft originally developed Exchange Server for its own internal use to replace its UNIX-based email system. As a result, the first commercial release of Exchange Server started at version 4.0 in 1996. However, Exchange Server didn't gain market momentum until 1997 when Exchange Server 5.5 was released. Exchange Server 5.5 had full support for SMTP as well as the International Telecommunication Union (ITU) X.400 and X.500 standards. ***X.400*** defines the rules for sending email today, whereas ***X.500*** defines the structure and use of directory services such as Novell eDirectory and Microsoft ***Active Directory (AD)***. In addition, Exchange 5.5 made efficient use of ***public folders***, which were storage areas on the email server that could be used to store email and other types of message data such as newsgroup postings for easy organization and sharing among email recipients.

Exchange 5.5 also introduced the OWA web-based email interface to allow remote clients the ability to check their email with their web browser. For fast storage and retrieval of email, Exchange 5.5 stores mailboxes in an email ***database*** on the hard drive of the Exchange server.

Exchange Server 2000 was released shortly after Windows 2000 and added better clustering support, larger email database sizes, and the ability to combine email databases into ***storage groups*** for better database management. It was also the first version of Exchange Server that required the Microsoft Active Directory service.

Exchange Server 2007 is closely integrated with the Active Directory service. For more information on Active Directory, refer to Lesson 2, "Working with Active Directory."

Exchange Server 2003 followed the release of Windows Server 2003 and had tools that could easily upgrade Exchange Server 5.5 and 2000 email servers. As a result, many organizations that deployed Exchange Server 5.5 did not upgrade their email servers until Exchange Server 2003 was available. In addition to the features in previous versions, Exchange Server 2003 added support for disaster recovery using the ***recovery storage group (RSG)***, as well as ActiveSync and spam filtering. However, Exchange Server 2003 could be installed only on 32-bit versions of Windows 2000 Server and Windows Server 2003.

Exchange Server 2007 offers many different tools and features compared to previous versions of Exchange Server as will be discussed in the next section.

What's New in Exchange Server 2007

Exchange Server 2007 contains many new features and improvements that make it Microsoft's most advanced email server today. Understanding these features and improvements is essential before deploying Exchange Server 2007 in a Windows network environment.

Like previous versions of Exchange Server, Exchange Server 2007 comes in two editions: Standard and Enterprise. The Enterprise edition contains more support for hardware and extra features that are unavailable in the Standard edition.

Exchange Server 2007 has a vastly different structure compared to previous versions of Exchange Server.

Although you can download a trial 32-bit (x86) version of Exchange Server 2007 for testing purposes, the commercial version only runs on 64-bit (x86-64) computers with a 64-bit version of Windows Server 2003. Because previous versions of Exchange ran only on 32-bit computers, organizations can no longer perform in-place upgrades to Exchange Server 2007. Instead, organizations must purchase new hardware to run Exchange Server 2007 and migrate existing mailboxes to the new servers.

XREF If you want to install Exchange Server 2007 on a 64-bit version of Windows Server 2008, you must install Exchange Server 2007 Service Pack 1 (SP1) or greater. See Lesson 3, "Deploying Exchange Server 2007" for more information.

Exchange Server 2007 has several new features that make it an attractive choice for email relay. These features include:

1. Enhanced performance.

   Because Exchange Server 2007 only runs in 64-bit production environments, it can take advantage of more than 4 GB of physical RAM. Having more than 4 GB of RAM allows Exchange Server to speed up Input/Output (I/O) requests to hard disks as well as support more email databases and storage groups.

   Exchange Server 2007 is limited to 5 databases and storage groups on a single server for Standard edition and 50 databases and storage groups on a single server for Enterprise edition. For comparison, Exchange Server 2003 was limited to 1 database and storage group for Standard edition or 20 databases and 4 storage groups for Enterprise edition.

   Databases also have a faster structure in Exchange Server 2007 than in previous versions of Exchange Server. The smallest writable unit within an email database is called a *page*. A larger database page size increases the likelihood that an entire email will be read using a single I/O request. The 8 KB page size used in Exchange Server 2007 databases is twice the page size used in previous versions of Exchange and adds to the overall speed of Exchange Server.

2. Unlimited database size.

   Previous versions of Exchange Server had a maximum database size of 16 terabytes (TB). Exchange Server 2007 database sizes are theoretically unlimited. In practice, the maximum database size on Exchange Server 2007 is only limited by hardware capability and backup requirements. This allows an email database to grow at the same pace as an organization's email needs.

3. Fax and voice mail integration.

   Using the **Unified Messaging (UM)** feature of Exchange Server 2007, you can integrate voice mail and faxes into your email system. Users can then configure call answering or access their voice mail, faxes, and email from Outlook, Entourage, OWA, or a smart phone running the Windows Mobile operating system.

   Similarly, you can use **Outlook Voice Access (OVA)** to access your mailbox from a telephone. Your emails and calendar appointments can be read to you over the phone line, or you can send or forward email messages using the voice recognition feature of OVA.

4. Improved management tools.

   Exchange Server 2007 has consolidated and refined its graphical tools used for managing the Exchange server as well as provided a new scriptable command-line interface.

⊕ **MORE INFORMATION**

When configuring previous versions of Exchange Server, you typically used a graphical utility such as Exchange Administrator (Exchange 5.5) or Exchange System Manager (Exchange 2000 and 2003). Neither of these utilities exist in Exchange Server 2007.

The new *Exchange Management Console (EMC)* in Exchange Server 2007 uses the new and more intuitive Microsoft Management Console (MMC) version 3.0 interface. This interface has four panes as shown in Figure 1-7.

Figure 1-7

The Exchange Management Console

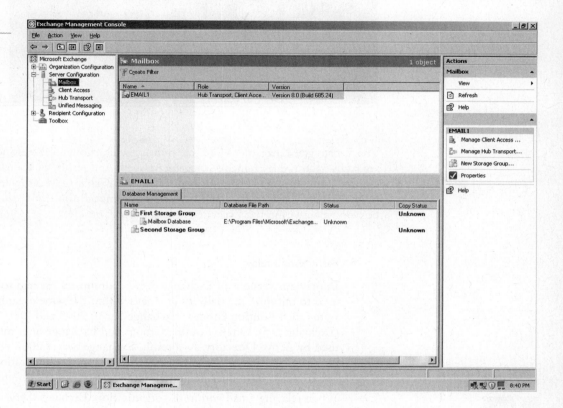

The Console Tree allows you to navigate to different areas of the utility, whereas the Action Pane displays common task shortcuts that correspond to the object highlighted in the Console Tree. You can use the Result Pane to view properties for an object in the Console Tree and the Work Pane to modify those properties.

The Exchange Management Console also provides a centralized graphical interface for administration. To manage email settings for individual users in Exchange Server 2000 and 2003, you needed to open the properties of user accounts in the Active Directory Users and Computers console. All of these tasks can now be done within the Exchange Management Console in Exchange Server 2007.

In addition to the Exchange Management Console, Exchange Server 2007 offers the *Exchange Management Shell (EMS)*, which is a snap-in for the Windows *PowerShell* scripting language. The Exchange Management Console has almost 400 Exchange-specific commands called *cmdlets* that may be used to configure and manage Exchange Server 2007. For standardization and easy recall, cmdlets are verb-noun combinations that define the action that is performed (verb) followed by the object or area that is affected (noun). For example, the **Remove-PublicFolder** cmdlet can be used to remove a public folder on an Exchange server, whereas the **Set-Mailbox** cmdlet can be used to set parameters for a user's mailbox. In addition, cmdlets may be combined in useful ways using UNIX-style data redirection or stored in reusable script files to automate complex tasks. An example of the Exchange Management Shell interface is shown in Figure 1-8.

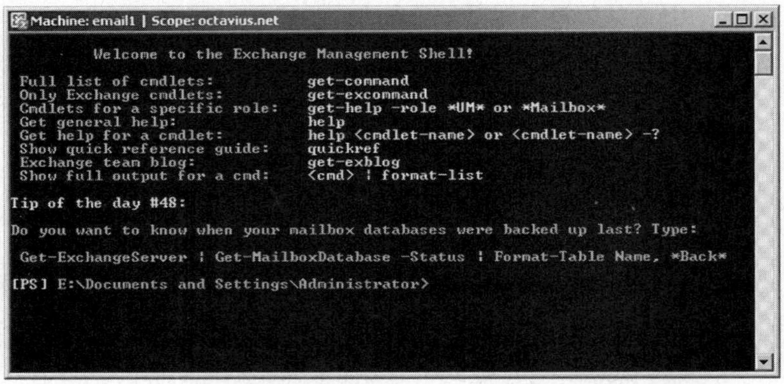

Figure 1-8

The Exchange Management Shell

> **TAKE NOTE***
>
> The Exchange Management Console translates all actions to PowerShell commands that are run within the Exchange Management Shell. As a result, all Exchange Management Console functions may be performed within the Exchange Management Shell. In addition, the Exchange Management Shell can perform some administrative functions that cannot be performed within the Exchange Management Console.

X REF

The configuration of Active Directory sites is discussed in Lesson 2, "Working with Active Directory."

TAKE NOTE*

Spam is often referred to as junk email. Although it is often used to advertise a product or service, spam includes any email that is unsolicited and not part of normal business or personal communications.

5. Faster email relay.

In previous versions of Exchange Server, administrators had to define objects that were used to optimize the delivery of emails within the same organization. These objects were called Routing Groups (Exchange Server 2000 and 2003) and Exchange Sites (Exchange 5.5). Often, Routing Groups and Exchange Sites mirrored the *site* structure used by Active Directory. As a result, Exchange Server 2007 no longer creates Routing Groups or Exchange Sites. Instead, it uses the site configuration from Active Directory to determine how email should be routed.

When relaying email within the organization, Exchange Server 2007 minimizes the number of email servers that need to process email by looking up the Active Directory site configuration and calculating the quickest route to the destination email server. Email is then routed directly to the destination email server.

For faster email relay outside the organization, Exchange Server 2007 no longer relies on the SMTP service within the Internet Information Services (IIS) component of Windows. Instead, Exchange Server 2007 ships with its own SMTP service that is optimized to work directly with the new components in Exchange Server 2007.

6. Enhanced email protection.

Exchange Server 2007 comes with improved email filtering to reduce the number of malicious and *spam* messages. Emails that have been scanned by antivirus software are tagged before they are routed within the organization, giving destination computers better control over emails that may be malicious and should be scanned locally for viruses. In addition, Exchange Server 2007 can now use the Junk Email Filter Lists from its Outlook 2003, Outlook 2007, and Entourage clients to filter emails at the server level.

7. Managed folder support.

Today, many organizations require that important emails be saved for legal or business reasons. In Exchange Server 2007, you can use the ***Messaging Records Management (MRM)*** feature to create a specific folder within a user's mailbox called a ***managed folder***.

You can then specify custom settings for managed folders that prevent emails from being deleted by the Exchange server for a certain period of time. Users can then store important emails in their managed folder to satisfy the needs of their organization.

8. Better user experience.

Exchange also boasts several improvements that are geared toward the user. The OWA interface now supports ActiveSync and has additional functions as well as a new design that work together to make it easier to use. Outlook and Entourage clients will notice more reliable and efficient calendaring functionality as well as the ability to customize how Out of Office messages are sent.

9. Improved clustering support.

In Exchange Server 2003, you could provide redundancy for your entire email server by installing a second Exchange server and configuring Windows Cluster Services to create an Exchange Server *cluster*. Both of the Exchange servers, or *nodes*, needed to share the same external storage device for storing emails and had to run in one of two cluster modes. In Active/Passive mode, one of the Exchange servers (the active node) was active and in use on the network, while the other node (the passive node) was only used if the active node became unavailable (a process called *failover*). In Active/Active mode, each node was actively used. Failover would occur if one of the active nodes became unavailable, and the other Exchange server would handle twice its normal load.

The main downside of failover is that it only protects against the failure of a server and not the data on the shared storage device. As a result, Exchange Server 2007 introduces several new types of clustering based on existing clustering methods used on database servers.

In *Cluster Continuous Replication (CCR)* and *Standby Continuous Replication (SCR)*, you can configure Exchange Server 2007 to replicate its email data continuously to another Exchange server on a local or remote network. CCR requires that the target Exchange server be installed in the same cluster whereas SCR does not. Because each Exchange server maintains its own storage, the email data is protected when a failure occurs.

Similarly, you can configure Exchange Server 2007 to replicate its email data continuously to another local hard drive as a form of backup in case the main hard disk fails. This is called *Local Continuous Replication (LCR)*.

10. Role-based deployment.

To make the deployment of Exchange Server easier in organizations that deploy several email servers, Exchange Server 2007 introduces five *server roles* that define the functions that will be available on a particular email server. In smaller organizations, a single server can be configured with several server roles. However, in larger organizations, you can spread different server roles across multiple email servers to enhance email security and speed up email relay. The five server roles in Exchange Server 2007 are discussed in the next section of this lesson.

TAKE NOTE*

Support for Active/Active mode clustering has been discontinued with Exchange Server 2007. You can still use Active/Passive mode clustering with Exchange Server 2007 by creating a *Single Copy Cluster (SCC)*.

TAKE NOTE*

To use SCR, you must have Exchange Server 2007 SP1.

➕ MORE INFORMATION

Some features that were available in previous versions of Exchange Server are no longer available in Exchange Server 2007. The most important of these include the creation of direct connectors to other email systems such as Novell GroupWise, Lotus Notes, and legacy X.400 MTA. Messages sent to these systems must be relayed across the Internet with all other public email. If you need to create connectors to these systems, you must use an Exchange Server 2003 computer within your organization.

Exchange Server 2007 Roles

Server roles are used by Exchange Server 2007 to refine the services that are available on a particular email server. This allows administrators to adapt Exchange Server 2007 to the particular environment in which it will be used. Before you deploy Exchange Server 2007, you must have a good understanding of the five server roles and how they may be used together within an organization.

As mentioned in the previous section, one of the key differences between Exchange Server 2007 and previous versions of Exchange Server is its role-based architecture. Exchange Server 2007 introduces five server roles that are specifically designed to help email administrators better control how Exchange Server 2007 relays email internally within their own organization. In addition, server roles make it easier for email administrators to deploy multiple Exchange servers within the same organization as well as grow their email infrastructure. Table 1-1 lists the five server roles available in Exchange Server 2007.

Table 1-1

The five server roles in Exchange Server 2007

SERVER ROLE	DESCRIPTION
Client Access Server (CAS)	Allows email clients access to their mailboxes using OWA (HTTP/HTTPS), POP3, IMAP4, Outlook Anywhere (RPC over HTTP/HTTPS), ActiveSync, and MAPI (RPC).
Mailbox	Responsible for hosting and providing access to the databases that contain mailboxes and public folders.
Hub Transport (Hub)	Handles all email relay within the organization and is functionally equivalent to the MTA and MDA in a generic email system. The Hub role is integrated with the Active Directory service and uses Exchange Server 2007 configuration stored in Active Directory to direct and restrict email flow.
Edge Transport (Edge)	Functionally equivalent to the smart host role in a generic email system although it is optional. It offers antivirus and antispam protection to provide extra security at the edge or perimeter of your network. All email sent to or received from the Internet passes through servers that hold this role. For added security, the Edge role cannot directly access Active Directory. Instead, only the information from Active Directory that is used to filter emails is sent from Hub servers to Edge servers via a special protocol called EdgeSync.
Unified Messaging (UM)	Allows users to access email, voice mail, and fax messages from a MAPI client, OWA, smart phone, or telephone. It is optional.

A single Exchange server can run all of the server roles simultaneously with the exception of the Edge role, which must run on its own Exchange server.

X REF

Server roles are chosen during the installation of Exchange Server 2007. For more information on the installation of Exchange Server 2007, refer to Lesson 3, "Deploying Exchange Server 2007."

By default, Exchange Server 2007 installs the CAS, Mailbox, and Hub roles to allow email access, storage, and relay as shown in Figure 1-9.

Figure 1-9

The Default Exchange Server Roles

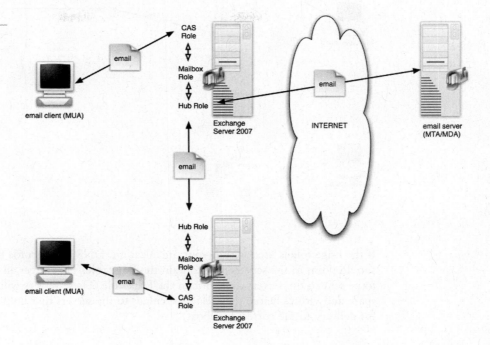

The Hub role performs all internal and external email relay. Internal email is sent to the correct destination email servers using recipient information in Active Directory. Before external email is sent, the Hub role must use DNS MX records to locate the destination email server. Similarly, MX records must exist in DNS for at least one email server in your organization that contains the Hub role to allow external email servers the ability to relay email to your organization. In addition, nearly all organizations use a firewall between their internal networks and the Internet. As a result, you also need to ensure that incoming SMTP/ESMTP traffic (TCP/IP port 25) is allowed to reach the servers that perform the Hub role.

In larger organizations that have more demanding email relay requirements, you can divide the CAS, Mailbox, and Hub roles among several email servers. These servers can be placed strategically to allow for improved email performance. For example, placing servers that have the CAS role close to client computers will speed up email access times.

One of the main problems that organizations face today is security. For email systems, incoming email from the Internet may be malicious (contain viruses) or unsolicited (spam).

As a result, many organizations install antivirus and antispam software on their email servers. However, this software uses a great deal of server resources and will adversely affect the performance of the email server as a result. After installing antispam and antivirus software on an Exchange server that is running the CAS, Mailbox, or Hub role, clients will notice that it takes longer to access the server, obtain email from their mailbox, use their calendar, and send email to others in the same organization.

To solve this problem, you can implement an Exchange server that is running the Edge role on the perimeter of your network to filter Internet-based email traffic using antivirus and antispam software. Figure 1-10 shows how an Edge role may be used to alter email relay.

Figure 1-10

Using the Edge Server Role

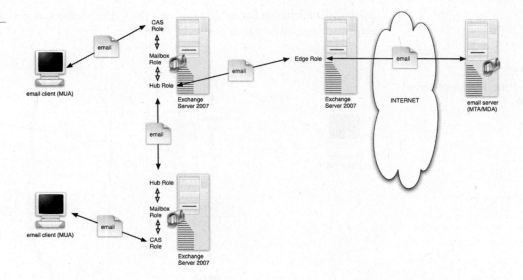

If the Edge role is used within your organization, DNS MX records for your organization should point to the servers that contain the Edge role. This forces all incoming Internet email to be sent to the servers that contain the Edge role. These servers will then filter emails for spam and viruses before they relay the emails to the servers that hold the Hub transport role for delivery to the correct mailbox.

TAKE NOTE* Larger organizations will likely have multiple servers that contain the Edge role. For round robin load balancing, DNS MX records for these servers should have the same priority number.

The Edge role only deals with Internet-based email and does not affect internal email processed by the CAS, Mailbox, and Hub roles. Because most email sent by an organization is addressed to internal recipients, you will obtain better email performance by using the Edge role to protect Internet-based email rather than installing antivirus and antispam software on other server roles.

TAKE NOTE* Although the Edge role cannot coexist on the same computer as other server roles, you can install the antivirus and antispam capabilities of the Edge role on an Exchange server that had the Hub role. However, this is not recommended for performance reasons.

Furthermore, the Edge role does not depend on Active Directory to function. As a result, Exchange servers that contain the Edge role do not need to be part of an Active Directory domain. However, the Edge role will need access to some configuration and user information in Active Directory to filter emails. This information is periodically sent to the Edge role server from servers that run the Hub role using a special protocol called *EdgeSync*.

➕ **MORE INFORMATION**

To obtain information using EdgeSync, Windows Server 2003 computers that run the Edge role must be running the Active Directory Application Mode (ADAM) service. Similarly, Windows Server 2008 computers that run the Edge role must have the Active Directory Lightweight Directory Services (ADLDS).

You can optionally install one or more UM roles within your organization to allow voice mail, faxes, and email to be accessed by MAPI, OWA, and smart phone clients in your organization. UM functions as a relay between a company's existing internal telephone system, called a ***Private Branch eXchange (PBX)***, and the other email servers within your organization as shown in Figure 1-11.

Figure 1-11

Using the UM Server Role

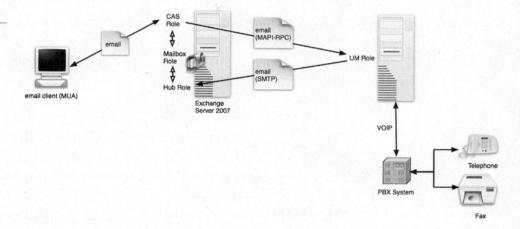

Incoming voice mail and fax messages recorded by the PBX are forwarded to a server running the UM role using the ***Voice Over IP (VOIP)*** protocol. The UM role then searches the Active Directory service to locate the users that match the telephone extension of the incoming voice mail or fax message. Once located, the UM role converts the voice mail or fax message to an email format and forwards it to the Hub role using SMTP for delivery to the correct mailbox.

To provide remote access to mailboxes from a phone line using OVA, the UM role also communicates directly with the CAS role using MAPI and the RPC protocol to access the appropriate information. This information is then converted to synthetic voice by the UM role and sent to the PBX system using VOIP.

SUMMARY SKILL MATRIX

IN THIS LESSON YOU LEARNED:

- Email is composed using an MUA on an email client and relayed to the recipients mailbox using MTAs and MDAs on email servers.

- For email to be routed across the Internet, MX records must exist in DNS to locate destination email servers that host mailboxes for recipients.

- Email clients and servers communicate using email protocols such as SMTP/ESMTP, IMAP4, POP3, HTTP, RPC, and ActiveSync. Different protocols are used to perform different parts of the email relay process.

- There were three widely used versions of Exchange Server before Exchange Server 2007: Exchange Server 5.5, Exchange Server 2000, and Exchange Server 2003. Each version has different features and support.

- Exchange Server 2007 offers better performance, additional security, enhanced tools, and more features than previous versions of Exchange Server.

- To enhance deployment and scalability, Exchange Server 2007 uses five server roles to define the services that are available on a particular Exchange server: CAS, Mailbox, Hub, Edge, and UM.

■ Knowledge Assessment

Fill in the Blank

Complete the following sentences by writing the correct word or words in the blanks provided.

1. The program used to send email on an email client is also called a _____.

2. Microsoft Outlook and Entourage typically connect to Exchange Server 2007 using RPC-based connections and _____.

3. The _____ and _____ protocols are often used to access email using a web browser.

4. An email server uses _____ and _____ records in DNS to determine the target email server to relay email to.

5. The _____ server role must be installed on its own Exchange server and cannot coexist with other server roles.

6. The Exchange Server 2007 feature that integrates voice mail and fax into an email system is called _____.

7. RPC over HTTP/HTTPS is called _____ in Exchange Server 2007.

8. _____ is a new type of clustering in Exchange Server 2007 that can be used to perform continuous backups of data to a local hard drive.

9. If a DNS server returns several MX records with different priorities, the one with the _____ priority is contacted first.

10. Exchange Management Shell is a command-based administration tool in Exchange Server 2007 that is based on _____.

Multiple Choice

Circle the letter that corresponds to the best answer.

1. Which of the following server roles in Exchange Server 2007 handles POP3 connections from client computers?
   a. CAS
   b. Hub
   c. Mailbox
   d. Edge

2. Outlook Web Access (OWA) relies on the _____ component of Windows.
   a. Site
   b. PowerShell
   c. IIS
   d. RPC

3. Which of the following email protocols encrypts data during transfer?
   a. ESMTPS
   b. IMAP4
   c. HTTP
   d. RPC

4. What DNS feature rotates the order of MX records before they are given to the email server that requested them?
   a. Failover
   b. MX ordering
   c. Priorities
   d. Round robin

5. Which of the following is not a valid email message format?
   a. Plain text
   b. RPC
   c. HTML
   d. Rich Text

6. Which of the following protocols can be used to obtain email from an email server? (Choose all that apply.)
   a. SMTP
   b. MAPI RPC
   c. POP3
   d. IMAP4

7. Which of the following priority numbers will most likely be assigned to the DNS MX record that is used to identify a smart host?
   a. 10
   b. 255
   c. 99
   d. 5

8. Which of the following is not a valid cmdlet structure?
   a. Get-PublicFolder
   b. Enable-MailboxDatabase
   c. Email-Send
   d. Update-Content

9. Which of the following allows Exchange Server 2007 to scale from small to large organizations? (Choose all that apply.)
   a. 64-bit architecture
   b. separation of roles
   c. unlimited database size
   d. support for new business requirements such as UM and MRM

10. What must be configured if your organization uses the Edge role?
    a. ActiveSync
    b. EdgeSync
    c. X.400
    d. MAPI

True/False

Circle T if the statement is true or F if the statement is false.

T | F   1. Servers that contain the Edge role access their configuration information from the Active Directory database.

T | F   2. Email systems typically adhere to the X.400 directory service standard.

T | F   3. Exchange servers store mailboxes in a database.

T | F   4. The Exchange Management Shell (EMS) can only perform a subset of the functions available in the Exchange Management Console (EMC).

T | F   5. IMAP4 was designed as a more robust replacement for POP3.

Matching

Match the term in Column 1 to its description in Column 2.

a. PBX

b. MTA

c. ActiveSync

d. Edge

e. Thunderbird

_____ 1. A server role that provides smart host capabilities in Exchange Server 2007.

_____ 2. A common Mail User Agent (MUA).

_____ 3. A software program that relays mail across computer networks such as the Internet.

_____ 4. Sends fax and voice mail to the Unified Messaging (UM) role.

_____ 5. An email protocol used by smart phones.

Review Questions

1. Outline the process and protocols used to relay email on the Internet.

2. Describe the protocols that email clients can use to obtain email from an email server as well as to send email to an email server.

■ Case Scenarios

Scenario 1-1: Creating a Proposal

You are the network administrator for a medium-sized organization. Currently, your organization has been using Windows 2000 servers running Exchange Server 2000 to provide email services. Your manager has asked you whether the organization should consider replacing its current Exchange servers with new servers that run Exchange Server 2007. Prepare a short proposal outlining the key benefits and costs associated with replacing the current Exchange server with several servers running Exchange Server 2007.

Scenario 1-2: Designing Server Roles

Your company has opened a new division that will employ 200 people and work under its own Internet identity. This new division will need a secure email system that allows internal Outlook clients to check their emails, fax, and voice mail. In addition, mobile clients require the ability to check their email from a telephone or smart phone. In a short memo, diagram the necessary server roles and email protocols that will need to be implemented in this new environment using Exchange Server 2007.

Working with Active Directory

LESSON SKILL MATRIX

TECHNOLOGY SKILL	OBJECTIVE DOMAIN
Describe the purpose and function of Active Directory.	Supplemental
Understand the structure of Active Directory.	Supplemental
Understand the function of groups, functional levels, sites, global catalog, and FSMO roles in an Active Directory environment.	Supplemental
Raise domain and forest functional levels.	Supplemental
Configure Active Directory sites.	Supplemental
Administer FSMOs, global catalog, and Trusts.	Supplemental
Create and manage OU, user, group, and computer objects.	Supplemental
Configure GPOs.	Supplemental

KEY TERMS

Active Directory Domains and Trusts
Active Directory Sites and Services
Active Directory Users and Computers
bridgehead server
container object
directory partitions
distribution group
domain
Domain Controller (DC)
domain functional level
Domain Naming Master
dynamic update
Flexible Single Master Operations (FSMO)
forest

forest functional level
forest root domain
global catalog (GC)
Globally Unique IDentifier (GUID)
Group Policy Objects (GPOs)
group scope
Infrastructure Master
Kerberos
leaf object
Lightweight Directory Access Protocol (LDAP)
PDC Emulator
RID Master
Schema Master
Security Accounts Manager (SAM)
security group

Security IDentifier (SID)
service record (SRV)
site link
site object
subnet object
tree
trust relationship
Universal Group Membership Caching (UGMC)
User Principal Name (UPN)

■ Understanding the Structure of Active Directory

THE BOTTOM LINE

Exchange Server 2007 is tightly integrated with the Active Directory service. As a result, the configuration of Active Directory often affects the deployment and configuration of Exchange Server 2007. Due to the close relationship between users and email, many organizations also require that Exchange Server administrators provide Active Directory administration as part of their job role. Therefore, it is important to understand the function and configuration of Active Directory as an Exchange Server administrator.

What is Active Directory?

Active Directory was introduced with Windows 2000 Server to provide access to user and computer information within a domain. Before examining the various procedures used to administer Active Directory, it is important to first understand its function and features.

Active Directory (AD) is a Windows directory service that stores and retrieves information about users and network resources. The information stored in AD is used by programs and services to validate the identity of users (a process called *authentication*) as well as restrict resource access for users (a process called *authorization*).

Directory services such as AD are designed for network environments where there are more than 10 computers and users require secure access to network resources such as shared files or printers. All client and server computers must be specifically configured to use a directory service. Computers that require the use of AD must be configured to join an AD *domain* as well as use a DNS server that contains records for computers within the domain.

When you use an AD network, you typically log on to a client computer that is part of an AD domain. The client computer then forwards your user logon information to a directory services server in your domain called a *Domain Controller (DC)* that validates your username and password and issues you a *token* that lists your user and group information. Your domain token is destroyed when you log out of your client computer and re-created when you log in again.

TAKE NOTE＊

To locate DCs, client computers must query their DNS server for *service records (SRV)* to identify the computers on the network that offer AD services.

＋ MORE INFORMATION

UNIX, Linux, Macintosh, Windows 2000, and later clients use the *Kerberos* ticket-based authentication protocol to log in to a DC and obtain a token. As a result, these tokens are often called *tickets*.

Each domain network resource contains an *Access Control List (ACL)*. The ACL lists the permissions that specific AD users have when accessing the resource. When you access a shared network resource, the server with the shared resource uses your token to verify your identity and enforce your permissions listed in the ACL. Provided that ACLs list only domain users, AD provides secure resource access because users not authenticated to the domain will be rejected when they attempt to access the resource.

TAKE NOTE＊

Because remote computers use your token to verify your identity, you are not prompted to log on to other domain computers. As a result, you only need to log on once to a DC to access all the resources that you have permission to within the domain. This feature is often called *single sign-on*.

AD objects contain an ACL. As a result, you can delegate control over different areas of the AD database to different administrators in your organization.

To allow computers to join domains and issue tokens to users, DCs must contain a **database** of **objects** such as user and computer accounts. This database is hierarchical and conforms to the International Telecommunication Union (ITU) X.500 standard. The AD service uses the **Lightweight Directory Access Protocol (LDAP)** to quickly access object information stored in the database.

Besides authentication and authorization, AD contains a powerful administrative feature called **Group Policy**. Group Policy can be used to automatically configure the software, security settings, and user interface on computers within an AD domain based on the location of the user or computer object within the AD database. Group Policy may also be used to deploy and remove software on domain computers.

Group Policy is often used to configure email client settings.

To configure Group Policy, administrators create **Group Policy Objects (GPOs)** that have the appropriate settings. A single GPO can be applied to thousands of users and computers within an organization. This reduces the time and effort that it takes to administer a large domain.

Understanding Objects

AD uses leaf objects to represent users and resources, as well as container objects to organize resources. When you work with AD, it is important to understand the different types of objects and their uses.

Exchange Server 2007 modifies the schema of AD to include new objects and attributes that are used to store email configuration for user objects.

The AD database can theoretically contain an unlimited number of objects. As a result, AD is scalable to any size of organization.

The total list of all available object types (called **classes**) and their associated properties (called **attributes**) is stored in the AD **schema**. Members of the Schema Admins group in AD can modify the schema to include more object types and attributes.

Objects that represent a user, computer, or resource are called **leaf objects** and contain attributes that are used by applications. For example, the UM role of Exchange Server 2007 uses the telephone extension attribute within each user account object in AD to match incoming voice mail to the appropriate mailbox.

The default leaf object classes that exist in AD include:

- User accounts
- Group accounts
- Computer accounts
- Printers
- Shared folders

Alternatively, some AD objects can contain leaf objects and are primarily used to organize leaf objects for quick location, delegation of administration, and the use of Group Policy. As a result, these objects are called **container objects** and provide the main structure of AD. There are three main container objects:

- Domains
- Organizational units (OUs)
- Sites

A domain object represents a particular organization or business unit and is given a unique DNS domain name as a result. Domain objects can contain leaf objects as well as OUs.

OUs are similar to folders on a hard drive. While folders on a hard drive can contain files or subfolders, OUs can contain leaf objects or other OUs called **child OUs**. Nearly all AD objects are organized into OUs within a domain. Figure 2-1 shows a domain called octavius.net that uses OUs to organize leaf objects by division (East and West) as well as by department (Accounting, Marketing, and Production).

Figure 2-1

The Octavius Domain Structure

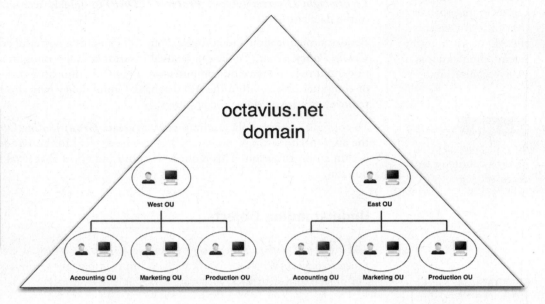

TAKE NOTE*

There is no limit to the number of child OUs that can be created under a single parent OU. However, for performance reasons, you should create no more than five levels of child OUs under a parent OU.

TAKE NOTE*

Although each object in AD has a unique name, it is also identified by a variable-length number called a *Security IDentifier (SID)* that is used to identify the object in an ACL, as well as a 128-bit number called a *Globally Unique IDentifier (GUID)* that is used to guarantee its uniqueness in the AD database.

Because objects within the AD database are organized hierarchically and searched using LDAP, each object must have a unique LDAP name called a *distinguished name (DN)*. DNs identify leaf objects using the *common name (CN)* prefix. For example, the DN for a user account called bob in the Accounting OU under the West OU shown in Figure 2-1 would be: CN=bob,OU=Accounting,OU=West,DC=octavius,DC=net

Site objects represent physical locations. A site object can contain DC computer accounts and is primarily used to control the replication of AD data between physical locations. We discuss site objects in more depth later in this lesson.

Understanding Forests and Trusts

To accommodate all sizes of organizations, AD creates a forest for each organization that contains one or more trees. Each tree can contain one or more domains that share a common DNS name structure. Trust relationships are automatically created between domains in a forest to allow resource access across domains. Understanding the AD forest and trust structure is vital when administering DCs.

Domain objects are the base unit of organization in AD. Each domain has a unique DNS name that represents the name of the organization or business unit. In small organizations, there is typically one business unit for the entire organization. However, larger organizations can contain several individual business units.

To accommodate large organizations, AD creates a *forest* that can contain multiple domains that are part of the same organization. When the first DC in an organization is created, it creates the forest as well as the first domain in the forest called the *forest root domain*. As additional DCs are added, they can be configured to participate in the forest root domain or they can be used to create additional domains within the same forest. Figure 2-2 depicts a typical forest.

TAKE NOTE*

Although each domain in a forest must have at least one DC to hold the AD database for that domain, you should install additional DCs in each domain. This allows for fault tolerance if a single DC fails as well as provides load balancing for authentication requests. There is no limit to the number of DCs that can be installed in a single domain.

Figure 2-2

Octavius Forest Structure

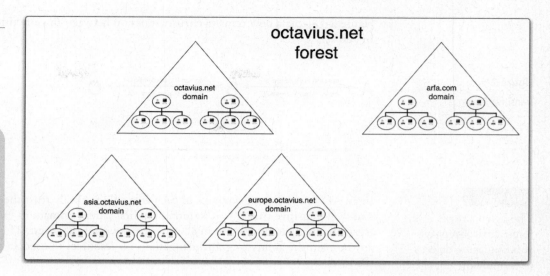

In Figure 2-2, octavius .net is typically referred to as a *parent domain*, whereas asia.octavius .net and europe.octavius .net are called *child domains*.

Trust relationships do not give permissions to resources. Instead, they allow users to access resources in other domains that an administrator has granted them permission to. Without trust relationships, permissions on domain resources may only be given to users in the same domain.

Some business units are related and will likely contain a portion of the same DNS name. In Figure 2-2, the octavius.net domain represents the main offices of the Octavius organization in North America, whereas the asia.octavius.net and europe.octavius.net subdomains represent the Asian and European offices of the Octavius organization. Because all three domains share the same core domain name, we refer to them as the octavius.net *tree*.

If an organization contains business units that have different public identities or DNS names, these units will be represented by separate trees in the forest. Although the arfa.com domain in Figure 2-2 is part of the Octavius organization, it is part of the arfa.com tree.

Each domain in a forest maintains its own security, administrator user accounts, and resources. To allow users in a domain (the source domain) to access resources that they have permission to in another domain (the target domain), the target domain must trust the source domain. This is called a *trust relationship* or simply a *trust*.

Trust relationships are represented by arrow symbols in a forest diagram. Figure 2-3 shows how trust relationships are drawn between two fictitious domains (domain A and domain B).

Figure 2-3

One-Way Trusts

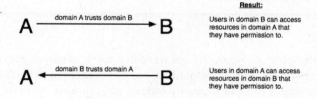

The trust relationships shown in Figure 2-3 are called *one-way trusts*. If users in each domain require access to resources in the other domain, then a *two-way trust* can be used as shown in Figure 2-4.

Figure 2-4

Two-Way Trusts

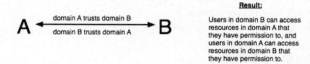

To reduce the number of trust relationships that need to be created in large forests, trust can be *transitive*. If domain A trusts domain B using a transitive trust, and domain B trusts domain C using a transitive trust, then it is assumed that domain A trusts domain C as well. Users in domain C can then access resources that they have permission to in domain A.

Figure 2-5 depicts how transitive trusts function between three fictitious domains (domain A, B, and C).

Figure 2-5

Transitive Trusts

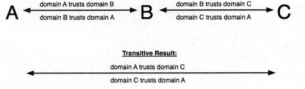

TAKE NOTE*

The default trusts in a forest are self-repairing and cannot be deleted or modified.

In an AD forest, parent domains in each tree automatically trust their child domains using two-way transitive trusts. Furthermore, the first parent domain in each tree automatically trusts the first parent domain in all other trees within the forest. This allows administrators in any domain the ability to grant permissions on resources to users in any other domain within the forest.

Figure 2-6 shows the default trust relationships for the octavius.net forest.

Figure 2-6

Default Trusts for the Octavius Forest

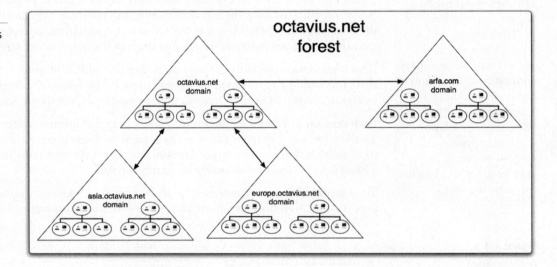

Although the trusts in Figure 2-6 are transitive, users in europe.octavius.net must first contact the octavius.net domain before they access resources in the arfa.com domain. To speed up resource access, you can manually create a trust directly between the europe.octavius.net and arfa.com domains. This trust is called a ***shortcut trust*** and will prevent the octavius.net domain from being contacted when users in europe.octavius.net access resources in arfa.com.

TAKE NOTE*

External trusts to an NT4 domain must be one-way and nontransitive.

You can also create trusts to entities outside of your forest. For example, ***external trusts*** can be made between a domain in your forest and an NT4 domain and a domain in another Windows forest. Similarly, ***realm trusts*** can be made between a domain in your forest and a UNIX Kerberos Realm, and ***cross forest trusts*** can be made between two Windows Server 2003 machines and newer forests.

Understanding Groups

Global, domain local, and universal security groups are used to simplify permissions assignments on resources within your forest. In order to successfully manage authorization in a forest, you must first understand the different group types and scopes available as well as their intended usage.

You can assign permissions on resources within your domain to user accounts in your domain or to user accounts in remote domains that you trust via a trust relationship. However, assigning permissions to specific user accounts is a time consuming and inefficient process in organizations that have several user accounts that require access to the same resources.

To organize and simplify the assignment of permissions on resources, you should place several user account objects in a group object and assign permissions to the group object for the resource. This approach also minimizes the number of entries in the ACL on each resource and increases the speed of resource access. For example, to grant 50 users access to a particular resource, placing those users in a group and assigning permissions on the resource to the group results in a single entry in the ACL.

There are two main types of group accounts in AD:

- Security groups
- Distribution groups

Distribution groups are designed for email distribution only and contain an email address attribute as a result. When you send email to a distribution group, it is sent to the user accounts that are members of the group.

Like distribution groups, *security groups* can be used for email distribution. Unlike distribution groups, security groups can be assigned permissions to resources and are the main group type used in AD as a result.

To accommodate resource access across domains in a forest, AD further defines three *group scopes*:

- Global
- Domain local
- Universal

Although these group scopes may be applied to both distribution and security groups, they mainly serve to simplify permissions assignment across the forest using security groups. Consequently, each security group scope has a different application within the AD forest as described in Table 2-1.

Table 2-1

Active Directory security group scopes

Group Scope	Allowed Group Members	Domains That Can Use the Group
Global	Objects (users accounts, computer accounts, group accounts) from the same domain as the global group	Any domain in the forest
Domain local	Objects (users accounts, computer accounts, group accounts) from any domain in the forest	Only the domain to which the domain local group belongs
Universal	Objects (users accounts, computer accounts, group accounts) from any domain in the forest	Any domain in the forest

TAKE NOTE *

The process of adding a group to the membership list of another group is called *group nesting.*

Global security groups may be assigned permissions to resources or added as a member to another group in any domain within the forest. However, global groups can only contain objects from the same domain in which the global group was created. Alternatively, domain local groups may be assigned permissions to resources or added as a member to another group in the same domain but can contain objects from any domain in the forest. Universal groups are unrestricted; they can be assigned permissions to resources, added as a member to another group in any domain within the forest, and can contain any object in the forest.

If used properly, these three group scopes organize the assignment of permissions across an entire forest. At minimum, user accounts in each domain should be added to global groups based on job function.

For example, each domain could contain a global group called Sales-GG. The Sales-GG group can then be assigned permissions to resources in the same domain or in other domains within the forest.

To simply the assignment of permissions to all sales users in the forest, you could create a universal group called Sales-U and add the Sales-GG groups from each domain to its membership list. If you assign permissions to the Sales-U group, all sales users in the forest will receive the permissions.

TAKE NOTE *

In order to use universal groups or nest groups of the same type, your domain must be running at the Windows 2000 Native function level or higher. Functional levels are discussed in the next section.

Additionally, you can create domain local groups for specific resources to make permissions assignments easier to identify. For example, if all sales users in the forest must use a printer in your domain called HPLaserJet6, you could create a domain local group called HPLaserJet6-DL and add the Sales-U group as a member. By simply assigning print permission to the HPLaserJet6-DL group, you will have given print permission to all sales users within the organization.

This approach is often called *AGUDLP*:

A—**A**dd users to

G—**G**lobal groups based on job function. Add global groups to

U—**U**niversal groups for forestwide use. Add universal groups to

DL—**D**omain **L**ocal groups that are matched to a particular resource. Assign

P—**P**ermissions to the domain local group.

> ➕ **MORE INFORMATION**
>
> Computers that do not participate in AD contain user accounts and group accounts in the Windows Registry that are only used on the local computer. Although these local user accounts and local groups do not exist in the AD database, users who log in to a domain from a client computer can still choose to log in using a local user account rather than authenticate to the domain. In this case, domain resources are unavailable and the user can only access resources that grant access to their local user account and local groups.
>
> Furthermore, when a computer joins a domain, domain groups are automatically added as members to the default local groups. For example, the Domain Users group is added to the local Users group and the Domain Admins group is added to the local Administrators group on each domain computer. This gives domain users the same abilities as local users and domain administrators the same abilities as local administrators on each domain computer.

Understanding Functional Levels

Domains in an AD forest use functional levels to maintain backwards compatibility to Windows NT4 domains or previous versions of AD. Changing your domain functional level affects the features of both AD and Exchange Server 2007. Thus, it is important to understand AD functional levels when supporting Exchange Server 2007 in an AD environment.

Windows domains were first introduced with Windows NT4 Server, yet NT4 domains did not use AD. Instead, Windows NT4 domains stored user, group, and computer accounts in a nonhierarchical database called the **Security Accounts Manager (SAM)**. A read-write copy of the SAM was stored on a single **Primary Domain Controller (PDC)** in each NT4 domain. All additional NT4 DCs were called **Backup Domain Controllers (BDCs)** and obtained a copy of the SAM from the PDC so that they could authenticate users.

AD was introduced with Windows 2000 Server and was a major departure from the SAM structure used in Windows NT4. Although Windows Server 2003 and Windows Server 2008 also use AD, they contain additional AD features that are unavailable in previous versions.

Many organizations have based their network infrastructure on Windows NT4 and Windows 2000 domains in the past. As a result, you can migrate these domains to Windows Server 2003 and 2008 by upgrading or replacing older DCs with new ones. However, this migration may take several months or years. Consequently, domains within your organization can contain a mixture of Windows NT4, Windows 2000, Windows Server 2003, and Windows Server 2008 DCs.

To account for the diverse features and structure between each version of DC, each AD domain contains **domain functional levels** that allow different levels of backwards compatibility by allowing different types of DCs to participate in domain authentication. The domain functional levels for Windows Server 2003 AD domains are described in Table 2-2.

Table 2-2

Windows Server 2003 domain functional levels

DOMAIN FUNCTIONAL LEVEL	DC OPERATING SYSTEMS SUPPORTED WITHIN THE DOMAIN
Windows 2000 Mixed	Windows NT4, Windows 2000, Windows Server 2003
Windows NT4 Interim	Windows NT4, Windows Server 2003
Windows 2000 Native	Windows 2000, Windows Server 2003
Windows Server 2003	Windows Server 2003

By default, Windows Server 2003 AD domains are in the Windows 2000 Mixed functional level to allow backwards compatibility with Windows NT4 and Windows 2000 DCs. By raising the domain functional level to the Windows 2000 Native functional level, you prevent NT4 DCs from participating in domain authentication and enable several Windows 2000 specific features such as the ability to use universal groups. Similarly, to enable the new features introduced in Windows Server 2003 AD, you must raise your domain functional level to the Windows Server 2003 functional level.

⚠ **WARNING** Raising a functional level is a one-way operation. You cannot return to the previous functional level once it has been raised.

Domain functional levels only determine the types of DCs that can participate in a particular domain. A domain at the Windows Server 2003 functional level can only contain Windows Server 2003 DCs but can still contain clients that run previous versions of Windows such as Windows NT4 and Windows 2000.

Windows Server 2008 AD does not allow backwards compatibility with Windows NT4 domains. Table 2-3 lists the domain functional levels available in Windows Server 2008.

Table 2-3

Windows Server 2008 domain functional levels

Domain Functional Level	DC Operating Systems Supported within the Domain
Windows 2000 Native	Windows 2000, Windows Server 2003, Windows Server 2008
Windows Server 2003	Windows Server 2003, Windows Server 2008
Windows Server 2008	Windows Server 2008

TAKE NOTE*

Exchange Server 2007 requires that you upgrade your domain functional level to Windows 2000 Native or higher.

By default, Windows Server 2008 AD uses the Windows 2000 Native functional level for backwards compatibility. To take advantage of new features introduced with Windows Server 2003 AD, you must raise your domain to the Windows Server 2003 functional level. Similarly, to enable the new features introduced with Windows Server 2008 AD, you must raise your domain to the Windows Server 2008 functional level.

In a forest that contains multiple domains, each domain may operate at a different functional level. Those domains that have a higher functional level can take advantage of the latest features in AD. Some features of AD require minimum domain functional level of all domains within the forest. As a result, AD contains *forest functional levels* that define the type of DCs allowed within all domains in the forest. Tables 2-4 and 2-5 show the forest functional levels used by Windows Server 2003 AD and Windows Server 2008 AD, respectively.

Table 2-4

Windows Server 2003 forest functional levels

Forest Functional Level	DC Operating Systems Supported within the Forest
Windows 2000	Windows NT4, Windows 2000, Windows Server 2003
Windows Server 2003 Interim	Windows NT4, Windows Server 2003
Windows Server 2003	Windows Server 2003

Table 2-5

Windows Server 2008 forest functional levels

Forest Functional Level	DC Operating Systems Supported within the Forest
Windows 2000 Native	Windows 2000, Windows Server 2003, Windows Server 2008
Windows Server 2003	Windows Server 2003, Windows Server 2008
Windows Server 2008	Windows Server 2008

TAKE NOTE*

Cross forest trusts require that both forests apply the Windows Server 2003 forest functional level or higher.

To raise your forest functional level, you must first raise your domain function levels. For example, to raise the forest function level to Windows Server 2003, all domains in your forest should first be raised to the Windows Server 2003 domain functional level. As with domain functional levels, you cannot revert to a previous forest functional level once it has been raised.

Understanding Sites and Replication

Information is replicated between DCs in a domain and forest when new information is added to the AD database or existing information is modified or removed. To control replication within an organization, AD uses site and site link objects. Furthermore, Exchange Server 2007 uses AD sites to control the flow of internal email within an organization.

To ensure the continuous operation of AD if a DC fails, most organizations deploy more than one DC in each domain within a forest. Each DC in a domain will contain a copy of the AD database. To ensure that DCs in the same domain can authenticate users using the same AD database, changes made to the AD database on one DC are replicated to other DCs.

To understand how AD replication works, you must first understand the structure of the AD database stored on each DC. There are three main sections of the AD database called *directory partitions*:

- Schema partition
- Configuration partition
- Domain partition

The schema partition contains the AD schema and must be identical on all DCs in the forest to ensure that objects can be interpreted by any DC. If a change is made to the schema partition, such as the addition of a new object class, the schema partition changes must be replicated to all other DCs in the forest.

Like the schema partition, the configuration partition must be identical on all DCs in the forest as it stores the structure and layout of the AD forest. If you change the structure of the forest by adding a new domain or trust relationship, the configuration partition will be replicated to all other DCs in the forest.

All objects within a particular domain are stored in the domain partition on the DCs. Because of this, the domain partition is the largest directory partition and typically contains thousands of objects. Replicating the domain partition to all DCs in the forest would prove too bandwidth intensive and would increase the size of the AD database unnecessarily. As a result, when a change is made to the domain partition on a DC, such as the addition of a user account object, it is replicated to other DCs in the same domain only. Because each domain maintains its own domain objects, you must contact DCs in a remote domain when you need access to information that is stored within an object in the remote domain.

On a fast network such as a LAN, AD replication occurs quickly. However, many organizations have multiple physical locations that are linked by relatively slow WAN connections via the Internet. Frequent AD replication across these slow WAN connections will consume a great deal of the available bandwidth and likely slow down the organization's access to the Internet.

One way to reduce the impact of AD replication on bandwidth is to ensure that each location within your organization has its own domain. In this case, only replication of schema and configuration changes will occur across the slow WAN connections to DCs in other domains within the forest. Administrators can simply ensure that changes made to the schema or forest structure occur after normal business hours to minimize the impact of any replication outside of the domain.

Unfortunately, using one domain per location is more costly to implement and manage over time. Alternatively, you can implement AD *site objects* to optimize the replication that occurs across slow WAN links between the physical locations within your organization.

TAKE NOTE*

Although changes to the schema and configuration are replicated to all other DCs in the forest, these changes are relatively infrequent. Alternatively, changes to the domain partition are relatively frequent and replicated only to DCs within the same domain.

Consider the octavius.net domain shown in Figure 2-7. DC1 and DC2 contain a copy of all objects in the octavius.net domain yet are physically located at the western offices of the Octavius organization in Cupertino, California. Similarly, DC3 and DC4 contain a copy of the objects in the octavius.net domain. However, they are located in the eastern offices of the Octavius organization in Boston, Massachusetts.

Figure 2-7

Octavius.net Domain Controller Locations

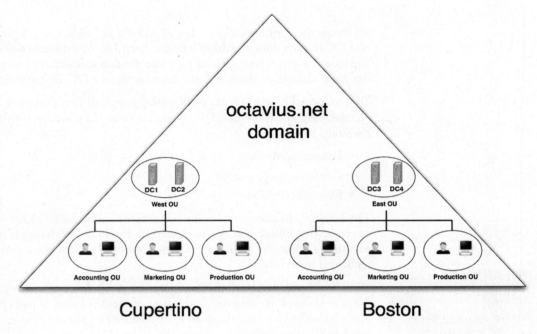

When an AD object such as a user account is created or modified on DC3 in Boston, it is immediately replicated to DC1, DC2, and DC4. Replication to DC4 will take only a few moments on the Boston network, but will take considerably longer to traverse the Internet from Boston to Cupertino in order to reach DC1 and DC2. Assuming that AD objects are modified several hundred times per hour, replication to DC1 and DC2 will likely congest the slow WAN connections in both Boston and Cupertino.

Furthermore, objects created by administrators in Boston will likely be used primarily by the DCs in Boston. For example, if an administrator creates a user account on DC3 for a new hire at the Boston office, only DC3 and DC4 will need to query the user account object to perform authentication unless the user travels to Cupertino.

By creating AD sites that represent the Cupertino and Boston locations, you can create a *site link* object between the Cupertino and Boston sites that specifies when replication should occur. Figure 2-8 shows the octavius.net domain configured using sites.

The site link between the Cupertino and Boston sites shown in Figure 2-8 can be configured to schedule replication for certain times or accumulate AD database changes for a certain period of time before replicating them all at once to reduce the effects on WAN bandwidth.

Figure 2-8

Octavius.net Site Structure

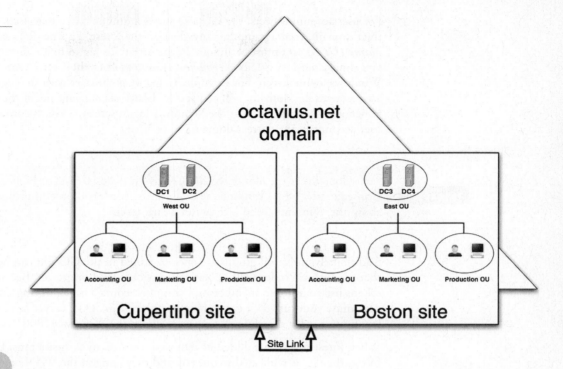

To save bandwidth, replication between sites only occurs between a single DC in each site called a ***bridgehead server***. Although AD automatically chooses a DC to become the bridgehead server in each site, you can manually specify the bridgehead server for each site.

Assume that the Cupertino-Boston site link is configured to replicate every hour between 9:00 p.m. and 3:00 a.m., which is after normal business hours in both locations. In this case, a new user account object created on DC3 will immediately replicate to DC4 but will not replicate to DC1 and DC2 until after 9:00 p.m. Because the user account is for a Boston user, the replication delay to Cupertino is negligible.

There is no limit to the number of sites and site link objects that may be created in an AD forest. In large organizations that have several offices, you will likely create many sites and site link objects. In this case, you can change the ***cost*** value on each site link to encourage the use of certain replication paths. If there are multiple site link objects between a source and destination domain, AD will use the site link objects that have the lowest cost between both domains.

It is important to create your AD site structure carefully. Exchange Server 2007 uses the AD site structure to control how email is relayed within your organization.

Understanding Global Catalog

The global catalog provides quick object access to universal groups and UPNs within an AD forest. After configuring AD sites, you should carefully consider the placement of global catalog servers within your organization to allow quick authentication and resource access. Additionally, Exchange Server 2007 contacts the global catalog to search for email recipients within the organization when relaying email.

For fast resource access in remote domains, you should always ensure that client computers can easily reach a GC server by placing the GC on at least one DC in each site within the forest.

Because forests can grow very large, a list of all object names in the forest is stored on at least one DC to aid in locating objects in the AD. This list is called the ***global catalog (GC)*** and is hosted on the first DC in the forest by default. The GC is similar to a telephone book. Where a telephone book allows you to quickly locate a telephone number, the GC allows you to quickly locate an object in a remote domain.

For user account objects, the GC also stores a unique name that users can use to log in to their domain from a computer anywhere in the forest. This name is called a *User Principal Name (UPN)* and must be unique in the forest. To log in to a remote domain using a UPN, you simply need to specify *username@domainname* in the User Name dialog box at the Windows logon screen. For example, to log in as the user with the login name bob in the asia.octavius.net domain, you can specify bob@asia.octavius.net at the Windows logon screen. When a UPN is specified at the Windows logon screen, a GC is contacted to locate the right user account in the correct domain.

> **TAKE NOTE***
>
> Only domains at the Windows 2000 Native functional level or higher can access the GC. Consequently, UPNs can only be used during the logon process if the domain is at or above the Windows 2000 Native functional level.

Additionally, universal groups are entirely stored in the GC and can be accessed by domains that are at the Windows 2000 Native functional level or greater. Because authentication tokens list your group membership, you must contact a GC during the logon process to determine your universal group membership. Thus, a GC server is necessary to complete the logon process for domains that are at or above the Windows 2000 Native functional level.

When forest objects are added or removed, the GC in each site must be updated. In a large forest, the GC is replicated frequently and may congest the WAN bandwidth in small branch locations. To solve this problem, you should avoid placing the GC on DCs in sites that have limited WAN bandwidth. For these sites, they must still contact a GC in another site to complete the logon process if the domain is at the Windows 2000 Native functional level.

To speed up the logon process for sites in a Windows 2000 Native functional level domain that do not have a GC, you should enable *Universal Group Membership Caching (UGMC)* on the site to allow DCs in the site the ability to cache the universal group memberships for user accounts. In this case, a remote GC must be contacted the first time a user authenticates to the domain to verify universal group memberships and populate the cache. On subsequent logons, the DC in the site simply uses the universal group membership information for the user stored in the cache to complete the logon process.

> **TAKE NOTE***
>
> Even if a GC is unavailable, domain administrators can still log in to a domain that is at or above the Windows 2000 Native functional level.

Understanding FSMO Roles

> Flexible Single Master Operations (FSMO) roles provide specific functions within an AD domain and forest. It is important to understand the placement and function of FSMO roles in order to optimize the performance of AD as well as troubleshoot AD problems.

In any AD environment, certain domain and forest functions must be coordinated from a single DC. These functions are called *Flexible Single Master Operations (FSMO)*. A DC can hold a single FSMO role or can hold all FSMO roles for its domain or forest.

Table 2-6 lists the two forestwide FSMO roles that must be present on a single DC in the forest, as well as the three domainwide FSMO roles that must be on a single DC in each domain within the forest.

Table 2-6

Forestwide and Domainwide FSMO Roles

FSMO ROLE	NUMBER PER DOMAIN OR FOREST	FUNCTION
Schema Master	1 per forest	Replicates changes made to the AD schema to all DCs in the forest. In order to modify the AD schema, the DC that holds the Schema Master FSMO role must be available.
Domain Naming Master	1 per forest	Permits the addition of new domains and removal of existing domains. Before a new domain is added to the forest, the DC that holds the Domain Naming Master FSMO is contacted to ensure that the name is unique. The Domain Naming Master also ensures that the updated forest configuration is replicated to all DCs in the forest. For best performance, the DC that contains the Domain Naming Master FSMO role should also contain the GC.
PDC Emulator	1 per domain	Emulates an NT4 PDC for backwards compatibility to NT4 BDCs that exist in a Windows 2000 Mixed functional level domain. In addition, the PDC Emulator coordinates user password changes and synchronizes time among the computers in a domain.
RID Master	1 per domain	Issues unique **Relative IDentifiers (RIDs)** to DCs within the domain. RIDs are unique numbers that are used to create Security Identifiers (SIDs) for newly created objects in the domain. Because the RID Master generates the RIDs used by all the DCs in a domain when creating new objects, SIDs are guaranteed to be unique among domain objects. The RID Master FSMO generates blocks of 500 RIDs for each DC in the domain. When a DC has exhausted its supply of RIDs, it contacts the RID Master FSMO to obtain another 500.
Infrastructure Master	1 per domain	Coordinates group membership as well as the use of GUIDs and DNs between the current domain and other domains in the forest. Because the GC performs similar functions, the Infrastructure Master FSMO role should be placed on a DC that does not contain the GC.

By default, the first DC installed in the forest contains all five FSMO roles and the first DC installed in all additional domains contains the three domainwide FSMO roles. However, if one of these DCs fail, several FSMO roles will be unavailable. As a result, you should move the default FSMO roles to different DCs for fault tolerance.

It is important to ensure that the DCs that contain FSMO roles are available at all times. For example, if the PDC Emulator FSMO role is unavailable, users could receive an incorrect time that may prevent them from logging in to their domain because the Kerberos authentication protocol requires that the time on a client and DC be no more than five minutes different. Additionally, if the RID Master FSMO is unavailable, you could receive an error message when attempting to create a new object in the AD database.

If a DC that holds an FSMO role fails, you can force another DC to assume the FSMO role. To do this, you must *seize* the FSMO role from a DC that is online. To bring the failed DC back online, you should first reinstall the operating system and configure it as a new DC in the existing domain.

TAKE NOTE*

Exchange Server 2007 extends the AD schema. As a result, it is important to ensure that the first Exchange Server 2007 computer deployed can contact the DC that holds the Schema Master FSMO role. It is good practice to move the Schema Master FSMO role to a DC close to the computer that will become the first Exchange server to reduce installation problems and speed the installation process.

■ Installing Active Directory

THE BOTTOM LINE

AD consists of several services and components that run on a Windows Server. To deploy AD in your organization, you must first prepare your servers and network environment as well as run the Active Directory Installation Wizard. Following installation, you should ensure that all components were installed successfully before configuring AD. Alternatively, you can remove AD from a DC to restore it to its previous state.

Preparing for Installation

The common American proverb "failing to plan is planning to fail" is true for any AD installation. To reduce the chance that an AD installation will fail, you should ensure that you have the necessary prerequisites before beginning the installation.

Although you can install Exchange Server 2007 SP1 on a Windows Server 2008 computer, Exchange Server 2007 was originally designed to interoperate in a Windows Server 2003 AD environment. As a result, we will focus on the installation and configuration of Windows Server 2003 AD in this lesson.

Before you begin the installation of AD on a Windows Server 2003, it is important to ensure that you have the necessary prerequisites:

TAKE NOTE*

You cannot install AD on a computer running the Web Edition of Windows Server 2003.

- A computer running the Standard Edition, Enterprise Edition, or Datacenter Edition of Windows Server 2003 or Windows Server 2003 R2 with the latest service packs and updates installed. This computer should use the NTFS file system for its system volume and contain at least 250 MB of free space on the NTFS file system for use by AD.
- A DNS server on the network that supports SRV records and is configured with a zone for the AD domain. Alternatively, this DNS server can be created and configured automatically on the first DC in a domain during AD installation.

TAKE NOTE*

To support AD, your DNS server must support the ***Berkeley Internet Name Domain (BIND)*** version 4.9.6 standard to allow SRV record support. To also allow the automatic creation and updating of SRV records using the DNS ***dynamic update*** protocol, your DNS server should support BIND version 8.1.2. Windows Server 2003 DNS supports BIND version 8.1.2 standard.

TAKE NOTE*

For performance reasons, it is considered a poor practice to install AD on a server that provides other business-critical services such as web, email, file, print, or database services.

- A network interface that is connected to a TCP/IP network and configured to use the appropriate DNS server. If you are installing a new forest or tree in an existing forest, you can automatically install and configure DNS on your computer during the AD installation. In this case, you should specify your own IP address in the Preferred DNS server dialog box within TCP/IP properties to ensure that DNS is installed on your computer regardless of whether an external DNS server on the Internet holds a zone for your domain.
- A user account that is a member of the local Administrators group on the Windows Server 2003 computer. To join an existing domain, you also require a user account that is a member of the Domain Admins group in the existing domain. Similarly, to create a new domain in an existing forest, you will also require a user account that is a member of the Enterprise Admins group in the forest root domain.

CONFIGURE DNS BEFORE ACTIVE DIRECTORY INSTALLATION

GET READY. Turn on the computer, and log in as the Administrator user account. Close any windows that appear on the desktop.

1. Click **Start, Control Panel,** and then click **Network Connections.** A list of your network connections will appear on the right-hand menu.

2. Click the network connection that is connected to your TCP/IP network. If you have a single network interface, this is called **Local Area Connection** by default. The network interface property screen appears.

3. Highlight **Internet Protocol (TCP/IP)**, and click **Properties**. The Internet Protocol (TCP/IP) Properties screen appears.

4. Ensure that the **Preferred DNS server** dialog box lists the IP address of a DNS server on your network that is configured with a zone for the AD domain that you wish to install on your computer. If you are installing a new forest or tree and plan to automatically install and configure DNS during AD installation, ensure that the computer's IP address is listed in the Preferred DNS server dialog box as shown in Figure 2-9.

Figure 2-9

Preparing DNS for Active Directory Installation

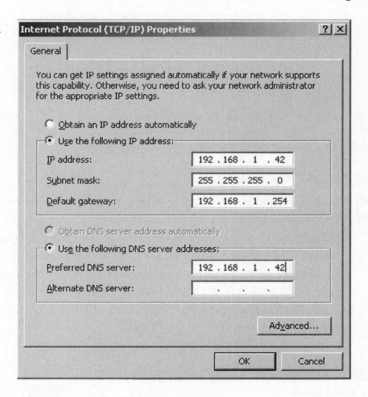

5. Click **OK** to close the Internet Protocol (TCP/IP) Properties screen.
6. Click **OK** to close the network interface property screen.

Performing the Installation

If you have verified the prerequisites for AD, the installation of a DC will likely proceed without any problems. The methods used to install a DC in a new forest and existing forest are almost identical. Although this section will discuss both methods, we will focus on creating the first DC in a new forest.

When you install AD on a new Windows Server 2003 computer, you must run the *Active Directory Installation Wizard*. This wizard may be used to install an additional DC in an existing domain, a new domain in an existing tree, a new domain in a new tree, or a new domain in a new forest.

ANOTHER WAY

You can use the IP address 127.0.0.1 to refer to your local computer. Instead of entering your computer's IP address in the Preferred DNS server dialog box shown in Figure 2-9, you can instead enter 127.0.0.1 in the Preferred DNS server dialog box to achieve the same effect.

To start the Active Directory Installation Wizard, you can simply run the **dcpromo.exe** program from a command window or the Run dialog box. Alternatively, you can use the *Configure Your Server Wizard* to start the Active Directory Installation Wizard by choosing the Domain Controller role when prompted as shown in Figure 2-10.

Figure 2-10

Configure Your Server Wizard

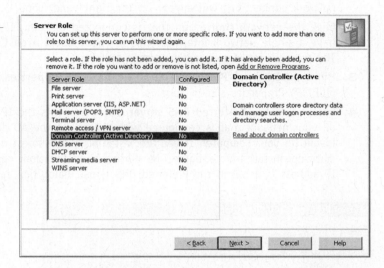

The Configure Your Server Wizard can be started from the Administrative Tools menu on the Windows Start menu or from the Manage Your Server window that appears after you log on to Windows Server 2003.

 INSTALL A NEW FOREST

GET READY. Turn on the computer, and log in as the Administrator user account. Close any windows that appear on the desktop.

1. Click **Start**, and then click **Run**. In the Run dialog box, type **dcpromo**, and press **Enter**. The Active Directory Installation Wizard appears.

2. Click **Next** at the Welcome page. You receive a warning indicating that Windows 95 and Windows NT4.0 SP3 clients are no longer supported in AD.

3. Click **Next** at the Operating System Compatibility page. The Domain Controller Type page appears as shown in Figure 2-11.

Figure 2-11

Specifying Domain Controller Type

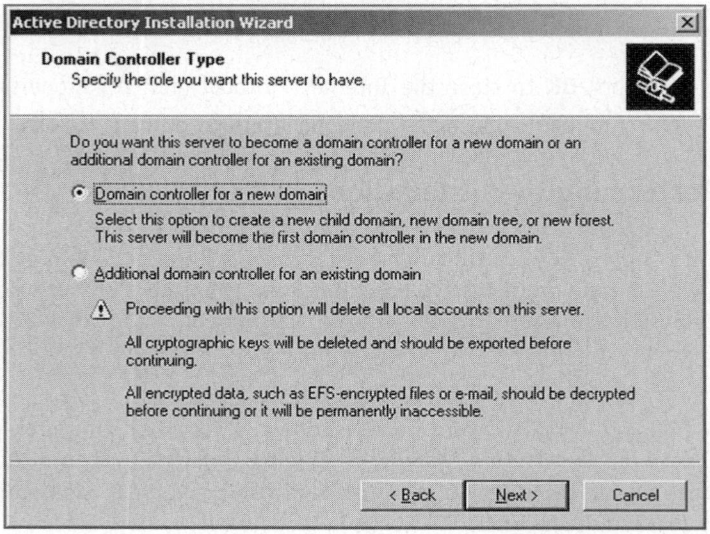

4. At the Domain Controller Type page ensure that **Domain controller for a new domain** is selected and click **Next**. The Create New Domain page is displayed.

➕ **MORE INFORMATION**

If you select **Additional domain controller for an existing domain** in Figure 2-11, you will be prompted to specify the DNS name of the target domain as well as the username and password for a user that is a member of the Domain Admins group in the target domain as shown in Figure 2-12.

Figure 2-12

Specifying the Domain Name and Credentials

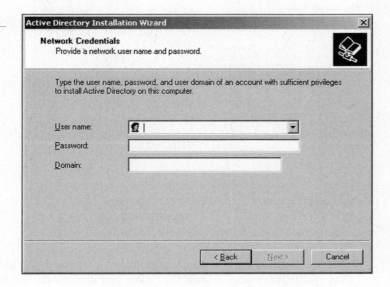

5. At Create New Domain page shown in Figure 2-13, ensure that **Domain in a new forest** is selected and click **Next**. The New Domain Name page appears.

Figure 2-13

Selecting a New Domain

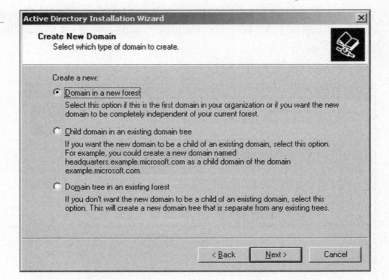

➕ **MORE INFORMATION**

If you select **Child domain in an existing domain tree** or **Domain tree in an existing forest** in Figure 2-13, you will be prompted to specify the DNS name of the new domain as well as the username and password for a user that is a member of the Enterprise Admins group in the target domain as shown in Figure 2-12.

6. At the New Domain Name page, enter the DNS name of the first domain in the forest as shown in Figure 2-14 and click **Next**. The Active Directory Installation Wizard takes a few moments to validate that no other domains exist on the network with the same name. In addition, the Active Directory Installation Wizard contacts the DNS server listed in TCP/IP properties to verify that a DNS zone is properly configured for the new domain. When this process completes, the NetBIOS Domain Name page is displayed.

Figure 2-14

Specifying the Domain Name

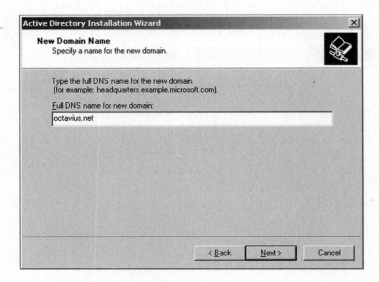

7. At the NetBIOS Domain Name page shown in Figure 2-15, review the NetBIOS name generated from your domain DNS name and click **Next**. The Database and Log Folders page appears.

 TAKE NOTE * By default, the NetBIOS domain name is generated from the first 15 characters of your DNS name before the first period. Windows 9x and NT4 clients use it when joining a domain or when locating a DC for authentication. Accordingly, if you change the default NetBIOS domain name, it is important to record it for future reference.

Figure 2-15

Specifying the NetBIOS Domain Name

TAKE NOTE *

In a production environment, you typically change the default location of the AD database and logs to a different hard drive. This allows for better performance because AD does not need to compete with the system drive when reading and writing data. The AD database and logs must reside on an NTFS partition.

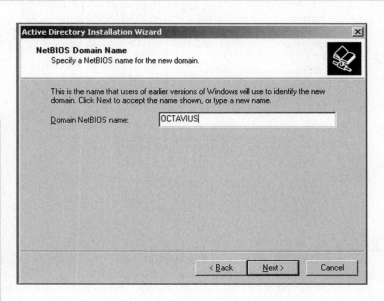

8. At the Database and Log Folders page, review the default location for the AD database and database logs as shown in Figure 2-16 and click **Next**. The Shared System Volume page is displayed.

Figure 2-16

Specifying the Database and
Log Location

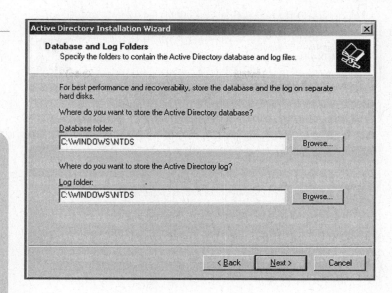

> **TAKE NOTE** *
>
> The SYSVOL shared
> folder is used to deploy
> GPOs to computers
> within the domain as
> well as perform replica-
> tion. It must reside on
> an NTFS volume and
> is typically stored on a
> separate hard drive in
> production environments
> to improve performance.

9. At the Shared System Volume page, review the default location for the SYSVOL
shared folder as shown in Figure 2-17 and click **Next**. Following this, the DNS
Registration Diagnostics page is displayed.

Figure 2-17

Specifying the SYSVOL Folder
Location

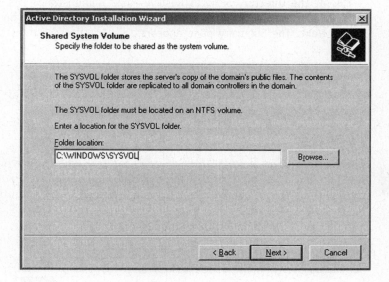

10. At the DNS Registration Diagnostics page, read the results of the DNS diagnostics
to identify whether the Preferred DNS server listed in TCP/IP properties is properly
configured to support SRV records for your domain. Because you are installing a
new forest and have not yet configured DNS, the diagnostic results indicate that
DNS is not installed on your DNS server (your computer) as shown in Figure 2-18.
As a result, ensure that **Install and configure the DNS server on this computer** is
selected and click **Next**. The Permissions page appears.

Figure 2-18

Selecting DNS Options

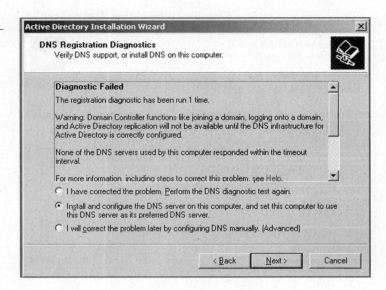

11. At the Permissions page, ensure that **Permissions compatible with Windows 2000 or Windows Server 2003 operating systems** is selected because we will not contain NT4 servers within our forest and click **Next**. The Directory Services Restore Mode Administrator Password page is displayed.

12. At the Directory Services Restore Mode Administrator Password page, enter a complex password in both password dialog boxes as shown in Figure 2-19 and click **Next**. The Summary page appears.

⚠ **WARNING** Because the Directory Services Restore Mode Administrator password is only set during DC installation, ensure that you write this password down in the event that you need to log in to your DC after it has been booted to Directory Services Restore Mode.

Directory Services Restore Mode does not load the AD and is typically used to repair problems with the AD database. You can enter this mode by pressing F8 during the boot process and selecting the Directory Services Restore Mode option from the menu that is displayed.

Figure 2-19

Specifying a Directory Service Restore Mode Password

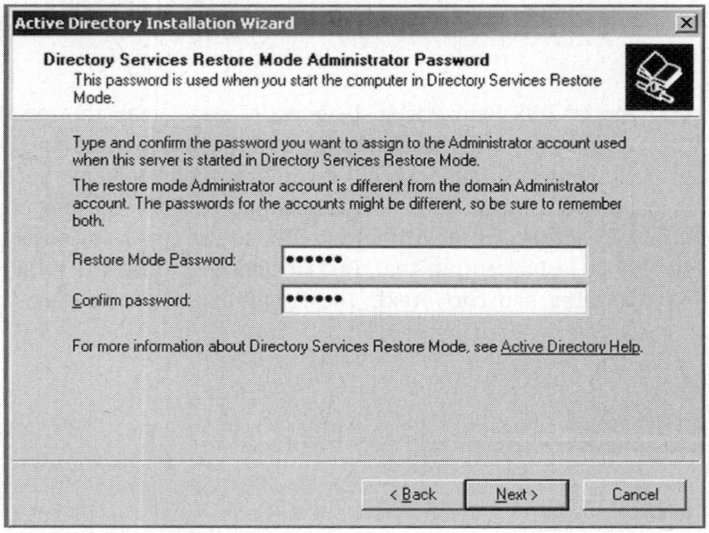

13. At the Summary page, review your installation choices and click **Next** to begin the installation of your DC. The installation typically takes 5 to 15 minutes depending on your hardware and will prompt you for your Windows Server 2003 CD in order to install the files required by the DNS server. After the installation has completed, click the **Finish** button.

14. To finish the installation process, click **Restart Now** on the screen that appears to restart your computer.

Verifying the Installation

After installing a new DC, you should ensure that your domain controller and DNS server are functioning properly before you configure sites, FSMOs, GC, and AD objects.

After the Active Directory Installation Wizard completes, you must reboot your computer to load the AD services. If successful, you should see your domain membership listed on the Computer Name tab of the System utility (**Start** > **Control Panel** > **System Properties**) as shown in Figure 2-20.

Figure 2-20

Verifying Domain Membership

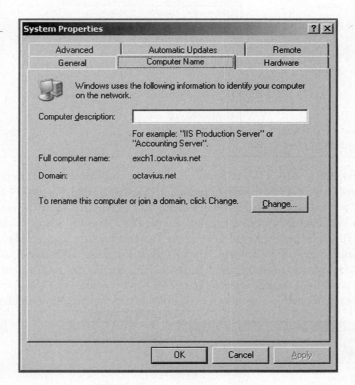

Although your domain membership may indicate the correct information, you should ensure that the AD services are running properly and that no problems were encountered during the installation.

To see any installation-related errors, you can view the **%systemroot%\debug\dcpromo.log** file in a text editor such as notepad.exe as shown in Figure 2-21.

Figure 2-21

Viewing the Active Directory Installation Log

TAKE NOTE*

The %systemroot% variable refers to the location of the Windows operating system directory. On most systems, it refers to C:\Windows.

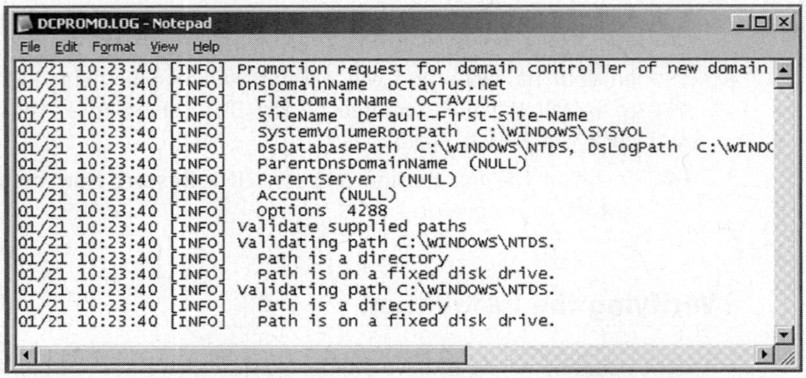

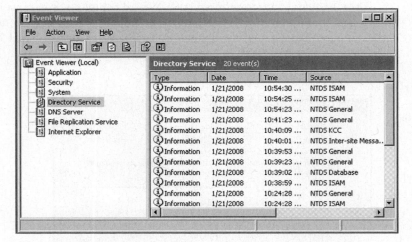

Additionally, you can use the Directory Service log in Event Viewer (**Start > Administrative Tools > Event Viewer**) to ensure that no errors were encountered during the initialization of AD services at boot time as shown in Figure 2-22.

Figure 2-22

Viewing the Directory Service Log

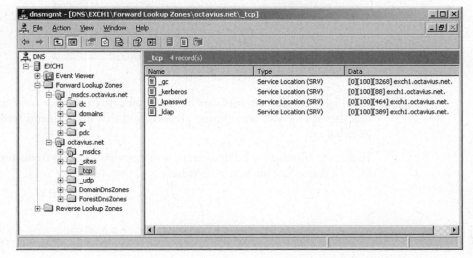

During the first boot following AD installation, your computer contacts the DNS server configured in TCP/IP properties using the DNS dynamic update protocol and creates the necessary SRV records used by clients when locating AD services. To verify the creation of SRV records on a Windows DNS server, simply open the DNS console (**Start > Administrative Tools > DNS**). Under your server object and the Forward Lookup Zones folder, you should see two zones for your domain (_msdcs.*domainname* and *domainname*) with several subfolders if the dynamic update protocol was successful. The subfolders contain SRV records that describe the services available on DCs in your domain. Figure 2-23 shows the two zones created on the EXCH1 server for the octavius.net domain, as well as the SRV records in the _tcp subfolder of the octavius.net zone.

Figure 2-23

Verifying SRV Record Creation

If you do not see any subfolders or SRV records in the DNS console, simply restart the Net Logon service on your DC to rerun the DNS dynamic update process. To restart the Net Logon service, simply open the Services console (**Start** > **Administrative Tools** > **Services**), right click the Net Logon service in the list and select **Restart**. Alternatively, you can restart the Net Logon service from a command window or Run dialog box using the following commands:

net stop netlogon

net start netlogon

If restarting the Net Logon service does not create SRV records, you should ensure that the zone for your domain supports DNS dynamic updates. On a Windows DNS server, simply right click your *domainname* zone in the DNS console and click Properties to view the status of your DNS zone as shown in Figure 2-24.

Figure 2-24

Specifying Dynamic Updates on a Zone

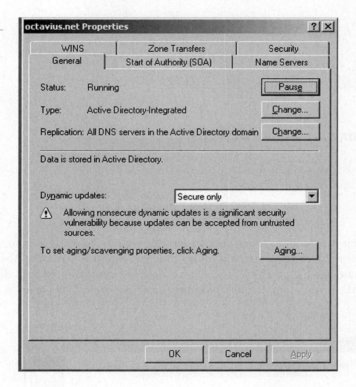

If the Dynamic updates drop-down box is set to None, then you need to change it to allow dynamic updates. Secure dynamic updates are chosen by default if DNS is installed during the Active Directory Installation Wizard and use the Kerberos protocol to ensure that only domain computers are allowed to create records on the DNS server.

TAKE NOTE *

If you used a nonWindows DNS server that does not support dynamic updates to host the DNS zones used by AD, you can manually import the SRV records listed in the %systemroot%\system32\config\netlogon.dns file into the zone file on the nonWindows DNS server.

The dynamic update protocol is not limited to the creation of SRV records in DNS. Computers running Windows 2000 and later in the domain use the dynamic update protocol to automatically create A records for their computers. In large domains, this can create numerous records in the DNS zone and slow down DNS queries as a result. Consequently, you should click on the **Aging** button shown in Figure 2-24 to configure the automatic deletion of outdated DNS records that were added with dynamic update as depicted in Figure 2-25.

Figure 2-25

Enabling DNS Aging and Scavenging

Removing Active Directory

To remove AD from an existing DC, you can simply run the Active Directory Installation Wizard again.

There may be times when you need to remove AD from a DC in your domain such as the decommissioning of a server. In this case, you can simply run the Active Directory Installation Wizard again on the DC. The Active Directory Installation Wizard detects the configuration of AD on the computer and prompts you to remove AD as shown in Figure 2-26.

Figure 2-26

Removing Active Directory

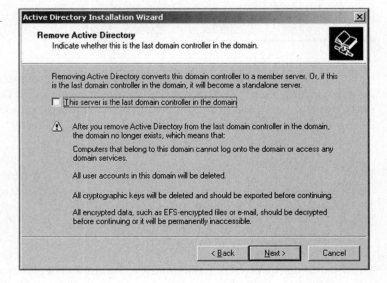

After removing AD from your DC, the computer will still be joined to the domain and will still contain a computer account in the domain unless you select **This server is the last domain controller in the domain** from Figure 2-26.

TAKE NOTE* If the removal of AD fails or you receive an error message during the Active Directory Installation Wizard, you can force the removal of AD by running the **dcpromo/forceremoval** command from a command window or the Run dialog box.

■ Configuring Active Directory

THE BOTTOM LINE Following a successful AD deployment, there are several tasks that you should perform to ensure that AD functions properly. More specifically, you should ensure that your domains and forest run at the highest functional level, as well as create a site structure that allows for efficient replication. Additionally, you should examine the placement of FSMOs and GC to optimize AD performance and reliability and create trusts that allow fast resource access between child domains as well as resource access to foreign domains, forests, and Kerberos realms.

Raising Functional Levels

The domain and forest functional level affects the type of DCs that are allowed in the domain and forest. As a result, raising your domain and forest functional level will allow you to use additional features that are available in more recent versions of AD.

By default, new AD domains are set to the Windows 2000 Mixed functional level for backwards compatibility. In general, you should always ensure that all domains and the forest run at the highest possible domain functional level to allow for the most functionality from AD.

Before deploying Exchange Server 2007, you need to ensure that all domains that will contain Exchange Server or email recipients are raised to the Windows 2000 Native functional level or higher.

 RAISE THE DOMAIN FUNCTIONAL LEVEL

GET READY. Turn on the computer, and log in as the Administrator user account. Close any windows that appear on the desktop.

1. Click **Start**, **Administrative Tools**, and **Active Directory Domains and Trusts**. The Active Directory Domains and Trusts console appears.

2. In the left pane, right click the object that represents your AD domain and select **Raise Domain Functional Level** from the menu. The Raise Domain Functional Level window appears as shown in Figure 2-27.

Figure 2-27

Raising the Domain Functional Level

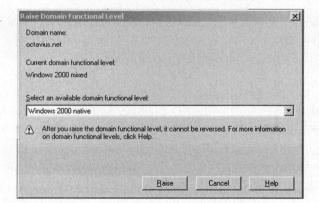

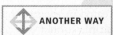 **ANOTHER WAY** You can also raise the domain functional level by right clicking your domain object in the Active Directory Users and Computers console and selecting Raise Domain Functional Level from the menu.

3. Select the appropriate domain functional level from the drop-down box shown in Figure 2-27 and click **Raise**. You will receive a warning indicating that the action is irreversible.

4. Click **OK** to confirm the action.

5. Click **OK** again to close the Raise Domain Functional Level dialog box.

 RAISE THE FOREST FUNCTIONAL LEVEL

GET READY. Turn on the computer, and log in as the Administrator user account. Close any windows that appear on the desktop.

1. Click **Start, Administrative Tools**, and **Active Directory Domains and Trusts**. The Active Directory Domains and Trusts console appears.

2. In the left pane, right click Active Directory Domains and Trusts and select **Raise Forest Functional Level** from the menu. The Raise Forest Functional Level window appears as shown in Figure 2-28.

Figure 2-28

Raising the Forest Functional Level

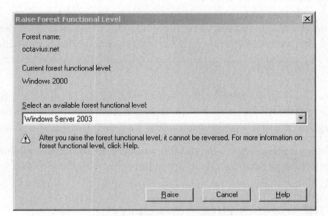

3. Select the appropriate forest functional level from the drop-down box shown in Figure 2-28 and click **Raise**. You will receive a warning indicating that the action is irreversible.

4. Click **OK** to confirm the action.

5. Click **OK** again to close the Raise Forest Functional Level dialog box.

Configuring Sites

After creating a new domain or forest, you should ensure that you create site and subnet objects that represent the physical locations within your organization. Following this, you should configure site link objects between sites to allow for efficient replication.

By default, AD creates a single site called Default-First-Site-Name that includes all DCs in the forest that hold a copy of the AD database. As a result, AD assumes that all DCs are on the same fast LAN and changes between DCs are replicated frequently.

If your organization spans multiple physical locations, you should create multiple site objects that represent each location and move DC objects to the appropriate site.

To ensure that new DCs that are added to the forest are automatically associated with the correct site, you should create ***subnet objects*** that represent the physical TCP/IP subnets that are available in each site. When a DC is added to the forest, the IP address on its network interface is associated with the correct subnet object and a DC object is created in the site that the subnet object is coupled with. A single site can be associated with multiple subnet objects if the site has several different interconnected LANs.

TAKE NOTE*

Instead of creating a new site object for the first site in your organization, you can simply rename Default-First-Site-Name.

Once sites and subnets have been configured, you can create site link objects that connect two or more sites together. Site link objects contain the restrictions used when AD data is replicated between bridgehead servers in different sites.

The protocol used to replicate between DCs is called the *inter-site transport*. Although most replication uses an inter-site transport that uses RPCs over the IP protocol, you can configure SMTP to replicate the AD schema and configuration between domains in the same forest. By default, AD creates a default site link object called DEFAULTIPSITELINK that connects all sites using the IP inter-site transport.

To configure sites, you can use the ***Active Directory Sites and Services*** console (**Start** > **Administrative Tools** > **Active Directory Sites and Services**). Figure 2-29 shows the default site structure following the installation of the first DC (EXCH1) in the octavius.net organization.

TAKE NOTE*

If you wish to configure subnet objects, you must coordinate the TCP/IP configuration within the organization to ensure that each location uses a different TCP/IP subnet.

Figure 2-29

Default Site Structure

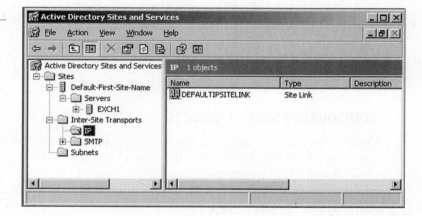

CONFIGURING SITE OBJECTS

Site configuration relies on the details of your actual organization. Although the following exercises use the octavius.net organization introduced in this lesson as an example, they can be performed on any forest for practice. Octavius.net contains two physical locations (Cupertino and Boston) that are linked to each other via the Internet.

 CONFIGURE SITE OBJECTS

GET READY. Turn on the computer, and log in as the Administrator user account. Close any windows that appear on the desktop.

1. Click **Start**, **Administrative Tools**, and **Active Directory Sites and Services**. The Active Directory Sites and Services console appears.

2. In the left pane, expand Default-First-Site-Name. Underneath Default-First-Site-Name, expand the Servers folder. Note that an object representing your DC exists within the Default-First-Site-Name site.

3. Right click Default-First-Site-Name and select **Rename** from the menu. Type **Cupertino** beside the site object and press **Enter**.

4. Right click the Sites folder and select **New Site** from the menu. The New Object—Site window appears.

5. Type **Boston** in the Name dialog box. Next, click on **DEFAULTIPSITELINK** to ensure that the new site uses the default site link object as shown in Figure 2-30 and click **OK**. An Active Directory window appears.

Figure 2-30

Creating a New Site

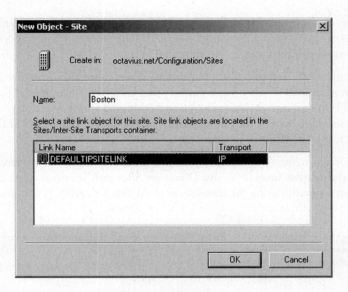

6. Click **OK** to close the Active Directory window.

CONFIGURING SUBNET OBJECTS

Octavius.net has three subnets across the Cupertino and Boston locations. The Cupertino site has a single LAN that uses the 10.1.0.0 subnet. The Boston site has two LANs that use the 10.2.0.0 and 10.3.0.0 subnets.

 CONFIGURE SUBNET OBJECTS

GET READY. Turn on the computer, and log in as the Administrator user account. Close any windows that appear on the desktop.

1. Click **Start**, **Administrative Tools**, and **Active Directory Sites and Services**. The Active Directory Sites and Services console appears.
2. Right click the Subnets folder and select **New Subnet** from the menu. The New Object—Subnet window appears as shown in Figure 2-31.

Figure 2-31

Creating a New Subnet

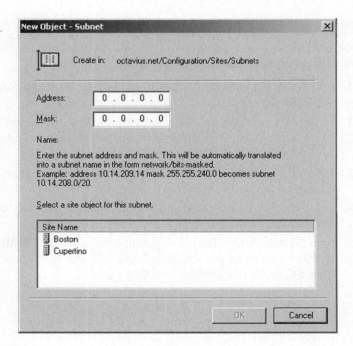

3. In the Address dialog box, enter the IP network **10.1.0.0**. In the Mask dialog box, enter the subnet mask **255.255.0.0**. Next, highlight the **Cupertino** site to associate the 10.1.0.0 network with the Cupertino site and click **OK**.

4. Again, right click the Subnets folder and select **New Subnet** from the menu. In the Address dialog box, enter the IP network **10.2.0.0**. In the Mask dialog box, enter the subnet mask **255.255.0.0**. Next, highlight the **Boston** site to associate the 10.2.0.0 network with the Boston site and click **OK**.

5. Again, right click the Subnets folder and select **New Subnet** from the menu. In the Address dialog box, enter the IP network **10.3.0.0**. In the Mask dialog box, enter the subnet mask **255.255.0.0**. Next, highlight the **Boston** site to associate the 10.3.0.0 network with the Boston site and click **OK**.

CONFIGURING SITE LINK OBJECTS

Octavius.net has different administrative staff members in the Cupertino and Boston locations who are responsible for creating objects for use within their own location. As a result, object replication can occur after business hours without affecting normal operations. You need to ensure that replication only occurs every hour between 9:00 p.m. and 3:00 a.m. Monday to Friday and hourly on weekends.

 CONFIGURE SITE LINK OBJECTS

GET READY. Turn on the computer, and log in as the Administrator user account. Close any windows that appear on the desktop.

1. Click **Start**, **Administrative Tools**, and **Active Directory Sites and Services**. The Active Directory Sites and Services console appears.

2. In the left pane, expand Inter-Site Transports and highlight the **IP** folder. Note the DEFAULTIPSITELINK object within the IP folder.

3. Right click the DEFAULTIPSITELINK object in the right page and select **Delete** from the menu. When prompted to confirm the deletion, click **Yes**.

4. Right click the IP folder in the left pane and select **New Site Link** from the menu. The New Object—Site Link window appears as shown in Figure 2-32.

Figure 2-32

Creating a New Site Link

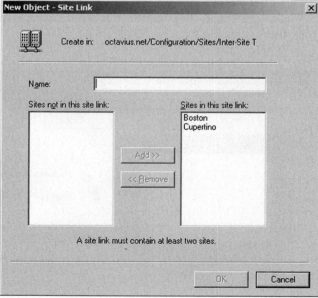

5. Type **Cupertino-to-Boston** in the Name dialog box. Ensure that the Boston and Cupertino sites are included within the site link as shown in Figure 2-32 and click **OK**.

6. Right click the Cupertino-to-Boston site link in the right pane and select **Properties** from the menu. The Cupertino-to-Boston Properties screen appears a shown in Figure 2-33.

Figure 2-33

Configuring Site Properties

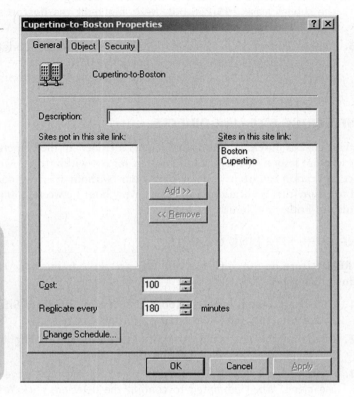

TAKE NOTE*

Because we only have a single site link that can be used to connect the Cupertino and Boston sites, there is no need to modify the cost of this site link to influence the use of a particular site link.

7. Enter **60** in the Replicate every dialog box instead of the default value of 180.

8. Click the **Change Schedule** button. The Schedule for Cupertino-to-Boston window appears.

9. Use your mouse to highlight the cells that indicate 3:00 a.m. to 9:00 p.m. Monday to Friday and choose **Replication Not Available** as depicted in Figure 2-34 and click **OK**.

Figure 2-34

Specifying a Replication Schedule

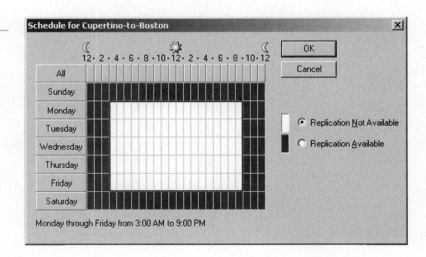

10. Click **OK** to close the Cupertino-to-Boston Properties screen.

CONFIGURING THE PREFERRED BRIDGEHEAD SERVER

Although several DCs will be added to the octavius.net forest in the coming months, you wish to ensure that EXCH1 in the Cupertino site is always used to perform replication using the IP inter-site transport between Cupertino and Boston. The procedures in this section can be used on any server object within the Active Directory Sites and Services console.

 CONFIGURE THE PREFERRED BRIDGEHEAD SERVER

GET READY. Turn on the computer, and log in as the Administrator user account. Close any windows that appear on the desktop.

1. Click **Start**, **Administrative Tools**, and **Active Directory Sites and Services**. The Active Directory Sites and Services console appears.

2. In the left pane, expand Cupertino. Underneath Cupertino, expand the Servers folder. Right click the EXCH1 object and select **Properties** from the menu. The EXCH1 Properties screen is displayed as shown in Figure 2-35.

Figure 2-35

Specifying the Preferred Bridgehead Server

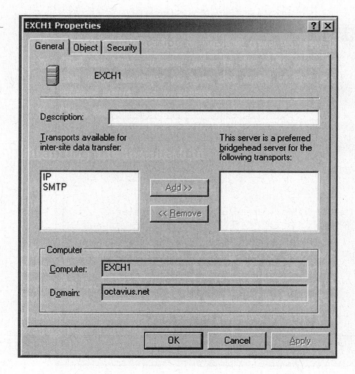

3. By default, all replication protocols are listed in the left dialog box. Highlight **IP** in the left dialog box and click the **Add** >> button to move it to the right dialog box. This will ensure that EXCH1 is used as the bridgehead server for the Cupertino site.

4. Click **OK** to close the EXCH1 Properties screen.

Configuring the Global Catalog

Configuring GC is important to ensure the normal operation of AD and guarantee fast object queries. As a result, it is important to configure GC on the appropriate DCs within your organization.

For best performance, you should ensure that all sites within your organization have at least one DC that contains the GC. Additionally, you must ensure that a GC exists in each site that contains an Exchange server.

If you have a site that is connected to other sites via a slow WAN connection that is ill-suited to GC replication traffic, you may instead choose to enable UGMC on the site to allow fast user logons to a Windows 2000 Native functional level or higher domain.

 ADD THE GLOBAL CATALOG TO A DOMAIN CONTROLLER

GET READY. Turn on the computer, and log in as the Administrator user account. Close any windows that appear on the desktop.

1. Click **Start**, **Administrative Tools**, and **Active Directory Sites and Services**. The Active Directory Sites and Services console appears.

2. In the left pane, expand the site that contains your DC object. Underneath the site, expand the Servers folder and expand your DC object to expose the NTDS Settings object. Right click **NTDS Settings** and select **Properties** from the menu. The NTDS Settings Properties screen is displayed as shown in Figure 2-36.

Figure 2-36

Adding the Global Catalog

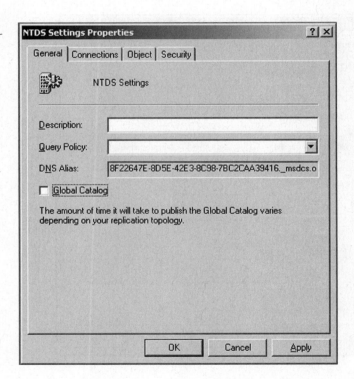

3. Place a check mark in the Global Catalog checkbox and click **OK** to close the NTDS Settings Properties screen.

 ENABLE UNIVERSAL GROUP MEMBERSHIP CACHING ON A SITE

GET READY. Turn on the computer, and log in as the Administrator user account. Close any windows that appear on the desktop.

1. Click **Start**, **Administrative Tools**, and **Active Directory Sites and Services**. The Active Directory Sites and Services console appears.

2. In the left pane, highlight the site that should use UGMC. Right click the **NTDS Settings** object in the right pane, and select **Properties** from the menu. The NTDS Site Settings Properties screen is displayed as shown in Figure 2-37.

Figure 2-37

Enabling Universal Group
Membership Caching

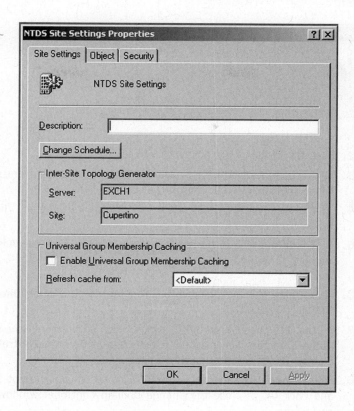

3. Place a check mark in the Enable Universal Group Membership Caching checkbox and click **OK** to close the NTDS Site Settings Properties screen.

Configuring FSMO Roles

FSMO roles provide critical operations in an AD forest and domain. You should become accustomed with the tools used to view and change FSMO roles in order to optimize the performance and reliability of AD.

By default, the forestwide FSMO roles exist on the first DC in the forest and the domainwide FSMO roles exist on the first DC in each domain. After installing new forests, domains, and DCs, you should consider moving the FSMO roles to a DC that is highly visible on the network to allow FSMOs to function normally. You can view and change FSMO roles using one of the following utilities:

- Active Directory Schema MMC snap-in (Schema Master)
- Active Directory Domains and Trusts (Domain Naming Master)
- Active Directory Users and Computers (PDC Emulator, RID Master, Infrastructure Master)

If the DC that holds an FSMO fails, you must use the **ntdsutil.exe** command on a running DC to forcefully seize and assume the FSMO role.

 VIEW AND CHANGE THE SCHEMA MASTER

GET READY. Turn on the computer, and log in as the Administrator user account. Close any windows that appear on the desktop.

1. Click **Start**, **Run**, and type **regsvr32 schmmgmt.dll** in the Run box to register the Active Directory Schema snap-in. If successful, you will see the RegSvr32 window shown in Figure 2-38.

Figure 2-38

Registering the Schema DLL

2. Click **OK** to close the RegSvr32 window.

3. Next, click **Start**, **Run**, type **mmc** in the Run box, and press **Enter** to open the Microsoft Management Console (MMC).

4. In the MMC, click **File** and select **Add/Remove Snap-in**. The Add/Remove Snap-in window appears.

5. Click **Add** and select **Active Directory Schema** from the Add Stand-alone Snap-in window. Click **Add** and then click **Close** to close the Add Stand-alone Snap-in window.

6. Click **OK** in the Add/Remove Snap-in to add the Active Directory Schema to the MMC.

7. In the left pane of the MMC, expand Active Directory Schema. Next, right click Active Directory Schema and select **Change Domain Controller** from the menu. The Change Domain Controller window appears.

8. Select **Specify Name**, enter the DNS name of your current DC in the dialog box and click **OK** to close the Change Domain Controller window.

9. Right click Active Directory Schema and select **Operations Master** from the menu. The Change Schema Master window appears as shown in Figure 2-39.

Figure 2-39

Viewing and Changing the
Schema Master

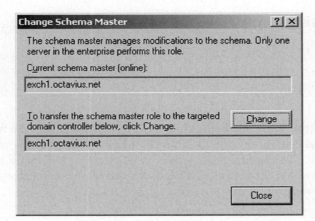

10. Observe the name of the DC that currently holds the Schema Master FSMO role. If the Schema Master DC is online, you can transfer the role to your DC (listed in the second dialog box). To do this, click the **Change** button shown in Figure 2-39 and click **Yes** when prompted to confirm the change.

11. Click **Close** to close the Change Schema Master window.

VIEW AND CHANGE THE DOMAIN NAMING MASTER

GET READY. Turn on the computer, and log in as the Administrator user account. Close any windows that appear on the desktop.

1. Click **Start**, **Administrative Tools**, and **Active Directory Domains and Trusts**. The Active Directory Domains and Trusts console appears.

2. In the left pane, right click Active Directory Domains and Trusts and select **Connect to Domain Controller** from the menu. The Connect to Domain Controller window appears.

3. Select your DC from the list and click **OK** to close the Connect to Domain Controller window.

4. In the left pane, right click Active Directory Domains and Trusts and select **Operations Master** from the menu. The Change Operations Master window appears as shown in Figure 2-40.

Figure 2-40

Viewing and Changing the Domain Naming Master

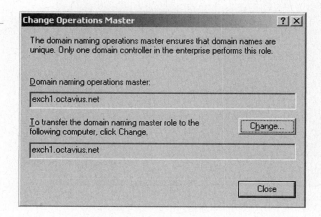

5. Observe the name of the DC that currently holds the Domain Naming Master FSMO role. If the Domain Naming Master DC is online, you can transfer the role to your DC (listed in the second dialog box). To do this, click the **Change** button shown in Figure 2-40 and click **Yes** when prompted to confirm the change.

6. Click **Close** to close the Change Operations Master window.

⊙ VIEW AND CHANGE THE DOMAINWIDE FSMO ROLES

GET READY. Turn on the computer, and log in as the Administrator user account. Close any windows that appear on the desktop.

1. Click **Start, Administrative Tools,** and **Active Directory Users and Computers.** The Active Directory Users and Computers console appears.

2. In the left pane, right click the object that represents your domain and select **Connect to Domain Controller** from the menu. The Connect to Domain Controller window appears.

3. Select your DC from the list and click **OK** to close the Connect to Domain Controller window.

4. In the left pane, right click the object that represents your domain and select **Operations Masters** from the menu. The Operations Master window appears as shown in Figure 2-41. Note that there are three tabs for each of the three domain-wide FSMO roles.

Figure 2-41

Viewing and Changing the
Domainwide FSMO Roles

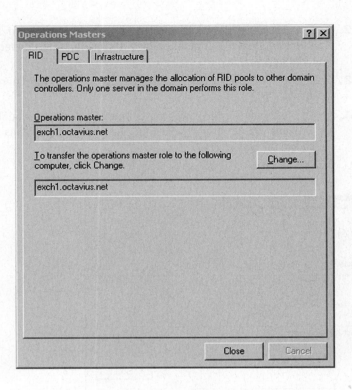

5. Observe the name of the DC that currently holds the RID Master FSMO role. If the RID Master DC is online, you can transfer the role to your DC by clicking the **Change** button and clicking **Yes** when prompted to confirm the change.

6. Click on the PDC tab and observe the name of the DC that currently holds the PDC Emulator FSMO role. If the PDC Emulator DC is online, you can transfer the role to your DC by clicking the **Change** button and clicking **Yes** when prompted to confirm the change.

7. Click on the Infrastructure tab and observe the name of the DC that currently holds the Infrastructure Master FSMO role. If the Infrastructure Master DC is online, you can transfer the role to your DC by clicking the **Change** button and clicking **Yes** when prompted to confirm the change.

8. Click **Close** to close the Operations Master window.

SEIZE A FAILED FSMO ROLE

GET READY. Turn on the computer, and log in as the Administrator user account. Close any windows that appear on the desktop.

1. Click **Start**, **Run**, type **ntdsutil** in the Run dialog box, and press **Enter**. The ntdsutil.exe prompt appears in a command window.

2. At the ntdsutil.exe prompt, type **roles** and press **Enter** to open the FSMO maintenance prompt.

3. At the FSMO maintenance prompt, type **connections** and press **Enter** to open the server connections prompt.

4. At the server connections prompt, type **connect to server DC** where *DC* is the DNS name of your current DC and press **Enter**. Type **quit** at the server connections prompt, and press **Enter** to return to the FSMO maintenance prompt.

5. At the FSMO maintenance prompt, type one of the following commands to seize the appropriate FSMO role and press **Enter**. You will be presented with the Role Seizure Confirmation Dialog window as shown in Figure 2-42.

- Seize PDC
- Seize RID Master
- Seize schema Master
- Seize infrastructure Master
- Seize domain naming Master

Figure 2-42

Seizing an FSMO Role

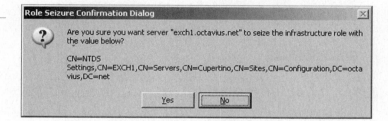

6. Click **Yes** to confirm the role seizure.
7. Type **qui**t at the FSMO maintenance prompt, and press **Enter** to return to the ntdsutil.exe prompt.
8. Type **quit** at the ntdsutil.exe prompt, and press **Enter** to close ntdsutil.

Configuring Trusts

You may be required to create a trust relationship between domains in order to speed up authentication and resource access within your own forest to allow group membership and resource access to a remote forest, domain or Kerberos realm. As a result, you should understand how to set up additional trust relationships in your forest.

Two-way transitive trusts are automatically created between the first domains in each tree within a forest as well as between parent domains and their child domains. This gives administrators in a domain the ability to assign permissions to users and groups in other domains within the forest. In addition, trust relationships allow users and groups to become members of groups in another domain within the same forest.

Although the default trusts in a forest cannot be managed using Windows utilities, you can use the Active Directory Domains and Trusts console (**Start** > **Administrative Tools** > **Active Directory Domains and Trusts**) to create additional shortcut trusts between domains in different trees to speed up performance. In addition, the Active Directory Domains and Trusts console can be used to create trusts to domains, forests, and Kerberos realms outside of your forest to allow for remote permissions assignment or group membership.

Before creating a trust relationship, you should ensure that your computer can contact a DC in the target domain, forest, or Kerberos Realm. This often involves ensuring that the DNS server listed in TCP/IP properties for members of the domain is configured to forward requests for the target domain to a DNS server that holds the necessary A or SRV records for the target domain. On a Windows DNS server, you can simply open the DNS console (**Start** > **Administrative Tools** > **DNS**), and highlight the Forwarders tab of your DNS server properties to add a forwarder entry as shown in Figure 2-43.

Figure 2-43

Configuring a DNS Forwarding Entry

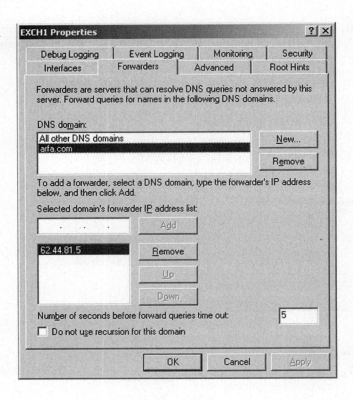

The DNS server configured in Figure 2-43 will forward any DNS name resolution requests for arfa.com to the DNS server with the IP address 62.44.81.5.

Once you are able to resolve names in the target domain successfully, you can right click the object that represents your domain in the Active Directory Domains and Trusts console, choose **Properties**, and highlight the Trusts tab as shown in Figure 2-44.

Figure 2-44

Manually Configuring Trust Relationships

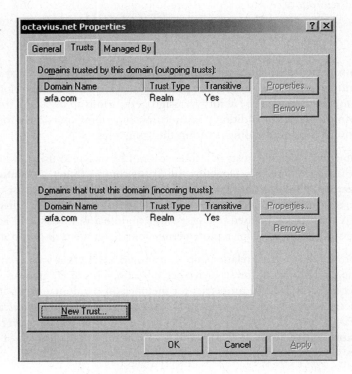

TAKE NOTE* Manually created trusts can become corrupted over time. You can check the validity of a trust in the Active Directory Domains and Trusts console by selecting the **Properties** button beside a trust shown in Figure 2-44.

Figure 2-44 already indicates that a two-way realm trust has been created between your domain and arfa.com (outgoing trust) as well as between arfa.com and your domain (incoming trust). To create additional trusts, you can click on the **New Trust** button shown in Figure 2-44 to open the New Trust Wizard. After specifying the name of the target domain, forest, or Kerberos realm in the New Trust Wizard, the options available will be specific to the type of trust available. You may be prompted for the style of trust (transitive or nontransitive), as well as the direction of the trust (one-way outgoing, one-way incoming, two-way). If you create a one-way incoming or two-way trust, you must contact the remote DC to configure the trust and will need to enter a password to validate the trust or a username and password of the remote Administrator to automatically create the trust.

■ Managing Active Directory Objects

THE BOTTOM LINE The creation and management of OU, user, computer, and group objects is a common daily administrative task for AD and Exchange administrators. In addition, Group Policy is often used to configure the settings applied to users and computers within AD including email configuration. Consequently, it is important to understand the procedures and utilities used to manage AD objects and Group Policy.

Creating and Managing Organizational Units

Before creating objects within a domain, you should ensure that a suitable OU structure exists to organize those objects.

OUs are primarily used to organize objects within a domain and may be created or managed using the Active Directory Users and Computers console (**Start** > **Administrative Tools** > **Active Directory Users and Computers**). The OUs that you create for your domain will depend on the requirements of the organization. As a result, new domains only contain a single Domain Controllers OU by default to contain DC computer accounts. All other objects such as user, computer, and group accounts are organized into default folders and should be moved to the appropriate OUs after they have been created.

Figure 2-45 shows the default Domain Controllers OU and folder structure for the octavius .net domain as well as additional East and West OUs that were created by the domain administrator to suit the organization. The East and West OUs contain subordinate OUs for each of the major departments in octavius.net.

To rename, move, or delete an OU, you can simply right click the OU within the Active Directory Users and Computers console and select the appropriate option. Before deleting an OU, ensure that the objects within the OU have been moved to another location.

TAKE NOTE* OU icons can be easily differentiated from folder icons in the Active Directory Users and Computers console because OU icons contain a picture of a book.

Figure 2-45

Octavius.net Organizational
Unit Structure

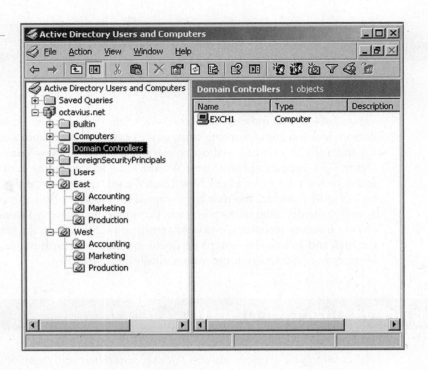

⊖ CREATE A NEW ORGANIZATIONAL UNIT

GET READY. Turn on the computer, and log in as the Administrator user account. Close any
windows that appear on the desktop.

1. Click **Start**, **Administrative Tools**, and **Active Directory Users and Computers**.
   The Active Directory Users and Computers console appears.
2. In the left pane, right click the object that represents your AD domain and
   select **New** followed by **Organizational Unit** from the menu. The New Object—
   Organizational Unit window appears as shown in Figure 2-46.

Figure 2-46

Creating a New
Organizational Unit

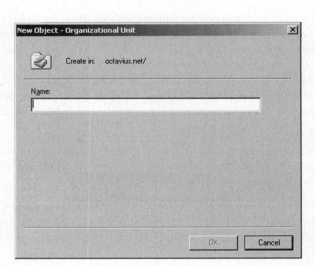

3. Type the name of the OU in the Name dialog box and click **OK**.

Creating and Managing Users

Exchange server relies on the information stored within user accounts when relaying email to mailboxes within the organization and when sending emails outside the organization. In order to manage Exchange Server 2007, it is important to first understand how to create and manage user accounts.

User account objects in AD store a great deal of information that is used by various programs and services. As with OUs, you can create user accounts using the Active Directory Users and Computers console (**Start** > **Administrative Tools** > **Active Directory Users and Computers**). When you create a user account, you need only specify the user's name, UPN, and password information. However, when you view the properties of a user account by right clicking the user account object and selecting **Properties** from the menu, you can navigate the several tabs to specify several more attributes as shown in Figure 2-47 for the user Bob Jones.

Figure 2-47

Editing User Attributes

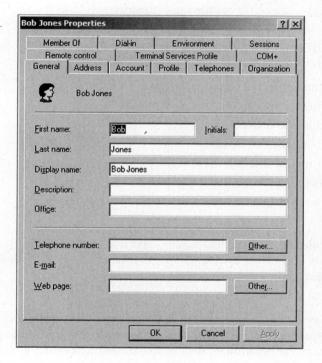

If you need to change the attributes of several user accounts simultaneously, simply select each user account object in Active Directory Users and Computers while holding down the **Ctrl** key on the keyboard, right click the selection, and choose **Properties**. This opens the Properties for Multiple Items window as shown in Figure 2-48. Not all user attributes are available in the Properties for Multiple Items window because many attributes are user specific.

Figure 2-48

Editing the Attributes for Multiple Users

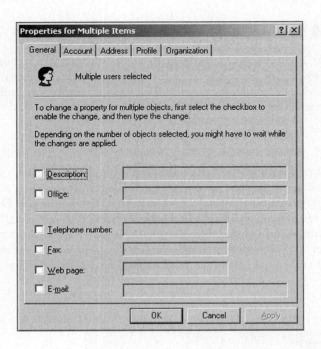

As with OU objects, most user maintenance can be performed by right clicking the user account object and selecting the appropriate option. This includes:

- Renaming the user account
- Moving the user account
- Deleting the user account
- Disabling the user account
- Resetting the user password
- Adding the user account to a group
- Copying the user account

 TAKE NOTE *

If you accidentally delete a user account and re-create it, you must reassign all permissions to resources because the deleted user's SID is never reused. As a result, you should disable user accounts rather than delete them when possible.

To save time and ease management, many administrators create a sample user account for a specific department called a *user account template* that contains attributes that are common to all users in the department, such as account restrictions and group membership. When creating users in the future, you can then copy the template user account for that department and supply only the unique user information for the particular user.

CREATE A USER ACCOUNT

GET READY. Turn on the computer, and log in as the Administrator user account. Close any windows that appear on the desktop.

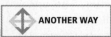 **ANOTHER WAY**

Instead, right click your domain object to create a new user account directly under the domain object. However, this is considered poor organization for AD objects.

1. Click **Start**, **Administrative Tools**, and **Active Directory Users and Computers**. The Active Directory Users and Computers console appears.

2. In the left pane, locate the OU object that should contain the user account. Right click the OU object and select **New** followed by **User** from the menu. The New Object—User window appears as shown in Figure 2-49.

Figure 2-49

Creating a New User

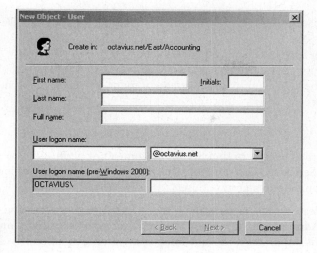

TAKE NOTE *

By default, AD domains require complex passwords for user accounts. These passwords must be at least six characters long and contain three of the four different types of characters (uppercase, lowercase, numbers, symbols).

3. Supply the appropriate information in the First name, Initials, and Last name fields as necessary.

4. In the User logon name dialog box, select a logon name that is unique in your domain and ensure that the correct domain name is listed next to it. This will become the UPN for the user account.

5. Observe the User logon name (preWindows 2000) that must be used if the user logs into the domain from a Windows 9x or NT4 client computer, and click **Next**. You will see the screen shown in Figure 2-50.

Figure 2-50

Specifying User Password Configuration

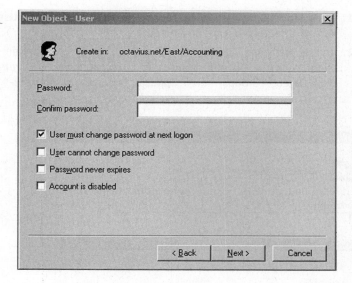

6. Supply the appropriate password information and options for your user account and click **Next**. You will be presented with a summary of your selections.

7. Click **Finish** to create the user account object.

Creating and Managing Groups

Groups are important to reduce the time and effort needed to administer resources in an AD and Exchange Server environment. Consequently, it is important to understand how groups can be created and managed using Active Directory Users and Computers.

Every domain contains a Domain Admins security group in the default Users folder in the Active Directory Users and Computers console that allows members to administer the domain. In addition, the forest root domain contains an Enterprise Admins group that allows forestwide administration and a Schema Admins group that allows modification of the AD schema. The first Administrator account in the forest automatically belongs to all three groups.

AD uses group objects to simplify the assignment of permissions to multiple user accounts. Exchange Server can also use groups to simplify email administration for multiple users or relay information to a group of users.

You can create group accounts using the Active Directory Users and Computers console (**Start** > **Administrative Tools** > **Active Directory Users and Computers**). When creating a group it is important to use a naming convention that accurately describes the group. For example, **Accounts Payable GG East** can be used to easily indicate a Global Group that contains Accounts Payable users in the East division of the organization.

Once created, you can modify the properties of the group and change its type or scope or group membership. Groups can contain user, group, and computer objects as members. To, rename, move, or delete a group, you can right click the group within the Active Directory Users and Computers console and select the appropriate option.

CREATE A NEW GROUP

GET READY. Turn on the computer, and log in as the Administrator user account. Close any windows that appear on the desktop.

Deleting a group does not delete the members of the group.

1. Click **Start**, **Administrative Tools**, and **Active Directory Users and Computers**. The Active Directory Users and Computers console appears.
2. In the left pane, locate the OU object that should contain the group account. Right click the OU object and select **New** followed by **Group** from the menu. The New Object—Group window appears as shown in Figure 2-51.

Figure 2-51

Creating a New Group

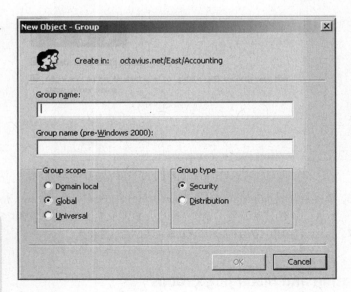

Instead, right click your domain object to create a new group account directly under the domain object. However, this is considered poor organization for AD objects.

3. Supply a name in the Group name dialog box and select the appropriate group scope and type. Observe the Group name (preWindows 2000) that must be used if the user logs in to the domain from a Windows 9x or NT4 client computer, and click **OK**.

➜ ADD MEMBERS TO A GROUP

ANOTHER WAY

If you want to add the current group as a member of another group, you can highlight the **Member Of** tab shown in Figure 2-52.

GET READY. Turn on the computer, and log in as the Administrator user account. Close any windows that appear on the desktop.

1. Click **Start**, **Administrative Tools**, and **Active Directory Users and Computers**. The Active Directory Users and Computers console appears.

2. In the left pane, locate the group object that you wish to modify. Right click the group object and select **Properties**. Highlight the **Members** tab of the group's properties as shown in Figure 2-52.

Figure 2-52

Modifying Group Membership

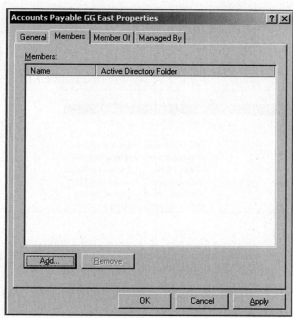

3. Click the **Add** button. The Select Users, Contacts, Computers, or Groups window appears as shown in Figure 2-53.

Figure 2-53

Searching for Objects

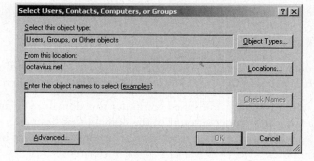

4. If you plan to add computer accounts to your group, you must select the **Object Types** button, place a checkbox beside Computers in the Object Types window, and click **OK**.

5. In the Select Users, Contacts, Computers, or Groups window, you can supply the name of the object or search for the object by clicking the **Advanced** button, supplying optional search criteria, and clicking the **Find Now** button to view an object list as depicted in Figure 2-54.

Figure 2-54

Listing Available Objects

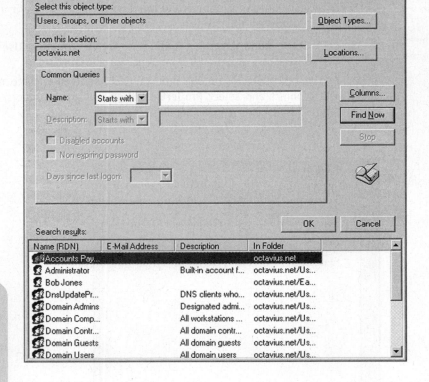

6. Select the appropriate object from the list and click **OK** to return to the Select Users, Contacts, Computers, or Groups window.

7. Click **OK** to return to the group properties window.

8. Click **OK** to modify the group membership.

Creating and Managing Computers

Computer objects are used to provide Kerberos authentication and Group Policy for most computers within your domain. Consequently, it is important to understand how to create and administer computer objects in AD.

Computer objects exist for all Windows NT-based computers within a domain. Although Windows 9x computers can join a domain, they are not represented by computer objects.

When you join a Windows NT-based computer to a domain, you are prompted for the username and password of a user account in the domain that has rights to add computer objects to AD. This user account is then used to create a computer object in the domain that represents the computer.

By default, computer objects are created in the default Computers folder in the domain and named according to the NetBIOS name of the computer. You should always move computer objects to the appropriate OU after they have been created for organization and assignment of Group Policy.

Alternatively, you can create computer objects named after the NetBIOS name of each client computer before the computers are joined to the domain to save time and ensure that the computer accounts are located in the correct OU before the client computer joins the domain. This process is called *prestaging* computer objects.

TAKE NOTE*

Administrators can create an unlimited number of computer objects within a domain, whereas nonadministrative user accounts have the ability to add up to 10 computer accounts in the domain.

Although the location of computer objects determines the GPOs that the associated computers receive, computer objects are primarily used by the Kerberos authentication protocol. Each computer object contains a system-generated password that is synchronized to the associated client computer and used to secure the Kerberos protocol between the client and DC during authentication. This system-generated password is changed every 14 days and may occasionally become unsynchronized. If a computer object becomes unsynchronized, the client computer will no longer be able to authenticate any user to the domain. In this case, you can right click the computer object in the Active Directory Users and Computers console and select **Reset Account**. Following this, you must remove the domain membership on the computer and then rejoin it to the domain so that it can resynchronize with the associated computer object.

Similarly, to move or delete a computer object, you can right click the computer object within the Active Directory Users and Computers console and select the appropriate option.

⊙ PRESTAGE A COMPUTER OBJECT

GET READY. Turn on the computer, and log in as the Administrator user account. Close any windows that appear on the desktop.

TAKE NOTE*

Only Windows 2000 and later computers can use Group Policy and Kerberos authentication.

1. Click **Start**, **Administrative Tools**, and **Active Directory Users and Computers**. The Active Directory Users and Computers console appears.

2. In the left pane, locate the OU object that should contain the computer account. Right click the OU object and select **New** followed by **Computer** from the menu. The New Object—Computer window appears as shown in Figure 2-55.

Figure 2-55

Creating a Computer Object

⬙ ANOTHER WAY

Instead, you can right click your domain object to create a new computer account directly under the domain object. However, this is considered poor organization for AD objects.

3. Supply the NetBIOS name of the client computer in the Computer name dialog box and select the user that is allowed to join the computer to the domain and use this computer object. For a Windows NT4 computer, the NetBIOS name must match the name in the Computer name (preWindows 2000) dialog box and you must select **Assign this computer account as a preWindows 2000 computer**. If the

computer is a Windows NT4 BDC, you must additionally select **Assign this computer account as a backup domain controller**. Click **Next** to view the Managed window shown in Figure 2-56.

Figure 2-56

Specifying a Managed Computer Object

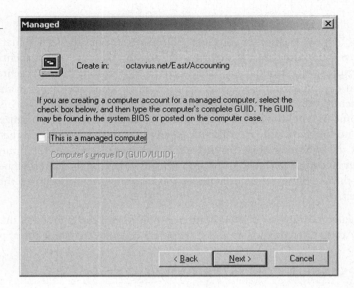

4. If the computer will be installed using Remote Installation Services (RIS) or Windows Deployment Services (WDS), then you should select **This is a managed computer** and enter the GUID that is stored in the BIOS of the client computer and used to perform remote installations.

5. Click **Next** to review your configuration options.

6. Click **Finish** to create the computer account.

RESET A COMPUTER OBJECT

GET READY. Turn on the computer, and log in as the Administrator user account. Close any windows that appear on the desktop.

1. Click **Start**, **Administrative Tools**, and **Active Directory Users and Computers**. The Active Directory Users and Computers console appears.

2. In the left pane, locate the appropriate computer object. Right click the computer object and select **Reset Account**.

3. Click **Yes** when prompted to confirm the reset.

4. Click **OK** to close the confirmation dialog box. Following this step, you must configure the client computer to remove domain membership and then reconfigure the client computer to join the domain again. For Windows 2000 and later computers, you can configure domain membership on the Computer Name tab of System properties in the Control Panel.

5. On the client computer, click **Start**, **Control Panel**, and **System**. The System Properties window appears.

6. Highlight the **Computer Name** tab and click the **Change** button. The Computer Name Changes window appears.

7. Select **Workgroup** and supply a temporary workgroup name that is less than 15 characters long and click **OK**. Enter the credentials of a valid domain user account when prompted and click **OK**.

8. Click **OK** when prompted to reboot your computer. Click **OK** to close the System Properties dialog box and reboot your computer.

9. After your client computer has rebooted, click **Start**, **Control Panel**, and **System**. The System Properties window appears.

10. Highlight the **Computer Name** tab and click the **Change** button. The Computer Name Changes window appears.

11. Select Domain, enter the FQDN of the domain and click **OK**. Enter the credentials of a valid domain user account when prompted and click **OK**.

12. Click **OK** to close the System Properties window and reboot your computer.

Configuring Group Policy

By configuring Group Policy, Active Directory can be used to configure user and computer settings within your domain.

Group Policy is a versatile administrative tool in AD that can be used to apply software and configure settings on computers within the domain using GPOs. To function, GPOs must be linked to a site, domain, or OU that contains user or computer accounts.

GPO settings are stored in one of two sections within a GPO: the *Computer Configuration* and the *User Configuration*. Windows 2000 or later computers apply the Computer Configuration from all GPOs that are linked to a site, domain, or OU object that contain their computer account. Similarly, when domain users log in to a Windows 2000 or later computer, they apply the User Configuration from all GPOs that are linked to a site, domain, or OU object that contains their user account.

A single user or computer object may receive the settings from several GPOs. To prevent conflicts in the event that two GPOs contain different values for the same setting, GPOs are applied to user and computer objects based on the link in the following order:

1. Site
2. Domain
3. Parent OU
4. Child OUs

Thus, if the User Configuration section of a GPO linked to your domain has a setting that conflicts with the same setting in the User Configuration section of a GPO that is linked to the OU that contains your user account, you will receive the setting that is configured in the GPO that is linked to the OU that contains your user account.

There are two default GPOs in each AD domain. The Default Domain Policy GPO is linked to the domain object and applies to all users and computers in the domain by default. The Default Domain Controllers Policy GPO is linked to the Domain Controllers OU and applies to DC computer accounts.

To create and manage additional GPOs that are linked to a domain or OU object, you can right click the domain or OU object in the Active Directory Users and Computers console, select **Properties**, and highlight the Group Policy tab as shown in Figure 2-57.

Figure 2-57

Managing Group Policy Objects

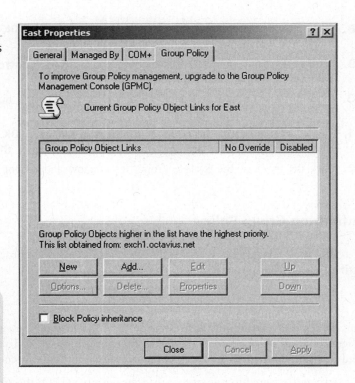

ANOTHER WAY

The *Group Policy Management Console (GPMC)* is a comprehensive tool used to manage GPOs that are linked to sites, domains, and OUs. You can download the GPMC from Microsoft's Web site.

To create a new GPO, you can click the **New** button shown in Figure 2-57. Alternatively, you can link an existing GPO to the current domain or OU object by selecting the **Add** button and selecting the appropriate GPO.

To create and manage GPOs that are linked to sites objects, you can access the properties of a site object in the Active Directory Sites and Services console and select the **Group Policy** tab. The options available are identical to those in Figure 2-57.

To edit a GPO, simply click on the Edit button shown in Figure 2-57 to open the *Group Policy Object Editor* depicted in Figure 2-58. Using the Group Policy Object Editor, you can select the appropriate configuration options under the User Configuration or Computer Configuration section.

Figure 2-58

Modifying Group Policy Object Settings

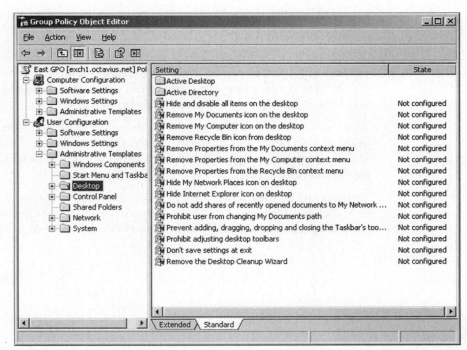

The Administrative Templates sections under the User Configuration and Computer Configuration can be expanded to include additional configuration options available for various software packages. Many software manufacturers allow you to download and install *administrative templates* that can be imported into a GPO and used to configure settings for their software applications.

To import an additional administrative template into a GPO, right click Administrative Templates under the User Configuration or Computer Configuration shown in Figure 2-58, select **Add/Remove Templates**, and specify the templates that you wish to add. Figure 2-59 shows a GPO with the Microsoft Outlook 2007 administrative template added.

Figure 2-59

Configuring Administrative Templates

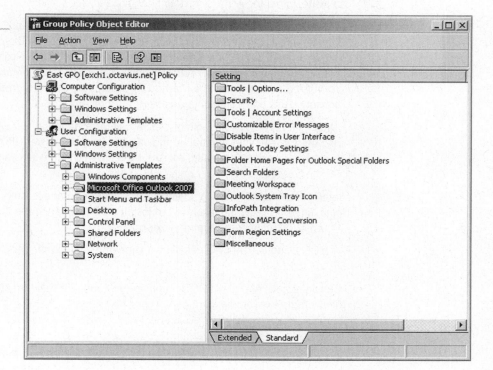

SUMMARY SKILL MATRIX

IN THIS LESSON YOU LEARNED:

- AD is maintained on DCs that contain a database of objects for a domain within a tree in a forest. Each DC also contains a copy of the object schema and forest configuration.

- Leaf objects represent users and network resources, whereas container objects are used to organize leaf objects within an AD database. Most leaf objects can be created using the Active Directory Users and Computers console.

- Domains in a forest provide their own security and use trust relationships to allow the assignment of permissions on resources to users in remote domain. Two-way transitive trusts exist by default between parent and child domains in a forest as well as between the parent domains of each tree in the forest. Additional trusts can be manually created using the Active Directory Domains and Trusts console.

- AD uses security groups with scopes that are global, universal, or domain local to organize the assignment of permissions in the forest.

- Functional levels are used to represent the level of backwards compatibility allowed in a domain and forest. You can raise your functional level to reduce backwards compatibility and enable new domain features. You can raise your domain and forest functional level using the Active Directory Domains and Trusts console.

- Site and subnet objects are used to represent different locations within an AD forest. You can create site link objects between sites that specify restrictions for replication. Site, subnet, and site link objects can be managed using the Active Directory Sites and Services console.

- The GC is a database of all object names, UPNs, and universal groups in the forest. It is used to speed forestwide searching, allow remote logins, maintain universal group membership, and allow logins for Windows 2000 Native and higher functional level domains. You can specify the placement of GC using the Active Directory Sites and Services console.

- UGMC allows for fast user logins in sites that do not contain a GC and may be configured on a site within the Active Directory Sites and Services console.

- FSMO roles provide special functions in an AD forest and domain. Each forest contains a Schema Master FSMO that may be configured using the Active Directory Schema MMC snap-in, as well as a Domain Naming Master FSMO that may be configured using Active Directory Domains and Trusts console. Similarly, each domain contains a PDC Emulator, RID Master, and Infrastructure Master FSMO that may be configured using the Active Directory Users and Computers console.

- Group Policy is a powerful administrative tool for configuring software and settings on computers within your domain using GPOs. You can administer GPOs using the Active Directory Users and Computers console, the Active Directory Sites and Services console, and the GPMC.

- Before installing AD, you should ensure that you have the necessary operating system, login, and DNS requirements. You can install a DC by running the Configure Your Server Wizard or by running the dcpromo.exe command.

- After installing AD on a DC, you should verify the addition of the AD services and DNS SRV records.

- You can remove AD from a DC by running the Configure Your Server Wizard or by running the dcpromo.exe command.

■ Knowledge Assessment

Fill in the Blank

Complete the following sentences by writing the correct word or words in the blanks provided.

1. To begin an AD installation, you can run the _____ command.

2. The authentication protocol used by Windows 2000 and later computers in a domain is called _____.

3. The _____ FSMO role is responsible for time synchronization across the domain.

4. To complete the authentication process in a domain that is at the Windows 2000 Native functional level or higher, a _____ must be contacted.

5. Following an AD installation, you should verify the existence of _____ records on the DNS server that holds the zone for the AD domain.

6. The letters _____ represent the general principle used when assigning users to groups in a large forest.

7. To view the DC that holds the Schema Master FSMO role, you must use the _____ MMC snap-in.

8. A(n) _____ is an LDAP name used to describe each object within AD.

9. To speed up resource access across child domains in your forest, you can create _____ trusts.

10. To enable Universal Group Membership Caching, you must use the _____ console.

Multiple Choice

Circle the letter that corresponds to the best answer.

1. You receive an object-related error when attempting to create a new user account within your domain. What FSMO role should you ensure is online to complete the addition of the user account?
   a. PDC Emulator
   b. Domain Naming Master
   c. Infrastructure Master
   d. RID Master

2. You plan on promoting an existing Windows Server 2003 computer to become an additional domain controller in your domain. To which group must the user account you specify during the AD installation belong at minimum?
   a. Domain Users
   b. Domain Admins
   c. Enterprise Admins
   d. Schema Admins

3. Which of the following utilities must you use to seize an FSMO role?
   a. ntdsutil.exe
   b. dcpromo.exe
   c. Active Directory Domains and Trusts
   d. Active Directory Sites and Services

4. Which of the following are container objects in the AD database? (Choose all that apply.)
   a. Group policy
   b. Site
   c. Domain
   d. OU

5. Which of the following objects is used to locate the correct site for a newly installed DC?
   a. Site link
   b. Subnet
   c. Locator
   d. Bridgehead

6. Several users called you today stating that they could not change their passwords. After investigating, you also noticed that the time on their computers was also incorrect. Which of the following FSMO roles may be unavailable?
   a. PDC Emulator
   b. RID Master
   c. Infrastructure Master
   d. Schema Master

7. Which of the following DCs are allowed to participate in a Windows 2000 Native mode domain? (Choose all that apply.)
   a. Windows NT4 Server
   b. Windows 2000 Server
   c. Windows Sever 2003
   d. Windows Server 2008

8. A single user within your organization calls you for help after having trouble logging on to the domain. After further investigation, you notice that the user is able to log on to the domain from another computer and that no users are able to successfully log on to the domain from the user's original computer. What is most likely the cause of the problem?
   a. The time on the computer is incorrect and must be changed
   b. The user account has been disabled and must be enabled
   c. The user account has been locked and must be unlocked
   d. The computer account for the user's computer has become corrupted and must be reset

9. You wish to create a group that will contain the Marketing staff within your own domain. This group will be assigned permissions to resources in other domains within your forest. What is the most appropriate scope for this new group?
   a. Local
   b. Global
   c. Domain local
   d. Universal

10. When attempting to remove AD from an existing DC that you wish to decommission, you receive an error message. Which switch to the dcpromo.exe command will allow you to remove this DC from the domain?
    a. /force
    b. /remove
    c. /forceremoval
    d. /f

True/False

Circle T if the statement is true or F if the statement is false.

T F **1.** Tokens are issued to users following authentication and used to provide access to resources that list the user in their ACL.

T F **2.** When a domain functional level is set to Windows 2000 Interim, only Windows 2000 and later DCs are allowed to participate in domain authentication.

T F **3.** Global groups may only be used in the local domain but can contain objects from any domain in the forest.

T F **4.** Computer objects may be managed using the Active Directory Users and Computers console.

T F **5.** By default, two-way transitive trusts are between all domains in a forest.

T F **6.** To control replication, you configure the properties of site link objects.

T F **7.** When possible, you should ensure that each site in the forest contains a DC that contains the GC role.

T F **8.** You can configure Group Policy using the Active Directory Domains and Trusts console.

T F **9.** The Domain Naming Master FSMO role should be on a DC that contains the GC.

T F **10.** A single AD domain can contain an unlimited number of objects.

Review Questions

1. Explain why it is important to create sites after deploying your first domain in the forest.
2. Detail reasons why understanding the function and location of your FSMO roles will help you troubleshoot AD problems.
3. Give some reasons why each AD site should contain a DC that hosts the GC.
4. Explain why AD domains are a security and replication boundary.

■ Case Scenarios

Scenario 2-1: Designing a Forest

You are the network administrator for a shipping company with locations in the United States, Canada, and Japan. There are five offices in the United States, three offices in Canada, and three offices in Japan. In a short memo, diagram a sample forest, domain, and OU structure that will accommodate this organization.

Scenario 2-2: Planning for Sites, GC, and FSMO Roles

In the forest diagram that you created for the company described in Scenario 2-1, label the appropriate sites that should be created to ensure efficient replication. Assuming that each site has a minimum of two DCs, label the location of GC servers and FSMO roles.

Deploying Exchange Server 2007

LESSON SKILL MATRIX

TECHNOLOGY SKILL	OBJECTIVE DOMAIN	OBJECTIVE DOMAIN NUMBER
Meeting Active Directory Requirements	Prepare the infrastructure for Exchange installation.	1.1
Preparing Legacy Exchange Servers	Prepare the infrastructure for Exchange installation.	1.1
Meeting Hardware Requirements	Prepare the servers for Exchange installation.	1.2
Meeting Software Requirements	Prepare the servers for Exchange installation.	1.2
Performing a Graphical Installation	Install Exchange.	1.3
Performing an Unattended Installation	Install Exchange.	1.3
Finalizing the Installation	Install Exchange.	1.3

KEY TERMS

Exchange Best Practices Analyzer
Exchange organization
Just a Bunch of Disks (JBOD)
link state
migration

Parallel Advanced Technology Attachment (PATA)
Redundant Array of Independent Disks (RAID)
routing groups
Serial Advanced Technology Attachment (SATA)

Small Computer Systems Interface (SCSI)
Storage Area Network (SAN)
Windows Server Update Services (WSUS)

■ Preparing for an Exchange Server 2007 Installation

THE BOTTOM LINE

Email infrastructures are among the largest systems within organizations today and should be planned carefully as a result. The deployment of Exchange Server 2007 is no exception to this rule. Before you deploy Exchange Server 2007 in your organization, you will need to plan server roles as well as prepare the appropriate hardware and software. In addition, you will need to prepare AD as well as any legacy Exchange servers for the deployment of Exchange Server 2007.

Planning Exchange Roles

> Fundamental to a successful Exchange Server 2007 deployment is the proper planning of Exchange server roles. More specifically, you should focus on the number of Exchange servers required for your organization as well as the number and type of server roles that should be placed on each Exchange server.

Before deploying Exchange Server 2007, you should carefully consider the number and placement of server roles within your organization. In most small organizations, a single Exchange server with the Mailbox, Hub Transport, and CAS roles will usually be adequate for the current email requirements. As a result, a typical Exchange Server 2007 installation includes these roles by default.

Because Exchange servers that hold the Mailbox, Hub Transport, and CAS roles can provide email storage, access, and routing, they are easily scalable. As small organizations grow, they can introduce additional Exchange servers with these same roles to service different areas within the organization as shown in Figure 3-1.

Figure 3-1

Scaling the Default Server Roles

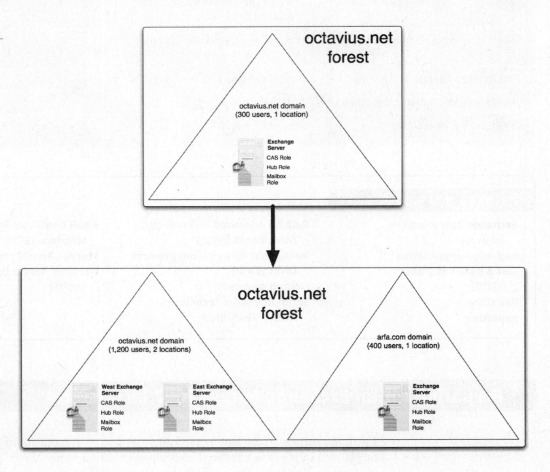

In Figure 3-1, the Octavius organizat ion expanded from a single domain, single location, 300-user structure to a multiple domain, three location, 1,600-user structure by adding two additional Exchange servers. Each Exchange server provides email storage and access for clients within their location, as well as internal and external email routing.

In larger organizations, it is more efficient and cost effective to deploy Exchange servers that have specific server roles and that are strategically placed within an organization to optimize email storage, access, and routing. These Exchange servers need only contain the hardware necessary to support their function. Figure 3-2 depicts an octavius.net domain that contains a diverse Exchange infrastructure spanning two locations.

Figure 3-2

Separating Server Roles

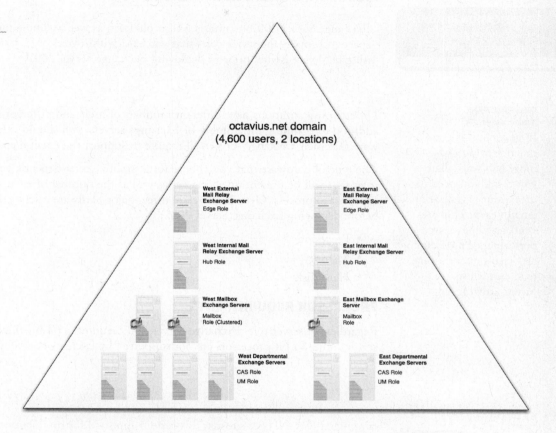

In Figure 3-2, email storage is provided by the Mailbox Exchange servers in the East and West offices. In addition, each location has several Departmental Exchange servers that provide email access to clients in each department. To support internal and external email relay as well as ensure that inbound and outbound email is filtered for viruses and spam, there are separate Exchange servers in each location that provide the Hub role and the Edge role.

Ultimately, the number and placement of Exchange server roles will depend on the needs and structure of your organization, but should support current email requirements and allow for future growth. In addition, the design of your Exchange infrastructure must obey the following rules:

- There must be at least one Hub role per AD site to allow for email relay between Exchange servers in different sites.
- The CAS role should have fast access to the Mailbox role. If the CAS and Mailbox roles are on different servers, you should ensure that the network that separates them has at least 100 Mbps of bandwidth.
- Clustered Mailbox roles cannot share hardware with other roles.
- Edge roles cannot share hardware with other roles.

Although it is not restricted, it is poor practice to install any Exchange role on a server that contains other network functions such as a DC, database server, file server, print server, or proxy server. These functions will require additional resources over time as the company grows and will likely reduce the performance of your Exchange server. Furthermore, if you install Exchange on a DC, you will not be able to change the domain membership or remove AD from the DC until Exchange is removed first.

Meeting Hardware Requirements

Exchange Server 2007 requires a 64-bit platform as well as ample memory and hard disk space to support the server roles that will exist within your organization. As a result, planning hardware is vital prior to deploying Exchange Server 2007.

Different organizations have different numbers of users and different email requirements. In addition to planning the number of Exchange servers, you should carefully consider the hardware that each Exchange server will require to support the email demands of the organization.

The type of hardware that you choose for a specific server depends on the Exchange server roles that will be present on the server as well as the number of emails that the server is expected to process. Overall, there are three major hardware categories that you must consider before deploying Exchange Server 2007:

- Processor
- Memory
- Hard disk

PROCESSOR REQUIREMENTS

Regardless of server role, Exchange Server 2007 requires a 64-bit Intel 64 or AMD64 processor. Itanium 64-bit processors are not supported by Exchange Server 2007.

Although Exchange Server 2007 can be installed on a 32-bit Intel or AMD processor running at 800 MHz or greater, this is not supported for production environments and is intended for product testing only. However, you can install the Exchange management tools on a 32-bit computer to perform remote administration of a computer running a 64-bit version of Exchange Server 2007.

Most server-class computers today ship with a variety of configurations and can contain multiple processors or processors with multiple cores. As a result, it is difficult to determine the minimum number of processors and processor cores required for an Exchange server. In general, the number of processors and processor cores is largely dependent on the number of emails that are sent within your organization as well as the server roles on each Exchange server. Server roles that perform numerous calculations are likely to require multiple processors with multiple cores.

For example, servers that host the Edge role will require multiple processors or processor cores to support the calculation required by the antivirus and antispam software. Similarly, servers that host the CAS role and provide access to email using encrypted protocols such as POP3S will likely require multiple processors or processor cores to handle the calculations needed for the encryption and decryption. Similarly, servers that contain multiple server roles will perform more calculations and will likely require multiple processors or processor cores.

MEMORY REQUIREMENTS

Due to its 64-bit architecture, Exchange Server 2007 can use more than 4 GB of physical RAM. However, the recommended minimum RAM requirements vary depending on the server role as described in Table 3-1.

Table 3-1

Exchange Server 2007 RAM requirements

EXCHANGE SERVER ROLE	RECOMMENDED MINIMUM RAM
Edge Transport (Edge)	1 GB per core (2 GB minimum)
Hub Transport (Hub)	1 GB per core (2 GB minimum)
Unified Messaging (UM)	1 GB per core (2 GB minimum)
Client Access Server (CAS)	2 GB per core (2 GB minimum)
Mailbox	2 GB plus 5 MB per mailbox

If an Exchange server will contain multiple server roles, you should add the appropriate minimum RAM requirements shown in Table 3-1. Thus an Exchange server that hosts the Edge, Hub, CAS, and Mailbox server roles should have at least 8 GB of RAM plus 5 MB per mailbox.

In addition, the amount of RAM on an Exchange server holding the Mailbox server role relates to the number of storage groups used to store email. A server with 2 GB of RAM that hosts the Mailbox server role will adequately support up to 4 storage groups. However, to properly support 50 storage groups, the server hosting the Mailbox server role should have 26 GB of RAM.

In addition to physical RAM requirements, each Exchange server should contain an adequate amount of virtual memory. The amount of virtual memory in Windows is determined by the size of the paging file. In general, you should ensure that the paging file size for any Exchange server is equal to the amount of physical RAM plus 10 MB.

By default, the paging file exists on the Windows system partition. Although not required for Exchange Server 2007, you should move the paging file to a different hard disk. This increases overall system performance because paging requests will not compete with Windows I/O requests on the same hard disk. However, by moving the paging file to another hard disk, Windows cannot create automatic memory dumps in the event of a system crash. Normally, this is not a problem in most environments, but should be considered if your organization has a Microsoft support contract because automatic memory dumps can be sent to Microsoft support for analysis.

MODIFY THE PAGING FILE

GET READY. Turn on the computer, and log in as the Administrator user account. Close any windows that appear on the desktop.

1. Click **Start**, **Control Panel**, and then click **System**. The System Properties window appears.

2. Highlight the **Advanced** tab. In the Performance section, click the **Settings** button to open the Performance Options window.

3. Highlight the **Advanced** tab. In the Virtual memory section, click the **Change** button to open the Virtual Memory window.

4. Select the appropriate hard drive partition in the selection window at the top of the screen and ensure that **Custom size** is selected.

5. Specify an initial and maximum size for your paging file in the dialog boxes and click **Set**. The initial size for your paging file must be set to the minimum paging file size required by Exchange Server 2007.

6. Click **OK** to close the Virtual Memory window. Click **OK** again to close the Performance Options window and click **OK** once again to close the System Properties window.

TAKE NOTE*

Exchange Server 2007 SP1 has a more efficient storage engine. As a result, you only need 15 GB of RAM to support 50 storage groups in Exchange Server 2007 SP1.

TAKE NOTE*

To move your paging file to a different hard drive, simply specify a **Custom size** for a partition on the target hard drive in the Virtual Memory window and specify **No paging file** for the Windows system partition.

HARD DISK REQUIREMENTS

All hard disk partitions that will be used by Exchange Server 2007 must be formatted using the NTFS file system. For installation, Exchange Server 2007 requires a minimum of 1.2 GB of free disk space as well as an additional 200 MB of free space on the Windows system partition.

In addition, Exchange Server 2007 will require ample storage for email queues and storage groups. The amount of space required for the email queues and storage groups depends on the number of emails that your organization typically sends, the average size of email attachments, and whether your organization archives email over time. Because hard disk space is generally inexpensive today, it is best practice to double your maximum expected space requirements to allow for future growth.

To speed email relay, storage, and retrieval, you should ensure that your hard disks have fast transfer rates. **Small Computer Systems Interface (SCSI)** and **Serial Advanced Technology Attachment (SATA)** hard disks generally have faster transfer rates than **Parallel Advanced Technology Attachment (PATA)** hard disks. Many organizations today store important server information such as Exchange mailboxes on external hard disks that can be shared by several servers. This configuration is called a **Storage Area Network (SAN)** and typically involves SCSI or SATA hard disks in an external drive enclosure that are linked to one or more servers with a fast connection.

Furthermore, many servers and SAN devices use several hard disks simultaneously to speed up data transfer and provide fault tolerance in the event of a hard disk failure. This configuration is called a **Redundant Array of Independent Disks (RAID)** and is a good form to use for any Exchange server in your organization that hosts the Mailbox role. Although RAID configurations may be handled by software running on the Windows operating system, it is most often implemented by the hard disk controller on the computer to reduce the strain on the computer's processor and improve performance.

➕ MORE INFORMATION

The three most common RAID implementations are called RAID 0, RAID 1, and RAID 5. RAID 0 configurations are not fault tolerant if a single hard drive fails and include **spanning** and **striping**.

RAID 0 spanning is also called **Just a Bunch of Disks (JBOD)** and consists of two or more hard disks that are seen as one large continuous volume. Thus, if you had two 250 GB hard disks, you could create one volume that is 500 GB in size. When the free space on the first disk is exhausted, the second hard disk is used to store data.

RAID 0 striping also creates a single large volume, but divides data equally among two or more hard disks to speed up read-and-write operations. For example, if you have three hard disks in a RAID 0 striping configuration, a file that is saved to the hard disk would be divided into three sections. Each section is written to a different hard disk concurrently, which allows the file to be saved in one-third the time. This same file can then be read in one-third of time for the same reason. Because RAID 0 speeds read-and-write access, it is appropriate for the Hub, Edge, UM, and CAS roles. The Mailbox role should provide fault tolerance for its email and public folder databases and is better suited for RAID 1 and RAID 5.

RAID 1 is called **mirroring** and provides fault tolerance in the case of a hard disk failure. In this RAID configuration, all information is written to two separate hard disks at the same time. If one hard disk fails, then the system automatically uses the other hard disk exclusively. Because each hard disk contains identical data, no data is lost by the failure of a single hard drive, and the failed hard drive can be replaced and reconfigured as a RAID 1 after working hours.

RAID 5 is called **striping with parity** and is the most common RAID configuration used today. It is similar to striping because it creates a single volume and divides data, yet it requires a minimum of three hard disks. In a RAID 5 configuration that uses three hard disks, files are split into two sections and saved to two of the hard disks. Parity information that can be used to regenerate the file if half of it is missing is saved on the remaining hard disk. During each write operation, the parity information is rotated among all three drives. Thus, if a single hard drive fails, the parity information can be used to quickly generate the missing data. Similarly, in a RAID 5 configuration that uses four hard disks, files are divided into three sections and saved to three different hard disks while the parity information is saved to the remaining hard disk. If a single hard disk fails, then the parity information can be used to regenerate the data that was missing. Because parity information is only written to a single hard drive during a normal write operation, the parity information takes up less overall space in RAID 5 configurations that use more hard disks.

In larger systems, RAID levels are often combined. For example, RAID 15 refers to a RAID 5 stripe with parity configuration that is mirrored (RAID 1) to another RAID 5 stripe with parity, and RAID 10 refers to a RAID 0 stripe that is mirrored (RAID 1) to another RAID 0 stripe.

Meeting Software Requirements

Exchange Server 2007 requires a 64-bit Windows Server 2003 operating system or later. In addition, you must install several software components before deploying Exchange Server 2007. The number and type of software components depends on the server roles that will be hosted on the Exchange Server 2007 computer.

TAKE NOTE*

You should always ensure that your Windows operating system is updated with the latest service pack and contains the latest patches from Microsoft.

Exchange Server 2007 relies on several software components. First and foremost, Exchange Server 2007 must be installed on a computer running the Windows Server 2003, Windows Server 2003 R2, or Windows Server 2008 operating system with the latest updates. If you plan on providing cluster capabilities on Exchange Server 2007, you must use the Enterprise or Datacenter Edition of Windows Server 2003, Windows Server 2003 R2, or Windows Server 2008.

In addition to the operating system software requirements, Exchange Server 2007 also requires several supporting software components:

- Windows PowerShell Version 1.0 or later
- .NET Framework Version 2.0 or later
- MMC Version 3.0 or later

INSTALL EXCHANGE SERVER 2007 PREREQUISITE SOFTWARE ON WINDOWS SERVER 2003

GET READY. Turn on the computer, and log in as the Administrator user account. Close any windows that appear on the desktop.

1. Obtain and install PowerShell 1.0 for your platform. You can download PowerShell 1.0 for your platform from www.microsoft.com/downloads.

ANOTHER WAY

Rather than searching the Microsoft Download Web site for software, it is easier to enter a search string into a search engine Web site such as Google.com. For example, entering the phrase **powershell download** into Google.com will present you with a direct link to the download page for the latest version of PowerShell from the Microsoft download Web site. This method will work for any software packages that you need to download in this lesson.

2. Obtain and install the .NET Framework 2.0 and the .NET Framework 2.0 SP1 packages for your platform. You can download these packages from www.microsoft.com/downloads.

ANOTHER WAY

If you have Windows Server 2003 R2 or later, the .NET Framework 2.0 package is available using the **Add/Remove Windows Components** section of **Add or Remove Programs** in Control Panel. However, after adding this component using Control Panel, you must download the .NET Framework 2.0 SP1 patch.

3. Ensure that you have the MMC Version 3.0 installed on your computer. You can download the MMC Version 3.0 for your platform from www.microsoft.com/downloads.

Depending on the server roles that are required on your Exchange Server 2007 computer, you may need to install additional Windows software components. These components are listed in Table 3-2.

Table 3-2

Prerequisite software required by server roles

SERVER ROLE	REQUIRED SOFTWARE
Client Access Server (CAS)	IIS (including the WWW service and ASP.NET components) RPC over HTTP proxy
Mailbox	IIS (including the WWW service and COM + components)
Hub Transport (Hub)	No additional software components are required
Edge Transport (Edge)	ADAM SP1 for computers running Windows Server 2003 or Windows Server 2003 R2 Active Directory Lightweight Directory Services (AD LDS) for computers running Windows Server 2008
Unified Messaging (UM)	Windows Media Encoder Windows Media Audio Voice Codec Core XML Services (MSXML) Version 6.0 or later

TAKE NOTE*

If you install IIS on your computer, you must ensure that the SMTP and NNTP components are not selected before installing Exchange Server 2007.

INSTALL ROLE-BASED PREREQUISITE SOFTWARE FOR EXCHANGE SERVER 2007 ON WINDOWS SERVER 2003

GET READY. Turn on the computer, and log in as the Administrator user account. Close any windows that appear on the desktop.

1. Click **Start**, **Control Panel**, and then click **Add or Remove Programs**. The Add or Remove Programs window appears.

2. Click **Add/Remove Windows Components** tab. After a few moments, the Windows Components Wizard window appears.

3. Place a checkmark beside **Application Server**. This installs IIS with the default components including the WWW service and COM + components. The SMTP and NNTP components are not installed by default.

4. Highlight Application Server and click **Details**. In the Application Server window, place a checkmark beside **ASP.NET** and click **OK**.

5. Highlight Networking Services and click **Details**. In the Networking Services window, place a checkmark beside **RPC over HTTP Proxy** and click **OK**.

6. Click **Next** to install the components. Insert your Windows Server 2003 installation media when prompted and click **OK**. After the installation has finished, click **Finish** and close the Add or Remove Programs window.

7. Obtain and install ADAM for your platform. You can download ADAM for your platform from www.microsoft.com/downloads.

8. Obtain and install the MSXML 6.0, Windows Media Encoder, and Windows Media Audio Voice Codec packages for your platform. You can download these packages for your platform from www.microsoft.com/downloads.

CERTIFICATION READY?
Prepare the infrastructure for Exchange installation.
1.1

Meeting Active Directory Requirements

Before installing the first Exchange Server 2007 computer in your forest, you must ensure that AD is properly prepared. This involves meeting Schema Master and GC requirements as well as running several commands from the Exchange Server 2007 installation media to prepare the forest and domains for Exchange Server 2007 objects.

Although Exchange Server 2007 operates closely with AD, you must take several steps to prepare your AD forest for the installation of the first Exchange server.

All domains that will contain Exchange Server 2007 computers or email recipients must be running at the Windows 2000 Native or higher functional level.

Furthermore, Exchange Server 2007 requires constant access to the GC. Accordingly, you must ensure that at least one GC server exists in each site that will contain Exchange Server 2007 computers. Moreover, all GC servers used by Exchange Server 2007 must be running Windows Server 2003 SP1 or Windows Server 2003 R2 or later.

Before the installation of the first Exchange Server 2007 computer in the forest, the AD schema must be extended to include new objects. To extend the AD schema, Exchange Server 2007 requires that the DC that contains the Schema Master FSMO role must be running Windows Server 2003 SP1 or Windows Server 2003 R2 or later.

Once you have satisfied the functional level, GC, and Schema Master requirements, you must perform several tasks to prepare AD for Exchange Server 2007 objects. These tasks must be performed in the following order:

1. Prepare legacy permissions.
2. Prepare the Active Directory schema.
3. Prepare the first domain.
4. Prepare all other domains.

TAKE NOTE*
Depending on the size and complexity of your forest, each of these tasks may take a considerable amount of time because the changes may need to replicate to other DCs within the domain and forest.

Although the Exchange Installation Wizard will prompt you to perform these tasks when you install the first Exchange Server 2007 computer in your forest, it is best to perform these actions beforehand for flexibility in large forests as well as to ensure that any problems that arise can be remedied before the installation of Exchange Server 2007. To prepare your AD forest and domains before installing Exchange Server 2007, you can run the **setup.com** program from the root of the Exchange Server 2007 installation media with the appropriate switches.

PREPARING LEGACY PERMISSIONS

ANOTHER WAY

To save typing, you can use the **/pl** switch in place of the **/PrepareLegacy ExchangePermissions** switch.

For any domains in the forest that currently have Exchange 2000 or Exchange Server 2003 deployed, you must prepare the permissions on those domains for the addition of Exchange Server 2007. To prepare all domains, you can run the **setup /PrepareLegacy ExchangePermissions** command as shown in Figure 3-3 from the root of the Exchange Server 2007 installation media while logged in as a user that is a member of the Enterprise Admins group. Alternatively, if you wish to prepare a single domain only, you can log in as a user that is a member of the Domain Admins group and run the command **setup /PrepareLegacyExchangePermissions:** *domainname* from the root of the Exchange Server 2007 installation media where *domainname* is the DNS name of the appropriate domain in your forest.

Figure 3-3

Preparing Legacy Permissions

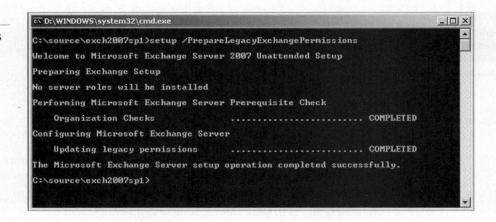

PREPARING THE ACTIVE DIRECTORY SCHEMA

ANOTHER WAY

To save typing, you can use the **/ps** switch in place of the **/PrepareSchema** switch.

Before the first Exchange Server 2007 computer is installed in your forest, you must extend the AD schema to include new Exchange Server 2007 object classes and attributes. To do this, you must log on as a user that is a member of the Enterprise Admins and Schema Admins groups to a computer that is in the same domain and site as the DC that holds the Schema Master FSMO role. Next, you can run the command **setup /PrepareSchema** command as shown in Figure 3-4 from the root of the Exchange Server 2007 installation media.

Figure 3-4

Preparing the Active Directory Schema

```
D:\WINDOWS\system32\cmd.exe                                      _□×

C:\source\exch2007sp1>setup /PrepareSchema

Welcome to Microsoft Exchange Server 2007 Unattended Setup

Preparing Exchange Setup

No server roles will be installed

Performing Microsoft Exchange Server Prerequisite Check

    Organization Checks          ..................... COMPLETED

Configuring Microsoft Exchange Server

    Extending Active Directory schema
    Progress                     ..................... COMPLETED

The Microsoft Exchange Server setup operation completed successfully.

C:\source\exch2007sp1>
```

PREPARING THE FIRST DOMAIN

TAKE NOTE*

Because the Exchange organization is stored in the configuration partition of AD, you can only create one Exchange organization per AD forest in Exchange Server 2007.

After extending the AD schema, you can prepare the first domain for the addition of the first Exchange Server 2007 computer and create an *Exchange organization*. The Exchange organization defines the scope of management for Exchange server and is typically set to the same name as the AD forest.

To prepare the first domain for Exchange Server 2007 and create the Exchange organization, you can log in to a DC in the domain as a user that is a member of the Enterprise Admins group and run the command **setup /PrepareAD /OrganizationName:***name* command from the root of the Exchange Server 2007 installation media where *name* is the name of the Exchange organization. The preparation of the first domain in the Octavius Exchange organization is shown in Figure 3-5. The Exchange organization name must only contain alphanumeric characters. No special characters, symbols, or punctuation characters are allowed.

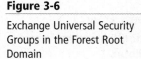

To save typing, you can use the **/p** switch in place of the **/PrepareAD** switch as well as the **/on** switch in place of the **/OrganizationName** switch.

Figure 3-5

Preparing the First Active Directory Domain and Exchange Organization

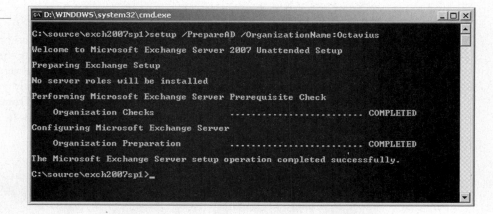

If you are adding Exchange Server 2007 to an existing Exchange Server 2003 environment, an Exchange organization already exists in the AD forest. As a result, you do not need to specify the **/OrganizationName** switch to the **setup** command. However, you still need to be logged in as a user that is a member of both the Enterprise Admins group and the Exchange Server 2003 Full Administrator role.

After preparing the first domain for Exchange Server 2007, you will notice a new OU called Microsoft Exchange Security Groups in the Active Directory Users and Computers console as shown in Figure 3-6. This OU contains the following universal security groups:

- **Exchange Organization Administrators**—Contains administrative user accounts that can administer all components of Exchange.
- **Exchange Public Folder Administrators**—Contains administrative user accounts that can administer Exchange public folders.
- **Exchange Recipient Administrators**—Contains administrative user accounts that can administer AD user accounts and manage user mailboxes.
- **Exchange Servers**—Contains the computer accounts for all Exchange servers.
- **Exchange View-Only Administrators**—Contains administrative user accounts that can read Exchange configuration information for auditing purposes.
- **ExchangeLegacyInterop**—Used to maintain interoperability between Exchange Server 2007 and Exchange Server 2003 computers in the forest.

Figure 3-6

Exchange Universal Security Groups in the Forest Root Domain

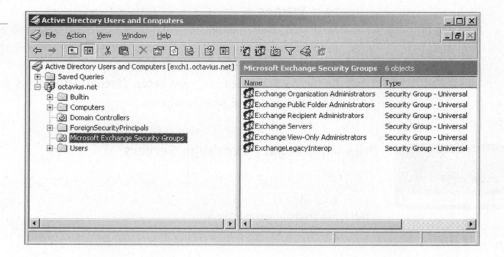

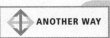 **ANOTHER WAY** To save typing, you can use the **/pd** switch in place of the **/PrepareDomain** switch as well as the **/pad** switch in place of the **/PrepareAllDomains** switch.

PREPARING ALL OTHER DOMAINS

After preparing the first domain for Exchange Server 2007, you can prepare other domains in the forest as a member of the Enterprise Admins group by using the command **setup.exe/ PrepareDomain:** *domainname* from the root of the Exchange Server 2007 installation media where *domainname* is the name of the target domain. Alternatively, you can prepare all other domains in the forest using the command **setup.exe /PrepareAllDomains** from the root of the Exchange Server 2007 installation media as shown in Figure 3-7.

Figure 3-7

Preparing All AD Domains

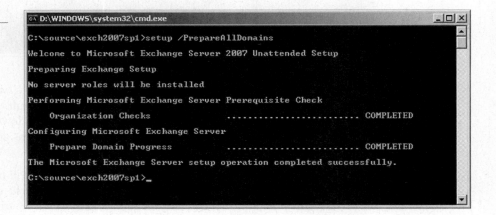

➔ PREPARE A FOREST FOR EXCHANGE SERVER 2007

GET READY. Turn on the computer, and log in as the Administrator user account in the forest root domain. Close any windows that appear on the desktop.

1. Click **Start**, and then click **Command Prompt**. The Command Prompt window appears.
2. Navigate to the root of your Exchange Server 2007 installation media using the appropriate command at the command prompt. For example, if your installation media is identified as D drive in My Computer, simply type **D:** at the command prompt and press **Enter.**
3. At the command prompt, type **setup /PrepareLegacyExchangePermissions** and press **Enter.**
4. At the command prompt, type **setup /PrepareSchema** and press **Enter.**
5. At the command prompt, type **setup /PrepareAD /OrganizationName:**name where *name* is the name of your Exchange organization and press **Enter.**
6. At the command prompt, type **setup /PrepareAllDomains** and press **Enter.**
7. Close the command prompt window.

Preparing Legacy Exchange Servers

If your organization contains legacy Exchange Server 2003 or Exchange 2000 servers, you must take additional steps to ensure that Exchange Server 2007 can coexist with them in the same Exchange organization.

XREF

Creating and moving mailboxes will be covered in Lesson 4, "Configuring a New Exchange Server" and Lesson 5, "Working with Recipient Objects."

Many organizations that plan to deploy Exchange Server 2007 already have an existing Exchange server infrastructure in place. Due to hardware requirements, you cannot perform an in-place upgrade of previous versions of Exchange to Exchange Server 2007.

Instead, you must introduce Exchange Server 2007 servers to your existing Exchange environment. Following this, you can gradually move the mailbox and public folder resources on the legacy Exchange servers to servers running Exchange Server 2007 and retire the legacy Exchange servers. This process is called *migration* and may take several weeks or months to perform depending on the size and complexity of your organization.

Before adding an Exchange Server 2007 computer to your legacy Exchange infrastructure, you must ensure that AD has been prepared as described in the previous section. Furthermore, you must ensure that:

- No Exchange 5.5 or earlier servers exist within your organization,
- Servers running Exchange Server 2003 have Exchange Server 2003 SP2 or greater, and
- Servers running Exchange 2000 have Exchange 2000 SP3 or greater.

Instead of using AD site objects, Exchange Server 2003 and Exchange 2000 use *routing groups* to identify different physical locations within the same Exchange organization. Internal email in an Exchange Server 2003 or Exchange 2000 infrastructure is routed between routing groups using a *link state* software transport. If your existing Exchange Server 2003 or Exchange 2000 infrastructure contains two or more routing groups, you must disable link state before introducing your first Exchange Server 2007 computer. You can disable link state by adding a REG_DWORD called **SuppressStateChanges** with a value of **1** to the registry key **HKEY_LOCAL_MACHINE\SYSTEM\CurrentControlSet\Services\RESvc\Parameters** on all Exchange Server 2003 and Exchange 2000 servers.

 DISABLE LINK STATE ON A LEGACY EXCHANGE SERVER

GET READY. Turn on the Exchange Server 2003 or Exchange 2000 computer, and log in as the Administrator user account. Close any windows that appear on the desktop.

1. Click **Start** and then click **Run**. In the Run dialog box, type **regedit** and press **Enter**. The Registry Editor window appears.

2. Expand **HKEY_LOCAL_MACHINE\SYSTEM\CurrentControlSet\Services\RESvc\Parameters**.

3. Right click the Parameters key in the left pane and click **New, DWORD Value**. Type **SuppressStateChanges** in the Name field and press **Enter**.

4. Double click the **SuppressStateChanges** value. In the Edit DWORD Value window, type **1** in the Value data dialog box and click **OK**.

5. Close the Registry Editor window and reboot the computer to reload the Windows registry.

Running the Exchange Best Practices Analyzer

You can run the Exchange Best Practices Analyzer to ensure that you have correctly installed prerequisite software and performed the necessary AD preparation prior to the installation of Exchange Server 2007.

Exchange Server 2007 comes with a utility called the *Exchange Best Practices Analyzer* tool that can help you tune the performance of your Exchange servers and detect configuration errors. After you have prepared the AD forest for the installation of the first Exchange Server 2007 computer, you can download and run the Exchange Best Practices Analyzer to verify that all software and AD prerequisites have been met as well as gauge the size and complexity of your AD forest.

When you run the Exchange Best Practices Analyzer, you are prompted to check for updates and the name of a DC in your forest to connect to. Following this, you can specify a new Exchange 2007 Readiness Check scan as shown in Figure 3-8.

Figure 3-8

Specifying Scan Options

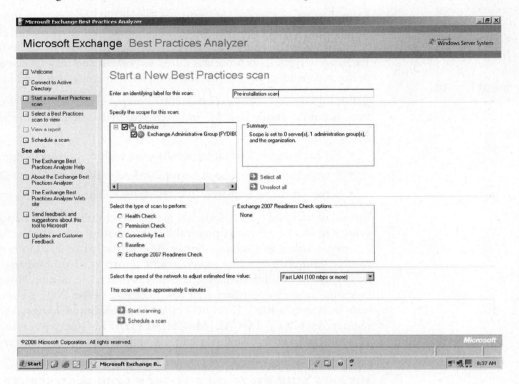

Once you complete a scan by clicking the **Start scanning** link in Figure 3-8, you can view one of several reports to identify the readiness of your AD forest for an Exchange Server 2007 installation. If your AD domain is ready for Exchange Server 2007 installation, the default List Reports view shown in Figure 3-9 should indicate no warnings or errors.

Figure 3-9

Viewing Scan Results

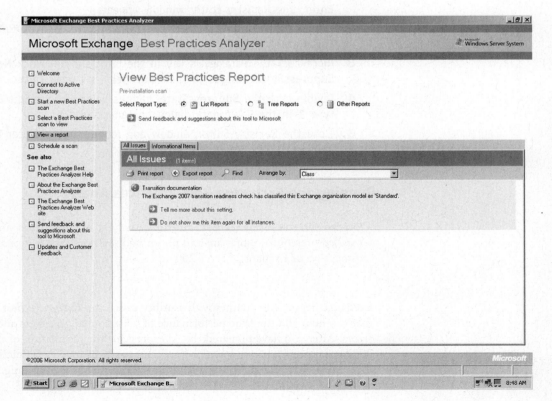

The report shown in Figure 3-9 also indicates that the AD forest uses the Standard *Exchange organization model.* There are four Exchange organization models that describe the relative size and complexity of the AD forest: simple, standard, large, and complex. You can use these Exchange organization models to gauge the complexity required when planning your Exchange Server 2007 server roles.

 RUN THE EXCHANGE BEST PRACTICES ANALYZER

GET READY. Turn on the computer, and log in as the Administrator user account. Close any windows that appear on the desktop.

1. Ensure that you have downloaded and installed the latest version of the Exchange Server 2007 Best Practices Analyzer from **www.microsoft.com/downloads**.

2. Click **Start, All Programs, Microsoft Exchange**, and then click **Best Practices Analyzer Tool**. The Microsoft Exchange Best Practices Analyzer window appears.

3. On the Welcome page, click **Download the latest updates**. Any updates for the Exchange Best Practices Analyzer will be automatically downloaded and installed. Next, click **Select options for a new scan**.

4. On the Connect to Active Directory page, ensure that the name of your DC is listed in the Active Directory server dialog box and click **Connect to the Active Directory server**. If you receive an Authentication error, click **Show advanced login options**, specify the appropriate user information and click **Connect to the Active Directory server**.

5. On the Start a New Best Practices scan page, type a descriptive name for your scan in the dialog box, select **Exchange 2007 Readiness Check** and click **Start scanning**.

6. On the Scanning Completed page, click **View a report of this Best Practices scan**.

7. On the View Best Practices Report page, note any warnings regarding your AD structure if present and click **Transition documentation** to view your Exchange organization model. Next, highlight the **Informational Items** tab to view your AD summary.

 TAKE NOTE*

You can print or export your reports using the **Print report** and **Export report** buttons in the summary window or select **Tree Reports** to view detailed reports regarding your AD forest.

8. Close the Microsoft Exchange Best Practices Analyzer window.

■ Installing Exchange Server 2007

↓
THE BOTTOM LINE

After properly preparing for Exchange Server 2007 deployment, the installation process is straightforward. To install Exchange Server 2007 from the installation media, you can run the setup.exe for graphical mode or the setup.com for unattended mode. Following the installation of Exchange Server 2007, you should verify that all components were correctly installed as well as license and update your Exchange servers.

CERTIFICATION READY?
Install Exchange.

1.3

Performing a Graphical Installation

Once you have satisfied the necessary hardware, software, and AD prerequisites, you can start the Exchange Server 2007 installation and select the server roles that should be installed on your email server.

To start an Exchange Server 2007 graphical installation, simply log in to the server using a user account that is a member of the Enterprise Admins group and run the **setup.exe** program from the root of the Exchange Server 2007 installation media.

During the installation, you must select the server roles that will be hosted on the Exchange server. A typical Exchange Server 2007 installation adds the Client Access Server, Hub Transport, and Mailbox roles, whereas a custom Exchange Server 2007 installation allows you to select specific roles. If you select the Edge Transport role or a Mailbox role that is clustered, you cannot add any additional roles to the Exchange server.

The installation procedure is identical for 32-bit and 64-bit versions of Exchange Server 2007 and Exchange Server 2007 SP1. In this lesson and throughout this text, we will focus on Exchange Server 2007 SP1.

 INSTALL EXCHANGE SERVER 2007 SP1

GET READY. Turn on the computer, and log in as the Administrator user account. Close any windows that appear on the desktop.

1. Navigate to the root of the Exchange Server 2007 media and double click the **setup.exe** file. After a few moments, the Exchange Server 2007 welcome screen appears as shown in Figure 3-10.

Figure 3-10

Exchange Server Setup
Welcome Screen

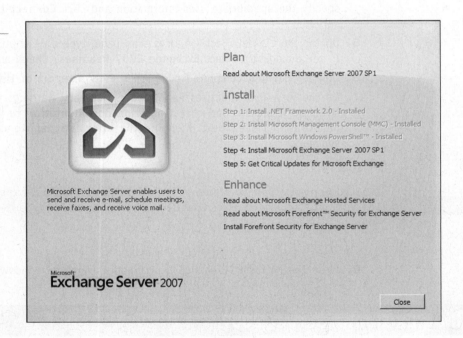

 If you have installed the Exchange Server 2007 prerequisite software, the links for Steps 1, 2, and 3 will be unavailable as depicted in Figure 3-10. If these links are available, they direct you to the Microsoft Download Web site.

2. Click **Step 4: Install Microsoft Exchange Server 2007 SP1**. The Exchange Server 2007 SP1 Setup wizard appears as shown in Figure 3-11.

Figure 3-11

Starting the Exchange Server 2007 Installation

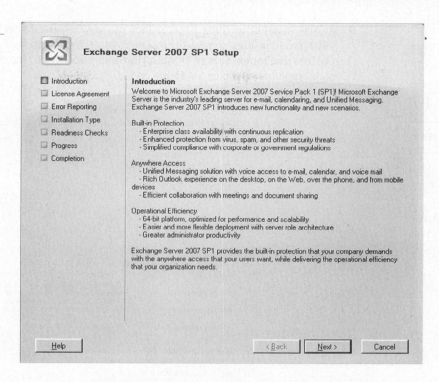

3. At the Introduction page, click **Next**. The License Agreement page appears.

4. At the License Agreement page, select **I accept the terms in the license agreement** and click **Next**. The Error Reporting page appears.

5. At the Error Reporting page, ensure that **No** is selected and click **Next**. The Installation Type page appears as shown in Figure 3-12.

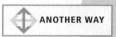

ANOTHER WAY

You may instead select **Yes** at the Error Reporting page to participate in Microsoft's quality assurance program. However, this will require added bandwidth and is not recommended for classroom use.

Figure 3-12

Specifying the Installation Type

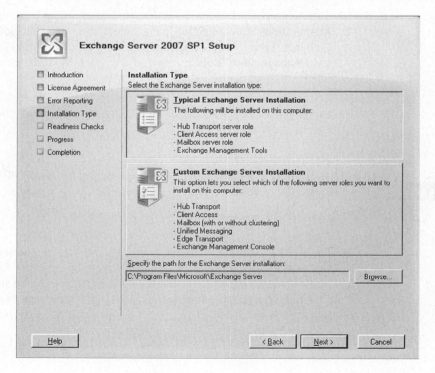

6. At the Installation Type page, select the volume and folder that Exchange Server 2007 program files should be installed to at the bottom of the screen. Next, select **Custom Exchange Server Installation** and click **Next**. The Server Role Selection page appears as shown in Figure 3-13.

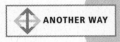
ANOTHER WAY

If you select **Typical Exchange Server Installation** from the Installation Type page, the installation program will install the Hub Transport, Client Access, and Mailbox roles as well as the Exchange Management Tools.

Figure 3-13

Selecting Individual Server Roles

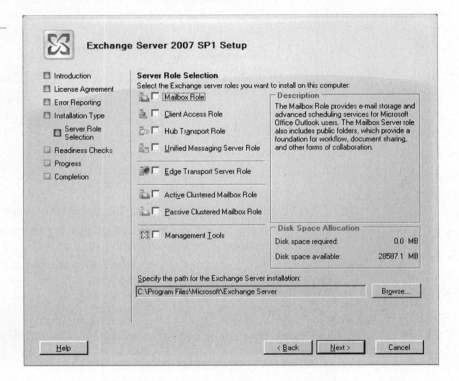

7. At the Server Role Selection page, select the roles that you require on your Exchange Server 2007 computer based on your preinstallation plan. Next, ensure that **Management Tools** is selected and click **Next**. If you selected the Mailbox role, the Client Settings page appears.

8. At the Client Settings page, select **Yes** to allow Entourage and Outlook 2003 and earlier MAPI clients access to your Exchange server and click **Next**. The Readiness Checks page appears.

TAKE NOTE *

A public folder database is required by Entourage and Outlook 2003 or earlier clients when connecting to your Exchange server using MAPI. If you select **Yes** at the Client Settings page, a default public folder database is created on your Exchange server.

9. Review the Readiness Checks page for any errors or warnings. If you have not met the proper software, hardware, and AD requirements, the Readiness Checks page will display errors that describe the component that must be installed or the action that must be taken before you are allowed to continue the Exchange Server 2007 installation as shown in Figure 3-14. Once you have corrected the errors, you can click **Retry** to perform the readiness checks again.

Figure 3-14

A Failed Readiness Check

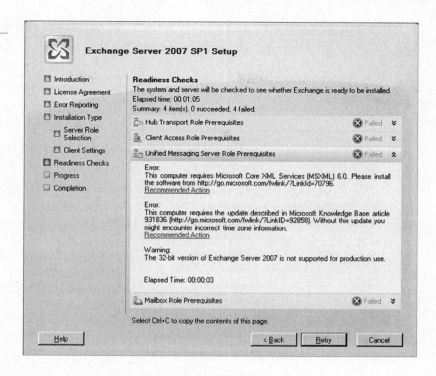

10. Once the Readiness Checks page is free of errors, you can click the **Install** button shown in Figure 3-15 to begin the Exchange Server 2007 installation.

Figure 3-15

Completing the Readiness Checks

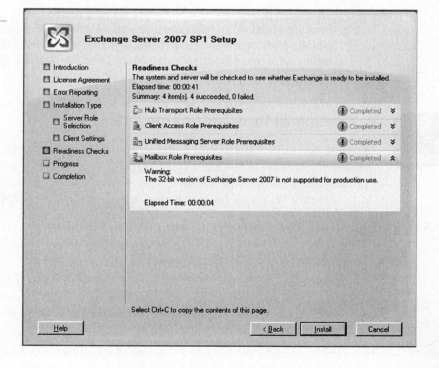

TAKE NOTE*

Figure 3-15 indicates the warning that you receive when you install the 32-bit version of Exchange. Although the installation will proceed, the 32-bit version should not be used in a production environment.

11. At the end of the Exchange Server 2007 installation, you will be presented with the Completion page shown in Figure 3-16.

Figure 3-16

Completing the Exchange Server Installation

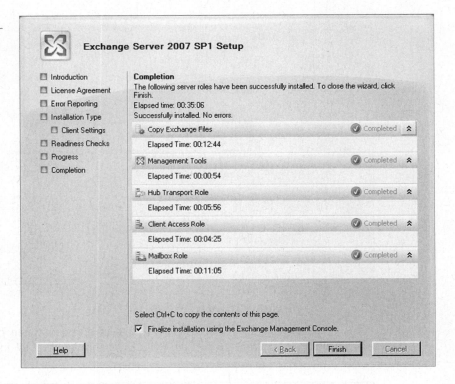

12. Deselect **Finalize installation using the Exchange Management Console** and click **Finish**. A window will appear indicating that some Exchange Server 2007 settings require that you reboot your computer. Click **OK** to close the window.

13. Reboot your computer.

Performing an Unattended Installation

Unattended installations add flexibility to the deployment of Exchange Server 2007. For example, you could use an unattended installation command within a script file that is run at a remote site or schedule an unattended installation command to run at a later time using the Windows Task Scheduler. To perform an unattended installation, you must supply the appropriate switches to the setup.com command in the root of the installation media.

TAKE NOTE*

If any software, hardware, or AD prerequisites have not been satisfied prior to performing an unattended installation, the setup program will fail and list the actions that need to be performed.

Unattended Exchange Server 2007 installations require the same information that a graphical installation requires. However, this information is specified using switches to the **setup.com** command from the root of the Exchange Server 2007 installation media by a user that is a member of the Enterprise Admins group.

For example, consider the following unattended installation command:

setup /mode:Install /roles:HubTransport,ClientAccess,Mailbox /EnableLegacyOutlook / TargetDir:D:\ExchangeServer2007

This command installs (**/mode:Install**) the Exchange Management tools, Hub, CAS, and Mailbox roles (**/roles:HubTransport,ClientAccess,Mailbox**) to the D:\ExchangeServer2007 directory (**/TargetDir:D:\ExchangeServer2007**) as well as creates a public folder database for Entourage and Outlook 2003 or earlier MAPI clients (**/EnableLegacyOutlook**).

If you do not specify a certain switch to the **setup.com** command, the default value will be assumed. Thus, the following command will install the Exchange Management tools, Hub, CAS, and Mailbox roles to the default directory (%systemroot%\Program Files\Microsoft\ Exchange Server\) without creating a public folder database for Entourage and Outlook 2003 or earlier MAPI clients.

setup /mode:Install /roles:HubTransport,ClientAccess,Mailbox

At minimum, you must specify the **/mode** switch to specify the type of installation as well as the **/roles** switch to specify the components to install.

Valid options to the **/roles** switch include:

- **Install** to install the specified roles
- **Uninstall** to remove the specified roles
- **Upgrade** to upgrade roles from Exchange Server 2003 to Exchange Server 2003 SP1

Valid options to the **/roles** switch include:

- **HubTransport**, **HT**, or **H** to specify the Hub Transport role
- **ClientAccess**, **CA**, or **C** to specify the CAS role
- **Mailbox**, **MB**, or **M** to specify the Mailbox role
- **EdgeTransport**, **ET**, or **E** to specify the Edge role
- **UnifiedMessaging**, **UM**, or **U** to specify the UM role

When you install any server role, the Exchange Management tools are automatically installed. If you only want to install the Exchange Management tools to the default location on a computer, you can specify **ManagementTools**, **MT**, or **M** as an option to the **/roles** switch as shown:

setup /mode:Install /roles:ManagementTools

> **TAKE NOTE**
> We have examined the most common switches to the setup.com command in this section. For a complete list of switches to the setup.com command, run the command **setup /?** from the root of the Exchange Server 2007 installation media.

Verifying the Installation

> After the installation process has completed, you should verify that all Exchange components were installed successfully before placing your Exchange server in a production environment. This involves reviewing your server configuration and folder structure as well as reviewing Exchange-related logs.

After installation, you should check the configuration of your system to ensure that there were no errors during the installation process. More specifically, you should perform the following tasks:

- Verify the addition of the Exchange management tools and server roles,
- Examine the Exchange folder structure, and
- Examine the Exchange logs.

VERIFYING EXCHANGE MANAGEMENT TOOLS AND SERVER ROLES

After installing the Exchange Server 2007, the Exchange Management Console MMC snap-in is added to the MMC and the Exchange Management Shell snap-in is added to PowerShell. You can open these utilities by selecting them from the Exchange Server menu (**Start**, **All Programs**, **Microsoft Exchange Server 2007**).

If the Exchange Management Shell snap-in was not properly added to PowerShell during the installation of the Exchange Management Tools, you can start PowerShell (**Start** > **All Programs** > **Windows PowerShell 1.0** > **Windows PowerShell**) and run the command **Add-PSSnapin Microsoft.Exchange.Management.PowerShell.Admin** to add it manually.

Similarly, if the Exchange Management Console snap-in was not added to the MMC during installation, you can open the MMC (**Start** > **Run** and type **mmc**), and manually add the Microsoft Exchange snap-in by selecting **File**, **Add/Remove Snap-in** from the MMC window.

Provided the Exchange Management tools were properly installed, you can verify the installation of server roles on your Exchange server by viewing the details pane for your server in the Exchange Management Console or by running the command **get-ExchangeServer | Format-List** from the Exchange Management Shell.

If a particular server role or management tool was not installed properly, you can remove and reinstall the role. You will learn how to remove roles from your Exchange server at the end of this lesson.

 VERIFY EXCHANGE MANAGEMENT TOOLS AND SERVER ROLES

GET READY. Turn on the computer, and log in as the Administrator user account. Close any windows that appear on the desktop.

1. Click **Start**, **All Programs**, **Microsoft Exchange Server 2007**, and then click **Exchange Management Console**. The Exchange Management Console window appears.

2. Click **OK** to close the dialog box stating that you have unlicensed servers.

3. Highlight **Server Configuration** in the console tree pane and view your server object in the detail pane as depicted in Figure 3-17. The Role column next to your server object should list the roles that were successfully installed.

Figure 3-17

Verifying Server Roles Using the Exchange Management Console

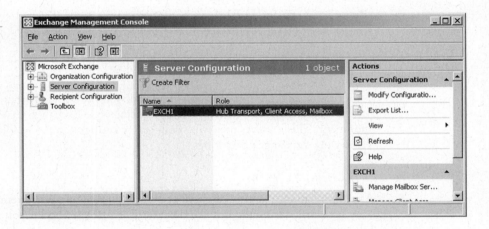

4. Close the Exchange Management Console.

 If you see a red circle icon next to Microsoft Exchange in the console tree pane, the Exchange Management Console cannot connect to the Exchange software on your server. If all Exchange-related services are running on your server, you may need to reinstall the Exchange management tools.

5. Click **Start**, **All Programs**, **Microsoft Exchange Server 2007**, and then click **Exchange Management Shell**. The Exchange Management Shell window appears.

6. At the command prompt, type **get-ExchangeServer | Format-List** and press **Enter** to view a server configuration similar to that shown in Figure 3-18. The ServerRoles section should list your installed server roles.

Figure 3-18

Viewing Server Configuration Using the Exchange Management Shell

7. Close the Exchange Management Shell.

EXAMINING THE EXCHANGE FOLDER STRUCTURE

During the Exchange Server 2007 installation, several new subdirectories are added to the installation directory depending on the roles you have installed. After installing Exchange Server 2007, you should verify the existence of these folders as well as become accustomed to their function for later use.

Figure 3-19 shows the folders present under the installation directory when you install Exchange Server 2007 in the default directory (%systemroot%\Program Files\Microsoft\ Exchange Server). Table 3-3 describes the function and contents of each of these folders.

Figure 3-19

Viewing the Exchange Folder Structure

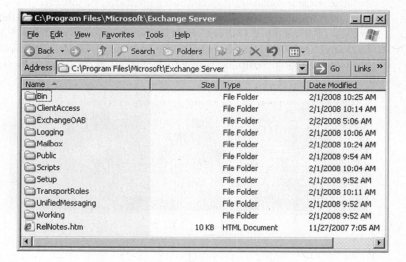

Table 3-3

Exchange Server 2007 installation directory subfolders

EXCHANGE SERVER ROLE	DESCRIPTION
Bin	Contains the programs and program components used by Exchange Server. This directory is present regardless of the server roles installed.
ClientAccess	Contains the configuration files used by the CAS role.
ExchangeOAB	Contains the Exchange offline address book used by the CAS role.
Logging	Contains Exchange server log files. This directory is present regardless of the server roles installed.
Mailbox	Contains the default storage groups and databases used by the Mailbox role for email and public folder storage.
Public	Contains configuration files and drivers used by the Edge and Hub roles when processing email for relay.
Scripts	Contains scripts that may be used to automate Exchange server administrative tasks. This directory is present regardless of the server roles installed.
Setup	Contains Exchange server configuration information. This directory is present regardless of the server roles installed.
TransportRoles	Contains the configuration used by the Hub and Edge roles when relaying and filtering email.
UnifiedMessaging	Contains the configuration files used by the UM role as well as the database used to store UM voice mail.

EXAMINING EXCHANGE LOGS

If you encountered error or warning messages during the Exchange Server 2007 installation process, you can obtain detailed information regarding the messages by viewing the Exchange setup log files. These log files are created in the %systemroot%\ExchangeSetupLogs\ folder and contain information regarding different parts of the installation process:

- ExchangeSetup.log lists the tasks that were performed during the Exchange Server 2007 installation process.
- ExchangeSetup.msilog lists the installation of files from the Exchange Server 2007 installation media.

Because these installation logs contain a great deal of information, you should use the Exchange Management Shell to search and display only messages that have the word "error" in them. For example, you can type **Get-SetupLog %systemroot%\ExchangeSetupLogs\ ExchangeSetup.log –error –tree** in the Exchange Management Shell to view only the errors from the ExchangeSetup.log file in a tree format as depicted in Figure 3-20.

Figure 3-20

Parsing the Exchange Setup Log

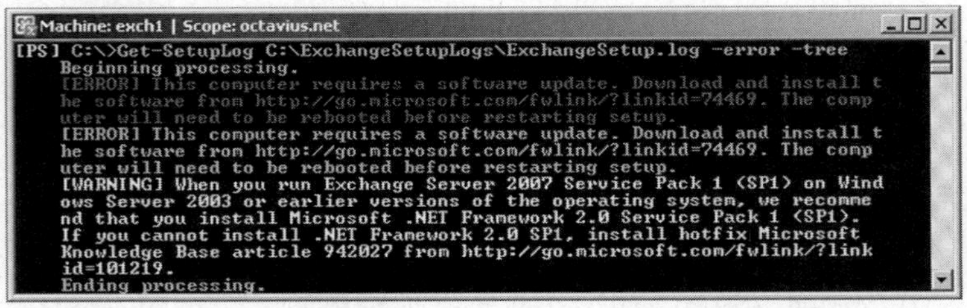

In addition to examining the Exchange setup log files for errors, you should also check for Exchange service errors. The services that comprise Exchange Server 2007 log information, warnings, and errors to the Windows Application Event Log. Exchange-related errors and warnings in the Windows Application Event Log often indicate configuration or installation-related problems.

 VIEW THE EXCHANGE SETUP LOGS AND APPLICATION EVENT LOG

GET READY. Turn on the computer, and log in as the Administrator user account. Close any windows that appear on the desktop.

1. Click Start, **All Programs**, **Microsoft Exchange Server 2007**, and then click **Exchange Management Shell**. The Exchange Management Shell window appears.

2. Type **Get-SetupLog %systemroot%\ExchangeSetupLogs\ExchangeSetup.log –error –tree** and press **Enter.** Once the log file has been parsed, view the results.

3. Type **Get-SetupLog %systemroot%\ExchangeSetupLogs\ExchangeSetup.msilog –error –tree** and press **Enter.** Once the log file has been parsed, view the results.

4. Close the Exchange Management Shell.

5. Click **Start**, **Administrative Tools**, and then click **Event Viewer**. The Event Viewer window appears.

6. Highlight **Application** in the left pane to view the Application Event Log.

7. Click the **Type** column twice in the right pane to sort the information, warning, and error messages by type and scroll to the top of the list. View any Exchange-related errors and warnings.

8. Close the Event Viewer window.

Finalizing the Installation

> Following a successful installation, you should enter the Exchange Server 2007 product key and update your Exchange Server software.

CERTIFICATION READY?
Install Exchange.
1.3

After a successful installation, Exchange Server 2007 is placed in a 120-day evaluation mode. To use Exchange Server beyond this period, you must enter the Exchange product key in the Exchange Management Console and restart the Microsoft Exchange Information Store service. Because the 32-bit version of Exchange Server 2007 is unsupported in production environments, you cannot purchase or enter a product key for it in the Exchange Management Console.

➕ MORE INFORMATION

You can also enter the Exchange Server product key in the Exchange Management Shell using the command **Set-ExchangeServer –Identity** *server_name* **–ProductKey** *xxxxx-xxxxx-xxxxx-xxxxx-xxxxx* where *server_name* is the name of the Exchange Server you wish to license and *xxxxx-xxxxx-xxxxx-xxxxx-xxxxx* is the 25-character Exchange product key. After entering this command, you must still restart the Microsoft Exchange Information Store service.

Because Exchange Server 2007 is a heavily used network resource, it is important to keep it updated to ensure that it maintains a high level of security and reliability. After installing Exchange Server 2007, you should periodically check for and install Exchange Server 2007 updates. By selecting **Step 5: Get Critical Updates for Microsoft Exchange** from the Exchange Server 2007 welcome screen shown earlier in Figure 3-10, you will be redirected to the Microsoft Update Web site where you can scan your computer for updates and install Exchange updates.

Alternatively, you can visit the Microsoft Update Web site manually using Internet Explorer to obtain Exchange updates or configure the *Automatic Updates* feature of Windows to ensure that your Exchange server receives updates on a regular basis.

In many organizations, administrators configure a *Windows Server Update Services (WSUS)* server to automatically download and distribute updates to computers within the organization. WSUS may also be used to update your Exchange servers within the organization.

 ENTER THE EXCHANGE PRODUCT KEY

GET READY. Turn on the computer, and log in as the Administrator user account. Close any windows that appear on the desktop.

1. Click **Start**, **All Programs**, **Microsoft Exchange Server 2007**, and then click **Exchange Management Console**. The Exchange Management Console window appears.
2. Click **OK** to close the dialog box stating that you have unlicensed servers.
3. In the console tree pane, highlight **Server Configuration**.
4. In the result pane, highlight your server. Next, click **Enter Product** Key in the action pane. The Enter Product Key window appears.
5. Input your product key in the Product Key dialog box and press **Enter**.
6. Close the Exchange Management Console. You must now restart the Microsoft Exchange Information Store service to enable the product key.
7. Click **Start**, **Administrative Tools**, and then click **Services**. The Services window appears.
8. Right click **Microsoft Exchange Information Store** in the right pane and click **Restart**.
9. Close the Services window.

> **ANOTHER WAY**
>
> You can also restart the Microsoft Exchange Information Store by typing the command **net stop "Microsoft Exchange Information Store" /y** followed by the command **net start "Microsoft Exchange Information Store" /y** from a Windows command prompt.

 UPDATE EXCHANGE SERVER 2007

GET READY. Turn on the computer, and log in as the Administrator user account. Close any windows that appear on the desktop.

1. Navigate to the root of the Exchange Server 2007 media and double click the **setup.exe** file. After a few moments, the Exchange Server 2007 welcome screen appears.
2. Click **Step 5: Get Critical Updates for Microsoft Exchange**. Internet Explorer opens and directs you to the Microsoft Update Web site. Follow the instructions on the Web site to scan for and apply any updates that are required by your version of Windows and Exchange Server 2007.
3. Close all windows on your desktop.
4. Click **Start**, **Control Panel**, and then click **System**. The System Properties window appears.
5. Highlight the **Automatic Updates** tab and select **Automatic (recommended)**. Select an appropriate time for downloading updates and then click **OK**.

■ Changing and Removing Exchange Server 2007

> **↓ THE BOTTOM LINE**
>
> After deploying Exchange Server 2007, you may need to add additional server roles to an Exchange server or remove existing server roles. Before changing or removing Exchange Server 2007, you should first understand the associated restrictions and procedures.

Over time, you may need to add server roles to an existing Exchange server to provide extra functionality. Alternatively, you may need to remove server roles from an Exchange server to change your server role structure, improve performance, or decommission an Exchange server.

TAKE NOTE * You must be a member of the Exchange Organization Administrators group to add and remove server roles on existing Exchange servers. By default, the Administrator account in the forest root domain is a member of this group.

To perform these tasks, you can simply select Microsoft Exchange Server 2007 in the Add or Remove Programs tool as shown in Figure 3-21.

Figure 3-21

Changing and Removing Exchange Server

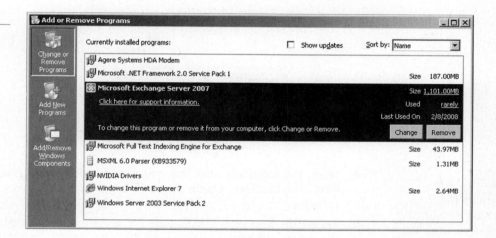

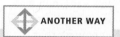 **ANOTHER WAY**

To start the Exchange Setup wizard in Maintenance mode and add server roles to your existing Exchange server, you can also run the **setup.exe** command from the root of your Exchange Server 2007 installation media.

When you click the **Change** button beside Microsoft Exchange Server 2007 in Figure 3-21, the Exchange Setup wizard starts in Maintenance mode and allows you to add server roles to your existing Exchange server. Similarly, clicking the **Remove** button in Figure 3-21 will start the Exchange Setup wizard and allow you to remove server roles from your Exchange server.

Alternatively, you can use the **/mode:Install** and **/mode:Uninstall** switches of the **setup.com** command to add and remove server roles from an existing Exchange server respectively. For example, to remove the CAS role from your Exchange server, you could run the following command from the root of your Exchange Server 2007 installation media:

setup /mode:Uninstall /roles:ClientAccess

TAKE NOTE * Before you remove the Mailbox role, you must ensure that all mailbox and public folder databases have been removed or moved to other Exchange servers.

 ADD ADDITIONAL SERVER ROLES TO EXCHANGE SERVER 2007

GET READY. Turn on the computer, and log in as the Administrator user account in the forest root domain. Close any windows that appear on the desktop.

1. Click **Start**, **Control Panel**, and then click **Add or Remove Programs**. The Add or Remove Programs window appears.

2. Highlight **Microsoft Exchange Server 2007** and click **Change**. The Exchange Server 2007 SP1 Setup window appears.

3. At the Exchange Maintenance Mode page, click **Next**. The Server Roles Selection page appears as depicted in Figure 3-22.

Figure 3-22

Adding Exchange Roles

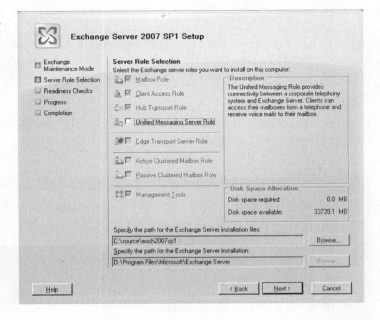

Figure 3-22

Adding Exchange Roles

TAKE NOTE

Only the roles that can be added to your Exchange server may be selected on the Roles Selection page. Because the Edge and Clustered Mailbox roles cannot share hardware with other roles, they cannot be selected.

4. Select the additional roles that you wish to add to your Exchange server and click **Next**. The Readiness Checks page will appear and check your system for prerequisite software.

5. Review the Readiness Checks page for any errors or warnings. If you have not met the proper software, hardware, and AD requirements for the role you wish to add, the Readiness Checks page will display errors that describe the component that must be installed or the action that must be taken before you are allowed to continue the Exchange Server 2007 installation. Once you have corrected the errors, you can click **Retry** to perform the readiness checks again.

6. Once the Readiness Checks page is free of errors, you can click the **Install** button to add the appropriate roles to your Exchange server.

7. On the Completion page, click **Finish**. A window will appear indicating that some Exchange Server 2007 settings require that you reboot your computer. Click **OK** to close the window.

8. Reboot your computer.

REMOVE SERVER ROLES FROM EXCHANGE SERVER 2007

GET READY. Turn on the computer, and log in as the Administrator user account in the forest root domain. Close any windows that appear on the desktop.

1. Click **Start**, **Control Panel**, and then click **Add or Remove Programs**. The Add or Remove Programs window appears.

2. Highlight **Microsoft Exchange Server 2007** and click **Remove**. The Exchange Server 2007 SP1 Setup window appears.

3. At the Exchange Maintenance Mode page, click **Next**. The Server Roles Selection page appears as depicted in Figure 3-23.

Figure 3-23

Removing Existing Server Roles

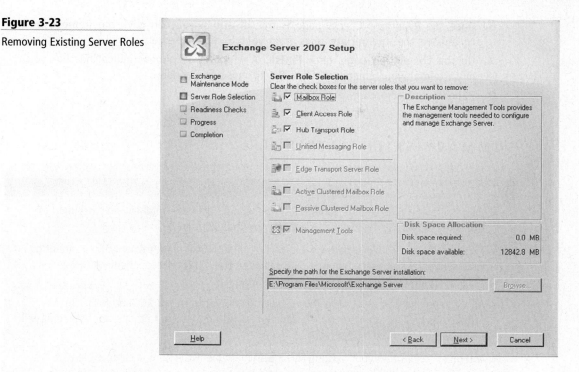

4. Select the additional roles that you wish to remove from your Exchange server and click **Next**. The Readiness Checks page will appear and check your system for prerequisite software.

5. Review the Readiness Checks page for any errors or warnings. If you are removing the Mailbox role and have not moved the mailbox and public folder databases to another server, you will see the error shown in Figure 3-24. Once you have corrected any errors, you can click **Retry** to perform the readiness checks again.

Figure 3-24

Mailbox Role Failed Readiness Checks

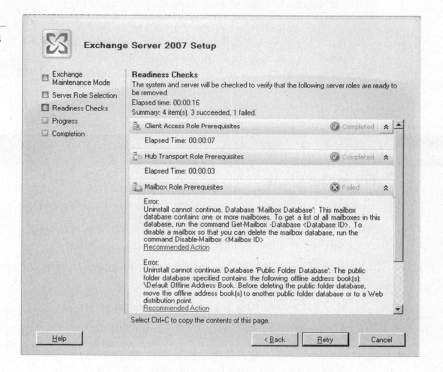

6. Once the Readiness Checks page is free of errors, you can click the **Remove** button to remove the appropriate roles from your Exchange server.

7. On the Completion page, click **Finish**. A window will appear indicating that you must reboot your computer. Click **OK** to close the window.

8. Reboot your computer.

SUMMARY SKILL MATRIX

IN THIS LESSON YOU LEARNED:

- Prior to deploying Exchange Server 2007, you should plan the number and placement of Exchange Server 2007 server roles within your organization.

- Exchange Server 2007 supports 64-bit Intel 64 and AMD64 platforms only. The amount of RAM and hard disk space required by Exchange Server 2007 is dependent on the server roles that will be hosted by the Exchange server.

- All Exchange servers must have PowerShell 1.0, .NET Framework 2.0, and MMC 3.0 installed as well as other software components that are specific to the server roles that will be hosted by the Exchange server.

- You must ensure that your existing AD and Exchange environment is compatible with Exchange Server 2007 prior to deployment. More specifically, you must prepare legacy Exchange servers, the AD schema, and AD domains prior to deploying AD. The Microsoft Exchange Best Practices Analyzer can help in Exchange server planning and preparation.

- You can install Exchange Server 2007 in graphical mode by running the **setup.exe** program or in unattended mode by using the appropriate switches to the **setup.com** program. During the installation, you must select the appropriate server roles for your Exchange server.

- Following an Exchange Server 2007 installation, you should review the installed Exchange components, Exchange setup logs, Application Event Log, as well as install an Exchange license and update your Exchange server.

- You can use the Add or Remove Programs utility in Control Panel to modify or remove server roles on existing Exchange servers.

■ Knowledge Assessment

Fill in the Blank

Complete the following sentences by writing the correct word or words in the blanks provided.

1. The recommended size of the paging file on your Exchange server is equal to the amount of RAM in your server plus _____ MB.

2. Fault tolerant RAID configurations are most appropriate for Exchange servers that host the _____ server role.

3. MSXML 6.0 or later is a software prerequisite for the _____ server role.

4. When an Exchange Server 2007 is added to the forest, its computer account is automatically added to the _____ universal security group in the forest root domain.

5. After you license your Exchange server, you must restart the _____ service for the changes to be applied.

6. If your existing Exchange Server 2003 infrastructure contains more than one routing group, you must disable _____ in the registry of the legacy Exchange server prior to deploying Exchange Server 2007.

7. To remove server roles from an existing Exchange Server 2007 computer, you must be a member of the _____ group.

8. To prepare the AD schema for the installation of the first Exchange Server 2007 computer, you can use the _____ command.

9. The Exchange organization name is usually the same as your _____ name.

10. To quickly view your server configuration from within the Exchange Management Shell, you can type the _____ command.

Multiple Choice

Circle the letter that corresponds to the best answer.

1. How much RAM is recommended for a quad-core Xeon computer that will run the Mailbox role only with 800 mailboxes?
   - **a.** 2 GB
   - **b.** 6 GB
   - **c.** 8 GB
   - **d.** 9 GB

2. How much RAM is recommended for a dual-core AMD64 computer that will run the Mailbox, CAS, and Hub roles and plans on hosting 200 mailboxes?
   - **a.** 2 GB
   - **b.** 6 GB
   - **c.** 8 GB
   - **d.** 9 GB

3. How much disk space do you require across all NTFS partitions to install the CAS and UM roles on a new Exchange server with one UM language pack?
   - **a.** 1.7 GB
   - **b.** 1.9 GB
   - **c.** 2.4 GB
   - **d.** 2.6 GB

4. Which of the following are requirements before running the **setup /PrepareSchema** command? (Choose all that apply.)
   - **a.** Your user account must be a part of the Enterprise Admins group
   - **b.** Your user account must be a part of the Schema Admins group
   - **c.** The DC that hosts the Schema Master FSMO must be on a computer running Exchange Server 2003 SP1 or Exchange Server 2003 R2.
   - **d.** Your Exchange server must be in the same AD site as the Schema Master FSMO

5. Which of the following Exchange server roles require the installation of IIS? (Choose all that apply.)
   - **a.** CAS
   - **b.** Mailbox
   - **c.** Hub
   - **d.** Edge

6. Which log in the Windows Event Viewer contains Exchange-related events?
   - **a.** Security
   - **b.** Directory Services
   - **c.** System
   - **d.** Application

7. Which of the following Exchange server roles requires that the RPC over HTTP proxy be installed?
   - **a.** CAS
   - **b.** Mailbox
   - **c.** Hub
   - **d.** Edge

8. Which of the following storage configurations use external hard disks that can be shared by multiple servers?
   - **a.** RAID
   - **b.** SAN
   - **c.** SCSI
   - **d.** PATA

9. Which of the following log files lists the tasks that were performed during the Exchange Server 2007 installation process?
   a. %systemroot%\ExchangeSetup.msilog
   b. %systemroot%\ExchangeSetup.log
   c. %systemroot%\ExchangeSetupLogs\ExchangeSetup.msilog
   d. %systemroot%\ExchangeSetupLogs\ExchangeSetup.log

10. Which of the following directories contains Exchange-related programs following a successful Exchange Server 2007 installation?
   a. %systemroot%\Program Files\Microsoft\Exchange Server\bin
   b. %systemroot%\Program Files\Microsoft\Exchange Server\OAB
   c. %systemroot%\Program Files\Microsoft\Exchange Server\Scripts
   d. %systemroot%\Program Files\Microsoft\Exchange Server\ExchangeMTA

True/False

Circle T if the statement is true or F if the statement is false.

T | F 1. A typical Exchange installation installs the CAS, UM, and Mailbox roles by default.

T | F 2. You must have at least one Hub role in each AD site that will contain Exchange servers or recipients.

T | F 3. Mailbox roles cannot share hardware with other roles.

T | F 4. Edge roles cannot share hardware with other roles.

T | F 5. All domains that will have Exchange servers or recipient objects must be set to Windows 2000 Native functional level or higher.

T | F 6. You must ensure that at least one DC in each domain that will contain Exchange servers hosts the GC.

T | F 7. To install the CAS role, you must ensure that the server contains the ASP.NET component of IIS.

T | F 8. All Exchange server roles require the .NET Framework 1.0 or later.

T | F 9. You cannot perform an in-place upgrade of Exchange Server 2003 to Exchange Server 2007.

T | F 10. Exchange Server 2007 cannot be installed on the Itanium 64-bit architecture.

Review Questions

1. Explain why smaller organizations are more likely to implement Exchange servers that contain multiple roles.

2. Give some reasons why the command **setup /PrepareAD /OrganizationName:***name* would fail (where ***name*** is the Exchange organization name).

■ Case Scenarios

Scenario 3-1: Planning Exchange Server Roles

You are the network administrator for a clothing retailer that has the following locations in the United States, Canada, and Europe:

Denver—500 users across two sites

Miami—1,100 users across three sites

Toronto—600 users in one site

Berlin—400 users in one site

London—800 users across two sites

All locations should perform virus and spam filtering on all incoming email as well as provide encrypted access for employees who check their email from home. In addition, Toronto and Miami require Unified Messaging functionality. Diagram a sample Exchange Server 2007 infrastructure for this organization that lists the number of Exchange servers required in each location and the roles that should be present on each Exchange server. Provide a rationale for all recommendations.

Scenario 3-2: Planning Exchange Hardware and Software

For the servers that you recommended in Scenario 3-1, detail the hardware and software required to support the Exchange Server 2007 server roles and user requirements in a short memo. Justify all of your decisions.

4 LESSON

Configuring a New Exchange Server

LESSON SKILL MATRIX

TECHNOLOGY SKILL	OBJECTIVE DOMAIN	OBJECTIVE DOMAIN NUMBER
Configuring the Hub Role	Configure Exchange Server roles.	1.4
Configuring the Edge Role	Configure Exchange Server roles.	1.4
Configuring the Mailbox Role	Configure Exchange Server roles.	1.4
Configuring the CAS Role	Configure Exchange Server roles.	1.4
Configuring Receive Connectors	Configure connectors.	3.1
Configuring Send Connectors	Configure connectors.	3.1
Configuring Microsoft Outlook	Configure client connectivity.	3.6
Configuring Microsoft Entourage	Configure client connectivity.	3.6
Configuring Microsoft Outlook Express and Windows Mail	Configure client connectivity.	3.6

KEY TERMS

accepted domain
administrative role
Cached Exchange Mode
connector
demilitarized zone (DMZ)
direct file access
Distributed Authoring and
   Versioning (DAV)
Exchange Organization
   Administrator

Exchange Public Folder
   Administrator
Exchange Recipient Administrator
Exchange Server Administrator
Exchange View-Only
   Administrator
mailbox database
Multipurpose Internet Mail
   Extensions (MIME)
perimeter network

permissions group
postmaster
public folder database
receive connector
screened subnet
Secure Password Authentication
   (SPA)
send connector
subscription file
WebReady

■ Configuring the Exchange Organization

THE BOTTOM LINE

Due to their purpose, email servers require a great deal of configuration after they are installed. Some of this configuration is specific to the individual servers and their server roles, whereas other configuration is based on the structure of the Exchange organization. Whether you deploy a new email infrastructure or add new servers to your existing email infrastructure, you should configure administrative roles to reflect your IT job role structure as well as create DNS records that other organizations can use to locate the appropriate email servers within your organization.

Configuring Exchange Administrator Roles

Assigning only the necessary permissions and rights to Exchange administrators within your organization helps secure your Exchange infrastructure. As a result, you should ensure that the correct administrative roles are granted to the administrative staff within your organization before configuring the various aspects of Exchange Server 2007.

In small organizations, there may be one or two network administrators who are responsible for the setup, configuration, and maintenance of your email servers. However, in larger organizations that span multiple locations, the administration of email servers is likely to be split among several different administrators. Each administrator will have different areas of responsibility and different administrative duties on the Exchange servers within the organization. Some administrators may require access to all Exchange servers within the organization, while other administrators may be responsible for one or two servers in their own locations.

Although the level of access that each administrator requires depends on the structure, needs, and culture of the organization itself, you should ensure administrators have the permissions and rights that they require to perform their job role without granting unnecessary permissions. To do this, you can assign administrative users and groups to various predefined ***administrative roles*** for the entire Exchange organization or for an individual Exchange server within the Exchange organization. These predefined administrative roles are listed in Table 4-1.

Table 4-1

Exchange Server 2007 administrative roles

ADMINISTRATIVE ROLE	SCOPE	PERMISSIONS
Exchange Organization Administrator	Organization-wide	Full permission to all components of Exchange as well as Exchange-related objects and information in AD.
Exchange Recipient Administrator	Organization-wide	Ability to modify the properties of any recipient object including users, contacts, groups, and public folders, as well as mailbox and UM settings for recipient objects.
Exchange Public Folder Administrator	Organization-wide	Ability to create and delete public folders as well as manage all public folder properties that are not related to specific recipient objects. This administrative role is only available in Exchange Server 2007 SP1 and later.
Exchange View-Only Administrator	Organization-wide	Ability to view all Exchange-related information on Exchange servers and within AD.
Exchange Server Administrator	Server specific	Full permission to administer all Exchange-related components on a specific Exchange server.

TAKE NOTE * In addition to having administrative role membership, you must also be a member of the local Administrators group on each Exchange server that you wish to administer.

To allow viewing of all Exchange-related information, the Exchange Public Folder Administrator and Exchange Recipient Administrator roles are members of the Exchange View-Only Administrator role by default. In addition, the Exchange Public Folder

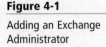

Administrator role and the Exchange Recipient Administrator role both contain the Exchange Organization Administrator role. This ensures that members of the Exchange Organization Administrator role always have the ability to perform the functions of the Exchange Public Folder Administrator and Exchange Recipient Administrator roles as well as the ability to view all Exchange-related information on Exchange servers and within AD.

Except for the Exchange Server Administrator role, all administrative roles are represented by universal security groups of the same name in the Microsoft Exchange Security Groups OU in the forest root domain. As a result, you can modify the membership of these groups in the Active Directory Users and Computers console to configure administrative roles.

Alternatively, you can use the Exchange Management Console to view, assign, or remove administrative roles. If you assign the Exchange Server Administrator role to a user or group, that user or group is also added to the Exchange View-Only Administrator role because the Exchange Server Administrator role is not a member of the Exchange View-Only Administrator role by default.

ADD AN EXCHANGE ADMINISTRATOR

GET READY. Turn on the computer, and log in as the Administrator user account. Close any windows that appear on the desktop.

1. Click **Start**, **All Programs**, **Microsoft Exchange Server 2007**, and then click **Exchange Management Console**. The Exchange Management Console window appears.
2. In the console tree pane, highlight **Organization Configuration**.
3. In the action pane, click **Add Exchange Administrator**. The Add Exchange Administrator window appears as shown in Figure 4-1.

Figure 4-1

Adding an Exchange Administrator

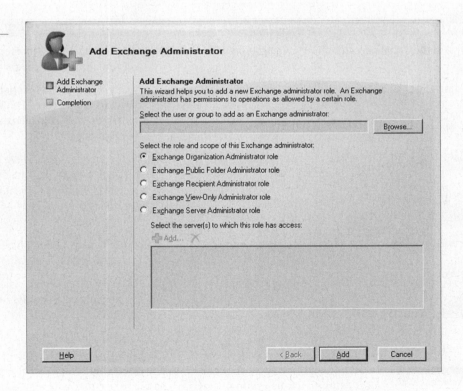

4. Click the **Browse** button, select the appropriate user or group and click **OK**.
5. Select the appropriate administrative role for the user or group. If you select the Exchange Server Administrator role, you must also click the **Add** button underneath Exchange Server Administrator role, select the Exchange server(s) that the role should apply to, and click **OK**.

THE COMMAND LINE WAY

You can also use the **Add-ExchangeAdministrator** and **Remove-ExchangeAdministrator** cmdlets in the Exchange Management Shell to add and remove administrative roles. For example, to assign the user with the logon name bob.jones to the Exchange Organization Administrator role for the Exchange organization called Octavius, you could run the following command in the Exchange Management Shell: **Add-ExchangeAdministrator -Role OrgAdmin -Identity Octavius\bob .jones**.

6. Click **Add**. The Completion page appears.
7. Click **Finish** to close the Add Exchange Administrator window.
8. Close the Exchange Management Console.

Configuring DNS Records

After deploying email servers within your organization, you should ensure that external organizations can relay email to your organization. This involves creating DNS records to represent the email servers within your organization that accept email.

Recall that DNS MX and A records are used to locate email servers for organizations on the Internet. The Exchange servers in your organization that host the Edge or Hub roles contact a DNS server when they need to resolve the names and IP addresses of foreign email servers to which they need to relay email.

Similarly, when foreign email servers need to relay email to your organization, they use DNS to resolve the names and IP addresses of the email servers within your organization. For this to occur, DNS must contain MX records that list the names of the Exchange servers in your organization that are configured to receive Internet email as well as A records that list the associated IP address of these servers.

Because the Edge role is responsible for processing incoming email from the Internet, you should ensure that MX and A records exist for each Exchange server in your organization that hosts the Edge role. If your organization has multiple Edge roles, you should balance the load of incoming email across all Exchange servers that host an Edge role using DNS round robin. To allow for DNS round robin, simply ensure that the MX records for each Exchange server have the same priority number.

If your organization does not contain the Edge role, then the Hub role is responsible for processing incoming Internet email. In this case, you must ensure that MX and A records exist for each Exchange server in your organization that contains the Hub role. If your organization has multiple Hub roles, you can also use DNS round robin to load balance the incoming email by ensuring that the MX records for your Exchange servers have the same priority number.

TAKE NOTE*

Because only the Edge and Hub roles process incoming Internet email, you do not need to create MX records for new Exchange servers that only host the CAS, Mailbox, or UM roles. If your organization uses the Edge role, then all incoming email must pass through the Edge role, and you do not need to create MX records for Exchange servers that host the Hub role.

TAKE NOTE*

Authoritative DNS servers can be queried by other DNS servers on the Internet provided that their domain is registered on the Internet by a Registrar. To register a domain using a Registrar, you can contact your ISP or visit www.internic.net.

If your organization uses a smart host to filter email before it is sent to your organization, you should ensure that an MX and A record exists for the smart host server and that its MX priority number is lower than the priority number used in the MX records for the Exchange servers that host the Edge or Hub role in your organization. This lower priority number will ensure that all email is first sent to the smart host server, which will be configured to forward email to the servers in your organization. If the smart host server is offline, then incoming email will be sent directly to the email servers in your organization that host the Edge or Hub role.

To create DNS MX and A records, you must first locate an ***authoritative DNS server*** for your organization's domain. An authoritative DNS server hosts the zone file that contains the DNS records for the domain that represents your organization. Other DNS servers on the Internet will query the authoritative DNS server for your organization's domain when they need to resolve the DNS MX and A records for your organization.

Some organizations pay their ISP to create and manage the authoritative DNS server for their DNS domain. In that case, you may need to contact the ISP to create the appropriate MX and A records. However, if your organization hosts its own authoritative DNS server, you can simply create the necessary MX and A records on your DNS server for the Exchange servers within your organization that contain the Edge or Hub role.

For Linux and UNIX-based DNS servers, creating MX and A records will likely involve editing the appropriate zone file located in the **/var/named** directory using a text editor or graphical utility. For Windows DNS servers, you can use the DNS console (**Start > Administrative Tools > DNS**) to create and manage DNS records.

If your DNS server supports dynamic update and your Exchange servers are configured to use the DNS server in TCP/IP properties, then A records for your Exchange servers will automatically be created on the DNS server. In this case, you will only need to create MX records for the appropriate Exchange servers within your organization.

⊕ CREATE MX AND A RECORDS ON AN AUTHORITATIVE DNS SERVER

GET READY. Turn on the computer, and log in as the Administrator user account. Close any windows that appear on the desktop.

1. Click **Start**, **Administrative Tools**, and then click **DNS**. The DNS console window appears.

2. Expand the **Forward Lookup Zones** folder under your server object in the left pane.

3. Right click the zone for your domain and select **New Host (A)** from the menu. The New Host window appears as shown in Figure 4-2.

Figure 4-2

Adding a DNS A Record

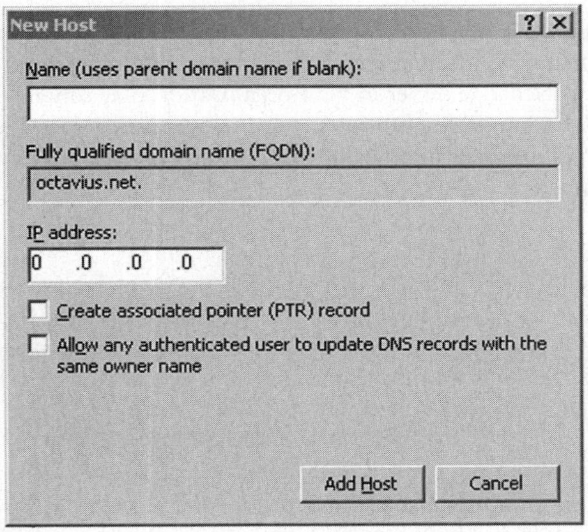

4. In the **Name** dialog box, type the host name of your Exchange server. Next, supply the appropriate IP address for the Exchange server in the **IP address** dialog box and click **Add Host**. Click **OK** to close the confirmation window and click **Done** to close the New Host window.

⚠ **WARNING** A common mistake when creating A records is to supply the FQDN in the **Name** dialog box instead of the host name. This will create an FQDN that contains subdomain names for your A record. To avoid this, double check the **Fully qualified domain name (FQDN)** field shown in Figure 4-2 after entering your host name to ensure that you have the correct FQDN.

5. Right click the zone for your domain and select **New Mail Exchanger (MX)** from the menu. The New Resource Record window appears as shown in Figure 4-3.

Figure 4-3

Adding a DNS MX Record

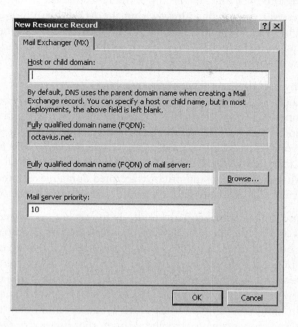

6. Verify that the authoritative DNS domain that your Exchange server will receive email for is listed in the **Fully qualified domain name (FQDN)** box. If your Exchange server will be configured to receive email for a subdomain, you must enter the appropriate subdomain in the **Host or child domain** dialog box. Normally this dialog box is left empty.

7. Next, supply the FQDN of the Exchange server in the **Fully qualified domain name (FQDN) of mail server** dialog box. If you wish to change the priority number from the default of 10, enter the appropriate priority number in the **Mail server priority** dialog box.

8. Click **OK** to create the MX record.

9. Close the DNS console.

 ANOTHER WAY

Instead of entering the FQDN of your email server, you can click the **Browse** button in Figure 4-3 and navigate to the A record for your email server.

■ Configuring Server Roles

 THE BOTTOM LINE

Most Exchange Server 2007 configuration depends on the server roles that are present on each email server within your organization. Although much of this configuration is discussed throughout this book, this section focuses on the configuration tasks that are commonly performed for server roles shortly after they have been added to the Exchange organization.

 REF

The structure and configuration of the UM role will be discussed in Lesson 12, "Providing for Mobile Access and Unified Messaging."

Configuring the Hub Role

After installation, the Hub role is configured to accept and route internal email within the organization. However, you should also configure the domains that the Hub role should accept email from, as well as configure a postmaster account for each server that hosts the Hub role in your organization to ensure that email problems are sent to the appropriate person.

CERTIFICATION READY?
Configure Exchange Server Roles.
1.4

CONFIGURING ACCEPTED DOMAINS

After installing the Exchange Server 2007, the Hub role is configured to receive emails that are addressed to an email address within the AD domain. For example, after installing the first Hub role in the octavius.net domain, the Exchange organization is set to accept email that is addressed to recipients in the octavius.net domain and reject email that is not addressed to a recipient in the octavius.net domain.

However, many organizations select additional domain name suffixes for email use by particular users within their organization. For example, the user bob.jones may be configured with the email address bob.jones@research.octavius.net to identify his membership in the research division of the organization. To allow for email that is addressed to bob.jones@research .octavius.net to be processed by your Hub servers, you must create an *accepted domain* for research.octavius.net that indicates that your Exchange organization is responsible for email that is sent to recipients in research.octavius.net. Once an authoritative accepted domain exists, the Hub server will locate the recipient by email address in AD and forward incoming email to the correct mailbox.

Similarly, some organizations contain multiple forests and must maintain separate Exchange organizations as a result. This is common practice when one company acquires another yet requires that both companies maintain their own identity. By default, email that is addressed to a domain in another forest is rejected by the Hub servers in your Exchange organization unless you create an accepted domain for the target domain name that specifies how email should be forwarded. If you want your Hub servers to forward email that is addressed to the target domain name directly, you must create an accepted domain that uses *internal relay*. Alternatively, you can create an accepted domain that uses *external relay* to force all email that is addressed to the target domain name to be forwarded to the appropriate email servers across the Internet by the Edge role. To forward email addressed to an accepted domain name to email servers outside the Exchange organization, the Hub and Edge roles must be able to resolve the MX records for the accepted domain name.

You can configure accepted domains within the Exchange Management Console by navigating to **Organization Configuration** > **Hub Transport** and selecting the **Accepted Domains** tab as shown in Figure 4-4.

> **TAKE NOTE** *
>
> If used, the Edge role also processes accepted domains. However, you cannot configure accepted domains for the Edge role. Instead, the Hub role replicates its accepted domain information to the Edge role using the EdgeSync protocol.

Figure 4-4

Viewing Accepted Domains

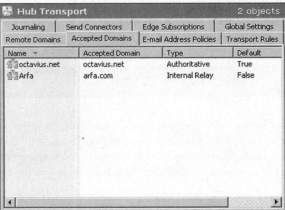

In Figure 4-4, emails that are addressed to recipients in the octavius.net domain are processed by the Hub servers, whereas emails addressed to recipients in the arfa.com domain are forwarded directly by the Hub server to the appropriate email server for the arfa.com domain using internal relay.

ADD AN ACCEPTED DOMAIN

GET READY. Turn on the computer and log in as the Administrator user account. Close any windows that appear on the desktop.

1. Click **Start, All Programs, Microsoft Exchange Server 2007,** and then click **Exchange Management Console.** The Exchange Management Console window appears.

2. In the console tree pane, expand **Organization Configuration** and highlight **Hub Transport**.

3. In the result pane, click the **Accepted Domains** tab.

4. In the action pane, click **New Accepted Domain**. The New Accepted Domain window appears as shown in Figure 4-5.

Figure 4-5

Creating a New Accepted Domain

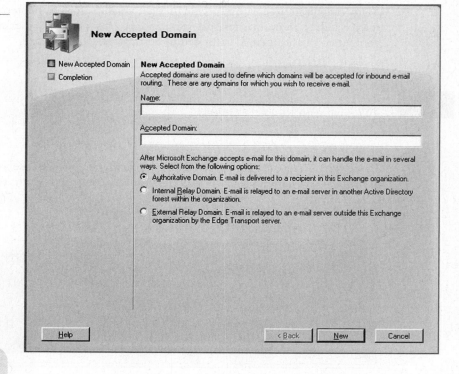

THE COMMAND LINE WAY

You can also use the **New-AcceptedDomain** and **Remove-Accepted Domain** cmdlets in the Exchange Management Shell to add and remove accepted domains. For example, to add the accepted domain for arfa.com shown in Figure 4-4, you could run the following command in the Exchange Management Shell: **New-AcceptedDomain -DomainName arfa.com -Name Arfa –DomainType InternalRelay.**

5. Type a name that represents the accepted domain in the **Name** dialog box. Next, type the domain name for the accepted domain in the **Accepted Domain** dialog box.

6. Select the appropriate method that should be used to handle email sent to the accepted domain:

   • **Authoritative Domain** is appropriate for domain names that are used by recipients who have mailboxes on your Exchange servers.

   • **Internal Relay Domain** allows your Hub role servers to directly forward email for the domain name to the appropriate email server by resolving its MX records.

   • **External Relay Domain** forces your Edge role servers to forward the email for the domain name to the appropriate email server on the Internet by resolving its MX records.

7. Click **New**. The Completion page appears.

8. Click **Finish** to close the New Accepted Domain window.

9. Close the Exchange Management Console.

CONFIGURING A POSTMASTER

Most email servers contain a special email address called the *postmaster* that represents the person who is responsible for the ongoing operation of the email server. Users who have problems sending or receiving email will see the postmaster email address on their delivery notifications and can send email to the postmaster to alert them to the problem.

In Exchange Server 2007, the relay of postmaster email is handled by the Hub role. Each server that hosts the Hub role can have a different postmaster, and the postmaster email address is not set by default.

To set the postmaster email address, you can use the **Set-TransportServer** cmdlet in the Exchange Management Shell. For example, to set the postmaster address on the server EXCH1 to Administrator@octavius.net, you could run the following command within the Exchange Management Shell:

Set-TransportServer–Identity EXCH1 –ExternalPostMasterAddress Administrator@octavius.net

Many organizations create a specific user and mailbox for postmaster email and set the postmaster address to postmaster@domainname. For this to occur, an existing mailbox must be configured to accept email addressed to postmaster@domainname.

 REF Configuring mailboxes with additional email addresses will be discussed in Lesson 5, "Working with Recipient Objects."

To view the postmasters configured for your organization, you can use the **Get-TransportServer | Format-List Name,ExternalPostMasterAddress** command within the Exchange Management Shell as shown in Figure 4-6.

Figure 4-6

Viewing Postmasters

Configuring the Edge Role

After installation, the Edge role is not functional until it is configured to participate in the Exchange organization. To do this, you must create a subscription file on each Edge role server and import it on a Hub role server within your site.

TAKE NOTE*

In a Windows Server 2008 AD environment, AD LDS is used instead of ADAM to obtain configuration information on an Edge role server.

Unlike other Exchange servers within your Exchange Organization, servers that host the Edge role cannot communicate directly with AD. Instead, these Edge role servers must use ADAM to periodically obtain AD and Exchange information using the EdgeSync protocol from a server that hosts the Hub role.

Most organizations have a ***perimeter network*** that is directly connected to the Internet via a firewall. Servers that must provide public access from other servers or clients on the Internet are typically placed in this perimeter network, whereas other servers that maintain sensitive resources are placed on the organization's internal LAN and configured to access the servers in the perimeter network through another firewall.

TAKE NOTE*

Perimeter networks are often called ***demilitarized zones (DMZs)*** or ***screened subnets***.

The Edge role in Exchange Server 2007 is intended for use within a perimeter network whereas all other roles are intended for use within the internal LAN. If your organization places an Edge role server in the perimeter network, it will need to communicate to a Hub role server on the internal LAN across a firewall as shown in Figure 4-7. For this to occur, you must open TCP port 50636 on the internal firewall to allow the EdgeSync protocol as well as ensure that the Edge role server can resolve the FQDN of the Hub role server and vice versa.

Figure 4-7

Edge Role Placement

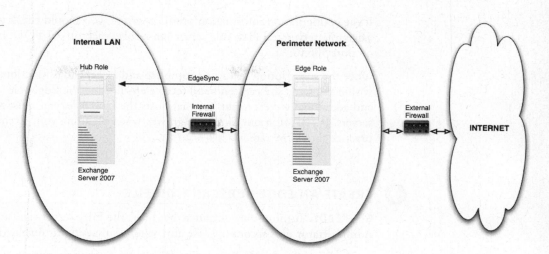

Once you have installed a server in the perimeter of your network that hosts the Edge role, you need to create an XML *subscription file* on the server. This subscription file is then imported into a server that hosts the Hub role to activate the EdgeSync protocol and allow email relay.

To create a subscription file on an Edge role server, you must run the following command in the Exchange Management Shell on the Edge role server:

New-EdgeSubscription–file *filename.xml*

Each server that hosts the Edge role must create its own subscription file, and the subscription file must be imported using the Exchange Management Console on a server that contains the Hub role within 24 hours of its creation. If you do not import the subscription file within 24 hours, you must create a new subscription file and import it within 24 hours.

After you have subscribed an Edge role server to a server that hosts the Hub role, you should run the **Start-EdgeSynchronization** command in the Exchange Management Shell on the Hub role server. This will force EdgeSync synchronization as well as verify that there are no EdgeSync-related errors as shown in Figure 4-8.

Figure 4-8

Forcing EdgeSync
Synchronization

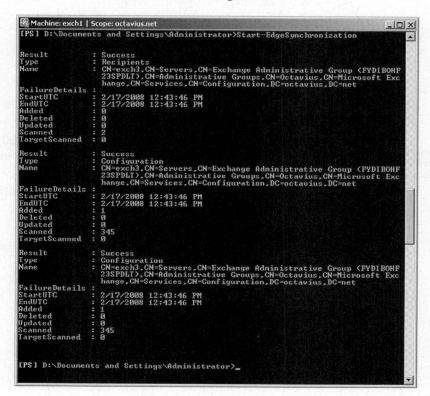

If the configuration information produces errors, you should check to ensure that both the Edge role server and Hub role server can resolve each other's FQDNs as well as communicate on port 50636.

Once the subscription process is complete and EdgeSync is functional, all Hub role servers within the same site can send and receive email using the Edge role server. However, if you add additional servers to the site that hosts the Hub role, you must resubscribe your Edge role servers. If you left room for future growth when planning your Exchange infrastructure, this practice should be rare.

CREATE AN EDGE SUBSCRIPTION FILE

GET READY. Turn on the computer that hosts the Edge server role, and log in as the Administrator user account. Close any windows that appear on the desktop.

1. Click **Start, All Programs, Microsoft Exchange Server 2007**, and then click **Exchange Management Shell**. The Exchange Management Shell window appears.

2. At the command prompt, type **New-EdgeSubscription–file "C:\EdgeSubscriptionExport .xml"** and press **Enter**.

> **TAKE NOTE***
>
> You can use any name for the file that you create with the **New-EdgeSubscription** command as long as you ensure that it contains the **.xml** extension. If you choose a different name for your subscription file, you must use that name when importing the subscription file into the Exchange Management Console in the next exercise.

3. When prompted to confirm the action, type **y** and press **Enter**.

4. Close the Exchange Management Shell.

5. Copy the C:\EdgeSubscriptionExport.xml file to removable media such as a memory stick or portable hard drive.

IMPORT AN EDGE SUBSCRIPTION FILE

GET READY. Turn on the computer that hosts the Hub role, and log in as the Administrator user account. Close any windows that appear on the desktop.

> **WARNING** This process must be completed within 24 hours of creating the Edge subscription file.

1. Click **Start, All Programs, Microsoft Exchange Server 2007**, and then click **Exchange Management Console**. The Exchange Management Console window appears.

2. In the console tree pane, expand **Organization Configuration** and highlight **Hub Transport**.

3. In the result pane, click the **Edge Subscriptions** tab.

4. In the action pane, click **New Edge Subscription**. The New Edge Subscription window appears as shown in Figure 4-9.

Figure 4-9

Importing an Edge Subscription File

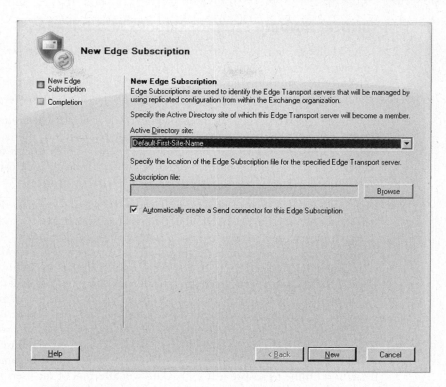

5. Select the appropriate AD site that your Edge role server should communicate with in the **Active Directory site** drop-down box.

6. Next, click **Browse**, navigate to and select the EdgeSubscriptionExport.xml file that you created on the Edge role server and click **OK**.

7. Click **New**. The Completion page appears.

8. Click **Finish** to close the New Edge Subscription window. The Edge subscription should appear under the Edge Subscriptions tab in the result pane.

9. Close the Exchange Management Console.

10. Click **Start**, **All Programs**, **Microsoft Exchange Server 2007**, and then click **Exchange Management Shell**. The Exchange Management Shell window appears.

11. At the command prompt, type **Start-EdgeSynchronization** and press **Enter**. Examine the output for errors.

12. Close the Exchange Management Shell.

THE COMMAND LINE WAY

Although you can import an Edge subscription file within the Exchange Management Console, you can also use the **New-EdgeSubscription** cmdlet in the Exchange Management Shell on a Hub role server. To import the C:\EdgeSubscriptionExport.xml file created earlier on an Edge role server into a Hub role server within the Cupertino site, you could run the following command in the Exchange Management Shell on the Hub role server:

New-EdgeSubscription -FileName 'C:\EdgeSubscriptionExport.xml' -Site 'Cupertino'

Configuring the Mailbox Role

After installation, Mailbox role servers contain a single storage group that contains a single mailbox database. Depending on installation choices, the Mailbox role server may also contain a database for public folders. To optimize information storage on your Mailbox role, you may need to move existing storage groups and databases or create new ones. In addition, these databases should enforce storage limits to prevent certain email recipients from using up all of the available space on your Mailbox role server before your databases are put into production.

CERTIFICATION READY?
Configure Exchange Server Roles.
1.4

UNDERSTANDING STORAGE GROUPS AND DATABASES

The Mailbox role is the most critical role in your Exchange organization because it stores and manages access to the mailboxes and public folders used to store vital company information. To ensure fast information access, Exchange Server 2007 uses a database storage engine that stores mailboxes in *mailbox databases* and public folders in *public folder databases*.

Because the size of a single mailbox or public folder database is unlimited in Exchange Server 2007, you can choose to create one mailbox database and one public folder database per server. However, as the size of a database grows, it becomes more difficult to search and manage. As a general rule, larger database sizes result in poorer Exchange performance and a greater likelihood that information within the database will get corrupted.

Because public folder databases typically store far less information than mailbox databases, you can only have one public folder database per Exchange server. However, you should create multiple mailbox databases on each Mailbox role server and divide mailboxes evenly among them. This optimizes database performance as well as provides for flexible recovery in the case of database corruption. Say, for example, that your Mailbox role server has four databases that contain the mailboxes for the users within your organization and each database has roughly the same number of mailboxes. If a single database becomes corrupted, then you can take the single database offline by dismounting it and then restore it from backup without affecting the other three databases. During the restore procedure, only one-quarter of all the users within the organization will be unable to access their mailboxes. Alternatively, if your Mailbox role server has only a single mailbox database and it becomes corrupted, taking the database offline to restore it from backup will affect all of the users within your organization.

The Standard edition of Exchange Server 2007 allows you to create up to 5 databases per server, whereas the Enterprise edition can create up to 50 databases on a single server.

All databases must be contained within a database storage group that is represented by a folder on a hard disk. Storage groups can contain up to five databases and are used to simplify database management because you can specify similar backup and maintenance schedules for each storage group.

Using the Standard edition of Exchange Server 2007, you can create only a single storage group on each Mailbox role server. As a result, if you create multiple databases on a Mailbox role server that runs Exchange Server 2007 Standard edition, you must place those databases in the same storage group.

Exchange Server 2007 Enterprise edition can create up to 50 storage groups on a single server. Because the Enterprise edition can also create up to 50 databases on a single server, each database can be located in its own storage group for more granular management. Because storage groups can be located on different hard disks, this allows for greater flexibility and fault tolerance in the event of a single hard disk failure.

TAKE NOTE* Microsoft recommends that you create one database per storage group in Exchange Server 2007 Enterprise edition.

MODIFYING THE DEFAULT STORAGE GROUPS AND DATABASES

When you install the Mailbox role on an Exchange server, a single mailbox database is created called **Mailbox Database.edb** and stored in a storage group called **First Storage Group** on the hard drive (%systemroot%\Program Files\Exchange Server\Mailbox\First Storage Group). If you chose to allow Entourage and Outlook 2003 and earlier MAPI clients the ability to access your Exchange server during the Exchange Server 2007 installation wizard, then a public folder database called **Public Folder Database.edb** is also created. If you are running the Enterprise edition of Exchange Server 2007, this public folder database will be stored in a separate storage group on the hard disk called **Second Storage Group** (%systemroot%\ Program Files\Exchange Server\Mailbox\First Storage Group).

Recall that Mailbox role servers are likely equipped with additional hard disks and that these additional hard disks are usually combined in some fault tolerant RAID such as RAID 1 or RAID 5. If your Mailbox role server has multiple hard disks or implements RAID, you should move the default storage groups and databases to another hard disk or RAID volume to improve performance and fault tolerance.

When information is stored in a database, it is first written to a transaction log in the storage group to improve performance and allow point-in-time recovery of information that is lost after being written to the database. By default, databases and transaction logs are stored in the same folder on the hard drive that comprises the storage group. However, when you move a storage group, you have the option to select a different folder for the database and transaction logs. Each of these folders still comprises the same storage group, but can be located on separate hard drives to improve performance and fault tolerance. In most cases, administrators store the database and transaction logs in the same folder to simplify organization and administration.

 MOVE THE DEFAULT STORAGE GROUPS

GET READY. Turn on the computer, and log in as the Administrator user account. Close any windows that appear on the desktop.

1. Click **Start**, **All Programs**, **Microsoft Exchange Server 2007**, and then click **Exchange Management Console**. The Exchange Management Console window appears.
2. In the console tree pane, expand **Server Configuration** and highlight **Mailbox**.
3. In the result pane, highlight your server object.
4. In the work pane, highlight **First Storage Group**.
5. In the action pane, click **Move Storage Group Path**. The Move Storage Group Path window appears as shown in Figure 4-10.

Figure 4-10

Moving a Default Storage Group

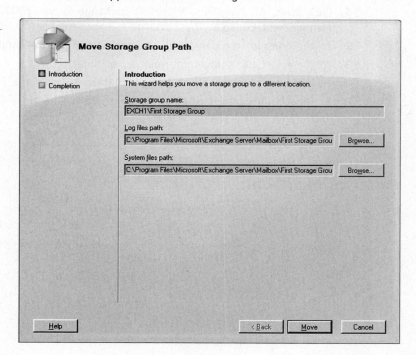

6. Beside the **Log files path** dialog box, click **Browse**. In the Browse For Folder window that appears, select the target hard disk and target folder that you wish to move the transaction logs to and click **OK**.
7. Beside the **System files path** dialog box, click **Browse**. In the Browse For Folder window that appears, select the target hard disk and target folder that you wish to move the storage group to and click **OK**. Normally, this is the same path chosen for the transaction logs.

TAKE NOTE*

If the target folder does not exist, you can click **Make New Folder** in the Browse For Folder window.

8. Click **Move**. When prompted to confirm that databases within the storage group will be unavailable during the move operation, click **Yes**. The Completion page appears.

9. Click **Finish** to close the Move Storage Group Path window. If your server is running Exchange Server 2007 Enterprise edition, and have created a public folder database during the installation, you should also move the Second Storage Group using the following steps.

10. In the work pane, highlight **Second Storage Group**.

11. In the action pane, click **Move Storage Group Path**. The Move Storage Group Path window appears as shown earlier in Figure 4-10.

12. Beside the **Log files path** dialog box, click **Browse**. In the Browse For Folder window that appears, select the target hard disk and target folder that you wish to move the transaction logs to and click **OK**.

13. Beside the **System files path** dialog box, click **Browse**. In the Browse For Folder window that appears, select the target hard disk and target folder that you wish to move the storage group to and click **OK**. Normally, this is the same path chosen for the transaction logs.

14. Click **Move**. When prompted to confirm that databases within the storage group will be unavailable during the move operation, click **Yes**. The Completion page appears.

15. Click **Finish** to close the Move Storage Group Path window.

16. Close the Exchange Management Console.

 MOVE THE DEFAULT MAILBOX AND PUBLIC FOLDER DATABASES

GET READY. Turn on the computer, and log in as the Administrator user account. Close any windows that appear on the desktop.

1. Click **Start**, **All Programs**, **Microsoft Exchange Server 2007**, and then click **Exchange Management Console**. The Exchange Management Console window appears.

2. In the console tree pane, expand **Server Configuration** and highlight **Mailbox**.

3. In the result pane, highlight your server object.

4. In the work pane, highlight **Mailbox Database** under the First Storage Group.

5. In the action pane, click **Move Database Path**. The Move Database Path window appears as shown in Figure 4-11.

Figure 4-11

Moving a Default Database

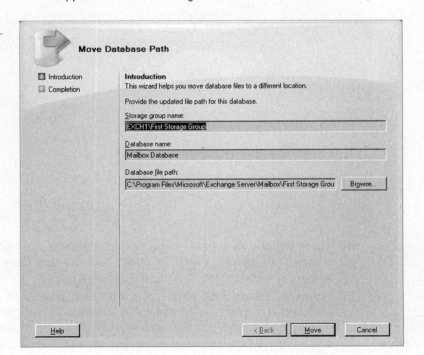

TAKE NOTE *

If you wish, you can provide a different file name for the database before you click **Save** in the Exchange Database window.

6. Beside the **Database file path** dialog box, click **Browse**. In the Exchange Database window that appears, select the target hard disk and target folder that you wish to move the database to and click **Save**. Normally, this is the same path chosen for the storage group and storage group transaction logs.

7. Click **Move**. When prompted to confirm that the database will be unavailable during the move operation, click **Yes**. The Completion page appears.

8. Click **Finish** to close the Move Database Path window. If you have created a public folder database during the installation, you should also move it to the appropriate storage group on another hard disk using the following steps.

9. In the work pane, highlight **Public Folder Database**. This database will be located under the First Storage Group if you are running Exchange Server 2007 Standard edition or under the Second Storage Group if you are running Exchange Server 2007 Enterprise Edition.

10. In the action pane, click **Move Database Path**. The Move Database Path window appears as shown earlier in Figure 4-11.

11. Beside the **Database file path** dialog box, click **Browse**. In the Exchange Database window that appears, select the target hard disk and target folder that you wish to move the database to and click **Save**. Normally, this is the same path chosen for the storage group and storage group transaction logs.

12. Click **Move**. When prompted to confirm that the database will be unavailable during the move operation, click **Yes**.

13. Click **Finish** to close the Move Database Path window.

14. Close the Exchange Management Console.

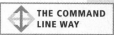
**THE COMMAND
LINE WAY**

You can also use the **Move-StorageGroupPath** and **Move-DatabasePath** cmdlets in the Exchange Management Shell to move storage groups and databases. For example, to move the transaction logs and storage group files for the First Storage Group on the server EXCH1 to the folder D:\SG1, you could run the following command in the Exchange Management Shell:

Move-StorageGroupPath–Identity 'EXCH1\First Storage Group' –LogFolderPath 'D:\SG1' –SystemFolderPath 'D:\SG1'

Similarly, to move the default Mailbox Database within the First Storage Group on the server EXCH1 to the same location, you could run the following command in the Exchange Management Shell:

Move-DatabasePath –Identity 'EXCH1\First Storage Group\Mailbox Database' –EdbFilePath 'D:\SG1\Mailbox Database.edb'

CREATING ADDITIONAL STORAGE GROUPS AND DATABASES

When you create new mailboxes, you have the ability to select the storage group and database that will store the mailbox data. This gives you the ability to divide up mailboxes among several different databases and storage groups on a single server to enhance performance and reliability. In addition, if you did not specify to create a public folder database during the Exchange installation, you will need to create a public folder database after installation to allow Entourage and Outlook 2003 and earlier MAPI clients the ability to access your Exchange server.

Accordingly, you almost always need to create additional storage groups and databases on a new Mailbox role server. As discussed earlier, by locating these storage groups and databases on a nonsystem hard disk that is part of a RAID, you can enhance the speed and fault tolerance of your databases.

REF Creating mailboxes will be discussed in Lesson 5, "Working with Recipient Objects."
Creating public folders will be discussed in Lesson 7, "Working with Public Folders."

CREATE A NEW STORAGE GROUP

GET READY. Turn on the computer, and log in as the Administrator user account. Close any windows that appear on the desktop.

1. Click **Start**, **All Programs**, **Microsoft Exchange Server 2007**, and then click **Exchange Management Console**. The Exchange Management Console window appears.
2. In the console tree pane, expand **Server Configuration** and highlight **Mailbox**.
3. In the detail pane, highlight your server object.
4. In the action pane, click **New Storage Group**. The New Storage Group window appears as shown in Figure 4-12.

Figure 4-12

Creating a New Storage Group

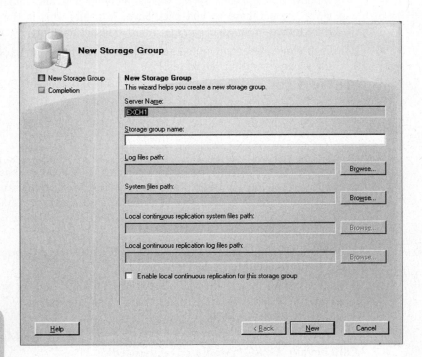

TAKE NOTE*

If the target folder does not exist, you can click **Make New Folder** in the Browse For Folder window.

X REF

Enabling storage groups for use with Local continuous replication will be discussed in Lesson 13, "Providing for High Availability."

5. In the Storage group name field, type a name for your storage group.
6. Beside the **Log files path** dialog box, click **Browse**. In the Browse For Folder window that appears, select the target hard disk and target folder that you wish to use for the transaction logs and click **OK**.
7. Beside the System files path dialog box, click **Browse**. In the Browse For Folder window that appears, select the target hard disk and target folder that you wish to use for the storage group and click **OK**. Normally, this is the same path chosen for the transaction logs.
8. Do not select any other options and click **New**.
9. Click **Finish** to close the New Storage Group window.
10. Close the Exchange Management Console

You can also use the **New-StorageGroup** cmdlet in the Exchange Management Shell to create a new storage group. For example, to create a new storage group called Third Storage Group on the server called EXCH1, and specify that transaction logs and storage group files should be stored in the folder D:\SG3, you could run the following command in the Exchange Management Shell:

THE COMMAND LINE WAY

New-StorageGroup –Server 'EXCH1' –Name 'Third Storage Group' –LogFolderPath 'D:\SG3' –SystemFolderPath 'D:\SG3'

Alternatively, you can use the **Get-StorageGroup** cmdlet to obtain information about an existing storage group or the **Set-StorageGroup** cmdlet to change its properties. To remove an existing storage group, you can use the **Remove-StorageGroup** cmdlet. For more information on the **New-StorageGroup, Get-StorageGroup**, **Set-StorageGroup,** and **Remove-StorageGroup** cmdlets, search for their names within Exchange Server 2007 Help.

⊙ CREATE A NEW MAILBOX DATABASE

GET READY. Turn on the computer, and log in as the Administrator user account. Close any windows that appear on the desktop.

1. Click **Start**, **All Programs**, **Microsoft Exchange Server 2007**, and then click **Exchange Management Console**. The Exchange Management Console window appears.

2. In the console tree pane, expand **Server Configuration** and highlight **Mailbox**.

3. In the result pane, highlight your server object.

4. In the work pane, highlight the storage group that should contain the new mailbox database.

5. In the action pane, click **New Mailbox Database**. The New Mailbox Database window appears as shown in Figure 4-13.

Figure 4-13

Creating a New Mailbox Database

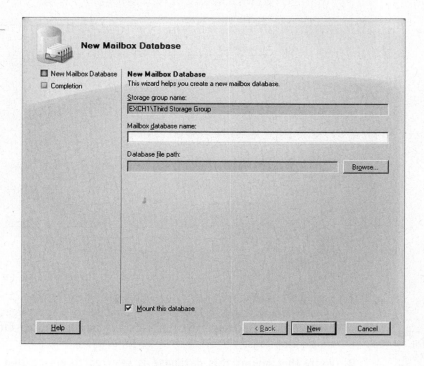

6. In the **Mailbox database name** field, type a name for your mailbox database.

7. Beside the **Database file path** dialog box, click **Browse**. In the Browse For Folder window that appears, select the target hard disk and target folder that you wish to

use and click **OK**. Normally, this is the same folder used for the storage group and transaction logs.

8. Verify that **Mount this database** is selected to ensure that the database will be available for use after creation and click **New**.

9. Click **Finish** to close the New Mailbox Database window.

10. Close the Exchange Management Console.

 CREATE A NEW PUBLIC FOLDER DATABASE

GET READY. Turn on the computer, and log in as the Administrator user account. Close any windows that appear on the desktop.

1. Click **Start**, **All Programs**, **Microsoft Exchange Server 2007**, and then click **Exchange Management Console**. The Exchange Management Console window appears.

2. In the console tree pane, expand **Server Configuration** and highlight **Mailbox**.

3. In the result pane, highlight your server object.

4. In the work pane, highlight the storage group that should contain the new mailbox database.

5. In the action pane, click **New Public Folder Database**. The New Public Folder Database window appears as shown in Figure 4-14.

Figure 4-14

Creating a New Public Folder Database

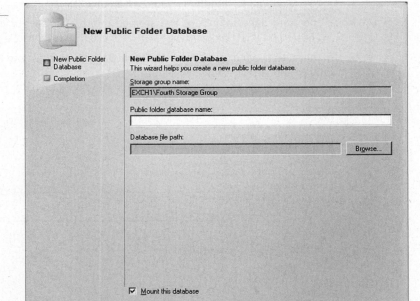

6. In the **Public folder database name** field, type a name for your mailbox database.

7. Beside the **Database file path** dialog box, click **Browse**. In the Browse For Folder window that appears, select the target hard disk and target folder that you wish to use and click **OK**. Normally, this is the same folder used for the storage group and transaction logs.

8. Verify that **Mount this database** is selected to ensure that the database will be available for use after creation and click **New**.

9. Click **Finish** to close the New Public Folder Database window.

10. Close the Exchange Management Console.

⚠ **WARNING** Remember that you can only create one public folder database per Mailbox role server. If you already have a public folder database, you will receive an error message when attempting to create one by clicking the **New** button.

THE COMMAND LINE WAY

You can also use the **New-MailboxDatabase** and **New-PublicFolderDatabase** cmdlets in the Exchange Management Shell to create new mailbox and public folder databases. For example, to create a new mailbox database called Mailbox Database 3 in the storage group called Third Storage Group on the server called EXCH1, and specify that the database file is stored as D:\SG3\Mailbox Database 3.edb, you could run the following command in the Exchange Management Shell:

New-MailboxDatabase–StorageGroup 'EXCH1\Third Storage Group' –Name 'Mailbox Database 3'– EdbFilePath 'D:\SG3\Mailbox Database 3.edb'

Similarly, to create a public folder database called Public Folder Database in the storage group called Fourth Storage Group on the server called EXCH1 and to specify that the database file is stored as D:\SG4\Public Folder Database.edb, you could run the following command in the Exchange Management Shell:

New-PublicFolderDatabase–StorageGroup 'EXCH1\Fourth Storage Group' –Name 'Public Folder Database'– EdbFilePath 'D:\SG4\Public Folder Database.edb'

Once you create a new public folder database using the Exchange Management Shell, you can mount it to make it available on the system using the **Mount-Database** cmdlet or later dismount it using the **Dismount-Database** cmdlet. To mount the databases created in the previous two examples, you could run the following commands within the Exchange Management Shell:

Mount-Database –Identity 'Mailbox Database 3'

Mount-Database –Identity 'Public Folder Database'

You can also use the **Get-MailboxDatabase** and **Get-PublicFolderDatabase** cmdlets to obtain information about an existing mailbox or public folder database. Additionally, the **Set-MailboxDatabase** and **Set-PublicFolderDatabase cmdlets** can be used to modify the properties of an existing mailbox or public folder database, and the **Remove-MailboxDatabase** and **Remove-PublicFolderDatabase** cmdlets can be used to remove a mailbox or public folder database. For more information on the cmdlets used in this section, simply search for their names within Exchange Server 2007 Help.

SETTING STORAGE LIMITS ON A NEW DATABASE

The main form of communication in many organizations today involves email, and email today often contains large attachments such as spreadsheets, presentations, and multimedia. Moreover, if users forget to remove unnecessary emails from their mailbox periodically, their mailboxes will grow continuously over time and use up the available space on your email servers. As a result, nearly all organizations impose some kind of user-based storage limit on email servers to prevent ambitious users from using up all of the available space on the Mailbox role servers. In general, you should enforce storage limits on your mailbox databases so that users are warned when they approach their limits and are not allowed to store emails once their limits have been reached.

To avoid problems, the best time to set up these email restrictions is immediately after creating a new mailbox database. If you highlight your mailbox database in the Exchange Management Console and select **Properties** from the action pane, you can set the default size restrictions for mailboxes that are stored in the mailbox database on the **Limits** tab as shown in Figure 4-15.

Figure 4-15 reflects limits that are appropriate for an organization that allocates a maximum of 1 GB (1048576 KB) for individual user mailboxes. When a user's mailbox reaches 900 MB (921600 KB), the user will receive a warning email at 1:00 a.m. from Exchange indicating that he is approaching his limit and should remove any unnecessary emails. When a user's mailbox reaches 950 MB (972800 KB), he will not be able to send any emails using Exchange server and will receive an additional warning email from Exchange at 1:00 a.m. However, the user will continue receiving emails from others until the mailbox size reaches 1 GB (1048576 KB). As this point, the user can no longer send or receive any emails until he reduces the size of his mailbox.

Figure 4-15

Modifying Mailbox Database Limits

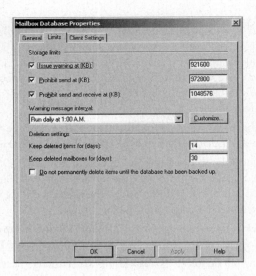

Storage limits can also be applied to public folder databases to prevent users from posting too much data to public folders. As with mailbox databases, to set limits on a public folder database, you can highlight it in the Exchange Management Console, select **Properties** from the action pane, and specify the appropriate settings on the **Limits** tab as shown in Figure 4-16.

Figure 4-16

Modifying Public Folder Database Limits

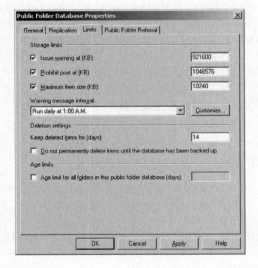

In Figure 4-16, users receive an email warning at 1:00 a.m. if they have posted more than 900 MB (921600 KB) to public folders within the public folder database. After storing 1 GB (1048576 KB) of data within the public folder database, users will receive an error if they attempt to post any additional data. In addition, users will receive an error message if they attempt to post a message or item that is larger than 10 MB (10240 KB) to a public folder that is stored in the public folder database.

THE COMMAND LINE WAY

You can also use the appropriate options alongside the **Set-MailboxDatabase** and **Set-PublicFolderDatabase** cmdlets in the Exchange Management Shell to set limits. For example, to set the limits shown in Figures 4-15 and 4-16, you could run the following commands in the Exchange Management Shell:

Set-MailboxDatabase –Identity 'Mailbox Database'– IssueWarningQuota '921600' –ProhibitSendQuota '972800'– ProhibitSendReceiveQuota '1048576'

Set-PublicFolderDatabase– Identity 'Public Folder Database'– IssueWarningQuota '921600'– ProhibitPostQuota '1048576'– MaxItemSize '10240'

Configuring the CAS Role

Because the CAS role provides client access to the databases maintained by the Mailbox role within your organization, it is important to ensure that the email protocols on the CAS role are properly configured after installation before you set up email clients. This involves enabling Outlook Anywhere, POP, and IMAP, as well as configuring options for OWA.

ENABLING EMAIL PROTOCOLS

Because MAPI takes full advantage of the features in email client programs such as Microsoft Outlook and Entourage, most organizations use the MAPI RPC protocol alongside these programs when configuring internal client computers for email access. In addition, mobile email access using a web browser or smart phone is becoming very popular in many organizations today. As a result, the CAS role is enabled for MAPI RPC, ActiveSync, and Outlook Web Access (OWA) connections by default after installation.

Although OWA is configured to allow client access using the HTTPS protocol, the SSL certificate that is used for HTTPS by IIS is not digitally signed and will give related warnings to users when they connect to OWA on the CAS role server using their web browser.

Providing signed SSL certificates to IIS for use with OWA is covered in Lesson 8, "Configuring Email Protocols and Transport Rules." The configuration of ActiveSync is discussed in Lesson 12, "Providing for Mobile Access and Unified Messaging."

Email client programs that connect to your Exchange servers from across the Internet often use POP3, IMAP4, or Outlook Anywhere (RPC over HTTP/HTTPS) protocols. However, these protocols are not enabled by default on the CAS role after installation.

To enable POP3, you simply need to enable and start the **Microsoft Exchange POP3** service in the Services console (**Start** > **Administrative Tools** > **Services**). After locating the Microsoft Exchange POP3 service in the Services console, right click the service, select **Properties,** and select a Startup type of **Automatic** to ensure that the service is automatically started at boot time as shown in Figure 4-17 . Following this, you can click the **Start** button in Figure 4-17 to start the service and allow POP3 clients access to the CAS role.

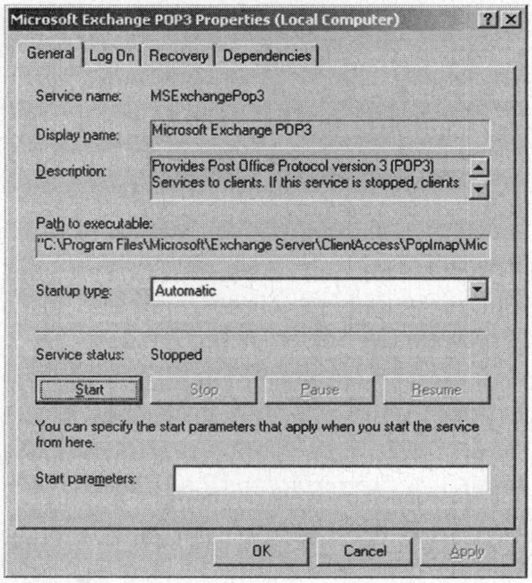

Figure 4-17

Enabling the POP3 Service

Microsoft Exchange POP3 Properties (Local Computer)	? X

General | Log On | Recovery | Dependencies |

Service name: MSExchangePop3

Display name: Microsoft Exchange POP3

Description: Provides Post Office Protocol version 3 (POP3) Services to clients. If this service is stopped, clients

Path to executable:
"C:\Program Files\Microsoft\Exchange Server\ClientAccess\PopImap\Mic

Startup type: Automatic

Service status: Stopped

[Start] [Stop] [Pause] [Resume]

You can specify the start parameters that apply when you start the service from here.

Start parameters:

[OK] [Cancel] [Apply]

As with POP3, you can enable the IMAP4 service by enabling and starting the Microsoft Exchange IMAP4 service in the Services console. The procedure for this is identical to the one for POP3.

If your organization has remote Outlook 2003 or later clients, you can enable the Outlook Anywhere protocol to obtain all the Exchange features available to MAPI clients. When used with HTTPS, Outlook Anywhere provides secure email access over the Internet using the RPC protocol. Before enabling Outlook Anywhere, secure access to Exchange using the RPC protocol, which requires that other encryption technologies such as IP Security (IPSec) or Virtual Private Networks (VPNs) be set up beforehand.

For extra security, remote Outlook Anywhere clients can connect to a secure proxy server such as ***Microsoft Internet Security and Acceleration (ISA) Server***, which can be configured to forward Outlook Anywhere traffic to your CAS role servers.

Before enabling Outlook Anywhere, you must install the **RPC over HTTP proxy** component of Windows. This was discussed in Lesson 3, "Deploying Exchange Server 2007."

 ENABLE OUTLOOK ANYWHERE

GET READY. Turn on the computer, and log in as the Administrator user account. Close any windows that appear on the desktop.

1. Click **Start**, **All Programs**, **Microsoft Exchange Server 2007**, and then click **Exchange Management Console**. The Exchange Management Console window appears.
2. In the console tree pane, expand **Server Configuration** and highlight **Client Access**.
3. In the action pane, click **Enable Outlook Anywhere**. The Enable Outlook Anywhere window appears as shown in Figure 4-18.

Figure 4-18

Enabling Outlook Anywhere

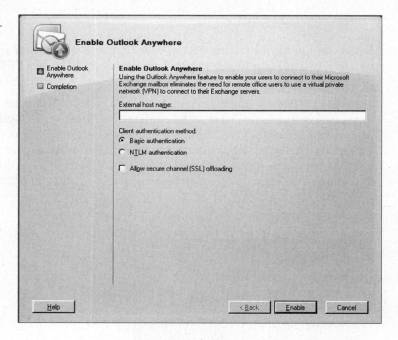

4. In the **External host name** field, type the FQDN of your CAS role server. Alternatively, if your Outlook Anywhere will be configured to connect via an ISA Server, enter the FQDN of your ISA Server in this field.
5. Select the appropriate authentication method:
   - **Basic authentication** transfers username and password information in plain text. This is adequate for use with Outlook Anywhere because the username and password are protected by HTTPS by default.
   - **NTLM authentication** does not transmit passwords across the network in plain text and is the recommended option as it offers additional protection.

6. If your CAS role server contains a bus mastering network card that supports SSL offloading, you can select **Allow secure channel (SSL) offloading** to ensure that the network card will perform the SSL encryption instead of the computer's processors.

7. Click **Enable**. At the Completion screen, click **Finish**.

8. Close the Exchange Management Console.

THE COMMAND LINE WAY

You can also use the **Enable-OutlookAnywhere** cmdlet in the Exchange Management Shell to enable Outlook Anywhere or the **Disable-OutlookAnywhere** cmdlet to disable Outlook Anywhere on a CAS role server. For example, to create enable Outlook Anywhere with NTLM authentication and no SSL offloading on the server EXCH1 and specify an external hostname of proxy1.octavius.net, you could run the following command in the Exchange Management Shell:

Enable-OutlookAnywhere -Server:'EXCH1' -ExternalHostName:'proxy1.octavius.net' -ExternalAuthenticationMethod:'NTLM' -SSLOffloading:$false

You can also use the **Get-OutlookAnywhere** cmdlet in the Exchange Management Shell to view the options that are configured for Outlook Anywhere. Alternatively, you can use several different options and arguments alongside the **Set-OutlookAnywhere** cmdlet to modify Outlook Anywhere options. For more information on the use of these cmdlets, simply search for them in Exchange Server 2007 Help.

CONFIGURING OWA OPTIONS

By providing access from anywhere on the Internet using a web browser, OWA provides flexibility and reliability for the users in your organization. However, this flexibility may also pose a threat to the security of your email system because there is no absolute way to ensure the identity of remote users. A malicious person could use someone else's username and password to access email using OWA from any location on the Internet. Similarly, if a user leaves her computer unattended in an Internet café while connected to OWA, others can gain access to company resources and sensitive information. In short, providing easy remote email access adds several potential security vulnerabilities.

To mitigate these security vulnerabilities, Exchange Server 2007 adds several enhancements to OWA. You can now restrict the user features that are available in OWA as well as the company file servers that OWA users are allowed to access. In addition, you can provide additional restrictions depending on computer location. When users connect to OWA on the CAS role server, they are prompted at the logon screen to select whether they are using a computer in a public or private location as shown in Figure 4-19.

Figure 4-19

OWA Logon Screen

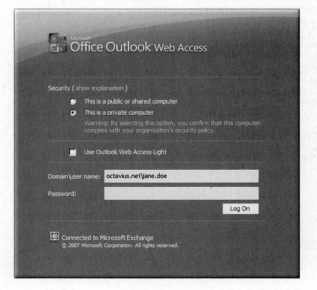

If users select **This is a public or shared computer** in Figure 4-19, you can specify options that prevent them from accessing file servers or the SharePoint infrastructure within your organization while using OWA. This will reduce the chance that a malicious person will gain access to sensitive information at an unattended computer.

To configure OWA options, you must navigate to **Server Configuration** > **Client Access** within the Exchange Management Console, select your CAS role server in the result pane and highlight the **Outlook Web Access** tab as shown in Figure 4-20.

Figure 4-20

Configuring OWA

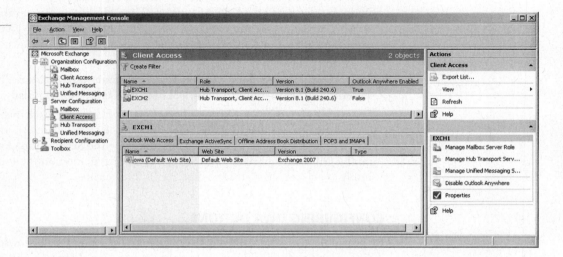

Most OWA configuration is performed within the properties of the owa (Default Web Site) object shown in Figure 4-20. On the Segmentation tab of owa (Default Web Site) properties, you can disable any unwanted OWA features as shown in Figure 4-21.

Figure 4-21

OWA Properties Segmentation Tab

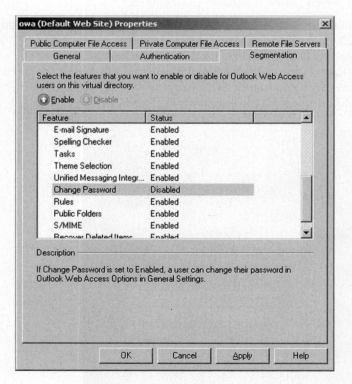

All OWA features are enabled by default. At minimum, most Exchange administrators disable the **Change Password** feature of OWA shown in Figure 4-21. This prevents a malicious user from changing a password using OWA on an unattended system and locking out the real user as a result.

You can also select the Remote File Servers tab of owa (Default Web Site) properties as shown in Figure 4-22 to specify the file servers that OWA users are allowed to access during their session. By default, OWA is blocked from accessing all file servers in the Unknown Servers section. In this case, you can click the **Allow** button in the Allow List section and provide the FQDNs of file servers that you wish OWA clients to access. Alternatively, you can select **Allow** in the drop-down box under the Unknown Servers section to allow access to all file servers by default and then click the **Block** button under the Block List section to provide the FQDNs of file servers that OWA clients should not access. If you specify the same FQDN in the Allow List and Block List sections, OWA clients will be blocked from accessing the server with that FQDN. If you modify the Allow List or Block List sections, you must also click the **Configure** button and add the domain names from all FQDNs to the list of internal servers that OWA uses when accessing network resources.

Figure 4-22

OWA Properties Remote File Servers Tab

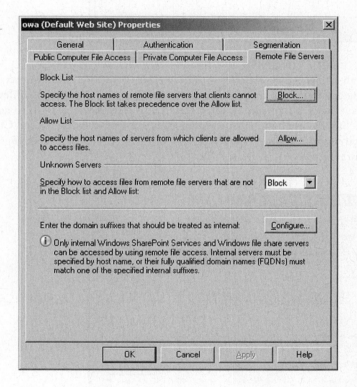

To set OWA options used when a user selects **This is a private computer** at the OWA logon screen shown in Figure 4-19, you can navigate to the Private Computer File Access tab shown in Figure 4-23.

As shown in Figure 4-23, OWA users are allowed to access email attachments (called *Direct file access*) as well as view certain document formats directly in their web browser using the *WebReady* feature of OWA by default. In addition, users are able to access file servers and SharePoint servers provided that they are allowed on the Remote File Servers tab shown earlier in Figure 4-22.

Figure 4-23

OWA Properties Private
Computer File Access Tab

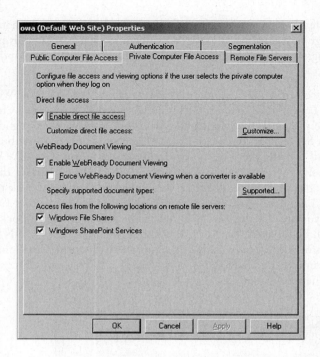

Because OWA users who are using a private computer are more secure than those who are using a public computer, it is safe to allow the default options unless you have a company policy that restricts remote file access. However, you may wish to control the way email attachments are handled for these OWA users by clicking on the **Customize** button and specifying the appropriate settings in the Direct File Access Settings window shown in Figure 4-24.

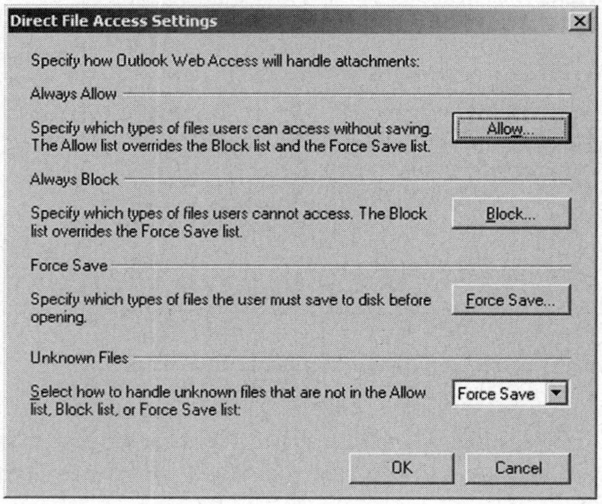

Figure 4-24

Specifying OWA Attachment
Settings

To specify the attachments that OWA users are allowed to open directly from their OWA session, you can click on the **Allow** button. Similarly, you can click the **Block** button to specify attachments that OWA users are not allowed to access or the **Force Save** button to specify attachments that OWA users must first save to their local computer before opening. For example, when you click the **Allow** button, the screen shown in Figure 4-25 appears and allows you to specify the file extensions (such as .avi or .bmp) or file types (GIF, Javascript) that are allowed.

Because email attachment formats are described by the *Multipurpose Internet Mail Extensions (MIME)* standard, you must use a MIME name when specifying file types in Figure 4-25. For example, to specify XML text files, the MIME name would be text/xml.

Figure 4-25

Allowing Attachment Types

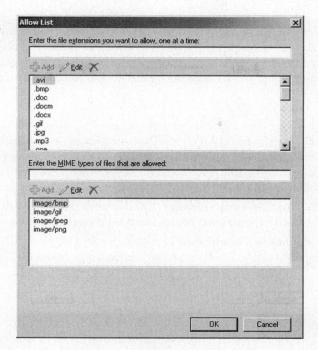

Once you have customized email attachment settings, you can choose to restrict the documents that are available for viewing with WebReady. By default, WebReady can be used to view Microsoft Word, PowerPoint, and Excel files as well PDF and rich text files. However, you can restrict this list by selecting the **Supported** button as shown in Figure 4-23.

By selecting the Public Computer File Access tab of owa (Default Web Site) properties, you can specify OWA options used when a user selects **This is a public or shared computer** at the OWA logon screen shown in Figure 4-19. The options and defaults on this tab are identical to the Private Computer File Access tab. However, you should restrict the default options. This will prevent users who access OWA from a public computer from having the same access level and abilities as those who access OWA from a private computer.

To prevent public OWA users from accessing file servers and SharePoint servers as well as downloading or viewing attachments that may contain sensitive company information, you could simply disable those features by deselecting them as shown in Figure 4-26.

Figure 4-26

OWA Properties Public Computer File Access Tab

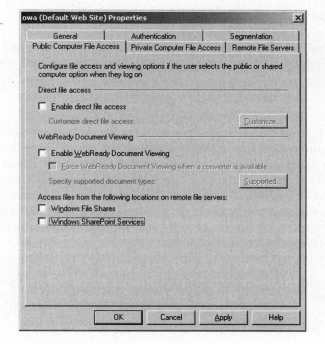

Although you can specify more restrictive options for public OWA users, the application of these restrictions relies on the user's ability to select the correct location at the OWA logon screen shown in Figure 4-19. If users select **This is a private computer** when they are at a public computer, they will be exposing their system to security vulnerabilities.

You can also use the **Set-OWAVirtualDirectory** cmdlet in the Exchange Management Shell to configure OWA options. For example, to enable WebReady document viewing for Private Computers on OWA for the Default Web Site on the server EXCH1, you could run the following command within the Exchange Management Shell:

Set-OWAVirtualDirectory -Identity 'EXCH1\owa (Default Web Site)' -ForceWebReady DocumentViewingFirstOnPrivateComputers

For more options that can be used alongside the Set-OWAVirtualDirectory cmdlet, simply search for Set-OWAVirtualDirectory within Exchange Server 2007 Help.

We will discuss the detailed configuration of the POP3/POP3S, IMAP4/IMAP4S, and HTTP/HTTPS protocols in Lesson 8, "Configuring Email Protocols and Transport Rules."

Configuring Email Relay

THE BOTTOM LINE

Exchange infrastructures can vary greatly in their composition and function because they are modeled after the needs of the organization. In addition to configuring new server roles that are deployed in your Exchange organization, it is vital to ensure that email is sent and received properly by Hub and Edge role servers. To do this, you must configure the appropriate connector objects that represent email flow within your organization and across the Internet.

Understanding Connectors

In any email system, specific objects form the basis for sending and receiving email. In order to understand how Exchange servers relay email internally and externally, you must first understand the concept of connector objects.

To relay email within your organization and across the Internet, your Hub and Edge role servers must have **connectors** that specify how to send and receive email. Connectors specify how your Exchange server should communicate with other Exchange servers, POP3 clients, IMAP4 clients, and external email servers. In addition, connectors are configured to match a certain type of traffic. **Receive connectors** are stored on a Hub or Edge role server and specify how to handle incoming traffic from other email servers or POP3 and IMAP4 clients. **Send connectors** are stored in AD and determine how to send email to other servers within the organization as well as across the Internet.

Previous versions of Exchange Server could create special connectors that allowed email to be relayed directly to nonExchange email servers that were part of your organization such as Novell GroupWise, Lotus Domino, and Microsoft Mail. In Exchange Server 2007, these special connectors are not available. Instead, email sent to these systems is relayed using SMTP alongside other outgoing email.

Configuring Receive Connectors

CERTIFICATION READY?
Configure Connectors.
3.1

Receive connectors contain the configuration information that allows Hub and Edge role servers to process inbound email from email clients and other servers. As a result, you should understand how to create and manage receive connectors to ensure that the email servers within your organization receive the email that is relayed to them.

TAKE NOTE*

Although Edge role servers can receive emails from the Internet and from within the organization by default, they must still be sub-scribed to a Hub role server before they are able to relay email.

When you install a new Edge role, a receive connector is automatically created that accepts email from the Hub role servers within your organization as well as incoming email from the Internet using the SMTP protocol on port 25.

Similarly, when you install a new Hub role, two receive connectors are automatically created. The first connector is called **Default**. It allows the Hub role server to receive email using SMTP on port 25 from POP3 and IMAP4 clients as well as from other Exchange servers within the organization. Because many POP3 and IMAP4 clients now use port 587 when sending email to the Hub role using SMTP, a second connector called **Client** is also created to allow SMTP connections from POP3 and IMAP4 clients on port 587.

CONFIGURING EXISTING RECEIVE CONNECTORS

To view the default receive connector on an Edge role server, you can simply navigate to **Edge Transport** within the Exchange Management Console, select your server object in the result pane and highlight the **Receive Connectors** tab as shown in Figure 4-27. On a Hub role server, you must navigate to **Server Configuration** > **Hub Transport** within the Exchange Management Console and select the appropriate server in the result pane as shown in Figure 4-28.

Figure 4-27

Viewing Receive Connectors on an Edge Role Server

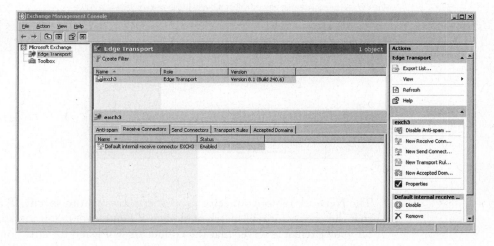

Figure 4-28

Viewing Receive Connectors on a Hub Role Server

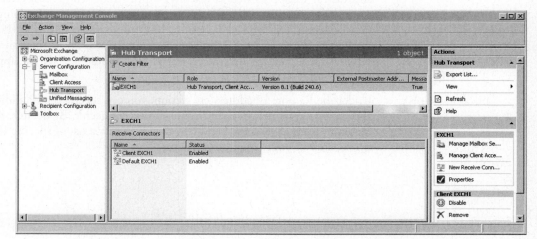

TAKE NOTE* You can temporarily prevent a receive connector from being used within the Exchange Management Console by selecting **Disable** in the action pane.

When you select **Properties** in the action pane for an existing connector, you can modify the connector settings. On the General tab of connector properties, you can specify the FQDN used when your email server responds to SMTP connection attempts as well as the maximum message size that your email server will accept as shown in Figure 4-29. If you select **Verbose** in the Protocol logging level drop-down box, information regarding all connections will be logged to files in the C:\Program Files\Microsoft\Exchange Server\TransportRoles\Logs\ProtocolLog\SmtpReceive directory. Because verbose logging will use a large amount of disk space, you should only enable it for a short period of time when troubleshooting a problem.

Figure 4-29

Receive Connector Properties General Tab

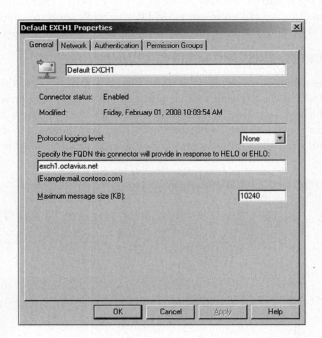

The Network tab of connector properties allows you to specify IP and port information that the connector will match as shown in Figure 4-30. You can specify the IP addresses on your Exchange server that the connector will listen for email on under the Local IP address(es) section as well as the SMTP port under the Port section. By default, receive connectors listen to all IP addresses on your server. If your Exchange server has multiple network interfaces, you may want to limit the connector to the IP address of a specific network interface on which you expect email. Similarly, if the connector should listen on a different port than 25 for SMTP traffic, you should specify the appropriate port under the Port section.

Under the Remote IP address(es) section, you can specify the IP addresses of remote computers and email servers that can send email to this connector. By default, receive connectors listen for email from any IP address, but you can specify a list of specific IP addresses to improve the security of your email infrastructure.

Figure 4-30

Receive Connector Properties
Network Tab

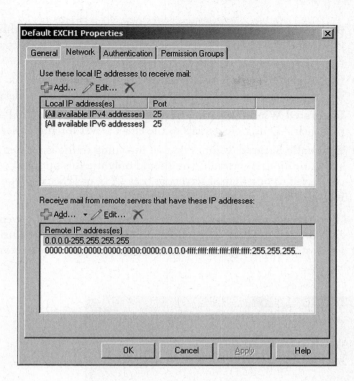

To provide additional security, many computers and email servers will attempt to authenticate to remote email servers before sending them email. The Authentication tab of receive connector properties allows you to specify the supported authentication protocols and mechanisms as shown in Figure 4-31.

Figure 4-31

Receive Connector Properties
Authentication Tab

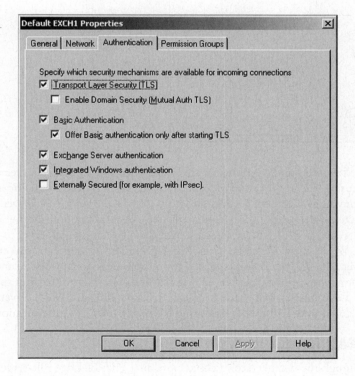

There are several different authentication options that can be selected:

- **Transport Layer Security (TLS)** is based on SSL and can be used to provide encrypted authentication, but requires a TLS certificate on both computers. Mutual Auth TLS is appropriate for providing security between organizations.

- **Basic Authentication** and Basic Authentication combined with TLS is appropriate for POP3 and IMAP4 clients that need to authenticate to your email server before sending email.
- **Exchange Server authentication** uses Kerberos to authenticate email servers and is used when relaying email internally within your organization by default.
- **Integrated Windows authentication** allows POP3 and IMAP4 clients to automatically pass their AD user credentials to the email server for authentication.
- **Externally Secured** assumes that all incoming traffic is secured and doesn't require authentication. As a result, you should only use this option if your network is privately connected to other email servers or uses VPN or IPSec encryption to secure all email transmission.

In addition to authentication, you must specify which users or remote computers can use each connector. These users and computers are represented using *permissions groups* that are configured using the Permissions Groups tab of connector properties as shown in Figure 4-32.

Figure 4-32

Receive Connector Properties Permissions Groups Tab

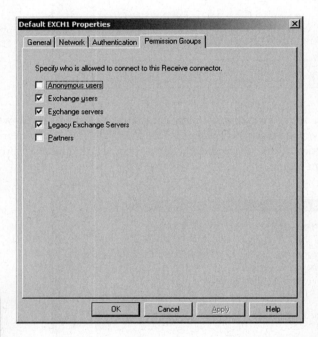

TAKE NOTE*

In order for a Hub or Edge role server to receive emails directly from the Internet, it must have a receive connector configured to accept the **Anonymous users** permissions group.

To allow users and computers to relay email to your Exchange server without authenticating using one of the authentication methods listed on the Authentication tab, you can select Anonymous users as a permissions group for the connector. However, this option is only selected if the receive connector needs to accept anonymous Internet email, as it also allows malicious users the ability to relay spam through your email server to protect their identities. By selecting Exchange users, POP3 and IMAP4 users can send email to your Exchange server after they have authenticated. Similarly, the Exchange server and legacy Exchange server options allow email from servers within your organization that run the Exchange 2007 Hub and Edge roles as well as from legacy Exchange 2000 and 2003 servers. The Partners option is only used for email that is sent using Mutual Auth TLS authentication.

TAKE NOTE*

You cannot create a receive connector that matches the same traffic specified by other receive connectors on the same server.

CREATING RECEIVE CONNECTORS

Although the default receive connectors on a Hub or Edge role server are configured appropriately to receive email from other servers as well as from POP3 and IMAP4 users, you may need to configure additional receive connectors on a new Hub or Edge role server. For example, if your organization uses port 7299 for internal email relay, you will need to create a new receive connector that allows for traffic from other Exchange servers on port 7299 using Exchange Server authentication.

To simplify specifying authentication methods and permissions groups, you are prompted to select one of the following intended use options when you create a new receive connector:

- **Internet** does not require authentication and is used for receiving email from the Internet because most public email servers do not authenticate when relaying email.
- **Internal** uses Exchange Server authentication and is used for receiving email from existing Exchange servers within your organization.
- **Client** requires Basic, TLS, or Integrated Windows authentication and is used for receiving emails from POP3 and IMAP4 users within your organization.
- **Partner** requires TLS authentication and is used for trusted email servers that are not directly part of your organization.
- **Custom** does not specify a default authentication method or apply to specific users or computers. After creating a custom receive connector, you must edit the connector properties to specify the appropriate authentication and permissions group options.

 CREATE A NEW CUSTOM RECEIVE CONNECTOR

GET READY. Turn on the Hub or Edge role computer, and log in as the Administrator user account. Close any windows that appear on the desktop.

1. Click **Start**, **All Programs**, **Microsoft Exchange Server 2007**, and then click **Exchange Management Console**. The Exchange Management Console window appears.
2. If you are creating a receive connector on an Edge role server, click **Edge Transport** in the console tree, select your server in the result pane and high-light the **Receive Connectors** tab in the work pane. Alternatively, if you are creating a receive connector on a Hub role server, expand **Server Configuration** in the console tree, click **Hub Transport** and highlight your server in the result pane.
3. In the action pane, click **New Receive Connector**. The New SMTP Receive Connec-tor window appears as shown in Figure 4-33.

Figure 4-33

Creating a New SMTP Receive Connector

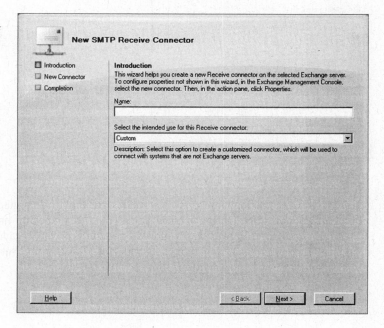

4. In the **Name** field, type a descriptive name for your receive connector. In the **Select the intended use for this Receive connector** drop-down box, ensure that Custom is selected and click **Next**. The Local Network settings page appears as shown in Figure 4-34.

Figure 4-34

Specifying Network Settings

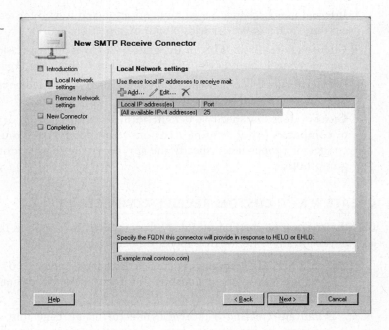

5. Type the FQDN of your server in the dialog box at the bottom of the screen and click **Edit**. The Edit Receive Connector Binding window appears as shown in Figure 4-35.

Figure 4-35

Editing Local Network Settings

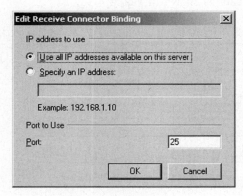

6. In the Port dialog box, type the SMTP port that the connector will use. If you wish to specify that the receive connector use a specific network interface on your server, select **Specify an IP address** and type in the IP address on the desired network interface. When finished, click **OK**. The Remote Network settings page appears as shown in Figure 4-36.

Figure 4-36

Specifying Remote Network Settings

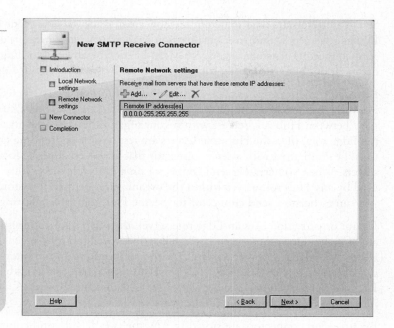

TAKE NOTE✱

You can click the **Add** button in Figure 4-35 to specify additional ports and network interfaces for the receive connector.

7. By default, email is accepted from all remote computers. To specify the computers that the connector will accept email from, you can click **Edit** and supply an alternate IP address range or click the arrow next to the Add button, select the appropriate criteria, and supply the appropriate information. When you have finished specifying the appropriate IP information, click **Next**. The New Connector page appears.

8. Review your selections and click **New**. The Completion page appears.

9. Click **Finish** to close the New SMTP Receive Connector window.

10. Close the Exchange Management Console.

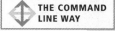

THE COMMAND LINE WAY

You can also use the **New-ReceiveConnector** cmdlet in the Exchange Management Shell to create receive connectors. For example, to create a custom receive connector called "SMTP for Port 7299" that accepts SMTP traffic on port 7299 on the network interface on your server with the IP 192.168.1.135 from other computers with IP addresses in the range 192.168.1.1 through 192.168.1.200, you could run the following command in the Exchange Management Shell:

New-ReceiveConnector -Name "SMTP for Port 7299" -Bindings 192.168.1.135:7299 -RemoteIPRanges 192.168.1.1-192.168.1.200

You can also use the **Get-Receive Connector** cmdlet to obtain information about the configuration of an existing receive connector, the **Set-ReceiveConnector** cmdlet to modify an existing receive connector, or the **Remove-ReceiveConnector** cmdlet to remove a receive connector. For more information on the usage of these cmdlets, search for them in Exchange Server 2007 Help.

Configuring Send Connectors

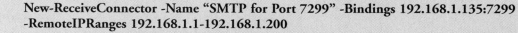

To relay email to other Exchange servers within your Exchange organization as well as to external email servers on the Internet, your Hub and Edge role servers must be configured with the appropriate send connectors. Understanding how to create and modify send connectors is essential for providing email relay within your organization.

CERTIFICATION READY?
Configure Connectors.

3.1

Send connectors are used to determine how email is relayed from your Exchange server to other Exchange servers within your organization or to external email servers on the Internet. Because send connectors are stored in AD, they can be used by any Hub or Edge role server within your organization, but are typically configured for use by specific Hub or Edge role servers.

By default, there are no explicit send connectors automatically created on a Hub server. However, hidden send connectors are built into Exchange Server 2007 to allow for email relay between Hub role servers within your organization. If your organization does not use the Edge role, then the Hub role servers are responsible for sending email to the Internet and must be configured with a send connector that allows email to be forwarded to external email servers. When you create a send connector on a Hub role server, that send connector can be used by any Hub role server within the organization because it is stored in AD. Alternatively, you can associate a send connector to specific Hub role servers during creation.

If your organization uses an Edge role server, then two send connectors are automatically created for the Edge role server when it subscribes to a Hub role server. The first send connector allows the Edge role server to send email to all locations on the Internet, whereas the second send connector allows the Edge role server to relay email to the Hub role servers within your Exchange organization. In short, these two default send connectors allow for Internet email functionality on your Hub and Edge role servers.

Because send connectors are stored in AD, the two default send connectors for each Edge role server are replicated from Hub role servers to the Edge role servers using EdgeSync. As a result, to modify a send connector for an Edge role server, you must modify the send connector on a Hub role server and allow the changes to propagate to the Edge role server.

CONFIGURING EXISTING SEND CONNECTORS

As with receive connectors, you must view the properties of a send connector in order to configure it. To locate the send connectors used by Hub and Edge role servers in your organization, you can navigate to **Organization Configuration** > **Hub Transport** within the Exchange Management Console and highlight the **Send Connectors** tab in the result pane as shown in Figure 4-37.

Figure 4-37

Viewing Send Connectors

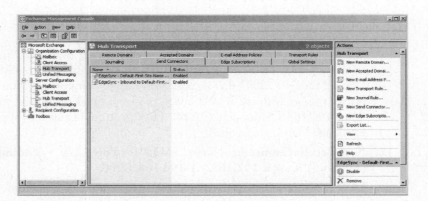

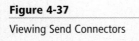 You can temporarily prevent a send connector from being used within the Exchange Management Console by selecting **Disable** in the action pane.

When you select **Properties** in the action pane for an existing connector, you can specify the FQDN used when your email server responds to SMTP connection attempts as well as the maximum message size that your email server will send on the General tab as shown in Figure 4-38. If you select **Verbose** in the **Protocol logging level** drop-down box, information regarding all connections will be logged to files in the C:\Program Files\Microsoft\ Exchange Server\TransportRoles\Logs\ProtocolLog\SmtpSend directory.

Figure 4-38

Send Connector Properties
General Tab

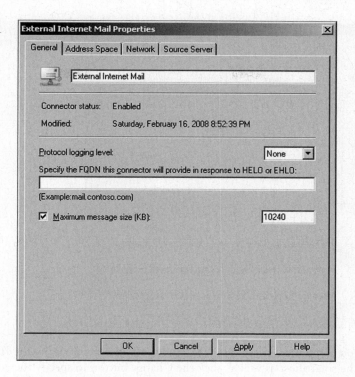

To specify the target DNS domains that the send connector will apply to, you must use the Address Space tab of send connector properties. The Address Space tab as shown in Figure 4-39 applies to all external DNS domains on the Internet (*). Alternatively, to control sent emails, you can specify certain domains on the Address Space tab for each connector and later specify that different Edge or Hub role servers use different connectors. If you add multiple DNS domains to the list, the lines with the lowest cost value are processed first. To specify that only Hub role servers in the same AD site can use the send connector, you can select the **Scoped Send connector** checkbox.

Figure 4-39

Send Connector Properties
Address Space Tab

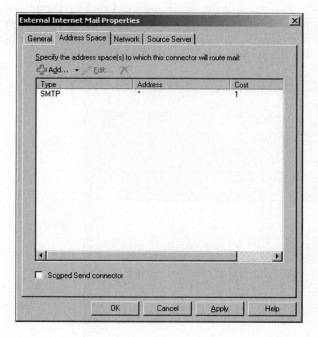

When locating target email servers to relay email to, Hub and Edge servers use DNS MX records by default. However, you can configure your Hub or Edge servers to forward outgoing email to a smart host using the Network tab of send connector properties as shown in Figure 4-40.

Figure 4-40

Send Connector Properties
Network Tab

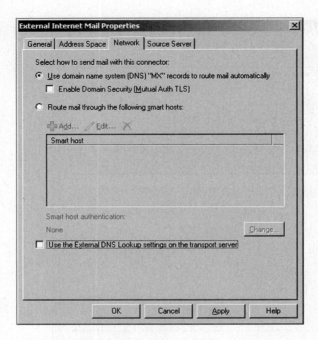

If you configure a smart host in Figure 4-40, you must specify the IP address or FQDN of the smart host as well as click the Change button to specify the authentication method required by the smart host server.

In some organizations, the internal DNS servers within the organization are not configured to resolve names on the Internet. In this case, it is important to ensure that you check **Use the External DNS Lookup settings on the transport server** in Figure 4-40. Following this, you must configure the IP address of at least one external DNS server that can resolve Internet DNS names on the **External DNS Lookups** tab of the Hub or Edge role server in the Exchange Management Console as shown in Figure 4-41. You can access the Edge role server properties by navigating to **Edge Transport** in the Exchange Management Console, highlighting your Edge role server in the details pane and clicking **Properties** in the action pane. To access the properties of a Hub role server, you can navigate to **Server Configuration > Hub Transport** in the Exchange Management Console, select your Hub role server in the details pane and click **Properties** in the action pane.

Figure 4-41

Exchange Server Properties
External DNS Lookups Tab

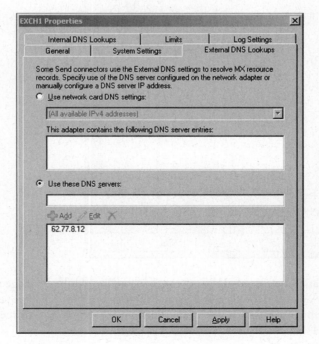

Once you have specified network settings, you can associate a send connector with specific servers on the Source Server tab of send connector properties as shown in Figure 4-42. Although you can add multiple servers to this list, you cannot add Hub role servers as well as Edge role servers to the same connector.

Figure 4-42

Send Connector Properties
Source Server Tab

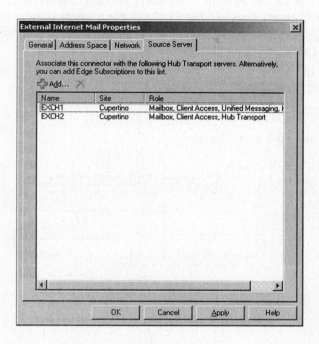

CREATING SEND CONNECTORS

By default, the Hub role servers within your organization can relay email internally. After subscribing an Edge role server to a Hub role server, the Hub role servers within your site can use the Edge role server to relay external Internet email using the default send connectors.

However, you will need to create send connectors on your Hub role servers if your organization does not use the Edge role or if you wish to customize email relay. By creating several send connectors that apply to different DNS domains and apply to different Edge or Hub servers, you can control which email servers relay email to particular DNS domains.

To simplify specifying the address space and source servers, you are prompted to select one of the following intended use options when you create a new send connector:

- **Internal** is used to route email through other Exchange servers within your organization. Because all Exchange servers in your Exchange organization can automatically relay email to one another using AD site information, you only need to select this option if you wish to customize internal email relay.

- **Internet** is used to send email to all domains on the Internet. This option is appropriate when creating send connectors for Hub role servers in your organization when the Edge role is not used.

- **Partner** is used to relay email to specific email servers that are not directly part of your organization.

- **Custom** does not specify a default address space or source server. This option allows you to specify all aspects of a send connector.

CREATE A NEW CUSTOM SEND CONNECTOR

GET READY. Turn on the Hub role computer, and log in as the Administrator user account. Close any windows that appear on the desktop.

1. Click **Start**, **All Programs**, **Microsoft Exchange Server 2007**, and then click **Exchange Management Console**. The Exchange Management Console window appears.

2. Expand **Organization Configuration** in the console tree, highlight **Hub Transport**, and click the **Send Connectors** tab in the result pane.

3. In the action pane, click **New Send Connector**. The New SMTP Send Connector window appears as shown in Figure 4-43.

Figure 4-43

Creating a New SMTP Send Connector

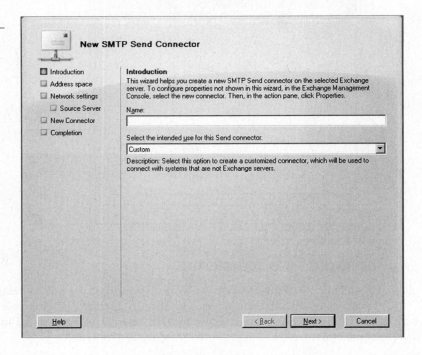

4. In the **Name** field, type a descriptive name for your send connector. In the **Select the intended use for this Send connector** drop-down box, ensure that Custom is selected and click **Next**. The Address space page appears as shown in Figure 4-44.

Figure 4-44

Specifying the Address Space

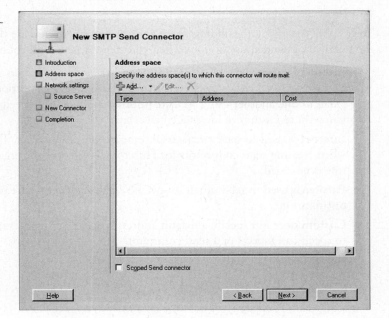

5. Click **Add**. The SMTP Address Space page appears as shown in Figure 4-45.

Figure 4-45

Adding an Address Space

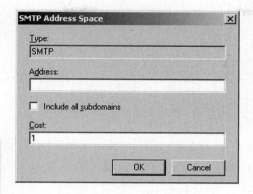

6. In the Address dialog box, type the DNS domain name that the send connector should apply to. Select **Include all subdomains** to apply the connector to all subordinate domains of the DNS domain name that you typed in the Address dialog box and click **OK** to close the SMTP Address Space window.

7. If you wish to apply the connector to the Hub servers in your AD site only, select **Scoped Send connector**. Click **Next**. The Network settings page appears as shown in Figure 4-46.

Figure 4-46

Specifying Network Settings

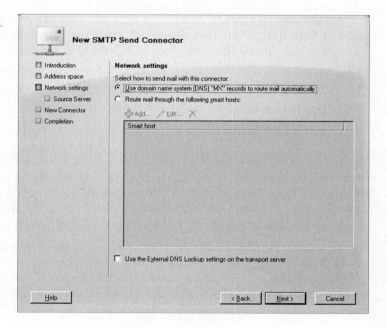

8. If email sent to the address space on this connector should be forwarded to a smart host, select **Route mail through the following smart hosts** and click **Add**. In the Add smart host window, specify the IP address or FQDN of your smart host and click **OK**.

9. If the connector should use an external DNS server listed in your Hub or Edge role server properties, click **Use the External DNS Lookup settings on the transport server**.

10. Click **Next**. The Source Server page appears as shown in Figure 4-47.

Figure 4-47

Specifying Source Servers

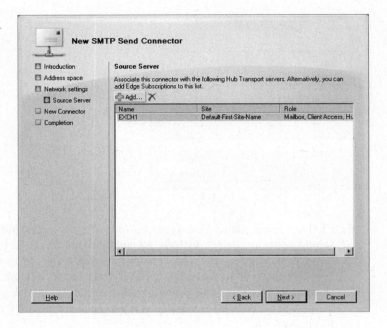

11. To apply the send connector to additional Hub or Edge role servers, click **Add**, select the appropriate servers and click **OK**. Alternatively, you can select any Hub or Edge role servers that should not apply the connector and press the red **X** icon to remove them. When finished, click **Next**. The New Connector page appears.

12. Review your selections and click **New**. The Completion page appears.

13. Click **Finish** to close the New SMTP Send Connector window.

14. Close the Exchange Management Console.

THE COMMAND LINE WAY

You can also use the **New-SendConnector** cmdlet in the Exchange Management Shell to create send connectors. For example, to create a custom send connector called "Internet SMTP Relay" that relays SMTP traffic addressed to all Internet DNS domains using any Exchange server, you could run the following command in the Exchange Management Shell:

New-SendConnector -Name "Internet SMTP Relay" -AddressSpaces*

You can also use the **Get-SendConnector** cmdlet to obtain information about the configuration of an existing send connector, the **Set-SendConnector** cmdlet to modify an existing send connector, or the **Remove-SendConnector** cmdlet to remove a send connector. For more information on the usage of these cmdlets, simply search for them in Exchange Server 2007 Help.

■ Configuring Clients

THE BOTTOM LINE

The configuration of an email system does not stop once the email servers have been prepared. For an email system to work, email clients must be configured to utilize the various email servers within your organization to send and receive email. Regardless of whether you are deploying Exchange for the first time or adding additional Exchange servers to your Exchange organization, you will likely need to configure new email clients or reconfigure existing clients in order for them to take advantage of your new email infrastructure.

Client Considerations

There is a wide variety of email client programs that can be used alongside different email protocols to access email servers from within the organization or from across the Internet. As a result, you should understand the different types of email client configurations possible before configuring email clients.

Configuring client computers varies tremendously in different situations. Email clients can be configured to interact with your email servers using a variety of different email protocols such as POP3 or MAPI RPC. Moreover, different email client programs support different protocols and protocol options. Although there are dozens of available different email client programs on the Internet, we restrict our discussion to Microsoft email client programs in this lesson. Table 4-2 lists these email client programs and their protocol support.

Table 4-2

Common email client programs

Email Client Program	Email Protocols Supported
Microsoft Outlook 2003 Microsoft Outlook 2007	MAPI RPC POP3/POP3S IMAP4/IMAP4S SMTP/SMTPS and ESMTP/ESMTPS Outlook Anywhere (RPC over HTTP/HTTPS) HTTP/HTTPS (to OWA and Windows Live Hotmail only)
Microsoft Entourage 2004 Microsoft Entourage 2008	MAPI RPC POP3/POP3S IMAP4/IMAP4S SMTP/SMTPS and ESMTP/ESMTPS HTTP/HTTPS (to OWA and Windows Live Hotmail only)
Microsoft Outlook Express Windows Mail	POP3/POP3S IMAP4/IMAP4S SMTP/SMTPS and ESMTP/ESMTPS HTTP/HTTPS

TAKE NOTE *

By default, Exchange Server 2007 configures encryption for all POP3, IMAP4, and HTTP connections in favor of greater security. Consequently, you will need to specify the appropriate POP3S, IMAP4S, or HTTPS protocol options within the client email program.

Although most email client programs support multiple email protocols, the protocol that you choose to configure is largely dependent on whether client computers are on the same LAN as your Exchange servers or whether they connect remotely from across the Internet.

Users within an organization typically use the Microsoft Office suite and connect to Exchange servers using a fast LAN. As a result, you will likely configure the MAPI RPC protocol for these clients because it works closely with Microsoft Outlook and Entourage to allow for advanced user features such as time scheduling. This configuration is referred to simply as **Exchange** or **Exchange Server** in Microsoft Outlook and Entourage because the email client connects directly to the Exchange server using the MAPI RPC protocol.

For remote email clients, you will likely set up the email client to connect to the Exchange server using the POP3, IMAP4, SMTP, HTTP, or Outlook Anywhere protocols.

If your remote email clients have Microsoft Outlook installed as part of the Microsoft Office suite, they can be configured to use Outlook Anywhere to take full advantage of the same features that they are accustomed to when connecting with Microsoft Outlook in the office.

In other situations, email clients will usually be configured to use the POP3 or IMAP4 protocol. POP3 and IMAP4 are designed for receiving email only. When you configure an email client to use POP3 or IMAP4, you must specify the name or IP address of a CAS role server within your organization that has the POP3 or IMAP4 services started. However, you must also specify the name or IP address of a Hub role server within your organization that has a receive connector to allow the email client program to send emails using SMTP. Newer email client programs use port 587 for SMTP whereas older email client programs use port 25. In most cases, by selecting the advanced or detailed configuration sections of an email client program, you can configure the port that the email account will use. This port should match the port used by a receive connector on the appropriate Hub role server.

In addition, when you configure an SMTP server for your POP3 or IMAP4 account, you can optionally select *Secure Password Authentication (SPA)* to protect SMTP authentication using a modified NTLM authentication mechanism designed specifically for email clients that are members of your domain.

Although you can configure most email client programs to use HTTP or HTTPS to connect to your Exchange servers, it connects using the OWA components within IIS. Rather than configuring an email client to use HTTP, it is much simpler to advise remote clients to enter a URL in their web browser. Because Exchange Server 2007 uses HTTPS for OWA by default, users can enter the URL **https://CAS_server/exchange/username** in their web browser to connect to OWA where CAS_server is the name or IP address of a CAS role server in your organization that has OWA configured and the username is the logon name of the user. Depending on the configuration of IIS, you may be prompted to log in to the web server before you are able to log in to OWA as shown earlier in Figure 4-19.

ANOTHER WAY

You can also use **https:// CAS_server/exchange** or **https://CAS_server/owa** within the URL dialog box of a web browser to gain access to OWA. In both cases, OWA will use your logon credentials to determine which mailbox you require access to.

Configuring Microsoft Outlook

The most common email client that you will set up in organizations is Microsoft Outlook. Microsoft Outlook is bundled with the Microsoft Office suite and allows users to send and receive email using any protocol.

CERTIFICATION READY?
Configure client connectivity.
3.6

Microsoft Outlook is part of the Microsoft Office program suite and currently the most common email client program used to connect to Exchange servers in organizations. Because most organizations deploy the Microsoft Office suite on the computers on the internal LAN, Outlook is often configured to use the MAPI RPC protocol to connect to Exchange servers. The two most recent versions of the Microsoft Office suite are Microsoft Office 2003, which includes Outlook 2003, and Microsoft Office 2007, which includes Outlook 2007.

When you start Outlook 2003 or Outlook 2007 for the first time, the Office Startup wizard appears and allows you to configure a MAPI RPC, Outlook Anywhere, POP, IMAP, or HTTP email account. To set up POP, IMAP, or HTTP accounts afterward, you can select **Account Settings** from the **Tools** menu in Outlook. Alternatively, you can set up any type of email account afterward by navigating to **Start** > **Control Panel** > **Mail**.

If you are configuring a MAPI RPC account in Outlook 2003 or later, you will be able to select *Cached Exchange Mode*. Selecting this option will cache Exchange-related information to the client computer's hard drive to speed performance. However, if the Exchange administrator makes configuration changes on the Exchange server, those changes will not take effect until the next time Outlook is started.

The steps for configuring email accounts in Outlook 2003 and Outlook 2007 are very similar. As a result, we will focus on configuring Outlook 2007 and note any differences.

CONFIGURE A NEW ACCOUNT IN MICROSOFT OUTLOOK 2007

GET READY. Turn on the client computer, and log in as the appropriate domain user account if necessary. Close any windows that appear on the desktop.

1. Click **Start**, **All Programs**, **Microsoft Office**, and then click **Microsoft Office Outlook 2007**. If the Office 2007 Startup wizard appears, click **Next**. Select **No** and click **Next**. Select **Continue with no e-mail support** and click **Finish**.

2. Close Outlook 2007.

3. Click **Start**, **Control Panel**, **Mail**. At the Mail Setup—Outlook window, click **E-mail Accounts**. If prompted to enable RSS feeds, click **Yes**. The Account Settings window appears as shown in Figure 4-48.

Figure 4-48

Outlook Account Settings

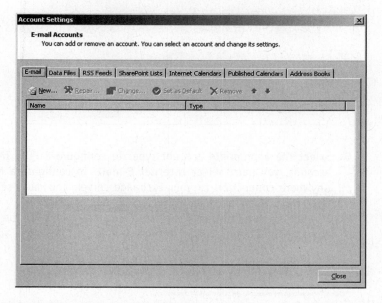

In Outlook 2003, you are prompted to **Add a new e-mail account** when you click **E-mail Accounts** at the Mail Setup—Outlook window. Following this, you must select the type of email account (**Microsoft Exchange Server** using MAPI RPC, **POP3**, **IMAP**, or **HTTP**). Following this, the configuration options for each protocol are nearly identical to those in Outlook 2007.

TAKE NOTE*

4. In the Account Settings window, click **New**. The Add New E-mail Account window appears as shown in Figure 4-49.

Figure 4-49

Adding a New Outlook Account

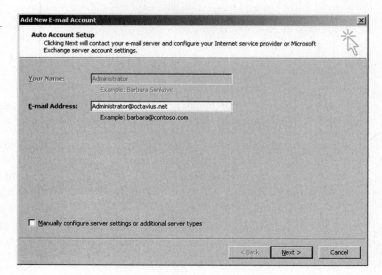

5. Select **Manually configure server settings or additional server types** and click **Next**. The Choose E-mail Service page appears as shown in Figure 4-50.

Figure 4-50

Specifying the Account Type

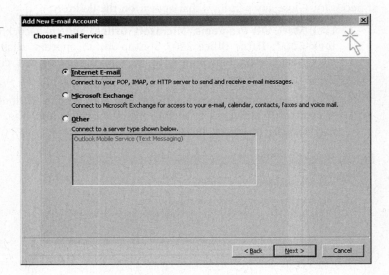

6. Select the appropriate account type. To configure a POP, IMAP, or HTTP-based account, you must select **Internet E-mail**. To configure a MAPI RPC or Outlook Anywhere connection to your Exchange server, you must select **Microsoft Exchange**. Click **Next** when finished.

7. If you selected Internet E-mail in Figure 4-50, you will be prompted to supply the correct information on the Internet E-mail Settings page shown in Figure 4-51.

Figure 4-51

Configuring POP, IMAP, and HTTP Settings

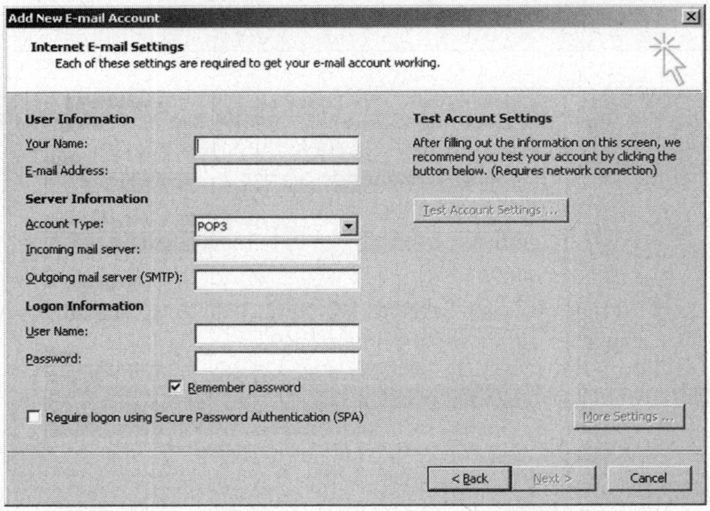

After supplying your name and email address, you must select either **POP**, **IMAP**, or **HTTP** in the **Account Type** drop-down box.

a. If you select POP or IMAP as the account type, you must specify the FQDN or IP address of a CAS role server running the associated POP or IMAP service in the **Incoming mail server** dialog box. In addition, to send email you must supply the FQDN or IP address of a Hub role server in the **Outgoing mail server (SMTP)** dialog box.

b. If you selected HTTP as the account type, you will be allowed to select your HTTP service provider (i.e., Hotmail, OWA) as well as the associated URL.

Most email servers require authentication, so you must supply the appropriate username and password in the Logon Information section. If your email client is part of a Windows domain, you can also select **Require logon using Secure Password Authentication (SPA)** to provide additional security when sending email to your SMTP server.

After you have provided the required information, you can optionally click the **More Settings** button to specify different port numbers, credentials for outgoing SMTP traffic, and encryption. Because Exchange Server 2007 uses POP3S and IMAP4S by default, you must click **More Settings**, highlight the Advanced tab, and select the appropriate option to configure SSL. Figure 4-52 shows an SSL configuration for POP3S.

Figure 4-52

Configuring Advanced
Account Settings

The Advanced tab for a POP connection also allows you to optionally configure POP3 to leave copies of email on the server just as IMAP4 does. Figure 4-52 has this option configured as well. Once you click **OK** in Figure 4-52, you can click **Test Account Settings** as shown in Figure 4-51 to ensure that the email servers can be successfully contacted from your computer.

8. Alternatively, if you selected Microsoft Exchange in Figure 4-50, you will be prompted to supply the FQDN or IP address of a CAS role server as well as your domain user account on the Microsoft Exchange Settings page shown in Figure 4-53.

Figure 4-53

Adding an Exchange
Account

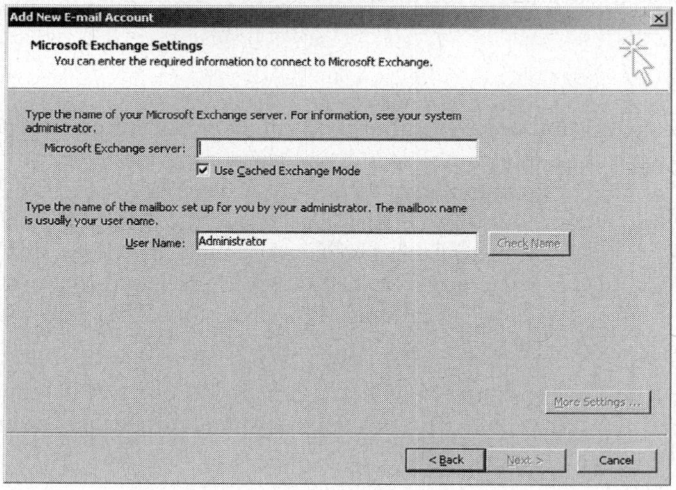

To store a copy of the user's mailbox on the local computer for fast access, ensure that the **Use Cached Exchange Mode** box is selected. Following this, you can click **Check Name** to verify the connection to the Exchange server. If the connection attempt is successful, the FQDN of the server and the user account will be underlined in the Microsoft Exchange Settings window.

To enable Outlook Anywhere, you must click **More Settings** and select **Connect to Microsoft Exchange using HTTP** on the **Connection** tab as shown in Figure 4-54. Following this you must click on the **Exchange Proxy Settings** button and specify the name of the Exchange server or ISA Server computer that is configured to accept Outlook Anywhere connections.

Figure 4-54

Configuring Outlook Anywhere Settings

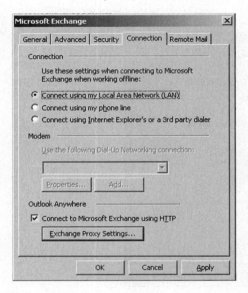

9. When finished specifying account settings, click **Next**. The Congratulations! screen appears.

10. At the Congratulations! screen, click **Finish** to close the Add New E-mail Account window.

11. Close the Mail Setup—Outlook window.

Configuring Microsoft Entourage

CERTIFICATION READY?
Configure client connectivity.
3.6

> For Macintosh users, Microsoft Entourage provides a robust email client that can connect to Exchange servers within your organization.

In many organizations, Macintosh computers will be used in departments that perform desktop publishing, graphics, and specialized programs that run only on UNIX-based platforms. These computers will likely run the Microsoft Office 2004 or Microsoft Office 2008 program suites that are analogous to the Microsoft Office 2003 and Microsoft Office 2007 program suites available for PCs. Although the Microsoft Office suites for Macintosh include the same Microsoft Word, Microsoft Excel, and Microsoft PowerPoint programs that PC users use, Microsoft Entourage is used instead of Microsoft Outlook as the main email client program.

The steps for configuring email accounts in Entourage 2004 and Entourage 2008 are nearly identical. As a result, we will focus on configuring Entourage 2008 and note any differences.

➔ CONFIGURE A NEW ACCOUNT IN MICROSOFT ENTOURAGE 2008

GET READY. Turn on the Macintosh client computer, and log in as the appropriate domain user account if necessary. Close any windows that appear on the desktop.

1. Click the Microsoft Entourage icon on the Macintosh OS X dock to open Microsoft Entourage 2008. Alternatively, you can navigate to **Macintosh HD**, **Applications**, **Microsoft Office 2008**, and then click **Microsoft Entourage** to open Microsoft Entourage 2008. If an Account Setup Assistant window appears, close the window.

2. Select the **Tools** menu and click **Accounts**. The Accounts window appears as shown in Figure 4-55.

Figure 4-55

Entourage Accounts Window

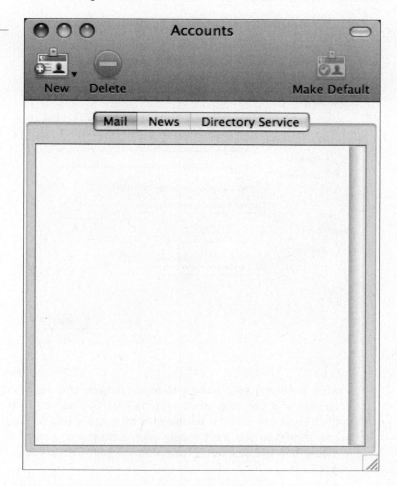

3. In the Account window, click **New**. If the Account Setup Assistant window appears, click **Configure Account Manually**, click **Cancel**, and click **New** from the Account window again. The New Account window appears as shown in Figure 4-56.

Figure 4-56

Adding a New Entourage Account

TAKE NOTE✱

To configure a MAPI RPC account in Entourage 2004, you must first select the **Exchange** tab from the Account window before clicking the **New** button. The Exchange tab is not used in Entourage 2008.

4. Select the appropriate email protocol in the Account type drop-down box. You can select from POP, IMAP, Exchange (MAPI RPC or HTTP/HTTPS), or Windows Live Hotmail (HTTP/HTTPS). The Edit Account window appears.

5. If you selected POP as the account type in Figure 4-56, you will be prompted to supply the correct POP service information as shown in Figure 4-57.

Figure 4-57

Configuring POP Settings

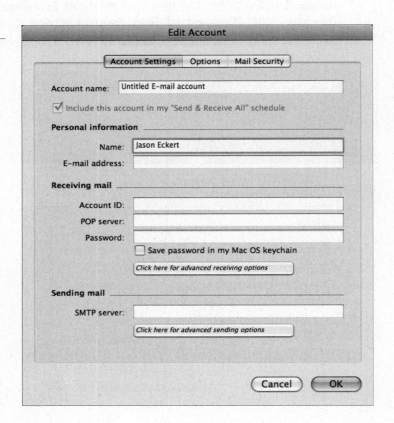

After supplying your name and email address, you must supply the FQDN or IP address of a CAS role server running the POP3 service in the **POP server** dialog box. Email can only be downloaded after the client has authenticated to the CAS role server, so you must supply your username or email address in the **Account ID** dialog box and supply the password for your user account in the **Password** dialog box.

To prevent Entourage from prompting you for your password each time it is started, you must select **Save password in my Mac OS keychain**.

In addition, to send email you must supply the FQDN or IP address of a Hub role server in the **SMTP server** dialog box and click **Click here for advanced sending options** to specify the user account name and password used to authenticate when sending to your Hub role server.

You do not need to configure encryption for a POP3 account because Entourage detects whether POP3S is used and automatically configures it. However, to configure other POP3 options such as whether to leave a copy of email on the server, you can click the **Options** tab shown in Figure 4-57 and configure the appropriate options.

6. If you selected IMAP as the account type in Figure 4-56, you will be prompted to supply the correct IMAP service information as shown in Figure 4-58.

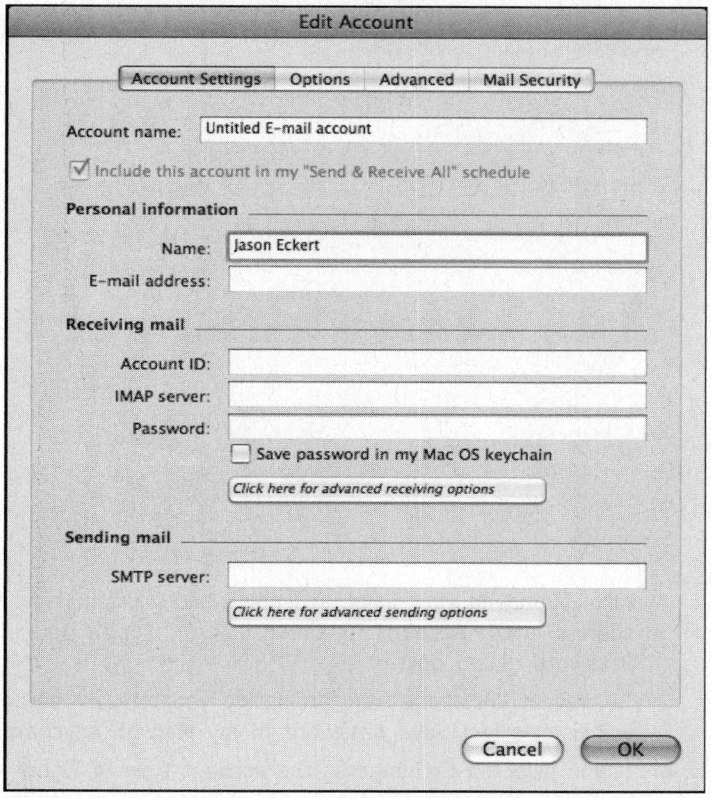

Figure 4-58

Configuring IMAP Settings

After supplying your name and email address, you must supply the FQDN or IP address of a CAS role server running the IMAP4 service in the **IMAP server** dialog box. Email can only be downloaded after the client has authenticated to the CAS role server, so you must supply your username or email address in the **Account ID** dialog box and supply the password for your user account in the **Password** dialog box.

To prevent Entourage from prompting you for your password each time it is started, you must select **Save password in my Mac OS keychain**.

In addition, to send email you must supply the FQDN or IP address of a Hub role server in the **SMTP server** dialog box and click **Click here for advanced sending options** to specify the user account name and password used to authenticate when sending to your Hub role server.

You do not need to configure encryption for an IMAP4 account because Entourage detects whether IMAP4S is used and automatically configures it. However, to configure other IMAP4 options, such as the use of public folders, you can click the **Options** tab shown in Figure 4-58 and configure the appropriate options.

7. If you selected Windows Live Hotmail as the account type in Figure 4-56, you will be prompted to supply the correct information regarding your Hotmail account as shown in Figure 4-59.

Figure 4-59

Configuring HTTP Settings

Figure 4-59

Configuring HTTP Settings

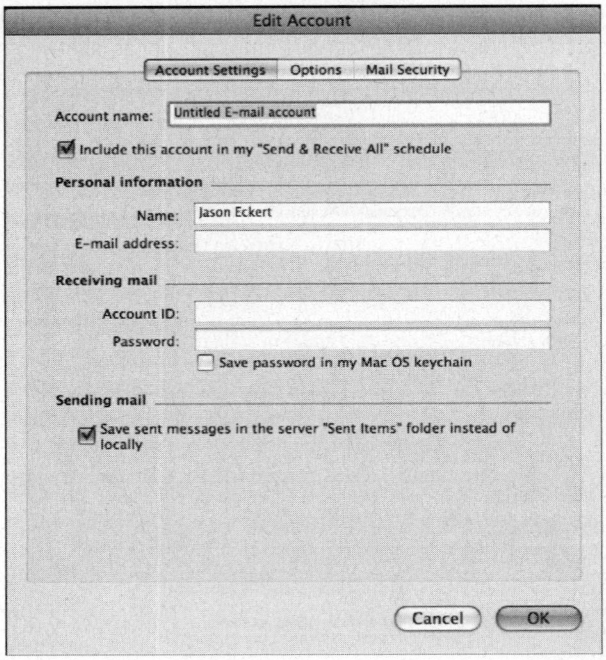

TAKE NOTE*

To configure a Windows Live Hotmail account, you must have a Windows Live Plus membership.

After supplying your name and email address, you must supply your Hotmail email address in the **Account ID** dialog box and supply your Hotmail password in the **Password** dialog box.

To prevent Entourage from prompting you for your password each time it is started, you must select **Save password in my Mac OS keychain**.

8. If you selected Exchange as the account type in Figure 4-56, you will be prompted to supply the correct information regarding your Exchange server and user account as shown in Figure 4-60.

Figure 4-60

Configuring Exchange Settings

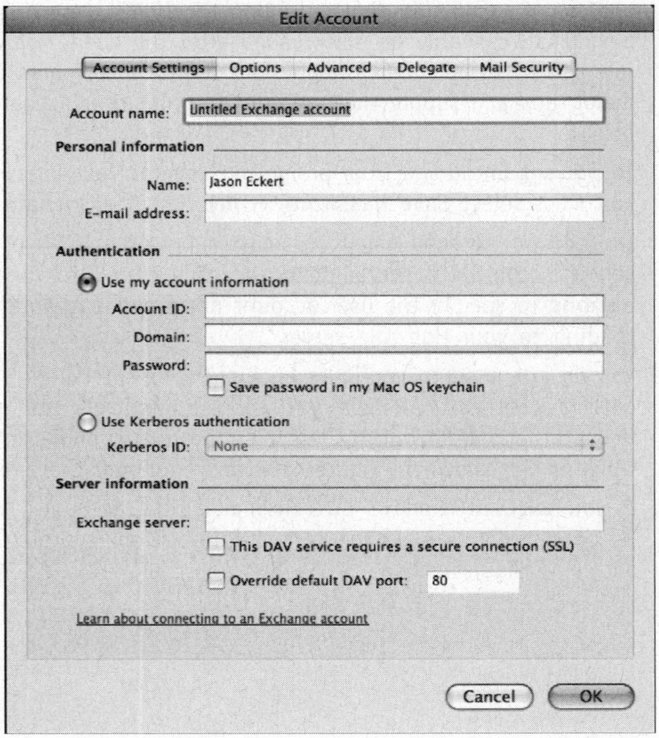

After supplying your name and email address, you must supply your domain credentials. If you select **Use my account information**, you must supply your domain user account name in the **Account ID** dialog box, the DNS name of your Windows domain in the **Domain** dialog box, and your domain user account password in the **Password** dialog box.

To prevent Entourage from prompting you for your password each time it is started, you must select **Save password in my Mac OS keychain**. Alternatively, if your Macintosh computer is a member of an AD domain in your forest, you can simply select **Use Kerberos authentication** and choose your user account from the **Kerberos ID** drop-down box.

Following this, you supply the name of your CAS role server. If you enter the FQDN of your CAS role server in the Exchange server dialog box, Entourage will use the MAPI RPC protocol to send and retrieve email. However, you can also enter the URL for OWA on your CAS role server (**http://FQDN_of_CAS_server/exchange**) to config-ure Entourage to use HTTP/HTTPS when sending and receiving email using the web-based *Distributed Authoring and Versioning (DAV)* service that is part of OWA.

Exchange Server 2007 uses encryption for all DAV and MAPI connections, so you must also select **This DAV service requires a secure connection (SSL)**.

9. After you have specified the appropriate information for your POP, IMAP, Exchange, or Windows Live Hotmail account, click **OK** to close the Edit Account window.

10. Close the Accounts window.

Configuring Microsoft Outlook Express and Windows Mail

For home users, Microsoft Outlook Express and Windows Mail allow for the remote access of email using POP, IMAP, or HTTP. Because most Windows operating systems come with either of these programs, you will likely need to configure them at some point or cre-ate documentation to allow home users the ability to set up their own accounts to connect to the organization's email servers.

Unlike Microsoft Outlook and Entourage, Microsoft Outlook Express is a part of the Internet Explorer application package. As a result, it is shipped with nearly all Microsoft operating sys-tems such as Windows 98, Windows 2000, Windows XP, and Windows Server 2003.

If your organization has users who require company email access from their PC at home, you will likely need to provide them with instructions on how to configure their Microsoft Outlook Express clients to send and receive email using your organization's Exchange serv-ers and the POP or IMAP protocols. Alternatively, these clients can use OWA to access their email or configure Outlook Express to retrieve email using OWA.

Windows Vista uses an improved version of Microsoft Outlook Express called Windows Mail. Unlike Outlook Express, Windows Mail is not part of the Internet Explorer applica-tion package and is available exclusively for Windows Vista clients. The steps for configur-ing email accounts in Microsoft Outlook Express and Windows Mail are virtually identical. As a result, we will focus on configuring Microsoft Outlook Express because it has a larger install base.

CONFIGURE A NEW ACCOUNT IN MICROSOFT OUTLOOK EXPRESS

GET READY. Turn on the client computer, and log in as the appropriate domain user account if necessary. Close any windows that appear on the desktop.

1. Click **Start**, **All Programs**, and then **Outlook Express**. If you are prompted to make Outlook Express the default mail client on your computer, deselect **Always perform this check when starting Outlook Express** and click **No**. The Outlook Express window appears.

TAKE NOTE*

To configure an Exchange account type in Microsoft Entourage 2008, you must be running the Standard edition of Microsoft Office 2008 or greater.

CERTIFICATION READY?
Configure client connectivity.
3.6

2. Select the **Tools** menu, click **Accounts**. The Internet Accounts window appears as shown in Figure 4-61.

Figure 4-61

Configuring Outlook Express Accounts

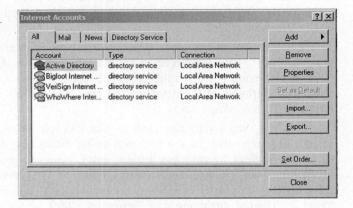

3. Click the **Add** button and select **Mail** from the side menu. The Internet Connection Wizard window appears as shown in Figure 4-62.

Figure 4-62

Setting the Display Name

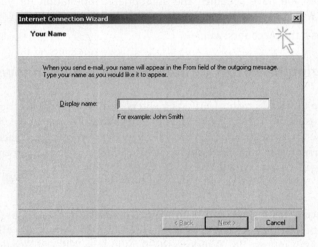

4. Type your name in the **Display name** dialog box and click **Next**. The Internet E-mail Address page appears as shown in Figure 4-63.

Figure 4-63

Setting the E-mail Address

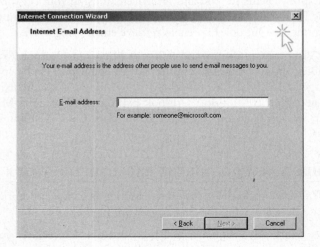

5. Type your email address in the **E-mail address** dialog box and click **Next**. The E-mail Server Names page appears as shown in Figure 4-64.

Figure 4-64

Configuring POP and IMAP
Settings

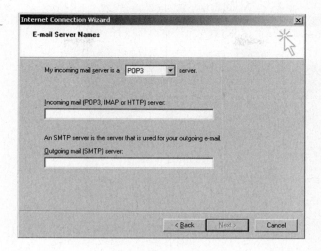

6. Select the appropriate account type (**POP**, **IMAP**, **HTTP**) in the drop-down box.

7. Specify the FQDN or IP address of a CAS role server running the associated POP, IMAP, or HTTP (OWA) service in the **Incoming mail (POP3, IMAP, HTTP) server** dialog box.

   a. If you selected a POP or IMAP account type, you must also supply the FQDN or IP address of a Hub role server in the **Outgoing mail (SMTP) server** dialog box in order to send email.

   b. If you selected HTTP as the account type, you will also be allowed to select your HTTP service provider (**Hotmail**, **MSN**, **Other**) as well as the associated URL as shown in Figure 4-65. To configure Outlook Express to use OWA, you must select the **Other** provider and specify the OWA URL in the **Incoming mail (POP3, IMAP, HTTP) server** dialog box.

Figure 4-65

Configuring HTTP Settings

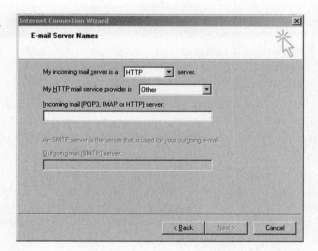

8. When finished specifying account settings, click **Next**. The Internet Mail Logon screen appears as shown in Figure 4-66.

9. Enter your user account name in the **Account name** dialog box and the associated password in the **Password** dialog box. Unless the computer is a public computer, ensure that **Remember password** is selected to prevent Outlook Express from prompting for credentials each time it is opened. If your email client is part of a Windows domain, you can also select **Logon using Secure Password Authentication (SPA)** to provide additional security when sending email to your SMTP server.

Figure 4-66

Configuring Authentication

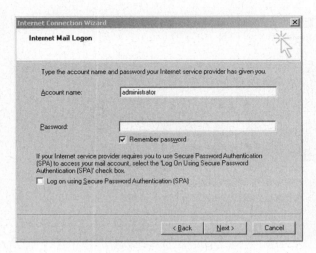

10. Click **Next** when finished. The Congratulations page appears.

11. Click **Finish** to close the Internet Connection Wizard window. After you have added a POP3 or IMAP4 account, it is not configured for encryption (POP3S or IMAP4S). Exchange Server 2007 uses encryption by default, so you must configure the properties of the account in the Internet Accounts window afterward.

12. Highlight your POP3 or IMAP4 account in the Internet Accounts window and click **Properties**. On the Advanced tab, select **This server requires a secure connection (SSL)** for the appropriate protocol and click **OK**.

13. Close the Internet Accounts window.

SUMMARY SKILL MATRIX

IN THIS LESSON YOU LEARNED:

- Administrative roles are used to grant permissions to AD and Exchange Server 2007. You should ensure that administrative user accounts are members of the appropriate administrative role within your Exchange organization.

- To allow foreign email servers on the Internet to relay email to your Exchange servers, you should ensure that DNS MX records exist for your domain name. Depending on your email structure, MX records can resolve to the IP address of your Hub role servers, Edge role servers, or smart hosts.

- To accept and process email addressed to domain names that are not part of your AD structure, you must configure accepted domains on your Hub role servers. Email sent to accepted domain names can be sent to mailboxes within your organization or forwarded to email servers outside of your organization by Hub or Edge role servers.

- Each Hub role server can be configured with a postmaster email address that users can email if problems arise with email relay.

- Before an Edge role server can relay email, it must be subscribed to a Hub role server in the same AD site. To subscribe an Edge role server, you can create a subscription file that must be imported into a Hub role server within 24 hours.

- Email is stored in mailbox databases within storage groups on Mailbox role servers within your organization. To speed performance and provide fault tolerance, you should create additional storage groups and mailbox databases on different hard disks, as well as move the default storage groups and mailbox databases to another hard disk.

- Public folders are also stored within public folder database within storage groups on Mailbox role servers within your organization. Although you can only have one public folder database per Exchange server, this database should be moved to a different hard disk for performance and fault tolerance.

- You can configure storage limits on public folder and mailbox databases to ensure that storage space is not exhausted quickly.

- By default, a new CAS role server allows MAPI RPC, ActiveSync, and OWA connections from client computers. However, you can enable POP3, IMAP4, and Outlook Anywhere support after installation.

- To ensure security for remote users, you should configure OWA options shortly after installing a new CAS role server. You can configure different OWA options for public and private remote users.

- Connectors are used to represent email relay within your organization.

- Receive connectors are created on Hub and Edge role servers to accept SMTP email from other servers and POP or IMAP clients. Default receive connectors are created on Hub and Edge role servers.

- Send connectors are created on Hub servers to allow for email relay within the organization as well as to email servers across the Internet. Send connectors are automatically created on Edge servers once they are subscribed to a Hub role server. Hub role servers contain hidden send connectors by default that allow them to relay email to other internal Exchange servers.

- After modifying your Exchange infrastructure, you will likely need to configure client email programs. Microsoft Outlook and Entourage are part of the Microsoft Office suite and are typically used to provide MAPI RPC connections to Exchange for internal client computers. Microsoft Outlook Express and Windows Mail are bundled with most Microsoft operating systems and are often used to connect to Exchange remotely using the HTTP, POP, and IMAP protocols.

■ Knowledge Assessment

Fill in the Blank

Complete the following sentences by writing the correct word or words in the blanks provided.

1. Exchange Server Enterprise edition can create up to _____ databases per Mailbox role server.

2. The _____ of a send connector determines the DNS domains that the connector can relay email to.

3. After creating a subscription file on an Edge role server, you must import the subscription file into a Hub role server in the same site within _____ hours.

4. After installing a new Edge server role, you must create _____ records in _____ to allow other organizations to relay email to your organization.

5. Microsoft _____ is an email client program that is included with the Microsoft Office program suite for Macintosh computers.

6. To enable the POP3 and IMAP4 services, you must use the _____ console.

7. You can set the maximum message and mailbox size limits using the Limits tab of _____ properties.

8. You would like to ensure that all internal email addressed to your partner organization arfa.com is forwarded directly to the appropriate email servers by your Hub servers. To do this, you must create an accepted domain for arfa.com that uses _____ relay.

9. To access OWA, you can specify the URL https://servername/_____ within a web browser.

10. Edge role servers are typically installed on a _____ network.

Multiple Choice

Circle the letter that corresponds to the best answer.

1. When configuring OWA options, which selections will improve the security of your OWA clients? (Choose all that apply.)
   a. Disabling the change password feature of OWA.
   b. Disabling WebReady content viewing.
   c. Specifying more restrictive options on the Private Computer File Access tab than on the Public Computer File Access tab.
   d. Restricting the attachments that OWA users can download.

2. What intended use should you select in the New SMTP Receive Connector wizard if you wish to create a connector to match SMTP traffic from other Exchange servers within your organization?
   a. Internet
   c. Client
   b. Internal
   d. Custom

3. Which intended use should you select in the New SMTP Send Connector wizard if you wish to create a connector that applies to all domains on the Internet?
   a. Internet
   c. Custom
   b. Internal
   d. Partner

4. Which of the following email client programs has support for the MAPI RPC protocol? (Choose all that apply.)
   a. Windows Mail
   c. Microsoft Outlook Express
   b. Microsoft Outlook
   d. Microsoft Entourage

5. Which port do newer email client programs use when sending email using SMTP?
   a. 23
   c. 110
   b. 25
   d. 587

6. What could you select when setting up an Outlook 2003 or later client to allow Exchange account information to be cached to the local computer?
   a. Use Cached Exchange Mode
   b. Use security for this connection (SSL)
   c. This DAV port requires a secure connection (SSL)
   d. Enable Client Side Caching

7. Which of the following protocols are enabled by default on a new CAS role server? (Choose all that apply.)
   a. HTTP/HTTPS (OWA)
   c. ActiveSync
   b. POP3/POP3S
   d. MAPI RPC

8. Which of the following authentication methods on a receive connector are appropriate for POP3 and IMAP4 clients?
   a. Basic
   c. Integrated Windows
   b. Exchange Server
   d. TLS

9. How many databases can be created on an Exchange Server 2007 Standard edition computer?
   a. 1
   c. 50
   b. 5
   d. 255

10. Which of the following Exchange administrative roles is server specific?
   a. Exchange Organization Administrator
   b. Exchange Public Folder Administrator
   c. Exchange Server Administrator
   d. Exchange View-Only Administrator

True/False

Circle T if the statement is true or F if the statement is false.

T | F **1.** Because there are no explicit send connectors created on a new Hub role server, it is unable to relay email to other Exchange servers within the organization.

T | F **2.** POP and IMAP are commonly configured on email clients that connect remotely to a Microsoft Exchange server.

T | F **3.** You can configure accepted domains within the Exchange Management Console on a Hub or Edge role server.

T | F **4.** Send connectors can be created on a Hub or Edge role server.

T | F **5.** When enabling Outlook Anywhere, the external host name typically points to a server that is running Microsoft ISA Server.

T | F **6.** To allow POP and IMAP clients to send email, your Hub role servers must be configured with the appropriate receive connector.

T | F **7.** Members of the Exchange Organization Administrator role can administer any server within the organization.

T | F **8.** Windows Mail is an improved version of Microsoft Outlook and is included with the Windows Vista operating system.

T | F **9.** If your organization uses smart hosts, the DNS MX records for your organization should point to them using a lower priority number.

T | F **10.** Permissions groups are used to determine the users and computers that a send connector applies to.

Review Questions

1. Explain why creating multiple storage groups and mailbox databases on a single Mailbox role server provides for greater manageability and fault tolerance.

2. Explain how you can use the **Use the External DNS Lookup settings on the transport server** option on your send connectors to improve the security and performance of your email relay.

■ Case Scenarios

Scenario 4-1: Configuring an Alternate SMTP Port

As a security precaution, you have been instructed to ensure that all SMTP traffic within your organization from POP and IMAP clients be sent on port 805 rather than port 25. In a short memo, describe the steps required to allow SMTP traffic on port 805 on the Hub role servers within your organization.

Scenario 4-2: Configuring Email Clients

Your organization has recently decided to allow employees to access their company email from home after working hours using the POP3 protocol. In addition, home users will be allowed to send email using the company's SMTP servers. It is your responsibility to provide the necessary information to the people in your organization who wish to configure their home computers for POP3 email access. Assuming that employees use a variety of different operating systems and email client programs, list the steps and information that people in your organization can likely follow to set up their home computers.

Working with Recipient Objects

LESSON SKILL MATRIX

Technology Skill	Objective Domain	Objective Domain Number
Working with Mailbox Users	Configure recipients.	2.1
Working with Mail Users and Mail Contacts	Configure recipients.	2.1
Implementing an Exchange Resource Forest	Configure recipients.	2.1
Working with Mail-Enabled Groups	Configure mail-enabled groups.	2.2
Working with Resource Mailboxes	Configure resource mailboxes.	2.3
Moving Mailboxes	Move mailboxes.	2.5
Configuring Resource Booking Policies	Configure policies.	3.4

KEY TERMS

Active Directory Migration Tool
  (ADMT)
alias
Automatic Booking
Book-In Policy
Calendar Attendant
dynamic distribution group
Exchange resource forest
expansion server

Full Access permission
In Policy
linked mailbox user
mail contact
mail user
mail-enabled universal
  distribution group
mail-enabled universal security
  group

master account
Out Policy
recipient object
Resource Booking Attendant
resource mailbox
Send As permission
Send On Behalf permission

■ Understanding Recipient Objects

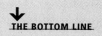
THE BOTTOM LINE

Recipient objects represent the entities within your organization that use your Exchange servers for email relay and access. Before you understand how to create, configure, and manage recipient objects, you must first understand the various types of recipient objects and their usage within the organization.

When you send email, you provide a target email address in the form alias@domain where the *alias* represents the person or entity that should receive the email and domain represents the DNS domain used by the organization. Although the alias portion of an email typically represents a user within your organization or other organizations on the Internet, it can also represent a group of people, a folder, or a resource. In short, the alias portion of an email address represents the recipient of the email sent to that email address.

In general, recipients are simply objects within Exchange or Active Directory (AD) that contain an email address within your organization that Exchange can relay email to.

There are nine major types of *recipient objects* that can be created in Exchange Server 2007. Table 5-1 lists the major recipient object types and their features.

Table 5-1

Exchange Server 2007 recipients

RECIPIENT OBJECTS	DESCRIPTION
Mailbox user	User accounts within AD that have an email address within the organization as well as a mailbox on a Mailbox role server within the organization. Any email sent to a mailbox user is sent to the mailbox for the mailbox user.
Mail user	User accounts within AD that have an email address within the organization, but do not have a mailbox on any Mailbox role server within the organization. Instead, mail users have a second, external email address that is attached to their AD user account. Any email sent to the email address of a mail user within your organization is forwarded using the external email address to the appropriate email server on the Internet.
Mail contact	Objects within AD that contain an email address within the organization as well as an external email address. Any email sent to the email address of a mail contact within your organization is forwarded using the external email address to the appropriate email server on the Internet. Because mail contacts are not user account objects, they cannot be used to log in to an AD domain.
Mail-enabled universal distribution group	Universal distribution groups in AD that have an email address within the organization. Any email sent to a mail-enabled universal distribution group is forwarded to all recipient objects within the group.
Mail-enabled universal security group	Universal security groups in AD that have an email address within the organization. Any email sent to a mail-enabled universal security group is forwarded to all recipient objects within the group. In addition, mail-enabled universal security groups can be assigned permissions to domain resources such as files and printers.
Dynamic distribution group	Contains an email address within the organization as well as a set of criteria used to automatically determine its group membership. Any email sent to a dynamic distribution group is forwarded to all recipient objects that match the appropriate criteria.
Resource mailbox	Used to simplify resource scheduling when creating meeting requests using the Calendaring feature of MAPI clients such as Outlook. More specifically, resource mailboxes are disabled mailbox users that represent rooms or equipment. Like other mailbox users within your organization, resource mailboxes have an email address within the organization that is used by the Calendaring feature of MAPI clients when scheduling resource usage.
Linked mailbox user	Allows a user in one forest to access a mailbox in another forest across a trust relationship. Linked mailbox users are typically used when Exchange Server 2007 is deployed in a separate forest for security reasons or when several different forests require a single uniform Exchange infrastructure.
Mail-enabled public folder	Public folder objects that contain an email address within the organization. Any emails that are sent to a mail-enabled public folder are stored within the public folder itself.

X REF

Mail-enabled public folders will be discussed in Lesson 7, "Working with Public Folders." All other recipient objects will be discussed in this lesson.

To create and manage all recipient objects within your organization, you must be a member of the Exchange Recipient Administrator or Exchange Organization Administrator role. Members of the Exchange Public Folder Administrator role are able to create and manage mail-enabled public folders within your organization.

■ Working with Mailbox Users

THE BOTTOM LINE

Mailbox users are the most common recipient objects that Exchange administrators work with because they represent users within an organization that have both a user account in AD and a mailbox on an Exchange server. In addition, mailbox users have the most configuration and management options. To work with mailbox users, you must understand how to create them, remove them, configure their properties, and manage their permissions.

CERTIFICATION READY?
Configure recipients.

2.1

Creating Mailbox Users

Mailbox users may be created using the Exchange Management Console or the Exchange Management Shell. During creation, you must specify an existing user account or create a new one as well as specify the mailbox settings and alias for the mailbox user.

Because most members of your organization require a mailbox hosted by email servers within your organization, mailbox users are the most common type of recipient object that you will create in Exchange Server 2007. All mailbox users require an AD user account that is connected to a mailbox within a mailbox database on a Mailbox role server within your organization.

Depending on your organization's structure and policies, Exchange administrators may also be responsible for creating AD user accounts. In that case, you can create and associate a mailbox to a new AD user account at the same time by creating a new mailbox user in the Exchange Management Console. Alternatively, if your organization separates administrative duties and requires that different administrators create new AD user accounts and mailboxes, you can simply create a mailbox and associate it to an existing AD user account in the Exchange Management Console.

Regardless of whether you are creating a new mailbox user or mailbox enabling an existing AD user, you will be prompted to supply the alias used when creating the email address for the mailbox user. Although the alias does not need to match the login name of the user, it usually does for consistency.

 CREATE A MAILBOX USER

GET READY. Turn on the computer, and log in as the Administrator user account. Close any windows that appear on the desktop.

1. Click **Start**, **All Programs**, **Microsoft Exchange Server 2007**, and then click **Exchange Management Console**. The Exchange Management Console window appears.

2. In the console tree pane, expand **Recipient Configuration** and highlight **Mailbox**.

3. In the action pane, click **New Mailbox**. The New Mailbox window appears as shown in Figure 5-1.

Figure 5-1

Creating a New Mailbox User

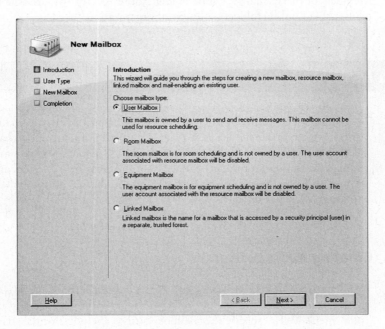

4. Select **User Mailbox** and click **Next**. The User Type page appears as shown in Figure 5-2.

Figure 5-2

Specifying the User Type

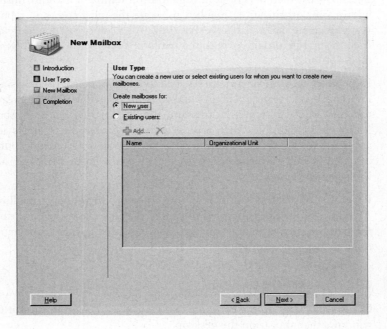

5. If you wish to create a new AD user with an associated mailbox, ensure that **New user** is selected. Alternatively, you can choose to mailbox enable an existing AD user. To mailbox enable an existing user, select **Existing users**, click the **Add** button, select the appropriate user in the Select User window that appears and click **OK**.

6. Click **Next**. If you selected New user on the User Type page, you will be prompted to specify the AD user account information on the User Information page as shown in Figure 5-3.

Figure 5-3

Adding User Information

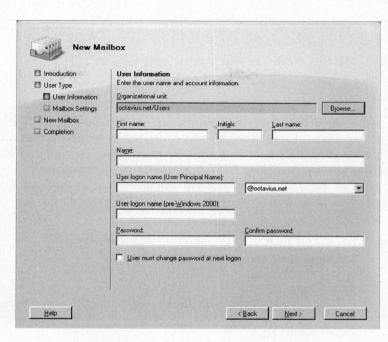

TAKE NOTE*

If you selected **Existing users** on the User Type page, you will skip entering the account information shown in Figure 5-3.

7. By default, the user will be created in the default Users folder in your current domain. Because users are rarely created in this folder, you should click **Browse**, select the appropriate Organizational Unit (OU), and click **OK**. All other account settings on this page are similar in function to the settings that you choose when creating a new user account in the Active Directory Users and Computers console as discussed in Lesson 2. When finished entering the user account information, click **Next**. The Mailbox Settings page appears as shown in Figure 5-4.

Figure 5-4

Configuring Mailbox Settings

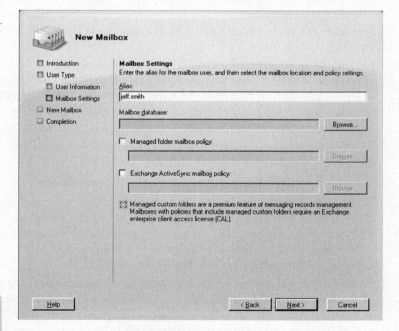

X REF

Managed folder policies will be discussed in Lesson 6, "Address Lists, Policies, and Bulk Management." ActiveSync policies will be discussed in Lesson 12, "Providing for Mobile Access and Unified Messaging."

8. At the Mailbox Settings page, ensure that the **Alias** dialog box contains the recipient name that should appear in the email address. For example, in Figure 5-4, the email address for the user will be jeff.smith@domain.

9. Click **Browse** next to the Mailbox database dialog box, select the Mailbox database in the Select Mailbox Database window that appears, and click **OK**.

10. If you have created a Managed folder mailbox policy or an ActiveSync mailbox policy that you wish to apply to this mailbox user, you can select the associated checkboxes in Figure 5-4 and click the related **Browse** buttons to select them.

11. Click **Next**. The New Mailbox page appears.

12. Review the summary of your settings and click **New**. The Completion page appears.

TAKE NOTE*

The completion page of most configuration wizards in Exchange Server 2007 displays a command that may be used to perform the same actions from within the Exchange Management Shell that you have executed during the wizard. When creating a new mail box user and associated AD user account, the password that you specify is not shown within this command for security reasons. Instead, you will see the value 'SystemSecurity SecureString' in place of all passwords specified within an Exchange Server 2007 wizard.

13. Click **Finish** to close the New Mailbox window.

14. Close the Exchange Management Console.

THE COMMAND LINE WAY

You can also use the **Enable-Mailbox** cmdlet in the Exchange Management Shell to create a mailbox for an existing AD user or the **New-Mailbox** cmdlet to create a new AD user and associated mailbox.

For example, to create a mailbox in the Mailbox Database within the First Storage Group on the server EXCH1 for the existing user with the logon name jeff.smith in the domain octavius.net, you could run the following command in the Exchange Management Shell:

Enable-Mailbox 'jeff.smith@octavius.net'– Database 'EXCH1\First Storage Group\ Mailbox Database'

Alternatively, to create a new AD user for Jeff Smith (logon name = jeff.smith) within the East OU in the octavius.net domain, require that Jeff must change his password on the next logon and create an associated mailbox in the Mailbox Database within the First Storage Group on the server EXCH1, you could run the following command in the Exchange Management Shell:

New-Mailbox -UserPrincipalName 'jeff.smith@octavius.net' –Alias 'jeff.smith' –Database 'EXCH1\First Storage Group\Mailbox Database' –Name 'Jeff Smith' –OrganizationalUnit 'octavius.net/East' –FirstName 'Jeff' –LastName 'Smith' –DisplayName 'Jeff Smith' –ResetPasswordOnNextLogon $true

After entering the previous command within the Exchange Management Console, you will be prompted to type an initial password for Jeff Smith. Alternatively, you could run the following command before creating the user:

$password = Read-Host 'Enter password' –AsSecureString

This command will prompt you for a password and store it in the $password variable. Next, you can use this $password variable when creating several mailbox users in the Exchange Management Shell. For example, to create the Jeff Smith user described earlier and set the initial password to the value of the $password variable, you could run the following command in the Exchange Management Shell:

New-Mailbox –UserPrincipalName 'jeff.smith@octavius.net' –Alias 'jeff.smith' –Database 'EXCH1\First Storage Group\Mailbox Database' –Name 'Jeff Smith' –OrganizationalUnit 'octavius.net/East' –FirstName 'Jeff' –LastName 'Smith' –DisplayName 'Jeff Smith' –ResetPasswordOnNextLogon $true –password $password

Configuring Mailbox Users

The configuration of mailbox users can be performed by accessing the properties of the mailbox user within the Exchange Management Console or by running the appropriate cmdlet within the Exchange Management Shell.

Provided that you are a member of the Exchange Organization Administrator or Exchange Recipient Administrator role, you can administer the properties of all mailbox users within the organization, regardless of which Mailbox role server stores their associated mailbox.

To view all mailbox users within your organization, you can navigate to **Recipient Configuration** > **Mailbox** within the Exchange Management Console. Because there may be hundreds or thousands of mailbox users within your organization, you can narrow the list of users shown in the Exchange Management Console by selecting **Create Filter** from the detail pane and specifying the appropriate information. For example, to see the mailbox users on the server called EXCH1, you could specify Server Equals EXCH1 as shown in Figure 5-5 and click **Apply Filter**.

Figure 5-5

Applying Mailbox User Filters

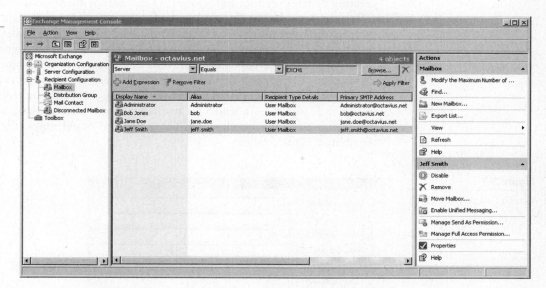

You can add/specify multiple criteria to your view filter in Figure 5-5 by clicking **Add Expression** or remove your filter by selecting **Remove Filter**.

Once you have located the appropriate mailbox user, you can highlight it in the detail pane and select **Properties** from the action pane to view its properties. The properties for the Jeff Smith mailbox user are shown in Figure 5-6.

Figure 5-6

Mailbox User Properties

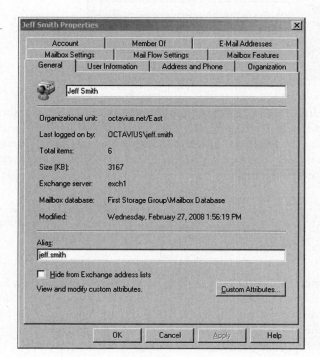

The General tab of mailbox user properties displays the information about the location of the AD user account as well as the location and contents of the mailbox itself. In Figure 5-6, the mailbox for Jeff Smith has 6 items that take up 3167 KB of space on the Mailbox Database in the First Storage Group on the server exch1. In addition, you can modify the alias used to generate the email address for the mailbox user or hide the user from any email address lists that are generated by Exchange to represent groups of mail recipients.

By clicking the **Custom Attributes** button shown in Figure 5-6, you can store up to 15 custom attributes in the mailbox user that may be used later when searching for users or creating dynamic distribution groups. These custom attributes are simply text labels that reflect the job role, project, subdepartment, or status of the mailbox user. You can use these custom attributes to store information that is not normally stored in the properties of a user account. For example, the first custom attribute could represent the team within the organization, the second custom attribute could represent the project, and the third custom attribute could represent the location of the project. If Jeff Smith is part of the TASU team working on the project called Athena in Chicago, you could enter the custom attributes shown in Figure 5-7. To search for mailbox users who are working on project Athena, you can then create a filter as shown earlier in Figure 5-5 and supply the expression Custom Attribute 2 Equals Athena.

Figure 5-7

Adding Custom Attributes

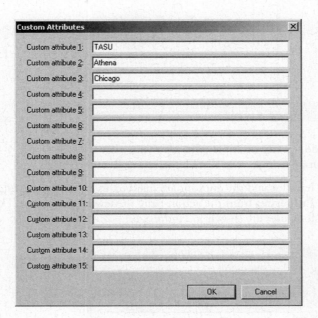

The User Information, Address and Phone, Organization, Member Of, and Account tabs of mailbox user properties contain information about the mailbox user such as logon name, group membership, full name, contact information, and department. This information is taken from the existing AD user account if the account was mailbox enabled, but must be entered manually if the user account was created alongside the mailbox.

TAKE NOTE* Although the Member Of tab lists the groups that the mailbox user is a member of, you cannot modify group membership using it.

The remaining tabs within the properties of a mailbox user contain Exchange-specific configuration for the mailbox user and mailbox. To view and modify the SMTP email address for the mailbox user, you can use the E-Mail Addresses tab. By default, a single email address is added in the form alias@domain. However, you can add additional email addresses to allow the recipient to receive email sent to multiple email addresses.

Figure 5-8 shows the E-Mail Addresses tab for the user Jeff Smith in the octavius.net domain. Because the alias for Jeff Smith is jeff.smith, the SMTP address jeff.smith@octavius.net was added automatically using an email address policy. An additional address, jsmith@octavius .net was added afterward to reflect the email address format that was used by the octavius .net domain in the past. If a remote sender with the old contact information for Jeff Smith addresses email to jsmith@octavius.net, it will still be sent to the mailbox for Jeff Smith. Because the jeff.smith@octavius.net address is bold in Figure 5-8, it will be used as the sending address when Jeff Smith sends or replies to email. Hence, when Jeff Smith replies to an email that was addressed to jsmith@octavius.net, the reply will list jeff.smith@octavius.net as the sender instead of jsmith@octavius.net. The sending address is always defined from the alias set on the mailbox user. To change the sending address, you can deselect **Automatically update e-mail addresses based on e-mail address policy**, shown in Figure 5-8, highlight another email address, and click **Set as Reply**.

Figure 5-8

Configuring Email Addresses

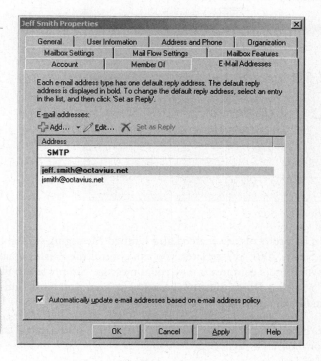

X REF

Email address policies will be discussed in Lesson 6, "Address Lists, Policies, and Bulk Management."

Additional addresses are also used when users change their legal surname after marriage. For example, if Sue Wong (sue.wong@octavius.net) changes her surname to Richards, you can modify the alias for Sue Wong's mailbox user to sue.richards on the General tab of her mailbox user properties. This will assign a default SMTP email address of sue.richards@octavius .net and automatically add a secondary SMTP address of sue.wong@octavius.net to ensure that she receives email that is still sent to sue.wong@octavius.net. When Sue Richards replies to any emails that were sent to sue.wong@octavius.net, the reply email will be from sue .richards@octavius.net, and the original sender can then update his or her contact list.

Many organizations specify a postmaster of postmaster@domain on their Hub role servers. To ensure that email sent to postmaster@octavius.net is sent to Jeff Smith, you could set postmaster@octavius.net as the postmaster email address on your Hub role servers and then add the address postmaster@octavius.net as an additional email address on the E-Mail Addresses tab of Jeff Smith's mailbox user object.

X REF

Configuring postmaster addresses and accepted domains on Hub role servers was discussed in Lesson 4, "Configuring a New Exchange Server."

Although there is no limit to the number of additional SMTP addresses that you can create for a single mailbox user, you should keep the number to a minimum for manageability and performance. Furthermore, if you add an additional email address that has a different domain, you must add an authoritative accepted domain for the domain on the Hub transport servers within your organization to ensure that your Hub servers will accept email for the domain and forward it to the appropriate mailbox.

To control the protocols and features that the mailbox user is allowed to use, you can enable or disable the appropriate protocols or features on the Mailbox Features tab shown in Figure 5-9.

Figure 5-9

Specifying Mailbox Features

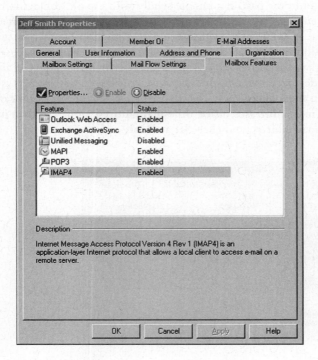

By default, all protocols are enabled and Unified Messaging is disabled. If you are running Exchange Server 2007 SP1 or later, you can control the default email format used when POP or IMAP users compose a new email message. Simply select POP3 or IMAP4 as shown in Figure 5-9, click **Properties**, uncheck **Use protocol default**, and select the appropriate default email format:

- **Text.** Emails are composed in plain text, which means email can be processed by any client or mobile device.
- **HTML.** Emails are composed in HTML format.
- **HTML and alternative text.** Emails can consist of HTML and plain text components.
- **Enriched text.** Emails are composed using Rich Text Format (RTF).
- **Enriched text and alternative text.** Emails can consist of RTF and plain text components.

The Mailbox Settings tab of mailbox user properties shown in Figure 5-10 can be used to change the mailbox settings for the mailbox user. In the properties of Messaging Records Management, you can specify a managed folder mailbox policy or modify the one chosen during the creation of the mailbox user. Similarly, in the properties of Storage Quotas, you can override the mailbox size limits and deleted item retention period set on the mailbox database as shown in Figure 5-11.

In Figure 5-11, deleted items will be retained for the default period of 14 days, and users will receive a warning email when their mailbox reaches 900 MB (921600 KB). When a user's mailbox reaches 950 MB (972800 KB), he will receive an additional warning email and will not be able to send any emails using Exchange. However, the user will continue receiving emails from others until the mailbox size reaches 1 GB (1048576 KB). As this point, the user can no longer send or receive any emails until he reduces the size of his mailbox.

You can configure default mailbox size limits on the Limits tab of mailbox database properties as discussed earlier in Lesson 4, "Configuring a New Exchange Server."

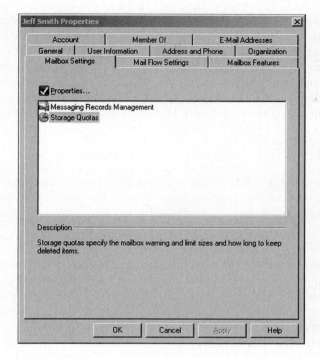

Figure 5-10

Configuring Mailbox Settings

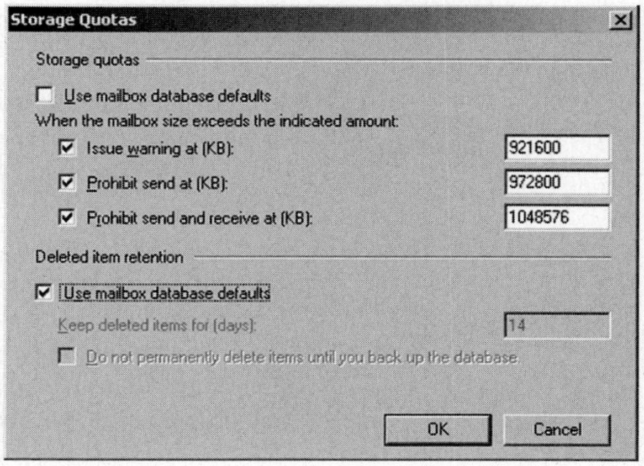

Figure 5-11

Configuring Mailbox Storage Quotas

To allow for greater flexibility and more granular control, you can also alter settings for mail relay on an individual user basis. This information is used by the Mailbox, CAS, and Hub role servers within your organization and can be configured using the Mail Flow Settings tab of mailbox user properties. Figure 5-12 displays the Mail Flow Settings tab for Jeff Smith.

When you access the properties of Delivery Options in Figure 5-12, you can specify **Send On Behalf permission**, forwarding options, and recipient limits as shown in Figure 5-13.

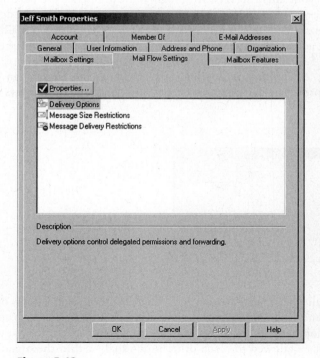

Figure 5-12

Configuring Mail Flow Settings

Figure 5-13

Configuring Delivery Options

By default, when Jeff Smith sends email, the From field in the email displays his primary email address (jeff.smith@octavius.net). However, because Bob Jones and Jane Doe have Send On Behalf permission to Jeff Smith's mailbox, they can compose a new email from their own account in Outlook or Entourage, choose the option to view the From box, and then change the contents of the From box to jeff.smith@octavius.net. When the email is sent, it will appear as though it was sent from "Bob Jones on behalf of Jeff Smith" if the email was composed by Bob Jones or from "Jane Doe on behalf of Jeff Smith" if the email was composed by Jane Doe.

TAKE NOTE *Mailbox users can also grant Send On Behalf permissions themselves from within Outlook by specifying the appropriate users on the **Delegates** tab of **Tools** > **Options**, or from within Entourage by specifying the appropriate users on the **Delegates** tab of account properties.*

In addition, email that is sent to Jeff Smith's mailbox is forwarded to Sue Wong as well as Jeff Smith's mailbox using the Forwarding address section of Figure 5-13. *Forwarding* is often used when an employee leaves the organization to ensure that emails are sent to the mailbox user who will act as a replacement. In addition, forwarding is also a method of monitoring emails from users within your organization. In this case, you should ensure that the email is delivered to both the forwarding address and mailbox if the user should not be made aware of the monitoring.

In the early days of email, it was not uncommon to send out mass emails that contained hundreds of recipients for advertising purposes. Today, this activity may be negatively interpreted as spam and can be limited by specifying the maximum number of recipients within the Recipient limits section of Delivery Options. As shown in Figure 5-13, any emails with more than 50 recipients that are sent by Jeff Smith will be returned as undeliverable.

Emails with large attachments are difficult to relay and can slow down the email servers within your organization. As a result, you should always restrict the maximum size of emails that are relayed by your email servers. Although you can restrict the maximum message size within the properties of a send or receive connector on the Hub and Edge role servers within your organization, you can also restrict the size of emails on a mailbox user basis. To do this, you can access the properties of Message Size Restrictions on the Mail Flow Settings tab. Figure 5-14 shows the message size restrictions for the mailbox user Jeff Smith. By preventing Jeff Smith from sending or receiving emails larger than 10 MB (10240 KB), you will improve the performance of the Hub and Edge role servers within your organization.

Figure 5-14

Restricting Message Sizes

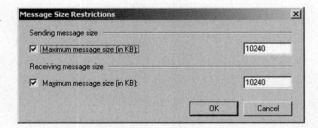

You can also specify the allowed senders for an individual mailbox user. This is often useful when email communication within your organization must be restricted to specific users. Research and development teams are an example of this because information within the team must not be allowed to reach other individuals within the organization by accident.

To specify allowed senders for a mailbox user, you can access the properties of Message Delivery Restrictions in the Mail Flow Settings tab of mailbox user properties as shown in Figure 5-15 for the user Jeff Smith. In Figure 5-15, Jeff Smith allows messages from all authenticated senders except for Billy Martin.

Figure 5-15

Configuring Allowed Senders

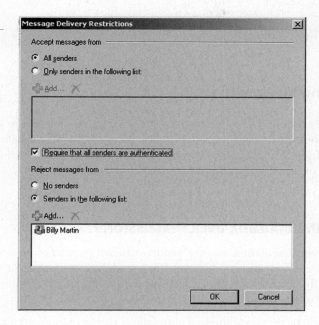

You can also modify the properties of a mailbox user using the **Set-Mailbox** cmdlet within the Exchange Management Shell. For example, to set the maximum size for sent email to 10 MB (10485760 bytes) for the user Jeff Smith, you could run the following command within the Exchange Management Shell:

Set-Mailbox 'jeff.smith@octavius.net' -MaxSendSize 10485760

When you identify the object that you wish to modify within the Exchange Management Console, you can use a variety of different formats. For example, you can identify Jeff Smith using his display name (Jeff Smith), logon name (jeff.smith), or LDAP name (CN=Jeff Smith, OU=East, DC=octavius, DC=net). Because the Exchange Management Shell supports UNIX-style redirection, you can use the pipe (|) symbol to send the name of the object to the appropriate cmdlet. As a result, the following commands perform the same action as the one described earlier:

THE COMMAND LINE WAY

Set-Mailbox –Identity 'Jeff Smith' –MaxSendSize 10485760

Set-Mailbox –Identity 'jeff.smith' –MaxSendSize 10485760

Set-Mailbox –Identity 'CN=Jeff Smith, OU=East, DC=octavius, DC=net' –MaxSendSize 10485760

'jeff.smith@octavius.net' | Set-Mailbox –MaxSendSize 10485760

'Jeff Smith' | Set-Mailbox –MaxSendSize 10485760

'jeff.smith' | Set-Mailbox –MaxSendSize 10485760

'CN=Jeff Smith, OU=East, DC=octavius, DC=net' | Set-Mailbox –MaxSendSize 10485760

All future cmdlet examples will vary the syntax used to identify recipient objects. This will ensure that you become accustomed to the different formats available within the Exchange Management Shell.

These examples only modified a single attribute of the Jeff Smith mailbox user (MaxSendSize). To see other options that can be used alongside the SetMailbox cmdlet to modify other properties of a mailbox user, search for Set-Mailbox within Exchange Server 2007 Help.

To view the settings that you have configured for a mail user, you can use the **Get-Mailbox** cmdlet. For example, the following command within the Exchange Management Shell lists the properties of the Jeff Smith mail user described earlier:

Get-MailUser 'jeff.smith@octavius.net' | format-list

Managing Mailbox Users

After you create and configure the properties for mailbox users, you must manage them over time. This involves granting or denying permissions as well as disabling or removing the mailbox user. In addition, you may need to reconnect the mailbox for a disabled or deleted user to a new or existing mailbox user at a later time.

MANAGING MAILBOX USER PERMISSIONS

Although you can grant a user the Send On Behalf permission to another mailbox user, the Send On Behalf permission does not allow senders to mask their identity. Email sent using the Send On Behalf permission will always list the real sender in the From field or preview pane within the email client.

However, there are two additional permissions that an administrator can grant on a mailbox user to allow other users the ability to assume that user's identity. These permissions are the *Send As permission* and the *Full Access permission*.

The Send As permission is nearly identical to the Send On Behalf permission. However, the Send As permission hides the identity of the original sender. For example, if you grant Bob Jones the Send As permission to the Jeff Smith mailbox user account, Bob Jones can compose a new email from his own account in Outlook or Entourage, choose the option to view the From box, and then change the contents of the From box to jeff.smith@octavius.net. However, when the email is sent, it will appear as though it was sent from Jeff Smith. The recipients of the email message will not know that the email was actually sent from Bob Jones on Jeff Smith's behalf.

You can also grant the Send As permission to a group for a mailbox user to allow all members of the group the ability to send emails as that user. This is often used if your organization requires several users to send certain emails using a single identity. Say, for example, that the Octavius organization creates a dummy mailbox user with the email companyevents@ octavius.net and grants Send As permission to several users or groups for this dummy mailbox user. In this case, any user with Send As permission to this dummy mailbox user can send companywide emails regarding special events using a consistent single identity of companyevents@octavius.net.

TAKE NOTE*

You should only grant the Send As permission if another person must be trusted to send email using the sole identity of another user.

➔ MANAGE SEND AS PERMISSIONS FOR A MAILBOX USER

GET READY. Turn on the computer, and log in as the Administrator user account. Close any windows that appear on the desktop.

1. Click **Start, All Programs, Microsoft Exchange Server 2007,** and then click **Exchange Management Console.** The Exchange Management Console window appears.
2. In the console tree pane, expand **Recipient Configuration** and highlight **Mailbox.**
3. In the result pane, select the user you wish to manage Send As permissions for.
4. In the action pane, click **Manage Send As Permission.** The Manage Send As Permission window appears as shown in Figure 5-16.

Figure 5-16

Managing Send As Permission

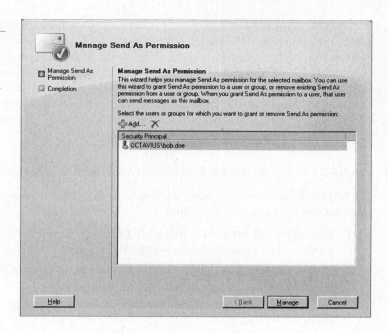

5. To remove the Send As Permission granted to an existing user or group listed in the Security Principle dialog box, highlight the user or group and click the red **X** icon. Alternatively, to grant the Send As permission to a user or group, click **Add**, select the appropriate user or group in the Select User or Group dialog box that appears, and click **OK**.

6. Click **Manage**. The Completion page appears.

7. Click **Finish** to close the Manage Send As Permission window.

8. Close the Exchange Management Console.

THE COMMAND LINE WAY

You can also use the **Add-ADPermission** cmdlet in the Exchange Management Shell to assign Send As permission to a user or group for a mailbox user. For example, to grant Send As permission to Bob Jones (logon name = bob.jones@octavius.net) for the mailbox user Jeff Smith located in the East OU of the octavius.net domain (LDAP name: CN= Jeff Smith, OU=East, DC=octavius, DC=net), you could run the following command in the Exchange Management Shell:

Add-ADPermission –Identity 'CN=Jeff Smith, OU=East, DC=octavius, DC=net' –User 'octavius.net\bob.jones' –ExtendedRights 'Send-as'

Similarly, you can use the **Remove-ADPermission** cmdlet to remove Send As permissions for a mailbox user. For example, to remove the Send As permission added in the previous example, you could run the following command in the Exchange Management Shell:

Remove-ADPermission –Identity 'CN=Jeff Smith,OU=East,DC=octavius,DC=net' –User 'octavius.net\bob.jones' –InheritanceType 'All' –ExtendedRights 'Send-as' –ChildObjectTypes $null –InheritedObjectType $null –Properties $null

Although the Send As permission allows a delegate the ability to send emails as another mailbox user, it does not allow the delegate to view the emails within that user's mailbox. In some organizations, an assistant or colleague must be able to send and receive emails using another user's identity when that user is on a business trip, vacation, or sick leave. To do this, you can grant the Full Access permission to the assistant or colleague for the target mailbox user. Users with Full Access permission to a target mailbox user can open the target mailbox alongside their own mailbox from within Outlook or Entourage. As a result, they will receive emails sent to the target mailbox user and can respond to them using the identity of the target mailbox user.

You can also grant the Full Access permission to a group for a mailbox user to allow all members of the group the ability to receive and send emails as that user. This is often used if your organization has an information mailbox that several users need to have full control of. For example, the Octavius organization can create a dummy mailbox user with the email address hr@octavius.net and grant Full Access permission to the human resources group within the organization. Members of the human resources group will be able to receive emails sent to hr@octavius.net and will be able to reply to the ones that they are individually responsible for in their departments.

 MANAGE FULL ACCESS PERMISSIONS FOR A MAILBOX USER

GET READY. Turn on the computer, and log in as the Administrator user account. Close any windows that appear on the desktop.

1. Click **Start**, **All Programs**, **Microsoft Exchange Server 2007**, and then click **Exchange Management Console**. The Exchange Management Console window appears.

2. In the console tree pane, expand **Recipient Configuration** and highlight **Mailbox**.

3. In the result pane, select the user that you wish to manage Full Access permissions for.

4. In the action pane, click **Manage Full Access Permission**. The Manage Full Access Permission window appears as shown in Figure 5-17.

Figure 5-17

Managing Full Access Permission

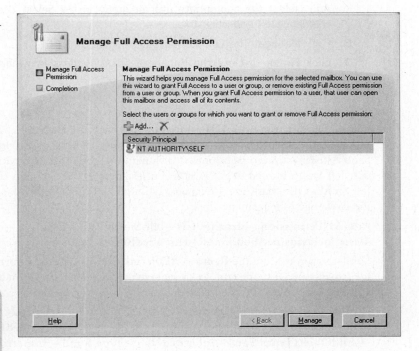

TAKE NOTE*

Do not remove the default **NT AUTHORITY\SELF** security principle shown in Figure 5-17. This security principle is required to allow mailbox users full access to their own mailbox.

5. To remove the Full Access permission granted to an existing user or group listed in the Security Principle dialog box, highlight the user or group and click the red **X** icon. Alternatively, to grant the Full Access permission to a user or group, click **Add**, select the appropriate user or group in the Select User or Group dialog box that appears, and click **OK**.

6. Click **Manage**. The Completion page appears.

7. Click **Finish** to close the Manage Full Access Permission window.

8. Close the Exchange Management Console.

THE COMMAND
LINE WAY

You can also use the **Add-MailboxPermission** cmdlet in the Exchange Management Shell to assign Full Access permission to a user or group for a mailbox user. For example, to grant Full Access permission to Bob Jones (logon name = bob.jones@octavius.net) for the mailbox user Jeff Smith located in the East OU of the octavius.net domain (LDAP name: CN=Jeff Smith, OU=East, DC=octavius, DC=net), you could run the following command in the Exchange Management Shell:

Add-MailboxPermission –Identity 'CN=Jeff Smith,OU=East,DC=octavius,DC=net' –User 'octavius.net\bob.jones' –AccessRights 'FullAccess'

Similarly, you can use the **Remove-MailboxPermission** cmdlet to remove Full Access permissions to a user or group for a mailbox user. For example, to remove the Full Access permission added in the previous example, you could run the following command in the Exchange Management Shell:

Remove-MailboxPermission –Identity 'CN=Jeff Smith, OU=East, DC=octavius, DC=net' –User 'octavius.net\bob.jones' –InheritanceType 'All' –AccessRights 'FullAccess'

Users who have Full Access permission to the target user's mailbox must manually add the target mailbox to the properties of their Exchange account within Outlook or Entourage. To do this from within Outlook 2007, you can navigate to **Tools** > **Account Settings**, double click on your Exchange account, click the **More Settings** button, and add the appropriate mailbox to the Mailboxes section on the Advanced tab shown in Figure 5-18.

Figure 5-18

Adding Additional Mailboxes to an Exchange Account in Outlook 2007

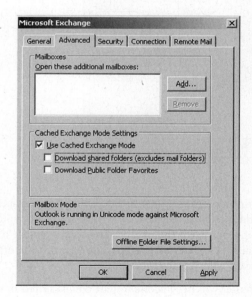

DISABLING, REMOVING, AND RECONNECTING MAILBOX USERS

When you navigate to **Recipient Configuration** > **Mailbox** within the Exchange Management Console and highlight a mailbox user in the detail pane, you are given the **Disable** or **Remove** options in the action pane.

If you choose to disable a mailbox user, all Exchange-related properties within the AD user account are removed, but the user account is not removed from AD. In general, you should disable mailbox users if the AD account no longer needs email access yet the AD account must still exist for domain authentication.

Alternatively, if you choose to remove a mailbox user, the AD user account is removed completely and the associated user will no longer be able to authenticate to the domain. This option is typically used to save time if the administration of Exchange and AD are performed by the same person. If a user account and mailbox must be removed when a user leaves the organization, then both tasks can be done at the same time from within the Exchange Management Console. Otherwise, the mailbox user would need to be disabled in the Exchange Management Console and the associated user account would need to be removed in the Active Directory Users and Computers console.

Regardless of whether you disable or remove an existing mailbox user, the mailbox is not removed immediately. Instead, the mailbox is simply disconnected and marked for deletion. You can view the disconnected mailboxes within your organization by navigating to **Recipient Configuration > Disconnected Mailbox** within the Exchange Management Console.

By default, disconnected mailboxes are automatically removed after 30 days, but you can change this interval by accessing the Limits tab of mailbox database properties as shown in Figure 5-19. To view the properties of a mailbox database, simply navigate to **Server Configuration > Mailbox** in the Exchange Management Console and select the appropriate server in the detail pane. You can then highlight the appropriate mailbox database in the work pane and click **Properties** in the action pane.

Figure 5-19

Configuring Deletion Settings on a Mailbox Database

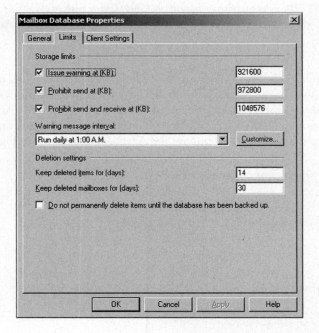

When users leave your organization, the associated mailbox user accounts are either disabled or removed. In addition, the email addresses for those users are typically added as secondary email addresses in the properties of the mailbox users who replace them in their job roles. This allows future emails from external contacts addressed to the original user to be sent to the mailbox of the person who replaced them.

In some cases, the new user will need access to past emails stored in the mailbox of the original mailbox user who left the organization. You can reconnect the original user's mailbox to the new user account after you create an AD user account for them.

TAKE NOTE*

Alternatively, you can disable the AD user account for a user who has left the organization and create a new mailbox user for the person who will act as a replacement. Following this, you can grant the new user Full Access permission to the existing mailbox and add it as a secondary mailbox within Outlook or Entourage as discussed earlier. This will allow the replacement user to receive and reply to emails that are sent to the original user.

DISABLE A MAILBOX USER

GET READY. Turn on the computer, and log in as the Administrator user account. Close any windows that appear on the desktop.

1. Click **Start**, **All Programs**, **Microsoft Exchange Server 2007**, and then click **Exchange Management Console**. The Exchange Management Console window appears.

2. In the console tree pane, expand **Recipient Configuration** and highlight **Mailbox**.

3. In the result pane, select the appropriate mailbox user, and click **Disable** in the action pane. When prompted to confirm the action, click **Yes**.

4. Close the Exchange Management Console.

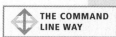 THE COMMAND LINE WAY

You can also use the **Disable-Mailbox** cmdlet in the Exchange Management Shell to disable a mailbox user. To disable Jeff Smith (email address jeff.smith@octavius.net), you could run the following command in the Exchange Management Shell:

Disable-Mailbox 'jeff.smith@octavius.net'

 REMOVE A MAILBOX USER

GET READY. Turn on the computer, and log in as the Administrator user account. Close any windows that appear on the desktop.

1. Click **Start**, **All Programs**, **Microsoft Exchange Server 2007**, and then click **Exchange Management Console**. The Exchange Management Console window appears.

2. In the console tree pane, expand **Recipient Configuration** and highlight **Mailbox**.

3. In the result pane, select the appropriate mailbox user and click **Remove** in the action pane. When prompted to confirm the action, click **Yes**.

4. Close the Exchange Management Console.

 THE COMMAND LINE WAY

You can also use the **Remove-Mailbox** cmdlet in the Exchange Management Shell to remove a mailbox user from AD and mark the mailbox for deletion. To remove the user Jeff Smith (logon name = jeff.smith) in the octavius.net domain, you could run the following command in the Exchange Management Shell:

Remove-Mailbox –Identity 'octavius.net\jeff.smith'

The Exchange Management Shell allows for additional options when removing users. For example, to remove the mailbox immediately from the mailbox database without waiting the default time period of 30 days, you can append **–Permanent $true** to the Remove-Mailbox command.

 RECONNECT A MAILBOX

GET READY. Turn on the computer, and log in as the Administrator user account. Close any windows that appear on the desktop.

1. Click **Start**, **All Programs**, **Microsoft Exchange Server 2007**, and then click **Exchange Management Console**. The Exchange Management Console window appears.

2. In the console tree pane, expand **Recipient Configuration** and highlight **Disconnected Mailbox**.

3. In the result pane, select the appropriate mailbox and click **Connect** in the action pane. The Connect Mailbox window appears as shown in Figure 5-20.

Figure 5-20

Connecting a Disconnected
Mailbox

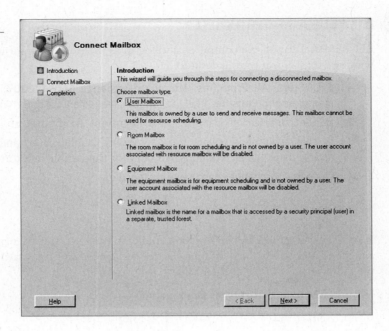

4. Select the type of mailbox that you wish to reconnect. To reconnect a user mailbox, ensure that **User Mailbox** is selected and click **Next**. The Mailbox Settings
   page appears as shown in Figure 5-21.

Figure 5-21

Specifying Mailbox Settings

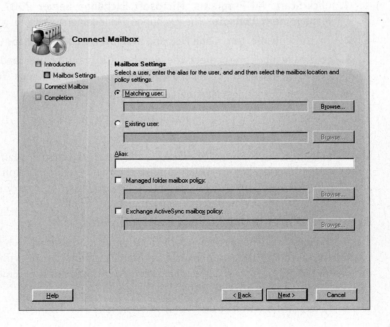

5. If you wish to reconnect the mailbox to an AD user of the same name, select
   Matching user, click **Browse**, select the user account in the Select User window, and
   click **OK**. Alternatively, to reconnect the mailbox to a different AD user, select **Existing
   user**, click **Browse**, select the user account in the Select User window, and click **OK**.

6. Ensure that the correct alias is listed in the Alias dialog box. You can optionally
   specify a managed folder or ActiveSync policy by selecting the associated checkboxes in Figure 5-21 and clicking the related **Browse** buttons to select them.

7. Click **Next**. The Connect Mailbox page appears.

8. Click **Connect**. The Completion page appears.

9. Click **Finish** to close the Connect Mailbox window.

10. Close the Exchange Management Console.

THE COMMAND LINE WAY

You can also use the **Connect-Mailbox** cmdlet in the Exchange Management Shell to reconnect a mailbox. Before you reconnect a mailbox using the Exchange Management Shell, you must first obtain the GUID for the appropriate mailbox on the Mailbox role server by running the following command within the Exchange Management Shell on the Mailbox role server:

Get-MailboxStatistics | Where {$_.DisconnectDate -ne $null} | format-list

Next, you can locate the value in the **MailboxGuid** field for the appropriate disconnected mailbox and use it alongside the **Connect-Mailbox** cmdlet. For example, to reconnect the mailbox for Jeff Smith (MailboxGuid = 390fa663-db30-46b3-adf4-0dc752fb4e6s) within the Mailbox Database in the First Storage Group on the Mailbox role server exch1.octavius.net to the AD user Jeff Smith (logon name = jeff.smith) with an alias of jeff.smith, you could run the following command in the Exchange Management Shell:

Connect-Mailbox –Identity '390fa663-db30-46b3-adf4-0dc752fb4e6s' -Database 'exch1 .octavius.net\First Storage Group\Mailbox Database' –User 'octavius.net\jeff.smith' –Alias 'jeff.smith'

■ Working with Mail Users and Mail Contacts

THE BOTTOM LINE

For users within your organization who do not require a mailbox hosted on an Exchange server, you can create mail users or mail contacts to represent them so that they can participate in your Exchange infrastructure. Because mail users and mail contacts often represent external email recipients, they are configured to forward email to an external email server. In addition to configuring mailbox users, Exchange administrators must understand how to configure mail users and mail contacts in any Exchange organization.

CERTIFICATION READY?
Configure recipients.
2.1

Creating Mail Users and Mail Contacts

You can create mail users and mail contacts within the Exchange Management Console or the Exchange Management Shell. As with creating mailbox users, you can choose to create a new mail user or mail enable an existing AD user account. Similarly, you can create a new mail contact or mail enable an existing AD contact.

Nearly all organizations employ external members who are contracted to provide essential services within the organization, yet are employed directly by another organization. Often, these external members do not require a mailbox in your organization because they already have a mailbox on an email server within their home organization.

Because email is often a primary form of communication between all members of an organization regardless of whether they are directly employed or not, it is important to accommodate external members within your Exchange infrastructure.

TAKE NOTE*

Only create mail users if the contract member requires an AD user account to access network resources. If the contract member does not require an AD user account, you can create a mail contact to represent them.

If external members require access to network resources, you will need to create AD user accounts for them as well as grant permissions to the appropriate resources for their user accounts. However, instead of creating mailboxes for these users within your organization, you can create email addresses for them that are used to forward email to their organization's email server. User accounts that are used to provide email forwarding in this scenario are called *mail users*.

Alternatively, if external members will not require access to network resources or the ability to authenticate to the domains in your AD forest, you can simply create a *mail contact* for them that contains an email address used to identify them within the organization. When email is sent to the mail contact, Exchange will simply forward it to the external organization's email server.

Regardless of whether you create a mail contact or mail user, you must specify the external email address for the user as well as an alias that will be used to create an email address for the member within the organization. For example, if you create a mail contact or mail user in the octavius.net domain for Kelly Armstrong using an alias of kelly.armstrong and specifying the external email address of karmstrong@mips-in.com, then the mail contact or mail user for Kelly Armstrong will have a primary email address of karmstrong@mips-in.com, secondary email address of kelly.armstrong@octavius.net, and an external email address of karmstrong@ mips-in.com. Other users within the organization will quickly find kelly.armstrong when searching for email addresses within their domain using their email client programs. However, when email is sent to kelly.armstrong@octavius.net, it is simply forwarded to karmstrong@ mips-in.com using external email relay.

By default, when you create a new mail user, an associated AD user is created as well. Alternatively, you can choose to mail enable an existing AD user account to create a new mail user. This is appropriate for organizations with separate AD and Exchange administrators and administrative duties.

Similarly, when you create a new mail contact, an associated AD contact object is created as well. If your organization separates AD and Exchange administrative duties, you can choose to mail enable an existing AD contact object that another administrator has created to create a new mail contact.

 CREATE A MAIL USER

GET READY. Turn on the computer, and log in as the Administrator user account. Close any windows that appear on the desktop.

1. Click **Start**, **All Programs**, **Microsoft Exchange Server 2007**, and then click **Exchange Management Console**. The Exchange Management Console window appears.
2. In the console tree pane, expand **Recipient Configuration** and highlight **Mail Contact**.
3. In the action pane, click **New Mail User**. The New Mail User window appears as shown in Figure 5-22.

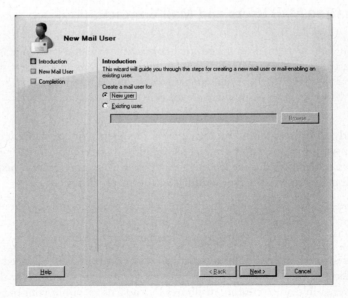

4. If you wish to create a new AD user that is mail enabled, ensure that **New user** is selected. Alternatively, you can choose to mail enable an existing AD user. To mail enable an existing user, select **Existing user**, click the **Browse** button, select the appropriate user in the Select User window that appears, and click **OK**.
5. Click **Next**. If you selected New user on the previous screen, you will be prompted to specify the AD user account information as shown in Figure 5-23.

Figure 5-23

Adding Mail User Information

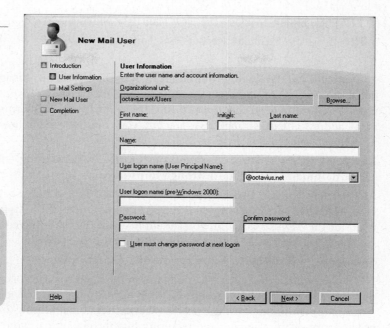

6. By default, the user will be created in the default Users folder in your current
domain. Because users are rarely created in this folder, you should click **Browse**,
select the appropriate OU, and click **OK**. All other account settings on this page
are similar in function to the settings that you choose when creating a new user
account in the Active Directory Users and Computers console as discussed in Lesson 2.
When finished entering the user account information, click **Next**. The Mail Settings
page appears as shown in Figure 5-24.

Figure 5-24

Adding Mail User Settings

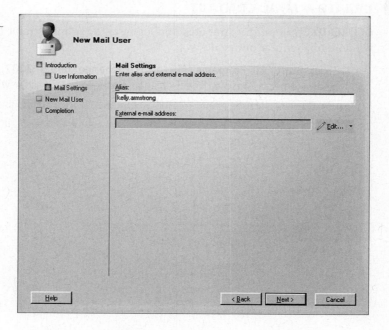

7. At the Mail Settings page, ensure that the **Alias** dialog box contains the recipient
name that should appear in the email address. For example, in Figure 5-24, the
email address for the user will be kelly.armstrong@domain.

8. Click **Edit** next to the External email address dialog box, type in the external SMTP
email address for the mail user in the SMTP Address window that appears and click **OK**.

9. Click **Next**. The New Mail User page appears.

10. Review the summary of your settings and click **New**. The Completion page appears.

11. Click **Finish** to close the New Mail User window.

12. Close the Exchange Management Console.

THE COMMAND LINE WAY

You can also use the **Enable-Mailbox** cmdlet in the Exchange Management Shell to mail enable an existing AD user. For example, to mail enable the Kelly Armstrong user in the East OU of the octavius.net domain and specify an alias of kelly.armstrong and external email address of karmstrong@mips-in.com, you could run the following command in the Exchange Management Shell:

Enable-MailUser –Identity 'octavius.net/East/Kelly Armstrong' –Alias 'kelly.armstrong' –ExternalEmailAddress 'karmstrong@mips-in.com'

Alternatively, you can create a new mail user and associated AD user account using the **New-MailUser** cmdlet within the Exchange Management Shell. To specify an initial password for the AD user account, you should first run the following command within the Exchange Management Shell and supply the appropriate password when prompted:

$password = Read-Host 'Enter password' –AsSecureString

Next, you can run the following command in the Exchange Management Shell to create the mail user and AD user account for Kelly Armstrong (alias and logon name = kelly .armstrong) within the East OU in the octavius.net domain, using an external email address of karmstrong@mips-in.com and requiring that the default password supplied earlier be changed on the next logon:

New-MailUser -Name 'Kelly Armstrong' -FirstName 'Kelly' -LastName 'Armstrong' –DisplayName 'Kelly Armstrong' -OrganizationalUnit 'octavius.net/East' –UserPrincipalName 'kelly.armstrong@octavius.net' -Password $password -ResetPasswordOnNextLogon $true –ExternalEmailAddress 'karmstrong@mips-in.com'

CREATE A MAIL CONTACT

GET READY. Turn on the computer, and log in as the Administrator user account. Close any windows that appear on the desktop.

1. Click **Start**, **All Programs**, **Microsoft Exchange Server 2007**, and then click **Exchange Management Console**. The Exchange Management Console window appears.

2. In the console tree pane, expand **Recipient Configuration** and highlight **Mail Contact**.

3. In the action pane, click **New Mail Contact**. The New Mail Contact window appears as shown in Figure 5-25.

Figure 5-25

Creating a New Mail Contact

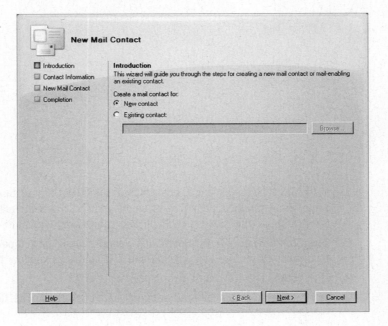

4. If you wish to create a new AD contact object that is mail enabled, ensure that **New contact** is selected. Alternatively, you can choose to mail enable an existing AD contact object. To mail enable an existing contact object, select **Existing contact**, click the **Browse** button, select the appropriate user in the Select Contact window that appears, and click **OK**.

5. Click **Next**. The Contact Information page appears as shown in Figure 5-26.

Figure 5-26

Adding Contact Information

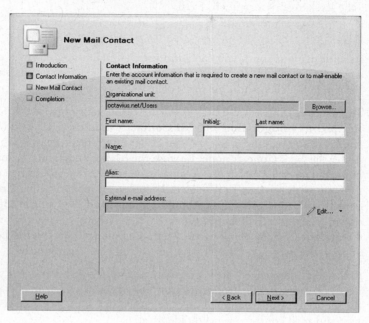

TAKE NOTE *

If you selected **Existing contact** in Figure 5-25, you will only be allowed to change the alias and external email address information shown in Figure 5-26.

6. If you chose New contact in Figure 5-25, the mail contact will be created in the default Users folder in your current domain. Because objects are rarely created in this folder, you should click **Browse**, select the appropriate OU, and click **OK**. For a new contact, you should also enter the name information for the contact.

7. Ensure that the **Alias** dialog box contains the recipient name that should appear in the email address. For example, if the alias is kelly.armstrong, the email address for the mail contact will be kelly.armstrong@domain.

8. Click **Edit** next to the External e-mail address dialog box, type in the external SMTP email address for the mail contact in the SMTP Address window that appears, and click **OK**.

9. Click **Next**. The New Mail Contact page appears.

10. Review the summary of your settings and click **New**. The Completion page appears.

11. Click **Finish** to close the New Mail Contact window.

12. Close the Exchange Management Console.

You can also use the **Enable-MailContact** cmdlet in the Exchange Management Shell to mail enable an existing contact object within AD. For example, to mail enable the Kelly Armstrong contact object in the East OU of the octavius.net domain and specify an alias of kelly.armstrong and external email address of karmstrong@mips-in.com, you could run the following command in the Exchange Management Shell:

Enable-MailContact –Identity 'octavius.net/East/Kelly Armstrong' -Alias 'kelly .armstrong' –ExternalEmailAddress 'karmstrong@mips-in.com'

THE COMMAND
LINE WAY

Alternatively, you can use the **New-MailContact** cmdlet to create a new mail contact. For example to create a mail contact for Kelly Armstrong (alias = kelly.armstrong) within the East OU in the octavius.net domain using an external email address of karmstrong@ mips-in.com, you could run the following command in the Exchange Management Shell:

New-MailContact -Name 'Kelly Armstrong' -FirstName 'Kelly' -LastName 'Armstrong' -OrganizationalUnit 'octavius.net/East' -Alias 'kelly.armstrong' -ExternalEmailAddress 'karmstrong@mips-in.com'

Configuring Mail Users and Mail Contacts

Because mail users and mail contacts do not have mailboxes within the organization, there are fewer configuration options for them compared to mailbox users. Like mailbox users, the configuration of mail users and mail contacts is performed using the properties of the recipient object in the Exchange Management Console or the appropriate cmdlet within the Exchange Management Shell.

As with mailbox users, you can administer all mail users and mail contacts within your organization provided you are a member of the Exchange Organization Administrator or Exchange Recipient Administrator role.

To view all mail users and mail contacts within your organization, you can navigate to **Recipient Configuration > Mail Contact** within the Exchange Management Console. As with viewing mailbox users, you can also create filters to narrow the list of objects displayed under the Mail Contact node. Because the Mail Contact node contains both mail user and mail contact recipient objects, you should create a filter to display only the types of objects that you wish to view. To display only mail users, you can click **Create Filter** in the detail pane, specify **Recipient Type Details Equals Mail User** in the appropriate expression drop-down boxes, and click **Apply Filter**. Alternatively, to display only mail contacts, you can click **Create Filter** in the detail pane, specify **Recipient Type Details Equals Mail Contact** in the appropriate expression drop-down boxes, and click **Apply Filter**.

Once you have located the appropriate mail user or mail contact, you can highlight it in the detail pane and select **Properties** from the action pane to view its properties. The properties for the Kelly Armstrong mail user are shown in Figure 5-27; however, the properties of a mail user and mail contact are nearly identical.

Figure 5-27

Mail User Properties

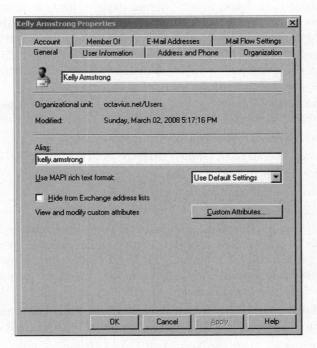

Like the General tab of mailbox user properties, the General tab in the properties of a mail user or mail contact displays the location of the AD object as well as allows you to change the alias, hide the object from email address lists, and create up to 15 custom attributes for use when searching for objects or creating dynamic distribution groups. However, instead of displaying mailbox information, the General tab in the properties of a mail user or mail contact allows you to control whether the mail user or mail contact can send emails from a MAPI client within the organization using rich text format by selecting **Always** or **Never** in the associated drop-down box.

Both mail users and mail contacts have Address and Phone, Organization, and Member Of tabs that contain information about the mail user. Mail users also have User Information and Account tabs that contain information from AD regarding the associated user account. Similarly, mail contacts have a Contact Information tab that lists information regarding the AD contact object. The information from these tabs is taken from the existing AD user or contact object if the object was mail enabled, but must be entered manually if the mail user or mail contact was created by Exchange.

The E-Mail Addresses tab for a mail user or mail contact lists the primary external email address as well as the internal secondary email address generated using the alias. In Figure 5-28, the Kelly Armstrong mail user has an external SMTP email address of karmstrong@mips-in .com that is marked as the primary address so that emails sent by the mail user contain karmstrong@mips-in.com within the From field of the email. Because the mail user was created in the octavius.net domain, a secondary email address of kelly.armstrong@mips-in.com was generated from the alias to allow internal users to quickly locate and send mail to the mail user.

Figure 5-28

Configuring Mail User Email Addresses

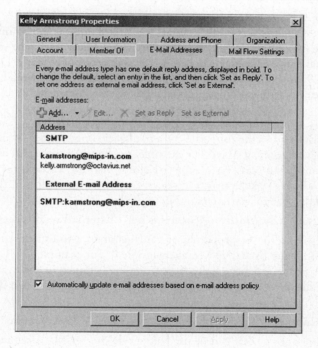

As with mailbox users, you can add additional email addresses to the E-Mail Addresses tab of a mail user or mail contact as well as change the alias. However, you cannot remove the external email address. If the external email address needs to be changed, you can highlight it and click the **Edit** button to modify it.

Because mail users and mail contacts do not have mailboxes, there are no Mailbox Settings or Mailbox Features tabs as seen in the properties of a mailbox user. In addition, the Mail Flow Settings tab of a mail user or mail contact can only be used to limit message size and delivery as shown in Figure 5-29.

Figure 5-29

Configuring Mail Flow Settings

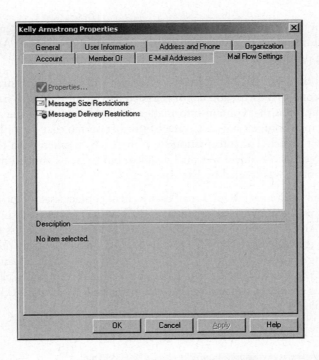

If you access the properties of Message Size Restrictions as shown in Figure 5-29, you can specify the maximum size for messages received by your Exchange servers for forwarding to the external email address. By accessing the properties of Message Delivery Restrictions in Figure 5-29, you can specify allowed senders for a mail user or mail contact. These settings are identical to those specified for a mailbox user as shown earlier in Figure 5-15.

THE COMMAND LINE WAY

You can also modify the properties of a mail user using the **Set-MailUser** cmdlet within the Exchange Management Shell. For example, to change the external email address to kellya@ mips-in.com for the existing mail user Kelly Armstrong in the octavius.net domain (internal email address = kelly.armstrong@octavius.net), you could run the following command within the Exchange Management Shell:

Set-MailUser 'kelly.armstrong@octavius.net' –ExternalEmailAddress 'kellya@mips-in.com'

Similarly, to modify the properties of a mail contact, you can use the **Set-MailContact** cmdlet within the Exchange Management Shell. For example, to change the display name to Kelly Armstrong for the Kelly Armstrong mail contact in the octavius.net domain (internal email address = kelly.armstrong@octavius.net), you could run the following command within the Exchange Management Console:

Set-MailContact 'kelly.armstrong@octavius.net' –DisplayName 'Kelly Armstrong'

To see more options that can be used alongside the Set-MailUser and Set-MailContact cmdlets, search for Set-MailUser and Set-MailContact within Exchange Server 2007 Help.

To view the settings that you have configured for a mail user, you can use the **Get-MailUser** cmdlet. Similarly, the **Get-MailContact** cmdlet can be used to view settings for a mail contact. For example, the following command within the Exchange Management Shell lists the properties of the Kelly Armstrong mail user described earlier:

Get-MailUser 'kelly.armstrong@octavius.net' | format-list

Managing Mail Users and Mail Contacts

As with mailbox users, you can disable or remove mail users and mail contacts. These tasks can be done using the Exchange Management Console, the Active Directory Users and Computers console, or the appropriate cmdlets within the Exchange Management Shell.

Unlike mailbox users, you cannot grant Send As permission or Full Access permission to a mail user or mail contact. However, you can disable or remove a mail user and mail contact in much the same way you would disable or remove a mailbox user.

If you disable a mail user, all Exchange-related properties within the AD user account are removed, but the user account is not removed from AD. In general, you should disable mail users if users within your organization no longer need to contact the mail user, yet the AD account must still exist for domain authentication.

Similarly, if you disable a mail contact, the Exchange-related properties within the AD contact object are removed, but the contact object is not deleted.

Alternatively, if you choose to remove a mail user or mail contact, the associated AD user account or contact object is removed completely. This option is often used when the contract for a mail user or mail contact has expired. Because mail users and mail contacts do not have associated mailboxes, you can also remove them by deleting their objects directly in the Active Directory Users and Computers console.

 DISABLE A MAIL USER OR MAIL CONTACT

GET READY. Turn on the computer, and log in as the Administrator user account. Close any windows that appear on the desktop.

1. Click **Start, All Programs, Microsoft Exchange Server 2007**, and then click **Exchange Management Console.** The Exchange Management Console window appears.

2. In the console tree pane, expand **Recipient Configuration** and highlight **Mail Contact.**

3. In the result pane, select the appropriate mail user or mail contact and click **Disable** in the action pane. When prompted to confirm the action, click **Yes.**

4. Close the Exchange Management Console.

THE COMMAND LINE WAY

You can also use the **Disable-MailUser** cmdlet in the Exchange Management Shell to disable a mail user. To disable Kelly Armstrong (internal email address kelly.armstrong@ octavius.net), you could run the following command in the Exchange Management Shell:

Disable-MailUser 'kelly.armstrong@octavius.net'

Similarly, you can use the **Disable-MailContact** cmdlet in the Exchange Management Shell to disable a mail contact. To disable Kelly Armstrong (internal email address kelly.armstrong@ octavius.net), you could run the following command in the Exchange Management Shell:

Disable-MailContact 'kelly.armstrong@octavius.net'

 REMOVE A MAIL USER OR MAIL CONTACT

GET READY. Turn on the computer, and log in as the Administrator user account. Close any windows that appear on the desktop.

1. Click **Start, All Programs, Microsoft Exchange Server 2007**, and then click **Exchange Management Console.** The Exchange Management Console window appears.

2. In the console tree pane, expand **Recipient Configuration** and highlight **Mail Contact.**

3. In the result pane, select the appropriate mail user or mail contact and click **Remove** in the action pane. When prompted to confirm the action, click **Yes.**

4. Close the Exchange Management Console.

You can also use the **Remove-MailUser** cmdlet in the Exchange Management Shell to remove a mail user from AD. To remove the user Kelly Armstrong (logon name = kelly .armstrong) in the octavius.net domain, you could run the following command in the Exchange Management Shell:

Remove-MailUser –Identity 'octavius.net\kelly.armstrong'

Similarly, you can use the **Remove-MailContact** cmdlet in the Exchange Management Shell to remove a mail contact from AD. To remove the contact Kelly Armstrong (logon name = kelly.armstrong) in the octavius.net domain, you could run the following command in the Exchange Management Shell:

Remove-MailContact –Identity 'octavius.net\kelly.armstrong'

■ Working with Mail-Enabled Groups

THE BOTTOM LINE

Mail-enabled groups are used to streamline the sending of email to multiple recipients within an organization. As a result, you should create mail-enabled groups after deploying a new Exchange organization and as organizations grow and change over time. In addition, you should understand how to manage and configure mail-enabled groups to ensure that they reflect the needs of users and the organization.

CERTIFICATION READY?
Configure mail-enabled groups.
2.2

Working with Mail-Enabled Universal Groups

Mail-enabled universal groups are simply universal security or distribution groups that have an email address and contain other recipient objects as members. You can create, configure, and manage them using the Exchange Management Console and Exchange Management Shell.

CREATING MAIL-ENABLED UNIVERSAL GROUPS

Creating mail-enabled groups simplifies and organizes the sending of email to multiple recipients. Nearly all organizations are made up of several different departments, teams, projects, and business units. By creating mail-enabled groups to represent these entities and adding the appropriate mailbox users, mail users, and mail contacts to these groups, you can enhance the productivity of the users within your organization. For example, when these users need to communicate to all the members of a specific department, they could send an email to the mail-enabled group for that department. All members of the department will receive a copy of the email message and can reply to it individually.

TAKE NOTE*

In general, it is considered good form to create mail-enabled groups within your organization to represent even the smallest groups of users who share the same function, location, or job role. This allows for the greatest flexibility when sending emails.

You can create security groups and distribution groups within AD that have global, domain local, or universal scope. Security groups may be assigned permissions and rights to network resources, whereas distribution groups cannot. Exchange Server 2007 allows you to mail enable both security groups and distribution groups, however, these groups must have universal scope. If you create a *mail-enabled universal security group*, it can be used to assign permissions and rights to network resources as well as to send email to a group of recipient objects. However, if you create a *mail-enabled universal distribution group*, it can only be used when sending email to a group of recipient objects. In general, you should create mail-enabled universal security groups if the members within the group require the same access to network resources. This allows administrators to use the mail-enabled universal security groups to simplify the assignment of permissions on resources. If the mail-enabled groups should only be used by Exchange, you should create them as mail-enabled universal distribution groups.

Mail-enabled universal security and distribution groups can contain any recipient object other than dynamic distribution groups. This includes other universal security and distribution groups.

To save administration, you can create and mail enable a new universal security or distribution group within the Exchange Management Console. Alternatively, you can choose to mail-enable an existing universal security or distribution group that was created previously. As with creating other recipient objects, you must specify an appropriate alias for the group object during creation that will be used to generate the email address that others will use when contacting group members.

 ### CREATE A MAIL-ENABLED UNIVERSAL GROUP

GET READY. Turn on the computer, and log in as the Administrator user account. Close any windows that appear on the desktop.

1. Click **Start**, **All Programs**, **Microsoft Exchange Server 2007**, and then click **Exchange Management Console**. The Exchange Management Console window appears.

2. In the console tree pane, expand **Recipient Configuration** and highlight **Distribution Group**.

3. In the action pane, click **New Distribution Group**. The New Distribution Group window appears as shown in Figure 5-30.

Figure 5-30

Creating a New Universal Distribution Group

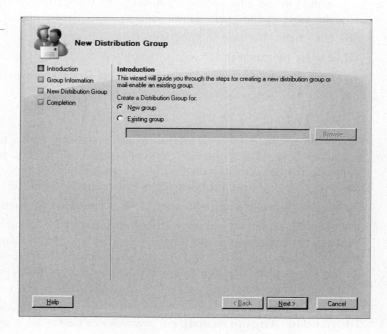

4. If you wish to create a new universal group that is mail enabled, ensure that **New group** is selected. Alternatively, you can choose to mail enable an existing universal group. To mail enable an existing universal group, select **Existing group**, click the **Browse** button, select the appropriate universal security or distribution group in the Select Group window that appears, and click **OK**.

5. Click **Next**. The Group Information page appears as shown in Figure 5-31.

Figure 5-31

Specifying Group Information

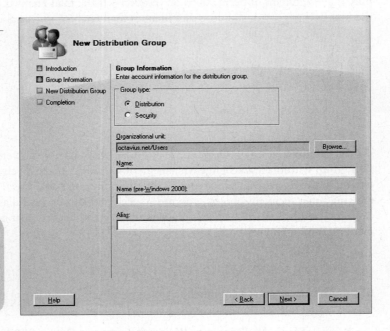

TAKE NOTE *

If you selected **Existing group** in Figure 5-30, you will only be allowed to change the alias field shown in Figure 5-31.

6. If you chose New group in Figure 5-30, the universal group will be created in the default Users folder in your current domain. Because objects are rarely created in this folder, you should click **Browse**, select the appropriate OU, and click **OK**. For a new universal group you should select the appropriate type (**Distribution** or **Security**) as well as supply an appropriate name in the **Name** dialog boxes.

7. Ensure that the **Alias** dialog box contains the appropriate group name that should appear in the email address. Normally, for simplicity and organization, the alias is the same as the group name.

8. Click **Next**. The New Distribution Group page appears.

9. Review the summary of your settings and click **New**. The Completion page appears.

10. Click **Finish** to close the New Distribution Group window.

11. Close the Exchange Management Console.

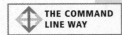

You can also use the **Enable-DistributionGroup** cmdlet in the Exchange Management Shell to mail enable an existing universal group object within AD. For example, to mail enable the Marketing universal group in the East OU of the octavius.net domain and specify an alias of marketing, you could run the following command in the Exchange Management Shell:

Enable-DistributionGroup –Identity 'octavius.net/East/Marketing' –Alias 'marketing'

Alternatively, you can use the **New-DistributionGroup** cmdlet to create a new mail contact. For example to create a new mail-enabled universal distribution group called Marketing in the East OU of the octavius.net domain with a Pre-Windows 2000 name of Marketing and an alias of marketing, you could run the following command in the Exchange Management Shell:

New-DistributionGroup –Name 'Marketing' –SamAccountName 'Marketing' –Type 'Distribution' –OrganizationalUnit 'octavius.net/East' –Alias 'marketing'

CONFIGURING MAIL-ENABLED UNIVERSAL GROUPS

Mail-enabled groups are displayed under the **Recipient Configuration** > **Distribution Group** node within the Exchange Management Console and can be administered by members of the Exchange Organization Administrator or Exchange Recipient Administrator role.

If your organization has several mail-enabled groups, you can create a filter to narrow the list of objects displayed under the Distribution Group node. To display only mail-enabled universal security groups, you can click **Create Filter** in the detail pane, specify **Recipient Type Details Equals Mail-Enabled Universal Security Group** in the appropriate expression drop-down boxes, and click **Apply Filter**. Alternatively, to display only mail-enabled universal distribution groups, you can click **Create Filter** in the detail pane, specify **Recipient Type Details Equals Mail-Enabled Universal Distribution Group** in the appropriate expression drop-down boxes, and click **Apply Filter**.

Once you have located the appropriate mail-enabled universal group, you can highlight it in the detail pane and select **Properties** from the action pane to view its properties. The properties options of mail-enabled universal security groups that you can configure are identical to the properties options of a mail-enabled universal distribution group. The properties of the Marketing mail-enabled universal group are shown in Figure 5-32.

Figure 5-32

Universal Distribution Group
Properties

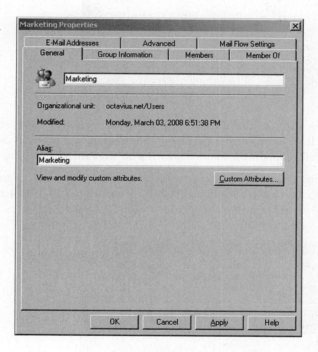

The General tab in the properties of a mail-enabled universal group displays the location of the AD object as well as allows you change the alias and create up to 15 custom attributes for use when searching for the mail-enabled universal group or creating dynamic distribution groups.

The E-Mail Addresses tab of a mail-enabled universal group lists the primary email address for the group that was automatically generated using the alias. As with other recipient objects, you can create additional email addresses for a mail-enabled universal group.

In addition, the Mail Flow Settings tab of a mail-enabled universal group is identical to the Mail Flow Settings of a mail user or mail contact. You can specify the maximum size for incoming messages that are forwarded to the mail-enabled universal group as well as specify allowed senders for the mail-enabled universal group.

Because a mail-enabled universal group can be a member of other groups, the property sheet has a Member Of tab that lists the groups that contain the mail-enabled universal group. However, this list is not modifiable because group membership can only be changed on the parent group. To add members to your mail-enabled universal group or remove existing members, you can use the Members tab shown in Figure 5-33.

Figure 5-33

Configuring Members

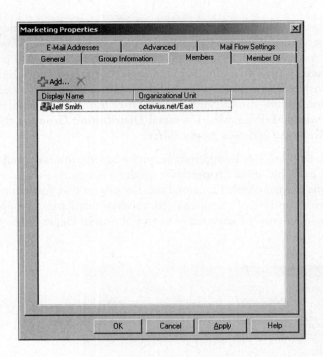

After a new mail-enabled universal group has been created, there are no members by default. However, if you mail-enable an existing universal group, the mail-enabled universal group will automatically contain the mail recipients who were members of the group beforehand.

After adding members to your mail-enabled universal group, it is good form to enter a description for your group that will be displayed when a MAPI client such as Outlook or Entourage views the group's properties as shown in Figure 5-34.

Figure 5-34

Configuring Group Information

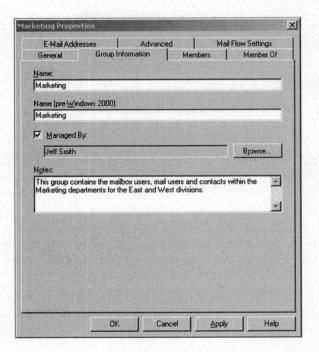

You can also select a recipient to act as the ***group manager***. The group manager is typically the person who is responsible for the operation of the department or team within the organization that the group represents. If mail sent to a mail-enabled universal group is rejected by one of its members, a nondelivery report is generated and sent to the sender by default. For mail-enabled universal groups that have several members, there is a greater possibility that the sender will receive multiple nondelivery reports. To prevent this, you can force nondelivery reports to be sent to the group manager by selecting **Send delivery reports to group manager** on the Advanced tab of mail-enabled universal group properties as shown in Figure 5-35. The group manager can then contact the Exchange administrator to investigate delivery problems.

Figure 5-35

Specifying Advanced
Distribution Group Information

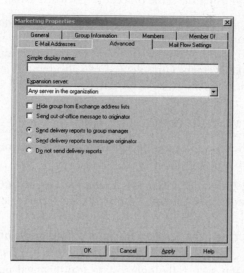

You can specify a display name on the Advanced tab to be used in delivery reports as well as hide the group from address lists and prevent the sender from receiving out-of-office messages from group members.

The *expansion server* is the Exchange server that is responsible for looking up the group membership within AD before routing email addressed to the group. By default, the nearest Hub role server provides this function, but you can choose a specific expansion server in the drop-down box in Figure 5-35.

THE COMMAND LINE WAY

You can add members to a mail-enabled universal group using the **Add-Distribution GroupMember** cmdlet and remove existing members using the **Remove-DistributionGroup Member** cmdlet. For example, to add Kelly Armstrong (email address kelly.armstrong@octavius .net) as a member of the Marketing mail-enabled universal group (email address = marketing@ octavius.net), you could run the following command within the Exchange Management Console:

Add-DistributionGroupMember –Identity 'marketing@octavius.net' –Member 'kelly .armstrong@octavius.net'

You can also modify the properties of a mail-enabled universal group using the **Set-Distribution Group** cmdlet within the Exchange Management Shell. For example, to change the display name to Marketing Group for the Marketing mail-enabled universal group within the octavius .net domain (email address = marketing@octavius.net), you could run the following command within the Exchange Management Console:

Set –DistributionGroup –Identity 'marketing@octavius.net' –DisplayName 'Marketing Group'

To see more options that can be used alongside the Set-DistributionGroup cmdlet, search for Set-DistributionGroup within Exchange Server 2007 Help.

To view the properties that you have configured for a mail-enabled universal group, you can use the **Get-DistributionGroup** cmdlet. For example, the following command within the Exchange Management Shell lists the properties of the Marketing distribution group:

Get-DistributionGroup –Identity 'marketing@octavius.net' | format-list

MANAGING MAIL-ENABLED UNIVERSAL GROUPS

To prevent a mail-enabled universal group from being used to relay mail to its members, you can simply disable it. Disabling a mail-enabled universal group will remove all Exchange-related properties within the AD universal group account, but the universal group, its membership list, and its members are not removed. After disabling a mail-enabled universal group, you can mail enabled it again using the same procedure discussed earlier in this lesson.

Alternatively, if you choose to remove a mail-enabled universal group, the universal group is removed completely from AD. If you need to recreate the mail-enabled universal group in the future, you will need to add the appropriate members again. Although they can be removed within the Exchange Management Console, you can also remove mail-enabled universal groups by deleting their objects in the Active Directory Users and Computers console.

 DISABLE A MAIL-ENABLED UNIVERSAL GROUP

GET READY. Turn on the computer, and log in as the Administrator user account. Close any windows that appear on the desktop.

1. Click **Start**, **All Programs**, **Microsoft Exchange Server 2007**, and then click **Exchange Management Console.** The Exchange Management Console window appears.
2. In the console tree pane, expand **Recipient Configuration** and highlight **Distribution Group.**
3. In the result pane, select the appropriate mail-enabled universal group and click **Disable** in the action pane. When prompted to confirm the action, click **Yes.**
4. Close the Exchange Management Console.

THE COMMAND LINE WAY

You can also use the **Disable-DistributionGroup** cmdlet in the Exchange Management Shell to disable a mail-enabled universal group. To disable the Marketing mail-enabled universal group (email address = marketing@octavius.net), you could run the following command in the Exchange Management Shell:

Disable-DistributionGroup 'marketing@octavius.net'

 REMOVE A MAIL-ENABLED UNIVERSAL GROUP

GET READY. Turn on the computer, and log in as the Administrator user account. Close any windows that appear on the desktop.

1. Click **Start**, **All Programs**, **Microsoft Exchange Server 2007**, and then click **Exchange Management Console.** The Exchange Management Console window appears.
2. In the console tree pane, expand **Recipient Configuration** and highlight **Distribution Group.**
3. In the result pane, select the appropriate mail-enabled universal group and click **Remove** in the action pane. When prompted to confirm the action, click **Yes.**
4. Close the Exchange Management Console.

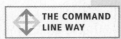
THE COMMAND LINE WAY

You can also use the **Remove-DistributionGroup** cmdlet in the Exchange Management Shell to remove a mail-enabled universal group. To remove the Marketing mail-enabled universal group (email address = marketing@octavius.net), you could run the following command in the Exchange Management Shell:

Remove-DistributionGroup 'marketing@octavius.net'

Working with Dynamic Distribution Groups

Dynamic distribution groups are better suited for sending email to multiple users if the list of users changes frequently. Unlike universal distribution groups, dynamic distribution groups use criteria to populate their membership when email is relayed to them. To work with dynamic distribution groups, you must understand how to create, configure, and manage them using the Exchange Management Console and the appropriate cmdlets within the Exchange Management Shell.

CREATING DYNAMIC DISTRIBUTION GROUPS

While mail-enabled universal groups simplify the sending of email to multiple recipients, their membership needs to be managed manually. This works well for mail-enabled universal groups that have a fixed membership. However, some organizational groups may have a membership that changes frequently. For these groups, creating and maintaining the membership of the associated mail-enabled universal groups can be time consuming.

For divisions, teams, and other entities within your organization that do not have a fixed membership, you can create a mail-enabled *dynamic distribution group*. Dynamic distribution groups automatically populate their group membership when they are used to relay email by searching AD for recipient objects that match certain criteria. These criteria are specified when you create the group and consist of two components:

- *Conditions* that match the value of an attribute within the recipient object such as Department or Custom Attribute 5
- A *filter* that specifies the location within AD that will be searched for recipient objects as well as the types of recipients to search for (contacts, mailbox users, etc.)

Say, for example, that you need to create a mail-enabled group that contains all of the full-time staff members who are part of the TASU project within the East Marketing department. In addition, your organization creates mailbox users for all full-time staff and stores the project name within the first Custom Attribute within each mailbox user. To perform this task, you could create a dynamic distribution group that specifies conditions that match the mail-enabled users within the East OU (and all subordinate OUs) whose Department attribute equals 'Marketing' and Custom Attribute 1 attribute equals 'TASU.' When email is sent to this group, Exchange performs a search for the appropriate mailbox users and forwards the email to each member.

Unlike other recipient objects, you only create a mail-enabled dynamic distribution group using Exchange tools. The alias that you specify for the mail-enabled dynamic distribution group will be used to generate the email address that others will use when contacting members of the dynamic distribution group.

 CREATE A DYNAMIC DISTRIBUTION GROUP

GET READY. Turn on the computer, and log in as the Administrator user account. Close any windows that appear on the desktop.

1. Click **Start, All Programs, Microsoft Exchange Server 2007**, and then click **Exchange Management Console**. The Exchange Management Console window appears.
2. In the console tree pane, expand **Recipient Configuration** and highlight **Distribution Group**.
3. In the action pane, click **New Dynamic Distribution Group**. The New Dynamic Distribution Group window appears as shown in Figure 5-36.

Figure 5-36

Creating a New Dynamic
Distribution Group

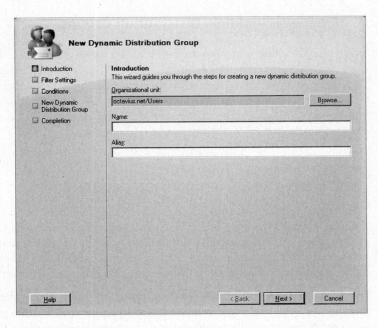

4. By default, the dynamic distribution group will be created in the default Users folder in your current domain. Because objects are rarely created in this folder, you should click **Browse**, select the appropriate OU, and click **OK**.

5. Next, supply an appropriate name for the dynamic distribution group in the **Name** dialog box as well as an appropriate alias used to generate the email address in the **Alias** dialog box. Normally the alias is the same as the group name for simplicity and organization.

6. Click **Next**. The Filter Settings page appears as shown in Figure 5-37.

Figure 5-37

Adding Filter Settings

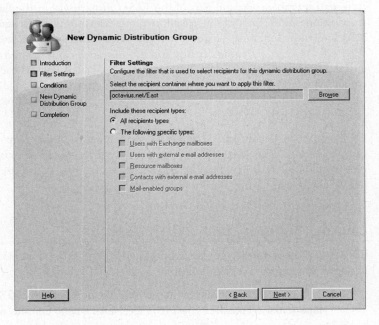

7. Click **Browse**. In the Select Organizational Unit window that appears, select the appropriate domain or OU that the dynamic distribution group will use when searching for recipients and click **OK**.

8. If you wish to restrict the types of recipient objects that the distribution group will apply to, select **The following specific types** and select the appropriate recipient types to include.

9. Click **Next**. The Conditions page appears as shown in Figure 5-38.

Figure 5-38

Adding Conditions

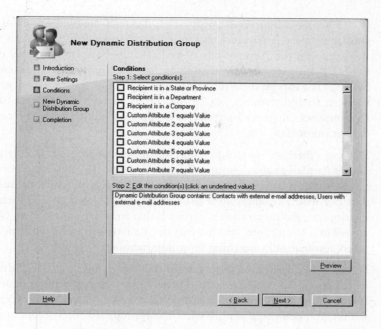

10. Select the recipient object attributes that the dynamic distribution group will match when searching for group members. Each attribute that you select will add a condition to the Step 2 dialog box. To add a value for each attribute, you must click **specified** within the condition that was added to the Step 2 dialog box, type in the appropriate value in the window that appears, click **Add,** and then click **OK**.

11. To test your settings by searching for the recipient objects that match your filter and conditions, you can click **Preview** in Figure 5-38 and review the information shown in the Dynamic Distribution Group Preview window. When finished reviewing the results, click **OK** to close the Dynamic Distribution Group Preview window.

12. Click **Next**. The New Dynamic Distribution Group page appears.

13. Review the summary of your settings and click **New**. The Completion page appears.

14. Click **Finish** to close the New Dynamic Distribution Group window.

15. Close the Exchange Management Console.

THE COMMAND LINE WAY

You can use the **New-DynamicDistributionGroup** cmdlet to create a new dynamic distribution group. For example, to create a new dynamic distribution group called External Marketing Members (alias = ext-marketing) within the Groups OU of the octavius.net domain that contains mail users and mail contacts within the Marketing department of the octavius.net domain, you could run the following command in the Exchange Management Shell:

New-DynamicDistributionGroup –Name 'External Marketing Members' –Alias 'ext-marketing' –OrganizationalUnit 'octavius.net/Groups' -IncludedRecipients 'MailUsers, MailContacts' –ConditionalDepartment 'Marketing' –RecipientContainer 'octavius.net'

To see more options that can be used alongside the New-DynamicDistributionGroup cmdlet, search for New-DynamicDistributionGroup within Exchange Server 2007 Help.

CONFIGURING DYNAMIC DISTRIBUTION GROUPS

As with mail-enabled universal groups, dynamic distribution groups are stored under the **Recipient Configuration** > **Distribution Group** node within the Exchange Management Console and can be administered by members of the Exchange Organization Administrator or Exchange Recipient Administrator role. To display only dynamic distribution groups under this node, you can click **Create Filter** in the detail pane, specify **Recipient Type Details Equals Dynamic Distribution Group** in the appropriate expression drop-down boxes, and click **Apply Filter**. Once you have located the appropriate mail-enabled universal group, you can highlight it in the detail pane and select **Properties** from the action pane to view its properties.

If you have configured the properties of a mail-enabled universal group, you will find similar properties within a dynamic distribution group. You can view the location of the group on the General tab as well as change the alias and set custom attributes. The E-Mail Addresses tab can be used to add additional email addresses, and the Mail Flow Settings tab can be used to set the maximum size for messages as well as specify allowed senders. In addition, on the Advanced tab you can add a group description to the Group Information tab as well as select a group manager that may be configured to receive delivery reports.

However, there are some differences between the properties of a dynamic distribution group and other mail-enabled groups. Because dynamic distribution groups cannot be a member of other group objects, there is no Member Of tab. Similarly, because the membership of a dynamic distribution group is not statically set, there is no Members tab. Instead, dynamic distribution groups contain a Filter tab that specifies the recipient object types and locations as well as a Conditions tab that lists the attributes that the dynamic distribution will match when automatically searching for group members.

Figure 5-39 displays the Filter tab for the Marketing-East-TASU dynamic distribution group, which applies to mailbox-enabled users within the East OU of the octavius.net domain. If this group needs to include additional recipient object types or apply to a different OU within AD, you could simply select the appropriate object types or click **Browse** and select a different OU.

Figure 5-39

Modifying Filter Settings

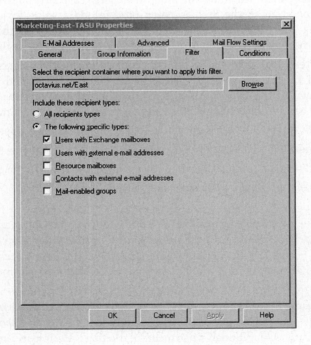

The Conditions tab of the Marketing-East-TASU dynamic distribution group shown in Figure 5-40 further specifies that recipient object members must have a Department attribute equal to Marketing as well as Custom Attribute 1 equal to TASU. To change the value of existing attributes, click on the related blue hyperlink in the Step 2 section and modify the value. For example, to modify the department in Figure 5-40, you would click on the **Marketing** hyperlink and supply a different value or add additional values. Alternatively, you can select additional attributes in the Step 1 section and modify the value in the Step 2 section in the same manner.

Figure 5-40

Modifying Configuration Settings

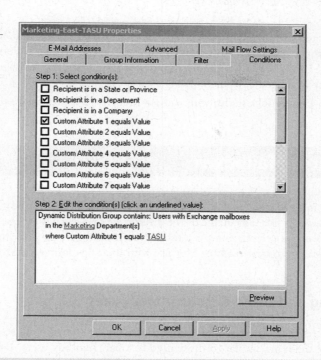

You can also modify the properties of a dynamic distribution group using the **Set-DynamicDistributionGroup** cmdlet within the Exchange Management Shell. For example, to add an additional condition to the Marketing-East-TASU dynamic distribution group that requires the Custom Attribute 2 to have a value of Chicago, you could run the following command within the Exchange Management Console:

Set-DynamicDistributionGroup –Identity 'Marketing-East-TASU' –Conditional CustomAttribute2 'Chicago'

To see more options that can be used alongside the Set-DynamicDistributionGroup cmdlet, search for Set-DynamicDistribution Group within Exchange Server 2007 Help.

To view the settings that you have configured for a dynamic distribution group, you can use the **Get-DynamicDistributionGroup** cmdlet. For example, the following command within the Exchange Management Shell lists the properties of the Marketing-East-TASU distribution group:

Get-DynamicDistributionGroup –Identity 'Marketing-East-TASU' | format-list

MANAGING DYNAMIC DISTRIBUTION GROUPS

Because dynamic distribution groups can only be created using Exchange tools, you cannot disable a dynamic distribution group and later mail enable it. Instead, to prevent the dynamic distribution group from being used, you must remove it entirely. If you need to recreate the same dynamic distribution group in the future, you will need to specify the appropriate filter and conditions again.

 REMOVE A DYNAMIC DISTRIBUTION GROUP

GET READY. Turn on the computer, and log in as the Administrator user account. Close any windows that appear on the desktop.

1. Click **Start**, **All Programs**, **Microsoft Exchange Server 2007**, and then click **Exchange Management Console**. The Exchange Management Console window appears.

2. In the console tree pane, expand **Recipient Configuration** and highlight **Distribution Group**.

3. In the result pane, select the appropriate dynamic distribution group and click **Remove** in the action pane. When prompted to confirm the action, click **Yes**.

4. Close the Exchange Management Console.

THE COMMAND LINE WAY

You can also use the **Remove-DynamicDistributionGroup** cmdlet in the Exchange Management Shell to remove a dynamic distribution group. To remove the Marketing-East-TASU dynamic distribution group, you could run the following command in the Exchange Management Shell:

Remove-DynamicDistributionGroup –Identity 'Marketing-East-TASU'

■ Working with Resource Mailboxes

↓ **THE BOTTOM LINE**

Many organizations deploy MAPI clients such as Outlook and Entourage. These clients are typically used to take advantage of the groupware features within Exchange Server 2007 such as advanced calendaring. As a result, you should become accustomed to the procedures used to create resource mailboxes for use with the calendaring features of MAPI clients.

CERTIFICATION READY?
Configure resource mailboxes.
2.3

Creating and Using Resource Mailboxes

Because resource mailboxes are similar in structure to mailbox users, the procedures used to create them are similar to those used to create mailbox users. Once created, Outlook and Entourage users can use them to hold information used to schedule a room or equipment resource. As with mailbox users, you can use the Exchange Management Console and Exchange Management Shell to create them.

Many organizations today take advantage of the calendaring features within Outlook and Entourage to schedule and manage meetings among email recipients. In a typical scenario, a user will send a new meeting request within Outlook or Entourage to other mail recipients within the organization that lists the time and locations of the meeting. The mail recipients can then choose to accept the meeting details, reject the meeting details, or propose an alternative time. Depending on the choices made within meeting requests, time will automatically be scheduled for each email recipient within the Calendar section of Outlook or Entourage. Additional meeting requests can be sent to change the details of a scheduled meeting or cancel it.

Exchange Server 2007 allows you to create recipient objects to represent rooms or equipment that can also be scheduled within a meeting request. These recipient objects are called *resource mailboxes*. When you create a new meeting request within Outlook or Entourage, you can click the **To** button to select recipient objects that should attend the meeting as well as the resources that the meeting will need as shown in Figure 5-41.

Figure 5-41

Adding Resources to a Meeting Request

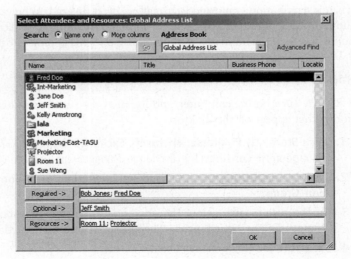

In Figure 5-41, the Resources dialog box contains two resource mailboxes to represent the need for Room 11 and a projector during the meeting. After selecting the appropriate recipient objects and resource mailboxes, the meeting request will list any room or equipment resource mailboxes within the Location field of the meeting request as shown in Figure 5-42. If the resource mailboxes listed within the email have *Automatic Booking* enabled, the sender will receive immediate notification if the room or equipment resources are already booked for that time when they click Send as shown in Figure 5-42. The sender can then reschedule the meeting as necessary.

Figure 5-42

Scheduling Resources in a Meeting Request

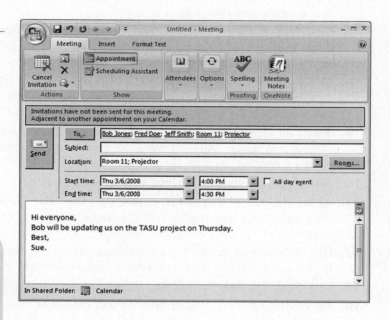

 **ANOTHER WAY**

Instead, add a resource mailbox to the **Required** or **Optional** dialog boxes shown in Figure 5-41. These resource mailboxes will then appear alongside other recipient objects within the **To** field shown in Figure 5-42.

Resource mailboxes are simply mailbox users with a disabled user account in AD and an associated mailbox within a mailbox database on a Mailbox role server within your organization to store meeting information. Because resource mailboxes do not represent users, it is considered good form to create a separate OU for them within your AD domain to allow for organization and quick access.

The process of creating a resource mailbox is nearly identical to that of creating a mailbox user. However, after the creation of a new resource mailbox, the corresponding user account in AD is disabled to prevent logons or mail retrieval. In addition, if you wish to use an existing user account within AD for the resource mailbox, that user account must first be disabled.

Before you create resource mailboxes, you should first create a naming convention for the rooms and equipment within your organization to allow for easy location within Outlook or Entourage. For example, your organization may use a naming convention of BuildingLocation-RoomNumber for rooms and BuildingLocation-Department-EquipmentName for equipment. Thus, Fairway204 could refer to room 204 within the building on Fairway Road, whereas Weber-Accounting-Epson2350Projector would refer to the associated Epson model 2350 projector within the Accounting department on Weber Street.

 CREATE A RESOURCE MAILBOX

GET READY. Turn on the computer, and log in as the Administrator user account. Close any windows that appear on the desktop.

1. Click **Start, All Programs, Microsoft Exchange Server 2007**, and then click **Exchange Management Console**. The Exchange Management Console window appears.

2. In the console tree pane, expand **Recipient Configuration** and highlight **Mailbox**.

3. In the action pane, click **New Mailbox**. The New Mailbox window appears as shown earlier in Figure 5-1.

4. To create a resource mailbox that represents a room number, select **Room Mailbox**. Alternatively, you can select **Equipment Mailbox** to create a resource mailbox that represents equipment or devices.

5. Click **Next**. The User Type page appears as shown earlier in Figure 5-2.

6. If you wish to create a resource mailbox alongside a new disabled AD user account, ensure that **New user** is selected. Alternatively, you can choose to use an existing AD user when creating a resource mailbox. To do this, select **Existing users**, click the **Add** button, select the appropriate user in the Select User window that appears, and click **OK**.

7. Click **Next**. If you selected New user on the User Type page, you will be prompted to specify the AD user account information on the User Information page as shown earlier in Figure 5-3.

8. By default, the user will be created in the default Users folder in your current domain. If you wish to store resource mailboxes in a different container, click **Browse**, select the appropriate OU, and click **OK**.

9. Supply an appropriate name in the Name dialog box as well as the two User logon name dialog boxes. Normally, the same name is used for all three dialog boxes. No other information need be supplied on this page.

10. Click **Next**. The Mailbox Settings page appears as shown earlier in Figure 5-4.

11. At the Mailbox Settings page, ensure that the **Alias** dialog box contains the same name that was specified in the Name dialog box on the User Information page.

12. Click **Browse** next to the Mailbox database dialog box, select the Mailbox database in the Select Mailbox Database window that appears and click **OK**.

13. Click **Next**. The New Mailbox page appears.

14. Review the summary of your settings and click **New**. The Completion page appears.

15. Click **Finish** to close the New Mailbox window.

16. Close the Exchange Management Console.

THE COMMAND LINE WAY

The **Enable-Mailbox** cmdlet in the Exchange Management Shell can also be used to create a resource mailbox from an existing disabled user account within AD. To create a room resource mailbox using the existing Room8 user in the East OU of the octavius .net domain, with an alias of Room8 and a mailbox within the Mailbox Database in the First Storage Group on the server EXCH1, you could run the following command in the Exchange Management Shell:

Enable-Mailbox –Identity 'octavius.net/East/Room8' –Alias 'Room8' –Database 'EXCH1\First Storage Group\Mailbox Database' –Room

Alternatively, to create a resource mailbox and associated AD user, you can use the **New-Mailbox** cmdlet. For example, to create an equipment resource mailbox with a Name, Logon Name, and Alias of 3M-Projector within the East OU of the octavius.net domain and create an associated mailbox in the Mailbox Database within the First Storage Group on the server EXCH1, you could run the following command in the Exchange Management Shell:

New-Mailbox –Name '3M-Projector' –Alias '3M-Projector' –UserPrincipalName '3M-Projector@octavius.net' –SamAccountName '3M-Projector' –OrganizationalUnit 'octavius.net/East' –Database 'EXCH1\First Storage Group\Mailbox Database' –Equipment

Configuring Resource Mailboxes

Although resource mailboxes contain the same properties as a regular mailbox user, most options are not configured because resource mailboxes are not used to gain access to the Exchange infrastructure. Instead, you typically configure resource information, automatic booking, and resource booking policies for use by others who schedule a resource using the resource mailbox. Although some of this configuration can be performed in the properties of the resource mailbox in the Exchange Management Console, most of it must be configured using cmdlets within the Exchange Management Shell.

CONFIGURING RESOURCE MAILBOX PROPERTIES

Because resource mailboxes are mailbox users, you can configure them under the **Recipient Configuration** > **Mailbox** node within the Exchange Management Console. Additionally, you can create a filter to narrow the list displayed in this node to specific room or equipment resource mailboxes only. Simply click **Create Filter** in the detail pane, specify **Recipient Type Details Equals Room Mailbox** or **Recipient Type Details Equals Equipment Mailbox** in the appropriate expression drop-down boxes, and click **Apply Filter**. Once you have located the appropriate resource mailbox, you can highlight it in the detail pane and select **Properties** from the action pane to view its properties.

The properties for a resource mailbox contain the same tabs as a mailbox user. However, because resource mailboxes are not used in the same manner as a mailbox user, the information on these tabs is not configured for a resource mailbox. Instead, resource mailboxes contain an additional Resource Information tab that can be used to list additional room or equipment attributes that will help users choose the appropriate resource when scheduling meetings. The Resource Information tab shown in Figure 5-43 indicates that Room 11 has a capacity of 16 seats and contains a projector, wireless network access, and a whiteboard.

Figure 5-43

Configuring Resource Information

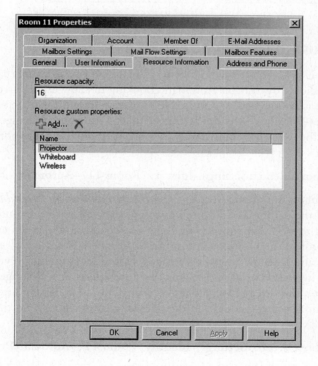

Before you can add custom properties to the Resource Information tab shown in Figure 5-43, you must create custom properties within the AD schema using the **Set-ResourceConfig** cmdlet in the Exchange Management Shell. For example, to create the Projector, Whiteboard, and Wireless custom properties for use with room resource mailboxes using the dc01.octavius. net DC, you could run the following command within the Exchange Management Shell:

Set-ResourceConfig –DomainController dc01.octavius.net –ResourcePropertySchema ('Room/Projector', 'Room/Whiteboard', 'Room/Wireless')

Although custom properties are often used to provide extra information for room resource mailboxes, you can create custom properties for equipment resource mailboxes by specifying **Equipment** in place of **Room** in the previous command. If you wish to create additional custom properties later on, you must also specify the existing properties alongside the Set-ResourceConfig command. Otherwise they will be overwritten.

When Outlook or Entourage users select resource mailboxes to add to a meeting request, they will see the capacity and custom properties under the Capacity and Description field of the selection dialog box as shown in Figure 5-44.

Figure 5-44

Viewing Resource Information

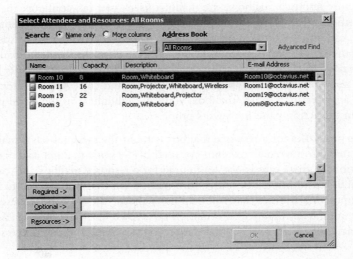

CONFIGURING AUTOMATIC BOOKING

In addition to adding capacity information and custom attributes to a new resource mailbox, you should also enable Automatic Booking to allow users to receive notification when a resource is double booked. To enable Automatic Booking on a resource mailbox, you must use the **Set- MailboxCalendarSettings** cmdlet within the Exchange Management Shell. For example, the following command will enable Automatic Booking on the Room 11 resource mailbox:

Set-MailboxCalendarSettings -Identity 'Room 11' –Automate –Processing:AutoAccept

After enabling Automatic Booking, the **Resource Booking Attendant** in Exchange Server 2007 will then automatically attempt to book the associated resources when a user sends a meeting request that contains resource mailboxes and return an error if the resource is already booked. In addition, Automatic Booking enables the **Calendar Attendant**, which automatically schedules meetings tentatively in a user's calendar even if the user is not currently logged on or accessing email using Outlook or Entourage. To turn off Automated Booking on the Room 11 mailbox, yet still allow the Calendar Attendant to run on the resource mailbox, you could run the following command within the Exchange Management Shell:

Set-MailboxCalendarSettings –Identity 'Room 11' –AutomateProcessing:AutoUpdate

Alternatively, to disable both the Resource Booking Attendant and Calendar Attendant components of Automatic Booking on the Room 11 resource mailbox, you can run the following command within the Exchange Management Shell:

Set-MailboxCalendarSettings –Identity 'Room 11' –AutomateProcessing:None

CONFIGURING RESOURCE BOOKING POLICIES

The **Set-MailboxCalendarSettings** cmdlet in Exchange Server 2007 may also be used to create *resource booking policies* that specify which users can automatically book a resource within a meeting request using Automatic Booking. There are three main types of policies that can be applied to users within your organization:

- In Policy
- Out Policy
- Book-In Policy

Users who are defined in an *In Policy* can request a resource, but the request must be approved by a delegate on the resource mailbox before the resource is booked for the time specified in the meeting request. To add jeff.smith@octavius.net and bob.doe@octavius.net to an In Policy for the Room 11 resource mailbox, you can run the following command within the Exchange Management Shell:

Set-MailboxCalendarSettings –Identity 'Room 11' –RequestInPolicy 'jeff.smith@octavius .net', 'bob.doe@octavius.net'

Alternatively, you could apply an In Policy to all users using the following command within the Exchange Management Shell:

Set-MailboxCalendarSettings –Identity 'Room 11' –AllRequestInPolicy:$true

Next, you can specify a delegate for the Room 11 resource mailbox with the ability to approve resource booking requests. This delegate can add the calendar for the resource mailbox to his own Exchange account within Outlook or Entourage and allow or deny booking requests. To set the delegate on the Room 11 resource mailbox to Billy Martin, you could run the following command within the Exchange Management Shell:

Set-MailboxCalendarSettings –Identity 'Room 11' –ResourceDelegates 'Billy Martin'

Alternatively, you can add users to an *Out Policy*. Users who are defined in an Out Policy can automatically book a resource without a delegate provided that there are no resource conflicts. If there is a resource conflict, the request is forwarded to the delegate for approval. To add jeff.smith@octavius.net and bob.doe@octavius.net to an Out Policy for the Room 11 resource mailbox, you can run the following command within the Exchange Management Shell:

Set-MailboxCalendarSettings -Identity 'Room 11' -RequestOutPolicy 'jeff.smith@ octavius.net', 'bob.doe@octavius.net'

Or you can instead apply an Out Policy to all users using the following command within the Exchange Management Shell:

Set-MailboxCalendarSettings –Identity 'Room 11' –AllRequestOutPolicy:$true

To allow the automatic booking of available resources without using a delegate, you can add those users to a *Book-In Policy*. To add jeff.smith@octavius.net and bob.doe@octavius.net to a Book-In Policy for the Room 11 resource mailbox, you can run the following command within the Exchange Management Shell:

Set-MailboxCalendarSettings –Identity 'Room 11' –BookInPolicy 'jeff.smith@octavius .net', 'bob.doe@octavius.net'

Alternatively, you could apply a Book-In Policy to all users using the following command within the Exchange Management Shell:

Set-MailboxCalendarSettings –Identity 'Room 11' –AllBookInPolicy:$true

To view the resource booking policy and Automatic Booking settings that you have configured for a resource mailbox, you can use the **Get-MailboxCalendarSettings** cmdlet. To view the settings for the Room 11 resource mailbox as a list, you can run the following command within the Exchange Management Shell:

Get-MailboxCalendarSettings –Identity 'Room 11' | format-list

➕ **MORE INFORMATION**

To see more options that can be used alongside the Set-MailboxCalendarSettings cmdlet to restrict users who schedule resources using resource mailboxes, search for Set-MailboxCalendarSettings within Exchange Server 2007 Help.

Managing Resource Mailboxes

Because resource mailboxes are similar in structure to mailbox users, the procedures and utilities used to manage them are identical.

Because resource mailboxes are simply mailbox users, the procedures and cmdlets used to manage them are identical to those used to manage mailbox users. Although you can grant the Send As and Full Access permissions for a resource mailbox, doing so will give unnecessary permissions to the resource mailbox and, as a result, is seldom done.

As with mailbox users, when you disable a resource mailbox, the associated user account is not deleted and the mailbox is marked for deletion. Similarly, when you delete a resource mailbox, the associated user account in AD is removed and the mailbox is marked for deletion. You can also reconnect the mailbox at a later time to an existing or new user account.

To perform these actions, refer to the procedures and cmdlets described within the "Managing Mailbox Users" section earlier in this lesson.

■ Moving Mailboxes

 THE BOTTOM LINE

There are a variety of different situations that will require the moving of mail boxes between Exchange servers within your organization or to other organizations. Understanding the procedures and utilities used to move mailboxes are key to performing as an Exchange administrator.

CERTIFICATION READY?
Move mailboxes.
2.5

As an Exchange administrator, you will be required to move mailboxes between mailbox databases, storage groups, and servers to meet a variety of different needs. When a user in one department relocates to another department, you may need to move the user's mailbox to a Mailbox role server in the other department to ensure fast email access. In addition, you may need to move mailboxes to provide load balancing for Mailbox access as your organization grows or to comply with structural change within the organization such as the combining of two departments. You can move mailboxes that are connected to mailbox users, linked mailbox users as well as resource mailboxes.

Although you can move mailboxes using the Exchange Management Console, the Exchange Management Shell allows you to specify more options when moving mailboxes. To move a mailbox, you must be a member of the Exchange Recipient Administrator role as well as a member of Exchange Server Administrator role and local Administrators group on the source and target Mailbox role servers at minimum.

After moving a mailbox, CAS role servers will automatically connect to the correct mailbox when providing access to email. However, the first time users access their mailboxes using OWA, they will need to wait several minutes while the OWA message table is rebuilt using the new mailbox location.

Moving Mailboxes Using the Exchange Management Console

If you need to move a small number of mailboxes within the same Exchange organization, the Exchange Management Console can provide a quick and easy-to-use interface.

By default, the Exchange Management Console allows you to move mailboxes with the same Exchange organization and AD forest only. The Exchange Management Console also allows mailboxes to be moved between Exchange servers within your organization running Exchange 2000 or Exchange Server 2003.

You can also move multiple mailboxes at the same time within the Exchange Management Console provided that they are to be moved to the same destination. To do this, you can navigate to **Recipient Configuration** > **Mailbox** and select the appropriate users while holding down the **Ctrl** key before selecting the **Move Mailbox** action. Alternatively, you can select a range of users by holding down the **Shift** key while selecting the first and last user.

After the move operation has completed, you should see the new mailbox location listed on the General tab of mailbox user properties as shown earlier in Figure 5-6.

 MOVE MAILBOXES USING THE EXCHANGE MANAGEMENT CONSOLE

GET READY. Turn on the computer, and log in as the Administrator user account. Close any windows that appear on the desktop.

1. Click **Start, All Programs, Microsoft Exchange Server 2007**, and then click **Exchange Management Console**. The Exchange Management Console window appears.

2. In the console tree pane, expand **Recipient Configuration** and highlight **Mailbox**.

3. In the result pane, select the appropriate mailbox(es) and click **Move Mailbox** in the action pane. The Move Mailbox window appears as shown in Figure 5-45.

Figure 5-45

Moving a Mailbox

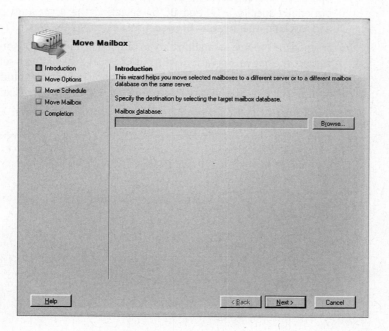

4. Click **Browse**, select the destination mailbox database in the Select Mailbox Database window and click **OK**. Click **Next** when finished. The Move Options page appears as shown in Figure 5-46.

Figure 5-46

Specifying Move Options

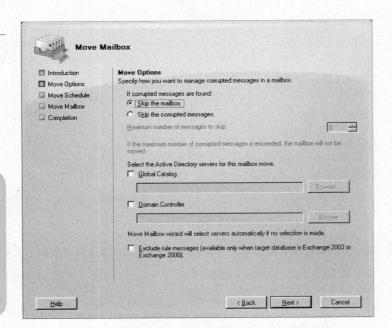

TAKE NOTE*

If you are moving a large mailbox, you must ensure that the mailbox does not exceed the storage limits on the target mailbox database. If it does, the move operation will fail.

5. By default, the move will fail if corrupted messages are detected in the mailbox during the move operation. Alternatively, you can select **Skip the corrupted messages** and specify the number of corrupted messages that you will skip before the move operation fails in the associated dialog box. Because a large number of corrupted messages usually indicate problems with the mailbox itself, you should keep this number to 10 or less.

6. The GC and DC used to provide and modify object information during the move operation are selected by default using the site information stored in AD. You can optionally specify a GC and DC by selecting the associated checkboxes in Figure 5-46 and clicking the related **Browse** buttons to select them.

7. If you are moving a mailbox to a target Exchange 2000 or Exchange Server 2003 server, the move operation will fail if you have mailbox settings that take up more than 32 KB of space. As a result, you should select **Exclude rule messages** to avoid problems if the destination server is not running Exchange Server 2007.

8. Click **Next**. The Move Schedule page appears as shown in Figure 5-47.

Figure 5-47

Scheduling a Move Operation

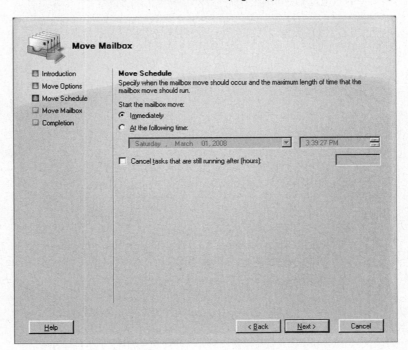

TAKE NOTE *

If you schedule a move operation, the Move Mailbox window remains open at the Move Mailbox page until the specified time is reached. If you want to move other mailboxes during this time, you must open another instance of the Exchange Management Console.

9. By default, the move operation will start immediately following the wizard. To schedule the move to occur at a different time, select **At the following time** and select the appropriate time from the drop-down boxes. Although the amount of time it takes to move a mailbox is large for larger mailboxes, network and service problems may pause a move operation indefinitely. To prevent this, you can click **Cancel tasks that are still running after (hours)** and supply the number of hours before a move operation is cancelled in the associated dialog box.

10. Click **Next**. The Move Mailbox page appears.

11. Click **Move**. Once the move operation has completed, the Completion page appears.

12. Click **Finish** to close the Move Mailbox window.

13. Close the Exchange Management Console.

Moving Mailboxes Using the Exchange Management Shell

To move several mailboxes, move mailboxes between forests, or perform advanced move operations, you must use the Move-Mailbox cmdlet within the Exchange Management Shell.

As with the Exchange Management Console, the Exchange Management Shell allows you to move mailboxes within your organization. However, the Exchange Management Shell can also be used to move mailboxes between forests and Exchange organizations as well as set advanced options for moving a mailbox.

To move mailboxes using the Exchange Management Shell, you can use the **Move-Mailbox** cmdlet. For example, to move the mailbox for Jeff Smith (email address = jeff.smith@ octavius.net) to the Mailbox Database in the Third Storage Group on the server exch2.octavius .net within the same Exchange organization, you can use the following command within the Exchange Management Shell:

Move-Mailbox 'jeff.smith@octavius.net' –TargetDatabase 'exch2.octavius.net\Third Storage Group\Mailbox Database'

By default, this mailbox move will assume the default values for all other move options that were specified when moving a mailbox using the Exchange Management Console. However, you can append options to the **Move-Mailbox** cmdlet to override these defaults as well as specify additional move options. Table 5-2 lists the most common options to the **Move-Mailbox** cmdlet.

Table 5-2

Common Move-Mailbox options

RECIPIENT OBJECTS	DESCRIPTION
-BadItemLimit 'n'	Specifies that the move operation will fail only after encountering more than *n* corrupted messages in the source mailbox.
-IgnoreRuleLimitErrors	Ignores mailbox rules during the move operation. This option can only be applied if the destination mailbox is on an Exchange 2000 or Exchange Server 2003 computer.
-GlobalCatalog 'FQDN'	Specifies that the global catalog (GC) server used during the move operation should be FQDN. It this is not specified, a GC server within the same site will be chosen.
-DomainController 'FQDN'	Specifies that the Domain Controller used during the move operation should be FQDN. It this is not specified, a Domain Controller within the same site will be chosen.

(continued)

Table 5-2 (*continued*)

RECIPIENT OBJECTS	DESCRIPTION
-ConfigurationOnly	Changes the location of the Exchange server in the mailbox user without moving the mailbox. This option is only used if the mailbox database has been moved previously to another server without updating the mailbox user properties.
-PreserveMailboxSizeLimit	Prevents the source mailbox from inheriting the mailbox size limits from the destination mailbox database during the move operation.
-RetryInterval 'hh:mm:ss'	Specifies the interval used to display status information during the move operation using the format hours:minutes:seconds (hh:mm:ss).
-RetryTimeout 'hh:mm'	Specifies the amount of time allowed for a mailbox move operation before it automatically fails using the format hours:minutes (hh:mm).
-AttachmentFilename 'arg'	Specifies the attachments that are allowed during the move. Typically *arg* is a wildcard such as '*.txt' to specify attachments that have a txt extension. Multiple *arg* values are allowed provided they are separated by commas.
-ExcludeFolders 'arg'	Specifies the folders that should be excluded from the move operation. To exclude the folder called Work from the move operation, *arg* should be set to '\Work'. Multiple *arg* values are allowed provided they are separated by commas.
-IncludeFolders 'arg'	Specifies the folders that should be included in the move operation. To include the contents of the Inbox folder only during the move operation, *arg* should be set to '\Inbox'. Multiple *arg* values are allowed provided they are separated by commas.
-Locale 'arg'	Specifies the locale of messages that should be included in the move operation.
-ContentKeywords 'arg'	Specifies the keywords that must be present in the message body or attachments for the message to be moved to the target mailbox. Multiple *arg* values are allowed provided they are separated by commas.
-SubjectKeywords 'arg'	Specifies the keywords that must be present in the message subject for the message to be moved to the target mailbox. Multiple *arg* values are allowed provided they are separated by commas.
-AllContentKeywords 'arg'	Specifies the keywords that must be present in the message subject, body, or attachments for the message to be moved to the target mailbox. Multiple *arg* values are allowed provided they are separated by commas.
-StartDate 'mm/dd/yyyy'	Specifies the earliest date for emails that should be included in the move operation using the format month/day/year (mm/dd/yyyy).
-EndDate 'mm/dd/yyyy'	Specifies the latest date for emails that should be included in the move operation using the format month/day/year (mm/dd/yyyy).

Thus, to move items newer than August 15, 2008, within the mailbox for Jeff Smith described in the previous example while preserving the original mailbox size limits and ensuring that five corrupted messages can be skipped before the move operation fails, you could run the following command within the Exchange Management Shell:

Move-Mailbox 'jeff.smith@octavius.net' –TargetDatabase 'exch2.octavius.net\Third Storage Group\Mailbox Database' –BadItemLimit'5' –PreserveMailboxSizeLimit -StartDate '08/15/2008'

You can also move a mailbox to another forest using the Exchange Management Shell. However, the **Move-Mailbox** cmdlet must be run from the target forest. To perform the move operation, you must also be a member of the Exchange Recipient Administrator role in both forests as well as a member of Exchange Server Administrator role and local Administrators group on the source and target Mailbox role servers at minimum.

Before running the **Move-Mailbox** cmdlet, you should create a variable within the Exchange Management Shell to store the credentials of the appropriate user in the source and target forests. To do this, you can enter the following commands within the Exchange Management Shell:

$SourceCredential = Get-Credential

$TargetCredential = Get-Credential

Following each of these commands, you will be prompted to supply the appropriate account and password information. This information will be stored in the $SourceCredential and $TargetCredential variables.

Next, you can run the Move-Mailbox cmdlet from the target forest to perform the move operation. For example, to move the mailbox for the user Jeff Smith in the octavius.net domain to the Mailbox Database within the First Storage Group on exch1.arfa.com in the arfa.com domain, you could run the following command in the Exchange Management Shell on an Exchange server within the arfa.com forest:

Move-Mailbox –Target Database 'exch1.arfa.com\First Storage Group\Mailbox Database' –Identity 'jeff.smith@octavius.net' –DomainController dc15.arfa.com –GlobalCatalog dc15.arfa.com "SourceForestGlobalCatalog dc2.octavius.net –NTAccountOU –OU=North, DC=arfa, DC=com" –SourceForestCredential $SourceCredential -TargetForestCredential $TargetCredential

For the move operation, the DC and GC server used in the target forest is dc15.arfa.com and the GC server used in the source forest is dc2.octavius.net. If you do not specify the DC and GC servers for the target forest, they will be chosen automatically from the site information within AD in the target forest. However, the source forest GC server must always be specified for the move operation to be successful.

In addition, the **Move-Mailbox** command creates a disabled user account of the same name in the target forest within the OU that you specify with the -**NTAccountOU** parameter. If a target mailbox already exists, you can instead use the –**AllowMerge** parameter to merge the source and target mailboxes.

If a mailbox needs to be moved between forests, the user account is often moved to the target forest first using the *Active Directory Migration Tool (ADMT)* in order to preserve account settings and SIDs. If the source user account does not need to be used following the mailbox move, you can also append the –**SourceMailboxCleanupOptions DeleteSourceNTAccount** option to the **Move-Mailbox** cmdlet to remove the source mailbox and AD user account.

■ Implementing an Exchange Resource Forest

THE BOTTOM LINE

To consolidate several Exchange infrastructures or to provide additional security, many organizations deploy Exchange in a separate resource forest to serve the email needs of other forests that comprise your organization. Mailbox users within the Exchange resource forest are created as linked mailbox users to allow users in other forests access to Exchange. You should become familiar with the process used to create a resource forest as well as the procedures and utilities used to create and manage linked mailbox users in the event that you need to deploy or work with Exchange resource forests.

CERTIFICATION READY?
Configure recipients.
2.1

Creating an Exchange Resource Forest and Linked Mailbox Users

Exchange resource forests are created in the same manner as any other forest and connect to other forests using one-way trust relationships. After deploying a resource forest, you must create linked mailbox users to allow email access for users in other forests. Linked mailbox users are created in the Exchange resource forest using the Exchange Management Console or Exchange Management Shell in much the same way that you create mailbox users.

Some organizations must maintain several different forests to allow for different security, business, or schema requirements. These organizations can choose to implement a single forest for use with Exchange only. This forest is called an *Exchange resource forest* and will contain all the mailboxes for users within all forests of the organization. Furthermore, because these mailboxes are linked to the appropriate user accounts in each forest for email access, they are called *linked mailbox users*.

Consider the three forests and domains shown in Figure 5-48. The octavius.net and alphamiata.net forests contain user accounts and function like most other forests. The arfa.com Exchange resource forest contains mailboxes that are linked to the user accounts in the octavius.net and alphamiata.net forests. Because the arfa.com forest trusts both the octavius.net and alphamiata.net forests, user accounts in the octavius.net and alphamiata.net forests can access the Exchange servers in the arfa.com forest when sending and receiving email.

Figure 5-48

The arfa.com Exchange Resource Forest Structure

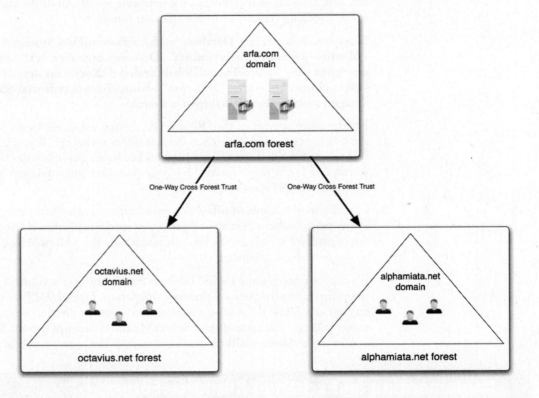

Linked mailbox users are simply mailbox users in an Exchange resource forest that have a disabled user account in the Exchange resource forest as well as a mailbox on a Mailbox role server in the Exchange organization for the Exchange resource forest. As a result, each user in the octavius.net and alphamiata.net forests shown in Figure 5-48 will have a matching user in the arfa.com forest that is disabled. Although users in the octavius.net and alphamiata .net forests can use an email client program to access their email from the Exchange servers in the arfa.com forest, they must supply the credentials for the user account in their own forest because the mailbox user that represents them in the arfa.com forest is disabled and only links to their user account in either the octavius.net or alphamiata.net forests.

The creation of forests and trust relationships were discussed earlier in Lesson 2, "Working with Active Directory."

To deploy an Exchange resource forest, you must ensure that one-way external or cross forest trusts are created so that the Exchange resource forest trusts all other forests. Next, you must create linked mailbox users in the Exchange resource forest that are linked to target user accounts in other trusted forests. These target user accounts are called *master accounts* and must be created in the target forest before a linked mailbox user is created in the Exchange resource forest.

CREATE A LINKED MAILBOX USER

GET READY. Turn on the computer in the Exchange resource forest, and log in as the Administrator user account. Close any windows that appear on the desktop.

1. Click **Start**, **All Programs**, **Microsoft Exchange Server 2007**, and then click **Exchange Management Console**. The Exchange Management Console window appears.

2. In the console tree pane, expand **Recipient Configuration** and highlight **Mailbox**.

3. In the action pane, click **New Mailbox**. The New Mailbox window appears as shown earlier in Figure 5-1.

4. Select **Linked Mailbox** and click **Next**. The User Type page appears as shown earlier in Figure 5-2.

5. If you wish to create a linked mailbox alongside a new disabled AD user account in the Exchange resource forest, ensure that **New user** is selected. Alternatively, you can choose to use an existing disabled AD user in the Exchange resource forest when creating a linked mailbox. To do this, select **Existing users**, click the **Add** button, select the appropriate user in the Select User window that appears, and click **OK**.

6. Click **Next**. If you selected New user on the User Type page, you will be prompted to specify information that will be used to create the disabled AD user account in the Exchange resource forest on the User Information page. Because the user account will be disabled, the password-related information is optional. For consistency and organization, the name information on this page should match the naming convention used for the AD user account in the target forest. For example, the information shown in Figure 5-49 will be used to create a user account for Adel Moore (logon name = adel.moore) in the arfa.com forest that will be later linked to the Adel Moore account in the octavius.net domain (logon name = adel.moore).

TAKE NOTE*

If you select **Existing users**, you will only be able to select existing users who are disabled within AD.

Figure 5-49

Creating a New Linked Mailbox User

New Mailbox

- [x] Introduction
- [x] User Type
- [x] User Information
- [ ] Mailbox Settings
- [ ] Master Account
- [ ] New Mailbox
- [ ] Completion

User Information
Enter the user name and account information.

Organizational unit:
| arfa.com/Octavius | Browse... |

First name: Adel   Initials: Last name: Moore

Name: Adel Moore

User logon name (User Principal Name):
adel.moore   @arfa.com

User logon name (pre-Windows 2000):
adel.moore

Password: ●●●●●●●●   Confirm password: ●●●●●●●●

- [ ] User must change password at next logon

Help   < Back   Next >   Cancel

TAKE NOTE*

If you selected **Existing users** on the User Type page, you will skip entering the account information on the User Information page shown in Figure 5-49.

7. By default, the user will be created in the default Users folder in the current domain of the Exchange resource forest. If you wish to store resource mailboxes in a different container, click **Browse**, select the appropriate OU and click **OK**. For organization, it is best to create OUs for each domain or forest that you will create linked mailbox users for. Because the target AD user account for Adel Moore is in the octavius.net domain, the Octavius OU was chosen as the location for the Adel Moore disabled AD user account in the arfa.com domain as shown in Figure 5-49.

8. Click **Next**. The Mailbox Settings page appears. Ensure that the **Alias** dialog box contains the alias that will be used to generate the email address for the linked mailbox user in the Exchange resource domain. The alias shown in Figure 5-50 for the Adel Moore linked mailbox user will generate an email address of adel.moore@ arfa.com.

Figure 5-50

Specifying Mailbox Settings

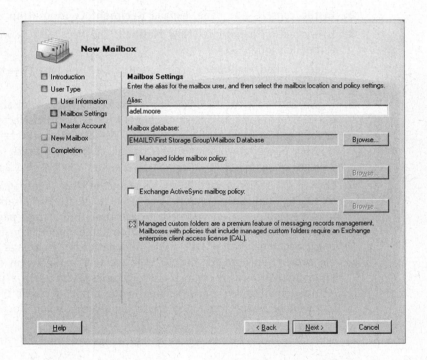

9. Click **Browse** next to the Mailbox database dialog box, select the appropriate Mailbox database in the Select Mailbox Database window that appears, and click **OK**.

10. If you have created a Managed folder mailbox policy or an ActiveSync mailbox policy that you wish to apply to the linked mailbox user, you can select the associated checkboxes in Figure 5-50 and click the related **Browse** buttons to select them.

11. Click **Next**. The Master Account page appears.

12. Click **Browse** next to the Trusted forest or domain dialog box, select the trusted domain that contains the target user account in the window that appears, and click **OK**. For the Adel Moore linked mailbox user described earlier, this domain is octavius.net as shown in Figure 5-51.

Figure 5-51

Specifying Master Account
Settings

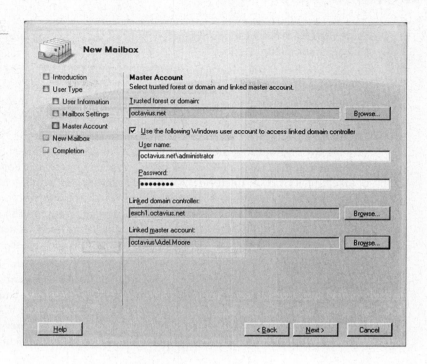

13. To ensure that the linked mailbox user is created successfully, you should select
Use the following Windows user account to access the linked domain controller
and specify the credentials of a user account in the target domain that is a member of the Domain Admins or Enterprise Admins group.

14. Click **Browse** next to the Linked domain controller dialog box, select a DC that is
in the same domain as the target user account in the window that appears, and
click **OK**.

15. Next, click **Browse** next to the Linked master account dialog box, select the target
user account in the window that appears, and click **OK**. For the Adel Moore linked
mailbox user, the Linked master account dialog box should display the octavius\
Adel.Moore account.

16. Click **Next**. The New Mailbox page appears.

17. Review the summary of your settings and click **New**. The Completion page appears.

18. Click **Finish** to close the New Mailbox window.

19. Close the Exchange Management Console.

**THE COMMAND
LINE WAY**

The **Enable-Mailbox** cmdlet in the Exchange Management Shell can also be used to create
a linked mailbox user using an existing disabled user account within the Exchange resource
forest. Before running the Enable-Mailbox cmdlet, you should first supply the credentials
of a Domain Admin or Enterprise Admin in the target domain by entering the following
command in the Exchange Management Console:

$TargetCredential = Get-Credential

Next, you can use the Enable-Mailbox cmdlet to create the linked mailbox user in the
Exchange resource forest. For example, to create a linked mailbox user from the existing
disabled user Adel Moore (alias and logon name = adel.moore) in Octavius OU in the
arfa.com domain within your Exchange resource forest, specify a mailbox in the Mailbox
database within the First Storage Group on the server EMAIL5, and link the mailbox
to the Adel Moore user account in the octavius.net domain (logon name = adel.moore)

using the DC exch1.octavius.net, you could run the following command in the Exchange Management Shell:

Enable-Mailbox –Identity 'arfa.com/Octavius/adel.moore' –Alias 'adel.moore' –Database 'EMAIL5\First Storage Group\Mailbox Database' –LinkedMasterAccount 'octavius.net\adel.moore' –LinkedDomainController 'exch1.octavius.net' –LinkedCredential $TargetCredential

Alternatively, you can use the **New-Mailbox** cmdlet after creating the $TargetCredential variable with the appropriate logon credentials to create the linked mailbox user in the Exchange resource forest alongside a disabled AD user account. For example, to create a linked mailbox user called Adel Moore (alias and logon name = adel.moore) in the Octavius OU of the arfa.com domain within your Exchange resource forest, specify a mailbox in the Mailbox database within the First Storage Group on the server EMAIL5, and link the mailbox to the Adel Moore user account in the octavius.net domain (logon name = adel.moore) using the DC exch1.octavius.net, you could run the following command in the Exchange Management Shell:

New-Mailbox –Name 'Adel Moore' –Alias 'adel.moore' –OrganizationalUnit 'arfa. com/Octavius' –UserPrincipalName 'adel.moore@arfa.com' –SamAccountName 'adel.moore' FirstName 'Adel' –LastName 'Moore' –Database 'EMAIL5\First Storage Group\Mailbox Database' –LinkedMasterAccount 'octavius.net\adel.moore' –LinkedDomainController 'exch1.octavius.net' –LinkedCredential $TargetCredential

Some organizations use Exchange resource forests to consolidate the existing Exchange organizations in several forests. This may be required after two or more organizations merge or when the IT departments within several different forests are combined into a single unit.

In this case, each forest that must be configured to use an Exchange resource forest will already have an Exchange infrastructure with mailbox users for several members of the organization. Luckily, the procedure for migrating to an Exchange resource forest is nearly identical to the procedure used to implement a new Exchange resource forest. To migrate to an Exchange resource forest, you must ensure that one-way external or cross forest trusts are created so that the Exchange resource forest trusts all other forests. Next, you must create linked mailbox users in the Exchange resource forest that are linked to master accounts in other trusted forests using the same procedure discussed earlier.

Because the master accounts in the target domain are already mailbox users, you can move the mailboxes for them in the target domain to the Exchange resource domain using the **Move-Mailbox** cmdlet in the Exchange Management Shell. The **Move-Mailbox** cmdlet must be run from an Exchange server in the Exchange resource forest with the –**AllowMerge** option.

Before running the Move-Mailbox cmdlet, you should specify the credentials for a user who is a member of the Domain Admins or Enterprise Admins group in the target domain by using the following command in the Exchange Management Console:

$TargetCredential = Get-Credential

Next, you can move the mailbox for a target user to the Exchange resource forest. For example, after creating the linked mailbox user for Adel Moore in the arfa.com domain, you can use the following command in the Exchange Management Shell to move the mailbox for the Adel Moore mailbox user in the octavius.net domain (logon name = adel.moore@octavius.net) to the Mailbox Database in the First Storage Group on the server EMAIL5 in the arfa.com domain.

Move-Mailbox 'octavius.net/adel.moore' –TargetDatabase 'EMAIL5\First Storage Group\Mailbox Database' –SourceForestGlobalCatalog 'exch1.octavius.net' –DomainController 'dc4.arfa.com' NTAccountOU 'OU=Octavius, DC=arfa, DC=com' –Sourceforestcredential $TargetCredential –AllowMerge

In this command, the linked mailbox user resides in the Octavius OU of the arfa.com domain in the Exchange resource forest. In addition, the GC server used in the target domain during the move was exch1.octavius.net and the DC used in the Exchange resource forest was dc4.arfa.com.

After the master account mailboxes for all linked mailbox users have been moved to Exchange servers in the Exchange resource forest, you can reconfigure email client programs to obtain email from the Exchange servers in the Exchange resource forest. Users can use the same domain credentials they use to log in to their domain to access email in the Exchange resource forest because the mailbox is linked to their domain AD user account.

Following this, you can disable the mailbox users in the target domains and decommission the Exchange servers. Disabling the mailbox users will not remove the associated user account in AD. As a result, users will still be able to authenticate and access email from the Exchange servers in the Exchange resource forest.

Configuring and Managing Linked Mailbox Users

The procedures used to configure and manage linked mailbox users are identical to those used to configure regular mailbox users. However, all configuration and management must be performed from within the Exchange resource forest.

The configuration and management of linked mailbox users is always performed in the Exchange resource forest. Because linked mailbox users are simply mailbox users who allow access from a master account in a trusted forest, you can configure them under the **Recipient Configuration > Mailbox** node within the Exchange Management Console. Additionally, you can create a filter to narrow the list displayed in this node to specific room or equipment resource mailboxes only. Simply click **Create Filter** in the detail pane, specify **Recipient Type Details Equals Linked Mailbox** in the appropriate expression drop-down boxes, and click **Apply Filter**. Once you have located the appropriate linked mailbox user, you can highlight it in the detail pane and select **Properties** from the action pane to view its properties.

The properties for a linked mailbox user are identical to those for a regular mailbox user and are configured in the same way using the same procedures and cmdlets. However, the E-Mail Addresses tab lists email addresses for the trusted domain as well as the domain in the Exchange resource forest as shown for the Adel Moore linked mailbox user in Figure 5-52.

Figure 5-52

Configuring Linked Mailbox
User Email Addresses

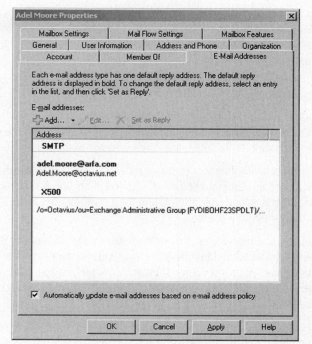

In Figure 5-52, the primary email address (adel.moore@arfa.com) was generated by the alias for the linked user account in the Exchange resource forest (arfa.com), whereas the secondary email address (Adel.Moore@octavius.net) reflects the domain that contains the linked master account (octavius.net). Thus, any email sent from Adel Moore will be addressed from adel.moore@ arfa.com. To maintain the original identity of octavius.net in sent emails, you could deselect **Automatically update e-mail addresses based on e-mail address policy**, highlight the Adel. Moore@octavius.net email address, and click **Set as Reply** as shown in Figure 5-52. In addition, an X500 address is added to allow DCs to locate the mailbox across the trust relationship.

To configure the other properties of a linked mailbox user, refer to the procedures and cmdlets described within the "Managing Mailbox Users" section earlier in this lesson.

You can grant the Send As and Full Access permissions for a linked mailbox user using the same procedures used with regular mailbox users. However, by default, linked mailbox users grant Send As and Full Access permission to the linked master account. These default permissions allow for mailbox access across forests and should not be removed. Similarly, to grant Send As or Full Access permission, you should select target users or groups in the trusted domains rather than in the Exchange resource forest. To grant Send As or Full Access permission to a linked mailbox user, refer to the procedures and cmdlets described within the "Managing Mailbox Users" section earlier in this lesson.

Disabling and removing linked mailbox users is also similar to disabling and removing regular mailbox users. When you disable a linked mailbox user, the link to the master account is removed and the mailbox is marked for deletion. However, the disabled user account in the Exchange resource forest is not deleted and the master account in the target domain is not deleted. When you delete a linked mailbox user, the link to the master account is removed, the mailbox is marked for deletion, and the disabled user account in the Exchange resource forest is deleted. However, the master account in the target domain is not deleted. As with mailbox users, you can reconnect a mailbox that is marked for deletion at a later time to a new or existing mailbox user or linked mailbox user. To disable, remove, or reconnect a linked mailbox user, refer to the procedures and cmdlets described within the "Managing Mailbox Users" section earlier in this lesson.

SUMMARY SKILL MATRIX

IN THIS LESSON YOU LEARNED:

- There are nine major recipient object types that contain email addresses within your organization: mailbox users, mail users, mail contacts, mail-enabled universal security groups, mail-enabled universal distribution groups, dynamic distribution groups, resource mailboxes, and mail-enabled public folders.

- Members of the Exchange Organization Administrator or Exchange Administrator role can create, configure, and manage all recipient objects using the Exchange Management Console as well as cmdlets within the Exchange Management Shell.

- Mailbox users are the most common recipient object. They consist of a mail-enabled user account and an associated mailbox. After creation, you can configure the mailbox settings, email addresses, and user information for a mailbox user, as well as disable, remove, or reconnect them to a mailbox.

- Mail users and mail contacts contain an external email address that internal organization email is forwarded to. Mail users are mail-enabled user accounts whereas mail contacts are mail-enabled contact objects within AD. After creation, you can configure email addresses and object information for mail users and mail contacts as well as disable or remove them.

- Mail-enabled universal groups are used when sending email to multiple recipient objects. Mail-enabled universal security groups can also be used to assign permissions and rights whereas mail-enabled universal distribution groups cannot. After creation, you can modify the group membership, group manager and expansion server settings for mail-enabled universal groups as well as disable or remove them.

- Instead of having a static group membership, dynamic distribution groups use criteria to match other recipient objects. These criteria are processed when email is sent to the dynamic distribution group and consist of a filter as well as several conditions. You can modify the filter and conditions for a dynamic distribution group after it has been created, as well as remove it entirely.

- Resource mailboxes are special mailbox users who are used to hold room or equipment resource scheduling information for use with the calendaring feature of Outlook and Entourage. Following creation, you can configure resource information, Automatic Booking, and resource booking policies for a resource mailbox. Like other mailbox users, resource mailboxes can also be disabled, removed, or reconnected.

- You can move mailboxes to other mailbox databases on the same server or another server using the Exchange Management Console or Move-Mailbox cmdlet within the Exchange Management Shell. The Move-Mailbox cmdlet offers more options than the Exchange Management Console and allows mailboxes to be moved between forests.

- To provide email services for multiple forests, or to consolidate email infrastructures, you can deploy an Exchange resource forest to hold Exchange servers that will be used by several forests across trust relationships. Linked mailbox users within the Exchange resource forest allow an associated master account in another forest access to email in a mailbox within the Exchange resource forest. Linked mailbox users are configured and managed like other mailbox users.

■ Knowledge Assessment

Fill in the Blank

Complete the following sentences by writing the correct word or words in the blanks provided.

1. When you configure a new linked mailbox user, you must specify a _____ to identify the remote user account that has the ability to access the mailbox.

2. The _____ US-cmdlet can obtain configuration information for a mail contact.

3. To prevent a mailbox user from using OWA, you can configure the appropriate option on the _____ tab of mailbox user properties.

4. To access the email within an additional mailbox in Outlook or Entourage, you must have _____ permission to the target mailbox.

5. To allow users to schedule a resource mailbox without the use of a delegate, you can create a _____ policy.

6. The default email address that is given to a recipient object is automatically generated from the _____ provided during creation and the domain name suffix of the domain the object was created in.

7. The _____ cmdlet may be used to create a new mailbox user.

8. When a member leaves the organization, you can configure _____ on the associated mailbox user to ensure that another mailbox user receives any email sent to that member.

9. To be notified immediately that a scheduled resource is unavailable when a meeting request is sent, the resource mailbox must have _____ enabled.

10. Before moving a mailbox to another forest in order to relocate an existing mailbox user, you should first migrate the user account to the target forest using the _____.

Multiple Choice

Circle the letter that corresponds to the best answer.

1. If a mailbox user within your organization legally changes his or her name, what actions should you perform on the recipient object? (Choose all that apply.)
   a. Modify the user information
   b. Modify the alias
   c. Change the primary email address
   d. Remove any secondary email addresses

2. Which of the following do dynamic distribution groups use to automatically populate their group membership? (Choose two answers.)
   a. conditions   b. scope
   c. filter   d. range

3. You are attempting to select custom properties within the properties of a resource mailbox, but none are displayed in the selection window. What should you do?
   a. Register them using the AD schema
   b. Configure them first using the Set-ResourceConfig cmdlet
   c. Add them as custom attributes first
   d. Create the custom properties first using the Object tab of resource mailbox properties

4. Which of the following recipient object types contain a disabled user account? (Choose all that apply.)
   a. mailbox users   b. linked mailbox users
   c. resource mailboxes   d. mail users

5. Which cmdlet can you use to reconnect a mailbox to an existing AD user?
   a. Enable-Mailbox
   b. New-Mailbox
   c. Connect-Mailbox
   d. Reconnect-Mailbox

True/False

Circle T if the statement is true or F if the statement is false.

T | **F** 1. By default, disconnected mailboxes are deleted after 30 days.

T | **F** 2. The Send On Behalf permission allows a user to send email using the sole identity of another user.

T | **F** 3. Exchange Recipient Administrators can create and manage all recipient objects within AD.

T | **F** 4. An Exchange resource forest is trusted by other forests using one-way cross forest or external trusts.

T | **F** 5. When you create an In Policy for a resource mailbox, users can automatically book the resource provided there are no conflicts.

T | **F** 6. When you disable a recipient object, the associated AD object is removed.

T | **F** 7. You can create a new mail-enabled universal security group using the SetDistributionGroup cmdlet within the Exchange Management Shell.

T | **F** 8. To provide an outside member of your organization an internal email address and the ability to log in to a domain, you can create a mail user.

T | **F** 9. The Move-Mailbox cmdlet within the Exchange Management Shell can only be used to move mailboxes within the same Exchange organization and forest.

T | **F** 10. The external email address for a mail user cannot be changed after the mail user has been created.

Review Questions

1. Explain why creating resource mailboxes will improve the productivity of your organization.

2. Explain how you can use custom attributes within recipient objects alongside dynamic distribution groups to simplify administration within Exchange Server 2007.

■ Case Scenarios

Scenario 5-1: Configuring an Exchange Resource Forest

Your organization has recently merged with another organization. During the merger, it was decided that both organizations will maintain separate forests and separate AD administrative staff but will combine their Exchange 2007 infrastructures into a single unit by deploying a new Exchange resource forest that will service both forests. You have been tasked with hiring the staff required to create and manage this new Exchange resource forest as well as create an action plan to migrate the existing Exchange infrastructures in both existing forests to the new Exchange resource forest.

In a short memo, describe the procedures that you will need to undertake to transition the current environment to an Exchange resource forest environment in a smooth and efficient manner.

Scenario 5-2: Managing Recipient Objects

Until recently, your organization has used mailbox users exclusively for all members of the organization including contract members. As a result, the available space on your Mailbox role servers is running low. During a meeting, your manager has asked you to provide possible solutions for this problem and recommend procedures to prevent it from happening in the future. You manager wants you to present this at the following meeting in one week.

Prepare a short presentation that you can present at this meeting that outlines some solutions to the disk space problem as well as some procedures that may be used to prevent the problem from reoccurring frequently in the future.

7 LESSON

Working with Public Folders

LESSON SKILL MATRIX

TECHNOLOGY SKILL	OBJECTIVE DOMAIN	OBJECTIVE DOMAIN NUMBER
Creating Public Folders	Configure public folders.	2.4, 3.5
Configuring Public Folders	Configure public folders.	2.4, 3.5
Configuring Mail-Enabled Public Folders	Configure public folders.	2.4, 3.5
Working with Multiple Public Folders	Implement bulk management of mail-enabled objects.	2.6

KEY TERMS

administrative permission
client permission
content replica
default public folder
  subtree
Folder Assistant

moderated public folder
moderator
Outlook Form Designer
public folder hierarchy
Public Folder Management
  Console

public folder referral
Send As permission
system public folder
  subtree
Top Level Hierarchy (TLH)

■ Understanding Public Folders

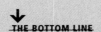

THE BOTTOM LINE

Public folders provide a flexible means of storing different types of items that email users work with on a regular basis as part of their job role. Consequently, many organizations configure public folders as part of their Exchange infrastructure. As an Exchange administrator, you will likely need to create, configure, and manage public folders within your organization.

Public folders are folders that Exchange users can use to share information such as emails, notes, file attachments, tasks, calendars, journals, forms, and contacts with other Exchange users. In addition, you can use public folders to archive emails or to provide access to company information or documents. By mail-enabling public folders, you can also use them to store emails that are sent to a specific email address. Furthermore, you can restrict access to public folders and their content or hide them from address lists.

Outlook and Entourage are the most common programs used to access public folders. When you set up an Exchange account within Outlook and Entourage, public folders are displayed alongside your normal email folders for you to access. Additionally, you can use Outlook Web Access (OWA) to access and use public folders.

TAKE NOTE*

In previous versions of Exchange Server, you could use public folders to provide newsgroups using the Network News Transfer Protocol (NNTP) for newsgroup clients such as Outlook Express. This feature is no longer available in Exchange Server 2007.

In many organizations, users are already familiar with email clients such as Outlook because they spend a great deal of time using it to support their job role. Because these users can access their email and public folders in the same client program, there is less of a learning curve in using public folders when compared to other technologies such as SharePoint and Groove 2007. However, although public folders provide an easy way of sharing or archiving files and information, they do not provide advanced document tracking features such as versioning. To provide these features, you will need to use other software that is specifically designed for document sharing such as SharePoint or Groove 2007. Similarly, technologies such as Messaging Records Management and message journaling are better suited for email archival when compared to public folders. Nonetheless, public folders provide a flexible mechanism for storing information and can prove very useful in many different situations.

Members of the Exchange Organization Administrator role or the Exchange Public Folder Administrator role can create, configure, and manage the public folders within your Exchange organization. To use the rights assigned to these roles, you must also be a local Administrator on the Mailbox server that contains the public folders.

■ Creating Public Folders

THE BOTTOM LINE

Although you can grant the ability to create public folders to others within your organization, you will likely need to create the initial public folder structure within your public folder databases. Public folders can be created within a public folder database on a Mailbox server within your organization using the Public Folder Management Console, Exchange Management Shell, Outlook, Entourage, or OWA.

CERTIFICATION READY?
Configure public folders.
2.4, 3.5

Before you create public folders, you must first have a public folder database on a Mailbox role server that will be used to store them. On the Client Settings page during the Exchange Server installation, you were asked whether your Exchange organization will have client computers that are running Outlook 2003 and earlier or Entourage. If you selected Yes, a public folder database was automatically created during the installation. This is because public folders are used to store Offline Address Books (OABs), Exchange client configuration information, and calendar scheduling (free/busy) information used by Outlook 2003 and earlier clients as well as Entourage 2004 and earlier clients that are configured to use an Exchange account. Alternatively, if you selected No on the Client Settings page, a public folder database was not created during installation, and you must first create and mount a public folder database as discussed in Lesson 4, "Configuring a New Exchange Server."

TAKE NOTE*

Instead of using public folders, Outlook 2007 and Entourage 2008 MAPI clients use the Autodiscover and Availability services within Exchange 2007 to obtain Offline Address Books, schedule calendar appointments, and obtain configuration information.

By default, mailbox users can connect to a single public folder database using Outlook, Entourage, or OWA. The public folder database that mailbox users will receive is configured on the Client Settings tab of mailbox database properties. For example, the mailboxes stored within the Mailbox Database shown in Figure 7-1 are configured to use the public folders stored in the Public Folder Database in the Second Storage Group on the server EXCH1.

Figure 7-1

Specifying a Public Folder
Database

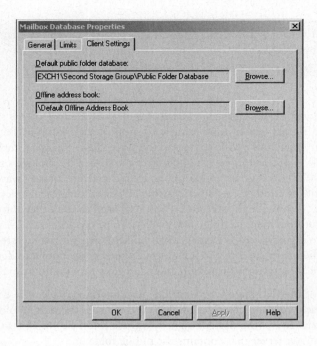

TAKE NOTE* Although mailbox users connect to a single public folder database by default, they will be able to see and access all of the public folders within the Exchange organization using *public folder referrals*. Public folder referrals are discussed in more detail later in this lesson.

Each new public folder database is configured to use the MAPI *Top Level Hierarchy (TLH)* tree structure. This allows you to create new public folders at the root of the database as well as under existing public folders.

In addition, MAPI TLH is divided into two subtrees. The *default public folder subtree* is used to store public folders for use by users, whereas the *system public folder subtree* stores the folders used to provide configuration, scheduling, and OAB information to MAPI clients. The folders under the system folder subtree cannot be accessed by users. They are automatically created and managed using Exchange Server and should not be modified.

TAKE NOTE* The default public folder subtree is also called the *Interpersonal Message (IPM) subtree*. The system folder subtree is often referred to using NON_IPM_SUBTREE.

You can create, configure, and manage public folders using Outlook, Entourage, or the *Public Folder Management Console* within the Exchange Management Console. To start the Public Folder Management Console, highlight the **Tools** node within the Exchange Management Console and double click **Public Folder Management Console** in the details pane. By default, the Public Folder Management Console displays the default public folder and system public folder subtrees on the current Exchange server as shown in Figure 7-2. You can manage any public folder database within the organization from within the Public Folder Management Console. Simply select **Connect to Server** in the action pane shown in Figure 7-2 and choose the appropriate server that contains the public folder database you wish to administer.

TAKE NOTE* The Public Folder Management Console is only available in Exchange Server 2007 SP1 or later.

Figure 7-2

Public Folder Management Console

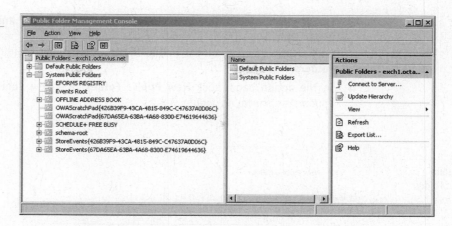

As shown in Figure 7-2, only the system public folders are created in a new public folder database. However, you can create new public folders under the default public folder subtree to match the needs of your organization. These folders can be created under the root (\) of the default public folder subtree or underneath existing public folders within the default public folder subtree. Figure 7-3 shows a public folder structure that has multiple levels within the public folder hierarchy under the root of the default public folder subtree.

TAKE NOTE *

In earlier versions of Exchange Server, you could create additional general-purpose public folder trees that could be accessed using OWA or NNTP clients. These general-purpose public folder trees are no longer supported in Exchange Server 2007, and all public folders that you create must reside under the default public folder subtree within a public folder database.

Figure 7-3

Viewing Public Folder Structure

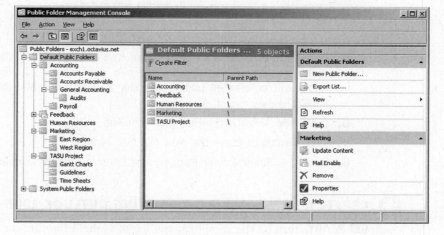

If you create a public folder within the Public Folder Management Console, it can only contain email and post items. Alternatively, if you create new public folders from within Outlook, Entourage, or OWA, you can select the type of content that will be allowed within the public folder.

 CREATE A NEW PUBLIC FOLDER USING THE PUBLIC FOLDER MANAGEMENT CONSOLE

GET READY. Turn on the computer, and log in as the Administrator user account. Close any windows that appear on the desktop.

1. Click **Start, All Programs, Microsoft Exchange Server 2007**, and then click **Exchange Management Console**. The Exchange Management Console window appears.

2. In the console tree pane, highlight **Tools** and double click **Public Folder Management Console** in the detail pane. The Public Folder Management Console window appears.

3. Expand **Default Public Folders** in the console tree pane and highlight the folder under which you wish to create a new public folder. To create a new public folder underneath the root of the public folder tree, simply highlight **Default Public Folders**.

4. In the action pane, click **New Public Folder**. The New Public Folder window appears as shown in Figure 7-4.

Figure 7-4

Creating a New Public Folder in the Public Folder Management Console

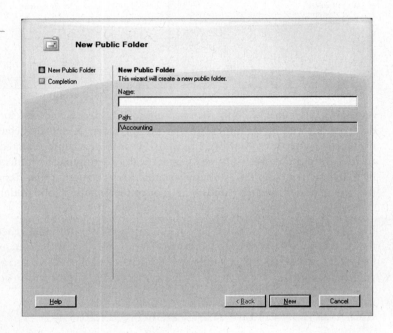

5. Type the name for the public folder in the Name dialog box. The Path dialog box should reflect the location for the new public folder. In Figure 7-4, the new public folder will be created underneath the Accounting public folder under the Default Public Folders root (\).

6. Click **New**. The Completion page appears.

7. Click **Finish** to close the New Mailbox window.

8. Close the Public Folder Management Console and the Exchange Management Console.

CREATE A NEW PUBLIC FOLDER USING OUTLOOK 2007

GET READY. Turn on the computer, and log in as the Administrator user account. Close any windows that appear on the desktop.

1. Click **Start**, **All Programs**, **Microsoft Office**, and then click **Microsoft Office Outlook 2007**. The Microsoft Outlook window appears.

2. Click on the Folder List icon in the lower left pane. In the Folder List window, expand **Public Folders**, **All Public Folders**.

3. Next, right click the folder under which you wish to create a new public folder and select **New Folder**. To create a new public folder underneath the root of the public folder tree, simply right click **All Public Folders** and select **New Folder**. The Create New Folder window appears as shown in Figure 7-5.

Figure 7-5

Creating a New Public Folder
in Outlook

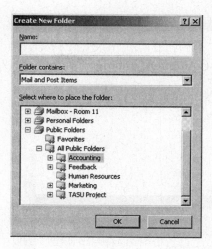

4. Type the name for the public folder in the **Name** dialog box. The dialog box at the bottom of the Create New Folder dialog box should reflect the location for the new public folder. To change this location, you can highlight the appropriate folder in this dialog box.

5. By default, public folders can store email and post items. To modify the type of items that should be stored in the public folder, you can select one of the following in the **Folder contains** drop-down box:

- **Calendar Items**
- **Contact Items**
- **InfoPath Form Items**
- **Journal Items**
- **Mail and Post Items**
- **Note Items**
- **Task Items**

6. Click **OK**. Close Microsoft Outlook.

CREATE A NEW PUBLIC FOLDER USING ENTOURAGE 2008

GET READY. Turn on the Macintosh computer, and log in as the Administrator user account. Close any windows that appear on the desktop.

1. Click the Microsoft Entourage icon on the Macintosh OS X dock to open Microsoft Entourage 2008. Alternatively, you can navigate to **Macintosh HD**, **Applications**, **Microsoft Office 2008**, and then click **Microsoft Entourage** to open Microsoft Entourage 2008. The Microsoft Entourage 2008 window appears.

2. In the left pane, expand **Public Folders**, **All Public Folders.**

3. Next, right click the folder under which you wish to create a new public folder and select **New Folder**. To create a new public folder underneath the root of the public folder tree, simply right click **All Public Folders** and select **New Folder**. The Create New Folder window appears as shown in Figure 7-6.

Figure 7-6

Creating a New Public Folder
in Entourage

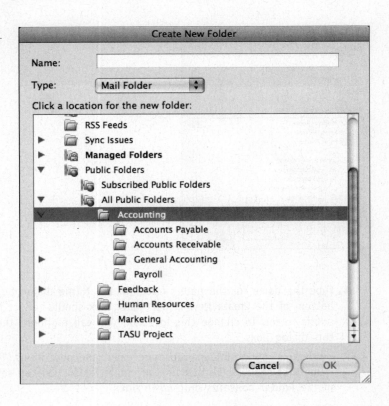

4. Type the name for the public folder in the **Name** dialog box. The dialog box at the bottom of the Create New Folder dialog box should reflect the location for the new public folder. To change this location, you can highlight the appropriate folder in this dialog box.

5. By default, public folders can store email and post items. To modify the type of items that should be stored in the public folder, you can select one of the following in the **Type** selection box:

   • **Mail Folder**

   • **Calendar**

   • **Address Book**

6. Click **OK**. Close Microsoft Entourage.

CREATE A NEW PUBLIC FOLDER USING OWA

GET READY. Turn on the computer, and log in as the Administrator user account. Close any windows that appear on the desktop.

1. Open your web browser and enter the URL **http://*server*/public** where *server* is the FQDN or IP address of the Mailbox role server that hosts the public folder database in which you wish to create public folders. When prompted to log in, enter your username and password and click **OK**.

2. In the left pane, click **Public Folders**.

3. Next, right click the folder under which you wish to create a new public folder, select **Create New Folder** and then select the type of folder that you wish to create:

   • **Mail Folder**

   • **Calendar Folder**

   • **Contact Folder**

   • **Task Folder**

   • **Notes Folder**

To create a new public folder underneath the root of the public folder tree, simply right click **Public Folders**, select **New Folder**, and then select the appropriate folder type.

4. Type the name for the public folder in the dialog box that appears next to the new public folder icon in the left pane and press **Enter**.

5. Close your web browser.

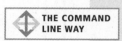
THE COMMAND LINE WAY

You can also use the **New-PublicFolder** cmdlet in the Exchange Management Shell to create a new public folder under the default public folder subtree. For example, to create a new public folder called Notes under the Accounting public folder under the root of the default public folder tree on the server EXCH2, you could run the following command in the Exchange Management Shell:

New-PublicFolder -Name 'Notes' -Path '\Accounting' -Server 'EXCH2'

If you omit the **–Path** option to the New-PublicFolder cmdlet, the new folder will be created under the root of the default public folder tree. Similarly, if you omit the **–Server** option to the New-PublicFolder cmdlet, the new public folder will be created in the public folder database on the closest Mailbox server. This server is located using site information stored in AD.

Once you have created public folders, you can view them using the **Get-PublicFolder** cmdlet. To view all of the public folders under the root (\), including subfolders, you can use the following command within the Exchange Management Shell:

Get-PublicFolder –Recurse | Format-List Name

Similarly, to view the details for public folder called Guidelines under the TASU Project public folder under the root (\) of the default public folder subtree on the server EXCH2, you could use the following command within the Exchange Management Shell:

Get-PublicFolder –Identity '\TASU Project\Guidelines' –Server 'EXCH2' | Format-List

Over time, you may need to monitor the size and number of items posted to a public folder. To do this, you can use the Get-PublicFolderStatistics cmdlet. To view the statistics for the TASU Project public folder under the root (\) of the default public folder subtree on the server EXCH2, you could use the following command within the Exchange Management Shell:

Get-PublicFolderStatistics –Identity '\TASU Project\Guidelines' –Server 'EXCH2' | Format-List

If you omit **–Identity '\TASU Project\Guidelines'** in the previous example, you will view statistics for all public folders on the server EXCH2.

■ Using Public Folders

↓
THE BOTTOM LINE

Nearly everyone today has used an email program to send email to others. However, understanding how to use public folders is somewhat less common because public folders are only used within organizations and business environments that deploy Exchange Server, Outlook, Entourage, and OWA. To understand how to configure public folders, you must first understand their basic usage and function.

Outlook, Entourage, and OWA are the main client email programs you can use to access public folders in Exchange Server 2007. For Outlook users, public folders are automatically added to the folder list under an Exchange account in the left pane as shown for the Jeff Smith mailbox user in Figure 7-7. Depending on your version and configuration of Outlook, you may need to select the Folder List icon at the bottom of the left pane to view the default public folder subtree underneath your mailbox folder list in Outlook.

An easy way to identify the Folder List icon is to move your mouse over each icon in the lower left area of the Outlook window and observe the description labels that appear. The Folder List icon will have a description label of **Folder List** or **View Folders** depending on your version of Outlook.

Figure 7-7

Viewing Public Folder Items in Outlook

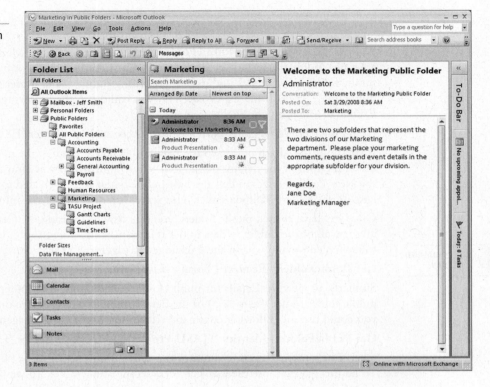

The **Mailbox—Jeff Smith** folder list normally contains the default email folders such as Inbox and Deleted Items, but has been collapsed in Figure 7-7 to show the public folders configured in the public folder database that is used by Jeff Smith's mailbox database. The root of the default public folder subtree is represented by the **All Public Folders** node in Figure 7-7. You can navigate the public folders underneath this node to view existing content. The Marketing folder highlighted in Figure 7-7 shows two meeting request emails from the Administrator regarding product presentations as well as a post item that welcomes visitors to the marketing public folder. You can double click any item within a public folder to view it or simply highlight it to view its contents in the right pane (reading pane) as shown with the welcome post in Figure 7-7.

To add existing items to a public folder, you can simply locate them in your mailbox folder list, right click them, and select Move to folder. You can then browse to an existing public folder and click **OK** to move the item to that public folder. This is often used for public folders that are designed to store copies of emails regarding company events or public folders used to archive important items. Provided that the public folder was created in Outlook and configured to contain the appropriate content, you can move email, post items, calendar items, contacts, tasks, notes, and journal items to a public folder. Email and post items are two of the most commonly configured content types used for public folders.

Alternatively, you can choose to add a new item to a public folder by selecting the appropriate public folder and clicking **New** in the upper left corner of Outlook. If your public folder is configured to contain email and post items, clicking **New** in the upper left corner will create a new post item by default as shown in Figure 7-8. However, you can select the drop-box icon to the right of the **New** button to select other item types. Post items are simply messages that can contain a subject line and message as well as attachments such as files and pictures. By clicking **Post** as shown in Figure 7-8, the post item will be stored in the appropriate public folder for others to view or respond to. After highlighting a post item, users can click **Reply** (shown in Figure 7-7) to reply to the original sender via email or the **Post Reply** button to post a related reply within the public folder itself.

Figure 7-8

Creating a New Post

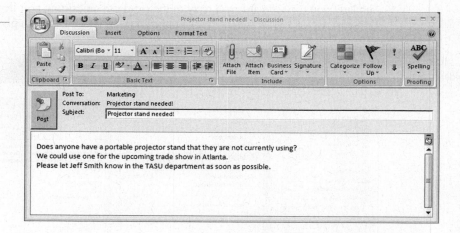

After creating an Exchange account in Entourage, you will see public folders alongside the other default mail folders provided that you manually specified a public folder server when you set up the Exchange account. To specify a public folder server for an Exchange account within Entourage, you can navigate to **Tools** > **Accounts**, double click your Exchange account and click the **Advanced** tab as shown in Figure 7-9.

Figure 7-9

Specifying a Public Folder Server in Entourage

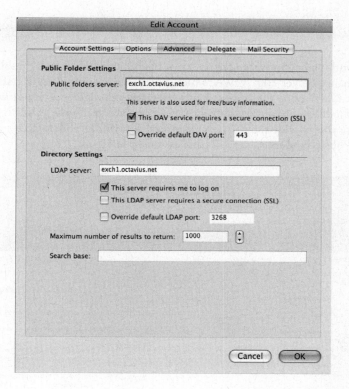

The server name or IP address that you specify in the Public folders server dialog box in Figure 7-9 does not need to be the same server configured on the Client Settings tab of the user's mailbox database as shown earlier in Figure 7-1. If you select a different server, then Entourage will locate the public folder database on that particular server. In addition, you must select **This DAV service requires a secure connection (SSL)** because all public folder access between Entourage and Exchange 2007 must be encrypted using SSL.

After you specify a public folder server in Entourage, the default public folder subtree will appear under the **All Public Folders** node within the left pane of Entourage as shown in Figure 7-10. As with Outlook, you can move items to public folders in Entourage as well as create a new post by clicking **New** or using the drop-down arrow to the right of **New** to select other message types. Similarly, you can send an email reply to the creator of an existing post item by clicking **Reply Directly** or post a related reply in the public folder by clicking **Post Reply** as shown in Figure 7-10.

Figure 7-10

Viewing Public Folder Items in Entourage

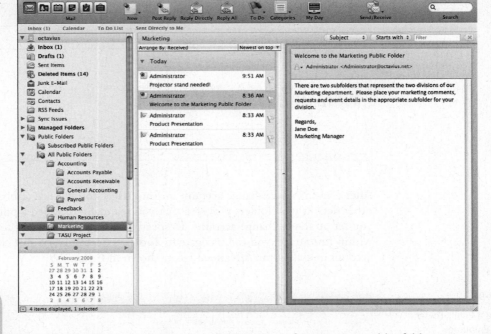

TAKE NOTE*

You can also access OWA using the URL **https://*server*/exchange** or **https://*server*/public** and specifying the appropriate credentials at the logon screen.

If Outlook or Entourage are not available options for accessing public folders, you can use Exchange Server 2007 OWA, which contains native support for public folders. Simply access your OWA using the address **https://*server*/exchange/*user_name*** where *server* is the FQDN or IP address of your Mailbox or CAS role server and *user_name* is your account name. Once you provide the correct credentials, you will be able to access public folders by clicking on **Public Folders** in the left pane as shown in Figure 7-11.

Figure 7-11

Viewing Public Folder Items in OWA

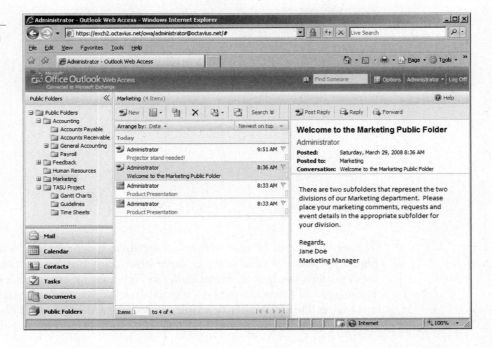

Although OWA is similar in functionality to Outlook and Entourage, you can only create new post items in a public folder by using the **New** button. However, you can perform most other public folder functions within OWA. For example, you can move existing items to a public folder within OWA as well as reply to public folder items using email with the **Reply** button or using a new post item with the **Post Reply** button.

■ Configuring Public Folders

↓ THE BOTTOM LINE Public folders host a wide variety of configuration options that make them useful in a variety of situations. After creating public folders, you will need to modify the permissions on them as well as configure folder options, replication, and limits to meet the needs of your organization.

CERTIFICATION READY?
Configure public folders.
2.4, 3.5

Configuring Client Permissions

Client permissions give mailbox users within your organization the ability to view and manage the content within public folders as well as create new public folder content. In most situations, you will need to modify the default client permissions on public folders using Outlook or the Exchange Management Shell to ensure that the mailbox users within your organization have only the necessary access to public folder content.

TAKE NOTE*

Outlook is the only client program that can be used to configure public folder properties such as client permissions. You cannot use OWA to configure the properties for a public folder, and Entourage can only be used to view the configuration of public folders.

After creating public folders, any mailbox user within your organization can view items within the public folder as well as add new items and manage their own items. Depending on the intended use of the public folder, this may not be desirable. For example, if your organization uses public folders to store information for a particular department, only certain mailbox users should be able to store and view the information in that public folder. As a result, you can set ***client permissions*** on a public folder to specify the permissions that users have to the content within the public folder.

Client permissions can be configured on a public folder using Outlook or the Exchange Management Shell. To configure client permissions on a public folder in Outlook, simply right click the appropriate public folder, select **Properties**, and highlight the **Permissions** tab as shown in Figure 7-12.

Figure 7-12

Configuring Client Permissions

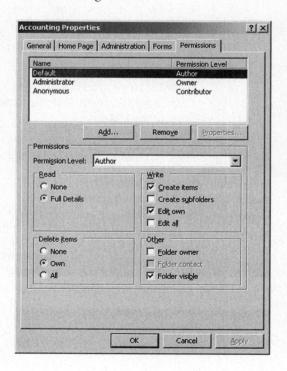

The client permissions for the Accounting public folder shown in Figure 7-12 can be used to determine whether a particular user can create, read, edit, and delete items within the Accounting public folder as well as create new public folders underneath the Accounting public folder. In addition, these client permissions can be used to determine whether the Accounting folder will be visible to the user in the default public folder subtree.

Because there can be many different combinations of client permissions, you can assign one of several *client permission levels* to a mailbox user or mail-enabled universal group as described in Table 7-1. These permission levels include common groups of client permissions that can be granted to a user or group.

Table 7-1

Public folder client permission levels

PERMISSION LEVEL	DESCRIPTION
None	Cannot view, create, modify, or delete any items within the public folder or view the public folder within the default public folder subtree.
Contributor	Can create new items in the folder, but cannot view other items in the folder or delete items. This permission level is appropriate when creating a drop-box folder that allows users to submit requests but not view or manage them afterwards.
Reviewer	Can view items within the folder only. This permission level is often assigned to users on public folders that provide information only.
Nonediting author	Can view and create items within the folder as well as delete items that they have created.
Author	Can view and create items within the folder as well as modify and delete items that they have created.
Publishing author	Can view and create items within the folder, create subfolders, as well as modify and delete items that they have created.
Editor	Can view, create, modify, and delete all items within the public folder.
Publishing editor	Can view, create, modify, and delete all items within the public folder as well as create subfolders.
Owner	Can view, create, modify, and delete all items within the public folder as well as create subfolders and modify the client permissions on the folder.
Custom	Used to designate a permission level that contains client permissions that have been manually specified.

The default client permission level granted to mailbox users is Author, which allows all other users to read all items in the folder as well as create and manage their own items. To restrict access to the content of a public folder, you should remove the **Default** user shown in Figure 7-12 or set the permission level to **None** for the **Default** user. Next, you can add the appropriate users or groups and assign the appropriate client permission level or custom client permissions.

Only mailbox users and mail-enabled universal groups within your Exchange organization can be assigned client permissions to public folders. When you click **Add** as shown in Figure 7-12 to add additional users or groups, you will not be able to select any mail users, mail contacts, and dynamic distribution groups.

In many organizations, the Exchange administrator does not handle the administration of public folder content and client permissions because it would be too time consuming. Instead, the manager of a department or project is often given the owner-client permission level. This user can then manage all content within the public folder, create subfolders, and assign client permissions to others as needed.

When you create a new public folder, it inherits its settings, including permissions, from its parent public folder. If you change the permissions on the parent public folder afterward, those permissions are not automatically set on its child public folders.

THE COMMAND LINE WAY

You can also use cmdlets within the Exchange Management Shell to manage client permissions on a public folder. To view existing client permissions on a public folder, you can use the **Get-PublicFolderClientPermission** cmdlet. For example, to view the existing client permissions on the Accounting public folder under the root of the default public folder subtree on the Mailbox server EXCH2, you could use the following command within the Exchange Management Shell:

Get-PublicFolderClientPermission –Identity '\Accounting' –Server 'EXCH2'

Similarly, you can use the **Add-PublicFolderClientPermission** cmdlet to add client permissions to a user or group. For example, to assign the author-client permission level to the mailbox user Jeff Smith to the same Accounting folder used in the previous example, you could execute the following command within the Exchange Management Shell:

Add-PublicFolderClientPermission –Identity '\Accounting' –Server 'EXCH2' –User 'Jeff Smith' –AccessRights 'Author'

To remove the client permissions for Jeff Smith to the Accounting public folder on EXCH2, you can use the **Remove-PublicFolderClientPermission** cmdlet in place of the **Add-PublicFolderClientPermission** cmdlet as shown in the following Exchange Management Shell command:

Remove-PublicFolderClientPermission –Identity '\Accounting' –Server 'EXCH2' –User 'Jeff Smith' –AccessRights 'Author'

When you use the **Remove-PublicFolderClientPermission** cmdlet, you will be prompted to confirm the removal.

Configuring Administrative Permissions

Unlike client permissions, administrative permissions allow users within your organization to administer various aspects of the public folders they have been granted access to. Administrative permissions can only be assigned using the Exchange Management Shell.

In addition to setting client permissions on a public folder to restrict content usage, you can also grant *administrative permissions* to users for individual public folders, which allows users to perform public folder administrative tasks. If you need to delegate the administration of public folders, it is good practice to grant administrative permissions to users for specific public folders rather than add them to the Exchange Public Folder Administrator role because Exchange Public Folder Administrator role members can modify the public folders on any public folder database within your organization.

The administrative permissions that can be granted to public folders in Exchange Server 2007 are listed in Table 7-2.

Table 7-2

Public folder administrative permissions

ADMINISTRATIVE PERMISSION	DESCRIPTION
None	Used to denote no administrative permissions on a public folder.
ModifyPublicFolderACL	Can modify the client permissions on a public folder (excluding client permissions for Administrative groups such as Domain Admins).
ModifyPublicFolderAdminACL	Can modify the client permissions on a public folder for Administrative groups such as Domain Admins.
ModifyPublicFolderDeleted-ItemRetention	Can modify the time period for deleted item retention within the properties of a public folder.
ModifyPublicFolderExpiry	Can modify expiry information within the properties of a public folder.
ModifyPublicFolderQuotas	Can modify quota limits within the properties of a public folder.
ModifyPublicFolderReplicaList	Can configure replication for a public folder.
AdministerInformationStore	Can modify all other properties for a public folder that are not granted by administrative permissions other than AllExtendedRights.
ViewInformationStore	Can view public folder properties.
AllExtendedRights	Can modify any public folder properties.

Administrative permissions can only be set and managed using cmdlets within the Exchange Management Shell. By default, members of the Exchange Public Folder Administrator role, the Exchange Organization Administrator Role, or the Domain Admins group can configure administrative permissions on public folders.

To view the existing administrative permissions on a public folder, you can use the **Get-PublicFolderAdministrativePermission** cmdlet. For example, to view the existing administrative permissions on the Marketing public folder under the root of the default public folder subtree on the Mailbox server EXCH1, you could use the following command within the Exchange Management Shell:

Get-PublicFolderAdministrativePermission –Identity '\Marketing' –Server 'EXCH1' | Format-List

You can also add the **–Owner** option to the **Get-PublicFolderAdministrativePermission** cmdlet to list the owner for a specific public folder. The owner of a public folder is the creator of the public folder. If a member of an administrative group such as Domain Admins creates a public folder, the group becomes the public folder owner.

To assign administrative permissions to a user or group for a public folder, you can use the **Add-PublicFolderAdministrativePermission** cmdlet. For example, to assign Fred Jones full administrative permission to the Marketing public folder used in the previous example, you could execute the following command within the Exchange Management Shell:

**Add-PublicFolderAdministrativePermission –Identity '\Marketing' –Server 'EXCH1'
–User 'Fred Jones' –AccessRights 'AllExtendedRights'**

Administrative permissions that are set on a public folder are not inherited by subfolders unless you add the **–InheritanceType 'All'** option to the **Add-PublicFolderAdministrative Permission** command.

To remove the administrative permissions that were assigned to Fred Jones in the previous example, you can simply replace the **Add-PublicFolderAdministrativePermission** cmdlet with the **Remove-PublicFolderAdministrativePermission** cmdlet as shown in the following Exchange Management Shell command. You will be prompted to confirm the removal.

**Remove-PublicFolderAdministrativePermission –Identity '\Marketing' –Server 'EXCH1'
–User 'Fred Jones' –AccessRights 'AllExtendedRights'**

Configuring Public Folder Options

From within Outlook, you can configure public folder options that affect how public folders appear within Outlook, Entourage, and OWA as well as the types of items that you can create within a public folder. In addition, you can use public folder options to modify public folder item processing or specify a public folder moderator.

In addition to setting client and administrative permissions, there are a number of options that can be configured within the properties of a public folder including view options, public folder moderators, processing options, and forms. Moreover, these options can only be configured by accessing the properties of the public folder within Outlook.

If you right click a public folder within Outlook and select **Properties**, you can provide a description for the public folder that will appear in Outlook, Entourage, or OWA as shown in the properties of the Time Sheets public folder in Figure 7-13. In addition, you can select view options or click the **Folder Size** button to view the size in KB used by the public folder and its subfolders.

Figure 7-13

Viewing Public Folder
Properties in Outlook

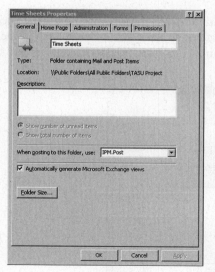

CONFIGURING FORMS

The General tab of public folder properties shown in Figure 7-13 allows you to select the default item type that is used when a user clicks the **New** button within Outlook, Entourage, or OWA. For public folders that allow email and post items, post items (IPM.Post) are created by default. However, you can also select a custom form that is based on an email message or post template. To create custom forms, you can use the *Outlook Form Designer* by navigating to **Tools** > **Forms** > **Design a Form** in the main Outlook window. Once your form has been designed, you can publish it and later select it using the drop-down box shown in Figure 7-13.

Say, for example, that your organization requires that project members post their time sheet information within the Time Sheets public folder. You could create a custom form called Time Sheet Form using the Outlook Form Designer to record the necessary information. Figure 7-14 shows a sample Time Sheet Form created in the Outlook Form Designer that is based on a standard post item template. After you are satisfied with the form layout, you can click the **Publish** button shown in Figure 7-14 and select the Time Sheets public folder.

Figure 7-14

Creating a New Custom Form

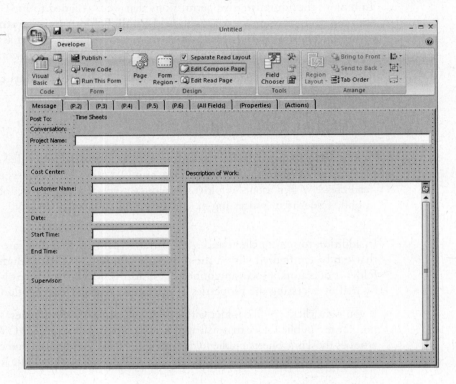

Now that you have published the Time Sheet Form to the Time Sheets folder, you can select Time Sheet Form as the default item type on the General Tab in the properties of the Time Sheets public folder shown in Figure 7-15. When project members need to post their time sheet

Figure 7-15

Specifying a Custom Form for a Public Folder

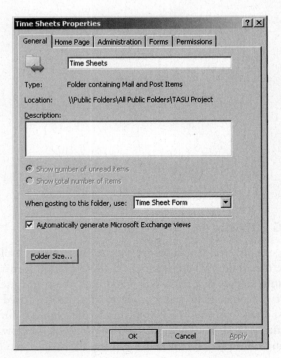

information, they simply select the Time Sheets folder in Outlook, Entourage, or OWA and click the **New** button. Instead of creating a new standard post item, they will receive the custom Time Sheets Form shown in Figure 7-16, where they can record the necessary time sheet information. When project members click the **Post** button in Figure 7-16, their time sheet information will be saved using the Time Sheet Form format as a post item within the public folder.

Figure 7-16

Creating a New Post Based on a Custom Form

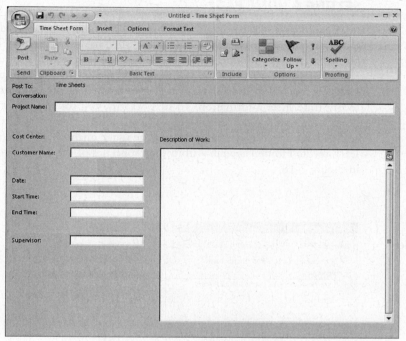

To ensure that project members do not see other time sheets, you could assign them contributor-client permissions to the Time Sheets folder. Similarly, to allow managers to view and manage the posted time sheets, you could assign them editor-client permission to the Time Sheets folder.

Although there can only be one default item type, a single public folder can contain multiple item types or forms. For example, if the Time Sheets public folder must contain post items based on the Time Sheet Form as well as standard post and message items, you can simply ensure that only those three item types are allowed on the Forms tab of public folder properties as shown in Figure 7-17.

Figure 7-17

Specifying Allowed Item Types and Forms

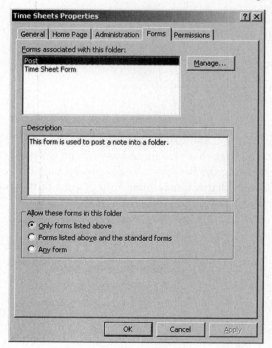

Because the Time Sheet Form is the default item type when creating a new item within the Time Sheets public folder, users must click the down arrow icon to the right of the **New** button in Outlook to select any additional item types such as standard post items or message items.

SETTING A HOME PAGE

Public folders can also contain a web page that is displayed instead of the item list within Outlook, Entourage, or OWA when the public folder is accessed. This is often useful when a public folder has subfolders that should be used for posting only certain types of information. Say, for example, that members of the TASU project in your company use public folders on a regular basis to store Gantt charts for project management, communicate guidelines, and record time sheet information. To support this, you could create a public folder called TASU Project that contains three subfolders: Gantt Charts, Guidelines, and Time Sheets. Next, you could create a web page that describes the usage of these subfolders and add the web page URL to the Home Page tab within the properties of the TASU Project public folder as shown in Figure 7-18.

Figure 7-18

Configuring a Public Folder Home Page

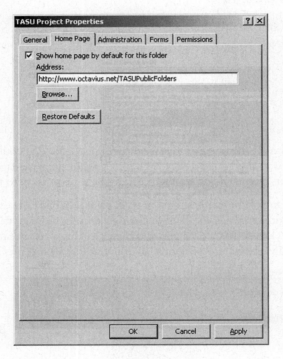

When Outlook, Entourage, and OWA users highlight the TASU Project public folder, they will be shown the web page that you created to indicate the public folder usage as shown in Figure 7-19. After reading the web page, TASU project members can then select the appropriate subfolder (Gantt Charts, Guidelines, Time Sheets) in the public folder list shown in Figure 7-19 to view and post items.

Figure 7-19

Viewing a Public Folder
Home Page

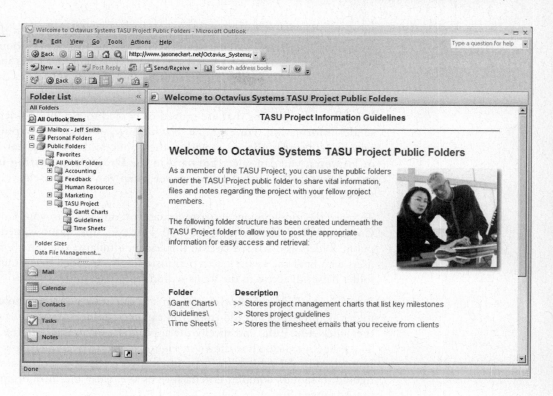

CONFIGURING ADMINISTRATIVE OPTIONS AND MODERATORS

The Administrative tab of public folder properties can be used to specify several different
public folder options as shown with the Feedback public folder properties in Figure 7-20.

Figure 7-20

Configuring Administrative
Options

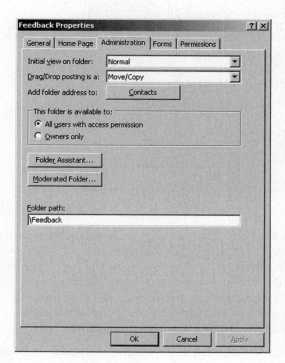

By default, items within public folders are listed in the order that they are posted unless you choose a different value in the **Initial view on folder** drop-down box. For example, to group similar items together when viewing public folder posts in the Feedback folder, you could select **Group by Subject** in the **Initial view on folder** drop-down box shown in Figure 7-20.

In addition, any items that are moved or copied to a public folder retain their original sender information. For example, if you move an email to the public folder that was sent by Jeff Smith, the email within the public folder will appear as if Jeff Smith added it. However, you can select **Forward** in the **Drag/Drop posting is a** drop-down box to ensure that you are listed as the sender when you move an email or other item to the public folder.

To make the public folder easier to locate, you can add it to your Contacts list by clicking the **Contacts** button shown in Figure 7-20. However, this option is used mainly by mail-enabled public folders as discussed later in this lesson. Similarly, you can allow public folder access to users who have the owner-client permission only, provided that all users who need to use the folder have full access to the items within the public folder.

By using the *Folder Assistant*, you can add rules that determine how new items within the folder are processed. To add rules, you can click **Folder Assistant** as shown in Figure 7-20, then click **Add Rule**, and specify the appropriate information in the Edit Rule dialog box. The Edit Rule dialog box shown in Figure 7-21 forwards any emails that contain the word **important** in the subject line (case insensitive) to the user Bob Jones. Rules can also be configured to contain complex criteria such as size, date, and form of information by selecting the **Advanced** button in Figure 7-21.

Figure 7-21

Adding a Folder Assistant Rule

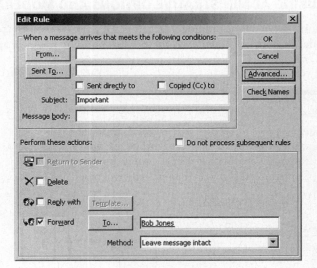

You can also use the Folder Assistant to create a *moderated public folder*. Any new items that are posted to a moderated public folder are automatically forwarded to a specific user called the *moderator* for review. The moderator will receive the item in his or her mailbox. After reviewing the item to ensure that it meets minimum standards and does not contain any profanity, the moderator can then copy or move the item into the public folder for others to access. You can specify multiple users or a group as moderators for a single public folder if several people must share the moderator responsibility.

To create a Feedback moderated public folder, simply click the **Moderated Folder** button as shown in Figure 7-20 and supply the appropriate information in the Moderated Folder window. The Moderated Folder window shown in Figure 7-22 forwards all new items posted to the folder to Adel Moore. Because Adel Moore is also listed in the Moderators dialog box, she can also move items back to the public folder after reviewing them.

Figure 7-22

Configuring a Moderated
Public Folder

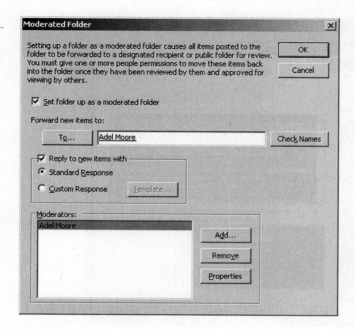

Any users who post a new item to the Feedback public folder will receive the following standard message to indicate that a moderator must first approve new items before they are posted:

Thank you for your submission. Please note that submissions to some folders or discussion groups are reviewed to determine whether they should be made publicly available. In these cases, there will be a delay before approved submissions can be viewed by others.

Alternatively, you can select **Custom Response** as shown in Figure 7-22 and click the **Template** button to modify the default message.

Configuring Public Folder Replication and Referrals

To ensure that public folders may be accessed across your Exchange organization, public folder databases replicate public folder lists and provide referrals to other public folder databases. In addition, you can configure the content of public folders to replicate between the public folder databases on the Exchange servers within your organization. You can configure public folder referrals and replication using the Public Folder Management Console and the Exchange Management Shell.

Recall that mailbox users who use an Exchange account in Outlook, Entourage, or OWA connect to the public folder database that is configured in their mailbox database properties. However, these same users will see all of the public folders within your Exchange organization under the All Public Folders node within Outlook or Entourage under the Public Folders section of OWA because public folder databases replicate their public folder lists to other public folder databases within the organization. The public folder list for a public folder database is called the *public folder hierarchy* and is replicated to all other public folder databases every 15 minutes by default. To modify replication of the public folder hierarchy, navigate to **Server Configuration** > **Mailbox** within the Exchange Management Console, access the properties of a public folder database, and highlight the Replication tab as shown in Figure 7-23.

Figure 7-23

Configuring Replication
Options for a Public Folder
Database

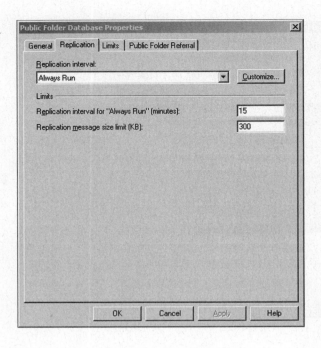

To restrict replication to specific times, you can select a different **Replication interval** or click **Customize** to specify when public folder hierarchy replication will occur. Alternatively, you could use a **Replication interval** of **Always Run** as shown in Figure 7-23 and specify a different interval in the **Replication interval for "Always Run" (minutes)** dialog box. Public folder hierarchies are replicated using emails that are sent between Mailbox role servers. By default, if there is more than 300 KB of information, additional emails will be sent to relay the extra information. However, you can change this size limit using the **Replication message size limit (KB)** dialog box in Figure 7-23.

When you create new public folders, the public folder hierarchy will be automatically replicated to all other public folder databases according to the information that you specified on the Replication tab of the public folder database.

 **ANOTHER WAY**   You can also replicate the public folder hierarchy immediately by selecting the **Public Folders** node in the Public Folder Management Console and clicking **Update Hierarchy** in the action pane.

Once the public folder hierarchy has replicated, mailbox users who are configured to use a different public folder database will see the new public folder in their own public folder hierarchy and can access your new public folder using a ***public folder referral***. By using public folder referrals, Mailbox role servers can redirect mailbox users to the appropriate public folder database that contains the correct public folder.

Using public folder referrals to access public folder content can be quite slow, especially if the target public folder database is on a remote Mailbox role server. As a result, you can configure frequently used public folders to replicate their item content to another public folder database. Mailbox users who are configured to use a target public folder database will now no longer need to use public folder referrals to access the information in the public folder because their public folder database contains a copy of the items. Public folders that are replicated between public folder databases are called ***content replicas***. When new items are created in a content replica, the new items are replicated to all other content replicas.

To configure content replication for a public folder, you can highlight the public folder in the detail pane within the Public Folder Management Console, click **Properties** from the action pane and add the appropriate public folder databases to the Replication tab. The Marketing public folder shown in Figure 7-24 replicates its contents between the public folder databases on the servers EXCH1 and EXCH2.

Figure 7-24

Configuring Public Folder
Content Replication

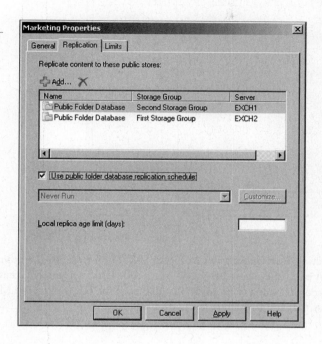

By default, public folders use the same schedule for replication specified on the Replication tab in the properties of their public folder database. However, for some public folders, you may need to deselect **Use public folder database replication schedule** and select or configure a different replication schedule. You can also configure the local public folder so that old items are automatically removed after a certain period of time using the **Local replica age limit (days)** dialog box in Figure 7-24. This will reduce the overall size of the local public folder as well as bandwidth that is needed to replicate its contents to other public folder databases.

Once you have configured content replication, you can highlight the public folder in the Public Folder Management Console and select **Update Content** from the action pane to replicate the contents immediately. Following this, new items that are added to the public folder will be replicated automatically using the schedule that you specified on the Replication tab of public folder properties.

Although content replicas reduce the number of public folder referrals, their replication will also use network bandwidth. As a result, it is important to keep the number of content replicas to a minimum. By default, if a mailbox user is given a public folder referral to a public folder that has content replicas, that mailbox user will be connected to the closest content replica using the site information stored in Active Directory (AD). Alternatively, you can manually choose the replicas that your Mailbox role server will refer mailbox users to using the Public Folder Referral tab of public folder database properties as shown in Figure 7-25.

Figure 7-25

Configuring Referrals on a
Public Folder Database

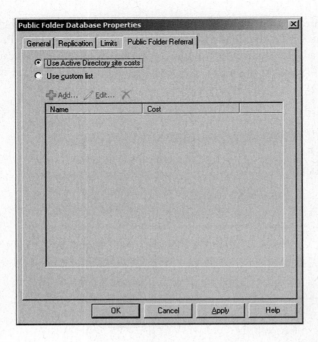

After selecting **Use custom list** in Figure 7-25, you can add the appropriate Mailbox servers and assign each one a cost between 1 and 100. Users who need access to a public folder that is not stored on your public folder database will be referred to the Mailbox server with the lowest cost that holds the desired public folder.

THE COMMAND
LINE WAY

You can also use cmdlets within the Exchange Management Shell to configure and manage public folder replication. To configure the replication of the public folder hierarchy on your public folder databases, you can use the **Set-PublicFolderDatabase** cmdlet. For example, to specify that the public folder hierarchy in the Public Folder Database on your Exchange server replicates between 6:00 p.m. Saturday and 8:00 a.m. Sunday at 15-minute intervals and allows you to view the existing client permissions on the Accounting public folder under the root of the default public folder subtree on the Mailbox server EXCH2, you could use the following command within the Exchange Management Shell:

Set-PublicFolderDatabase –Identity 'Public Folder Database' –ReplicationSchedule 'Saturday.6:00PM-Sunday.8:00AM'

You can use different time formats alongside the **–ReplicationSchedule** option. For example, **'Sun.18:00-Sun.8:00'** would also specify replication between 6:00 p.m. Saturday and 8:00 a.m. Sunday, and **'Always'** would replicate at all times at 15-minute intervals. If your organization has multiple public folder databases and referrals are often granted to content in other databases, you can also use the **–CustomReferralServerList** option to manually specify the servers used during referrals and their costs. To configure the Public Folder Database on your Exchange server to send public folder referrals only to the server EXCH1 (cost=5) and EXCH2 (cost=10), you could run the following command:

Set-PublicFolderDatabase –Identity 'Public Folder Database' -CustomReferralServerList 'EXCH1:5','EXCH2:10'

To replicate the public folder hierarchy immediately, you can use the **Update-PublicFolderHierarchy** cmdlet. For example, to replicate the public folder hierarchy on the server EXCH1, you could run the following command in the Exchange Management Shell:

Update-PublicFolderHierarchy –Server 'EXCH1'

Additionally, you can configure content replicas for public folders using the **Set-PublicFolder** cmdlet. For example, to add replicas of the Marketing public folder under the root of the default public folder subtree on your Mailbox role server to the servers EXCH1 and EXCH2 using the replication schedule defined in your public folder database, you could execute the following command within the Exchange Management Shell:

Set-PublicFolder –Identity '\Marketing' –Replicas 'EXCH1,EXCH2' -UseDatabase ReplicationSchedule $true

If you decide to later specify a different replication schedule for the Marketing public folder of 7:00 to 9:00 p.m. on Saturday, you can run the following command within the Exchange Management Shell:

Set-PublicFolder –Identity '\Marketing' –ReplicationSchedule 'Saturday.7:00PM-Saturday.9:00PM'

The time formats that you can use following the **–ReplicationSchedule** option to the **Set-PublicFolder** cmdlet are identical to those for the same option in the **Set-PublicFolderDatabase** cmdlet. In addition, you can manually force content replication of a public folder by using the **Update-PublicFolder** cmdlet. To replicate the contents of the Marketing folder under the root of the default public folder subtree on the server EXCH1, you can run the following command within the Exchange Management Shell:

Update-PublicFolder –Identity '\Marketing' –Server 'EXCH1'

The Exchange Management Shell can also be used to control public folder replication across the entire Exchange organization. You can use the **Suspend-PublicFolderReplication** cmdlet without any options or arguments to temporarily stop all public folder replication in your Exchange organization. Afterwards, you can run the **Resume-PublicFolderReplication** cmdlet to resume public folder replication in your Exchange organization.

For a full list of options to the cmdlets mentioned in this section, search for the appropriate cmdlet in the Exchange Server 2007 Help.

Configuring Public Folder Limits

As with mailboxes, you can specify space usage and deletion limits for public folders to save space on the Mailbox servers within your organization. Public folder limits can be configured using the Public Folder Management Console or the Exchange Management Shell.

Depending on their usage and function, public folders may contain a large number of items, and these items could utilize a large amount of storage space on the Mailbox role servers within your organization. Some organizations implement a dedicated Mailbox role server that only contains a public folder database to store the public folders within the organization. This prevents public folder growth from affecting the mailbox databases used to store emails.

Other organizations that are unable to implement a dedicated public folder server store their public folder databases on the same Mailbox role servers that host mailbox databases. In this situation, it is good practice to store the public folder database and mailbox databases on each Mailbox role server on separate hard disks or RAID arrays. This prevents public folders from using hard disk space that may be required for email storage.

Regardless of public folder database structure, you should implement storage limits for the public folders within a public folder database to prevent unnecessary disk space usage. Although you can implement these storage limits using the Limits tab of the public folder database as discussed in Lesson 4, "Configuring a New Exchange Server," they are often configured on a public folder level because different public folders will likely require different storage limits.

To configure storage limits for a single public folder, highlight the public folder in the detail pane within the Public Folder Management Console, click **Properties** in the action pane and highlight the Limits tab. By default, public folders are configured to use the limits set on the Limits tab of their public folder database, but you can override this by supplying the appropriate values as shown for the Feedback public folder in Figure 7-26.

Figure 7-26

Configuring Public Folder
Limits

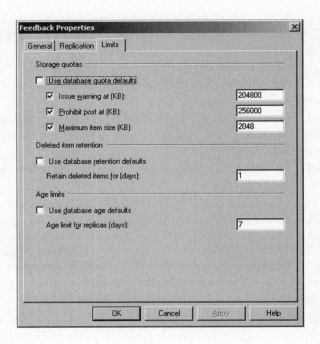

In Figure 7-26, the maximum size of a posted item is 2 MB (2048 KB). In addition, when
the total size of the posts in the Feedback folder reaches 200 MB (204800 KB), the owner of
the public folder receives an email indicating that the limit has been reached. When the total
size of posts reaches 250 MB (256000 KB), users receive an error message when attempting
to add items to the public folder and the public folder owner receives an additional email
from the system indicating the limit.

The owner of a public folder is the creator of the public folder. If a member of an administrative group such as Domain Admins creates a public folder, the group becomes the public
folder owner. If the Marketing public folder exists under the root of the default public folder
subtree on the server EXCH1, you can use the following command within the Exchange
Management Shell to view its owner:

**Get-PublicFolderAdministrativePermission –Identity '\Marketing' –Server 'EXCH1'
–Owner | Format-List**

Figure 7-26 also indicates that items received from content replicas of the Feedback public folder
are automatically deleted after 7 days to save space. Items that are deleted from a public folder are
not permanently deleted immediately. Instead, public folder databases retain deleted items for 14 days
by default. You can override this limit by specifying the appropriate number on the Limits tab of a
public folder. The Feedback public folder shown in Figure 7-26 retains deleted items for 1 day.

TAKE NOTE*

To recover deleted items from within Outlook or Entourage, simply navigate to **Tools >
Recover Deleted Items** and select the deleted items that you wish to recover. To recover
deleted items within OWA, click **Options** in the upper right corner, select **Deleted Items**
under the Options section in the left pane, and select the deleted items that you wish to
recover.

THE COMMAND
LINE WAY

You can also use the **Set-PublicFolder** cmdlet within the Exchange Management Shell
to configure public folder limits. For example, to set the same limits for the \Feedback
folder shown in Figure 7-26, you could use the following command within the Exchange
Management Shell:

**Set-PublicFolder –Identity '\Feedback' –MaxItemSize '2048' –StorageQuota '204800'
–PostStorageQuota '256000' –AgeLimit '7' –RetainDeletedItemsFor '1'**

Configuring Mail-Enabled Public Folders

↓
THE BOTTOM LINE

Public folders can be configured as recipient objects to accept email that is addressed to them. Instead of storing email in a mailbox database, public folders store email as items within their public folder database. You can mail-enable public folders and later manage them using the Public Folder Management Console or the Exchange Management Shell.

CERTIFICATION READY?
Configure public folders.
2.4, 3.5

Although you can store email within public folders, emails must be posted, moved, or copied to the public folder using Outlook, Entourage, or OWA. As a result, public folders are not recipient objects in their default configuration.

However, by mail enabling a public folder, you convert it to a recipient object that contains an email address. When you send email to the email address associated with the public folder, the emails are automatically posted to the public folder or sent to a moderator if a moderator is configured on the public folder. As a result, mail-enabled public folders do not require mailboxes.

Because mail enabled public folders are recipient objects, they will also have an associated object in AD as well as appear in the Global Address List. Moreover, mail-enabled public folders can be added to mail-enabled groups and custom address lists like any other recipient object.

There are several common uses for mail-enabled public folders. Some organizations use mail-enabled public folders to archive key emails. When users compose a new email that requires archiving, they can add the mail-enabled public folder to the **To** dialog box alongside other recipients. When the email is sent, a copy will be sent to the mail-enabled public folder recipient object and automatically stored in the public folder.

In addition, incoming email addressed to the mail-enabled public folder will also be stored in the public folder. Say, for example, that the Octavius organization encourages users who access their company Web site to send comments and feedback to feedback@octavius.net. By creating a public folder called Feedback and configuring it as a mail-enabled public folder with the email address feedback@octavius.net, the Feedback public folder will collect feedback emails from Web site users. Periodically, mailbox users within your organization who have the necessary client permissions to the public folder can view the feedback items within the folder, delete inappropriate items, and respond to other items as needed. In addition, you can configure *Send As permission* on the public folder to give certain mailbox users the ability to reply to email items within the folder as feedback@octavius.net. These mailbox users can then open an email item within a public folder using Outlook or Entourage, click the **Reply** button and specify feedback@octavius.net in the **From** dialog box. When the email is sent, it will appear as though it was from feedback@octavius.net rather than the actual mailbox user's email address.

 MAIL ENABLE A PUBLIC FOLDER

GET READY. Turn on the computer, and log in as the Administrator user account. Close any windows that appear on the desktop.

1. Click **Start, All Programs, Microsoft Exchange Server 2007**, and then click **Exchange Management Console**. The Exchange Management Console window appears.
2. In the console tree pane, highlight **Tools** and double click **Public Folder Management Console** in the detail pane. The Public Folder Management Console window appears.
3. Expand **Default Public Folders** in the console tree pane and highlight the folder that you wish to mail enable in the detail pane.
4. In the action pane, click **Mail Enable**.
5. Close the Public Folder Management Console and the Exchange Management Console.

TAKE NOTE*

To remove all email-related configuration for a mail-enabled public folder, you can select **Mail Disable** from the action pane.

THE COMMAND LINE WAY

You can also use the **Enable-MailPublicFolder** cmdlet within the Exchange Management Shell to mail enable an existing public folder. For example, to mail enable the Feedback public folder under the root of the default public folder subtree on your current Exchange server, you could run the following command within the Exchange Management Shell:

Enable-MailPublicFolder –Identity '\Feedback'

Alternatively, you can remove all email-related attributes from a public folder by using the **Disable-MailPublicFolder** cmdlet. For example, to remove all email attributes from the Feedback public folder used in the previous example, you could run the following command within the Exchange Management Shell:

Disable-MailPublicFolder –Identity '\Feedback'

CONFIGURE SEND AS PERMISSION FOR A MAIL-ENABLED PUBLIC FOLDER

GET READY. Turn on the computer, and log in as the Administrator user account. Close any windows that appear on the desktop.

1. Click **Start**, **All Programs**, **Microsoft Exchange Server 2007**, and then click **Exchange Management Console**. The Exchange Management Console window appears.

2. In the console tree pane, highlight **Tools** and double click **Public Folder Management Console** in the detail pane. The Public Folder Management Console window appears.

3. Expand **Default Public Folders** in the console tree pane and highlight the folder that you wish to configure Send As permission for in the detail pane.

4. In the action pane, click **Manage Send As Permission**. The Manage Send As Permission screen appears as shown in Figure 7-27.

Figure 7-27

Configuring Public Folder Send As Permissions

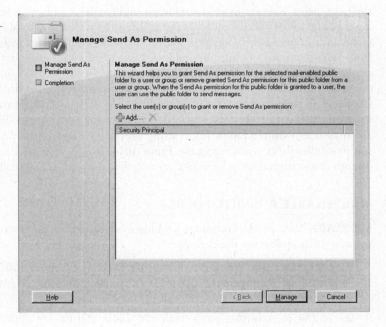

5. Click **Add**. Select the appropriate user or group in the Select User or Group window that appears and click **OK**.

6. Click **Manage**. The Completion page appears.

7. Click **Finish**. Close the Public Folder Management Console and the Exchange Management Console.

THE COMMAND
LINE WAY

You can also use the **Add-ADPermission** cmdlet within the Exchange Management Shell to grant the Send As permission to a user or group for a public folder. The following command will assign Jeff Smith the Send As permission to the Feedback public folder when executed in the Exchange Management Shell:

Add-ADPermission –Identity 'Feedback' -User 'Jeff Smith' -ExtendedRights 'Send As'

It is important that you do not specify the path to the public folder when using the **Add-ADPermission** cmdlet as it only searches AD for the object name. To list the users and groups that have Send As permission for the Feedback public folder, you can use the **Get-ADPermission** cmdlet as shown:

Get-ADPermission –Identity 'Feedback' | Format-List User,ExtendedRights

Use the **Remove-ADPermission** cmdlet from within the Exchange Management Shell as shown to remove the Send As permission granted to Jeff Smith for the Feedback folder. You will be prompted to confirm the removal.

Remove-ADPermission –Identity 'Feedback' -User 'Jeff Smith' -ExtendedRights 'Send As'

You can access the properties of a mail-enabled public folder within the Public Folder Management Console; you will see the same General, Replication, and Limits tabs present in all public folder properties. However, you will also see Exchange General, E-Mail Addresses, Member Of, and Mail Flow Settings tabs as shown in Figure 7-28. These tabs contain the same recipient object attributes that you have examined in Chapter 5, "Working with Recipient Objects."

Figure 7-28

Mail-Enabled Public Folder
Properties

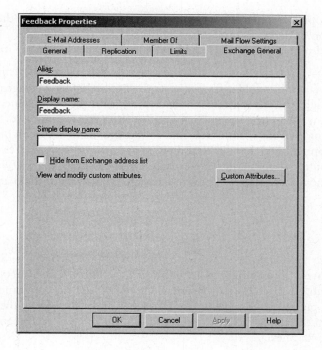

On the Exchange General tab, you can set the Alias and Display Name information as well as specify up to 15 custom attributes and hide the public folder from address lists. The Member Of tab lists groups to which the mail-enabled public folder belongs, and the E-Mail Addresses tab lists the email addresses used by the public folder. Unless modified, the default email address policy automatically assigns an email address of alias@domainname to the public folder. The Mail Flow Settings tab allows you to configure delivery options such as forwarding and Send On Behalf permission as well as message size restrictions and allowed senders.

To set any email-related properties for a public folder, you can also use the **Set-MailPublicFolder** cmdlet within the Exchange Management Shell. For example, to set the first custom attribute to TASU and the maximum item send limit to 2048 KB for the TASU Project public folder under the root of the default public folder subtree on your current Exchange server, you could run the following command within the Exchange Management Shell:

Set-MailPublicFolder –Identity '\TASU Project' –CustomAttribute1 'TASU' –MaxSendSize '2048'

You can also use the **Get-MailPublicFolder** cmdlet to obtain email-related information for a public folder. For example, the following command in the Exchange Management Shell will display the name and first custom attribute set on each public folder in the public folder database on your Exchange server:

Get-MailPublicFolder | Format-List Name,CustomAttribute1

Removing Public Folders

Provided that you have the appropriate permission, you can remove public folders and their contents using the Public Folder Management Console, the Exchange Management Shell, Outlook, Entourage, or OWA.

TAKE NOTE*

You must first mail disable a mail-enabled public folder before removing it.

Although public folder are typically created by users who have the appropriate client permission underneath an existing public folder, only members of the Exchange Public Folder Administrator or Exchange Organization Administrator roles can remove a public folder.

To remove a public folder from within the Public Folder Management Console, you can highlight the appropriate public folder within the detail pane, select **Remove** in the action pane, and click **Yes** to confirm the action when prompted. Alternatively, you can delete a folder from within Outlook, Entourage, or OWA by right clicking it, selecting the appropriate **Delete** or **Delete Folder** option, and clicking **Yes** to confirm the deletion. When you remove a public folder using Outlook, Entourage, OWA, or the Public Folder Management Console, all subfolders and the items within them are automatically removed as well.

THE COMMAND LINE WAY

To remove a public folder from within the Exchange Management Shell, you can use the **Remove-PublicFolder** cmdlet. However, the **Remove-PublicFolder** cmdlet does not remove subfolders unless the **–Recurse** option is specified. For example, to remove the Feedback public folder and all of its subfolders under the root of the default public folder subtree on the server EXCH2, you could run the following command in the Exchange Management Shell:

Remove-PublicFolder –Identity '\Feedback' –Server 'EXCH2' –Recurse

After running this command, you will be prompted to confirm each deletion or press **A** to confirm all deletions. To test the removal of the Feedback public folder to see if you will receive any errors without actually removing the public folder, you can append the **–WhatIf** option to the previous command.

■ Working with Multiple Public Folders

THE BOTTOM LINE

Like the recipient objects introduced in Chapter 5, "Working with Recipient Objects," you can create, configure, and manage multiple public folders using bulk management commands within the Exchange Management Console or by selecting several public folders within the Public Folder Management Console.

CERTIFICATION READY?
Implement bulk management of mail-enabled objects.
2.6

You can apply the bulk management techniques that you learned in Lesson 6, "Address Lists, Policies, and Bulk Management" to public folders and mail-enabled public folders. For most tasks, you can create CSV files and use the **Import-CSV** cmdlet within the Exchange Management Shell to send the information in the CSV file to the appropriate public folder cmdlet.

For example, to create the public folder structure shown in Figure 7-29, you could first create a CSV file called **C:\Public Folders.csv** that has two fields as shown in Figure 7-30. The first field could be called Name and list the names of each new public folder whereas the second field could be called Path and list the path that the public folder should be created under. Because public folder names can contain spaces, you should enclose each name and path within double or single quotes to ensure that the CSV file is processed correctly. In addition, public folders that need to be created under the root of the default public folder tree should list a path of "\".

Figure 7-29
Viewing Public Folder Structure

Public Folder Management Console
File Action View Help
Public Folders - exch1.octavius.net
Default Public Folders
Accounting
Accounts Payable
Accounts Receivable
General Accounting
Audits
Payroll
Feedback
Human Resources
Marketing
East Region
West Region
System Public Folders
Default Public Folders... 4 objects
Create Filter
Name
Parent Path
Accounting
Feedback
Human Resources
Marketing
Actions
Default Public Folders
New Public Folder...
Export List...
View
Refresh
Help
Accounting
Update Content
Mail Enable
Remove
Properties
Help

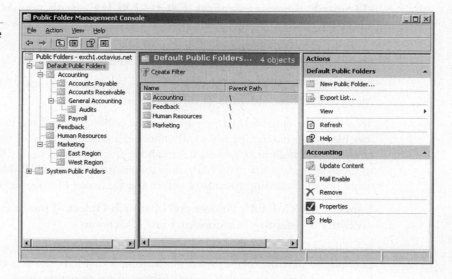

Figure 7-30
New Public Folders.csv File

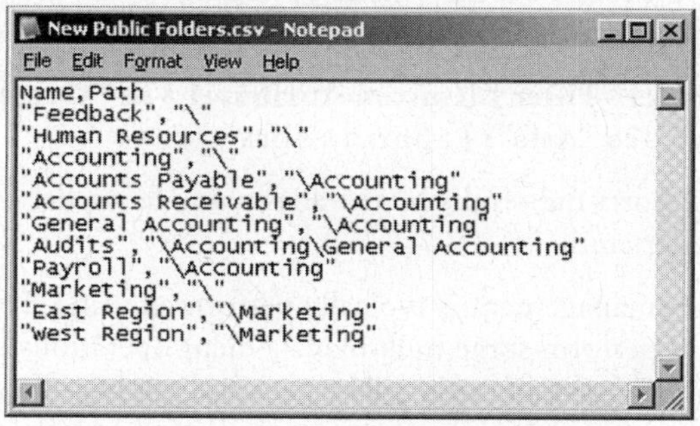

New Public Folders.csv - Notepad
File Edit Format View Help
Name,Path
"Feedback","\"
"Human Resources","\"
"Accounting","\"
"Accounts Payable","\Accounting"
"Accounts Receivable","\Accounting"
"General Accounting","\Accounting"
"Audits","\Accounting\General Accounting"
"Payroll","\Accounting"
"Marketing","\"
"East Region","\Marketing"
"West Region","\Marketing"

Next, you could run the following command within the Exchange Management Shell on the appropriate Mailbox role server to create the public folder structure:

Import-CSV 'C:\New Public Folders.csv' | ForEach-Object –Process { New-PublicFolder –Name $_.Name –Path $_.Path }

Once created, you can configure or manage these new public folders using bulk management commands. Because most cmdlets that configure and manage public folders require the path of the public folder, you could create a CSV file that lists each folder's path as shown in Figure 7-31 with the **C:\Public Folders.csv** file.

Figure 7-31

Public Folders.csv File

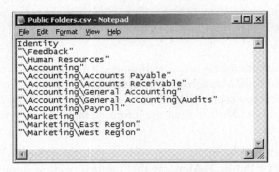

Next, to add content replicas for the public folders listed in the **C:\Public Folders.csv** file on the servers EXCH2 and EXCH3 and set a replication schedule between 10:00 p.m. Saturday and 6:00 a.m. Sunday, you could run the following command within the Exchange Management Shell:

Import-CSV 'C:\Public Folders.csv' | ForEach-Object –Process { Set-PublicFolder –Identity $_.Identity –Replicas 'EXCH2,EXCH3' –ReplicationSchedule 'Saturday.10:00PM-Sunday.6:00AM' }

In addition, you could use the following command in the Exchange Management Shell to mail enable the public folders listed in the **C:\Public Folders.csv** file:

Import-CSV 'C:\Public Folders.csv' | ForEach-Object –Process { Enable-MailPublicFolder –Identity $_.Identity }

To modify the email-related properties of the public folders listed in the **C:\Public Folders .csv** file, you must use the Set-MailPublicFolder cmdlet instead of the Set-PublicFolder cmdlet in the bulk management command. For example, to set the first custom attribute to Octavius for the mail-enabled public folders listed in the **C:\Public Folders.csv** file, you could use the following command within the Exchange Management Shell:

Import-CSV 'C:\Public Folders.csv' | ForEach-Object –Process { Set-MailPublicFolder –Identity $_.Identity –CustomAttribute1 'Octavius'

Not all public folder bulk management commands require the creation of a CSV file. For example, to view the mail-enabled public folders that have the first custom attribute set to Octavius or Arfa, you could use the **–Filter** option alongside the Get-MailPublicFolder cmdlet as shown in the following command:

Get-MailPublicFolder –Filter { (CustomAttribute1 –eq "Octavius") –or (CustomAttribute1 –eq "Arfa") } –SortBy Alias

This command also sorts the results by the alias name using the **–SortBy** option to the Get-MailPublicFolder cmdlet.

TAKE NOTE*

You can also create PowerShell scripts to manage public folders and mail-enabled public folders using the same syntax discussed in Lesson 6, "Address Lists, Policies, and Bulk Management."

Although most bulk management is typically performed using Exchange Management Shell commands, you can perform some bulk management operations using the Public Folder Management Console. You can optionally create and apply a filter in the detail pane of the Public Folder Management Console to narrow the list of public folders. Next, you can highlight several public folders within Public Folder Management Console while holding down the Shift or Ctrl keys and select **Update Content**, **Mail Enable**, **Mail Disable,** or **Remove** from the action pane to perform the related action.

SUMMARY SKILL MATRIX

IN THIS LESSON YOU LEARNED:

- Public folders provide a flexible means of storing email, calendar, journal, note, post, form, and task items within your organization for access by Outlook, Entourage, and OWA mailbox users. Public folders are also used to store calendaring, configuration information, and OABs for Outlook 2003, Entourage 2004, and earlier MAPI clients.

- Public folders are created within the default public folder subtree in a public folder database on the Mailbox role servers within your organization. The system public folder subtree stores public folders used internally by Exchange and should not be modified.

- When using OWA or an Exchange account in Outlook or Entourage, mailbox users automatically connect to the public folder database configured within their mailbox database properties.

- To create, configure, and manage public folders, you must be a member of the Exchange Public Folder Administrator role or the Exchange Organization Role as well as a local Administrator on the Mailbox role server that holds the public folder database.

- Client permissions are used to restrict access to public folder content whereas administrative permissions may be used to delegate administrative control to public folders.

- Custom forms can be used alongside public folders to create items that meet organizational needs.

- Public folders can contain custom view options as well as a home page that identifies the contents of subfolders.

- You can use the Folder Assistant to create filters that control the processing of items that are added to public folders. In addition, public folders may be configured to forward email to moderators who approve content before it is posted.

- Public folder hierarchies are replicated among the public folder databases within your organization. Users who need to connect to remote public folders are automatically referred to them by their public folder database server. You can also configure public folders to replicate their contents to other public folder databases as well as restrict the times for replication.

- To conserve space within a public folder database, you can specify limits for each public folder as necessary.

- Public folders may be mail enabled in order to receive email from other recipient objects. These emails are stored within the public folder alongside other items.

- The Public Folder Management Console is a graphical utility that may be used to create, configure, and manage public folders. It provides an alternative to the public folder cmdlets available within the Exchange Management Shell. In addition to these utilities, public folders can be created, configured, and removed within Outlook, Entourage, and OWA client utilities. Public folder options such as forms, home pages, view options, filters, and moderators can only be configured using Outlook clients.

- You can use the Public Folder Management Console or cmdlets within the Exchange Management Shell to perform bulk management of public folders. Public folder bulk management also supports the use of CSV files and the creation of PowerShell scripts.

■ Knowledge Assessment

Fill in the Blank

Complete the following sentences by writing the correct word or words in the blanks provided.

1. Before using public folders within _____, you must first configure a public folder server within the properties of the Exchange account.

2. The _____ is a graphical utility that may be used to create, configure, and manage public folders and is only available in Exchange Server 2007 SP1 and later.

3. To configure new public folder administrative permissions, you must use the _____ cmdlet within the Exchange Management Shell.

4. The _____ client permission grants all permissions to the content within public folders except for the ability to modify permissions.

5. To grant all administrative permissions on a public folder to a user, you can assign the _____ administrative permission to that user.

6. The _____ tab of public folder properties within Outlook may be used to configure how items are processed when moved or copied to a public folder.

7. When emails are sent to a mail-enabled public folder, they are stored within the public folder or forwarded to a _____, if one is configured.

8. To force content replication for a specify folder, you can select the appropriate folder within the Public Folder Management Console and select the _____ action.

9. You can specify a maximum item size for public folder posts on the _____ tab of public folder properties within the Public Folder Management Console.

10. The _____ can be used to create rules that specify how new posted items are processed within a public folder.

Multiple Choice

Circle the letter that corresponds to the best answer.

1. When you create a new public folder using the Public Folder Management Console, which of the following item types can be created in the public folder by default? (Choose all that apply.)
   a. email
   b. post
   b. calendar
   d. note

2. Which of the following client permission levels allows you to add items to a public folder but not view or manage other items that are in the public folder?
   a. contributor
   c. publishing author
   b. author
   d. editor

3. You wish to ensure that Bob Jones can modify the permissions that are set on the Comments public folder but not modify any permissions that have been assigned to Exchange administrators. Which administrative permission should you assign to Bob Jones for the Comments public folder?
   a. ModifyPublicFolderClientPermissions
   b. ModifyPublicFolderPermissions
   c. ModifyPublicFolderAdminACL
   d. ModifyPublicFolderACL

4. Which of the following MAPI clients use public folders to obtain OABs and calendaring information? (Choose all that apply.)

- **a.** Entourage 2004b
- **b.** Outlook 2007
- **c.** Outlook 2003
- **d.** Entourage X

5. Which of the following Exchange Management Shell commands will display all the public folders under the default public folder subtree on your current Exchange server?

- **a.** List-PublicFolder "\"
- **b.** Get-PublicFolder "\"
- **c.** List-PublicFolder –All
- **d.** Get-PublicFolder –Recurse | Format-List Name

6. You have recently opened a post item within a public folder using your Outlook MAPI client and wish to reply to the person who created the post item. Which button can you use to reply to the creator of the post item by posting a reply post item to the public folder rather than emailing the sender?

- **a.** Reply
- **b.** Post Reply
- **c.** Create Reply
- **d.** New

7. The arfa.com organization has a mail-enabled public folder called HRComments that stores comments and questions from users within the organization. As an HR manager, you plan on replying to some of these comments and questions but do not wish to let the sender know that the reply came from your email address. What permission must you have to the public folder to reply to comments and questions as HRComments@arfa.com?

- **a.** Owner
- **b.** Send As
- **c.** Send On Behalf
- **d.** Full Control

8. Your public folder database is quickly using the available space on your Mailbox server. After some investigation, you notice that many of the public folders contain items that are several weeks old. You would like to ensure that items older than 7 days are automatically deleted from the public folders within the public folder database. What should you do?

- **a.** Specify a **Local replica age limit** of 7 days on the Replication tab of public folder properties
- **b.** Check **Items must be deleted after 7 days** in the properties of the public folder database.
- **c.** Apply a filter that deletes items after 7 days on the **Administration** tab of public folder properties in Outlook
- **d.** Configure a maximum retention limit of 7 days using the **Set-PublicFolder** cmdlet.

9. You wish to create a custom form for use with a public folder. All new posts should use this form by default. Which of the following actions should you perform to provide this functionality? (Choose all that apply. Each answer provides a part of the solution.)

- **a.** Publish the form to the appropriate public folder.
- **b.** Specify the new form on the General tab of public folder properties within Outlook.
- **c.** Add the form to the Allowed Forms section on the Forms tab of public folder properties within the Public Folder Management Console.
- **d.** Create a new form using the Outlook Form Designer.

10. Which of the following cmdlets can be used to mail enable a public folder?

- **a.** Mail-Enable
- **b.** Mail-EnablePublicFolder
- **c.** Enable-PublicFolder
- **d.** Enable-MailPublicFolder

True/False

Circle T if the statement is true or F if the statement is false.

T   F   1. Each Exchange server within your organization can only have a single public folder database that contains a single public folder tree.

T   F   2. The public folder hierarchy is replicated between all Exchange folders within your Exchange organization by default.

T   F   3. You can only specify a single moderator within the properties of a public folder.

T   F   4. Client permissions are used to provide access to the content within a public folder as well as the ability to create subfolders.

T   F   5. The owner of a public folder is the person who created the public folder by default.

T   F   6. A mail-enabled public folder can be deleted using the **Remove-PublicFolder** cmdlet within the Exchange Management Shell.

T   F   7. Public folder home pages must be configured using an Outlook client.

T   F   8. Although multiple forms may be associated with a public folder, only one form may be selected as the default post item.

T   F   9. Public folder content replicas are configured within the properties of the public folder database.

T   F   10. You can configure size limits for a public folder using the Public Folder Management Console, Outlook, or the Exchange Management Shell.

Review Questions

1. Explain the purpose of the system public folder subtree within public folder databases.
2. Explain how content replicas may be used to improve public folder performance and reliability as well as reduce network traffic.

■ Case Scenarios

Scenario 7-1: Designing a Public Folder Proposal

As a new Exchange administrator within your organization, you are shocked to find that public folders are not used for collaboration or storage by any users within the organization. Moreover, the other Exchange administrators do not understand the benefits of using public folders and have only deployed public folder databases to fit the needs of older MAPI clients that require them for normal operation.

Prepare a proposal that you can present to the other Exchange administrators during the next department meeting that outlines some of the benefits of using public folders as well as the configuration options that may be used to control public folder usage.

Scenario 7-2: Implementing a Public Folder Structure

After hearing your proposal in Scenario 7-1, your department has approved the deployment of public folders and asked you to create and configure public folders for content sharing for each of the departments within your organization. Until the exact public folder needs of each department are determined over the next few weeks, you will start by creating a single public folder for each department and granting permissions for all users within the department so that they can add and manage their own items. Over the next few weeks, public folder users will email their public folder needs to a public folder using the email comments@domainname. Items within this folder will be read by all members of your IT department and used to determine the next steps to implementing additional public folders within your organization.

Explain how you would perform these actions using the various utilities available in Exchange Server 2007.

Configuring Email Protocols and Transport Rules

LESSON SKILL MATRIX

TECHNOLOGY SKILL	OBJECTIVE DOMAIN	OBJECTIVE DOMAIN NUMBER
Configuring Transport Rules	Configure transport rules and message compliance.	3.3
Configuring Client Access Protocols	Configure client connectivity.	3.6
Configuring the SMTP Protocol	Configure client connectivity.	3.6

KEY TERMS

Autodiscover service
Availability service
basic authentication
bounce message
Delivery Status Notification
  (DSN)
digest authentication
Edge Rules Agent

forms-based authentication
iCalendar
Integrated Windows
  Authentication
message classification
Non-Delivery Notification (NDN)
Non-Delivery Receipt (NDR)
Non-Delivery Report (NDR)

Out of Office Assistant
remote domain
Spam Confidence Level (SCL)
transport rule
Transport Rules Agent
Windows Rights Management
  Services
X.509 certificate

■ Configuring Client Access Protocols

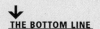

THE BOTTOM LINE

The CAS role servers within your Exchange organization provide access to email using a variety of different protocols including POP3, IMAP4, HTTP, MAPI, and Outlook Anywhere. The protocols used depend on the location of the email client computer as well as the email client programs used by users to access email. Moreover, each protocol offers unique configuration options that support its usage within the organization. Accordingly, a fundamental understanding of client access protocol configuration is key to deploying Exchange within any organization.

Configuring POP3 and IMAP4

CERTIFICATION READY?
Configure client
connectivity.
3.6

POP3 and IMAP4 are commonly used to obtain email from Internet clients. You can configure the ports, authentication, encryption, protocol limits, and calendaring options used by these protocols on the CAS role servers within your organization. To configure the POP3 and IMAP4 protocols, you can use either the Exchange Management Console or cmdlets within the Exchange Management shell.

POP3 is the oldest and most common email protocol used by Internet email clients. Most ISPs offer POP3 services to their home and business clients, and all email client programs have built-in POP3 support.

POP3 is designed to download email from an email server to a client for viewing. Because POP3 only downloads email and does not open a persistent connection between the email client and server, POP3 is appropriate for clients with slow dial-up modem connections to the Internet.

When a POP3 client connects to an email server, it first checks for any new email since the last connection and then downloads it. Although this frees up space on the email server, it was designed for obtaining email from a single client computer. Say, for example, that you connect to your email server and download all of the email that you received during the day using POP3. Later, you connect to your email server from a different POP3 client and download any new emails you received since the last connection. These new emails are only stored on the POP3 client computer and not on the original computer that you used earlier. As a result, the emails you received during the day are spread across two different client computers and no longer remain on the email server.

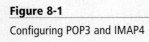

X REF

Configuring Outlook, Outlook Express, Entourage, and Windows Mail POP3 clients to store copies of email on the email server was covered in Lesson 4, "Configuring a New Exchange Server."

To prevent this, most POP3 clients let you choose whether to allow email to remain on the email server after it has been downloaded. However, in most clients such as Outlook, Outlook Express, Entourage, and Windows Mail, this is not the default behavior and you must manually configure the account properties to allow emails to remain on the email server.

IMAP4 is a more sophisticated protocol than POP3. Instead of downloading email from the email server, it simply views emails that are stored on the email server using a persistent connection. Any emails viewed over an IMAP4 connection are cached to the email client and updated when the email client later reconnects to the email server. Say, for example, that you view emails over an IMAP4 connection and your IMAP4 email client caches those viewed emails to the client computer's hard drive. Next, you delete those same emails using a different MAPI client and then return to your IMAP4 client. When your IMAP4 client reconnects to the email server, it will notice that those items were moved to the Deleted Items folder and will update its own cache to match.

In addition, to save bandwidth, IMAP4 clients only view the headers of emails from the email server. The contents of the email are only retrieved from the email server and cached on the client computer when the email is opened.

Another important IMAP feature is native public folder support. Most IMAP clients also allow you to specify only those public folders that you want your IMAP client to synchronize automatically and download new items from to save bandwidth and storage.

After enabling the POP3 and IMAP4 services on your CAS role servers as discussed in Lesson 4, "Configuring a New Exchange Server," you can configure how CAS role servers respond to POP3 and IMAP4 requests. To do this within the Exchange Management Console, simply navigate to the **Server Configuration** > **Client Access** node, highlight the appropriate CAS role server in the detail pane, and select the **POP3 and IMAP4** tab in the work pane as shown in Figure 8-1. You must be a member of either the Exchange Organization Administrator role or the Exchange Server Administrator role for the CAS role server to configure POP3 and IMAP4 settings.

Figure 8-1

Configuring POP3 and IMAP4

Client Access			2 objects
Create Filter			
Name ▲	Role	Version	Outlook Anywhere Enabled
EXCH1	Hub Transport, Client Acc...	Version 8.1 (Build 240.6)	True
EXCH2	Hub Transport, Client Acc...	Version 8.1 (Build 240.6)	False

EXCH1

| Outlook Web Access | Exchange ActiveSync | Offline Address Book Distribution | POP3 and IMAP4 |

Protocol Name ▲
IMAP4
POP3

You can only configure POP3 and IMAP4 within the Exchange Management Console using Exchange Server 2007 SP1 or later. If you run the original release of Exchange Server 2007, you must use cmdlets within the Exchange Management Shell to configure POP3 and IMAP4.

To configure the POP3 or IMAP4 protocols, you can highlight **POP3** or **IMAP4** in the work pane as shown in Figure 8-1 and select **Properties** from the action pane. The properties for both the POP3 and IMAP4 protocols are nearly identical. On the General tab of POP3 or IMAP4 properties, you can configure the banner that email client programs will receive when they first connect to the POP3 or IMAP4 server as shown for the properties of POP3 in Figure 8-2.

Figure 8-2

Configuring POP3 General Settings

Although most email client programs do not display this message to the user, it is usually added to log files on the client computer and may assist in troubleshooting POP3 and IMAP4 connectivity problems. If the banner string shown in Figure 8-2 appears in the log file, it indicates that the email client program was able to successfully establish a connection to the POP3 service on the Exchange server. Because POP3 uses TCP port 110, you could also run the command **telnet server 110** (where server is the IP address or FQDN of the CAS role server) from a Windows command prompt on a client computer. If you see the banner string listed in Figure 8-2, the client computer is able to successfully interact with the POP3 service on your Exchange server. Alternatively, you could test an IMAP4 connection using the command **telnet server 143** (where server is the IP address or FQDN of the CAS role server) from a Windows command prompt on a client computer because IMAP uses TCP port 143 by default.

On the Binding tab of POP3 or IMAP4, you can configure your CAS role server to only listen on network interfaces that are configured with specific IP addresses as well as specify the ports that will be used by POP3 or IMAP4 connections. Figure 8-3 shows the default options on the Binding tab of POP3 properties, whereas Figure 8-4 shows the default options on the Binding tab of IMAP4 properties.

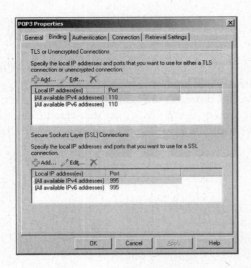

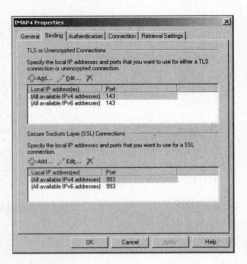

Figure 8-3

Configuring POP3 Interfaces and Ports

Figure 8-4

Configuring IMAP4 Interfaces and Ports

By default, the POP3 and IMAP4 services in Exchange Server 2007 are configured to listen to all IP addresses (IPv4 and IPv6) that are configured on network interfaces in your Exchange server.

POP3 email clients that do not use encryption typically contact the POP3 service on a CAS role server using TCP port 110. Similarly, IMAP4 email clients that are not configured for encryption use TCP port 143 when communicating with a CAS role server. However, you can configure email clients to encrypt POP3 or IMAP4 emails using either Secure Socket Layer (SSL) or Transport Layer Security (TLS).

SSL is the traditional technology used to provide encryption for POP3 and IMAP4 connections. SSL uses TCP port 995 for POP3S and TCP port 993 for IMAP4S by default. TLS is an enhanced version of SSL that can be used by newer email clients such as Outlook 2007 and Entourage 2008. Unlike SSL, TLS uses the same port as unencrypted traffic (TCP port 110 for POP3S and TCP port 143 for IMAP4S) by default.

Most Exchange servers only have a single network interface and contain clients that use the standard port numbers for POP3 and IMAP4. As a result, it is unnecessary to modify the settings on the Binding tab in most environments. However, if your Exchange server has several network interfaces and only services POP3 and IMAP4 clients on one of them using a nonstandard port, you can edit the default lines shown in Figure 8-3 and Figure 8-4 to reflect this. Simply click **Edit** in the appropriate section and specify a single IP address that the POP3 or IMAP4 service should bind to as well as a different port number to match the port number used by the POP3 or IMAP4 email clients.

X REF

Configuring certificates for use with SSL and TLS encryption is covered in Lesson 9, "Configuring Security."

In previous versions of Exchange Server, you needed to obtain an *X.509 certificate* in order to perform SSL or TLS encryption alongside the POP3 or IMAP4 service. However, Exchange Server 2007 automatically generates a sample X.509 certificate for use with SSL or TLS when you select the CAS role during the Exchange Server installation. This certificate is named according to your CAS role server's computer name and specified on the Authentication tab of both POP3 and IMAP4 properties. Figure 8-5 shows the Authentication tab of POP3 properties for the computer EXCH1. This sample certificate is only intended to provide support for SSL and TLS immediately following installation and should be replaced with a proper certificate.

Figure 8-5

Configuring Authentication

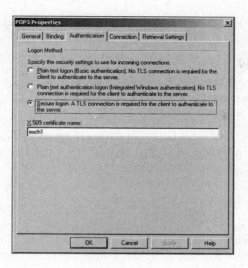

Moreover, POP3 and IMAP4 clients must authenticate before obtaining email from a CAS role server. When a client authenticates to a CAS role server, the CAS role server contacts Active Directory (AD) to complete the authentication process. If the username and password supplied by the user are authenticated by AD, then the CAS role server will allow access to email for that user.

In Exchange Server 2007, clients are required to encrypt their logon credentials using TLS (Secure logon) as shown in Figure 8-5. If you select **Plain text logon (Basic authentication)** in Figure 8-5, email client programs will transmit the user's logon credentials to the CAS role server in plain text. In this case, anyone who can obtain a copy of the network traffic could potentially see the username and password of the user and should only be configured if the email client program does not support any other authentication method. Alternatively, if you select **Plain text authentication logon (Integrated Windows authentication)** in Figure 8-5, email client programs will encrypt the user's logon credentials using an NTLM hash or Kerberos before sending them to the CAS role server. However, this method requires that the email client computer be joined to the same AD domain as the Exchange server.

To modify connection settings for POP3, you can edit the default values on the Connection tab of POP3 properties as shown in Figure 8-6. Similarly, you can modify the default values on the Connection tab of IMAP4 properties to configure IMAP4 connections as shown in Figure 8-7.

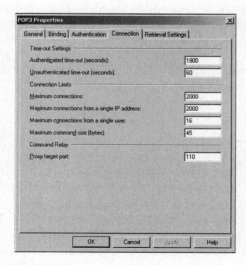

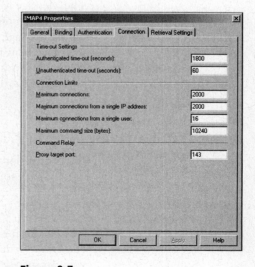

Figure 8-6

Configuring POP3 Connection Settings

Figure 8-7

Configuring IMAP4 Connection Settings

By default, POP3 and IMAP4 each allow up to 2,000 simultaneous connections per CAS role server. Although these 2,000 connections can be from a single IP address, only 16 of them can be from a single user. Furthermore, authenticated sessions will automatically end after 15 minutes (1,800 seconds) of inactivity, and unauthenticated sessions will automatically end after 60 seconds of inactivity. Unauthenticated sessions typically refer to the time period before a POP3 or IMAP4 client authenticates to the CAS role server.

By default, the POP3 service accepts POP3 requests that contain commands that are 45 bytes of size or less, whereas the IMAP4 service accepts IMAP4 requests that are up to 10 KB (10,240 bytes) in size. If your CAS role server receives a POP3 or IMAP4 request for email that resides in a mailbox on an Exchange 2003 server within your organization, it will redirect the request to the appropriate Exchange 2003 server using the port specified in the **Proxy target port** dialog box in Figure 8-6 and Figure 8-7.

The Retrieval Settings tab of POP3 or IMAP4 properties allows you to select the default email message format, sort order (Ascending or Descending), and calendar retrieval options for POP3 or IMAP4 connections. The Retrieval Settings tab of the default POP3 object is shown in Figure 8-8.

> **TAKE NOTE** *
>
> You can configure the **Maximum connections** in Figure 8-6 and Figure 8-7 to accept up to 25,000 POP3 and IMAP4 connections per CAS role server.

Figure 8-8

Configuring Calendar and Format Settings

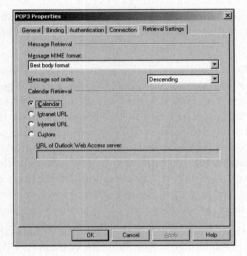

The Message MIME format drop-down box shown in Figure 8-8 allows you to select the same email message formats that you can configure within the properties of POP3 or IMAP4 on the Message Features tab of mailbox user properties as discussed in Lesson 5, "Working with Recipient Objects." By default, POP3 and IMAP4 email messages allow for Best body format, but you can choose Text, HTML, HTML and alternative text, Enriched text, as well as Enriched text and alternative text.

> **TAKE NOTE** *
>
> If you specify POP3 and IMAP4 options on the Message Features tab within the properties of a mailbox user, those options will take precedence over any POP3 and IMAP4 options that you specify on your Exchange server.

The default method to obtain calendar information using POP3 or IMAP4 is the universal *iCalendar* standard. However, if you have Outlook 2007 or Entourage 2008 clients or later, you can specify that they obtain calendar information from an Intranet or Internet URL. Alternatively, you can select **Custom** in Figure 8-8 and specify the URL for OWA to obtain calendar information.

THE COMMAND LINE WAY

You can also use the **Set-POPSettings** cmdlet in the Exchange Management Shell to manage POP3 settings for the CAS role servers within your Exchange organization. Similarly, the **Set-IMAPSettings** cmdlet can be used to manage IMAP4 settings for the CAS role servers within your Exchange organization. For example, to set the maximum number of POP3 and IMAP4 connections to 25,000 on the server EXCH1, you could run the following commands in the Exchange Management Shell:

Set-POPSettings -Server 'EXCH1' –MaxConnections '25000'

Set-IMAPSettings -Server 'EXCH1' –MaxConnections '25000'

If you omit the **–Server** option to the cmdlets in the previous example, all CAS role servers will be affected. The Set-POPSettings and Set-IMAPSettings cmdlets can be used to configure any of the settings shown earlier within the properties of POP3 or IMAP4 in the Exchange Management Console. For more information on these cmdlets and their options, search for Set-POPSettings and Set-IMAPSettings within Exchange Server 2007 Help.

Configuring HTTP

Email clients typically access web-based email systems such as OWA using the Hypertext Transfer Protocol (HTTP). Like POP3 and IMAP4, you can configure protocol limits, ports, and authentication for HTTP as well as access restriction options and bandwidth limits. Although you can configure some HTTP options within the Exchange Management Console and Exchange Management Shell, some HTTP configuration must be performed using the Default Web site within the IIS Manager console.

Web-based email systems are fast becoming a common way of obtaining email on mobile computers because they only require a web browser. Client computers use their web browser to contact a web server that contains programs that allow you to retrieve and manage email from an email server as well as compose new emails that are sent by an email server. Moreover, web browsers communicate to these web servers using HTTP or HTTPS, which are unlikely to be restricted by firewalls. As a result, you can check email using a web-based email system from nearly any location and from free wireless connections when traveling with a mobile computer.

TAKE NOTE*

Although web-based email systems are common today, they are unlikely to replace email client programs because their interface, usability, and features are limited to those that can be displayed in a web page within the web browser. As a result, most organizations use web-based email systems as a backup method for obtaining email or for users who travel.

ANOTHER WAY

Recall that you can also use **https:// Mailbox_server/ exchange/username** or **https://Mailbox_server/ exchange** within the URL dialog box of a web browser to gain access to OWA.

In Exchange Server 2007, OWA is the program used alongside the Default Web site in IIS on each CAS role server to provide web-based email for clients with a web browser. OWA provides a Web site that allows users to obtain, manage, and compose emails that are then processed by the CAS role server that hosts OWA.

Moreover, the Default Web Site in IIS is configured to require SSL connections using an X.509 certificate that was generated during installation. As a result, users must use the URL https://CAS_server/owa in their web browser instead of http://CAS_server/owa when connecting to OWA in the default configuration. As with POP3 and IMAP4, the SSL certificate used by the Default Web Site is named for the server and only intended to provide support for HTTP+SSL (HTTPS) immediately following installation. Afterward, it should be replaced with a proper SSL certificate.

In Lesson 4, you learned how to configure OWA options such as WebReady document viewing and allowed file types using the **Server Configuration** > **Client Access** node within the Exchange Management Console. You can also configure the URL and authentication information used by OWA HTTPS clients by navigating to the same node within the Exchange Management Console as a member of the Exchange Organization Administrator role or the Exchange Server Administrator role for the CAS role server. Simply select the appropriate CAS role server in the detail pane, highlight **owa (Default Web Site)** under the Outlook Web Access tab in the work pane, and click **Properties** in the action pane. The General tab of owa (Default Web Site) properties allows you to set the default URL that internal and external clients will use when connecting to OWA as shown in Figure 8-9. For the server exch1.octavius .net shown in Figure 8-9, the default URL used by internal clients is https://exch1.octavius .net/owa. To allow for clients outside your organization to connect to OWA on your CAS role server using HTTPS, you must specify a URL in the External URL dialog box that users will use to connect. This URL must have a corresponding record in DNS and is automatically sent to the CAS role server in the HTTPS header from the web browser. If the CAS role server receives a different URL in the header, it will reject the HTTPS request. Consequently, if external HTTPS traffic must pass through a proxy server such as Microsoft ISA Server before it is forwarded to your CAS role servers, you must place the URL of the proxy server in the External URL dialog box in Figure 8-9 so that OWA does not reject the HTTPS request.

Figure 8-9

Configuring OWA URLs

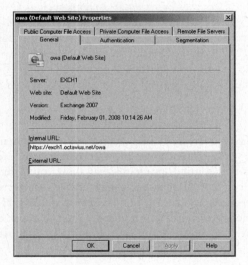

You can also configure the type of authentication method used by OWA on the Authentication tab of owa (Default Web Site) properties as shown in Figure 8-10. By default, OWA requires that users enter their credentials on the OWA logon form shown

Figure 8-10

Configuring OWA
Authentication

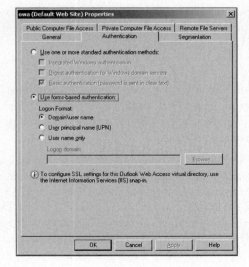

earlier in Figure 4-19. This type of authentication is called *forms-based authentication* and requires SSL. The default logon name format accepted on the OWA form is Domain\ username (i.e., octavius.net\jeff.smith) but you can modify the format to use the UPN (i.e., jeff.smith@octavius.net) or the username only (i.e., jeff.smith). If you choose the username only format, you must click the **Browse** button in Figure 8-10 and select the domain that will be used for logons.

If you select **Use one or more standard authentication methods** in Figure 8-10, you can choose different logon methods to use instead of the OWA logon form shown earlier in Figure 4-19. *Integrated Windows Authentication* automatically passes your username and password to the CAS role server using an NTLM hash or Kerberos and requires that the client computer be joined to the same domain as the CAS role server. *Digest authentication* uses a digital hash to protect the password when sending the username and password to the CAS role server. *Basic authentication* sends the username and password to the CAS role server unencrypted and is a poor security practice if you are not using SSL on your CAS role server to protect HTTP traffic.

TAKE NOTE*

To use digest authentication, user accounts must be configured to store passwords using reversible encryption on the Account tab of user account properties or within the Account Policies section of a GPO.

Because OWA uses the Default Web Site in IIS, you can configure other HTTP-related options within IIS Manager (**Start** > **All Programs** > **Administrative Tools** > **Internet Information Services (IIS) Manager**) provided that you are a member of the local Administrators group on the CAS role server. Expand the **Web Sites** folder under your CAS role server in IIS Manager, right click **Default Web Site**, and select **Properties**. On the Web Site tab of Default Web Site properties as shown in Figure 8-11, you can configure the port numbers and network interfaces used for HTTP connections. By default, HTTP connections are allowed on any IP address configured on network interfaces in your CAS role server. However, if your CAS role server has several network interfaces, you can direct IIS to only listen for HTTP connections on a single network interface by clicking **Advanced** and specifying a single IP address. Similarly, HTTP connections use TCP port 80 by default whereas HTTPS connections use TCP port 443. If the web browsers that connect to your CAS role servers use a nonstandard HTTP or HTTPS port, you can change these numbers. You can also modify the amount of time before idle HTTP sessions are automatically ended. The default is 120 seconds.

Figure 8-11

Configuring HTTP Interfaces and Ports

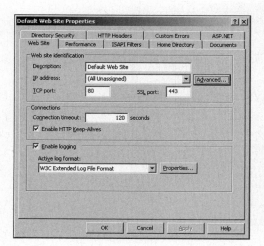

Additionally, you can limit the number of HTTP connections as well as the amount of bandwidth that HTTP traffic uses on your CAS role server using the Performance tab of Default Web Site properties as shown in Figure 8-12. Limiting the number and bandwidth of HTTP connections will prevent HTTP connections from adversely affecting the performance of other protocols on your CAS role server such as MAPI, POP3, and IMAP4.

Figure 8-12

Configuring HTTP Restrictions

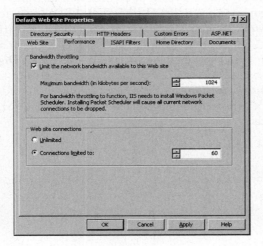

The Default Web Site listed in Figure 8-12 allows up to 60 concurrent HTTP or HTTPS connections and restricts the total bandwidth used by all 60 connections to 1024 KB per second. If you configure bandwidth throttling in Figure 8-12, you must also install the **Windows QoS Packet Scheduler**. To install the Windows QoS Packet Scheduler, you can navigate to the properties of your network interface (**Start** > **Control Panel** > **Network Connections** > **Connection_Name**), click the **Install** button and add the **QoS Packet Scheduler** service.

On the Directory Security tab of Default Web Site properties, you can configure authentication methods used by all virtual directories under the Default Web Site, IP address, and domain name restrictions, as well as the certificate used for SSL connections as shown in Figure 8-13. However, OWA authentication must be configured on the OWA virtual directory in the Exchange Management Console rather than within IIS Manager, and the default certificate configured in the Default Web Site should be replaced with a proper certificate.

Figure 8-13

Configuring Directory Security

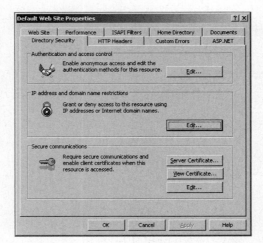

By default, all computers are allowed to connect to OWA on your CAS role server using HTTP/HTTPS. To restrict this, simply click the **Edit** button in the **IP address and domain name restrictions section** of Figure 8-13 and specify the appropriate information in the IP Address and Domain Name Restrictions window. You can specify computers by IP address, an IP network, or a domain name. In Figure 8-14, all computers are allowed to connect except for computers that have a DNS record in the arfa.com domain, computers that have an IP address on the 10.1.1.0 network (subnet mask 255.255.255.0), and the computer with the IP address 192.168.1.5. To restrict HTTP access to your CAS role server to certain computers only, you could instead select **Denied access** as shown in Figure 8-14 and add only those computers that require access.

Figure 8-14

Configuring IP Address and Domain Name Restrictions

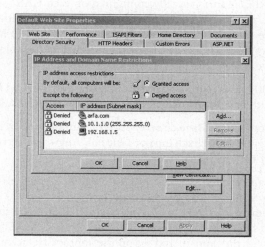

THE COMMAND LINE WAY

You can also use the **Set-OWAVirtualDirectory** cmdlet in the Exchange Management Shell to configure HTTP-related settings for OWA. For example, to configure digest authentication for OWA on the server EXCH1, you could run the following command in the Exchange Management Shell:

Set-OWAVirtualDirectory -Identity 'EXCH1\owa (Default Web Site)' -DigestAuthentication

For more information on the Set-OWAVirtualDirectory cmdlet and its options, search for Set-OWAVirtualDirectory within Exchange Server 2007 Help.

Configuring MAPI RPC and Outlook Anywhere

Exchange servers use the MAPI protocol to work closely with Entourage and Outlook clients within the local area networks (LANs) in your organization. As a result, MAPI RPC requires the least configuration of any email protocol. However, to use MAPI connections from remote networks using Outlook Anywhere, you will need to configure the Autodiscover and Availability services to allow for autoconfiguration, Online Address Book (OAB), and calendaring options using the Exchange Management Shell.

MAPI is similar to IMAP4 in structure and function. Like IMAP4, MAPI creates a persistent connection between the email client and server as well as allows for public folder support. However, MAPI protects the content of its emails so that they cannot be read in plain text when they are transferred across the network. In addition, because MAPI was developed by Microsoft, it contains additional features that work closely with Outlook and Entourage clients only.

Because MAPI connections are persistent and use RPCs to send information between the email server and client, they are appropriate for high-speed LAN use only. As a result, most Outlook and Entourage clients with an Exchange account (MAPI RPC) configured are within an organization and connect to the organization's Exchange servers using a LAN.

Email clients can also use MAPI RPC from across the Internet to connect to their Exchange server; however MAPI RPC must be contained within HTTP or HTTPS packets because most firewalls block RPC traffic. Outlook Anywhere is a protocol that tunnels MAPI RPC traffic within HTTP or HTTPS packets and is supported in Outlook 2003 and later MAPI clients.

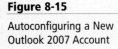

Enabling Outlook Anywhere on a CAS role server was covered in Lesson 4, "Configuring a New Exchange Server."

By default, MAPI RPC is automatically configured on each CAS role server. As a result, internal MAPI RPC clients can connect to all CAS role servers within your organization by default. However, to allow Outlook Anywhere (RPC over HTTP) MAPI clients to connect to your CAS role server from across the Internet, you must first enable the Outlook Anywhere protocol.

Exchange Server 2007 adds two new services that can only be used by Outlook 2007, Entourage 2008, and later MAPI clients: the Autodiscover and Availability services.

MAPI clients can contact the **Autodiscover service** running on Exchange Server 2007 to automatically configure a new Exchange or Outlook Anywhere account by simply specifying the email address of the recipient.

When configuring a new email account in Outlook 2007, you are first prompted to supply your email address in the Add New E-mail Account window as shown in Figure 8-15. By default, your domain username and primary email address are supplied at this window. If you click **Next** in Figure 8-15, Outlook 2007 will contact the Autodiscover service on an Exchange server for the domain and set up the appropriate account settings as shown in Figure 8-16. Alternatively, if you select **Manually configure server settings or additional server types** and click **Next**, you will need to manually enter your account configuration information.

Figure 8-15

Autoconfiguring a New Outlook 2007 Account

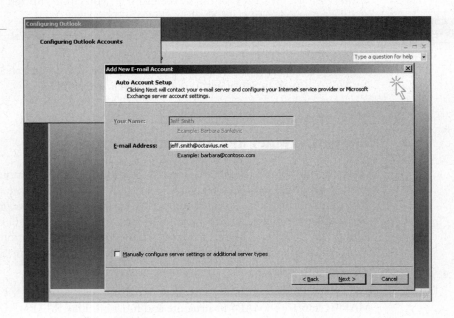

Figure 8-16

Completing the Autoconfigure
Process

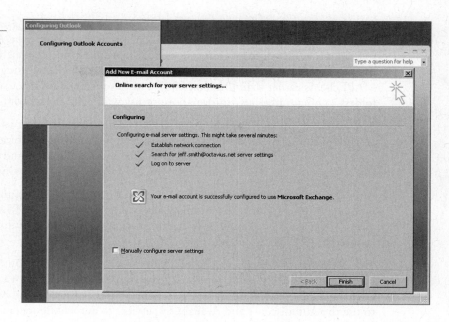

Similarly, when setting up a new Entourage 2008 account, you are first prompted to supply
your email address so that Entourage can use the Autodiscover service to configure your email
account settings as shown in Figure 8-17. Like Outlook 2007, Entourage 2008 also allows
you to configure account settings manually by clicking the **Configure Account Manually**
button shown in Figure 8-17.

Figure 8-17

Autoconfiguring a New
Entourage 2008 Account

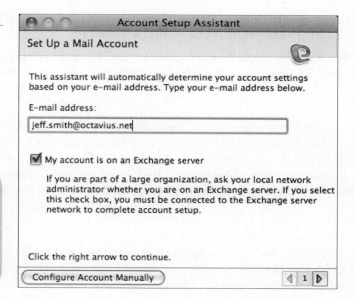

 X REF

Configuring new email
accounts in Outlook
2007 and Entourage
2008 was discussed in
Lesson 4, "Configuring a
New Exchange Server."

The Autodiscover service also reconfigures MAPI clients automatically when a mailbox is
moved. For example, if Jeff Smith's mailbox is moved to a different Mailbox role server at a
different site, Jeff Smith's MAPI client will automatically be configured to contact a new CAS
role server close to the Mailbox role server in the destination site.

In addition, the Autodiscover service allows Outlook 2007, Entourage 2008, and later MAPI
clients to obtain an OAB from the appropriate CAS role server directly. The MAPI client
connects to the Autodiscover service, locates the URL for the closest OAB, and downloads it
directly without relying on public folders. Previous versions of Outlook and Entourage must
still reply on system public folders to obtain OABs.

Similarly, these same MAPI clients can also take advantage of the *Availability service* in Exchange Server 2007. The Availability service is used alongside the Autodiscover service to obtain free/busy information for calendar scheduling. In previous versions of Exchange, the free/busy service provided this information to MAPI clients using system public folders. MAPI clients earlier than Outlook 2007 and Entourage 2008 must still rely on system public folders to obtain free/busy information for use with calendar scheduling.

The Autodiscover and Availability services are contacted using virtual directories under the Default Web Site in IIS on the CAS role servers within your organization. For the CAS role server exch1.octavius.net, the default URLs for the Autodiscover and Availability services are **https://exch1.octavius.net/Autodiscover** and **https://exch1.octavius.net/EWS**.

After an Exchange Server installation, the Autodiscover services on the CAS role servers within your organization are automatically configured with the URLs for automatic configuration, OAB, and Availability service information. However, this information is only available to internal MAPI RPC clients.

To enable the Autodiscover and Availability services for external Outlook Anywhere (RPC over HTTP) MAPI clients, you must specify an external URL for Outlook Anywhere, Exchange Web Services, and the OAB. Following this, Outlook Anywhere clients will be able to use the Autodiscover and Availability services to autoconfigure email accounts and obtain OABs and calendar scheduling information by connecting to the appropriate external URL.

The following commands within the Exchange Management Shell configure the Autodiscover and Availability services for Outlook Anywhere using the server exch1.octavius.net and the HTTPS protocol. In order to run these commands, you must be a member of the Exchange Organization Administrator role or the Exchange Server Administrator role for the CAS role server.

Set-OutlookAnywhere -Identity 'EXCH1' -ExternalHostname 'exch1.octavius.net'

Set-OABVirtualDirectory -Identity 'EXCH1\OAB (Default Web Site)' -ExternalURL 'https://exch1.octavius.net/OAB' -RequireSSL:$true

Set-WebServicesVirtualDirectory -Identity 'EXCH1\EWS (Default Web Site)' -ExternalURL 'https://exch1.octavius.net/EWS/Exchange.asmx' -BasicAuthentication:$True

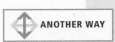
ANOTHER WAY

If you specified an external URL when you enabled Outlook Anywhere on your CAS role server, you do not need to execute the **Set-OutlookAnywhere** command afterward to set the external URL. Similarly, you can configure an OAB external URL in the properties of the **owa (Default Web Site)** object under the **Outlook Web Access** tab of **Server Configuration** > **Client Access** in the Exchange Management Console.

You can also test the functionality of the Autodiscover and Availability services using the **Test-OutlookWebServices** cmdlet within the Exchange Management Shell. For example, to determine whether the user Jeff Smith can access the CAS role server exch1.octavius.net using the Autodiscover and Availability services, you could run the following command within the Exchange Management Shell:

Test-OutlookWebServices –Identity 'Jeff Smith' –ClientAccessServer 'exch1.octavius.net' | format-list

If you omit the **–Identity** and **–ClientAccessServer** options to the **Test-OutlookWebServices** cmdlet, you will test the local CAS role server using the current user account.

■ Configuring the SMTP Protocol

THE BOTTOM LINE

The Hub role servers within your Exchange organization use the Simple Mail Transfer Protocol (SMTP) to receive emails from POP3 and IMAP4 clients as well as relay emails to other email servers. Although email relay is largely configured using send and receive connectors, you can use the Exchange Management Console or Exchange Management Shell to configure remote domains, transport settings, and SMTP limits to alter the relay of SMTP email within your organization.

CERTIFICATION READY?
Configure client connectivity.
3.6

SMTP is the protocol that email systems have largely been using since its formal standardization in 1982. As a result, it plays a vital role within any Exchange infrastructure. POP3 and IMAP4 clients send email to your Hub role servers using SMTP on TCP port 587 or 25, and Hub and Edge role servers relay email to other internal and external email servers using SMTP on TCP port 25.

The original SMTP protocol is only used by legacy email systems today. Instead, the newer Extended SMTP (ESMTP) protocol is used in its place and supports advanced functions such as authentication and encryption. In addition, these advanced functions are negotiated during an ESMTP session. When a computer starts an ESMTP connection to another computer, it first asks the other computer about the capabilities it supports and then adjusts its communication accordingly.

Nearly all email clients and email servers today support ESMTP and will fall back to using SMTP when communicating with other computers that do not support ESMTP. As a result, the term SMTP is commonly used when referring to either ESMTP or SMTP.

SMTP uses a series of text commands to send emails from one computer to another. Each time an SMTP command is sent, the other computer sends a reply to confirm that it received the SMTP command. Typical emails that are sent within an organization consist of over 20 separate SMTP commands.

As with POP3 and IMAP4, you can interact with the SMTP service on your Hub and Edge role servers using the **telnet.exe** command at a Windows command prompt. This is often useful in determining whether an email server supports SMTP or ESMTP. The first command in an SMTP session is HELO, whereas the first command in an ESMTP session is EHLO. Most email clients and servers today attempt an EHLO command when they communicate with SMTP. If successful, the other computer will respond with a list of the ESMTP features (such as authentication methods) that it supports. If the other computer only supports SMTP, then it will respond with an error code and the email client or server will then attempt a HELO command to see if the original SMTP protocol is supported.

If you type **telnet*server*25** (where *server* is the IP address or FQDN of the Hub or Edge role server), you will be able to type the EHLO command to see if the target email server supports ESMTP. Figure 8-18, shows the output from the **telnet exch1.octavius.net 25** command. The 220 line appears after running the telnet command to display the banner information from the SMTP service. The HELO command that was typed at the prompt afterward resulted in

Figure 8-18

Interacting with the SMTP Service

a 250 line that indicates that exch1.octavius.net supports SMTP. The EHLO command that was typed at the prompt following this resulted in several 250 lines that indicate the ESMTP features that exch1.octavius.net supports.

➕ **MORE INFORMATION**

To see a complete list of SMTP commands, search for "SMTP Commands and Definitions" on the Microsoft Technet Web site at http://technet.microsoft.com.

X REF

The configuration of send and receive connectors was covered in Lesson 4, "Configuring a New Exchange Server."

The Hub and Edge role servers within your Exchange organization process internal and external SMTP email using the information stored in send and receive connectors. However, you can also configure general SMTP protocol settings using various nodes within the Exchange Management Console.

By navigating to **Organization Configuration > Hub Transport** within the Exchange Management Console as a member of the Exchange Organization Administrator role, you can configure the processing of items sent to specific domains as well as SMTP transport settings.

Under the Remote Domains tab as shown in Figure 8-19, you can configure the processing of messages and message formats. After installation, there is a Default *remote domain* that applies to email that is sent to any external domain on the Internet (*). If you highlight the Default remote domain and click **Properties** in the action pane, you can configure the processing of Out of Office messages that are sent by Outlook or Entourage clients within your organization as shown in Figure 8-20.

Figure 8-19

Viewing the Default Remote Domain

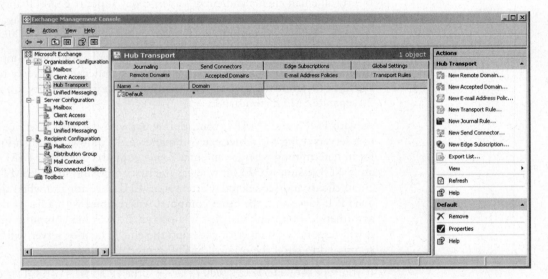

Figure 8-20

Configuring Out of Office Message Relay

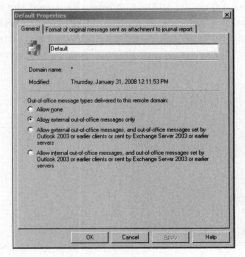

Out of Office messages are often used to give senders immediate notification that their email may not be read until a specified time when users go on vacation or business trips. Outlook and Entourage clients can use the ***Out of Office Assistant*** (**Tools** > **Out of Office Assistant** in Outlook and **Tools** > **Out of Office** in Entourage) to configure an autoreply message. If the user specifies that he or she is out of the office in the Out of Office Assistant, this message will automatically be sent in response to any emails that are received. Moreover, the Out of Office Assistant allows you to specify a different message for internal senders who are part of your Exchange organization and external senders who are not part of your organization.

By default, the Default remote domain allows Exchange Server 2007 Out of Office messages from Outlook 2007, Entourage 2008, and later clients to be relayed to external senders only. If your organization has Exchange 2000 or 2003 servers or MAPI clients that run an earlier version of Outlook or Entourage, you must select the appropriate option in Figure 8-20 to allow for internal or external Out of Office messages from legacy clients and servers.

If you select the **Format of original message sent as attachment to journal report** tab shown in Figure 8-21, you can also specify relay options such as whether to allow delivery reports, rich text, or automatic replies for the remote domain.

Figure 8-21

Configuring Message Relay and Formats

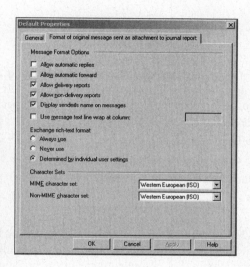

TAKE NOTE*

The **Format of original message sent as attachment to journal report** tab is mislabeled in Exchange Server 2007 SP1. The name of the tab should be **Message Format**, and the options specified on the tab apply to all SMTP email sent to the remote domain for which it applies.

If you wish to have different Out of Office or message format options for different external domains, you can create a new remote domain that applies to the correct external domain on the Internet and later specify the necessary options in the properties of the new remote domain. Any additional remote domains that apply to a specific domain will be used instead of the Default remote domain that applies to all domains on the Internet. For example, if you create a remote domain called Arfa that applies to all email sent to the arfa.com domain, its settings will always apply to emails that are sent to recipients in the arfa.com domain.

CREATE A NEW REMOTE DOMAIN

GET READY. Turn on the computer, and log in as the Administrator user account. Close any windows that appear on the desktop.

1. Click **Start, All Programs, Microsoft Exchange Server 2007**, and then click **Exchange Management Console**. The Exchange Management Console window appears.

2. In the console tree pane, expand **Organization Configuration** and highlight **Hub Transport**.

3. In the action pane, click **New Remote Domain**. The New Remote Domain window appears as shown in Figure 8-22.

Figure 8-22

Creating a New Remote Domain

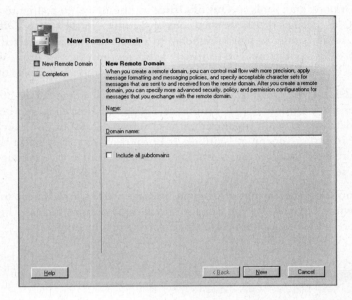

4. Type a name for your remote domain in the **Name** dialog box and type the FQDN of the remote domain in the **Domain name** dialog box. If the remote domain should apply to all subdomains of the FQDN that you specified in the Domain name dialog box, select **Include all subdomains**.

5. Click **New**. The Completion page appears.

6. Click **Finish** to close the New Remote Domain window.

7. Close the Exchange Management Console.

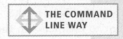

You can also use the **New-RemoteDomain** cmdlet within the Exchange Management Shell to create a new remote domain and the **Set-RemoteDomain** cmdlet to specify SMTP options for the remote domain. For example, to create a new remote domain called Arfa that applies to the arfa.com domain and all subdomains, you could run the following cmdlet within the Exchange Management Shell:

New-RemoteDomain -DomainName '*.arfa.com' -Name 'Arfa'

Next, to prevent Out of Office messages to this Arfa remote domain, you could run the following command within the Exchange Management Shell:

Set-RemoteDomain 'Arfa' –AllowedOOFType 'None'

You can also set Out of Office message options on an individual mailbox user using the **Set-Mailbox** cmdlet. For example, to allow all external Out of Office messages for the user Jeff Smith, you could run the following command within the Exchange Management:

Set-Mailbox –Identity 'Jeff Smith' –ExternalOOFOptions 'External'

Additionally, the **Get-RemoteDomain** cmdlet can be used to obtain the configuration information for an existing remote domain and the **Remove-RemoteDomain** cmdlet can be used to remove a remote domain. For more information on the remote domain cmdlets in this section, search for their names within the Exchange Server 2007 Help.

In addition to remote domain options, you can configure SMTP transport settings under the **Organization Configuration** > **Hub Transport** node within the Exchange Management Console. If you click the Global Settings tab in Figure 8-19, highlight **Transport Settings**, and click **Properties** in the action pane, you can configure the default maximum size for items that are sent and received as well as the default maximum recipients per message as shown in Figure 8-23.

Figure 8-23

Configuring General Transport Settings

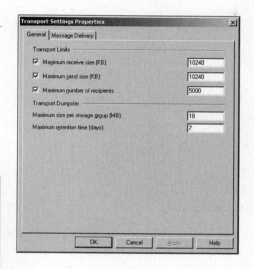

The Transport Dumpster settings shown in Figure 8-23 apply only to messages that have been sent from a mailbox that has been configured for Cluster Continuous Replication (CCR) and will be discussed in Lesson 13, "Providing for High Availability."

By default, incoming and outgoing SMTP messages can be 10 MB (10240 KB) in size and emails can be addressed up to 5,000 recipients. However, if you define the maximum receive size, maximum send size, and maximum number of recipients in the properties of a recipient object, it will override the limits that you set in the properties of Transport Settings.

On the Message Delivery tab of Transport Settings properties as shown in Figure 8-24, you can add the IP addresses of internal Hub role servers that will not participate in sender and spam filtering, as well as the **_Delivery Status Notification (DSN)_** codes that are allowed to be forwarded to recipient objects within your organization. DSNs are error messages that are sent by an email server to the sender of a message that could not be delivered. The DSN code is used to identify the type of error.

Figure 8-24

Configuring Message Delivery Options

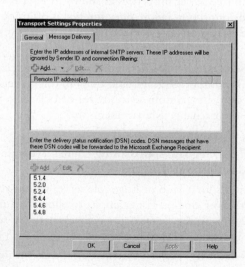

A DSN message is also called a **_Non-Delivery Report (NDR)_**, **_Non-Delivery Receipt (NDR)_**, **_Non-Delivery Notification (NDN)_**, or a **_bounce message_**.

Some SMTP settings can also be applied to individual Hub role servers within your organization. To configure these settings, you must be a member of the Exchange Organization Administrator role or the Exchange Server Administrator role on the Hub role server. Simply highlight the appropriate Hub role server in the detail pane under the **Server Configuration** > **Hub Transport** node within the Exchange Management Console and select **Properties** from the action pane. On the Limits tab of Hub role server properties, you can configure SMTP protocol parameters as shown in Figure 8-25.

Figure 8-25

Configuring SMTP Server Limits

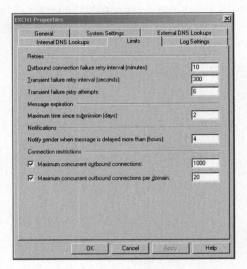

The default limits shown in Figure 8-25 indicate that the Hub role server will attempt to redeliver SMTP messages after 10 minutes if the first attempt could not be delivered due to network problems. If the redelivery fails, the Hub role server will attempt to redeliver the message up to 6 more times every 5 minutes (300 seconds). The senders of a message that is still stored in the SMTP queue after 4 hours will receive an email notification indicating that their email could not be delivered. If the email remains in the SMTP queue for 2 days, it will be automatically removed. In addition, the Hub role server allows for up to 1,000 concurrent SMTP sessions to other email domains on the Internet. However, only 20 concurrent SMTP sessions are allowed to the same email domain on the Internet.

You can also set SMTP limits on individual Edge role servers provided that you are a member of the local Administrators group on the Edge role server. Simply highlight **Edge Transport** in the console tree within the Exchange Management Console on the Edge role server, highlight the appropriate Edge role server in the detail pane, and select **Properties** from the action pane. The Limits tab of Edge role server properties contains the same configuration options as the Limits tab of Hub role server properties as shown in Figure 8-25. However, the default value for the Outbound connection failure retry interval is 30 minutes and the default value for the Transient failure retry interval is 600 seconds.

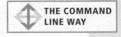

THE COMMAND LINE WAY

You can also use the **Set-TranportConfig** cmdlet within the Exchange Management Shell to configure the SMTP transport settings used by Hub role servers within your organization. For example, to set the maximum send size for SMTP relay, you could run the following cmdlet within the Exchange Management Shell:

Set-TransportConfig –MaxSendSize '20MB'

Similarly, you can run the **Get-TransportConfig** cmdlet to obtain the current SMTP transport settings used within your Exchange Organization.

To configure SMTP limits for a Hub or Edge role server within your organization, you can use the **Set-TransportServer** cmdlet. For example, to allow for a maximum of 300 outbound SMTP connections on the server exch1.octavius.net, you could run the following command within the Exchange Management Shell:

Set-TransportServer –Identity 'exch1.octavius.net' –MaxOutboundConnections '300'

To view SMTP settings for your Hub role servers you can also use the **Get-TransportServer** cmdlet. For more information on the Get-TransportConfig, Set-TransportConfig, Get-TransportServer, and Set-TransportServer cmdlets, simply search for their names within the Exchange Server 2007 Help.

■ Configuring Transport Rules

Transport rules may be used within an Exchange organization to modify the processing of email on the Hub and Edge role servers. Due to their complexity, you must first understand the application and features of transport rules before creating or managing them within your Exchange organization.

Understanding Transport Rules

Transport rules function differently on the Hub and Edge role servers within your organization. Each transport rule is comprised of conditions and exceptions that match emails as well as actions that determine how to process those emails. A wide variety of criteria, as well as several different email processing actions, may be used within conditions and exceptions. Before you create transport rules on the Hub and Edge role servers within your organization, you must first understand the various components of transport rules and their usage.

Because Hub and Edge role servers perform all email relay within an organization, they are the ideal location to apply rules that modify emails and alter email processing. These rules are called ***transport rules*** and can be used to provide several important email-related functions within an organization. For example, you can create transport rules to prevent the relaying of email that contains inappropriate keywords or confidential information. In addition, transport rules can be used to add legal disclaimers to certain email messages, such as those that are sent outside the organization. You can also configure transport rules to archive key emails, forward sensitive emails to another person for inspection, reject emails, log message information, or mark emails as spam messages.

Hub and Edge role servers within your organization maintain separate transport rules. When you configure transport rules on a Hub role server, those rules are stored within AD and used by the ***Transport Rules Agent*** on all Hub role servers within your organization. Only members of the Exchange Organization Administrator role can create and manage transport rules on the Hub role servers within your organization. Alternatively, when you configure transport rules on an Edge role server, those rules are stored on the local Edge role server and used by the ***Edge Rules Agent*** on that server only. If you have multiple Edge role servers within your organization, you must configure transport rules separately on each one. To create and manage transport rules on an Edge role server, you only need to be a member of the local Administrators group on the Edge role server.

Although transport rules can be used to perform a wide variety of functions on emails that are relayed by your Hub and Edge role servers, they contain a large set of configuration options as a result.

Transport rules are composed of three components: conditions, exceptions, and actions. The ***conditions*** of a transport rule are used to determine the emails that the transport rule applies to. Because the conditions of a transport rule can match a large number of emails, you can specify ***exceptions*** that exclude certain emails based on a certain criteria. For example, if you wish to create a transport rule that applies to all emails that have the keyword "Project" in their Subject line from users within the organization, you could specify a condition that matches any emails that have the word "Project" in their Subject line and specify an exception that excludes any emails from external senders.

If you specify multiple conditions within a single transport rule, emails must match all of the conditions for the transport rule to be applied. Alternatively, if you specify multiple exceptions, emails need only match a single exception to be excluded from the transport rule. In addition, the available conditions and exceptions are different for transport rules configured on a Hub role server and Edge role server.

Although the wording of conditions and transport rules in the Exchange Management Console is different to identify their application, the criteria used for conditions and criteria are the same. Table 8-1 lists the criteria that you can use for conditions and exceptions within a transport rule as well as the servers that they apply to.

Table 8-1

Criteria used within transport rule conditions and exceptions

CRITERIA	SERVER ROLE	DESCRIPTION
From people	Hub only	Matches emails with specific senders that you specify.
From a member of a distribution list	Hub only	Matches emails with senders who are members of a distribution group that you specify.
From users inside or outside the organization	Hub or Edge	Matches emails from internal or external senders (you must choose either internal or external).
Sent to people	Hub only	Matches emails with specific recipients that you specify.
Sent to a member of a distribution list	Hub only	Matches emails with recipients who are members of a distribution group that you specify.
Sent to users inside or outside the organization	Hub only	Matches emails sent to internal or external recipients (you must choose either internal or external).
Between members of one distribution list and another distribution list	Hub only	Matches emails that are sent between members of two different distribution groups that you specify.
When any of the recipients in the To field are people	Hub only	Matches emails with specific recipients you specify provided that those recipients are listed in the To field of the email.
When any of the recipients in the To field are members of a distribution list	Hub only	Matches emails sent to recipients provided that those recipients are listed in the To field of the email and are members of a distribution group that you specify.
When any of the recipients in the Carbon Copy (Cc) field are people	Hub only	Matches emails with specific recipients you specify provided that those recipients are listed in the Cc field of the email.
When any of the recipients in the Cc field are members of a distribution list	Hub only	Matches emails sent to recipients provided that those recipients are listed in the Cc field of the email and are members of a distribution group that you specify.
When any of the recipients in the To or Cc fields are people	Hub only	Matches emails with specific recipients that you specify provided that those recipients are listed in the To field or the Cc field of the email.
When any of the recipients in the To or Cc fields are members of a distribution list	Hub only	Matches emails sent to recipients provided that those recipients are listed in the To field or Cc field of the email and are members of a distribution group that you specify.
Marked with classification	Hub only	Matches emails that contain a specific classification that was selected in Outlook or Entourage before the message was sent.
When the Subject field contains specific words	Hub or Edge	Matches emails that contain specific word(s) within the Subject field of the email.
When the Subject field or the body of the message contains specific words	Hub or Edge	Matches emails that contain specific word(s) within the Subject field or body of the email.
When a message header contains specific words	Hub or Edge	Matches emails that contain specific word(s) within the message header of the email.

Table 8-1

CRITERIA	SERVER ROLE	DESCRIPTION
When the From address contains specific words	Hub or Edge	Matches emails that contain specific word(s) within the From field of the email.
When any recipient address contains specific words	Edge only	Matches emails that contain specific word(s) within the To, Cc, and Bcc fields of the email.
When the Subject field contains text patterns	Hub or Edge	Matches emails that contain specific text pattern(s) within the Subject field of the email. Text patterns are strings that may contain portions of a word, an entire word, or several words and other characters.
When the Subject field or the body of the message contains text patterns	Hub or Edge	Matches emails that contain specific text pattern(s) within the Subject field or body of the email. Text patterns are strings that may contain portions of a word, an entire word, or several words and other characters.
When the message header contains text patterns	Hub or Edge	Matches emails that contain specific text pattern(s) within the message header of the email. Text patterns are strings that may contain portions of a word, an entire word, or several words and other characters.
When the From address contains text patterns	Hub or Edge	Matches emails that contain specific text pattern(s) within the From field of the email. Text patterns are strings that may contain portions of a word, an entire word, or several words and other characters.
When text patterns exist in any recipient addresses	Edge only	Matches emails that contain specific text pattern(s) within the To, Cc, or Bcc fields of the email. Text patterns are strings that may contain portions of a word, an entire word, or several words and other characters.
When any attachment file name contains text patterns	Hub only	Matches emails that contain specific text pattern(s) within the file name of any attachment included in the email. Text patterns are strings that may contain portions of a word, an entire word, or several words and other characters.
With a spam confidence level (SCL) rating that is greater or equal to the limit	Hub or Edge	Matches emails that have been given a ***Spam Confidence Level (SCL)*** that is higher than a number that you specify. The SCL is a numerical value between 0 and 9 that indicates the likelihood that a email message is spam. SCL values are typically added by antispam software components within Exchange Server 2007. A message with an SCL of 0 is highly unlikely to be spam, whereas a message with an SCL of 9 is almost certainly spam.
When the size of any attachment is greater than or equal to the limit	Hub or Edge	Matches emails that have attachments that are larger than the size that you specify in KB.
Marked with importance	Hub only	Matches emails that are marked with Low, Normal, or High importance (you must choose a level). Outlook or Entourage users can choose an importance level for emails before they are sent.

The *actions* within a transport rule determine the actions that are performed on messages that match the transport rule. The allowed actions that you can contain within a transport rule on a Hub role server are different from the actions that you can contain within a transport rule on an Edge role server. Table 8-2 lists the actions that can be performed as well as the servers they apply to.

Table 8-2

Transport rule actions

ACTION	SERVER ROLE	DESCRIPTION
Log an event with message.	Hub and Edge	Adds an event to the Application event log on the local computer with a custom message that you specify.
Prepend the subject with string.	Hub and Edge	Adds a string that you specify to the beginning of the text in the Subject line of the email.
Apply message classification.	Hub only	Automatically applies a message classification to the email that you specify.
Append disclaimer text using font, size, color, with separator and fallback to action if unable to apply.	Hub only	Automatically adds text to the beginning or end of the email message using a specific font and color according to the settings and text that you specify.
Set the spam confidence level to value.	Hub and Edge	Automatically sets the SCL on the email to the value that you specify.
Set header with value.	Hub and Edge	Sets the message header field for messages to the text that you specify. If a message header field does not exist, it will be created with the text that you specify.
Remove header.	Hub and Edge	Removes the specified message header field.
Add a recipient in the To field addresses.	Hub and Edge	Adds an additional recipient that you specify to the To field of the email.
Copy message to addresses.	Hub and Edge	Adds an additional recipient that you specify to the Cc field of the email.
Blind carbon copy (Bcc) the message to addresses.	Hub and Edge	Adds an additional recipient that you specify to the Bcc field of the email.
Drop connection.	Edge only	Stops the SMTP connection from the remote email server without sending an NDR.
Redirect message to addresses.	Hub and Edge	Sends the email to a different recipient that you specify. The original recipient does not receive a copy of the email and no NDR is sent.
Put message in quarantine.	Edge only	Sends the email to the spam quarantine mailbox instead of sending it to the original recipient. You can configure the location of the spam quarantine mailbox by using the -QuarantineMailbox option to the **Set-ContentFilterConfig cmdlet.**
Send bounce message to sender with enhanced status code.	Hub only	Deletes the email message and sends an NDR to the original sender.
Reject the message with status code and response.	Edge only	Deletes the email message and sends an NDR to the original sender with a specific DSN code that you specify.
Silently drop the message.	Hub and Edge	Deletes the email message without sending any notification to the sender.

TAKE NOTE*

Windows Rights Management Services is an additional software component that must be installed on the servers and clients within your organization. For more information, search for Windows Rights Management Services at **http://technet.microsoft .com**.

Before you select the **Marked with classification** criteria or the **Apply message classification** action within a transport rule, you must first configure your Outlook clients to use *message classifications*. By default, there are several default message classifications that were originally designed to work alongside *Windows Rights Management Services* to restrict access to information. You can use these default message classifications alongside transport rules to restrict the processing of emails that contain specific classifications or create new message classifications that suit your organization's needs.

To create a new message classification called **Internal Use Only** that can be applied to emails that contain information that should not leave the organization, you could run the following command within the Exchange Management Shell:

New-MessageClassification -Name 'InternalUseOnly' -DisplayName 'Internal Use Only' -SenderDescription 'This category applies to information that should not be viewed by users who are not members of the organization.'

After creating a new message classification, OWA and Entourage 2008 MAPI users can then use this new classification when composing new emails. However, for Outlook MAPI clients, you must first export the message classification definitions to an XML file on your Exchange server. To create an XML file called C:\Classifications.xml that contains the message classifications from your Exchange server, simply run the following command within the Exchange Management Shell:

Export-OutlookClassification.ps1 > 'C:\Classifications.xml'

After you have created a message classifications XML file, you can copy it to each Outlook client computer and configure the appropriate registry keys to enable the message classifications.

CONFIGURE OUTLOOK 2007 TO USE MESSAGE CLASSIFICATIONS

GET READY. Turn on the computer, and log in as the Administrator user account. Close any windows that appear on the desktop.

1. Click **Start** and then click **Run**. Type **regedit** in the Run dialog box to open the Windows Registry Editor.

2. In the left pane, navigate to **HKEY_CURRENT_USER**, **Software**, **Microsoft**, **Office**, **12.0**, **Common**.

3. Right click **Common** in the left pane, select **New**, and then click **Key**. Supply the name **Policy** for the new key and press **Enter**.

4. Right click **Policy** in the left pane, select **New**, and then click **String Value**. Supply the name **AdminClassificationPath** for the new string value and press **Enter**.

5. Double click **AdminClassificationPath** in the right pane. In the Edit String window that appears, type the path to the message classifications XML file that you created on your Exchange server in the **Value data** dialog box and click **OK**. The Completion page appears. You must ensure that you use two backslash characters following the drive in the path name. For example, if the path name of the message classifications XML file is C:\Classifications.xml, you should type **C:\\Classifications.xml** in the **Value data** dialog box.

6. Right click **Policy** in the left pane, select **New**, and then click **DWORD Value**. Supply the name **EnableClassifications** for the new string value and press **Enter**.

7. Double click **EnableClassifications** in the right pane. In the Edit DWORD Value window that appears, type **1** in the **Value data** dialog box and click **OK**.

8. Right click **Policy** in the left pane, select **New**, and then click **DWORD Value**. Supply the name **TrustClassifications** for the new string value and press **Enter**.

9. Double click **TrustClassifications** in the right pane. In the Edit DWORD Value window that appears, type **1** in the **Value data** dialog box and click **OK**.

10. Close the Windows Registry Editor.

After configuring Outlook to use message classifications, you can add the appropriate message classification when composing a new email by selecting the icon shown in Figure 8-26.

Figure 8-26

Using Message Classifications
in Outlook 2007

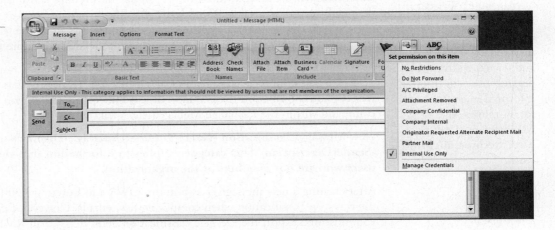

In Figure 8-26, the **Internal Use Only** message classification has been applied to the new email and the message classification description appears at the top of the email message. You can then create a transport rule on your Edge role servers to reject email messages that are sent to external recipients if the message contains the **Internal Use Only** message classification. To do this, you could create a transport rule on your Edge role servers that uses the **Marked with classification** criteria to match emails that use the **Internal Use Only** classification alongside the **Reject the message with status code and response** action.

When used alongside transport rules, message classifications provide a powerful and flexible way to restrict and process emails that are relayed by the Hub and Edge role servers within your organization.

Creating Transport Rules

You can create transport rules that provide email processing in a wide variety of environments for a wide variety of organizational needs. To create transport rules on a Hub or Edge role server, you can use either the Exchange Management Console or the Exchange Management Shell. Moreover, transport rules that are created on a Hub role server can be used by any Hub role server within your organization.

When you configure a transport rule for a Hub role server, that rule is applied to all Hub role servers within your organization to allow for email relay consistency. As a result, you can configure transport rules for Hub role servers using the **Organization Configuration > Hub Transport** node within the Exchange Management Console.

To configure transport rules within the Exchange Management Console on an Edge role server, you can navigate to the **Edge Transport** node. However, if you configure a transport rule for an Edge role server, that rule is applied to the local Edge role server only. If your organization has several Edge role servers that require the same transport rules, you can simply create the necessary transport rules on the first Edge role server and then use the **Export-TransportRuleCollection** cmdlet within the Exchange Management Shell to export the transport rules to an XML file that can later be imported to the other Edge role servers using the **Import-TransportRuleCollection** cmdlet.

To export the transport rules on the current Edge role server to the C:\EdgeRules.xml file, you could run the following command within the Exchange Management Shell:

Export-TransportRuleCollection C:\EdgeRules.xml

Next, you could copy the C:\EdgeRules.xml file to the same location on the other Edge role servers and run the following command within the Exchange Management Shell to import the transport rules:

Import-TransportRuleCollection C:\EdgeRules.xml

TAKE NOTE* You can also use a UNC path (\\servername\sharename) alongside the **Export-TransportRule Collection** and **Import-TransportRule Collection** cmdlets.

Due to the large number of conditions, exceptions, and actions that are available within a transport rule, there are many different applications for transport rules on both the Hub and Edge role servers within your organization. As a result, we will examine two common applications of transport rules within this section:

- The addition of a legal notice disclaimer to all outgoing emails using a transport rule that applies to the Hub role servers within your organization
- The configuring of message screening for all messages from external senders that contain communication regarding the TASU project within your organization.

⊕ CREATE A LEGAL NOTICE DISCLAIMER TRANSPORT RULE ON A HUB ROLE SERVER THAT APPLIES TO ALL EXTERNAL EMAILS

GET READY. Turn on the computer, and log in as the Administrator user account. Close any windows that appear on the desktop.

1. Click **Start**, **All Programs**, **Microsoft Exchange Server 2007**, and then click **Exchange Management Console.** The Exchange Management Console window appears.

2. In the console tree pane, expand **Organization Configuration** and highlight **Hub Transport**.

3. In the action pane, click **New Transport Rule**. The New Transport Rule window appears as shown in Figure 8-27.

Figure 8-27

Creating a New Transport Rule

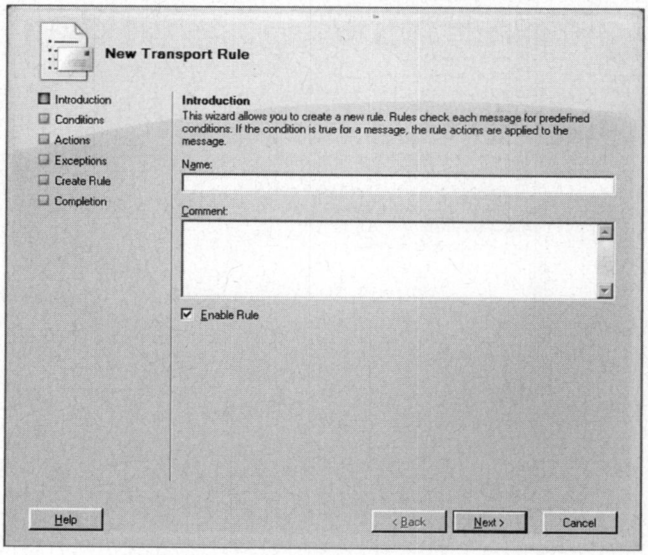

4. Supply an appropriate name for the transport rule in the **Name** dialog box as well as an appropriate description for the transport rule in the **Comment** dialog box. Verify that **Enable Rule** is selected to ensure that the transport rule is enabled after creation.

5. Click **Next**. The Conditions page appears as shown in Figure 8-28.

Figure 8-28

The Conditions Page

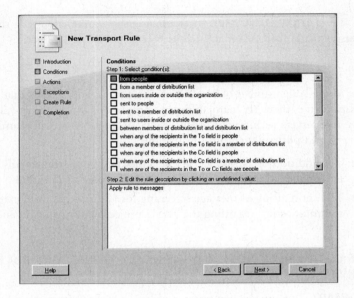

6. In the **Step 1: Select condition(s)** section, select **sent to users inside or outside the organization**. In the **Step 2: Edit the rule description by clicking an underlined value** click the **Inside** underlined word. In the Select scope window that appears, select **Outside** from the drop-down box and click **OK**. The Conditions screen will appear as shown in Figure 8-29.

Figure 8-29

Configuring Conditions

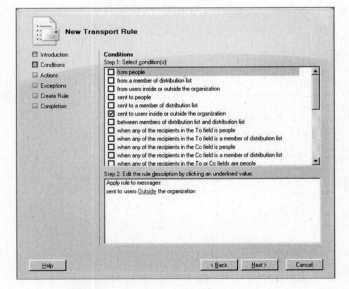

7. Click **Next**. The Actions page appears as shown in Figure 8-30.

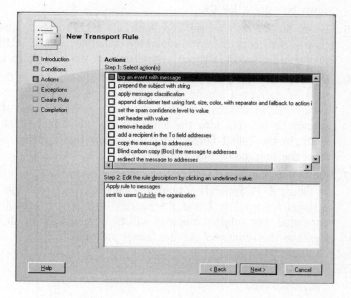

8. In the **Step 1: Select action(s)** section, select **append disclaimer text using font, size, color, with separator and fallback to action if unable to apply.**

9. In the **Step 2: Edit the rule description by clicking an underlined value** note that the disclaimer text is appended to emails with a separator line between the email and disclaimer text. In addition, the disclaimer text uses the smallest gray Arial font. If the disclaimer text cannot be inserted into the email message (i.e., if the message is encrypted), the email message will be wrapped as an attachment inside a new email that contains the disclaimer text.

10. Click the **disclaimer text** underlined words. In the Select disclaimer text window that appears, enter your legal disclaimer text in the **Disclaimer text** dialog box and click **OK**.

> **+ MORE INFORMATION**
>
> Because legal disclaimer messages have been used alongside emails for many years now, they are usually common between organizations. Following is a typical legal disclaimer message:
>
> **This transmission (including any attachments) may contain confidential information, privileged material (including material protected by the solicitor-client or other applicable privileges), or constitute nonpublic information. Any use of this information by anyone other than the intended recipient is prohibited. If you have received this transmission in error, please immediately reply to the sender and delete this information from your system. Use, dissemination, distribution, or reproduction of this transmission by unintended recipients is not authorized and may be unlawful.**

11. If you wish to attach the disclaimer to the beginning of the message, click the **append** underlined word. In the Select position window that appears, select **Prepend** from the drop-down box and click **OK**.

12. If you wish to use a font other than Arial for the disclaimer, click the **Arial** underlined word. In the Select font window that appears, select either **Courier New** or **Verdana** from the drop-down box and click **OK**.

13. If you wish to use a larger font size, click the **smallest** underlined word. In the Select font size window that appears, select the appropriate font size (**smaller, Normal, larger, largest**) from the drop-down box and click **OK**.

14. If you wish to change the font color, click the **Gray** underlined word. In the Select font color window that appears, select the appropriate font color from the drop-down box and click **OK**.

15. If you do not wish to use a separate line between the original email text and the disclaimer text, click the **with separator** underlined words. In the Select separator window that appears, select **without separator** from the drop-down box and click **OK**.

16. By default, legal disclaimers are wrapped around emails that cannot be modified such as encrypted emails. Alternatively, you can specify that the legal disclaimer be ignored in this case or that the message be rejected if the legal disclaimer cannot be inserted into the email. To do this, simply click the **wrap** underlined word. In the Select fallback action window that appears, select **ignore** or **reject** from the drop-down box and click **OK**.

17. When finished, your Actions page should resemble Figure 8-31. The Actions page in Figure 8-31 appends a sample legal disclaimer message to all messages using a larger red Arial font and a separator line. If the legal disclaimer cannot be appended, the original message will be wrapped as an attachment to a new email message that contains the disclaimer message.

Figure 8-31

Configuring Actions

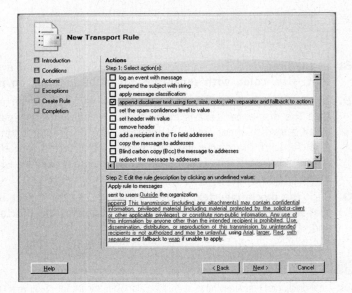

18. Click **Next**. The Exceptions page appears as shown in Figure 8-32.

Figure 8-32

The Exceptions Page

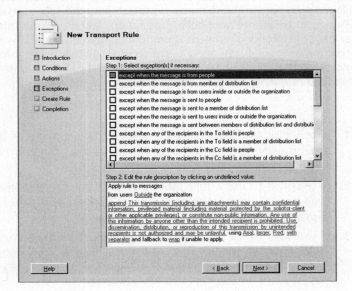

19. You can use the same process that you used on the Conditions tab to add criteria for emails that should be excluded from the transport rule. Because the legal notice disclaimer message should apply to all outgoing emails, you do not need to modify the Exceptions page.

20. Click **Next**. The Create Rule page appears.

21. Click **New**. The Completion page appears.

22. Click **Finish** to close the New Transport Rule window.

23. Close the Exchange Management Console.

 CREATE A MESSAGE SCREENING TRANSPORT RULE ON AN EDGE ROLE SERVER THAT APPLIES TO SPECIFIC RECIPIENTS

GET READY. Turn on the computer, and log in as the Administrator user account. Close any windows that appear on the desktop.

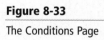

In this exercise, assume that you are the Exchange administrator for the octavius.net organization. The TASU project within your organization deals with confidential research that should not be sent to users outside of the organization. The project manager Jeff Smith intends to monitor all emails that leave the organization that mention the TASU project. To facilitate this, you need to create the appropriate transport rule on your Edge role servers.

1. Click **Start, All Programs, Microsoft Exchange Server 2007**, and then click **Exchange Management Console**. The Exchange Management Console window appears.

2. In the console tree pane, highlight **Edge Transport**.

3. In the action pane, click **New Transport Rule**. The New Transport Rule window appears as shown earlier in Figure 8-27.

4. Supply an appropriate name for the transport rule in the **Name** dialog box as well as an appropriate description for the transport rule in the **Comment** dialog box. Verify that **Enable Rule** is selected to ensure that the transport rule is enabled after creation.

5. Click **Next**. The Conditions page appears as shown in Figure 8-33.

Figure 8-33

The Conditions Page

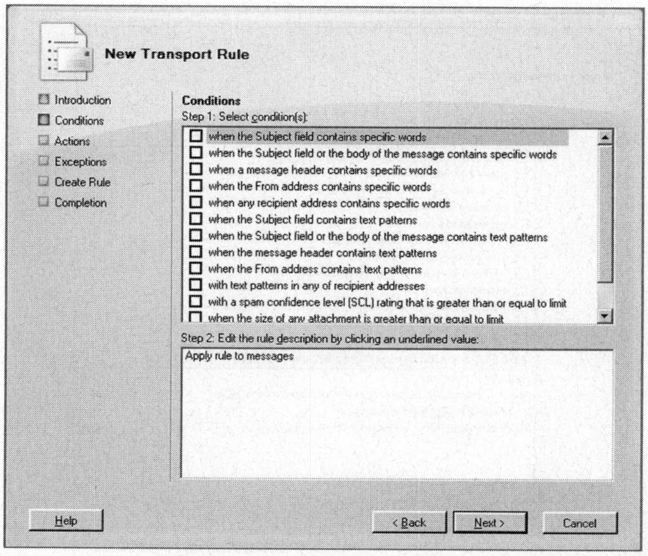

New Transport Rule

☐ Introduction
☑ Conditions
☐ Actions
☐ Exceptions
☐ Create Rule
☐ Completion

Conditions
Step 1: Select condition(s):

☐ when the Subject field contains specific words
☐ when the Subject field or the body of the message contains specific words
☐ when a message header contains specific words
☐ when the From address contains specific words
☐ when any recipient address contains specific words
☐ when the Subject field contains text patterns
☐ when the Subject field or the body of the message contains text patterns
☐ when the message header contains text patterns
☐ when the From address contains text patterns
☐ with text patterns in any of recipient addresses
☐ with a spam confidence level (SCL) rating that is greater than or equal to limit
☐ when the size of any attachment is greater than or equal to limit

Step 2: Edit the rule description by clicking an underlined value:

Apply rule to messages

Help   < Back   Next >   Cancel

6. In the **Step 1: Select condition(s)** section, select **when the Subject field or body of the message contains specific words**. In the **Step 2: Edit the rule description by clicking an underlined value** click the **specific words** underlined words. In the Specify words window that appears, type **TASU** in the dialog box, click **Add** and then click **OK**.

7. In the **Step 1: Select condition(s)** section, select **from users inside or outside the organization**. In the **Step 2: Edit the rule description by clicking an underlined value** click the **Inside** underlined word. In the Select scope window that appears, select **Outside** from the drop-down box and click **OK**. The Conditions screen will appear as shown in Figure 8-34.

8. Click **Next**. The Actions page appears as shown in Figure 8-35.

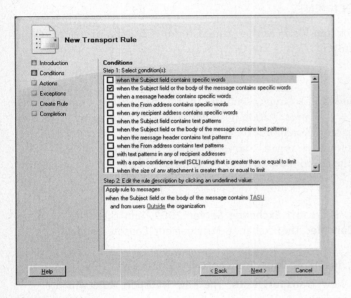

Figure 8-34

Configuring Conditions

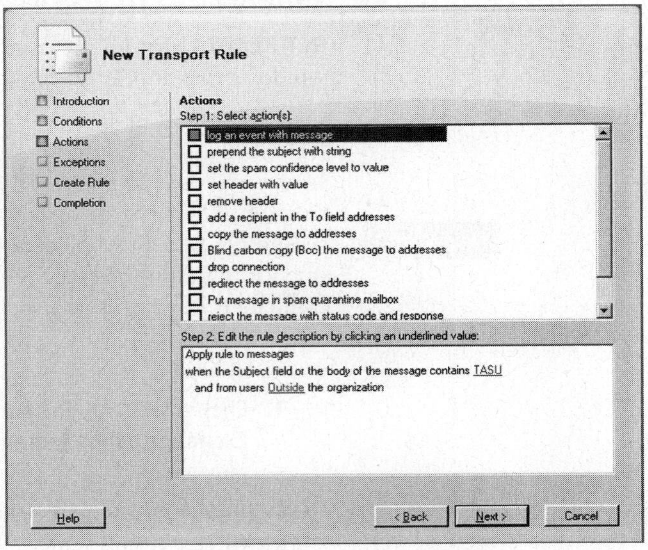

Figure 8-35

The Actions Page

9. In the **Step 1: Select action(s)** section, select **Blind carbon copy (Bcc) the message to addresses**. In the **Step 2: Edit the rule description by clicking an underlined value**, click the **addresses** underlined word. In the Select recipients text window that appears, type **jeff.smith@octavius.net** in the dialog box, click **Add** and then click **OK**. The Actions page should resemble Figure 8-36.

Figure 8-36

Configuring Actions

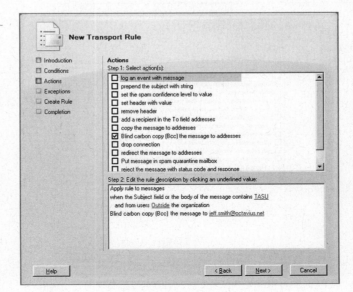

10. Click **Next**. The Exceptions page appears as shown in Figure 8-37.

Figure 8-37

The Exceptions Page

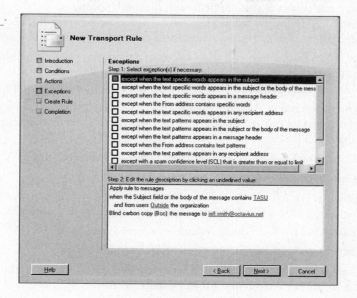

11. To exclude any emails that contain the word TASU that are sent to jeff.smith@octavius.net from being forwarded again to jeff.smith@octavius.net, select **except when the text specific words appears in any recipient address** in the **Step 1: Select action(s)** section. In the **Step 2: Edit the rule description by clicking an underlined value**, click the **specific words** underlined words. In the Specify words window that appears, type **jeff.smith@octavius.net** in the dialog box, click **Add**, and then click **OK**. The Exceptions page should resemble Figure 8-38.

Figure 8-38

Configuring Exceptions

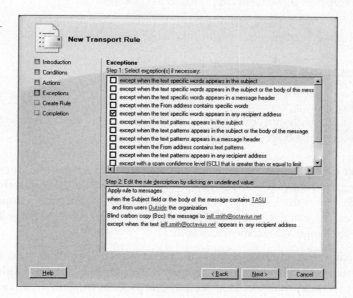

12. Click **Next**. The Create Rule page appears.

13. Click **New**. The Completion page appears.

14. Click **Finish** to close the New Transport Rule window.

15. Close the Exchange Management Console.

You can use the **New-TransportRule** cmdlet to create a new transport rule on a Hub or Edge role server. If this cmdlet is run from a Hub role server, the transport rule will be stored in AD for use by all Hub role servers. Alternatively, if this cmdlet is run from an Edge role server, the transport rule will be created on the local Edge role server only.

Say, for example, that you wish to create a transport rule that rejects emails that have the word TASU in the Subject field unless they are sent by Jeff Smith. Before creating this new transport rule, you must first define the conditions, exceptions, and actions using variables.

When executed in the Exchange Management Shell, the following commands create a condition variable called $Condition1 that matches emails that contain the word TASU in the Subject field:

$Condition1 = Get-TransportRulePredicate SubjectContains

$Condition1.Words = @('TASU')

Similarly, the following Exchange Management Shell commands create an exception variable called $Exception1 that excludes emails that are sent to Jeff Smith:

$Exception1 = GetTransportRulePredicate From

$Exception1.Addresses = @(Get-MailUser 'Jeff Smith')

To add an action variable called $Action1 that rejects messages and adds the text 'Only Jeff Smith can send TASU project emails.' to the NDR, you could execute the following Exchange Management Shell commands:

$Action1 = Get-TransportRuleAction RejectMessage

$Action1.RejectReason = 'Only Jeff Smith can send TASU project emails.'

Next, to create a new transport rule called Block TASU Project Emails using the conditions, exceptions, and actions defined earlier, you can execute the following Exchange Management Shell command:

New-TransportRule -Name 'Block TASU Project Emails' -Condition @($Condition1) -Exception @($Exception1) -Action @($Action1)

To learn more about creating transport rules using the Exchange Management Shell, search for New-TransportRule within Exchange Server 2007 Help.

THE COMMAND
LINE WAY

Managing Transport Rules

After creating transport rules on the Hub and Edge role servers within your organization, you can easily edit, disable, and remove them using the Exchange Management Console or Exchange Management Shell.

After configuring transport rules on your Hub role servers, you can view and manage them using the Transport Rules tab under the **Organization Configuration** > **Hub Transport** node within the Exchange Management Console. To manage transport rules on an Edge role server, you can navigate to the Transport Rules tab under the **Edge Transport** node within the Exchange Management Console.

To edit the conditions, exceptions, and actions for a transport rule, simply select the appropriate transport rule under the Transport Rules tab, and click **Edit Rule** in the action pane to start the Edit Transport Rule wizard. The pages in the Edit Transport Rule wizard are identical to the pages that you used to create the transport rule.

Alternatively, you can highlight a transport rule in the Exchange Management Console and select the **Disable Rule** action from the action pane to temporarily disable the rule or select the **Remove** action from the action pane to delete the transport rule. In general, it is good practice to disable transport rules if you are not sure whether the rule may be needed in the future. In addition, disabling a transport rule may be useful when troubleshooting an email relay problem. If disabling the transport rule did not solve the problem, the problem is not related to the actions defined within the transport rule. To enable a disabled transport rule, you can select the **Enable Rule** action from the action pane.

If you have created several transport rules on your Hub or Edge role servers, they will be given a priority number that is used to determine the order in which they are processed by the Hub or Edge role server. Hub and Edge role servers first process the transport rule that has a priority number of 0, followed by the transport rule that has a priority of 1, and so on. To speed up transport rule processing, you should ensure that the transport rules that frequently match emails are listed with a lower priority number than transport rules that rarely match emails. To change the priority number, highlight the transport rule in the Exchange Management Console, select the **Change Priority** action from the action pane, and specify the appropriate priority number.

**THE COMMAND
LINE WAY**

You can also use cmdlets within the Exchange Management Shell to manage transport rules on an Edge or Hub role server.

The **Get-TransportRule** cmdlet can be used to display the configuration of transport rules, and the **Set-TransportRule** cmdlet may be used to modify the configuration and priority of transport rules. Similarly, you can use the **Remove-TransportRule** cmdlet to remove transport rules or the **Disable-TransportRule** and **Enable-TransportRule** cmdlets to disable and enable transport rules respectively. For more information on the usage of these cmdlets, simply search for their names within the Exchange Server 2007 Help.

SUMMARY SKILL MATRIX

IN THIS LESSON YOU LEARNED:

- POP3 is the traditional email protocol used on the Internet to download email. IMAP4 is a newer email protocol used by Internet email clients that maintains a persistent connection to the email server for email viewing and provides support for additional features such as public folders.

- You can configure the authentication, encryption, ports, calendaring, and protocol limits used by both the POP3 and IMAP4 protocols using the name node within the Exchange Management Console or the appropriate cmdlets within the Exchange Management Shell. Only members of the Exchange Organization Administrator role or the Exchange Server Administrator role for the CAS role server are able to configure POP3 and IMAP4 settings.

- HTTP is used by email clients when accessing web-based email systems such as OWA. If you are a member of the Exchange Organization Administrator role or the Exchange Server Administrator role for the CAS role server that hosts OWA, you can configure some settings for HTTP such as authentication methods. Other HTTP settings such as protocol limits, ports, encryption, and access restrictions can be configured using the Default Web Site in IIS Manager provided that you are a member of the local Administrators group on the CAS role server.

- MAPI RPC is the most common email protocol used by Outlook and Entourage clients across a LAN. Outlook Anywhere provides MAPI RPC over HTTP for remote Outlook and Entourage clients. By default, MAPI RPC clients can take advantage of the Autodiscover and Availability services in Exchange Server 2007 to obtain autoconfiguration, OAB, and scheduling information. Alternatively, you must manually enable the Autodiscover and Availability services to work with Outlook Anywhere clients. To configure the Autodiscover and Availability services, you must be a member of the Exchange Organization Administrator role or the Exchange Server Administrator role for the CAS role server.

- SMTP is used by POP3 and IMAP4 clients as well as email servers to relay email. ESMTP is a newer implementation of SMTP that provides additional features such as authentication and encryption that are negotiated at the onset of an ESMTP connection. Most email client programs and email servers attempt to establish an ESMTP connection before falling back to an SMTP connection.

(continued)

- Provided that you are a member of the Exchange Organization Administrator role, you can configure SMTP transport settings as well as create and modify remote domains to control Out of Office message processing and SMTP message formats. In addition, you can modify the SMTP protocol limits on the Hub and Edge role servers within your organization. To modify SMTP protocol limits, you must be a member of the Exchange Organization Administrator role or the Exchange Server Administrator role for the Hub role server or a local Administrator on the Edge role server.

- By creating transport rules on the Hub and Edge role servers within your organization, you can modify the processing of email. Transport rules contains conditions and exceptions that are used to match emails as well as actions that may be used to delete, modify, monitor, or redirect emails.

- To create and manage transport rules on a Hub role server, you must be a member of the Exchange Organization Administrator role because transport rules are shared by all Hub role servers within the organization.

- To create and manage transport rules on an Edge role server, you must be a member of the local Administrators group on the Edge role server. Edge role transport rules are not shared by other Edge or Hub role servers within the organization. However, you can copy Edge role transport rules from one Edge role server to another to save time and administration.

■ Knowledge Assessment

Fill in the Blank

Complete the following sentences by writing the correct word or words in the blanks provided.

1. The _____ command in an ESMTP session determines the ESMTP features that the other computer supports.

2. The _____ service in Exchange Server 2007 allows for the autoconfiguration of MAPI account settings.

3. To configure the processing of Out of Office messages sent to a particular external email domain, you must create a new _____.

4. You can configure the maximum number of recipients in an SMTP message using the _____ tab of Transport Settings properties within the Exchange Management Console.

5. _____ is the default calendaring method used by POP3 and IMAP4 clients.

6. You can configure both POP3 and IMAP4 using the _____ node within the Exchange Management Shell.

7. If you configure bandwidth throttling for the HTTP protocol in the Default Web Site, you must also install the _____ in the properties of your network connection.

8. Transport rules use _____ and _____ to determine the emails that the transport rule should operate on.

9. The _____ cmdlet can be used to create additional message classifications that may be used to identify and process email using transport rules.

10. Transport rules that frequently match emails on your Hub and Edge role servers should be given a lower _____ number so that they are processed before other transport rules.

Multiple Choice

Circle the letter that corresponds to the best answer.

1. A Non-Delivery Report (NDR) is also referred to as a _____.
   a. Delivery Status Notification (DSN)
   b. Non-Delivery Receipt (NDR)
   c. Bounce message
   d. All of the above

2. What port should you configure on your IMAP4 clients so that they can connect to your Exchange server using SSL?
   a. 110
   b. 143
   c. 993
   d. 995

3. Which of the following protocols provides a persistent connection between the email client and server? (Choose all that apply.)
   a. IMAP4
   b. MAPI RPC
   c. POP3
   d. Outlook Anywhere

4. Which of the following email clients can use the Autodiscover and Availability services in Exchange Server 2007? (Choose all that apply.)
   a. Entourage 2004
   b. Outlook 2007
   c. Outlook 2003
   d. Entourage 2008

5. You configure digest authentication on your CAS role server, but HTTP clients are unable to connect using their credentials. What could be the problem?
   a. Digest authentication requires SSL.
   b. The AD user accounts are not configured to store passwords using reversible encryption.
   c. HTTP cannot use Digest authentication.
   d. The Default Web Site is not configured to use HTTP.

6. Which of the following protocols is best suited for remote clients who have dial-up Internet access?
   a. POP3
   b. IMAP4
   c. MAPI RPC
   d. HTTP

7. Which of the following cmdlets may be used to connect to the Autodiscover and Availability services for testing purposes?
   a. Connect-Autodiscover
   b. Get-OutlookConfiguration
   c. Get-Autodiscover
   d. Test-OutlookWebServices

8. Which of the following criteria can be used within a transport rule condition to match emails that have custom labels applied to them?
   a. When a message header contains specific words
   b. Marked with importance
   c. Marked with classification
   d. With a spam confidence level (SCL) rating that is greater than or equal to the limit

9. Which of the following transport rule actions can be used to send emails to another recipient and not to the original recipient listed in the email message?
   a. Redirect message to addresses
   b. Bcc the message to addresses
   c. Add a recipient in the To field addresses
   d. Copy message to addresses

10. Which of the following transport rule actions only apply to Edge role servers?
    a. Silently drop the message
    b. Reject the message with status code and response
    c. Send bounce message to sender with enhanced status code
    d. Put message in quarantine

True/False

Circle T if the statement is true or F if the statement is false.

T | F **1.** You can set Out of Office message options on an individual mailbox using the Exchange Management Shell.

T | F **2.** The Availability service can be used independently of the Autodiscover service.

T | F **3.** The first command in any ESMTP session is HELO.

T | F **4.** In order to run the **Set-IMAPSettings** cmdlet, you must be a member of the Exchange Organization Administrator role.

T | F **5.** Forms-based authentication is used by default for OWA and requires SSL.

T | F **6.** Integrated Windows Authentication encrypts logon credentials before sending them to the CAS role server.

T | F **7.** POP3 + TLS connections use port 995 by default.

T | F **8.** The X.509 certificate that is used for SSL and TLS connections alongside the POP3, IMAP4, and HTTP protocols is for temporary use only and should be replaced with a proper certificate for the organization.

T | F **9.** Transport rules must be configured separately on each Hub role server within your organization.

T | F **10.** In order to configure transport rules on the Edge role servers within your organization, you must be a member of the Exchange Organization Administrator role.

Review Questions

1. Explain how Exchange uses ESMTP to provide compatibility with other ESMTP and SMTP email systems.
2. Explain how the Autodiscover service may be used to reduce administrative effort within your organization.

■ Case Scenarios

Scenario 8-1: Selecting Email Protocols

Currently, your organization only allows internal access to the organization's email system using Outlook and Entourage clients and the MAPI RPC protocol. However, it has been decided that organization members should be allowed to connect to the organization's email system from home. For simplicity and administration, your organization will allow only a single protocol for home email clients. Because your organization uses public folders extensively and email is not to be downloaded to home email clients, you have narrowed your protocol selection to IMAP4 and Outlook Anywhere.

The IMAP4 and Outlook Anywhere protocols are similar in their purpose and function. Both protocols may be used to obtain email from remote clients using a persistent connection and both protocols support advanced features and public folders.

You must prepare a comparison of IMAP4 and Outlook Anywhere for your IT staff meeting tomorrow so that the members of your department can collectively decide on the protocol that will be allowed for home email clients. In a short memo, outline the pros and cons of using IMAP4 and Outlook Anywhere for home email access.

Scenario 8-2: Implementing Transport Rules

Your organization has recently discovered that important trade secrets have been leaked to competitors. It is believed that these trade secrets have been leaked unintentionally using regular email communication. As the Exchange administrator, you have been asked to determine whether Exchange Server 2007 can be used to minimize the chance that trade secrets are emailed to external recipients by accident. In a short memo, detail the various transport rules that can be created on the Hub and Edge role servers to address your organization's concerns.

9 LESSON

Configuring Security

LESSON SKILL MATRIX

TECHNOLOGY SKILL	OBJECTIVE DOMAIN	OBJECTIVE DOMAIN NUMBER
Protecting against Viruses and Spam	Configure the antivirus and antispam system.	3.2

KEY TERMS

asymmetric encryption
Certificate Revocation List (CRL)
Certificate Services
certificate template
Certification Authority (CA)
connection filtering
cryptography
digital signature
encryption algorithm
enrollment
Forefront Security for Exchange
    Server (FSE)

Forefront Server Security
    Administrator
host-based firewall
method of least privilege
multifactor authentication
network-based firewall
practical security
private key
public key
public key certificate
Purported Responsible Address
    (PRA)

Realtime Block List (RBL)
Security Configuration Wizard
    (SCW)
sender ID
sender reputation
Spam Confidence Level (SCL)
Subject Alternative Name (SAN)
symmetric encryption
thumbprint
trusted root
virus definition
Windows Firewall

■ Understanding Security

THE BOTTOM LINE

To protect the information that is stored on and relayed by email servers within your organization, you must implement various security technologies and configurations. However, you must first understand the various security threats and weaknesses that are common in email systems as well as the practices and procedures that can be used to minimize them.

No software is completely secure. There are always methods to manipulate software that is not desired or to access data that should not be accessed. However, the term *security* refers to the broad set of practices and procedures that you can use to minimize the chance that novice or advanced users will exploit your computer systems. Because these practices and procedures can take a great deal of time and money to implement, most organizations focus on implementing only those security practices and procedures that provide the most protection against exploits. This approach to security is called *practical security* and typically involves understanding the potential security risks for a particular organization, selecting the appropriate security technologies, and then implementing them. The security technologies, practices, and procedures selected will be relative to the level of risk as well as the amount of time and money that the organization can spend to protect against the risk. For example, financial institutions such as banks are more likely to have a larger security infrastructure than a manufacturing company because the likelihood and cost of a security breach is much higher.

Because email systems allow for communication, they also allow for unauthorized access to sensitive information. Sensitive information such as trade secrets could be sent to another person outside the organization within an email or as an attachment to an email. Moreover, sensitive information may be sent to others in the same organization who should not have access to it or be obtained by examining emails as they pass across networks. To minimize the possibility that this will happen, you can restrict access to the email system, encrypt email transfer, restrict email relay, limit permissions, control viruses and spam, stop unnecessary services, implement firewalls, and regularly update software.

RESTRICTING ACCESS TO THE EMAIL SYSTEM

Many organizations restrict access to the email system by preventing email access from outside the organization and forcing users to use an internal domain client computer to access email using a single protocol such as MAPI RPC. In addition, by implementing a policy whereby mailbox users must use complex passwords, change their password on a regular basis, and log in only during specific times, you minimize the chance that a member of your organization will guess another member's password and use it to exploit the email system. Similarly, by adopting a policy that requires mailbox users to be disabled when they leave the organization or take vacation will further prevent another member of the organization from using another user's email account. In organizations that require higher levels of security, users may be required to insert a **smart card** or use a **biometric thumbprint reader** on their workstation in addition to providing a username and password to log on to the domain or gain access to email. This approach to security is called **multifactor authentication** and minimizes the chances that unauthorized users will gain access to the computer system because multiple forms of authentication are required to do so.

ENCRYPTING EMAIL TRANSFER

Network protocol analyzers are commonly called **packet sniffers** because they capture (sniff) TCP/IP packets on the network.

Advanced users do not need to use another user's email account to view or send emails. Instead, they could use a **network protocol analyzer** program such as Wireshark to view the contents of POP3, IMAP4, HTTP, SMTP, and MAPI RPC traffic as it passes across a network from the client computer to the email server. To prevent this, you should always ensure that client computers access the email on their email server using encrypted versions of their email protocol. By default, MAPI RPC connections are encrypted and the default configuration of Exchange Server 2007 CAS role servers require POP3S, IMAP4S, HTTPS, and SMTPS using the default encryption certificate that is installed by Exchange. However, to allow for proper protocol encryption, you must replace the default encryption certificate on your Exchange servers with a signed certificate as discussed later in this lesson.

Recall that email servers relay email to other email servers across the Internet using SMTP. This email relay does not use encryption because it is too difficult to coordinate the usage of encryption certificates among all organizations in the world. However, because email servers relay SMTP email directly to the Internet from their organization's Internet connection to their ISP, it is unlikely that an advanced user will have the ability to view this SMTP traffic. Furthermore, today ISPs relay email directly to other ISPs on the Internet using private networks. Thus, the likelihood that an advanced user will be able to view unencrypted SMTP traffic as it passes from email server to email server across the Internet is very low.

Regardless, some organizations with higher security needs may encrypt email sent between partner organizations by creating special send and receive connectors in each organization that are configured to use TLS encryption alongside SMTP for email that is sent between the two organizations only. Still, other organizations may use general encryption technologies such as **Internet Protocol Security (IPSec)** or **Virtual Private Networks (VPNs)** to encrypt email traffic between partner organizations.

RESTRICTING EMAIL RELAY

Regardless of whether your organization encrypts Internet email relay, you should also ensure that the email servers within your organization only relay necessary emails. By creating transport rules to monitor, log, and restrict email relay, you can help prevent sensitive information from being sent to the wrong recipients. For example, because most sensitive information will be recorded in files such as spreadsheets, you could create a transport rule that prevents emails and attachments from being sent outside your organization if they contain keywords that represent sensitive information. In addition, you can create transport rules that only allow certain users to send email to outside organizations or other users within the organization. This is important in preventing corporate fraud. For example, by preventing people in the Purchasing department (who create purchase orders for equipment and supplies) from communicating via email to users within the Accounts Payable department (who pay bills that have been received from other companies that are purchased from), you minimize the chance that someone in the Purchasing department will work with someone in the Accounts Payable department to commit fraud by agreeing to purchase equipment for noncorporate use.

LIMITING PERMISSIONS

TAKE NOTE*

You can use the Exchange Best Practices Analyzer tool introduced in Lesson 3, "Deploying Exchange Server 2007" to check the permissions assigned to Exchange servers. Access the **Best Practices Analyzer** under the **Toolbox** node within the Exchange Management Console and select a **Permission Check** scan type when prompted.

Many exploits that occur within organizations today are the result of poor permission assignments. Members of your organization should only have the permissions that they need to access data and no more. This practice is called the *method of least privilege.* For example, executive salary information may be stored within the HR public folder. If the Exchange Administrator or public folder owner does not modify the permissions to allow only HR staff to view the information in the public folder, then everyone within the organization will have access to the executive salary information due to the default permissions that are set on new public folders.

CONTROLLING VIRUSES AND SPAM

Viruses are small programs or program fragments that perform a wide variety of unwanted activities on your system. Some viruses slow the performance of your system whereas other viruses destroy valuable data. Still other viruses may be used to provide unauthorized access to your system by sending information to the Internet that others can use to exploit your system. Modern viruses are configured to replicate from computer to computer when the file that holds the virus is opened. Some viruses spread via email and are called *email bombs* as a result. When the file or file attachment that contains the email bomb is opened, the virus obtains a list of any email addresses it can find within your email client program (i.e., contact lists) and sends email to those recipients on your behalf along with the email bomb virus.

The best protection against viruses within your organization is antivirus software. Because most viruses are spread by email, installing antivirus software on the Edge or Hub role servers within your organization and regularly updating the virus database of your Edge or Hub role server will minimize the number of viruses within your organization. However, no antivirus software will catch every single virus. As a result, it is also important that you educate users about how to identify viruses and instruct them to delete any emails that appear to contain viruses. Because viruses are usually contained within email attachments, you should advise users to first determine whether an attachment is safe to open. In general, users should only open attachments if:

* They expected to receive the attachment, and it is from a trusted sender.
* The attachment is not an executable program (executable programs typically have a file extension of .exe, .bat, .vbs, .com, .ini, or .reg).
* The attachment does not have a suspicious filename (e.g., click_to_win.exe) or a file extension that does not match the filename (e.g., picture_of_ocean.vbs).

Spam, or junk mail, is simply unsolicited email from organizations on the Internet called *spammers*. In most cases, spam emails are from companies that you have never heard of or contacted in the past. Because different spam messages are often emailed to the same recipient and spammers trade their recipient lists with other spammers, you could receive hundreds of spam messages per day in your Inbox. Large numbers of spam messages waste time and productivity within organizations and are often cited as a primary reason why organizations change their email address formats.

Although spam messages can contain viruses, most spam messages are designed to sell questionable products, illegal services, and pornographic material. Consequently, spam is illegal in many regions and countries.

In addition, many spam messages contain hyperlinks that are used to verify that your email address exists to external organizations. These organizations will likely use this information to send more spam. Other spam messages attempt to lure users into filling out forms on Internet Web sites that contain their personal information. This information is often used to commit fraud or gain unauthorized access to a system because users often use personal information when generating account passwords. This type of spam is called a ***phishing attack***.

To minimize the number of spam messages that your organization receives, it is important to install antispam software on the Edge or Hub role servers within your organization. However, because spam messages are often designed to resemble legitimate emails, antispam software cannot prevent all spam messages from entering your recipient's mailboxes. As a result, it is important to educate your users so that they can identify spam messages. Following this, it is vital that users understand that they should not respond to spam messages or click on any hyperlinks within the spam message itself.

A message is likely spam if it:

- Is from someone you do not know through a freely obtainable Internet account (e.g., hotmail, gmail, or yahoo);
- Is from scrambled, sales-oriented, or random-generated recipients (e.g., w8C4rsa29846@hotmail.com or freequote@offers.com);
- Requests sensitive information using hyperlinks in the email itself that do not reflect the organization that sent the email;
- Contains a message that asks for help or assistance from an unknown person or organization;
- Contains an empty **To:** field; or
- Contains sales- or service-oriented information in the subject line (e.g., Make Quick Cash, Free Offer, Find Old Classmates).

The configuration of antivirus and antispam software is discussed later in this lesson.

STOPPING UNNECESSARY SERVICES AND IMPLEMENTING FIREWALLS

To gain access to a server, network users must interact with a network service that is running on the server. Each network service listens for incoming network traffic on specific port number(s) and processes any traffic that matches its port number(s). For example, the POP3 service on a CAS role server listens to TCP port 110 for unencrypted and TLS POP3 requests and TCP port 995 for SSL POP3 requests. If the POP3 service is stopped, then any incoming network traffic sent to the CAS role server on TCP port 110 or 995 will be discarded because there is no service that will respond to the request.

Similarly, if all services that listen to port numbers are stopped on a particular server, there is no possible way for a network user to access or exploit the server. However, to function, servers must provide certain network services to network users. Malicious network users can interact with these running network services to exploit the system if there is a weakness in the network service itself. Although many network services provide a high level of security, malicious network users will attempt to interact with all possible network services on your Exchange servers in hopes of finding a weakness. By stopping unnecessary services on your Exchange servers, you reduce the number of network services that malicious network users can attempt to exploit and hence reduce the ***attack surface*** of your Exchange servers. For example, if your CAS role server does not service POP3 clients, stopping the POP3 service and setting its startup type to Disabled will prevent malicious network users from interacting with your server via the POP3 service.

Another way to reduce the attack surface of your Exchange servers is to implement firewalls. Firewalls are software programs that prevent unnecessary network traffic from reaching computer systems. There are two main types of firewalls that you can use to protect Exchange Server: host-based firewalls and network-based firewalls.

A *host-based firewall* runs as a software component on the server itself to restrict incoming traffic destined for specific port numbers. However, host-based firewalls do not restrict outgoing traffic from the server itself and the associated responses from other servers. For example, if you implement a host-based firewall on your CAS role server that prevents traffic on TCP port 110 and 995, no network users can connect to your CAS role server on those ports regardless of whether the POP3 service is running. However, your CAS role server can connect to other servers using TCP port 110 and 995 and receive the associated responses through the firewall.

While host-based firewalls protect individual servers, **network-based firewalls** protect traffic passing from one network to another. As a result, they are typically comprised of software components on routers. By restricting network traffic on TCP port 110 and 995 from passing through your network-based firewall into your LAN, you prevent external network users from interacting with the POP3 services running on any server in your LAN. However, in this case, internal network users can still connect to the POP3 services running on any server in the LAN that does not have a host-based firewall that restricts POP3 traffic.

The configuration of services and firewalls is discussed in the next section of this lesson.

PERFORMING REGULAR SOFTWARE UPDATES

Although you can reduce the attack surface on your Exchange servers, malicious network users can still interact with those services that the server must host and attempt to locate a security loophole. Most network-based attacks attempt to interact with network services on servers in ways that the original developer of the network service did not expect. These types of attacks are commonly called *buffer overruns* and are designed to locate flaws in network services that allow a malicious network user unauthorized access to the system. The only solution to a network service weakness that can be exploited using a buffer overrun is to update the network service software to a newer version that does not contain the flaw. Program updates are continually created and released when weaknesses are found in network services. Consequently, it is important to update the software on your Exchange servers on a regular basis to ensure that the network services on them are not vulnerable to new buffer overrun attacks.

Although you can update Exchange Server 2007 using the setup program or the Windows Update Web site, you can also configure a *Windows Server Update Services (WSUS)* server on your network to automate the deployment of updates to the servers and workstations in your organization.

■ Reducing the Exchange Attack Surface

 THE BOTTOM LINE

A key component to any secure email system is the reduction of enabled services and open ports to minimize the number of ways that malicious users can interact with your email servers. You can achieve this by disabling unused services or by implementing host-based and network-based firewalls.

As mentioned in the previous section, reducing the attack surface is fundamental to ensuring that Exchange Server network exploits are minimized. The attack surface of a computer is simply the sum total of all the ways that a network user can interact with network services running on the computer. By stopping unnecessary services and implementing firewalls to restrict access to network services, you can minimize the attack surface on the Exchange servers within your organization. To perform these tasks, you must at a minimum be a member of the local Administrators group on the Exchange server.

You can stop unnecessary network services on an Exchange server by navigating to **Start** > **Administrative Tools** > **Services** in Windows, right clicking the appropriate network service in the Services window, and selecting **Stop** from the menu. To prevent the service from starting at boot time, you can also access the properties of the appropriate network service in the Services window and set its Startup type to **Disabled** as shown for the Telnet service in Figure 9-1.

Figure 9-1

Disabling a Service

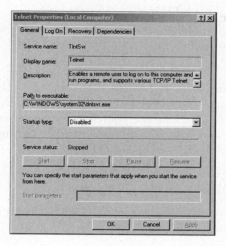

In addition to stopping unnecessary network services on your Exchange servers, you can implement a host-based firewall such as ***Windows Firewall*** to prevent all network requests from entering your Exchange server unless they are on a specific port number or destined for a specific service that your Exchange server provides. By default, host-based firewalls block inbound access to all protocols and allow exceptions for the protocols that you specify based on the program name or port number for a particular service. Table 9-1 lists common port numbers that are used by Exchange Server protocols.

Table 9-1

Common port numbers associated with Exchange Server protocols

PROTOCOL	PORT NUMBERS
ADAM (EdgeSync)	TCP 50389 (ADAM LDAP)
	TCP 50636 (ADAM LDAP with SSL)
HTTP (Outlook Web Access)	TCP 80 (unencrypted HTTP)
	TCP 443 (HTTP with SSL)
IMAP4	TCP 143 (unencrypted IMAP4 or IMAP4 with TLS)
	TCP 993 (IMAP4 with SSL)
MAPI RPC	UDP 135 (for service discovery)
	Random port number (for MAPI RPC data)
Outlook Anywhere	TCP 593 (for service discovery)
	TCP 80 (unencrypted HTTP)
	TCP 443 (HTTP with SSL)
POP3	TCP 110 (unencrypted POP3 or POP3 with TLS)
	TCP 995 (POP3 with SSL)
SMTP/ESMTP	TCP/UDP 25 (Internet email relay, legacy client access)
	TCP/UDP 587 (Client access)

If you use a host-based firewall on your Exchange server, you may need to open more ports than those listed in Table 9-1 if your server hosts additional network services. For example, if your Exchange server runs the DNS service, you will also need to open TCP and UDP port 53 to allow other computers to query your DNS service.

TAKE NOTE*

In case you disable too many network services or restrict too many ports, it is good practice to first configure the attack surface on a test Exchange server in a test environment before performing the same actions in a production environment.

The ***Security Configuration Wizard (SCW)*** component of Windows can be used to disable unused services as well as configure Windows Firewall on the Exchange servers within your organization to minimize the attack surface. Moreover, Exchange Server 2007 comes with templates that can be imported into the SCW to customize SCW settings for each server role.

⊕ INSTALL AND RUN THE SECURITY CONFIGURATION WIZARD TO REDUCE THE EXCHANGE SERVER ATTACK SURFACE

GET READY. Turn on the computer, and log in as the Administrator user account. Close any windows that appear on the desktop.

TAKE NOTE*

You must have Windows Server 2003 SP1 or Windows Server 2003 R2 or later to install the SCW.

1. Click **Start**, **Control Panel**, and then click **Add or Remove Programs**. When the Add or Remove Programs window appears, click **Add/Remove Windows Components** to open the Windows Components Wizard.

2. On the Windows Components page, select **Security Configuration Wizard** and click **Next**.

3. Click **Finish** to close the Windows Components Wizard. Close the Add or Remove Programs window.

4. Click **Start** and then click **Run**. In the Run dialog box, type **scwcmd register/ kbname:Ex2007KB/kbfile: "%programfiles%\Microsoft\Exchange Server\Scripts\ Exchange2007.xml"** and click **OK**. This command registers the Exchange Server 2007 services and features with the SCW.

5. Click **Start**, **Administrative Tools**, and then click **Security Configuration Wizard**. When the Security Configuration Wizard window appears, click **Next**. The Configuration Action screen appears as shown in Figure 9-2.

Figure 9-2

Creating a New Security Policy

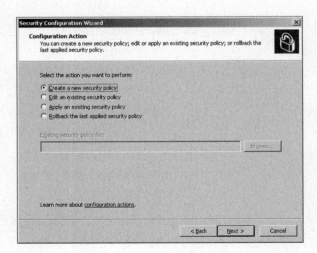

6. At the Configuration Action screen, ensure that **Create a new security policy** is selected and click **Next.** The Select Server screen appears as shown in Figure 9-3.

Figure 9-3

Selecting a Server

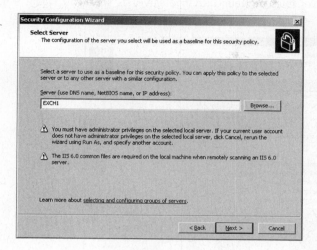

7. At the Select Server screen, type the NetBIOS name, IP address, or FQDN of the Exchange server that you wish to analyze. Alternatively, you can click **Browse**, select your server in the Select Computer window that appears, and click **OK.** If you select a different server than the local computer on which you are running the SCW, you must ensure that your local computer has IIS 6.0 installed.

8. When finished, click **Next.** The SCW will take a few moments to analyze the Exchange server on the Processing Security Configuration Database page. When it is finished, click **View Configuration Database** to open the SCW Viewer window.

9. In the SCW Viewer, expand the appropriate Exchange Server 2007 roles that are present on your Exchange server to view information regarding the installed services as well as the programs that listen on ports. Figure 9-4 shows the Exchange 2007 Hub Transport role expanded.

Figure 9-4

Viewing Server Details in the SCW Viewer

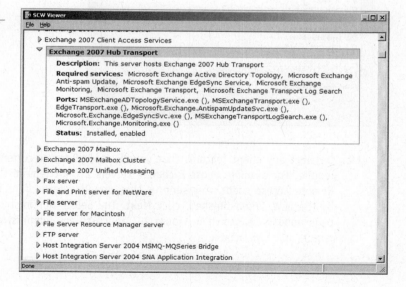

10. When finished, close the SCW Viewer window and click **Next** on the Processing Security Configuration Database page. When the Role-Based Service Configuration page appears, click **Next**. The Select Server Roles page appears and lists the installed server roles on your Exchange server as shown in Figure 9-5.

Figure 9-5

Selecting Server Roles

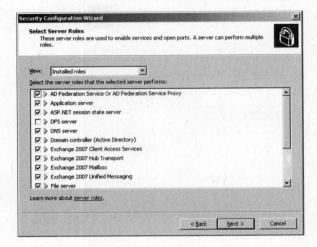

11. Deselect any server roles that your Exchange server currently has but does not require. For example, most Exchange servers do not require the Telnet server or File server services. Any services that you select here will be disabled by the SCW. When finished, click **Next**. The Select Client Features page appears and lists any client programs that are enabled on your Exchange server as shown in Figure 9-6.

Figure 9-6

Selecting Client Features

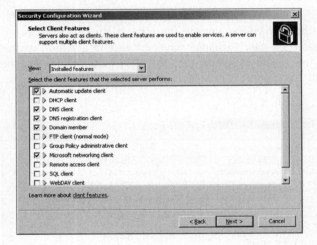

12. Deselect any client features that your Exchange server currently has but does not require. For example, most Exchange servers do not require the FTP client or the Remote access client. Any services that provide these client features will be disabled by the SCW. When finished, click **Next**. The Select Administration and Other Options page appears as shown in Figure 9-7 and lists any administrative programs that require network access.

Figure 9-7

Selecting Administration
and Other Options

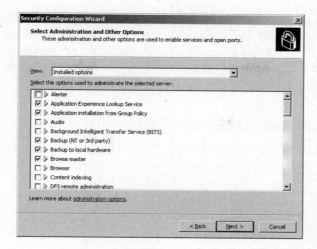

13. Deselect any administrative options that your Exchange server does not require. Any services associated with the administrative options that you deselect will be set to disabled by the SCW. Click **Next**. The Select Additional Services page appears as shown in Figure 9-8 and lists any third-party or additional Windows components that require network access.

Figure 9-8

Selecting Additional Services

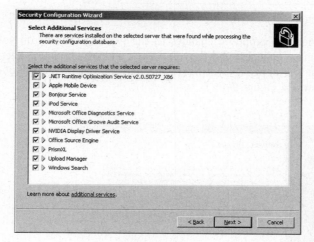

14. Deselect any additional software services that your Exchange server does not require. Any services associated with the additional software that you deselect will be set to disabled by the SCW. Click **Next**. The Handling Unspecified Services page appears as shown in Figure 9-9.

Figure 9-9

Handling Unspecified Services

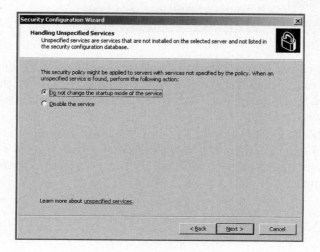

15. By default, any services that were not detected by the SCW are left unchanged. However, you can optionally select **Disable the service** as shown in Figure 9-9 to disable any services that were not listed previously during the SCW. When finished, click **Next**. The Confirm Service Changes window appears as shown in Figure 9-10.

Figure 9-10

Confirming Service Changes

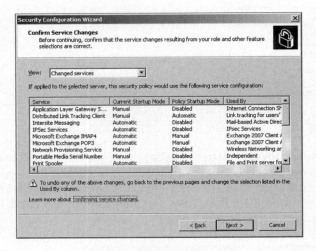

16. Review the proposed changes to the existing services on your computer. If you wish to make changes, you can click **Back** and modify your selections on the appropriate pages. Otherwise, click **Next**. The Network Security Configuration page appears as shown in Figure 9-11.

Figure 9-11

Specifying Network Security Options

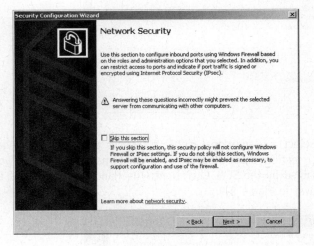

17. By default, the SCW enables Windows Firewall and blocks any incoming traffic that is not specifically allowed according to your selections in the remaining pages of the SCW. If you do not wish to enable Windows Firewall, select **Skip this section** as shown in Figure 9-11.

18. Click **Next**. If you did not select **Skip this section** as shown in Figure 9-11, the Open Ports and Approve Applications page appears and lists the ports that match the enabled network services on your Exchange server as shown in Figure 9-12.

Figure 9-12

Specifying Open Ports
and Approved Applications

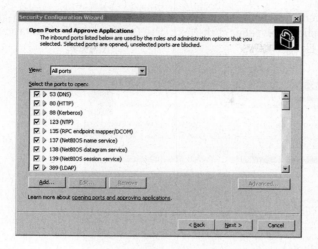

19. Deselect any ports that represent services that network computers should not use
    when contacting your Exchange server. For other services, you can specify the net-
    work interfaces that the service should be listed on as well as the remote clients
    that are allowed to interact with the service. Highlight the appropriate service and
    click **Advanced**. On the Remote Address Restrictions tab in the window that appears,
    you can choose to restrict access to specific remote hosts or networks that you
    specify by clicking **Add**. The **Remote Address Restrictions** tab shown in Figure 9-13
    allows access to the DNS service for all computers on the 10.0.0.0 network as well
    as the host 192.168.1.55. If your Exchange server has multiple network interfaces,
    you can specify that the service only listen to requests from remote clients on a
    single network interface using the **Local Interface Restrictions** tab as shown in
    Figure 9-14. When finished specifying Advanced options, click **OK** to return to the
    Open Ports and Approve Applications page.

> **TAKE NOTE** *
>
> When you click **Add** as shown in Figure 9-13, you can also require remote clients to use
> IPSec encryption or signing when interacting with the service. Exchange servers typically
> host several connections to clients and other servers. Because IPSec requires more resources
> per connection than SSL or TLS, IPSec is not a recommended option for securing traffic
> on your Exchange server.

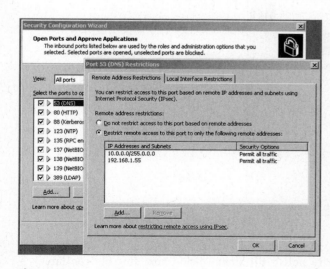

Figure 9-13

Configuring the DNS Port

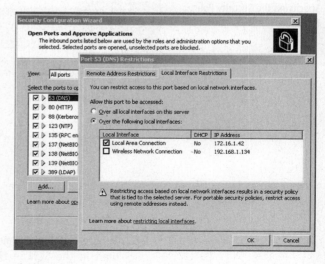

Figure 9-14

Specifying Network Interfaces for the DNS Port

20. When you are finished selecting port options on the Open Ports and Approve Applications page, click **Next**. The Confirm Port Configuration page appears as shown in Figure 9-15.

Figure 9-15

Confirming Port Configuration

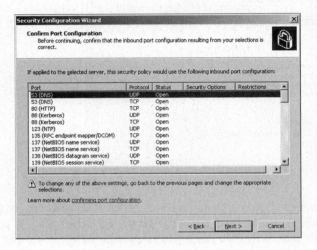

21. Review the port selections for Windows Firewall. If you wish to make changes, you can click **Back** and modify your selections on the previous page. Otherwise, click **Next**.

 The SCW also allows you to specify registry keys that will prevent communication from unsecure clients, configure auditing of key events, as well as configure the usage of IIS. Because these parts of the SCW do not directly affect the attack surface of your Exchange server, we will skip their configuration.

22. At the Registry Settings page, select **Skip this section** and click **Next**.

23. At the Audit Policy page, select **Skip this section** and click **Next**.

24. At the Internet Information Services page, select **Skip this section** and click **Next**. When the Save Security Policy page appears, click **Next**. The Security Policy File Name page appears as shown in Figure 9-16.

Figure 9-16

Specifying the Security Policy File Name

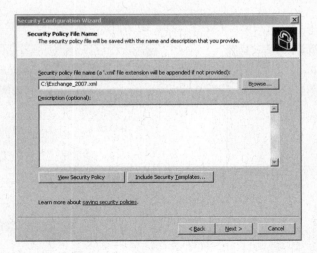

25. Supply the path name to an XML file that will store the settings that you configured in the SCW in the **Security policy file name** dialog box. This file can later be applied to other Exchange servers by running the SCW and selecting **Apply an existing security policy** on the Configuration Page as shown earlier in Figure 9-2.

TAKE NOTE *

After you have applied a security policy, you can run the SCW again and select **Rollback the last applied security policy** as shown earlier in Figure 9-2 to undo the settings configured by the security policy.

You can optionally supply a description of the policy in the **Description** dialog box. Click **View Security Policy** to review security policy settings or click **Include Security Templates** to add existing Windows security templates to the security policy.

26. When finished, click **Next**. Click **OK** to close the window that indicates that a reboot will be required after applying the policy. The Apply Security Policy window appears.

27. By default, the SCW does not apply the policy. To apply the policy immediately to your system, select **Apply now** and click **Next**. After the security policy is applied to your Exchange server, click **Next**. The Completing the Security Configuration Wizard page appears.

28. Click **Finish** to close the Security Configuration Wizard.

When reducing the attack surface of your Exchange servers, it is also important to restrict the network traffic that is allowed to pass into your LANs and reach your Exchange servers using network-based firewalls. Network-based firewalls typically offer advanced filtering options that are unavailable in host-based firewalls. For example, network-based firewalls can restrict traffic based on source and destination IP address, network, and MAC address as well as by protocol and port number. Although you can implement a Windows server running the ***Routing and Remote Access Service (RRAS)*** to perform routing and network-based firewall functionality within your organization, most organizations use network devices, such as hardware-based routers, to perform routing and network-based firewall functions for performance and cost purposes. These hardware-based routers often support ***Network Address Translation (NAT)***. NAT allows outgoing traffic from a network but only allows incoming network traffic that has been specifically configured to be forwarded to a particular computer on the internal network.

Network-based firewalls work together with host-based firewalls to provide a practical level of security for your network. If, for example, your organization has a single Exchange server on the internal LAN that hosts the Hub, CAS, and Mailbox roles as well as an Edge role server in the perimeter network that is used to filter inbound and outbound emails. Also, users within your organization use MAPI RPC within the internal LAN to obtain and send email using the internal Exchange server and can use IMAP4 with SSL (IMAP4S) from home clients to obtain email from the organization's CAS role email server across the Internet. In this situation, you can use network and host-based firewalls to reduce the attack surface of your Exchange servers as shown in Figure 9-17.

Figure 9-17

Firewall Configuration

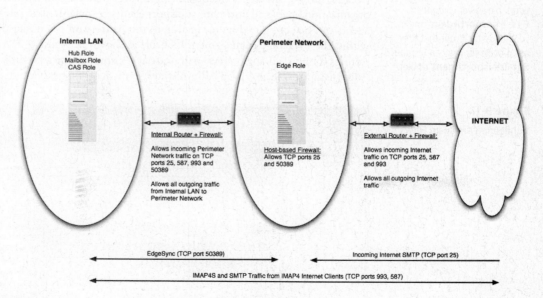

The firewall on the external router shown in Figure 9-17 is configured to allow only incoming SMTP (TCP port 25 for Internet email and TCP port 587 for IMAP4 client emails) and IMAP4S (TCP port 993) traffic to pass from the Internet into the perimeter network, but all outgoing Internet traffic is allowed. Similarly, the firewall configured on the internal router is configured to allow only SMTP

(TCP port 25 for email relay from the Edge role server and TCP port 587 for IMAP4 client emails), IMAP4S (TCP port 993), and EdgeSync (TCP port 50389) to pass from the perimeter network to the internal LAN, but allow all traffic from the internal LAN to pass to the perimeter network. Additionally, a host-based firewall on the Edge role server will prevent malicious users from interacting with services other than SMTP (TCP port 25) and EdgeSync (TCP port 50389). Because MAPI RPC clients must contact their CAS role server using a random port number, a host-based firewall is not configured on the Exchange server within the LAN.

■ Protecting against Viruses and Spam

THE BOTTOM LINE

Spam messages and viruses are two of the most common problems that plague organizations today. By implementing antispam filters and antivirus software on key Exchange servers within your organization, you will minimize the amount of spam messages and viruses that are passed into your organization. Consequently, you will also minimize the time wasted by spam messages and virus infections as well as enhance the email experience for the users within your organization.

CERTIFICATION READY?
Configure the antivirus and antispam system.
3.2

Configuring Antispam Filters

Exchange Server 2007 may be used to protect against spam messages that are received from the Internet. Edge role servers within your organization automatically have several antispam agents enabled to combat incoming spam messages. Understanding how to configure these antispam agents is key to ensuring that most spam messages are removed before entering the organization while allowing legitimate email messages to reach the intended recipients.

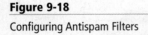
MORE INFORMATION

Antispam transport agents are used in addition to transport agents that provide for transport rules and journaling. You can view the list of all transport agents and the order in which they are applied on a Hub or Edge role server using the **Get-TransportAgent** cmdlet. To change the order that they are processed, you can use the **Set-TransportAgent** cmdlet.

To reduce the number of spam messages, Exchange Server contains several different ***antispam transport agents*** that email must pass through before reaching a mailbox. Each antispam transport agent is designed to filter emails based on different criteria such as sender, recipient, or email content.

Because most spam enters the organization from the Internet, Edge role servers within your organization enable all antispam transport agents by default. The settings for most of these agents can be configured by navigating to the **Anti-spam** tab under the **Edge Transport** node within the Exchange Management Console as shown in Figure 9-18. To modify antispam settings for an Exchange server, you must at a minimum be a member of the Exchange Server Administrator role and local Administrators group on that server.

Figure 9-18

Configuring Antispam Filters

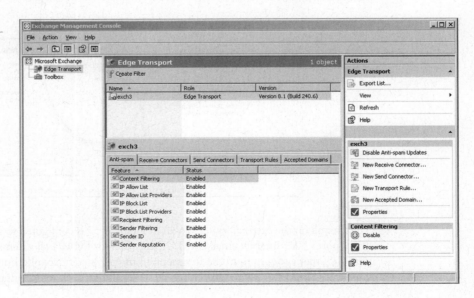

Each of the antispam features listed in Figure 9-18 can be disabled by highlighting the feature and selecting Disable from the action pane. Similarly, updated spam information and programs are automatically downloaded from the Microsoft Update Web site using the Automatic Updates feature of Windows and applied to your Edge role server. To prevent the automatic downloading of updates, you can select **Disable Anti-spam Updates** in the action pane shown in Figure 9-18.

If your organization does not use an Edge role server, you can enable a limited number of antispam transport agents on your Hub role servers by using the **Set-TransportServer** cmdlet within the Exchange Management Shell. For example, to enable the antispam transport agents on the server exch1.octavius.net, you could run the following command within the Exchange Management Shell:

Set-TransportServer –Identity 'exch1.octavius.net' –AntispamAgentsEnabled $true

After enabling the antispam transport agents on your Hub role server, you must restart the Exchange Server Transport service. Following this, you will see an Anti-spam tab under the **Server Configuration** > **Hub Transport** node within the Exchange Management Console. Unfortunately, the only antispam features that you can configure on your Hub role servers are the IP Allow List and IP Block List features shown earlier in Figure 9-18.

Configuring antispam settings is an art. Strict antispam settings will prevent some legitimate emails from reaching recipients whereas lenient antispam settings will allow some spam messages to reach recipients. As a result, it is important to continually refine your spam restrictions to ensure that members of your organization receive critical emails but only the occasional spam message.

FILTERING SPAM BY EMAIL CONTENT

To configure spam filtering by email content, you can highlight **Content Filtering** as shown in Figure 9-18 and select **Properties** from the action pane. On the **Custom Words** tab of Content Filtering Properties, you can specify a list of noncase-sensitive words or phrases that will be used to label messages as spam or not spam. As shown in Figure 9-19, any email messages that have "fast money," "make money," "no obligation," or "viagra" in the message body or subject line will be labeled as spam unless they contain "TASU" or "TPS Report."

On the Exceptions tab of Content Filtering Properties, you can add recipients within your organization who should be exempt from content filtering. This is appropriate for users who receive critical or time-sensitive emails that should never be accidentally removed by content filtering. As illustrated by Figure 9-20, any email addressed to **adel.moore@octavius.net** or **jeff.smith@octavius.net** will not be examined by the content filtering antispam transport agent.

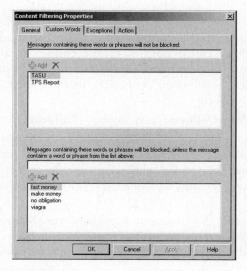

Figure 9-19

Specifying Custom Words

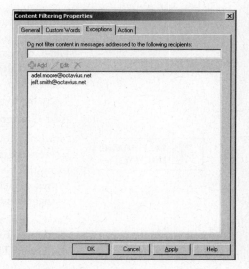

Figure 9-20

Specifying Exceptions

In addition to the words and phrases specified on the Custom Words tab of Content Filtering Properties, Exchange Server 2007 maintains a list of words and phrases that are commonly used within spam messages. These words and phrases are updated regularly and contain rankings that are used to determine the **Spam Confidence Level (SCL)**. The SCL is a number between 0 and 9 that represents the likelihood that a particular email is spam. An SCL of 0 is not likely to be spam whereas an SCL of 9 is almost certainly spam. Emails that contain words with a high-spam ranking and emails that contain multiple spam-related words are likely to have a high SCL. On the Action tab of Content Filtering Properties, you can configure how your Edge role server processes emails that have a certain SCL.

As shown in Figure 9-21, emails with an SCL of 9 are automatically deleted and an NDR is not sent to the original sender whereas emails with an SCL of 7 or 8 are automatically deleted and an NDR is sent to the original sender. Emails with an SCL of 5 or 6 are redirected to the quarantine mailbox (**spam-quarantine@octavius.net**) and an NDR is sent to the original sender. The quarantine mailbox is simply a mailbox that you create on a Mailbox role server to store potential spam messages. If an important email is accidentally sent to the quarantine mailbox due to content filtering, you can access the quarantine mailbox and forward it to the user who requested it.

> **TAKE NOTE** *
>
> The quarantine mailbox will accumulate many emails over time. As a result, you should create the quarantine mailbox in a separate mailbox database and ensure that the quarantine mailbox is monitored and emptied regularly.

Figure 9-21

Configuring Content Filter Actions

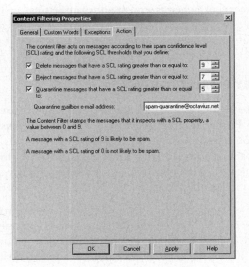

You can also use cmdlets within the Exchange Management Shell to configure content filtering. The **Add-ContentFilterPhrase** cmdlet can be used to add custom words, the **Get-ContentFilterPhrase** cmdlet can view existing custom words and the **Remove-ContentFilterPhrase** cmdlet can remove custom words. For example, to block messages that contain the phrase "easy money," you could run the following command within the Exchange Management Shell:

Add-ContentFilterPhrase –Phrase 'easy money' –Influence BadWord

Similarly, you can configure content filtering actions and exceptions using the **Set-ContentFilterConfig** cmdlet or view existing content filtering actions and exceptions using the **Get-ContentFilterConfig** cmdlet. For example, to configure the same settings shown earlier in Figure 9-21, you could use the following command within the Exchange Management Shell:

Set-ContentFilterConfig -SclQuarantineEnabled:$true -SclRejectEnabled:$true -SclDeleteEnabled:$true -SclQuarantineThreshold 5 -SclRejectThreshold 7 -SclDeleteThreshold 9 -QuarantineMailbox spam-quarantine@octavius.net

Exchange Server 2007 can also populate the exceptions list used in content filtering from the data stored within the Safe Senders list that is part of the Junk E-Mail feature of

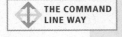

THE COMMAND LINE WAY

Outlook 2007 and Entourage 2008. This information is replicated to Edge role servers using the EdgeSync protocol and used to enhance content filtering. To do this, you can run the **Update-Safelist** cmdlet. For example, to update the Safe Senders from the user Jeff Smith, you can run the following command within the Exchange Management Shell:

Update-Safelist -Identity 'Jeff Smith'

Alternatively, you can update the Safe Senders from all mailbox users within the organization using the following commands within the Exchange Management Shell:

AdminSessionAdSettings.ViewEntireForest = $True

Get-Mailbox -ResultSize Unlimited | Where {$_.RecipientType -eq [Microsoft .Exchange.Data.Directory.Recipient.RecipientType]::UserMailbox } | Update-Safelist

For more information on the content filtering cmdlets in this section, search for their names within Exchange Server 2007 Help.

FILTERING SPAM BY IP ADDRESS

Often, several spam messages are sent from a single IP address. This IP address represents the server that has relayed the spam messages directly to your Edge role server and is typically an anonymous remailer. Anonymous remailers are SMTP servers that accept email from unauthenticated clients or other email servers and forward it to its destination. Most spammers send email through several anonymous remailers to hide their identity because most anonymous remailers are in countries that do not have laws that prevent their use. Some spammers take advantage of legitimate email servers on the Internet to send spam. As a result, you can choose to block the IP address of the legitimate email server for a specific time. After this time, the organization that owns the email server will have remedied its spam situation and will later be able to send email to your organization.

Because of this, one of the most effective methods to reduce spam messages is to filter messages by IP address. This is often called *connection filtering*. If you highlight **IP Block List** as shown in Figure 9-18 and select **Properties** from the action pane, you can specify the IP addresses or IP address ranges of spam senders (including anonymous remailers) as well as the time period for which to block them on the **Blocked Addresses** tab. As Figure 9-22 illustrates, any emails will be deleted that originate from the IP address 233.14.8.1 indefinitely because there is no Expiration date.

Figure 9-22

Configuring Blocked Addresses

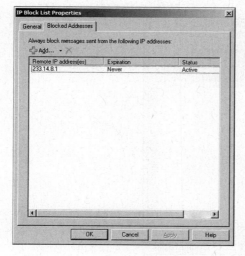

You can also provide IP addresses that should not be blocked by highlighting **IP Allow List** as shown in Figure 9-18, selecting **Properties** from the action pane, and adding the appropriate IP addresses or IP address ranges on the **Allowed Addresses** tab. IP addresses listed on the Blocked Addresses tab shown in Figure 9-22 take precedence over IP addresses listed on the Allowed Addresses tab. As illustrated by Figure 9-23, any messages from the IP address 64.114.88.12 and the IP address range 44.0.8.1 through 44.0.8.254 will be allowed unless they are also listed on the Blocked Addresses tab.

Figure 9-23

Configuring Allowed Addresses

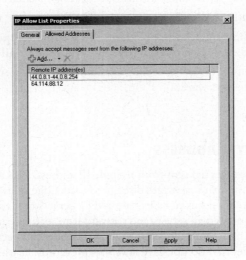

Blocking IP addresses is useful when you know the IP address of a sender that is propagating spam messages to your organization. However, determining the IP addresses to block is time consuming. As a result, many organizations subscribe to a *Realtime Block List (RBL)* provider that maintains a list of IP addresses of computers that are known to propagate spam. Your Edge role server can quickly query the RBL provider to see if certain sender's IP addresses are on the RBL. Any email from an IP address that is listed on an RBL is blocked from entering the organization. To configure one or more RBL providers, highlight **IP Block List Providers** as shown in Figure 9-18, select **Properties** from the action pane, and select the **Providers** tab. As Figure 9-24 illustrates, the MaxSecure RBL provider is used to determine whether incoming email messages are spam. If the IP address of the sender is not listed on the MaxSecure RBL, the Veritech RBL provider is queried. If the IP address of the sender is not listed on either RBL, the email is forwarded into the organization.

Figure 9-24

Specifying Block List Providers

You can modify the order that RBLs are queried by using the arrow icons shown in Figure 9-24. To add a new RBL provider, you can click **Add** and specify the name and domain name of the RBL provider in the Add IP Block List Provider window as shown in Figure 9-25. Some RBL providers provide different responses to identify whether the IP address is spam or not. For these RBL providers, you must enter the appropriate information under the Return status codes section in Figure 9-25. When an email is blocked because it is listed on an RBL, the sender receives an error message indicating the RBL that listed them. This allows legitimate organizations to contact the RBL and convince them to remove their IP address from the list. To customize the error message that is sent, you can click **Error Messages** shown in Figure 9-25.

Figure 9-25

Adding a Block List Provider

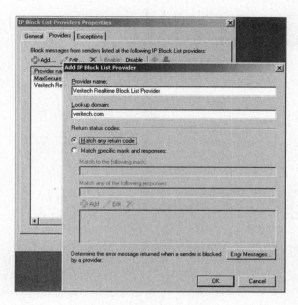

For users who receive critical or time-sensitive emails and should never be accidentally blocked by an RBL, you can add them to the Exceptions tab of IP Block List Providers properties. As shown in Figure 9-26, any email sent to the recipient **jeff.smith@octavius.net** will not be blocked even if the RBL lists the sender's IP address.

Figure 9-26

Specifying RBL Exceptions

Some RBL providers offer a list of secure IP addresses that are not used by spammers. You can configure your Edge role server to query this list. Navigate to the properties of **IP Allow List Providers** shown in Figure 9-18, and add the appropriate entries on the **Providers** tab as shown in Figure 9-27. The entries on the Providers tab shown in Figure 9-27 are added in much the same way that you added RBL providers in the properties of IP Block List Providers. However, if the same IP address is both allowed and blocked by an RBL provider, emails will be blocked from entering the organization.

Figure 9-27

Configuring Allow List Providers

You can also use cmdlets within the Exchange Management Shell to configure connection filtering. The **Add-IPBlockListEntry** and **Remove-IPBlockListEntry** cmdlets can be used to add and remove IP addresses to and from the IP block list respectively, whereas the **Add-IPAllowListEntry** and **Remove-IPAllowListEntry** cmdlets can be used to add and remove IP addresses to and from the IP allow list respectively. For example, to block the IP address 44.88.0.1 until 1:00 p.m. March 4, 2009, you could run the following command within the Exchange Management Shell:

Add-IPBlockListEntry –IPAddress '44.88.0.1' -ExpirationTime '3/4/2009 13:00'

Additionally, you can use the **Add-IPBlockListProvider** and **Remove-IPBlockListProvider** cmdlets to add and remove RBLs that are queried for blocked IP addresses respectively. Similarly, the **Add-IPAllowListProvider** and **Remove-IPAllowListProvider** cmdlets may be used to add and remove RBLs that are queried for allowed IP addresses. For example, to add the IP block list provider shown earlier in Figure 9-25, you could run the following command within the Exchange Management Shell:

Add-IPBlockListProvider –Name 'Veritech Realtime Block List Provider' –LookupDomain 'veritech.com'

You can also test RBL connections using the **Test-IPAllowListProvider** and **TestIPBlockListProvider** cmdlets or obtain connection filtering configuration using the **Get-IPBlockListEntry**, **Get-IPAllowListEntry**, **Get-IPBlockListProvider**, and **Get-IPAllowListProvider** cmdlets. For a complete list of connection filtering cmdlets and their usage, search for "connection filtering cmdlets" within Exchange Server 2007 Help.

FILTERING SPAM BY RECIPIENT

Recall that spammers often send email to common recipient names within the organization in hopes of contacting a valid recipient. When spammers obtain the address of a valid recipient (i.e., when a recipient clicks on a hyperlink within a spam message), they typically send multiple spam messages to that recipient. To filter spam by recipient, you can highlight **Recipient Filtering** shown in Figure 9-18, select **Properties** from the action pane, and specify the appropriate information on the **Blocked Recipients** tab as shown in Figure 9-28.

Microsoft®
Exchange Server 2007 **Configuring Security** | **377**

Figure 9-28

Specifying Blocked Recipients

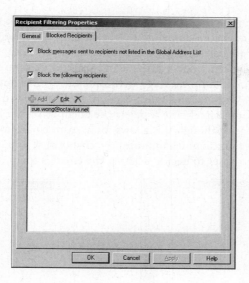

The Edge role server does not forward any messages to the Hub role servers within your organization unless the recipients are listed in the Global Address List (GAL). This prevents your Hub role servers from relaying unnecessary email and improves the performance of your Exchange infrastructure. In addition, email sent to the recipient **sue.wong@octavius.net** will not be forwarded to the Hub role servers. Blocking recipients is commonly done when users complain that they receive too many spam emails. By assigning the recipient a different email address on the E-mail Addresses tab of mailbox user properties and blocking the recipient's old email address using Recipient Filtering properties, you will prevent these spam messages from entering the organization.

 TAKE NOTE*

If you select **Hide from Exchange address lists** on the General tab of mailbox user properties, the mailbox user will not receive Internet email if **Block messages sent to recipients not listed in the Global Address List** is selected in Figure 9-28.

 THE COMMAND LINE WAY

You can also use the **Set-RecipientFilterConfig** cmdlet to configure recipient filtering or the **Get-RecipientFilterConfig** to view the configuration of recipient filtering. For example, to block emails sent to the recipients **sue.wong@octavius.net** and **adel.moore@octavius.net**, you could run the following command within the Exchange Management Shell:

Set-RecipientFilterConfig –BlockListEnabled $true –BlockedRecipients 'sue.wong@ octavius.net,adel.moore@octavius.net'

For more information on the Set-RecipientFilterConfig and Get-RecipientFilterConfig cmdlets, search for their names within Exchange Server 2007 Help.

FILTERING SPAM BY SENDER

Another way to identify spam messages is to examine the sender's email address within the email itself. Often the same sender (i.e., **sales@bestoffers.org**) is used in multiple spam messages. Similarly, spammers often use freely obtainable email accounts to send spam (e.g., hotmail.com email accounts). To prevent messages from entering your organization by sender email address, you can highlight **Sender Filtering** shown in Figure 9-18, select **Properties** from the action pane, and specify the appropriate information on the **Blocked Senders** tab.

As Figure 9-29 shows, **john.smith@averitech.org** as well as blank senders or senders in the bestoffers.org and hotmail.com domains are labeled as blocked senders. By default, emails from blocked senders are deleted and the sender receives an NDR. However, you can choose to label emails from blocked senders as spam and forward them to mailboxes within your organization by selecting **Stamp message with blocked sender and continue processing** as shown in Figure 9-30. Outlook and Entourage users will see a warning indicating that the message is spam and can then choose to reject the email using the Junk E-mail feature of Outlook and Entourage. Although this allows some spam emails to be processed by Exchange servers within your organization, it minimizes the chance that important emails will be rejected by allowing the mailbox user to decide whether the email is spam.

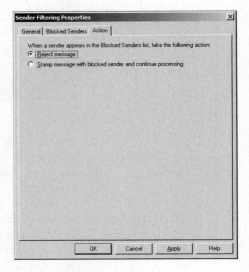

Figure 9-29

Specifying Blocked Senders

Figure 9-30

Configuring the Sender Filtering Action

Exchange Server 2007 also uses a complex *sender ID* algorithm that evaluates the senders listed within email header fields to calculate the *Purported Responsible Address (PRA)*. The PRA is a measure of the likelihood that a message is spam based on email header information. You can specify how Exchange deals with email messages that are likely spam due to their PRA value by navigating to the properties of **Sender ID** shown in Figure 9-18 and selecting the appropriate action on the **Action** tab as shown in Figure 9-31. By default, if Exchange determines that a message is likely spam due to the PRA, it adds a warning to the email and proceeds to deliver it to the appropriate mailbox. However, you can select **Reject message** shown in Figure 9-31 to prevent the message from being delivered and send an NDR to the sender. Alternatively, you can select **Delete message** as shown in Figure 9-31 to delete the message without sending an NDR to the sender.

Figure 9-31

Configuring the Sender ID Action

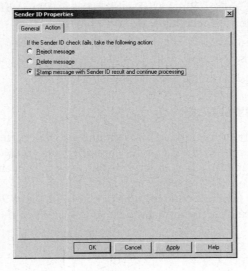

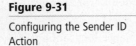

In addition to calculating the PRA, Exchange Server 2007 also monitors the SCL of emails that are determined to be spam and keeps track of the sender of the spam to determine the *sender reputation*. As the number of spam emails from a particular sender increases, the sender reputation declines. In addition, Exchange examines other aspects of the sender when determining the sender reputation including the SMTP traffic behavior and the DNS name of the sender.

You can configure sender reputation settings by highlighting **Sender Reputation** as shown in Figure 9-18 and selecting **Properties** from the action pane. On the **Sender Confidence** tab as shown in Figure 9-32, you can allow Exchange to test the sender's email server to determine whether it is an anonymous remailer. Email sent by an anonymous remailer automatically receives a poor sender reputation value.

Figure 9-32

Specifying an Open Proxy Test

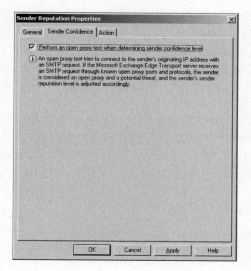

You can also control the processing of emails that have a poor sender reputation using the **Action** tab of Sender Reputation Properties as shown in Figure 9-33. By default, senders with a poor reputation are placed on the IP Block List for 24 hours if they have a poor sender reputation. The Sender Reputation Level Block Threshold value shown in Figure 9-33 is an arbitrary value that you can use to adjust how Exchange determines poor sender reputations. A higher threshold is more likely to give emails a poor sender reputation whereas a lower threshold is less likely to give emails a poor sender reputation.

Figure 9-33

Configuring Sender Reputation Action

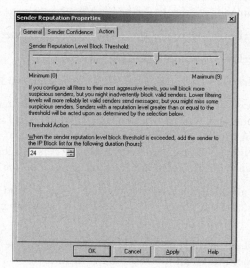

You can also use cmdlets within the Exchange Management Shell to configure sender filtering options. The **Set-SenderFilterConfig** cmdlet can be used to specify blocked senders and the **Get-SenderFilterConfig** cmdlet can be used to display blocked senders. For example, to reject emails from the same blocked senders as shown earlier in Figure 9-29, you could run the following command within the Exchange Management Shell:

Set-SenderFilterConfig –BlankSenderBlockingEnabled $true -BlockedDomainsAndSubdomains '*bestoffers.org,*hotmail.com' -BlockedSenders 'john.smith@averitech.org' –Action 'Reject'

The **Set-SenderIDConfig** cmdlet can be used to configure sender ID filtering and the **Get-SenderIDConfig** cmdlet can be used to view sender ID settings. For example, to reject messages that have an unacceptable PRA and send an NDR to the sender, you could run the following command within the Exchange Management Shell:

Set-SenderIDConfig -SpoofedDomainAction Reject

To configure and view sender reputation settings, you can use the **Set-SenderReputationConfig** and **Get-SenderReputationConfig** cmdlets respectively. For example, to set the same sender reputations settings shown in Figure 9-32 and Figure 9-33, you could run the following command within the Exchange Management Shell:

Set-SenderReputationConfig –OpenProxyDetectionEnabled $true -SrlBlockThreshold 6 -SenderBlockingEnabled:$true -SenderBlockingPeriod 24

For more information on these sender filtering cmdlets, search for their names within Exchange Server 2007 Help.

THE COMMAND LINE WAY

FILTERING SPAM BY ATTACHMENT

Edge role servers are automatically configured to filter emails based on the nature of the attachments that are included in the email. By default, Edge role servers filter email messages that contain common web application MIME types or common program extensions. However, you can modify this list or add entries that filter emails based on the name, extension, or MIME type of attachments using cmdlets within the Exchange Management Shell.

To view the current list of file names and MIME types that are filtered, you can run the **Get-AttachmentFilterEntry** cmdlet from within the Exchange Management Shell. There are over 60 file name extensions and MIME types that are filtered by default on an Edge role server.

Similarly, you can use the **Add-AttachmentFilterEntry** cmdlet to add a file name or MIME type to filter or you can use the **Remove-AttachmentFilterEntry** cmdlet to remove a file name or MIME type from being filtered. For example, to filter attachments called **readme.doc** as well as attachments that end with a **.bin** extension or have a JPEG image MIME type, you could run the following commands within the Exchange Management Shell:

Add-AttachmentFilterEntry –Name readme.doc –Type FileName

Add-AttachmentFilterEntry –Name *.bin –Type FileName

Add-AttachmentFilterEntry –Name image/JPEG –Type ContentType

All emails that are filtered by attachment are processed using the same action. By default, unacceptable attachments are removed from the email and the email is forwarded to the recipient within the organization with a notice indicating that the attachment was removed. You can use the **Get-AttachmentFilterListConfig** cmdlet to view the default action used for attachment filtering or the **Set-AttachmentFilterListConfig** cmdlet to modify the attachment filtering action.

For example, to reject all emails that have restricted attachments and send an NDR to the sender using a custom message, you could run the following command within the Exchange Management Shell:

Set-AttachmentFilterListConfig –Action Reject –RejectResponse "Your email has been rejected by octavius.net due to an unacceptable attachment."

Alternatively, you could configure emails that have restricted attachments to be deleted without sending an NDR using the following command within the Exchange Management Shell:

Set-AttachmentFilterListConfig –Action SilentDelete

To configure your Edge role server to delete restricted attachments from emails and forward them into the organization for delivery (the default action), you could run the following command within the Exchange Management Shell:

Set-AttachmentFilterListConfig –Action Strip

Configuring Forefront Security for Exchange Server Antivirus

Although there are many different antivirus software packages available on the market today that can be used alongside Exchange Server to remove viruses, Forefront Security for Exchange Server uses a variety of different virus-scanning engines and regular updates to minimize the number of viruses that enter your organization. In addition, Forefront Security for Exchange Server allows for advanced scanning options, manual virus scans, notifications, and detailed reporting.

Forefront Security for Exchange Server (FSE) is a powerful antivirus scanning and filtering software that can be used to scan email and public folder data that is processed by or stored on the Exchange servers in your organization.

At the time this was written, there were over 100,000 different active viruses for Windows operating systems and that number is continuously growing. This makes it more difficult to create an effective antivirus software program that catches all new viruses as they are released and is reflected by the large number of commercial antivirus software products available on the market today. One antivirus software product may not catch a specific newly released virus while another antivirus software product will. As a result, FSE uses several different licensed virus-scanning engines together from different antivirus companies to minimize the chance that a new virus will go undetected. These scanning engines are also configured to look for new *virus definitions* on the Internet every hour by default to protect against the latest virus attacks. FSE also allows you to customize the level to which virus-scanning engines analyze emails and attachments for viruses as well as the actions that can be performed on emails and attachments that contain viruses.

The functionality of FSE largely depends on the Exchange Server roles installed on the computer that hosts FSE. For example, if you install FSE on an Edge or Hub role server, it will scan email as it passes through the server. However, if you install FSE on a Mailbox role server, it will scan mailbox and public folder data stored on the Mailbox role server. To speed performance, FSE tags all messages that have been already scanned on one server role so that they are not scanned again when they reach other server roles within the organization that have FSE installed. For example, if an incoming email message is scanned by FSE on an Edge role server, the email message is not rescanned when it is passed to Hub or Mailbox role servers within your organization that host FSE unless you specify otherwise.

To install and manage FSE on an Exchange server, you must at a minimum be a member of the Exchange Server Administrator role and local Administrators group on that server.

INSTALLING FSE

Like other commercial antivirus software packages, Forefront is not free; it costs a great deal of money to keep antivirus programs and virus definitions updated to protect against new viruses. However, a 120-day evaluation of Forefront Security for Exchange Server is available for download from **www.microsoft.com/forefront/downloads.mspx**. At the end of the evaluation period, you can enter a valid license to continue using it rather than reinstalling a licensed version.

Forefront dramatically increases the processor and memory usage on your Exchange server. As a result, it is important to ensure that you allow for extra hardware during Exchange Server 2007 deployment to account for this. Microsoft recommends an additional 2 GB of RAM for Forefront in addition to the RAM required for server roles.

Any options chosen during the installation process can be modified afterward using the General Settings section within the FSE configuration utility.

INSTALL FOREFRONT SECURITY FOR EXCHANGE SERVER

GET READY. Turn on the computer, and log in as the Administrator user account. Close any windows that appear on the desktop.

You can select **Remote Installation** instead of **Local Installation** to perform an installation of Forefront on another computer across the network.

1. Navigate to the folder that contains the 120-day evaluation of FSE that you downloaded or the folder that contains the licensed copy of FSE and double click **setup.exe**. When the Welcome page appears, click **Next**.

2. On the License Agreement page, click **Yes**.

3. On the Customer Information page, enter your name and company in the appropriate dialog boxes and click **Next**.

4. On the Installation Location page, ensure that **Local Installation** is selected and click **Next**.

5. On the Installation Type page, ensure that **Full Installation** is selected and click **Next**. The Quarantine Security Settings page appears as shown in Figure 9-34.

Figure 9-34

Specifying Quarantine Settings

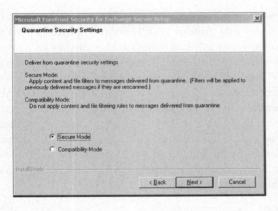

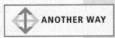

You can select **Client—Admin console only** instead of **Full Installation** to install the Forefront administration console only. This is often useful if you wish to remotely administer Forefront from a client computer. If there is a firewall between your client computer and Exchange server running Forefront, you must allow TCP port 135.

6. FSE is automatically configured to place infected messages in a quarantine folder. Messages can be moved from this quarantine folder if they need to be inspected for security reasons or if they were placed there accidentally. By default, FSE rescans any messages that are moved from the quarantine folder as shown in Figure 9-34. However, you can select **Compatibility Mode** if you do not want to rescan items that are moved from the quarantine folder. Click **Next**. The Engines page appears.

7. FSE uses up to five antivirus engines when scanning emails. The Microsoft Antimalware Engine is automatically chosen. Select up to four more antivirus engines as shown in Figure 9-35, and click **Next** when finished.

Figure 9-35

Selecting Virus-Scanning
Engines

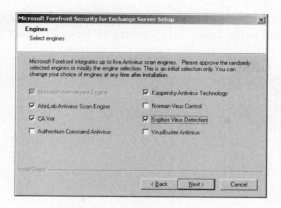

8. At the Engines Updates Required page, read the update information and click **Next**. The Proxy Server page appears as shown in Figure 9-36.

Figure 9-36

Specifying a Proxy Server

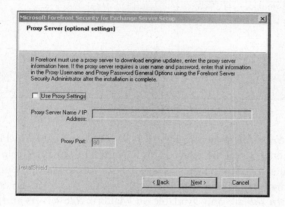

9. FSE must obtain virus updates by downloading them from the Internet. If your organization uses a proxy server to access the Internet, select **Use Proxy Settings** and supply the correct IP address or name of your proxy server as well as the port number in the dialog boxes provided and click **Next**. If your organization does not use a proxy server to obtain Internet access, click **Next**.

10. On the Choose Destination Location page, view the default destination folder that Forefront will be installed to. If you wish to change this location, click **Browse** and select a different folder and click **OK**. Click **Next**.

11. On the Select Program Folder page, view the default program folder on the Start menu that will be used to store the shortcut to the Forefront tools. If you wish to change this location, select an existing folder from the list or type a different name in the dialog box. Click **Next**.

12. At the Start Copying Files page, click **Next**.

13. At the Restart Exchange Transport Service page, click **Next** to restart the Exchange Transport Service to activate Forefront.

14. At the Recycling Exchange Transport Service page, click **Next**.

15. Click **Finish** to close the FSE setup window.

CONFIGURING FSE

After installing FSE, you can administer it using the *Forefront Server Security Administrator* utility (**Start** > **All Programs** > **Microsoft Forefront Server Security** > **Exchange Server** > **Forefront Server Security Administrator** by default). After opening Forefront Server Security

Administrator, you will be presented with the Scan Job Settings screen that may be used to configure email and public folder virus scanning as shown in Figure 9-37.

Figure 9-37

Configuring the Transport Scan Job

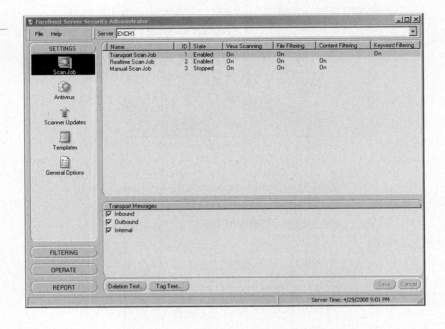

The *Transport Scan Job* shown in Figure 9-37 is only available on Hub and Edge role servers because it scans emails that are relayed through the Hub or Edge role server. At the bottom of Figure 9-37, you can configure the Transport Scan Job to scan inbound and outbound Internet emails as well email that is only sent internally within the organization. The *Realtime Scan Job* and *Manual Scan Job* are only available on Mailbox role servers and can be used to scan emails and public folders that are stored within databases on the Mailbox role server. The Realtime Scan Job automatically scans emails and public folder items as they are stored or retrieved, whereas the Manual Scan Job can be run manually to scan the contents of mailboxes and public folders. If you highlight Realtime Scan Job or Manual Scan Job shown in Figure 9-37, you can configure FSE to scan all or selected mailboxes and public folders as well as disable the scanning of mailboxes or public folders as shown in Figure 9-38.

TAKE NOTE*

By default, FSE does not rescan messages that have already been scanned by FSE on the same or other server roles.

Figure 9-38

Configuring the Realtime Scan Job

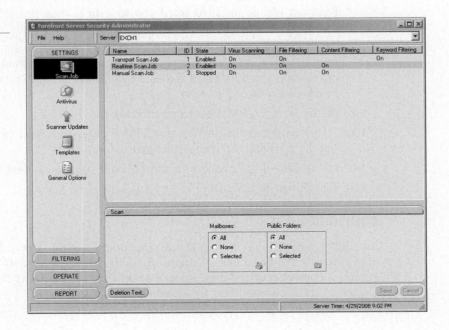

If you select **Antivirus** under the Settings section in the left pane shown in Figure 9-37, you can specify the virus-scanning engines used for each scan job as well as virus-scanning options as shown in Figure 9-39.

Figure 9-39

Configuring Antivirus Scanning

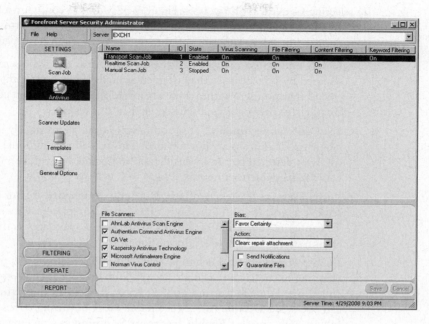

The Bias setting shown in Figure 9-39 determines how thorough each virus-scanning engine will be when scanning emails and attachments. There are five values for the Bias setting:

- **Max Certainty** (the most thorough and the most time consuming)
- **Favor Certainty**
- **Neutral**
- **Favor Performance**
- **Max Performance** (the least thorough and least time consuming)

When a virus is detected, the virus-scanning engines attempt to repair/remove the virus in the email or attachment (a process called *cleaning*). If the virus can be cleaned, the virus-free email is forwarded to the recipient. If the virus cannot be cleaned, the part of the email that contained the virus is replaced with a virus removal message or the attachment that contained the virus is deleted and replaced with another attachment that indicates the removal of a virus. However, you can modify this behavior by selecting a different Action as detailed in Figure 9-39. There are three possible Actions that can be used on virus-infected emails:

- **Skip: detect only** (which detects and labels viruses but does not remove them)
- **Clean: repair attachment** (the default action)
- **Delete: remove infection** (which removes the infected email or email attachment permanently)

Regardless of whether the virus can be cleaned or not, a copy of the virus-infected message is sent to the quarantine folder for later examination and, by default, a notification is not sent to the sender.

Other FSE settings can be configured by selecting the appropriate icon under the Settings section in the left pane shown in Figure 9-37. By selecting **Scanner Updates**, you can configure whether to download updated virus definitions for each virus-scanning engine and how often FSE should check for updates. By default, virus definitions are downloaded for all virus-scanning engines every hour. In the event of a new or serious virus attack, you can click the **Update Now** button on the Scanner Updates page to immediately update virus definitions.

To view additional scan jobs or modify existing scan job settings based on scan job templates, you can select the **Templates** icon in the left pane shown in Figure 9-37. To create a new scan job template, you can click **File** > **Templates** > **New** from the FSE window.

By selecting **General Options** from Figure 9-37, you can configure a large number of FSE scanning, logging, and diagnostic options as well as proxy server settings. Some of the more important options that you can configure on the General Options page include:

- **Delete encrypted compressed files.** This option will remove any files that could not be scanned by FSE because they were encrypted. If you enable this option, you must first ensure that no users within your organization use encryption certificates within their email client programs as discussed later in this lesson.

- **Scan on scanner update.** This option will rescan all previously scanned messages when new virus definitions are downloaded. This will allow additional viruses to be detected that were not detected before a virus definition update, but will also reduce the performance of your Exchange servers running FSE.

- **Purge Message if Message Body Deleted—Transport.** If your Edge role servers cannot remove a virus that is in the body of an email, it replaces the body with virus removal text. To configure your Hub role servers to delete these messages as they pass through the organization, you can select this option.

- **Enable Forefront for Exchange Scan.** This option allows you to enable or disable the scanning of emails as they pass through Hub or Edge role servers as well as the scanning of emails within mailboxes and public folders. By default, this setting is **Enable All**, but you can also select **Disable All**, select **Enable Store Scanning** to scan mailbox and public folders only, or select **Enable Transport Scanning** to scan email relayed on Hub and Edge role servers only.

FSE can also provide limited spam filtering for messages alongside the virus scanning provided by the Hub, Edge, and Mailbox role servers within your organization. Hub and Edge role servers can filter email based on keyword, attachment file name or extension, and sender. Mailbox role servers can filter email based on content (sender domain and subject line only), attachment file name or extension, and sender.

Although FSE maintains a regularly updated list of keywords, file names, and file extensions that should be filtered, you can add your own list of file names, file extensions, keywords, subject lines, sender domains, and allowed senders by navigating to the **Filter Lists** icon under the **Filtering** section in the left pane of the Forefront Server Security Administrator as shown in Figure 9-40.

Figure 9-40

Adding Entries to the Subject Lines Filter List

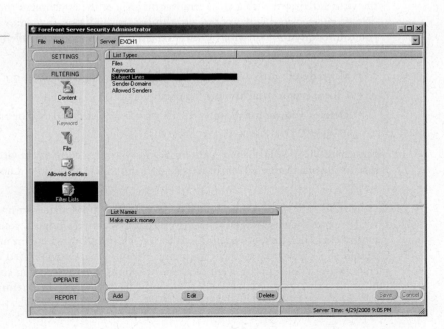

The subject line "Make quick money" was added to the list of subject lines shown in Figure 9-40. Following this, you can highlight the **Content** icon under the **Filtering** section shown in Figure 9-40 to configure how FSE handles emails that have a subject line of "Make quick money." As Figure 9-41 illustrates, if the Realtime Scan Job encounters the subject line "Make quick money," the email will be deleted immediately (**Purge: eliminate message**) and a copy will be sent to the quarantine folder for later examination if necessary.

Figure 9-41

Configuring Content Filtering

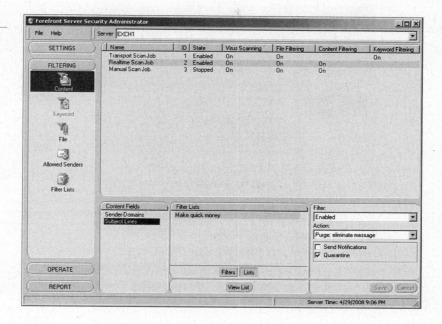

To run the Manual Scan Job in FSE, you can navigate to the **Run Job** icon under the **Operate** section in the left pane of the Forefront Server Security Administrator as shown in Figure 9-42, select the appropriate scanning options and click the **Start** button. Alternatively, the **Schedule Job** icon shown in Figure 9-42 can be used schedule a Manual Scan Job to run at a future time or on a regular basis, and the **Quick Scan** icon can be used to quickly scan certain mailboxes or public folders.

Figure 9-42

Running a Manual Scan Job

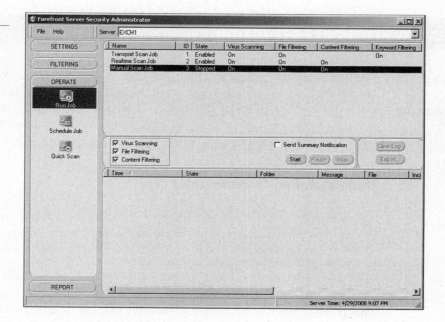

Undert he **Report** section in the left pane of the Forefront Server Security Administrator, you can configure email notifications and view detected viruses as well as the contents of the quarantine folder. By highlighting the **Notification** icon as shown in Figure 9-43, you can add specific email addresses to custom error messages that indicate when FSE-related events occur. For example, Figure 9-43 shows that **administrator@octavius.net** is emailed each time a new virus is detected.

Figure 9-43

Configuring Notifications

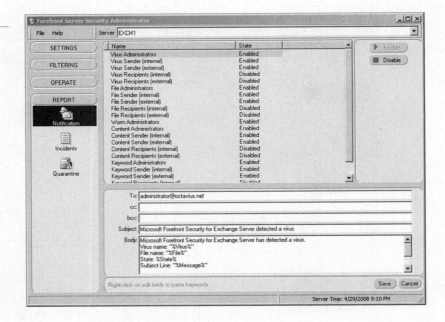

If you click the **Incidents** icon under the **Report** section shown in Figure 9-43, you can view the viruses that FSE has detected as well as a report that displays the number of viruses detected within emails and email attachments from mailboxes and public folders during a Realtime Scan Job or from a Transport Scan Job. Similarly, by clicking the **Quarantine** icon under the **Report** section shown in Figure 9-43, you can view quarantined messages as well as save quarantined items for later analysis or deliver them to their original destination if they were quarantined by mistake.

Configuring Protocol Encryption

THE BOTTOM LINE

The best protection against unauthorized access to network data is the use of protocol encryption. By encrypting email protocols using SSL or TLS, the data that passes across the network will be unreadable by malicious users. Before you can configure protocol encryption, you must first understand basic encryption terminology and features as well as how encryption works to secure data.

Understanding Cryptography

Cryptography uses keys and algorithms to scramble data so that it is unreadable by anyone other than the intended recipient. There are two main types of cryptography that may be used to encrypt data; each one is specialized for different uses.

Cryptography is the practice of protecting information so that only certain users can read it. *Encryption* is the cryptography process whereby files, emails, and other data are converted to a format that is unreadable called *ciphertext*. Users can then use a *decryption* process to decipher the ciphertext and make the data readable again. The readable data is often called *plaintext*.

To encrypt information, you must use an ***encryption algorithm***. An encryption algorithm is a mathematical formula or series of steps that can modify data. Because computers today can easily determine the steps in an encryption algorithm, nearly all encryption algorithms use a random component called a ***key*** to modify the steps within the algorithm. Suppose you create a simple encryption algorithm that multiplies a number by 2, subtracts 5, and then adds 3 to produce an encrypted number. If you perform this encryption algorithm on the number 20, you will obtain the number 38 as shown:

$$20 \times 2 - 5 + 3 = 38$$

Similarly, if you perform the same encryption algorithm on the number 44, you will obtain the number 86 as shown:

$$44 \times 2 - 5 + 3 = 86$$

With multiple examples, a simple computer program could easily determine the calculation used to encrypt the numbers. However, by multiplying each part of the equation by a random number called x, it becomes more difficult to determine the calculation (unless x is known). The equation now becomes:

$$plaintext \times 2(x) - 5(x) + 3(x) = ciphertext$$

If we assume that x is 5, then performing the encryption algorithm on the number 44 will produce the number 430 as shown:

$$44 \times 2(5) - 5(5) + 3(5) = 430$$

The x variable represents the encryption key. The larger the key, the more difficult it is to compare the plaintext and ciphertext to determine the encryption calculation. As a result, most keys are quite large. For example, if we use a key of 19827364 in the same encryption algorithm to encrypt the number 44, the resulting ciphertext (17051553304) will be very different than the original ciphertext (44) as shown:

$$44 \times 2(19827364) - 5(19827364) + 3(19827364) = 17051553304$$

In modern encryption algorithms, there are thousands of steps in the encryption algorithm and the randomly generated encryption keys are much larger than the key used in the previous example (19827364).

To decrypt the ciphertext in the previous example (17051553304), you could simply reverse the operations in the encryption algorithm using the same key (19827364) used to encrypt the original plaintext (44) as shown:

$$17051553304 - 3(19827364) + 5(19827364)/2(19827364) = 44$$

Because the encryption algorithm illustrated in the previous examples uses the same key to encrypt and decrypt, we call it a ***symmetric encryption*** algorithm. In symmetric encryption, a symmetric encryption algorithm is used alongside a key to encrypt plaintext. To decrypt ciphertext, the symmetric encryption algorithm is reversed and used alongside the same key. This process is illustrated in Figure 9-44.

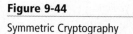

Figure 9-44

Symmetric Cryptography

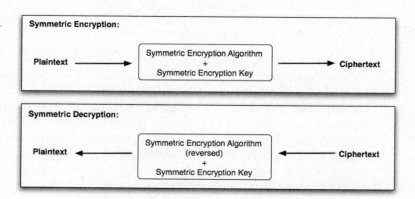

TAKE NOTE ✱

Each additional bit in the length of an encryption key doubles the strength of the encryption. For example, encryption that uses a 129-bit key is twice as difficult to decrypt as encryption that uses a 128-bit key.

Symmetric encryption is the simplest form of encryption used to protect information and the easiest encryption for modern computers to perform. As a result, symmetric encryption is ideal for encrypting large amounts of data quickly. The keys used by most symmetric encryption algorithms today are usually 128-bits or 256-bits long and are typically regenerated each time the encryption algorithm is used to encrypt information.

Unfortunately, symmetric encryption is ill suited to encrypting information that must be sent across a network because both the sender and recipient must first know the key. For example, if User A encrypts an email using symmetric encryption and sends it to User B, User B can only decrypt the file using the same key that was used to encrypt the file.

To solve this problem, you must use a method that allows User A to send the symmetric encryption key to User B across the network without allowing other users to view the symmetric encryption key. ***Asymmetric encryption*** addresses this problem by using different keys to encrypt and decrypt information.

In an asymmetric encryption algorithm, complex one-way mathematical functions are used to encrypt plaintext using a ***public key***, and a separate set of complex one-way mathematical functions are used to decrypt the associated ciphertext using a ***private key*** as illustrated in Figure 9-45. To provide this function, public and private keys must be generated at the same time on the same computer.

Figure 9-45

Asymmetric Cryptography

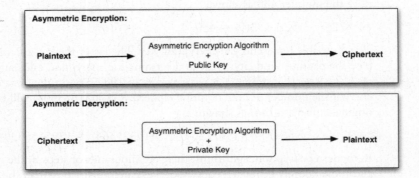

Each computer or user can generate a public/private key pair to use with asymmetric encryption. Public keys are normally given to any network user or computer that requests them. However, private keys are never disclosed.

Thus, if User A needs to send an encrypted message to User B, User A will first obtain User B's public key. Next, User A will encrypt the message using an asymmetric encryption algorithm alongside User B's public key. Because the resulting ciphertext was encrypted using User B's public key, only User B's private key can be used to decrypt it. As a result, User A can safely send the ciphertext across the network to User B and User B can use his or her own private key to decrypt the message.

➕ **MORE INFORMATION**

Although we normally encrypt plaintext using a public key and decrypt ciphertext using a private key, the key used to encrypt or decrypt is irrelevant as long as you have the other key. For example, if you encrypt plaintext using a private key, you can decrypt it using a public key.

Although asymmetric encryption works well across computer networks, it is much more difficult for computers to calculate. In addition, because public keys can be distributed to any user, longer key lengths are typically used to prevent malicious users from reverse-engineering the private key. Asymmetric encryption keys are typically 1024-bits or 2048-bits long. Due to this longer key length and complex encryption algorithm, asymmetric encryption is not suited for encrypting large amounts of information on modern computers today. For example, if it takes one second to encrypt a file using symmetric encryption, it would normally take about three minutes to encrypt the same file using asymmetric encryption.

Consequently, asymmetric encryption is often used to encrypt a small symmetric encryption key so that it can be sent to other users or computers across a network. The other users or computers can then decrypt the symmetric encryption key and use it for symmetric encryption. Because symmetric keys are typically small amounts of data that are 128-bits or 256-bits long, they can be encrypted using asymmetric encryption in less than one second on modern computers. The next section of this lesson examines how symmetric and asymmetric encryption work together for SSL and TLS.

Understanding SSL, TLS, and Certificates

SSL and TLS use the two different types of cryptography together to protect data transfer across the computer network. To ensure that malicious users cannot compromise the SSL and TLS encryption process, you must obtain a certificate from a Certification Authority.

Both SSL and TLS use symmetric encryption to protect data transfer and asymmetric encryption to protect the symmetric encryption key that is generated at the beginning of the SSL or TLS session. Exchange Server 2007 uses SSL and TLS to protect client email access using HTTP, POP3, IMAP4, and SMTP. Although most Internet email relay is unencrypted, Exchange Server 2007 can use TLS to protect SMTP email relay to other partner organizations on the Internet.

To use SSL or TLS, Exchange servers require a public and private key that will be used to protect the transmission of a symmetric key generated by the client computer for the HTTP, POP3, IMAP4, or SMTP session. Once the Exchange server and client computer have the same symmetric key, they will transfer information using symmetric encryption. This process is illustrated in Figure 9-46.

Figure 9-46

SSL and TLS Cryptography

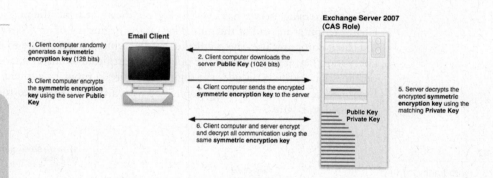

TAKE NOTE✱

As shown in Figure 9-46, Steps 2 through 5 use asymmetric cryptography, whereas Step 6 uses symmetric cryptography.

Unfortunately, there is one security weakness to the process shown in Figure 9-46. A malicious user could intercept the Exchange server public key as it is sent from the Exchange server to the email client computer and substitute his own public key in its place. The client computer would have no way of knowing whether the public key it received was from the Exchange server or the malicious user. After the email client generates a symmetric encryption key, encrypts it using the malicious user's public key, and sends it on the network, the malicious user could intercept the communication and decrypt the symmetric encryption key using the associated private key. This process is called a *man-in-the-middle attack*.

To prevent man-in-the-middle attacks, public keys are typically sent to a trusted third-party computer called a *Certification Authority (CA)* for endorsement before they are used for SSL and TLS. This process is called *enrollment* and is usually performed immediately after a public/private key pair has been generated. Once the CA verifies the identity of the user or computer that generated the public key, the CA creates a *public key certificate* that includes:

- The name of the certificate and its possible uses,
- The public key,

- A digital signature,
- A time period for which the certificate is valid (typically one year), and
- The location of the Certificate Revocation List (CRL).

The most important part of a public key certificate is the digital signature. The ***digital signature*** in the public key certificate is a hash of the public key that is encrypted using the private key of the CA itself. Any computer or user can request the public key of the CA (called the ***trusted root***) and decrypt the digital signature. If a digital signature can be decrypted by using the CA's public key, it proves that the CA's private key must have been used to create the digital signature. Additionally, this also proves that the CA verified the identity of the user or computer that generated the public key.

➕ **MORE INFORMATION**

A ***hash*** (also called a ***checksum***) is a small calculation that is performed based on the contents of a file or piece of information. Hashes are often used to determine whether a file has been modified in transit. After a file has been received from another computer, the hash value for the file is verified against another hash calculation to ensure that the contents have not been modified.

TAKE NOTE *

Remember that CAs do not generate public/private key pairs. They only generate public key certificates from a public key that was generated on another computer.

Once a CA creates a public key certificate, it returns the public key certificate to the computer that generated the public key so that it can be used for SSL or TLS. Because the CA only creates public key certificates and does not participate in the encryption process, it maintains a list of any issued public key certificates that should not be used in a ***Certificate Revocation List (CRL)***. The location of the CRL (typically a Web site) is listed within the certificate itself so client computers can check the CRL before using the public key in the certificate. Public key certificates are often added to the CRL when they are no longer used for a particular purpose or if the public key has been compromised by a malicious user.

Once an Exchange server has a public key certificate, it sends the public key certificate to the client computer instead of the public key at the beginning of an SSL or TLS session. Before the client computer uses the public key in the public key certificate to encrypt the symmetric encryption key, it first inspects the public key certificate to ensure that it is valid and not listed on the CRL and next decodes the digital signature to prove its authenticity and ensure that the hash matches the content of the public key within the public key certificate. This process is illustrated in Figure 9-47.

Figure 9-47

SSL and TLS Cryptography Using Certificates

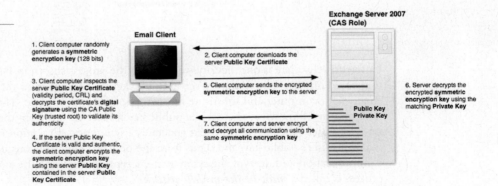

Configuring SSL and TLS Protocol Support

Although Exchange Server 2007 installs a self-signed certificate for use with SSL and TLS by default, you should replace this certificate with a CA-signed certificate from either a commercial CA or an enterprise CA within your organization.

By default, Exchange Server creates a public key certificate during installation that is digitally signed by the ***Windows Certificate API (CAPI)*** component of Windows on the Exchange server itself. As a result, this public key certificate is called a ***self-signed certificate***.

By default, this self-signed certificate is configured for use with all SSL/TLS-capable services that are installed on your Exchange server. You can use the **Get-ExchangeCertificate** cmdlet within the Exchange Management Shell to list the default self-signed certificate as well as the services for which it is enabled. Figure 9-48 shows the output of the Get-ExchangeCertificate cmdlet on the server exch2.octavius.net. The Services column in the output of the Get-ExchangeCertificate cmdlet lists the services using single characters IMAP4 (**I**), POP3 (**P**), UM (**U**), HTTP (**W**), and SMTP (**S**). Thus the characters **IP.WS** in the Services column shown in Figure 9-48 indicates that the default self-signed certificate on the server exch2.octavius.net can be used to provide SSL/TLS for IMAP4, POP3, HTTP, and SMTP connections. The services available on your Exchange server depend on the server roles installed. The Hub role installs the SMTP service, the Mailbox and CAS roles install the HTTP service, the CAS role installs the POP3 and IMAP4 services, and the UM role installs the UM services.

Figure 9-48

Viewing Certificate Uses

You can view the self-signed certificate on an Exchange server by navigating to the Default Web Site from within IIS Manager. If you right click the Default Web Site, click **Properties**, and highlight the **Directory Security** tab, you can select the **View Certificate** button to view the default self-signed certificate. The default self-signed certificate for the computer exch2.octavius .net is shown in Figure 9-49.

Figure 9-49

Viewing the Default Self-Signed Certificate

The red X icon shown in Figure 9-49 indicates that the computer does not have the trusted root (CA public key) used to verify the digital signature on the default self-signed certificate. As a result, when you use a web browser on the computer to access OWA on exch2.octavius.net, you will receive a certificate error as shown in Figure 9-50. Similarly, when you access a CAS role server using a POP3 or IMAP4 account that is configured for SSL or TLS, you will receive a similar warning about the default self-signed certificate as shown in Figure 9-51 using Outlook Express.

Figure 9-50

Internet Explorer Certificate Error

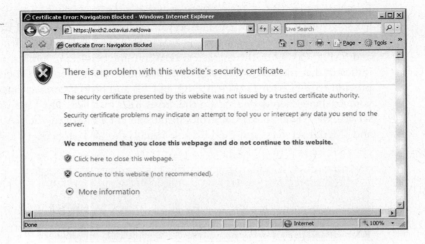

Figure 9-51

Outlook Express Certificate Error

Because the self-signed certificate generated during Exchange installation is not digitally signed by a CA, it is not trusted by email clients that connect to your Exchange servers. Instead, the default self-signed certificate was designed to provide SSL/TLS encryption immediately following Exchange installation only. As a result, you should replace the default self-signed certificate with a CA-signed public key certificate. This will prevent certificate errors on email clients as well as improve the security of SSL/TLS on your Exchange servers by preventing man-in-the-middle attacks.

There are many **commercial CAs** on the Internet, such as Verisign, eTrust, and Thawte that will issue public key certificates for a fee. Most client computers receive the trusted roots of these commercial CAs alongside web browser and operating system updates. This allows client computers to easily validate SSL or TLS public key certificates. As a result, paying a commercial CA to generate a public key certificate for SSL/TLS is commonly used if your servers need to perform SSL or TLS encryption with other computers on the Internet that are not part of your organization. For example, if your organization provides email access to home users, you would normally obtain a public key certificate that is signed by a commercial CA.

TAKE NOTE*

Commercial CAs are often called *public CAs*.

If your organization only uses SSL or TLS to encrypt communication between computers within the organization, then you can install a CA for use within your organization that can issue public key certificates for use with SSL/TLS. To ensure that each computer within your organization can verify the authenticity of these public key certificates, you must also import the trusted root of the organization's CA to each computer. You can import the trusted root certificate on each computer within your organization manually or by using a GPO.

Windows Server 2003 and 2008 have the ability to provide CA services within your organization using ***Certificate Services***. When you install Certificate Services, you can create an ***enterprise CA*** or ***stand-alone CA***. Only enterprise CAs can interoperate with AD and should be chosen to provide CA services within your Exchange organization. Moreover, large organizations can have several CAs configured in a CA hierarchy. The first CA deployed in a hierarchy is called the ***root CA***, and other CAs that participate in the hierarchy are called ***subordinate CAs***. In most organizations, only a single enterprise root CA is necessary for creating public key certificates.

You must at a minimum be a member of the Domain Admins group to install an enterprise CA. To configure certificates for use with an Exchange server, you must at a minimum be a member of the Exchange Server Administrator role and local Administrators group on that server.

TAKE NOTE

Each Exchange server that participates in SSL/TLS encryption requires a different certificate. The same CA normally issues each of these certificates.

INSTALL AN ENTERPRISE ROOT CA AND CONFIGURE CLIENT COMPUTERS WITH THE TRUSTED ROOT

GET READY. Turn on the computer, and log in as the Administrator user account. Close any windows that appear on the desktop.

1. Click **Start**, **Control Panel**, and then click **Add or Remove Programs**. When the Add or Remove Programs window appears, click **Add/Remove Windows Components** to open the Windows Components Wizard.

2. On the Windows Components page, select **Certificate Services** and click **Yes** to acknowledge that the computer's name and domain membership can no longer be changed. Click **Next**. The CA Type page appears as shown in Figure 9-52.

TAKE NOTE

Once you install Certificate Services on a computer to provide CA services, the computer's NetBIOS name, FQDN, and domain membership cannot be modified until you remove Certificate Services. This is because the name and domain membership of the CA are included in each public key certificate issued by the CA and used by computers to locate the CRL.

Figure 9-52

Creating an Enterprise Root CA

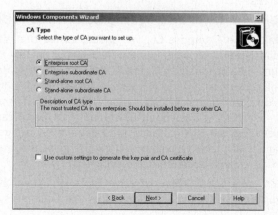

3. Ensure that **Enterprise root CA** is selected and click **Next**. The CA Identifying Information page appears as shown in Figure 9-53.

Figure 9-53

Adding CA Information

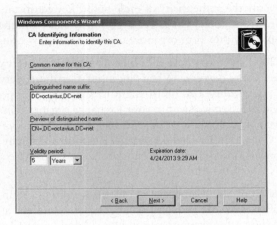

4. Type a descriptive name for your CA in the Common name for this CA dialog box. Normally the first CA in an organization is named for the organization. For example, Octavius Enterprise Root CA would be an appropriate common name for the Enterprise root CA in the Octavius organization.

5. By default, Enterprise root CAs generate their own public/private key pair for use when digitally signing public key certificates. The validity period for this public/ private key pair is 5 years by default, but you can change this value using the Validity period drop-down boxes shown in Figure 9-53.

The validity period for the CAs public/private key pair is used to determine the maximum validity period for public key certificates that are digitally signed by the CA. For example, if the CA certificate expires in April 2013, the CA cannot give a validity period beyond that date for any public key certificates that it digitally signs.

6. Click **Next**. After the CA public/private key pair is generated, the Certificate Database Settings page appears.

7. Review the default locations for the CA database and logs and click **Next**. When prompted to stop IIS to complete the installation of Certificate Services, click **Yes**.

8. Insert your Windows Server 2003 CD-ROM when prompted. When prompted to enable ASP, click **Yes**.

9. Click **Finish** to close the Windows Components Wizard window.

10. After installing an Enterprise CA, you should ensure that the computers within your organization obtain a copy of the CA trusted root so that they can validate the digital signatures on public key certificates that were issued by the CA. Although each client computer can obtain a copy of the trusted root by navigating to https:// *CA_name*/certsrv (where CA_name is the FQDN or IP address of the computer running Certificate Services) and selecting **Download a CA certificate, certificate chain, or CRL**, it would be too time consuming to perform on many computers. As a result, we will configure the Default Domain GPO to distribute the trusted root certificate for the CA to all domain computers automatically.

11. On your CA, click **Start**, **Administrative Tools**, and then click **Active Directory Users and Computers**. The Active Directory Users and Computers window appears.

12. Right click your domain in the left pane and click **Properties**. When the domain Properties window appears, highlight the **Group Policy** tab to view the Default Domain Policy as shown in Figure 9-54.

Figure 9-54

Viewing the Default Domain Policy

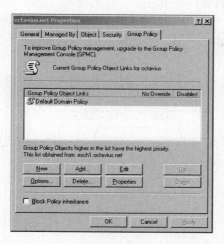

If you have the Group Policy Management Console (GPMC) installed, you will not see the Default Domain Policy in the screen shown in Figure 9-54. Instead, you will need to click the **Open** button on the Group Policy tab to open the GPMC and expand your forest and domain in the left pane to view the Default Domain Policy.

TAKE NOTE*

13. Highlight **Default Domain Policy** and click **Edit**. The Group Policy Object Editor appears.

If you have the GPMC installed, right click the Default Domain Policy in the left pane of the GPMC and select **Edit** to open the Group Policy Object Editor.

TAKE NOTE*

14. In the left pane of the Group Policy Object Editor, navigate to **Default Domain Policy** > **Computer Configuration** > **Windows Settings** > **Security Settings** > **Public Key Policies** > **Trusted Root Certification Authorities** as shown in Figure 9-55.

Figure 9-55

Configuring the Default Domain Policy

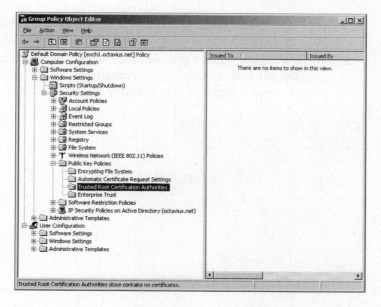

15. Right click **Trusted Root Certification Authorities** in the left pane and click **Import**. When the Certificate Import Wizard appears, click **Next**.

16. On the File to Import page, you must specify the trust root certificate of your CA. By default, the trusted root certificate is located on the root of C:\ on your CA and named *Server_CA-Name.crt*, where Server is the FQDN of your CA, and CA-Name is the name of your CA during installation. Figure 9-56 shows the location of the trusted root certificate for the Octavius Enterprise Root CA installed on exch1.octavius.net. Click **Browse**, select your trusted root certificate from C:\ in the Open window, and click **OK**. When finished, click **Next**.

Figure 9-56

Specifying a Trusted Root Certificate

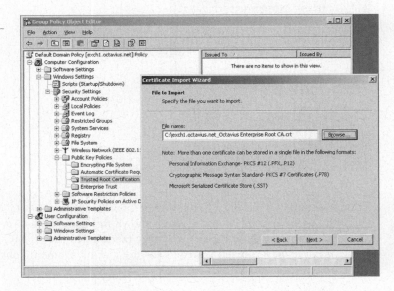

17. On the Certificate Store page, click **Next**. Click **Finish** to close the Certificate Import Wizard. Click **OK** to close the information dialog box.

18. Close the Group Policy Object Editor. Click **OK** to close the domain Properties window. Close the Active Directory Users and Computers window.

 REPLACE THE DEFAULT EXCHANGE SSL/TLS CERTIFICATE WITH A CERTIFICATE FROM AN ENTERPRISE CA

GET READY. Turn on the computer, and log in as the Administrator user account. Close any windows that appear on the desktop.

1. Click **Start**, **Administrative Tools**, and then click **Internet Information Services (IIS) Manager**. The Internet Information Services (IIS) Manager window appears.

2. In the left pane, expand your Exchange server and then expand **Web Sites**. Right click **Default Web Site** and select **Properties**. When the Default Web Site Properties window appears, highlight the **Directory Security** tab as shown in Figure 9-57.

Figure 9-57

Configuring Certificates in IIS Manager

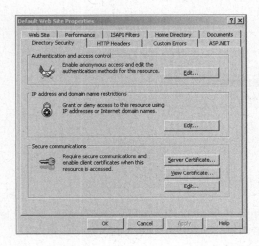

3. Click **Server Certificate**. When the Welcome to the Web Server Certificate Wizard page appears, click **Next** to start the IIS Certificate Wizard.

4. On the Modify the Current Certificate Assignment page, select **Remove the current certificate** as shown in Figure 9-58 and click **Next**. The Remove a Certificate page appears.

Figure 9-58

Removing an Existing Certificate

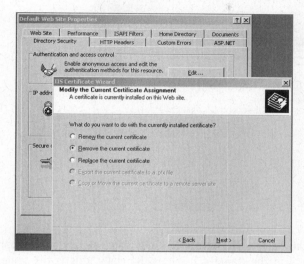

5. Review the details of the certificate that you are removing and click **Next**. Click **Finish** to close the IIS Certificate Wizard.

6. In the Default Web Site Properties window, click **Server Certificate**. When the Welcome to the Web Server Certificate Wizard page appears, click **Next** to start the IIS Certificate Wizard.

7. On the Modify the Current Certificate Assignment page shown in Figure 9-59, ensure that **Create a new certificate** is selected and click **Next**. The Delayed or Immediate Request page appears.

Figure 9-59

Creating a New Certificate

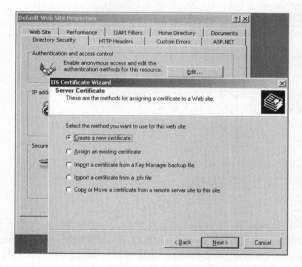

8. To enroll for a certificate from an Enterprise CA, ensure that **Send the request immediately to an online certification authority** is selected as shown in Figure 9-60 and click **Next**.

Figure 9-60

Sending a Certificate Request to an Enterprise CA

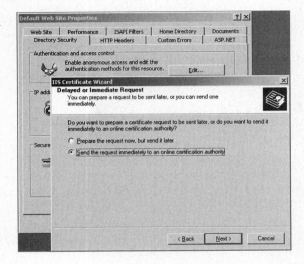

9. On the Name and Security Settings page, supply an appropriate name for your certificate in the **Name** dialog box. Normally, this is the same as the FQDN that email clients use when contacting your Exchange server for the server exch2.octavius.net as shown in Figure 9-61. You can optionally increase the key length to more than 1024 bits using the **Bit length** drop-down box, but this may exclude or reduce the performance of some SSL/TLS clients. Similarly, you can select the checkbox at the bottom of Figure 9-61 to select a different cryptographic algorithm provider, but this is necessary only for unusual situations. Click **Next** when finished.

Figure 9-61

Configuring the Certificate Name and Security

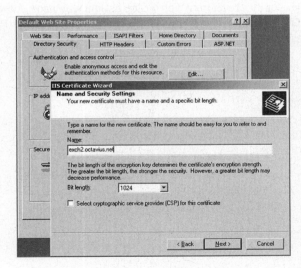

10. On the Organization Information page, supply the name of your organization in the **Organization** dialog box and supply the division name where your Exchange server resides in the **Organizational unit** dialog box. This division name is normally the same as the OU that contains the computer account for your Exchange server in AD. For example, if your Exchange server exists in the East OU of the Octavius organization, you could enter the values shown in Figure 9-62. Click **Next** when finished.

Figure 9-62

Specifying Organization
Information

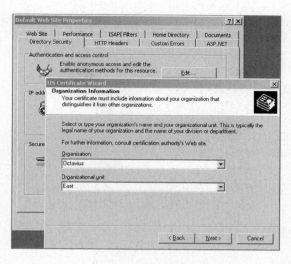

If you configure client
computers to contact
your Exchange server by
IP address or by using a
different name than the
one shown in Figure 9-63,
clients will receive a certificate error in their application that indicates that
the name on the SSL/TLS
certificate does not match
the server name.

Figure 9-63

Configuring a Common Name

11. On the Your Site's Common Name page, enter the FQDN or NetBIOS name that other
computers will use when contacting your Exchange server in the **Common name**
dialog box. For example, if you plan to configure client computers to contact exch2
.octavius.net, you would enter exch2.octavius.net in this dialog box as shown in
Figure 9-63. Click **Next** when finished.

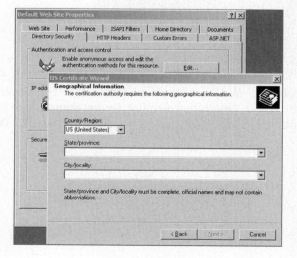

12. On the Geographical Information page, supply the appropriate information about your
Exchange server's physical location in the appropriate drop-down or dialog boxes
shown in Figure 9-64 and click **Next** when finished.

Figure 9-64

Specifying Geographical
Information

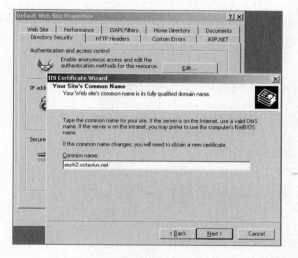

13. On the SSL Port page, ensure that port 443 is listed in the dialog box as shown in Figure 9-65 and click **Next.**

Figure 9-65

Specifying the SSL Port for HTTP

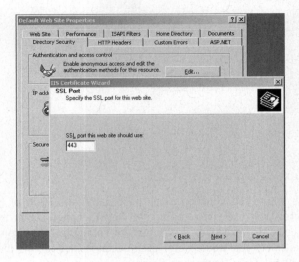

14. On the Choose a Certification Authority page, select your CA from the **Certification authorities** drop-down box as shown in Figure 9-66 and click **Next.**

Figure 9-66

Selecting an Enterprise CA

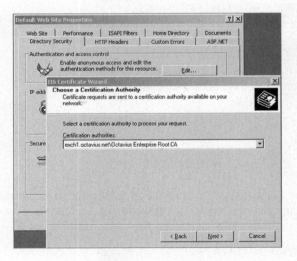

15. On the Certificate Request Submission page, review your certificate request settings and click **Next.** Click **Finish** to close the IIS Certificate Wizard.

16. In the Default Web Site Properties window, click **Edit** under the Secure communications section. Ensure that **Require secure channel (SSL)** and **Require 128-bit encryption** is selected as shown in Figure 9-67 and click **OK.**

Figure 9-67

Requiring SSL for HTTP

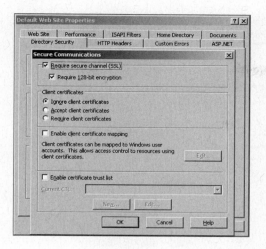

17. Click **OK** to close the Default Web Site Properties window and close IIS Manager.

 REPLACE THE DEFAULT EXCHANGE SSL/TLS CERTIFICATE WITH A CERTIFICATE FROM A COMMERCIAL CA

GET READY. Turn on the computer, and log in as the Administrator user account. Close any windows that appear on the desktop.

> **TAKE NOTE** ✻
>
> The process within IIS Manager for obtaining a certificate from a commercial CA is similar to that for obtaining a certificate from an Enterprise CA. As a result, we focus on the differences within this exercise.

1. Click **Start**, **Administrative Tools**, and then click **Internet Information Services (IIS) Manager**. The Internet Information Services (IIS) Manager window appears.

2. In the left pane, expand your Exchange server and then expand **Web Sites**. Right click **Default Web Site** and select **Properties**. When the Default Web Site Properties window appears, highlight the **Directory Security** tab as shown earlier in Figure 9-57.

3. Click **Server Certificate**. When the Welcome to the Web Server Certificate Wizard page appears, click **Next** to start the IIS Certificate Wizard.

4. On the Modify the Current Certificate Assignment page, select **Remove the current certificate** as shown earlier in Figure 9-58 and click **Next**. The Remove a Certificate page appears.

5. Review the details of the certificate that you are removing and click **Next**. Click **Finish** to close the IIS Certificate Wizard.

6. In the Default Web Site Properties window, click **Server Certificate**. When the Welcome to the Web Server Certificate Wizard page appears, click **Next** to start the IIS Certificate Wizard.

7. On the Modify the Current Certificate Assignment page shown earlier in Figure 9-59, ensure that **Create a new certificate** is selected and click **Next**. The Delayed or Immediate Request page appears.

8. To enroll for a certificate from a commercial CA, ensure that **Prepare the request now, but send it later** is selected as shown in Figure 9-68 and click **Next**.

Figure 9-68

Sending a Certificate Request to a Commercial CA

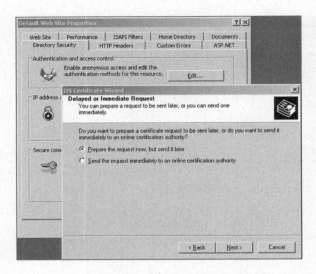

9. On the Name and Security Settings page, supply an appropriate name for your certificate in the **Name** dialog box (typically the FQDN of your Exchange server) and optionally modify the number of bits to use in the key as well as the cryptographic service provider as shown earlier in Figure 9-61.

10. On the Organization Information page, supply the appropriate organization and organizational unit names for your Exchange server as shown earlier in Figure 9-62 and click **Next**.

11. On the Your Site's Common Name page, enter the FQDN or NetBIOS name that other computers will use when contacting your Exchange server as shown earlier in Figure 9-63 and click **Next**.

12. On the Geographical Information page, supply the appropriate information about your Exchange server's physical location in the appropriate drop-down or dialog boxes as shown earlier in Figure 9-64 and click **Next**.

13. On the Certificate Request File Name page, enter the path to the text file that will contain the public key used to generate the certificate in the File name dialog box. The default name is c:\certreq.txt as shown in Figure 9-69. Click **Next** when finished.

Figure 9-69

Specifying the Certificate Request File Name

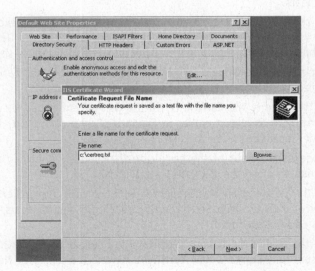

14. On the Request File Summary page, review your certificate request settings and click **Next**. Click **Finish** to close the IIS Certificate Wizard. Click **OK** to close the Default Web Site Properties window and close IIS Manager.

15. You must now contact the Web site for a commercial CA and request a certificate by following the steps outlined on the particular CA Web site. Part of this process will include

uploading the certificate request file (i.e., c:\certreq.txt) that contains your Exchange server's public key. In addition, you will be required to submit payment to the CA (typically using a credit card). The CA will then validate your identity using several methods (phone, records, physical meeting). After the validation process has completed (typically a few days), the CA will create a public key certificate file (with a .cer extension) that you can download from its Web site and import into IIS Manager.

16. Click **Start**, **Administrative Tools**, and then click **Internet Information Services (IIS) Manager**. The Internet Information Services (IIS) Manager window appears.

17. In the left pane, expand your Exchange server and then expand **Web Sites**. Right click **Default Web Site** and select **Properties**. When the Default Web Site Properties window appears, highlight the **Directory Security** tab as shown earlier in Figure 9-57.

18. Click **Server Certificate**. When the Welcome to the Web Server Certificate Wizard page appears, click **Next** to start the IIS Certificate Wizard.

19. On the Pending Certificate Request page, ensure that **Process the pending request and install the certificate** is selected as shown in Figure 9-70 and click **Next**.

Figure 9-70

Importing a Pending
Certificate Request

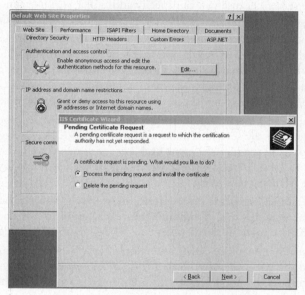

20. On the Process a Pending Request page, enter the path to the public key certificate file (*.cer) that you downloaded from the CA Web site in the **Path and file name** dialog box as shown in Figure 9-71 and click **Next**.

Figure 9-71

Specifying the Certificate File

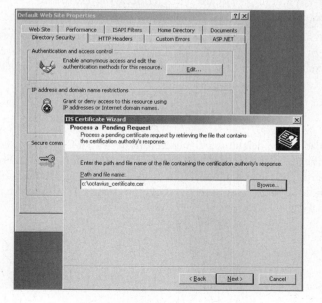

21. On the SSL Port page, ensure that port 443 is listed in the dialog box as shown earlier in Figure 9-65 and click **Next**.

22. Click **Next** on the Certificate Summary page. Click **Finish** to close the IIS Certificate Wizard.

23. In the Default Web Site Properties window, click **Edit** under the Secure communications section. Ensure that **Require secure channel (SSL)** and **Require 128-bit encryption** is selected as shown earlier in Figure 9-67 and click **OK**.

24. Click **OK** to close the Default Web Site Properties window and close IIS Manager.

THE COMMAND LINE WAY

You can also use cmdlets within the Exchange Management Shell to generate certificate requests and import them. To generate a certificate request that can be uploaded to a commercial CA for approval, you can use the **New-ExchangeCertificate** cmdlet. This is often useful if there are several names that Internet clients must use when contacting your Exchange server because you can specify additional FQDN names during the request that will be stored in the *Subject Alternative Name (SAN)* field of the certificate.

This is useful if you have remote Outlook or Entourage email clients. In order to use the Autodiscover service from a remote Outlook or Entourage client across a remote connection, you must also specify **autodiscover.domain** (where domain.com is your domain name) as an additional domain name during the certificate request or add the **–IncludeAutoDiscover** option to the New-ExchangeCertificate cmdlet.

For example, to generate a certificate request using a 1024-bit long key in the file c:\certreq.txt for the server exch2.octavius.net within Octavius organization (Country = US) that responds to the domain name exch2.octavius.net as well as the Subject Alternative Names exch2 and autodicover.octavius.net, you can use the following command in the Exchange Management Shell:

New-ExchangeCertificate -GenerateRequest $true -SubjectName 'C=US, O=Octavius, CN=exch2.octavius.net' -DomainName 'exch2,autodiscover.octavius.net' -PrivateKeyExportable $true –KeySize '1024' -Path 'c:\certreq.txt'

Next, you can upload the certificate request file (c:\certreq.txt) to a commercial CA and download the public key certificate file once the request has been approved. Following this, you can import the public key certificate using the **Import-ExchangeCertificate** cmdlet. To import the public key certificate file c:\octavius_certificate.cer and assign a friendly name of Exch2 Certificate, you could use the following command within the Exchange Management Shell:

Import-ExchangeCertificate -Path 'c:\octavius_certificate.cer' -FriendlyName 'Exch2 Certificate'

You can also use the New-ExchangeCertificate cmdlet to generate a new self-signed certificate or to request a certificate from an enterprise CA. For more information on the New-ExchangeCertificate and Import-ExchangeCertificate cmdlets, search for their names within Exchange Server 2007 Help.

After replacing the default self-signed certificate with a CA-signed certificate, you can view the new certificate by clicking on the View Certificate button on the Directory Security tab within the properties of the Default Web Site within IIS Manager as described earlier. The certificate should indicate that it was issued by the appropriate CA as shown for the SSL/TLS certificate shown in Figure 9-72 for the server exch2.octavius.net.

Figure 9-72

Viewing the CA-Signed
Certificate

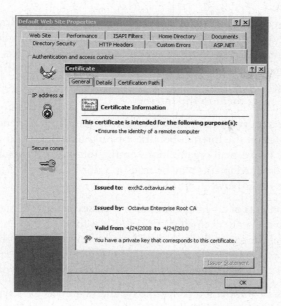

By default, the new CA-signed certificate is configured for use with the HTTP protocol as well as the POP3 and IMAP4 protocols if they were started on the Exchange server when the certificate was obtained. To configure this new certificate to be used for other protocols and services, you must first obtain the thumbprint for your new certificate by running the Get-ExchangeCertificate cmdlet as shown earlier in this section. Next, you can use the Enable-ExchangeCertificate cmdlet within the Exchange Management Shell to enable the certificate for use with other protocols and services. For example, to enable the command **Enable-ExchangeCertificate -Thumbprint** *thumbprint* **-Services 'IMAP, POP, UM, IIS, SMTP'** will enable the new CA-signed certificate with the specific *thumbprint* for use by IMAP4, POP3, UM, HTTP, and SMTP. However, because the HTTP protocol is already enabled after running the Web Certificate Wizard, you only need to enable any remaining protocols for use with a new CA-signed certificate. Figure 9-73 displays the Enable-ExchangeCertificate command needed to enable the exch2.octavius.net certificate for use with the additional protocols IMAP4, POP3, and SMTP as well as the output of the Get-ExchangeCertificate cmdlet afterward.

Figure 9-73

Enabling Certificate Use

When your public key certificate expires, you must renew the certificate or obtain a new one. If you are using a commercial CA, you typically obtain a new certificate using the same process discussed in this lesson. If you are using an enterprise CA, you can simply run the IIS Certificate Wizard again and select **Renew the current certificate** on the Modify the Current Certificate Assignment page shown earlier in Figure 9-58.

■ Configuring Email Encryption

THE BOTTOM LINE

You can also use certificates to encrypt emails within email client programs. This ensures that messages remain encrypted as they are passed through several different email servers on the Internet. In addition, you can digitally sign emails to prove their authenticity by configuring email client programs to use certificates.

In the previous section, you learned how to configure SSL and TLS encryption to encrypt OWA traffic between web browsers on client computers to CAS role servers using HTTPS. In addition, this same SSL and TLS encryption can be used to protect email transfer from CAS role servers to email clients using POP3S and IMAP4S as well as from email clients to Hub role servers using SMTPS. However, CAS and Hub role servers decrypt emails before processing them and relaying them to the Internet.

Most email servers on the Internet will accept only anonymous unencrypted SMTP email from other emails servers on the Internet because it would be too difficult to coordinate certificates and trusted roots between all organizations on the Internet. As a result, sensitive emails that are forwarded to Internet recipients may be read by a third-party who has access to the traffic on the Internet as it passes between email servers.

To protect the contents of an email message as it passes across the Internet, you must encrypt the email message on the sender's email client before it is forwarded to an email server. The encrypted message will simply be forwarded to the destination email server on the Internet alongside other emails, however its contents will not be readable. When the encrypted message is delivered to the destination email client, that email client can then decrypt the encrypted message.

This process uses a combination of symmetric and asymmetric encryption in much the same way that SSL and TLS does. The original email message is encrypted on the sender's email client using a randomly generated symmetric key and this symmetric key is then encrypted using the recipient's public key. When the message reaches the destination email client, the recipient decrypts the symmetric key using his private key and then proceeds to use the symmetric key to decrypt the contents of the email message. When the recipient replies to the email message, this process is reversed.

To encrypt individual emails, you must configure your email client with a public-private key pair. There are many different technologies that can generate public-private key pairs for use with email encryption between email client computers. If your organization does not have a CA, you can add a *Pretty Good Privacy (PGP)* or *GNU Privacy Guard (GPG)* key pair that you generated using a PGP or GPG utility to your email client program. However, because PGP and GPG do not use CA-signed keys, you must manually approve other users' PGP or GPG keys before you can use them to send encrypted emails.

+ MORE INFORMATION

PGP is licensed for commercial use, but GPG is freely obtainable. To obtain a copy of GPG, visit **http://gnupg.org.**

If your organization has a CA, you can simply add a CA-signed *user certificate* to your email client program and ensure that the destination computer contains the trusted root of the CA. To allow users to obtain user certificates from an enterprise CA, you must log in as a user who is a member of the Domain Admins group and grant the appropriate users the Read and Enroll permissions on a *certificate template* that can be used for email encryption. Users can then use the Certificates MMC snap-in to request a certificate. If the user account has Read and Enroll permissions to the certificate template, AD generates a public-private key pair within the user account and automatically sends the public key to the enterprise CA. Once the Enterprise CA digitally signs the certificate, it is returned to the user account. Users can then add this user certificate to their email client program and use it for email encryption.

+ MORE INFORMATION

You can also use Group Policy to automatically issue certificates to users within your organization using a process called *autoenrollment*. For more information on how to configure autoenrollment, search for autoenrollment at **http://technet.microsoft.com.**

Instead of configuring your email client program for encryption, you can configure it to digitally sign all emails. Your email client will encrypt a hash of each email that you send using your private key. Others on the Internet can then verify the digital signature using your public key and prove that the email was sent by you and not modified during transit. Digital email signing can be done regardless of whether you use a CA-signed certificate, PGP, or GPG.

CONFIGURE USER CERTIFICATE TEMPLATE PERMISSIONS

GET READY. Turn on the computer, and log in as the Administrator user account. Close any windows that appear on the desktop.

TAKE NOTE *

To perform these steps, you must already have an Enterprise CA installed within your forest.

1. On your Enterprise CA, click **Start** and click **Run**. In the run dialog box, type **certtmpl.msc** and press **Enter**. The Certificate Templates window appears.

2. In the right pane, right click **User** and click **Properties**. On the Security tab, ensure that Authenticated Users is allowed **Read** and **Enroll** permissions as shown in Figure 9-74.

Figure 9-74

Configuring a User Certificate Template

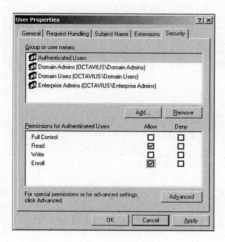

 TAKE NOTE *

If you wish to restrict the users who can obtain a user certificate, you can add the appropriate users as shown in Figure 9-74 and assign them Read and Enroll permissions instead.

3. Close the Certificate Templates window.

 TAKE NOTE *

If you configure the permissions on a different template than the one used in this exercise, you will need to add the template to the CA using the Certification Authority MMC snap-in (**Start** > **Administrative Tools** > **Certification Authority**).

 REQUEST A USER CERTIFICATE

GET READY. Turn on the computer, and log in as any user account. Close any windows that appear on the desktop.

1. Click **Start** and click **Run**. In the run dialog box, type **certmgr.msc** and press **Enter**. The Certificates—Current User window appears.

2. In the left pane, expand **Personal** and **Certificates**.

3. Right click **Certificates**, select **All Tasks**, and click **Request New Certificate**. When the Certificate Request Wizard window appears, click **Next**.

4. On the Certificate Types page, select **User** as shown in Figure 9-75 and click **Next**.

Figure 9-75

Creating a New Certificate Using a User Certificate Template

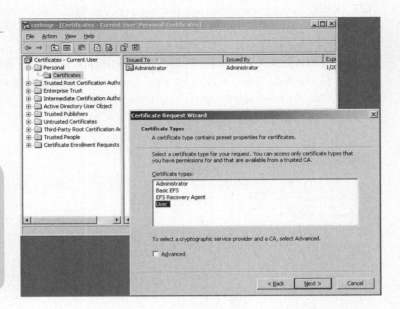

5. On the Certificate Friendly Name and Description page, supply an appropriate name for your certificate in the **Friendly name** dialog box as shown in Figure 9-76. Optionally, supply a description for your certificate in the **Description** dialog box and click **Next**.

Figure 9-76

Specifying a Friendly Name and Description

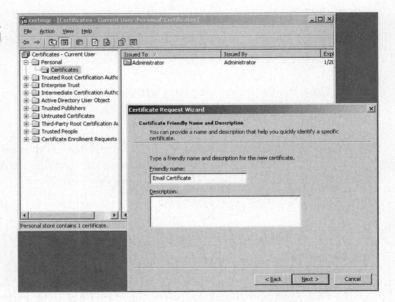

6. Click **Finish** to close the Certificate Request Wizard. Click **OK** to close the result dialog box. You should now see a new certificate listed in the right pane of the Certificate—Current User window.

7. Close the Certificate—Current User window.

Once you have obtained a user certificate, you can configure your email client to use this certificate for email encryption or digital email signing. For Outlook 2007, you can navigate to **Tools** > **Trust Center**. When the Trust Center window opens, you can click **E-mail Security** in the left pane and select the appropriate options to allow for email encryption and digital signing as shown in

Figure 9-77. To select the certificate used for email encryption and digital signing, you can click **Settings** as shown in Figure 9-77 and choose the appropriate certificate to list in the **Signing Certificate** and **Encryption Certificate** dialog boxes as shown in Figure 9-78.

Figure 9-77

Configuring Email Encryption and Digital Signing in Outlook 2007

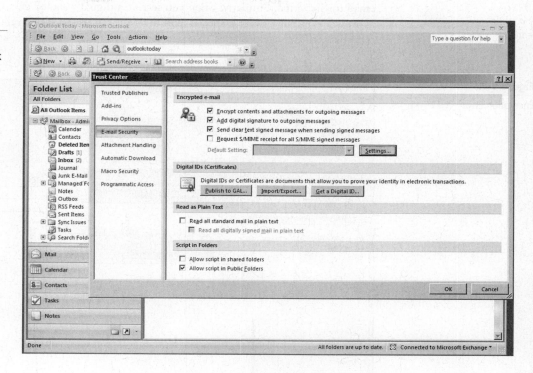

Figure 9-78

Selecting a Certificate in Outlook 2007

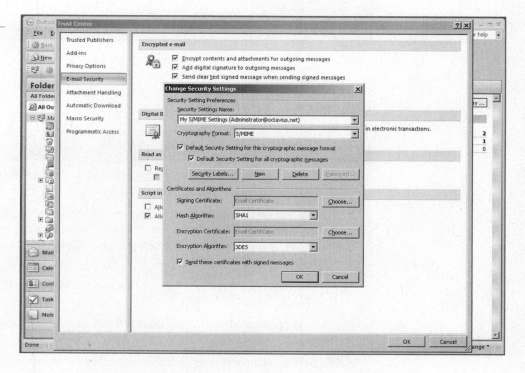

In previous versions of Outlook and in Outlook Express, you can configure email encryption and digital email signing by navigating to **Tool** > **Options** and selecting the **Security** tab. For Entourage clients, you can configure email encryption and signing by navigating to the **Mail Security** tab within the properties of the email account (**Tools** > **Accounts** in Entourage).

It is important to keep in mind that email encryption is a two-way process. If you enable email encryption in your email client program and attempt to send an encrypted email to a recipient who does not have a public-private key pair configured, you will receive an error message similar to the one shown in Figure 9-79 when attempting to send the email and will need to send the email unencrypted. Similarly, when you receive a digitally signed email, your email client program will typically display a special icon that you can use to see or validate the digital signature on the email message provided that you are able to obtain the public key of the sender.

Figure 9-79

Encryption Error

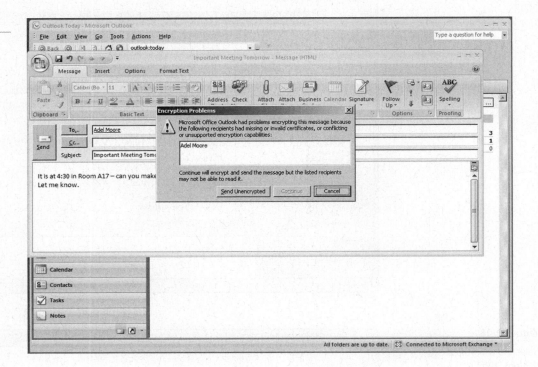

SUMMARY SKILL MATRIX

IN THIS LESSON YOU LEARNED:

- Practical security involves implementing practices and procedures that secure data according to organizational requirements.

- You can achieve practical security for your email system by restricting access to the email system, encrypting email transfer, restricting email relay, limiting permissions, minimizing viruses and spam, stopping unnecessary services, implementing firewalls, and updating software on a regular basis.

- You can minimize the chance that a malicious user will compromise your Exchange servers by reducing their attack surface.

- The SCW can be used to minimize the attack surface on an Exchange server by disabling unused services and implementing a host-based firewall.

- Network-based firewalls can be used to restrict the traffic that enters a network and thus reduce the Exchange attack surface.

- Antispam transport agents may be used to filter spam messages that enter your organization. These agents can filter spam messages by content, IP address, sender, recipient, and file attachment.

- Because nearly all spam enters your organization from the Internet, Edge role servers enable all antispam transport agents by default. You can optionally enable a limited number of antispam transport agents on Hub role servers.

- FSE is an antivirus software product that integrates with Exchange Server 2007 and uses up to five different antivirus-scanning engines that are updated on a regular basis. You can control the level of virus scanning as well as the processing of virus-infected files using FSE.

- When installed on a Hub or Edge role server, FSE scans messages that are relayed using a Transport Scan Job. Alternatively, FSE can scan mailboxes and public folders when installed on a Mailbox role server using the Realtime and Manual Scan Jobs.

- Cryptography protects data from access by unauthorized users by encrypting data using an algorithm and key. Symmetric cryptography uses the same key to encrypt and decrypt data, whereas asymmetric cryptography encrypts data using a public key and decrypts data using a private key. A digital signature is a hash that is encrypted using a private key. You can verify a digital signature using a public key.

- SSL and TLS use symmetric cryptography to encrypt email traffic on a network and asymmetric cryptography to protect the symmetric encryption key. To prevent a man-in-the-middle attack, public key certificates are used in place of public keys during the asymmetric encryption process.

- CAs create certificates by digitally signing public keys for other organizations. Commercial CAs are trusted by most applications, whereas enterprise CAs are trusted by an organization. You can install an enterprise CA within your organization to issue certificates for use with SSL and TLS. After obtaining a certificate, you can configure it for use with IMAP, POP, UM, HTTP, and SMTP.

- Email clients can be configured to encrypt the contents of emails before they are sent to an email server using user certificates. In addition, user certificates may be used to digitally sign emails that are sent by an email client.

■ Knowledge Assessment

Fill in the Blank

Complete the following sentences by writing the correct word or words in the blanks provided.

1. You can enable the _____ option in FSE to ensure that emails are rescanned following a virus definition update.

2. Filtering spam by IP address is commonly called _____.

3. The sum total of the number of ways that users can access your Exchange server is called the _____.

4. If you encrypt information using a public key, it must be decrypted using a _____.

5. The process of repairing a virus infection is called _____ .

6. To reduce the attack surface of a single Exchange server, you can run the _____ after registering the Exchange Server 2007 services.

7. The practice of limiting permissions is called _____.

8. You can configure content filtering to send copies of spam messages to a _____ mailbox.

9. You can obtain SSL and TLS certificates from a commercial or enterprise _____.

10. FSE can be configured to use up to _____ licensed antivirus engines for scanning emails.

Multiple Choice

Circle the letter that corresponds to the best answer.

1. Which of the following are good security practices with regards to Exchange? (Choose all that apply.)
   a. Limit access to email.
   b. Encrypt email traffic between clients and email servers.
   c. Ensure that client computers are regularly updated.
   d. Ensure that Exchange Server 2007 is regularly updated.

2. Which of the following scan jobs in FSE may be used to scan mailbox and public folder databases? (Choose all that apply.)
   a. Transport Scan Job
   b. Manual Scan Job
   c. Edge Scan Job
   d. Realtime Scan Job

3. After installing an enterprise CA within your organization, what must you install on all client computers so that they can validate CA-signed certificates?
   a. The CA private key
   b. The CA trusted root
   c. The CA digital signature
   d. The CRL

4. What must you obtain to configure digital email signing within Entourage?
   a. A CRL
   b. A digital signature
   c. A user certificate, PGP or GPG key pair
   d. A trusted root certificate

5. Which of the following bias settings would you configure within FSE to ensure that most viruses are detected?
   a. Favor Performance
   b. Max Certainty
   c. Max Performance
   d. Favor Certainty

6. Which of the following cmdlets may be used to update the Safe Senders list from an Outlook client?
   a. Set-ContentFilterConfig
   b. Update-Safelist
   c. Set-ContentList
   d. Update-ContentList

7. You have configured a CA-signed certificate for use with remote POP3 and IMAP4 clients. However, the autodiscover service on remote clients is unable to find your Exchange servers. How can you remedy the problem? (Choose two answers. Each answer is part of the solution.)
   a. Request a new SSL/TLS certificate using the New-ExchangeCertificate cmdlet
   b. Request a new SSL/TLS certificate using the Certificate Wizard
   c. Include an external URL in the certificate request
   d. Include a Subject Alternative Name (SAN) in the certificate request

8. Which of the following ports is used by EdgeSync traffic that is protected by SSL?
   a. 50636
   b. 443
   c. 995
   d. 993

9. Which of the following email addresses are likely from a spammer? (Choose all that apply.)
   a. bestoffer@acme.com
   b. A5829SGHW24@kei2.com
   c. julie@supersales.com
   d. hotbuys@hotmail.com

10. During the IIS Certificate Wizard, which value represents the URL of the Exchange server that users must use when accessing email?
    a. Organization
    b. Location
    c. Common name
    d. Subject Alternative Name (SAN)

True/False

Circle T if the statement is true or F if the statement is false.

T | F   **1.** Host-based firewalls may be used to filter traffic that enters a network.

T | F   **2.** Edge role servers have all antispam transport agents installed and enabled by default.

T | F   **3.** You can configure one or more RBLs to aid in filtering spam by IP address.

T | F   **4.** Attachment filtering can only be configured using cmdlets within the Exchange Management Shell on Hub role servers.

T | F   **5.** You can reduce the attack surface of a computer by enabling SSL or TLS encryption.

T | F   **6.** Educating users about how to identify spam and viruses is an important practice to minimize the spread of spam and viruses.

T | F   **7.** If the sender reputation is too low, the sender's IP address will be added to the IP Block List for 24 hours by default.

T | F   **8.** An SCL of 0 indicates that the email message is almost certainly spam, whereas an SCL of 9 indicates that the email message is not likely to be spam.

T | F   **9.** All asymmetric encryption must use the public key.

T | F **10.** By regularly updating the software on your Exchange servers, you minimize the chance of buffer overruns.

Review Questions

1. Explain why continuous configuration of antispam filters is necessary within an organization.
2. Explain how protocol encryption can be used to provide security for local and remote email clients.

■ Case Scenarios

Scenario 9-1: Reducing the Classroom Attack Surface

The services that you disable and the firewalls that you configure are ultimately dependent on your network environment and the configuration of your Exchange servers. For your classroom or home network, diagram your network(s), routers, proxy servers (if used), Exchange servers (and roles), and Internet configuration. On your diagram, label where you should place network- and host-based firewalls. In addition, label the protocols that each Exchange server must use for normal functionality. When finished, use the SCW to reduce the attack surface on your Exchange server(s) and configure network-based firewalls on your network router(s) or proxy server(s) to minimize your Exchange attack surface.

Scenario 9-2: Responding to a New Virus Attack

FSE can remove or clean viruses for which it has virus definitions. However, when a new virus is released, that virus will not be detected by FSE until a new virus definition update is released that identifies the virus. Explain what you would do in the event of a new virus attack. Detail how you would determine the attack has occurred, the first actions that you should perform to minimize the impact of the attack as well as the actions that you should take to remove the virus using FSE.

Appendix A
Exchange Server 2007 Configuration: Exam 70-236

OBJECTIVE DOMAIN	SKILL NUMBER	LESSON NUMBER
Prepare the infrastructure for Exchange installation.	1.1	3
Prepare the servers for Exchange installation.	1.2	3
Install Exchange.	1.3	3
Configure Exchange Server roles.	1.4	4, 12
Configure recipients	2.1	5
Configure mail-enabled groups.	2.2	5
Configure resource mailboxes.	2.3	5
Configure public folders.	2.4	7
Move mailboxes.	2.5	5
Implement bulk management of mail-enabled objects.	2.6	6, 7
Configure connectors.	3.1	4
Configure the antivirus and antispam system.	3.2	9
Configure transport rules and message compliance.	3.3	6, 8
Configure policies.	3.4	5, 6
Configure public folders.	3.5	7
Configure client connectivity.	3.6	4, 8
Monitor mail queues.	4.1	11
Monitor system performance.	4.2	11
Perform message tracking.	4.3	11
Monitor client connectivity.	4.4	11
Create server reports.	4.5	11
Create usage reports.	4.6	11
Configure backups.	5.1	10
Recover messaging data.	5.2	10
Recover server roles.	5.3	10
Configure high availability.	5.4	13

The *Microsoft Exchange Server 2007 Configuration* title of the Microsoft Official Academic Course (MOAC) series includes two books: a textbook and a lab manual. The exercises in the lab manual are designed for classroom use under the supervision of an instructor or a lab aide.

■ Classroom Setup

This course should be taught in a classroom containing networked computers where students can develop their skills through hands-on experience with Microsoft Exchange Server 2007. The exercises in the lab manual require the computers to be installed and configured in a specific manner. Failure to adhere to the setup instructions in this document can produce unanticipated results when the students perform the exercises.

Classroom Configuration

The following configurations and naming conventions are used throughout the course and are required for completing the labs as outlined in the lab manual.

The classroom network consists of a single instructor computer and several student computers. The student computers do not rely on the instructor computer for any labs in the lab manual. As a result, both the instructor computer and student computers have identical setup requirements. Furthermore, the instructor computer is optional; it may be used at the discretion of the instructor for demonstrating certain lab steps.

Each computer will need to have three fully updated instances of Windows Server 2003 SP2 hosted by three different virtual machines on the same computer using virtualization software such as:

- Microsoft Virtual PC
- Microsoft Virtual Server
- VMWare Server
- VMWare Workstation
- VMWare Fusion

This will allow both students and the instructor to interface with all three instances of Windows Server 2003 SP2 from the same computer during the exercises in this lab manual. Consequently, the host operating system that runs the virtualization software is irrelevant. Common host operating systems that can be used for virtualization include Windows 2000, Windows XP, Windows Server 2003, Windows Vista, Windows Server 2008, Linux, or Macintosh OS X.

Each computer that hosts the virtualization software should be configured with the correct IP information for classroom Internet access. Furthermore, the virtualization software on each computer should be configured to give Internet access to each virtual machine using NAT mode or Bridging mode.

Each instance of Windows Server 2003 SP2 hosted by the virtualization software should:

- Use the same password for the Administrator user for simplicity when switching from one virtual machine to another in the classroom environment.

- Have a different computer name that adheres to the following naming convention: StudentXX-A, StudentXX-B, and StudentXX-C, where XX is a unique number assigned by the instructor (typically the computer number within the classroom).

Include a single network interface that is configured with the correct IP address, subnet mask, and default gateway necessary to gain Internet access in the classroom. The network interface on StudentXX-A should also be configured with the DNS server used for Internet access within the classroom. The DNS server configured within the network interfaces on StudentXX-B and StudentXX-C should be the IP address of StudentXX-A.

Figure B-1 provides an example configuration for three instances of Windows Server 2003 on the first student computer using the 10.0.0.0 network, a classroom default gateway of 10.0.0.254, and a classroom DNS server of 10.0.0.253.

Figure B-1

A sample Student01 computer with three virtual machines

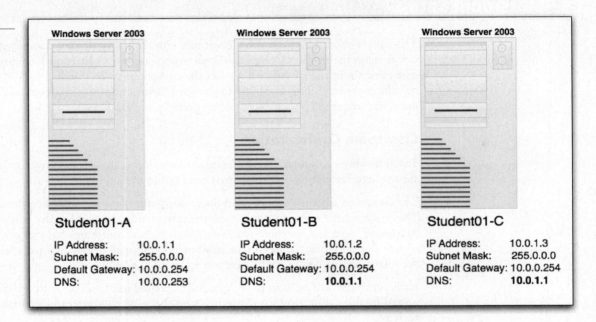

To support this classroom configuration, students configure their Windows Server 2003 virtual machines throughout the first three labs in the lab manual. Students configure the IP and name information for their virtual machines in Lab 1. In Lab 2, students configure the Active Directory service, and in Lab 3, students configure Exchange Server 2007 server roles.

The setup of the instructor computer, if used, will be identical to the student computer setup outlined in the lab manual. In addition, all labs within the lab manual are cumulative; before you begin a later lab, you must have completed all prior labs.

Classroom Computer Requirements

The host computer that will run the virtual machines in the classroom requires the following hardware and software:

Hardware Requirements

- Processor: 1 GHz (minimum); 2 GHz or faster (recommended)
- RAM: 2 GB (minimum); 4 GB or more (recommended)
  a. 2 GB of RAM leaves 512 MB for each of the three virtual machines plus 512 MB for the host OS
  b. 4 GB of RAM leaves 1024 MB of RAM for each of the three virtual machines plus 1024 MB of RAM for the host OS

- Disk space requirements: 40 GB (minimum); 80 GB or more (recommended)

    a. 40 GB leaves 10 GB for each of the three virtual machines plus 10 GB for the host OS

    b. 80 GB leaves 20 GB for each of the three virtual machines plus 20 GB for the host OS

- DVD-ROM drive
- Super VGA (800 x 600) or higher-resolution monitor
- Keyboard and mouse (or other pointing device)
- One network interface adapter

Software Requirements

- Microsoft Windows Server 2003, Enterprise edition
- Microsoft Exchange Server 2007, Enterprise edition

■ Classroom Computer Setup Instructions

Before you begin, do the following:

- Read this entire document.
- Verify that you have the Instructor CD provided with the course materials and the installation disk for Microsoft Windows Server 2003.

Installing Windows Server 2003

Using the following setup procedure, install Windows Server 2003 on each virtual machine.

> **TAKE NOTE** *
>
> Before you install Windows Server 2003, you must start and configure your virtualization software. This will depend on the virtualization software that you plan to use. Consult your virtualization software guide for more information.

 INSTALL WINDOWS SERVER 2003

> **TAKE NOTE** *
>
> These steps must be performed three different times in order to install three different virtual machines. It is unnecessary to provide the correct computer names and IP information during these steps since they will be configured during Lab 1 of the lab manual.

1. Boot the virtual machine from the Windows Server 2003 Installation disk. When you boot from the disk, the Windows Server 2003 Setup program starts.
2. At the Setup Notification screen, click **Enter**.
3. At the Welcome to Setup screen, click **Enter**.
4. At the Windows Licensing screen, press **F8** to accept the Windows Licensing Agreement.
5. At the partitioning screen, create a single partition that uses all of the space available to the virtual machine.
6. Select your C: partition and press **Enter** to install Windows Server 2003 on that partition.
7. Select **Format the partition using the NTFS file system** and press **Enter**. The partition will now be formatted and files will be copied to it. Following the copy operation, your virtual machine will be restarted.

8. Once the virtual machine has rebooted and the Windows environment has been loaded, click **Next** at the Regional and Language Options screen.

9. At the Personalize Your Software screen, enter your name in the Name box and your school or organization in the Organization box. Click **Next** when finished.

10. At the Your Product Key screen, enter the product key that came with your copy of Windows Server 2003. Click **Next** when finished.

11. At the Licensing Modes screen, ensure that **Per server** is selected and enter **50** in the concurrent connections box. Click **Next** when finished.

12. At the Computer Name and Administrator Password screen, enter the computer name **Student-A** if you are installing the first virtual machine, **Student-B** if you are installing the second virtual machine, or **Student-C** if you are installing the third virtual machine.

13. Enter the password of **secret** in both the Administrator password and Confirm password dialog boxes and click **Next** when finished. Click **Yes** when a message appears warning you about the simplicity of your password. Normally, you would select a complex password for Administrator in a production environment. However, we will use a simple password for convenience within the classroom environment.

14. At the Date and Time Settings screen, ensure that your date, time, and time zone are correct and click **Next**.

15. At the Networking Settings screen, ensure that **Typical settings** is selected and click **Next**.

16. At the Workgroup or Computer Domain screen, verify that **No, this computer is not on a network, or is on a network without a domain** is selected and click **Next**.

17. After the installation has completed, your virtual machine will automatically reboot. Remove the CD-ROM or DVD from your CD-ROM or DVD drive.

18. At the login dialog box, press Ctrl+Alt+Del and log in as the Administrator user (password > secret).

19. When the Manage Your Server screen appears, select the **Don't display this page at logon** checkbox in the bottom left hand corner of window and close the window.

20. Click **Start, All Programs, Activate Windows**. When the Activate Windows wizard appears, follow the directions to activate your copy of Windows Server 2003.

21. Install any updates needed to keep the operating system current.

Glossary

A

A (host) Records DNS records used to associate IP addresses to host names during DNS forward lookup.

accepted domain A domain for which Exchange Server 2007 can accept and relay email.

Access Control List (ACL) A collection of rules that define the access that all users and groups have to an object.

action An event that occurs following the processing of a rule or filter.

Active Directory (AD) Microsoft's directory service that automates network authentication, management, and security.

Active Directory Domains and Trusts A Windows utility that manages Active Directory trust relationships and domain functional levels.

Active Directory Installation Wizard The program used to install Active Directory on a Windows server.

Active Directory Migration Tool (ADMT) A utility that can migrate or move objects from one Active Directory domain and forest to another.

Active Directory Sites and Services A Windows utility that manages site objects and Global Catalog functionality for an Active Directory domain.

Active Directory Users and Computers A Windows utility that manages Active Directory objects.

active node The functional node of a Windows cluster.

active/passive server cluster A Windows cluster type that uses an active node to service client requests as well as a passive standby node that is used if the active node fails.

ActiveSync A protocol used to synchronize email and other items between a smartphone device and Microsoft Exchange Server.

ActiveSync policy A set of rules that restrict the functionality of a smartphone device that uses the ActiveSync protocol.

address list A list of email addresses available to users when locating email recipients.

administrative permission A level of access that allows one to administer a

component of Exchange Server 2007 such as public folders.

administrative role A level of access for administrators within Exchange Server 2007. Different administrative roles allow different abilities within the Exchange Organization.

administrative templates A file that contains configurable Group Policy items. Different third-party vendors release administrative templates that you can use within a Group Policy.

agent log A log that contains events from the antispam agents within Exchange Server 2007.

alert A configurable notification that is triggered when a particular event occurs on a system.

alias The primary name of a recipient object. It is normally the portion of an email address before the @ symbol.

antispam transport agent The Exchange Server component that performs spam filtering.

asymmetric encryption A type of cryptography that uses a public key and private key to encrypt and decrypt data.

attack surface The sum total of the ways that an attacker can interact with a target computer across the network.

attribute A configurable property within an object.

authentication The process by which Active Directory verifies that the user matches the user account employed to gain access.

authoritative DNS server A server that hosts a zone for a domain in the Domain Name Space.

authorization The process of determining whether an identified user or process is permitted access to a resource and the user's appropriate level of access.

Autodiscover service An Exchange Server 2007 service that allows client computers to easily discover and configure the appropriate email account on their email client programs.

autoenrollment A feature of Windows Server 2003 certificate services that allows the users and computers within

your organization to receive certificates from a Group Policy.

automated attendant A Unified Messaging component that provides user interface prompts on the organization's telephone system.

Automatic Booking A feature of Exchange Server 2007 calendaring that allows appointments to be scheduled automatically in other recipients calendars.

Automatic Speech Recognition (ASR) A feature of Unified Messaging that allows users to speak commands into their telephone to navigate their voicemail and email items as well as respond to or create new email items.

Automatic Updates A Windows component that automatically installs Windows updates from the Windows Update servers on the Internet.

Availability service An Exchange Server 2007 component that updates free/busy calendaring information for mailbox users.

B

Backup Domain Controller (BDC) A Windows NT4 domain controller that contains a read-only copy of the directory database.

backup job A set of files and objects that are backed up at the same time.

backup set A set of files and objects that are backed up, managed, and restored as a single unit.

basic authentication An authentication method that does not encrypt the username and password as it passes across the network.

batch file A file that contains commands that can be executed at a Windows command prompt.

Berkeley Internet Name Domain (BIND) The standard used for the Domain Name System.

biometric thumbprint reader A device that reads human thumbprints to provide authentication on a computer system.

BlackBerry Attachment Service A component of BlackBerry Enterprise Server that expands and sends attachments to BlackBerry smartphones.

BlackBerry Connect A software component that can be installed on many third-party smartphone devices to allow them to use the BlackBerry Infrastructure.

BlackBerry Desktop Manager utility A software program used to manage BlackBerry smartphone devices that are connected to the computer via a USB, serial or Bluetooth connection.

BlackBerry Enterprise Server (BES) A server software suite that allows Exchange Server 2007 to interact with the BlackBerry Infrastructure.

BlackBerry Infrastructure The hardware and software components that allow wireless providers to send and receive emails and other data to and from BlackBerry smartphone devices.

BlackBerry Manager utility The software program used to create and manage BlackBerry Enterprise Server objects.

BlackBerry Professional Server (BPS) An alternative to BlackBerry Enterprise Server designed for smaller organizations.

BlackBerry Server Configuration utility The software program used to configure the different components of the BlackBerry Enterprise Server.

Book-In Policy A scheduling policy that allows users to automatically schedule a resource mailbox.

bounce message An error message indicating that an email could not be delivered.

bridgehead server A domain controller that is responsible for intersite replication.

buffer overrun A software exploit that sends undesirable information to an application in order to gain unauthorized access to the system or deny others service to the application.

bulk management The process of creating and managing several objects at the same time.

C

Cached Exchange Mode A feature of Outlook 2003 and later that can store frequently used information, such as address lists, on the hard drive of the client computer for future access.

Calendar Attendant The Exchange Server 2007 software component that processes calendar meeting requests.

capacity planning The process of planning for present and future growth within an organization.

categorizer An Exchange Server 2007 component that analyzes incoming information such as emails and directs them to the appropriate software component for processing.

Certificate Revocation List (CRL) A list of blacklisted certificates on a Certification Authority. The CRL is made available to certificate users for validation purposes.

Certificate Services The component of Windows Server 2003 that provides Certification Authority functionality.

certificate template A collection of settings that represent the features and function of a certificate.

Certification Authority (CA) A server that validates and digitally signs public key certificates to prevent man-in-the-middle cryptography attacks.

checkpoint file A file that contains entries to indicate the successful application of changes to a database.

checksum A calculation that renders a number that uniquely represents the size and contents of a file or data string. It is also called a hash.

child domain A DNS or AD domain that contains an existing domain name prefixed by a subdomain name. For example, subdomain.domain.com is a child domain for domain.com.

ciphertext Data that has been encrypted by an encryption algorithm.

circular logging A database feature that reuses transaction log files instead of creating new ones when they reach their maximum size.

classes Object types.

cleaning The process of removing a virus from a virus-infected file.

cleanup agent The Exchange Server 2007 component that locates and removes deleted items from a mailbox.

Client Access Server (CAS) An Exchange Server 2007 server role that allows email clients to interact with Exchange Server 2007 to send and receive email and other information.

client permission A permission that is granted to a user to allow them access to the contents of a public folder in Exchange Server 2007.

client permission level A set of client permissions that are granted to a user.

cloned configuration An Edge role configuration that can be copied and configured on another Edge role server.

cluster A group of computers that are configured to work together for fault-tolerance or performance purposes.

Cluster Continuous Replication (CCR) A type of Exchange Server 2007 clustering that continuously copies mailbox database changes from an active cluster node to a passive cluster node. Following an active node failure, the Cluster Service changes the passive node to the active node.

Cluster Service The Windows service that can be used to create a fault-tolerant server cluster.

cmdlets Commands that can be executed within the Exchange Management Shell.

comma-separated values (CSV) file A file that lists information for an object on a line-by-line basis organized by comma-delimited fields that are defined at the beginning of the file.

commercial CA A CA that issues digitally signed certificates for a fee. It is also called a public CA.

committed A database change that has been successfully written from the transaction log to the database.

common name (CN) An LDAP component that identifies the name of the object.

Computer Configuration The portion of a Group Policy that applies to the computer account within the Active Directory domain.

condition A criteria that must be met for a rule or filter to apply.

configuration partition The part of the Active Directory database that stores domain and forest information.

Configure Your Server Wizard A Windows utility that allows you to configure Windows server roles such as DNS and Active Directory.

connection filtering An Exchange Server 2007 spam filter that can be used to reject emails based on the IP of the source email relay computer.

connector An object that represents a connection to another computer.

container object An Active Directory object that contains other Active Directory objects.

content replica A copy of a public folder and its contents that is replicated across the network.

copy backup A backup type that is used to copy specified files to a target location.

cost A number that represents the value of an object, link, or component. Objects, links, and components with lower costs are typically chosen before those with higher costs.

counter A performance statistic within the Windows Performance MMC snap-in.

counter log A file that records Windows performance information over a long period of time. Counter logs are configured in the Windows Performance MMC snap-in.

cross forest trust A trust relationship between two different Active Directory forests that are at the Windows Server 2003 forest functional level.

cryptography The study and process of restricting the access of information to those who require it.

D

database A file that organizes data into records that contain common fields.

decryption The process of decoding encrypted data.

default public folder subtree The hierarchical public folder structure available for storing user-defined public folders in a public folder database.

Delivery Status Notification (DSN) A message that contains information regarding the successful or unsuccessful delivery of an email message.

demilitarized zone (DMZ) A public network within an organization that is connected to both the Internet and the private corporate network via a firewall. It is also called a perimeter network or screened subnet.

Denial of Service (DoS) A type of network service attack that prevents users from accessing the network service normally.

dial tone recovery A high availability recovery method that can be used to switch the production database with a backup copy of the production database that is mounted to the Recovery Storage Group.

differential backup A backup type that backs up files that have changed since the last full (normal) backup. Differential backups do not reset the archive bit on each file following the backup procedure.

digest authentication A type of authentication that reversibly encrypts passwords before they are sent across a network.

digital signature A CA-signed hash of a public key that is used to validate certificates.

direct file access An Exchange Server 2007 feature that allows OWA users to access and save files to their local computer.

directory partitions Divisions of the Active Directory database.

directory services A suite of services that allows for centralized authentication.

Active Directory is an example of a directory services suite.

Directory Services Restore Mode A Windows mode that does not start the Active Directory database. You can boot to Directory Services Restore Mode by pressing F8 during the Windows boot sequence.

DirectPush The technology that notifies smartphones of new email items and PIM data within ActiveSync.

distinguished name (DN) An LDAP name that includes the name of an object and its location within the LDAP database.

Distributed Authoring and Versioning (DAV) A technology that allows the editing of Web content on remote servers.

distribution group A group type that can be used to relay email to the members of the group.

DNS name resolution The process of obtaining the IP address or name of a computer from the information stored on a DNS server.

domain A portion of the Domain Name Space.

Domain Controller (DC) A computer that hosts the Active Directory database.

domain functional level A mode that indicates the level of backwards-compatibility for Active Directory domain controllers.

domain local An Active Directory group scope that requires the group be assigned permissions to the local domain in which the group was created.

Domain Name System (DNS) A system that associates IP address to Fully Qualified Domain Names and vice versa.

Domain Naming Master An Active Directory FSMO role that enforces the uniqueness of domain names within a forest.

domain partition The portion of the Active Directory database that stores domain objects such as users and groups.

dynamic distribution group A group within Exchange Server 2007 that generates its membership from specific criteria.

dynamic update The process whereby a computer automatically creates or updates its DNS records on a DNS server.

E

E.164 A standard that defines the format of telephone numbers.

Edge Rules Agent An Edge role software component that can be used to control the relay of emails based on user-defined rules.

Edge Transport Role (Edge) An Exchange Server 2007 server role that provides security for all inbound and outbound email for an organization.

EdgeSync The protocol used to transfer configuration information from the Hub role servers to the Edge roles within your organization.

Electronic mail (email) Personal messages that are sent across a computer network such as the Internet.

email address policy A set of rules within an Exchange organization that defines how email addresses are automatically configured for recipient objects.

email bomb A spam or email message that is sent to several recipients.

email protocols An email delivery mechanism used by email clients and servers.

email queue A temporary storage location for emails that are relayed by an email server.

email relay The process of sending email from one computer to another.

Email Transfer Protocol (ETP) The protocol used between the BlackBerry Infrastructure and the BlackBerry Enterprise Server within your organization.

encryption The process of transforming data so that it can only be read by certain intended recipients.

encryption algorithm The mathematical formula used to perform encryption.

enrollment The process whereby a user or computer generates a public/private key combination and sends the public key to a Certification Authority for approval and digital signing.

enterprise CA A Windows Certification Authority that is integrated with the Active Directory service.

Event Viewer A Windows utility that logs system, application, and security events for later use.

exception A condition that should not be applied to a rule or filter.

Exchange Best Practices Analyzer A utility that can be used to analyze the performance, configuration, and health of an Exchange Server 2007 computer.

Exchange Management Console (EMC) The graphical Microsoft Management Console snap-in utility used to manage Exchange Server 2007.

Exchange Management Shell (EMS) The command-line utility used to manage Exchange Server 2007 using cmdlets.

Exchange organization An object that represents Exchange Server computers within the same organization and Active Directory forest.

Exchange Organization Administrator An Exchange Server 2007 administrative role that has all rights to the Exchange organization.

Exchange organization model A value that represents the relative complexity of the Exchange organization when analyzed in the Exchange Best Practices Analyzer utility.

Exchange Public Folder Administrator An Exchange Server 2007 administrative role that has all rights to manage public folder databases and their contents within the Exchange organization.

Exchange Recipient Administrator An Exchange Server 2007 administrative role that has all rights to manage recipient objects within the Exchange organization.

Exchange resource forest An Active Directory forest that contains resources that are used by another Active Directory forest across a trust relationship.

Exchange Server Administrator An Exchange Server 2007 administrative role that has rights to manage the databases and configuration of a specific Exchange server.

Exchange Troubleshooting Assistant A graphical software utility that can be used to diagnose and remedy various Exchange Server 2007 configuration, communication, and performance problems.

Exchange View-Only Administrator An Exchange Server 2007 administrative role that has the ability to view the properties of all objects within the Exchange organization.

expansion server The Hub role server that is responsible for generating the list of recipient objects within a dynamic distribution group.

Extended Simple Mail Transfer Protocol (ESMTP) The latest protocol used to relay email messages from POP3 and IMAP4 to email servers, as well as from email servers to other email servers across the Internet.

Extensible Storage Engine (ESE) The database engine used by Exchange Server 2007.

Extensible Storage Engine Utility A command line utility that may be used to defragment, analyze, and repair Exchange Server 2007 databases.

external relay Email relay to an email server in a remote organization across the Internet.

external trusts Trust relationships between two Active Directory domains or between an Active Directory domain and a Windows NT4 domain.

F

failover The process whereby a passive cluster node starts responding to client requests when the active cluster node fails.

file share witness A cluster node used to monitor other cluster nodes within a server cluster.

filter A series of restrictions that are applied to data as it passes through a server or application program.

Flexible Single Master Operations (FSMO) A domain controller role that provides a unique function within an Active Directory domain or forest.

Folder Assistant The Exchange Server 2007 component that creates and configures managed folders within mailboxes.

Forefront Security for Exchange Server (FSE) A Microsoft virus-scanning and spam-filtering software product for Exchange Server 2007.

Forefront Server Security Administrator The graphical utility used to manage FSE.

forest The largest container object within Active Directory.

forest functional level A mode that represents the level of backwards compatibility for legacy domain controllers within an Active Directory forest.

forest root domain The first domain within an Active Directory forest.

forms-based authentication A type of authentication that allows users to enter their credentials within a form on a web page that is secured with SSL.

forwarding The process of forwarding email to another recipient object automatically.

Full Access permission A permission granted to a user that gives the ability to view, manage, and send email to another user's mailbox.

full backup A backup of all files or objects regardless of their state.

full-text index An ordered list of the text within email fields to speed searching.

Fully Qualified Domain Names (FQDNs) Computer names within the Domain Name Space that include a host name followed by a domain name.

G

global An Active Directory group scope that allows the group to be assigned permissions and rights in any domain.

global catalog (GC) An Active Directory database and service that records user and group object information for the forest to ensure quick access and searching.

Globally Unique IDentifier (GUID) A unique number assigned to every Active Directory object.

GNU Privacy Guard (GPG) An open source version of the PGP protocol.

group manager A user that is responsible for the maintenance of a group.

group nesting The process of adding one group to another.

Group Policy The feature of the Active Directory service that can be used to install software or modify the settings on the computers within a domain.

Group Policy Management Console (GPMC) An MMC snap-in utility that can be used to manage all of the GPOs within an Active Directory forest.

Group Policy Object Editor The MMC snap-in utility that can be used to modify the settings within a GPO.

Group Policy Objects (GPOs) An object that contains a set of configuration settings that are applied to users and computers.

group scope The Active Directory domains that can assign permissions to an Active Directory group.

H

hard recovery A process where transaction logs are replayed after restoring a database from an online backup.

hash A calculation that renders a number that uniquely represents the size and contents of a file or data string. It is also called a checksum.

heartbeat A small network packet that is sent between cluster nodes.

high availability The practice where procedures and technologies are implemented to ensure that user interruption is minimized after the failure of a server.

host-based firewall A firewall located on a single computer that functions to limit the traffic passing from the network to the services that run on the computer itself.

Hub Transport Role (Hub) An Exchange Server 2007 server role that is responsible for relaying email within an Exchange Organization.

Hypertext Markup Language (HTML) The language used to format web pages.

Hypertext Transfer Protocol (HTTP) The protocol used to display web pages.

I

iCalendar A standard for calendar data exchange.

In Policy A scheduling policy that allows users to schedule a resource mailbox after they receive approval.

incremental backup A backup type that backs up files that have changed since the last incremental or full (normal) backup. Incremental backups clear the archive bit on each file following backup.

Information Store Integrity Checker A utility that can be used to check the high-level structural integrity of an Exchange mailbox database and fix any errors.

Infrastructure Master An FSMO role that updates group membership across domains within a forest.

instance An installed copy of an application that can be executed alongside other applications.

Integrated Windows Authentication An NTLM-based authentication mechanism used on web servers.

internal relay Email relay to another Exchange server within the same Exchange organization.

Internet Information Services (IIS) The Windows services that provide for the Web (HTTP), FTP, NNTP, and SMTP protocols.

Internet Message Access Protocol Version 4 (IMAP4) A common email access protocol that email clients can use to obtain email from an email server using a persistent connection.

Internet Protocol (IP) gateway A UM device that allows for communication between an IP network and PBX.

Internet Protocol Security (IPSec) A TCP/IP driver module that encrypts and decrypts IP data between two computers on a network.

Internet Service Provider (ISP) An organization that provides Internet access to other organizations.

Interpersonal Message (IPM) subtree The default public folder hierarchy used to contain user-created posts and items.

inter-site transport The protocol used to replicate Active Directory information between sites.

IT policy A BES object that can be used restrict the functionality of BlackBerry smartphones within your organization.

J

Journaling agent The Exchange Server 2007 software component that provides for message journaling.

Just a Bunch of Disks (JBOD) A series of hard disk drives that are treated as a single contiguous volume. JBOD is also known as RAID level 1 or spanning.

K

Kerberos The authentication protocol used by Active Directory.

key A unique piece of information that is used alongside encryption algorithms when encrypting data.

L

Last Restore Set option A restore option within Windows Backup that replays restored transaction logs following a database restore.

LCR storage group A storage group that is configured for LCR.

leaf object An object within Active Directory that does not contain other Active Directory objects.

Lightweight Directory Access Protocol (LDAP) The protocol used to search the Active Directory database.

link state A method used in Exchange Server 2003 and earlier when determining the best route for email to take when it is transferred between routing groups within the Exchange organization.

linked mailbox user A disabled mailbox user that is associated with a user account in another forest.

Local Continuous Replication (LCR) A high availability method that uses asynchronous log shipping and replay on a remote server.

local group A group stored within the registry of a Windows computer.

local user account A user account stored within the registry of a Windows computer.

local wipe The process of removing all user data from a mobile smartphone device.

log replay The process of adding the information from transaction log files to an Exchange database a second time.

log shipping A system that copies transaction log files from one database to another for backup purposes.

long-standing HTTPS request An HTTPS request that has an extended time-out value. Long-standing HTTPS requests are used by ActiveSync.

M

mail contact A recipient object that represents an external email recipient. It includes the external recipient's email address and personal information.

Mail Delivery Agent (MDA) The X.400 component that receives email from other email servers and delivers it to a recipient's mailbox.

Mail eXchanger (MX) records DNS records that list the email server for a particular DNS domain.

Mail Transfer Agent (MTA) The X.400 component that transfers email from one email server to another.

mail user A recipient object within Exchange Server 2007 that represents an Active Directory user account with an external email address.

Mail User Agent (MUA) The X.400 component that allows a client computer access to email on an email server.

mailbox database A database that stores email for mailbox users.

mailbox delivery queue A temporary storage location for email that is to be delivered to a mailbox on a Mailbox role server within your organization.

Mailbox Role An Exchange Server 2007 server role that stores mailbox and public folder databases as well as provides access to their contents.

mail-enabled universal distribution group A universal group object within Active Directory that functions as a recipient object within Exchange Server 2007.

mail-enabled universal security group A universal group object within Active Directory that can be used for permissions and rights assignments as well as functions as a recipient object within Exchange Server 2007.

managed custom folder A nondefault mailbox folder that is assigned a managed folder mailbox policy.

managed default folder A default mailbox folder that is assigned a managed folder mailbox policy.

managed folder A mailbox folder that is assigned a managed folder mailbox policy.

Managed Folder Assistant The Exchange Server 2007 component that is responsible for creating and updating managed folders within mailboxes.

managed folder mailbox policy A policy that contains managed folders that can be assigned to a mailbox.

man-in-the-middle attack A type of attack where a hacker intercepts and modifies network traffic while it is in transit.

Manual Scan Job An FSE scan that can be manually performed on mailbox and public folder databases.

MAPI clients Client computers that run software (such as Microsoft Outlook and Entourage) and can connect to Exchange Server 2007 using the MAPI protocol.

MAPI RPC The RPC-based, Microsoft-specific client access protocol designed to integrate Microsoft Outlook and Entourage with advanced features in Exchange Server 2007.

master account A user account that has the ability to access a mailbox in a resource forest.

memory leak A condition where a process on the system continuously consumes more and more available memory.

message classification A classification that can be applied to email messages within Microsoft Outlook and Entourage.

message dumpster A temporary location for deleted mailboxes on a Mailbox role server.

message journaling The process of archiving or copying email messages to another recipient's mailbox.

message tracking log A log file that records the messages that have passed through the email message queues on a Hub or Mailbox role server.

Messaging Application Programming Interface (MAPI) The RPC-based, Microsoft-specific client access protocol designed to integrate Microsoft Outlook and Entourage with advanced features in Exchange Server 2007. It is often referred to as MAPI RPC.

messaging compliance A set of procedures and practices that an organization uses to ensure that its messaging system meets legal requirements.

Messaging Records Management (MRM) An Exchange Server 2007 feature that allows organizations to easily store and archive messages for periods of time as required by law.

method of least privilege A practice where users are only granted the minimum necessary rights or permissions to servers, objects, and resources.

Microsoft Exchange Information Store The Exchange Server 2007 component that manages access to mailbox and public folder databases on a Mailbox role server.

Microsoft Internet Security and Acceleration (ISA) Server A Microsoft proxy server and firewall product.

migration The process of moving a user, configuration, or role to another location or computer.

mirroring A hard disk configuration where data is written to two identical hard disks simultaneously. It is often referred to as RAID level 1.

Mobile Data Service (MDS) A BES component that allows for the deployment of applications to BlackBerry smartphones.

moderated public folder A public folder that is configured to pass new posts to a moderator for approval before they are added to the public folder.

moderator A user that receives new public folder posts for approval.

multicast mode A NAT mode in which each network interface that is joined to the NAT cluster retains its original network hardware (MAC) address.

multifactor authentication A form of authentication where more than one proof of identity is required.

Multipurpose Internet Mail Extensions (MIME) A standard that defines different content formats for use on the Internet.

N

Network Address Translation (NAT) A type of routing that allows several computers on a private network to access a public network using a single IP address.

Network Attached Storage (NAS) A hard disk-based storage device that can be accessed across a computer network.

Network Load Balancing (NLB) A clustering process that evenly distributes network requests amongst several identically configured servers.

network protocol analyzer A software program that captures and analyzes network traffic. It is also called a packet sniffer.

network-based firewall A firewall that resides on a network router and serves to restrict the flow of traffic from one network to another.

node A computer that participates in a cluster.

Non-Delivery Notification (NDN) An error message indicating that an email could not be delivered.

Non-Delivery Receipt/Report (NDR) An error message indicating that an email could not be delivered.

nonprovisionable device A smartphone that can not be configured by all of the settings within an ActiveSync policy.

normal backup A backup of all selected files and objects regardless of their archive bit. It is often called a full backup.

O

object An entity that represents a person, place or thing.

Offline Address Book (OAB) A set of address lists that are cached to an email client's hard drive for use when the email client loses network connectivity to its email server.

offline backup A database backup that occurs when the database is not used by any services.

offline defragmentation A process whereby blank records within an offline database are removed to reduce database size and ensure that database records are contiguous.

one-way trust A trust relationship used by Active Directory to allow users in one domain the ability to access resources in another domain that they have permission to.

online defragmentation The process whereby a database engine removes data from a database while the database is being used by other processes.

Out of Office Assistant A component of Microsoft Outlook and Entourage that allows users to configure a message that is automatically sent as a reply to emails received by the user's mailbox when the users is not available.

Out Policy A scheduling policy that allows users to automatically schedule a resource mailbox if it is available. If it is unavailable, they must obtain approval.

Outlook Anywhere A protocol that allows MAPI clients to obtain email from their Exchange Server 2007 computer from across the internet using HTTPS. It is also called RPC over HTTP/HTTPS.

Outlook Form Designer A Microsoft Outlook utility that can be used to design a custom form template for use with emails or public folder posts.

Outlook Voice Access (OVA) A UM voice-controlled system that allows users the ability to access, reply, and manage their email via a telephone.

Outlook Web Access (OWA) A Web site and related services that are hosted by a CAS role server to provide access to email via a web browser.

over the air (OTA) A process that occurs across a wireless network.

P

packet sniffer A software program that captures and analyzes network traffic. It is also called a network protocol analyzer.

page The smallest manageable unit within a database.

page file A file that Windows writes information to that could not be written to physical memory. It is also called a swap file.

Parallel Advanced Technology Attachment (PATA) A hard disk technology that transfers information across a parallel interface cable to the computer.

parameter A piece of information used to configure an object, computer, or software component.

parent domain A DNS or AD domain that contains child domains. For example, domain.com is a parent domain for subdomain.domain.com.

passive mailbox database An inactive, standby mailbox database copy that can be used if the original mailbox database fails.

passive node An inactive, standby computer within a server cluster.

PDC Emulator An FSMO role that manages time synchronization, password changes, and BDC replication within an Active Directory domain.

performance baseline A standard level of performance for a computer.

performance object A performance category used within the Windows Performance MMC snap-in.

perimeter network A public network within an organization that is connected to both the Internet and the private corporate network via a firewall. It is also called a DMZ or screened subnet.

permissions group A group of permissions that can be granted as a single unit.

Personal Identification Number (PIN) A unique number that identifies a BlackBerry smartphone within the BlackBerry Infrastructure.

Personal Information Manager (PIM) An organizer data category that includes contacts, address lists, memos, calendars, and tasks.

phishing attack A network attack where fraudulent emails are sent to recipients with the intent of obtaining personal information.

pickup directory A directory that contains email for pickup by a transport agent in Exchange Server 2007

plaintext Data that has not been encrypted.

poison message queue A temporary storage location for email messages that

are potentially harmful to Exchange Server 2007.

Post Office Protocol Version 3 (POP3) A common email access protocol that can be used to download email from an email server.

postmaster A recipient object that users are directed to email when they encounter problems with their email functionality.

PowerShell A Windows command line management and scripting utility.

practical security A level of security that meets the needs of the organization.

premium journaling A type of email message journaling that journals messages that match a particular set of criteria.

prestaging The process of creating a computer object within Active Directory before the associated computer is joined to the Active Directory domain.

Pretty Good Privacy (PGP) A widely used technology used to encrypt and decrypt emails using asymmetric cryptography.

Primary Domain Controller (PDC) A Windows NT4 domain controller that contains a read-write copy of the directory database.

priority number A number that identifies the order for which DNS MX records should be processed following a DNS MX record lookup.

Private Branch eXchange (PBX) An internal telephone system within an organization.

private interface A network interface that does not receive client requests.

private key An asymmetric encryption key that can decrypt information that has been encrypted by the associated public key.

proactive monitoring A practice that involves monitoring servers and applications to ensure that problems can be identified shortly after they occur.

protocol log A log file on a Hub or Edge role server that contains SMTP and ESMTP information or each email that has been relayed.

public CA A CA that issues digitally signed certificates for a fee. It is also called a commercial CA.

public folder database A database that stores public folders and the related posts on a Mailbox role server.

public folder hierarchy A hierarchical structure used to organize public folders to ensure that users can quickly locate the information that they need.

Public Folder Management Console A graphical utility used to manage public

folders in Exchange Server 2007 SP1 and later.

public folder referral A process whereby a Mailbox role server directs a client to another public folder database on a different Mailbox role server to obtain public folder content.

public folder A folder that can be used to store email, posts, tasks, notes, memos, calendars, and journal items.

public interface A network interface that receives client requests.

public key An asymmetric encryption key that is typically used to encrypt data using an asymmetric encryption algorithm.

public key certificate An object that contains a CA-signed public key.

Public Switched Telephone Network (PSTN) The public telephone network.

Purported Responsible Address (PRA) An identification that determines the likelihood that an email is spam based on header information.

Q

Queue Viewer A graphical utility that may be used to view and mange the email queues on an Exchange Server 2007 computer.

R

reactive monitoring A practice where servers and applications are monitored following the detection of a problem to determine the nature of the problem and identify its cause.

realm trust An Active Directory trust relationship between a Windows domain and a UNIX Kerberos realm.

Realtime Block List (RBL) A list of blacklisted email relays and senders.

Realtime Scan Job An FSE scan that is immediately performed on items that are sent and received by mailboxes and public folders.

receive connector An object that represents how email is received by an Edge or Hub role server.

recipient An entity that is the target of an email.

recipient object An object that can receive email within Exchange Server 2007.

recovery storage group (RSG) A temporary storage group that can contain a restored backup copy of another database for use in disaster recovery and restore procedures.

Redundant Array of Independent Disks (RAID) A standard used to define the methods used to create volumes from several different hard disks.

Relative Identifier (RID) The unique component of a SID within a domain.

remote delivery queue An email queue that contains emails that are destined for remote domains on the Internet.

remote domain An Exchange Server 2007 object that represents a domain on the Internet that is not part of the organization.

Remote Procedure Call (RPC) A communication technology that allows commands to be executed on a remote computer.

remote wipe A process whereby the information on a smartphone device is removed using a command issued across a wireless network.

Research In Motion (RIM) The company that produces BlackBerry smartphone devices and hosts the BlackBerry Infrastructure.

Resource Booking Attendant The Exchange Server 2007 component that controls the resource booking process.

resource booking policy A set of rules that determines who can schedule resource mailboxes and whether approval is required.

resource mailbox A mailbox that is used for resource scheduling within MAPI clients.

Rich Text Format (RTF) A common cross-platform text format that allows for text formatting and styles.

RID Master An FSMO role that generates Relative Identifiers for objects within a domain.

roaming The process of switching to a different wireless infrastructure using a wireless device.

rogue process A process on a computer that consumes a large amount of CPU cycles.

root CA The first CA in a CA hierarchy.

round robin The process whereby a list of multiple DNS A records for a host are rotated for each name resolution request.

Routing and Remote Access Service (RRAS) The Windows server service that provides routing, VPN, and dial-in access.

routing groups Objects used within Exchange Server 2000/2003 to represent a set of Exchange server computers within the same site or fast LAN.

RPC over HTTP/HTTPS A protocol that allows MAPI clients to obtain email from their Exchange Server 2007 computer from across the internet using HTTPS. It is often called Outlook Anywhere in Exchange Server 2007.

S

schema The list of all object types and attributes within Active Directory.

Schema Master The FSMO role that has the ability to modify the Active Directory schema.

schema partition The portion of the Active Directory database that stores the Active Directory schema.

SCR source The original production database in an SCR configuration.

SCR target A standby database copy in an SCR configuration.

screened subnet A public network within an organization that is connected to both the Internet and the private corporate network via a firewall. It is also called a perimeter network or DMZ.

Secure Extended Simple Mail Transfer Protocol (ESMTPS) A version of the ESMTP protocol that uses cryptography.

Secure Hypertext Transfer Protocol (HTTPS) A version of the HTTP protocol that uses cryptography.

Secure Internet Message Access Protocol Version 4 (IMAP4S) A version of the IMAP4 protocol that uses cryptography.

Secure Password Authentication (SPA) An NTLM-based authentication mechanism used to authenticate an SMTP session with a remote SMTP server.

Secure Post Office Protocol Version 3 (POP3S) A version of the POP3 protocol that uses cryptography.

Secure Simple Mail Transfer Protocol (SMTPS) A version of the SMTP protocol that uses cryptography.

Secure Socket Layer (SSL) A technology used to provide encryption for a wide range of Internet protocols such as HTTP.

security The robustness of a computer, system or software program against unauthorized access.

Security Accounts Manager (SAM) The portion of the Windows registry that contains local user accounts and user accounts within a Windows NT4 domain.

Security Configuration Wizard (SCW) A Windows software utility that can be used to stop unneeded services, modify operating system security, and configure Windows Firewall.

security group An Active Directory group type that can be assigned permissions and rights to resources.

Security IDentifier (SID) A unique identifier assigned to a user account for use in permissions and rights assignments.

seeding The process of copying database contents to a standby database copy.

seize The process where a Windows domain controller forcibly obtains an FSMO role.

self-signed certificate A public key certificate that is digitally signed by the host that generated it.

Send As permission A permission that allows a mailbox user to send emails using another mailbox user in the From field.

send connector An object that represents how email is sent by an Edge or Hub role server.

Send On Behalf permission A permission that allows a mailbox user to send emails on behalf of another user in the From field.

sender The person or object that is listed in the From field of an email.

sender ID An email authentication technology that helps to reduce phishing attacks by verifying sender relay information.

sender reputation A measure used by the antispam agents on an Edge role server that identifies spam by combining several factors.

Serial Advanced Technology Attachment (SATA) A hard disk technology that transfers information across a serial interface cable to the computer.

server role A role that defines the functionality of an Exchange Server 2007 computer.

Server Routing Protocol (SRP) The protocol used to transfer information between the BlackBerry Infrastructure and a BlackBerry Enterprise Server.

service record (SRV) A DNS record that is used to list services that are available on a specific computer.

Session Initiation Protocol (SIP) A protocol used to establish multimedia and voice sessions across the Internet.

shared storage device A hard disk-based storage device that is connected to two or more cluster nodes.

shortcut trust A manually created trust relationship between two domains in the same Active Directory forest.

Simple Mail Transfer Protocol (SMTP) The legacy protocol used to relay email messages from POP3 and IMAP4 to email servers, as well as from email servers to other email servers across the Internet.

Single Copy Cluster (SCC) Two or more computers that are configured as a cluster using the Windows Cluster service.

single sign-on A feature of directory services such as Active Directory that allows users to authenticate to a single domain controller in order to access all of the required services on the network.

site A physical location within an organization.

site link An object that is used to represent the physical connection between sites.

site object An object that represents a physical location with a fast interconnect.

Small Computer Systems Interface (SCSI) A hard disk technology that is commonly used within server computers due to its fast transfer speed.

smart card A physical card that stores a private key used for multifactor authentication.

smart host A third-party email server that queues and filters email.

smartphone A mobile telephone device that offers data services such as email access and web browsing.

smartphone device identifier (ID) A number used to uniquely identify a smartphone device.

spam Unsolicited commercial email.

Spam Confidence Level (SCL) A number that represents the likelihood that an email message is spam. Higher SCL numbers represent higher spam liklihoods.

spammer A person or organization that sends spam messages on the Internet.

spanning A hard disk configuration that allows a single volume to span multiple hard disk drives. It is a form of RAID 0.

stand-alone CA A Windows CA that is not integrated with Active Directory.

standard journaling A type of message journaling in which a copy of all email messages for a mailbox database are sent to a specified mailbox.

Standby Continuous Replication (SCR) An Exchange Server 2007 configuration that performs log shipping from one mailbox database to a number of standby databases on different Mailbox role servers.

Storage Area Network (SAN) A series of network-available storage devices that are available to computers for storage via a fast interconnect.

storage group A storage area that is used to contain one or more public folder or mailbox databases as well as the associated transaction logs and system files.

streaming backup A backup method that does not take advantage of the Windows Volume Shadow Copy service.

striping A hard disk configuration that divides data so that it is evenly stored across several hard disks that operate as a single volume. It is a form of RAID 0.

striping with parity A type of striping that writes parity information to ensure that information can be recovered in the event of a single hard disk failure. It is also called RAID 5.

Subject Alternative Name (SAN) An additional name that is assigned to a public key certificate.

submission queue A temporary storage location for emails that have been submitted to a Hub or Edge role server for processing and relay.

subnet object An Active Directory object that represents an IP network used by a site object.

subordinate CA A CA that has been installed following the root CA in a CA hierarchy.

subscriber access number The number used by UM users when accessing OVA.

subscription file A file that contains the information used to activate and configure EdgeSync for an Edge role server.

swap file A file that Windows writes information to that could not be written to physical memory. It is also called a page file.

symmetric encryption A type of cryptography that uses a single key when encrypting and decrypting data.

System Monitor The Windows graphical performance monitoring utility within the Performance MMC snap-in.

system public folder subtree A public folder hierarchy used to store system information for MAPI clients such as offline address book information.

system state The configuration information used on a Windows computer, including the Windows registry, Active Directory, IIS metabase, and boot files.

T

tables The organizational unit used within a database. Each database table can contain rows (records) of information that are categorized by column (field).

Task Manager A small, graphical, real-time performance monitoring utility within Windows.

template recipient object A recipient object that is copied to create new recipient objects that share the same properties.

Text-to-Speech (TTS) engine A UM software component that translates text to spoken words that are sent to a telephone user.

threshold A value within a performance alert that triggers an event.

thumbprint A unique identifier for a public key certificate.

ticket A set of data used by Kerberos to provide authentication information to Active Directory domain members.

token A set of data used by NTLM to provide authentication information to Active Directory domain members.

Top Level Hierarchy (TLH) The default public folder hierarchy format used within Exchange Server 2007 public folder databases.

trace log A log file that is used to record system events within the Windows Performance MMC snap-in.

transaction log A file that temporarily stores information that must be written to a database.

transitive trust A trust relationship that can be used by other trust relationships.

Transport Layer Security (TLS) A security technology based on SSL that can be used to secure a wide range of network protocols such as SMTP and ESMTP.

transport rule A rule that can be used to modify the processing of email relay on an Edge or Hub role server.

Transport Rules Agent The Exchange Server 2007 component that is responsible for enforcing transport rules during email relay.

Transport Scan Job An FSE virus scan that runs in real time on a Hub or Edge role server to scan emails as they are relayed.

tree A group of Active Directory domains within the same forest that share the same domain name suffix.

trust An association between two Active Directory, NT4, or Kerberos domains that allows for remote resource access. It is also called a trust relationship.

trust relationship An association between two Active Directory, NT4, or Kerberos domains that allows for remote resource access. It is also called a trust.

trusted root The public key certificate of a CA. It is used to validate CA-signed certificates.

two-way trust A trust relationship used by Active Directory to allow users in one domain the ability to access resources in another domain that they have permission to and vice versa.

U

UM auto attendant A UM object that is used to process and respond to incoming telephone calls from a PBX.

UM dial plan A UM object that represents the configuration of the PBX systems within a single organization.

UM IP gateway A UM object that represents the IP address and configuration of an IP PBX gateway device within an organization.

UM mailbox policy A policy that is assigned to a mailbox user in Exchange Server 2007 to enable them for UM funtionality.

unicast mode A NAT mode in which each network interface that is joined to the NAT cluster uses the same virtual hardware (MAC) address.

Unified Messaging (UM) The Exchange Server 2007 component that allows for integration with an organization's PBX.

Uniform Resource Identifier (URI) A unique number used to identify resources on the Internet.

universal A type of Active Directory group scope that allows the group to be assigned rights and permissions within any native mode domain in the forest.

Universal Group Membership Caching (UGMC) A feature of an Active Directory site that allows domain controllers within the site to cache universal group memberships to speed logon times in a native mode domain.

unreachable queue A temporary location for email messages that could not be routed to their destination on a Hub or Edge role server.

user account template A user account that is copied to configure new users with the same settings.

user certificate A public key certificate that is assigned to a user account.

User Configuration The portion of Group Policy that is applied to users that log in to a domain computer.

User Principle Name (UPN) The unique name assigned to a user account in an Active Directory forest.

V

Virtual Private Networks (VPN) A virtual network that encrypts all traffic as it passes through an existing network.

virus definition An entry within antivirus software that provides the necessary information needed to detect the virus during a virus scan.

Voice Over IP (VOIP) A technology that allows spoken information to be sent across an IP network.

Volume Shadow Copy Service (VSS) A Windows services that can be used to efficiently back up open files.

W

WebReady Allows OWA users to access and view attachments in various formats such as Microsoft Office Word.

Windows Backup The file and service backup program in Windows Server 2003. You can use Windows Backup to back up and restore Exchange Server 2007.

Windows Certificate API (CAPI) The Windows API used to provide asymmetric cryptographic operations such as public and private key generation.

Windows Firewall A firewall software that ships with Windows XP and later operating systems.

Windows Mobile Device Center A Windows Vista software program that allows users to synchronize data from a mobile smartphone or PDA to their computer.

Windows QoS Packet Scheduler A Windows software component used for network bandwidth management and control.

Windows Rights Management Services A Windows service that works alongside applications to restrict access to sensitive information.

Windows Server Update Services (WSUS) A server software component that automates and simplifies the distribution of updates to the computers within your organization.

wireless provider A network provider that offers wireless service over long distances. There are many wireless providers in North America including AT&T, Rogers, and Bell.

X

X.400 A commonly used legacy email standard.

X.500 A commonly used directory service structure standard.

X.509 certificate A public key certificate that adheres to the X.509 standard for public key cryptography.

Z

zone A file or object that contains resource records for a portion of the Domain Name Space.

NOTES

NOTES

NOTES

NOTES

NOTES

NOTES